Reading Strategies and Practices

A Compendium, Fourth Edition

ROBERT J. TIERNEY
The Ohio State University

JOHN E. READENCE
University of Nevada, Las Vegas

ERNEST K. DISHNER
Pennsylvania State University at Harrisburg

Allyn and Bacon

Boston • London • Toronto • Sydney • Tokyo • Singapore

Series Editor: Virginia Lanigan
Marketing Manager: Ellen Mann
Production Administrator: Marjorie Payne
Editorial Assistant: Nicole De Palma
Cover Administrator: Linda Knowles
Composition/Prepress Buyer: Linda Cox
Manufacturing Buyer: Megan Cochran
Editorial-Production Service: Chestnut Hill Enterprises
Cover Designer: Karen Roehr

Copyright © 1995, 1990, 1985 by Allyn & Bacon
A Simon & Schuster Company
Needham Heights, Massachusetts 02194

A previous edition was published in 1980 under the title *Reading Strategies and Practice: A Guide for Improving Instruction,* Copyright © 1980 by Allyn and Bacon.

Library of Congress Cataloging-in-Publication Data
Tierney, Robert J.
    Reading strategies and practices : a compendium / Robert J.
Tierney, John E. Readence, Ernest K. Dishner — 4th ed.
      p. cm.
    Includes bibliographical references and index.
    ISBN 0-205-16285-1
    1. Reading.   2. Reading comprehension.   I. Readence, John E.,
1947–   . II. Dishner, Ernest K., 1943–   .   III. Title.
LB1050.T57   1995
428.4'3—dc20   94-18806

                                           CIP

This book is printed on acid-free, recycled paper.

Printed in the United States of America
10 9 8 7 6 5 4 3 2 1   99 98 97 96 95 94

Contents

Preface

This new edition of *Reading Strategies and Practices: A Compendium* represents a significant improvement over the earlier editions. Some of the changes that were made include the following:

- Addition of 17 new strategies and practices
- Addition of several new units, including Whole-Language and Literature-Based Approaches and Assessment Strategies for Classrooms, Teachers, and Students
- Revision of existing descriptions of strategies, especially the cautions and comments for each strategy
- Addition of several new strategies within existing units
- Discussion of each strategy in terms of current research findings, which addresses their utility

This book is a compendium of strategies; it is not a description of a single approach, nor is it intended to be eclectic. The inclusion of a strategy should not be perceived as our endorsement of that strategy. There are some strategies that we view as problematic; there are others about which we disagree.

We appreciate those of you who have used the book, especially those colleagues who gave us feedback for this revision. In addition, we appreciate the comments we received from the reviewers, James Crossman of Arizona State University and Marguerite Gillis of Southwest Texas State University. We hope you will find this new edition even more useful than its predecessors. Ideally, the book will stimulate reflection, discussion, evaluation, and intelligent use of instructional procedures. We especially want it to fill a void by being a ready reference for teachers and prospective teachers who want a clear, overall perspective of instructional procedures and who approach their teaching with a view to experimentation and decision making. The first, second, and third editions were used in numerous courses at the undergraduate and graduate level for such purposes; the new edition should have even greater utility. We also recommend the book to administrators and others concerned with reading improvement—including parents.

How to Use This Book

Intended Purposes

The purpose of this book is to afford the reader an active role in examining and evaluating instructional techniques. We do not expect readers to become familiar with all of the strategies or practices presented in the text, nor do we even advocate reading the text from cover to cover. Rather, we recommend reading it selectively and reflectively. Readers should select the units and strategies they wish to review and evaluate.

How Is This Book Organized?

For organizational purposes, the text is divided into 14 units. Within each unit we delineate our intent and provide recommendations as well as cautions for using various strategies and practices. The 14 units under which the strategies and practices have been classified are as follows:

Unit 1   Whole-Langauge and Literature-Based Approaches
Unit 2   Teaching Reading as a Language Experience
Unit 3   Response to Literature and Drama
Unit 4   Responding to Reading as Writers and Writing to Enhance Comprehension
Unit 5   General Frameworks
Unit 6   Discussion and Cooperative Learning
Unit 7   Comprehension Development and Thinking Critically
Unit 8   Meaning Vocabulary Strategies
Unit 9   Reading and Writing Across the Curriculum: Content Area Literacy
Unit 10 Studying
Unit 11 Intervention Programs for "At-Risk" Readers
Unit 12 Word Identification
Unit 13 Oral Reading
Unit 14 Assessment Strategies for Classrooms, Teachers, and Students

Some readers may disagree with the separation of teaching strategies and practices into these particular strands. This breakdown is intended as one viable method of organization; it is not suggested as a divinely inspired division of reading or curriculum.

The 14 units of this text describe 87 strategies and practices. As an aid to examining and evaluating these techniques, each unit provides the reader with an overview and a consistent organizational pattern. The following section describes how these aids might be used.

Unit Overview

At the beginning of each unit, an overview provides an introduction to the various strategies and practices presented in that section. This overview serves three essential purposes:

1. Since only selected strategies have been included within the various units, the overview provides information on the basis for selecting strategies.
2. Since several strategies could be classified into more than one unit, the overview provides information on the basis for the present classification.
3. The overview provides the reader with a brief orientation, which enables purposeful reading of each section and thus facilitates the evaluation, comparison, and intelligent selection of strategies and practices or their adaptations.

Strategies and Practices

In detailing the major features of the various strategies and practices, the discussion of each adopts the following framework:

Purpose

Rationale

Intended Audience

Description of the Procedure

Cautions and Comments

Where further information is desired, each unit provides an annotated list of references to guide readers in their research.

About the Authors

Robert J. Tierney is a professor at Ohio State University, where he is conducting research on reading-writing relationships and reading comprehension, as well as teaching graduate and undergraduate courses in language arts and reading. He received his Ph.D. from the University of Georgia and has been a member of the faculty at the University of Illinois, Harvard University, and the University of Arizona. A teacher, consultant, and researcher in both the United States and Australia, Dr. Tierney has written books and numerous articles dealing with theory, research, and practice.

John E. Readence received his M.A. at Ohio State University and his Ph.D. in reading education from Arizona State University. A teacher at both the public school and college levels and a consultant for numerous school districts, Dr. Readence has published many articles and textbooks in the education field. He has held positions at Kansas State University, the University of Georgia, and Louisiana State University, among others, and currently serves as Professor of Education at the University of Nevada, Las Vegas. His current instructional/research interests focus on content area literacy, teacher beliefs and practices, and reading comprehension and its assessment.

Ernest K. Dishner received B.S. and MA. degrees from East Tennessee State University and a doctorate in reading education from the University of Georgia. Since 1973 Dr. Dishner has held teaching and administrative positions at Arizona State University, Delta State University, the University of Northern Iowa, and Southwest Texas State University. Currently, Dr. Dishner serves as Professor of Education at Pennsylvania State University at Harrisburg. A former elementary and secondary reading teacher, Dr. Dishner has written articles in a variety of professional journals and coauthored or edited a number of college-level texts. His primary professional interests are in preservice and in-service teacher education and in content reading.

Whole-Language and Literature-Based Approaches

UNIT OVERVIEW

The originators of Whole-Language would be adamant that Whole-Language represents a view of literacy, learning, and teaching rather than a set of practices or any set approach. Nonetheless, the assumptions of Whole-Language have been used as the basis for suggesting certain practices that most educators have come to view as consistent with Whole-Language assumptions. The present unit describes Whole-Language, placing special emphasis on the assumptions that undergird this orientation, and then includes descriptions of a number of approaches that many Whole-Language educators tout. The strategies and frameworks described include: Theme-Based Units, Individualized Reading, Author-Reader Cycle, Sustained Silent Reading, Shared Book Experience, and Reading-Writing Workshop. Our inclusion of this set of strategies should not be viewed as a form of Whole-Language endorsement, as teachers may implement them in different ways, including some that may be inconsistent with Whole-Language tenets. In addition, many of the other units include strategies or approaches with various elements that might warrant their inclusion in this unit and their acceptance as practices that have the potential to be consistent with Whole-Language philosophy. Essentially, this same point was made by Altwerger, Edelsky, and Flores:

> First and foremost: Whole-Language is not practice. It is a set of beliefs, a perspective. It must become practice, but it is not the practice itself. Journals, book publishing, literature study, thematic science units and so forth do not make a classroom "Whole-Language." Rather these practices become Whole-Language-like because the teacher has particular beliefs and intentions. (1987, 145)

Whole-Language.   Whole-Language is a view of literacy, literacy-learning, and teaching that is driven by key assumptions about how students learn. Whole-Language has its antecedents in the student-centered notions of Dewey and the psycholinguistic assumptions of Kenneth Goodman, Smith, and others. In recent years, these assumptions have been used as the basis for suggesting classroom practices.

Theme-Based Units.   Theme-Based Units incorporates projects as a means of providing opportunities for learners to pursue integrated learning experiences wherein learners as individuals and members of different groups set goals, plan, research,

1

compose/construct, and share ideas gleaned from their exploration of topics and issues demanding the integration of resources and tools from different subject areas.

Individualized Reading.   Individualized reading, which centers on the child rather than on the material, seeks to counter the orientation away from individual characteristics. Based upon the notion of seeking, self-selection, and self-monitoring, Individualized Reading redirects reading instruction toward reading real books and toward students assuming responsibility for monitoring their own progress.

Author-Reader Cycle.   Like Whole-Language, the Author-Reader Cycle represents not so much a collection of strategies for reading and writing as an approach to learning. The Author-Reader Cycle, as explained in Harste, Short, and Burke (1988), uses literacy as a means for learning rather than as an end in itself. By engaging students as author in a cycle of experiences around the exploration of their worlds, writing serves as the backdrop for stimuli of, and in synergism with, reading, talk, and other ways of engaging students separately and together in shared explorations.

Sustained Silent Reading.   Sustained or uninterrupted Silent Reading is among the few strategies that have as their central focus opportunities for students to engage in sustained reading and to do so alongside others, including the teacher and sometimes others within a school, such as school personnel who provide services other than instruction.

Shared Book Experience.   Shared Book Experience adopts some of the features of early reading experiences between young children and their parents to the classroom. As described by Doake (1985) and Holdaway (1979), Shared Book Experience is intended as a means of establishing early reading experiences that capitalize on the children's natural prowess with stories and that dovetail story experiences with other language activities.

Reading-Writing Workshop.   The Reading-Writing Workshop represents a comprehensive approach to reading and writing that attempts to engage students in meaningful literacy activities and to develop strategic approaches to reading and writing. The workshop approach draws from holistic approaches to teaching and learning, including process writing and Whole-Language tenets and related strategies.

Reference:

B. Altwerger, C. Edelsky, and B. Flores. 1987. Whole-language: What's new? *The Reading Teacher* 27:144–154.

Whole-Language   ■

Purpose

Whole-Language is a view of literacy, literacy learning, and teaching that is driven by key assumptions about how students learn. In recent years, these assumptions have been used as the basis for suggesting classroom practices for students.

Rationale

Whole-Language has antecedents in the student-centered notion of Dewey, but its modern-day roots and articulation stem from the work of psycholinguists that began in the late sixties and early seventies. Early proponents of Whole-Language were Smith and Goodman. In an article entitled "On the psycholinguistic approach to teaching reading," they explained what remains as a key tenet—Whole-Language is a set of beliefs, not an approach. In this article, Whole-Language was synonymous with a "psycholinguistic approach." As they stated:

> . . . a "psycholinguistic approach" to reading would be the very antithesis of a set of instructional materials. . . . The child learning to read seems to need the opportunity to examine a large sample of language, to generate hypotheses about the regularity underlying it, and to test and modify these hypotheses on the basis of feedback that is appropriate to the unspoken rules that he happens to be testing.
>
> None of this can, to our mind, be formalized in a prescribed sequence of behaviorally stated objectives embalmed in a set of instructional materials, programmed or otherwise. The child is already programmed to learn to read. He needs written language that is both interesting and comprehensible and teachers who understand language-learning and appreciate his competence as a language-learner. (1971, 179–180)

This concern over making a distinction between beliefs and practice was stressed by Altwerger, Edelsky, and Flores. In response to the question "Whole-Language: What is it?" they stated:

> First and foremost: Whole-Language is not practice. It is a set of beliefs, a perspective. It must become practice, but it is not the practice itself. Journals, book publishing, literature study, thematic science units and so forth do not make a classroom "Whole-Language." Rather these practices become Whole-Language-like because the teacher has particular beliefs and intentions. (1987, 145)

Weaver (1990) further defines the beliefs and practices of Whole-Language as:

> . . . a way of thinking about children and their learning, a set of beliefs that increasingly guides instructional decision-making for those committed to this educational philosophy. Thus, if we talk about a whole language approach, we mean instructional practices that stem from this philosophy, not a system that can be embodied in sets of prepackaged materials. (P. 22)

Several key theoretical premises inform Whole-Language. In terms of assumptions about language, these premises seem aptly described by Altwerger, Edelsky, and Flores (1987), who suggest:

> Whole-Language is based on the following ideas: (a) language is for making meanings, for accomplishing purposes; (b) written language is language—thus what is true for language in general is true for written language; (c) the cuing systems of language (phonology in oral, orthography in written language, morphology, syntax, semantics, pragmatics)

are always simultaneously present in any instance of language use; (d) language use always occurs in a situation; (e) situations are critical to meaning making. (P. 145)

Gursky (1991) defines Whole-Language as:

... an entire philosophy about teaching, learning, and role of language in the classroom. It stresses that language should be kept whole and uncontrived and that children should use language in ways that relate to their own lives and cultures. In the whole language classroom, the final product—the "answer"—isn't as important as the process of learning to define and solve problems. Whole language advocates believe that the ideal classroom is a child centered one in which students enjoy learning because they perceive that the material has meaning and relevance to their lives. (P. 23)

In terms of assumptions about learning and teaching, Goodman and Goodman (1982) have offered several guidelines. In general, Whole-Language holds the view that teaching should be guided by what is known about language learning. The further teaching moves away from how students learn naturally, the more difficult the task is for students. In accordance with this view, a great deal of respect is given to the child's natural language learning processes and the fact that a child learns literacy from a very early age in a similar way to proficient readers. As Goodman and Goodman (1982) state:

In this method there are no pre-reading skills, no formalized reading readiness. Instead, learning is expected to progress from whole to part, from general to specific, from familiar to unfamiliar, from vague to precise, from gross to fine, from highly contextualized to more abstract. Children are expected to read, first, familiar meaningful wholes—easily predictable materials that draw on concepts and experiences they already have. These may be signs, cereal boxes, or books. From this perspective readiness is intrinsic when language is real. Children are ready when they see need and have confidence in themselves. By carefully building on what children already know, we assure their readiness. (P. 127)

In accordance with this view, Whole-Language does not support reading and writing curriculum that is overly structured or constrained by attempts to sequence a hierarchy of reading and writing experiences. The use of controlled vocabulary aimed at giving students control of a predetermined set of words is seen as being artificial, meaningless, and misdirected. Likewise, the isolation of skills and the tendency to teach skills to mastery are seen as inappropriate. As Goodman and Goodman (1982) state:

Learning to read is not learning to recognize words, it is learning to make sense of texts. In the whole-language program there is no separate phonics instructions. . . . Readers in a whole-language program do form rules for relating print to speech as they are reading meaningful texts. But these self-developed rules are not overlearned and artificial as they would be if they were imposed by a structured phonics program. (P. 127)

One of the key principles underlying Whole-Language is that language is learned best when the learner's focus is on use and meaning.

Whereas descriptions of Whole-Language principles may vary somewhat, they tend to focus on respect for the learner, for learning in meaningful situations, and for the learner's natural language-learning tendencies. In conjunction with these tendencies, Whole-Language values approximation, immersion, engagement, and exploration rather than mastery of conventions and piecemeal learning. In an attempt to summarize some of these key tenets, Goodman and Goodman offered the following list of selected principles:

1. Learning in school and out of school should not be different. In both situations learning should be functional and literacy should be an extension of natural language learning.
2. Function should be considered a necessary precondition for the development of form or learning about form.
3. Literacy development, including the learning of strategies, should occur during functional, meaningful, and relevant language use.
4. Literacy abilities are acquired by children from a very early age in conjunction with their personal and social development. They have already made strong beginnings in developing literacy and literacy learning principles before they come to school.
5. Teaching and learning do not have a one-to-one correspondence. "The teacher monitors development, provides relevant appropriate materials, and provides timely experiences to facilitate learning" (Goodman and Goodman 1982, 126). The learner extracts from that environment elements that are meaningful to him or her and expands upon those elements.
6. Risk taking is an essential part of language learning. Learners should be encouraged to speculate, predict, and generate their own hypotheses about meaning and meaning-making. Errors/mistakes should not be viewed as problematic but as an essential part of development.
7. Materials to be read and written should be functional rather than constrained by attempts to control texts and contexts artificially.
8. Fragmentation of language and language learning should be avoided.
9. Meaning should always be the focus, and learners should be urged to ask continually, "Does this make sense to me?"
10. Learning should proceed from the literacy base that the learner brings to school.

In an attempt to summarize some of the key tenets, researchers such as Goodman and Goodman (1982), Weaver (1990, 22–27), and Ruddell (1992, 613) offer the following list of selected principles for "language and literacy acquisition which serve to clarify the meaning of a whole language philosophy, define a whole language perspective, and guide the development of our instructional methodology" (Ruddell, 1992, 614).

1. Children, from a very early age, are active theory builders and hypothesis testers. Children grow and learn most readily when they actively pursue their own learning.
2. Materials to be read and written should be functional rather than constrained by attempts to control texts and contexts artificially. The driving force is children's need to obtain meaning; learners are encouraged to continually ask, "Does this make sense to me?"

3. Language performance is directly related to the language environment. Learning in and out of school should not be different. In both situations learning should be functional and literacy should be an extension of natural language learning. Learning should proceed from the literacy base that the learner brings to school.
4. Oral and written language acquisition are parallel and interactive in development. Fragmentation of language and language learning, learning part-to-whole, should be avoided.
5. Oral and written language development, including the learning of strategies, are directly related to and interactive with literacy acquisition and development.
6. Risk taking is an essential part of language learning. Learners, teachers, and students alike should become decision makers in the learning process. They are encouraged to speculate, predict, and generate their own hypotheses about meaning and meaning making. Errors/mistakes should not be viewed as problematic but as an essential part of development.
7. Ongoing and periodic assessment is intertwined with learning and teaching.
8. Interdisciplinary learning fosters the kinds of attitudes and behaviors needed in a technologically advanced, democratic society.

Cambourne (1988) presents a model of literacy learning (see Figure 1) that directly relates the Whole-Language philosophy with classroom instruction.

Intended Audience

Whole-Language is a view of literacy learning that is intended to guide literacy programs at any level.

Description of the Procedures

Rather than offering a prescription for practice, Whole-Language educators develop literacy learning environments based upon the needs and experiences of students and, within these environments, provide careful guidance that responds to the child's endeavors. In recent years, certain techniques and practices have become almost synonymous with Whole-Language. In an attempt to make Whole-Language more concrete, we will describe some of these techniques with the recognition that they should not be regarded as a formula for Whole-Language. For purposes of organization, we will discuss these techniques under three headings: Beginning Reading, Developing Reading, and Remediation or Revaluing.

Beginning Reading   Among the goals typically associated with a Whole-Language view of beginning reading are the following:

1. To build on children's developing awareness of functions of print, environmental reading, and informational reading
2. To create a literate environment in the classroom
3. To expand the learner's awareness of books
4. To expand the child's sense of style and form
5. To help the child develop strategies for making sense of print

FIGURE 1–1. A SCHEMATIC REPRESENTATION OF BRIAN CAMBOURNE'S MODEL OF LEARNING AS IT APPLIES TO LITERACY LEARNING

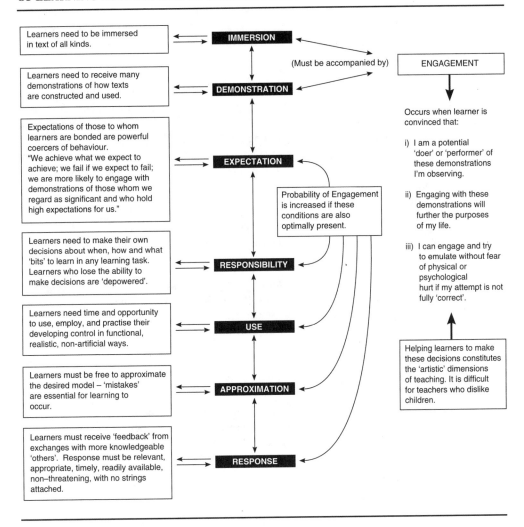

In accordance with these goals, a Whole-Language classroom is apt to be rich in print resources and lively in terms of meaningful/functional experiences with print. The classroom is likely to be surrounded by artwork, children's writings, class writings, books, and labels and other vehicles (charts, bulletin boards, menus, recipes) by which students can see, contribute to, and be part of a print environment. Excursions, simulations, role-playing, and so on, in which print is an integral part (e.g., a shopping list for a visit to a store, telephone messages) of the experience may be commonplace. Literature circles, writing centers, peer conferences, and reading areas are likely to be integral to providing the students with a sense of immersion, exploration, and opportunity to develop and use print.

Likewise, students' writing, dictated stories, shared book experiences, and assisted reading will likely be recurring activities as the teacher encourages student involvement with trade books (especially reading predictable books with familiar content and reading their own and each other's writing). The point is, "The children are growing into literacy under the guidance of their teachers. They are not carefully taken into it skill by skill" (Goodman and Goodman 1982, 129).

Developmental Reading   Goodman and Goodman (1982) suggest that there are three major "focal points" in using Whole-Language as students grow as readers. They are: (1) involving the students in lots of reading; (2) creating an environment that "accepts and encourages risk-taking"; and (3) maintaining a focus on meaning.

Based on these notions, a number of Whole-Language educators have proposed what they consider to be essential elements. For example, Watson and Crowley (1988) suggest that although not every classroom will look the same, the following similarities are likely to exist. As they state:

> In their own unique ways all whole-language teachers facilitate certain activities and procedures.
>
> 1. They find out about students' interests, abilities, and needs. And then they go an important step further—they use that information in planning curriculum.
> 2. They read to students or tell them stories every day.
> 3. They see to it that students have an opportunity to participate in authentic writing every day.
> 4. They see to it that students have an opportunity to read real literature every day.
> 5. They initiate discussions in which students consider the processes of reading and writing.
> 6. They know that kids can help other kids many times and in many ways that no one else can; therefore, they take advantage of the social nature of literacy (reading and writing) in order to promote it (Watson and Crowley 1988, 235).

In a similar vein, Andrea Butler (not dated) suggests that a balanced Whole-Language program typically includes all of the following elements:

- *Reading to children.* Quality literature, books owned by the children, and sometimes more demanding than those they read alone.
- *Shared book experience.* (For a discussion of this practice see Unit 3.)
- *Sustained silent reading.* (A discussion of this practice is provided in this unit.)
- *Guided reading.* This involves the teacher's working with a small group of children in the reading of picture books, short stories, or novels. In conjunction with the reading, the children are involved in independent reading, discussion, response activities, and sharing activities.
- *Individualized reading.* (A discussion of this practice is provided in this unit.)

- *Language experience.* (For a discussion of this see Unit 2.)
- *Children's writing.* Most of the guidelines emanating from Donald Graves's work in writing relate directly to Whole-Language.
- *Modeled writing.* Modeled writing involves the teacher's modeling good writing behavior. As Butler (not dated) states: "It involves composing in front of children, articulating the processes they are going through, and explaining why they are doing what they are doing. It can also take the form of teachers scribing as they and the students compose text collaboratively" (P. 30).
- *Opportunities for sharing.* Sharing time involves providing students the opportunity to present a finished product (response to reading, own writing, drama, report of play).
- *Content area reading and writing.* In the Whole-Language classroom the aforementioned activities extend to the content areas. As Butler states: " . . . the nine elements . . . do not just apply to the time allocated to the specific teaching of language. They apply all day in every content area."

Goodman and Goodman (1982) also emphasize that "Children are helped to broaden the scope and range of their reading and to build specific strategies which will be helpful with different kinds of texts" (P. 129). They go on to suggest the use of strategy lessons. (For an expanded discussion of strategy lessons, see Unit 12, Goodman's Reading Strategy Lessons.) Or, as Watson and Crowley suggest: "Strategy lessons take advantage of the strengths of a reader, and they are often brief and always to the point. Equally important, they lead to a discussion of the reading process." (P. 258) Apart from strategy lessons, a deliberate attempt is made to hold conferences with the children (either individually or in group) in an attempt to bring the reading to a conscious level. As Watson and Crowley (1987) contend:

> . . . Whole-Language teachers do talk about the reading process in both formal and informal ways with their students. They talk with students at the teachable moment—that is, when they need and can make immediate use of the information; furthermore, the teachers build on what readers are doing right, not what they doing wrong. Additionally, teachers bring reading to the students' awareness by discussing strategies involved in real reading . . . those strategies involve the reader's sampling from print, predicting . . . confirming . . . correcting . . . . instead of drilling on skills, children in Whole-Language classrooms are asked to reflect on the strategies they use. (P. 257)

Remediation or Revaluing   Goodman and Goodman (1982) argue that remedial programs enlist practices that tend to be in opposition to a Whole-Language view. For example, they suggest that remedial programs tend to focus on weaknesses rather than strengths, word-level rather than meaning-seeking strategies. In accordance with a Whole-Language view, they argue that instruction for troubled readers should focus on helping readers revalue themselves—that is, "help them to value what they can do and not be defeated by what they can't do, to trust themselves and their linguistic intuition . . .

specifics of a revaluing program include a great deal of Whole-Language, meaningful reading and of non-pressuring support" (P. 131).

Cautions and Comments

In our aforementioned discussion we attempted to highlight the notion that Whole-Language represents a viewpoint rather than a set approach. In presenting a description of key elements of Whole-Language, it should be reemphasized that Whole-Language is not a set of activities but a belief-driven approach that will and should vary. Certainly Whole-Language can be distinguished from approaches to reading that are highly structured and that presume a sequence of skills and strategies, including teaching suggestions that isolate separate skills and strategies. A useful comparison of Whole-Language with a decoding emphasis was developed by Reed and Ward (1982). It is shown in Figure 1–2.

One should not assume that a Whole-Language orientation is easy to achieve. As Altwerger, Edelsky, and Flores (1987) have explained, to become a Whole-Language teacher requires more than simply putting in place certain practices or activities. To achieve effective Whole-Language classrooms, teachers need to develop an understanding of some key facets of language learning, adopt an attitude of teaching as a continuous experiment, and open their eyes to what children are doing, can do, and might be sensitively guided to achieve.

Weaver points out that "many teachers prefer the safety of basals to the unpredictable vagaries of whole language." She emphasizes that "if teachers haven't made the shift in models of learning, they're going to take nice trade books and do all the awful things that have been done with basals, namely use the literature to teach isolated skills." (Gursky, 1990, 28) Smith (1992) concurs by saying "teachers could also mistake whole language as just another method rather than an entirely new approach to teaching. Such teachers still do not trust children to learn unless their attention is controlled and their progress monitored and evaluated" (P. 440).

Educators who do not fully understand the tenets of Whole-Language find that their concerns usually are among the many myths and misconceptions of what Whole-Language really is. Newman and Church (1990) and Weaver (1990) identify the following as the most frequently known myths associated with Whole-Language:

- Phonics, spelling, or grammar are not taught in Whole-Language classrooms
- Whole-Language means a literature-based curriculum
- Whole-Language is a way of teaching the language arts without integrating the other subject areas
- Teachers do not teach in Whole-Language classrooms
- A Whole-Language classroom is not structured
- Evaluation does not exist in Whole-Language classrooms
- "Anything goes" in a Whole-Language classroom
- Whole-Language teachers focus only on the process of learning

FIGURE 1–2.

Goals	Code Emphasis	Other Approaches*	Meaning Emphasis
What are the skills taught?	Subskills, e.g., sound-symbol correspondences, such as identification of initial and final vowels, consonants, syllables, and morphemes; dividing words into components and then sounding them out; understanding syntactic relationships; building a sight word vocabulary.		As they engage in communicative experiences, students acquire basic understandings of how language functions and is used. At the same time as students are involved in "total" reading experiences from the beginning, they become aware of what they are learning in terms of language conventions and discuss strategies they use as they read, write, and experience communication. The teacher's task is to capitalize upon and encourage the students to be their own informants.
Instruction *What is the order in which instruction takes place?*	Letter, sound, and word recognition taught first; comprehension skills become focus after students develop automaticity; preskills of a strategy are taught before the strategy itself is presented; high utility skills are introduced before less useful ones; easy skills are taught before more complex ones. Skilled comprehension strategies are taught beginning in the intermediate grades.		Students are encouraged to be active participants in their reading experiences. Rather than be taught subskills, they are provided experiences for understanding a variety of texts read for student self-initiated purposes. Students learn strategies and skills in conjunction with those communicative experiences. These experiences can emanate from the students' initial writing experience, from reading activities involving reading predictable texts, simple directions, stories, etc., or from print-related activities related to everyday activities (e.g., grocery lists, responding to signs and notices).
How are skills taught and practiced?	Subskills are taught in a specific sequence and are practiced until they are mastered. Complex skills are broken down into components. The teacher demonstrates the steps in a strategy and then provides structured practice in using the strategy. The students practice until they recognize when the strategy is called for in a situation. Practice includes a concentrated presentation of examples, with review across several lessons. Unison reading; individual oral responding, usually in small groups; game activities.		As children are involved in reading experiences for which they have self-propelled purposes, they are encouraged to consider the strategies they might use or do not use to achieve their reading goals. The teacher's task is to encourage the student to explore these learnings and try them or test them. Thus, skills/strategies are developed in conjunction with meaningful reading and learning experiences.

FIGURE 1–2. *(Continued)*

Goals	Code Emphasis	Other Approaches*	Meaning Emphasis
What kinds of learning experiences do students have?	Learning by practicing the same skill over and over again, gradually moving to more and more complex skills. Most children move through the various levels of a basal reader supplemented by high interest reading materials.		Learning is primarily experience based, using children's problems/purposes to direct selection of texts or using children's own written materials. Within these contexts, learning occurs through student discovery and exploration rather than teacher direction. Practice occurs naturally as students test their strategies in a variety of communication contexts. Practice involves testing as well as refining what is learned. Students are recognized as accomplished language learners who are apt to learn when experiences are meaningful and goals for learning are self-propelled.
What is the setting in which learning takes place?	Primarily in school, using a commercially published basal reader series and supplementary materials. Many classrooms have a reading corner where high-interest books are available to the children.		Children's experiences outside of school are used to create a functional, meaningful base for learning. Emphasis on taking the children into a variety of settings to build on their experience base. Classroom materials are many, varied, and predictable—they grow out of the children's and teacher's interests.
How is the learning situation structured?	Highly structured, with skills to be learned in a specific order.		The teacher serves as a group facilitator. The teacher arranges the environment, provides relevant, appropriate materials, and provides timely experiences to facilitate learning. The learner extracts from the environment those elements which are most meaningful.
	Some students will not be interested in learning. The teacher can show them that they can succeed in reading by designing lessons effectively, and that there is a reward in learning to read by using extrinsic rewards such as physical contact and by eventually developing intrinsic motivation in these students.		When language is functional, motivation to learn is high. Children know when they are successful because they have met their own needs. No external reward system is necessary.
	Children are divided into small groups based on their ability. More time is generally spent with low-ability groups. Continuing diagnosis allows for restructuring of groups based on needs of students.		Teachers work with children individually and in small groups. Much time is given to self-selected reading. Lessons tend to focus on developing strategies for getting meaning from print.

FIGURE 1–2. (*Continued*)

Goals	Code Emphasis	Other Approaches*	Meaning Emphasis
How do teachers respond to students' creativity?	Student creativity is not a focus of the beginning reading program.		The entire focus of the reading program is to build and maintain students' interest in reading. Students are encouraged to be as creative as they can be.
How are student "errors" viewed?	Specific skill deficits are diagnosed by the teacher based on identification of recurrent error patterns. The correction procedure involves praise for correct responses, modeling the correct response and leading the child (responding with the child), testing the child until he or she responds correctly every time, and giving the child a delayed test later in the lesson.		Self-exploration of problems on the part of students is a critical part of the learning process. Errors are accepted as a natural part of that process. Students' own motivation to learn results in the correction of errors. The teacher serves as a guide and facilitator in this process.
How is instruction in various skill areas or content areas coordinated or integrated?	This is highly individualized. It is recommended that teachers of intermediate children incorporate reading activities into all content area instruction; however, strategies for reading content materials are seldom taught.		Content areas are integrated within a problem-solving curriculum. Particular concern is given to the reading of content materials in mathematics, science, and social studies. Students work at the development of special strategies for reading and understanding these materials. Much emphasis is placed on written and oral language use together with reading.
Assessment			
How is learning assessed?	Children are tested, usually with informal reading inventories, at the beginning of the school year to determine their skill levels and to place them in the appropriate small groups. For ongoing evaluation, teachers use individual skills tests and have students read aloud individually.		Teachers observe and monitor the progress children are making in developing literacy. They observe students using language and informally apply their knowledge of language development to achieve an understanding of students' strengths and needs. Teachers evaluate the program on the basis of evidence that children have acquired and use comprehension strategies.

*These lines represent other possible approaches to reading instruction.

13

- There is little research supporting Whole-Language
- Whole-Language is a methodology
- Commercial whole-language materials make a Whole-Language teacher
- There is one right way to do Whole-Language
- Whole-Language is for the "super teacher"
- Change occurs only in the classrooms; administrators are not affected
- Whole-Language is another name for whole word, look-say method, and language experience approach
- Whole-Language teaching is a matter of teaching skills in context, rather than in isolation
- All you have to do to implement Whole-Language is to mandate it.

An ongoing challenge for Whole-Language teachers, according to Villaume and Worden (1993), "is the close examination of the student voices that emerge from classrooms" (P. 462). They state, "literate voices seek out and value different viewpoints in order to define their understandings of themselves and their world. Literate voices listen to others but do not expect to be told how to respond to exercises; their responses are personal, yet thoughtful. Literate voices are awake, alive, and stimulated by the complexity of the world around them" (P. 468).

Goodman (1992, 359–360) redefines the role of the teacher within a whole-language environment. He proclaims that "whole-language teachers must:

- Accept their status as professionals
- Have power (as professionals and faculties)
- Be supportive
- Reject certain traditional roles
- Seek to support learning, not control it
- Seek collaboration, not compete with peers and pupils
- Continually evaluate self, pupils, and the system in which they teach
- Assume professional roles as listed below:
  - The teacher as initiator
    The teacher invites students to participate in relevant and appropriate learning experiences
  - The teacher as mediator
    The teacher mediates learning, but does not dictate or interfere with the learning process
  - The teacher as kid watcher (Goodman, 1978)
    The teacher spends much time observing students in academic and social settings.

- The teacher as liberator

  The teacher must provide opportunities for students to take on more responsibility for their own learning. "They must seek to free the minds and creative energies of pupils for the greatest gains in their intellectual, physical, and social development" (P. 360).

- The teacher as curriculum maker

  The teacher must provide authentic experiences and a meaningful curriculum that builds upon "the personal and social experiences of the pupils" (P. 360).

Staab (1990) defines a successful Whole-Language teacher as:

. . . an individual who creates an exciting print environment and allows children to engage in meaningful literacy experiences. She continually provides mediation which means to lead from behind (Newman, 1990), thus discovering what a child is attempting to do and helping the child accomplish it. (P. 548)

Koepke (1991) further describes whole language teachers as:

. . . those individuals who declare their independence from the constraints of the centralized, highly regulated education system and share with students the power to make decisions about what is learned and how learning takes place. They need to be less like technicians, implementing programs and strategies without questioning their effectiveness, and more like explorers, observing and responding to students. (P. 36)

Gursky (1991) concurs by stating:

. . . the teacher is not an authoritarian, but a resource, a coach, and co-learner who shares power with the students and allows them to make choices. Learning in such a classroom is a social act, and children learn from and help each other. The challenge to the teacher is to adapt the curriculum and activities to the interest and talents of the children, to provide a content-rich environment, and to assure that they are constantly engaged in learning. The common techniques of whole language teaching—daily journal and letter writing, a great deal of silent and oral reading of real literature, and student cooperation, to name a few—are the philosophy in action. (P. 23)

Although an advocate for Whole-Language, Gursky (1991) does present cautions regarding the ongoing demands of Whole-Language teachers. He states, "Whole language teachers are constantly adapting as classroom events unfold; they guide rather than control; they watch for teaching opportunities and improvise and, while they acknowledge their role as far more fulfilling, it is also far more demanding" (P. 28).

Given these demands, it is not surprising that certain support groups have emerged in Canada and the United States that afford teachers interested in Whole-Language the opportunity to share. These groups are known by names such as TAWL (Teachers Applying Whole Language), CAWL (Children and Whole Language), and CEL (Child-centered, Experience-based Learning).

"More whole language groups are started for the same reason—because teachers want to teach the way students learn best. These teachers draw strength from each other, and through that strength, they gain confidence and power—power to change the way they teach." (Hood, 1989, 62)

Judging the validity of Whole-Language has been problematic. Certainly there are ample affidavits supporting the enthusiasm with which the approach has been embraced by teachers and students. In school situations in which students have received an overdose of skills and appear deprived of reading and writing, Whole-Language seems to have the potential to reestablish a set of more appropriate priorities. But several questions remain as to whether the current set of Whole-Language beliefs are valid and as to the relationship that should be in place between beliefs and practices. In past years the beliefs have been subjected to revision, reconsideration, or refinement as new understandings of language learning have emerged. The irony of Whole-Language may be that some of the practices being suggested—well-nigh tentatively—may constrain the ongoing reexamination and continued development of Whole-Language.

The authors of this compendium debated whether Whole-Language should be included in the book. Whole-Language is not an approach but a set of beliefs about readers, about learning to read, and about reading instruction. In the end, our decision to include Whole-Language was prompted by the attention that Whole-Language received in the late eighties and the number of teachers who asked the question "What is Whole-Language?" We hope the previous discussion offers at least a partial explanation.

Since students in a Whole-Language classroom "have an investment and an interest in their learning, they are encouraged to: (a) share in the decision making process, (b) suggest and negotiate projects, and (c) set their own goals as readers and writers. As a result, they become active participants in their literacy learning, they develop a sense of belonging, and learn to work responsibly and independently" (Weaver, 1991, 31).

Research confirms that learning within this supportive and nurturing environment can be successful and beneficial for special-needs students. For instance, Zucker (1993) identifies the following benefits her primary learning disabled students experienced. She states, "this type of environment:

- Focuses on language processes that directly target the basis of many learning difficulties
- Emphasizes a developmental approach that enables a more individualized format for students to find success
- Moves away from fragmentation of learning to a more meaningful, integrated approach to learning subject matter
- Permits multisensory language learning experiences that are meaningful, varied, and fun
- Enables collaboration among and between regular and special educators and related support personnel (P. 661)

Schulz's (1991) research confirms that two Down's syndrome first graders mainstreamed into a Whole-Language classroom have experienced growth in self-confidence and in learning. Ms. Niskanen (the receiving teacher) reports "they have learned as much from the other kids as from us. They also benefited from being totally immersed in words and books." Ms. Rounds (special educator) comments that "whole language has dispelled the myth that the only way retarded kids can learn is to repeat and repeat" (P. 34).

Ms. Curry, a teacher at the Dewey Center for Urban Education in Detroit, states,

> Every child is a whole language learner. Whole language happens to be wonderful for at-risk kids. I've seen whole language work for every child who comes into our doors. It doesn't matter what race, ethnic background, or what language they speak at home."
> (Ladestro, 1991, 43)

The success story of D'Alessandro's (1990) eight emotionally handicapped children can attest to the success of Whole-Language and supports the notion that all children can learn when immersed in authentic experiences. She reports,

> The full integration of the program takes place when the experiences gained from the reading are attached to personal experiences and become meaningful insights. This happens when writing is taught parallel to reading. (P. 292)

Technology, like children's literature, must be appreciated and cultivated within the Whole-Language classroom. Since "computers can serve as important tools for teaching and learning," (DeGroff, 572), DeGroff identifies six beliefs about technology that can be utilized within the classroom setting. These include:

- Social Interaction

  Computers can facilitate social interactions by utilizing student dyads. These dyads can be formed on an as-needed basis, or can be self selected.

- Whole and Meaningful Texts

  "Computers can be a medium for reading and writing whole and meaningful text" (P. 569). These texts can be in the form of notes, data, narratives, journal entries, and assignments.

- Real Purposes and Audiences

  "Computers facilitate reading and writing for real purposes when they involve whole and meaningful texts. In addition to opportunities for purposeful reading and writing, the experience of learning how to use computers provides opportunities for using purposeful oral language with real audiences" (P. 570).

- Process Approaches

  "Word processors offer many functions that have the power to facilitate writing process. Writers can easily revise and edit their drafts" (P. 570).

- Time and Choice

  "Teachers understand that children need time and choice in language learning. Software utilized in these classrooms are referred to as 'tools'—word processing software, database software, networking systems, and electronic mailing software" (P. 571).

- Risk Taking

  "If learners are to grow as language users, they must be encouraged and supported as risk takers. When they understand that change is easy with the word processor, they are willing to take chances with their writing" (P. 572).

References

Altwerger, B., C. Edelsky, and B. Flores. 1987. Whole-language: What's new? *The Reading Teacher* 27:144–154. Presents one of the most substantive discussions of what Whole-Language is and is not.

Balajthy, E. 1989. The printout: Holistic approaches to reading. *The Reading Teacher 42, 4,* 324. Provides eight guidelines supporting the implementation of technology in a literature-rich environment.

Baskwill, J., and P. Whitman. 1986. *Whole-language source book.* Toronto, Ont.: Scholastic. Presents a variety of ideas purported to be consistent with a Whole-Language viewpoint.

Butler, A. Not dated. *The elements of the whole-language program.* Crystal Lake, IL: Rigby. Describes in detail, including lesson plans, a Whole-Language approach.

———. Not dated. *Whole-language—a framework for thinking.* Crystal Lake, IL: Rigby. Discusses basic premises underlying Whole-Language.

Cambourne, B. 1988. *The whole story—natural learning and the acquisition of literacy in the classroom.* Auckland, New Zealand: Ashton Scholastic. An excellent reference supporting a model of literacy learning that defines seven conditions which must be present within a literate environment in order for learning to occur.

Crafton, L. 1994. *Challenges of holistic teachings: Answering the tough questions.* Norwood, MA: Christopher-Gordon. A resource for teachers that addresses key questions about holistic teaching.

D'Alessandro, M. 1990. Accommodating emotionally handicapped children through a literature-based reading program. *The Reading Teacher* 44:288–293. Describes how a special educator implemented a literature-based program to accommodate the personal, social, and academic needs of her elementary emotionally handicapped children.

DeGroff, L. 1990. Is there a place for computers in whole language classrooms? *The Reading Teacher, 43, 8,* pp. 568–572. Provides a guideline of how computers can be effectively implemented in a Whole-Language classroom.

Doake, D. 1987. *Changing the assumptions for literacy learning: A revolution in progress.* Monographs on Literacy Learning, Acadia University, Nova Scotia. Discusses the key assumptions underlying Whole-Language as well as practices that might emanate from these assumptions.

Edelsky, C. B. Altwerger, and B. Flores. 1991. *Whole language—What's the difference?* Portsmouth, NH: Heinemann. Clarifies Whole-Language from a theoretical and historical perspective.

Edelsky, C. 1991. *With literacy and justice for all.* Philadelphia, PA: The Farmer Press. "This volume documents the author's decade-long involvement with socially critical, holistic approaches to the everyday problems and possibilities facing teachers and language and literacy." (Editor's Introduction, p. viii).

Freeman, Y. S. and D. E. Freeman, 1992. *Whole language for second language learners.*

Portsmouth, NH: Heinemann. An informative text that provides practical ideas when applying the Whole-Language theory with second-language learners.

Goodman, K. 1986. *What's whole language?* Richmond Hill, Ont.: Scholastic-TAB. Represents a primary source for understanding the tenets of Whole-Language.

Goodman, K. S., Y. M. Goodman, and W. J. Hood. 1988. *The whole language evaluation book.* Portsmouth, NH: Heinemann. An edited volume of attempts by teachers to evaluate literacy in Whole-Language classrooms.

Goodman, K., and Y. Goodman. 1979. Learning to read is natural. In *Theory and practice of early reading,* vol. 1, edited by L. B. Resnik and P. A. Weaver. Hillsdale, NJ: Lawrence Erlbaum Associates. Discusses beginning reading development and the implications for teaching.

———. 1981. Twenty questions about teaching language. *Educational Leadership* 38:437–442. Addresses key questions about Whole-Language.

———. 1982. A whole language comprehension centered view of reading development. In *Basic skills: Issues and choices,* vol. 2, edited by L. Reed and S. Ward. St. Louis, MO: CEMREL, 125–134. Includes a thorough description of Whole-Language tenets and their implications.

Goodman, K. S. 1992. Why whole language is today's agenda in education. *Language Arts 69;* 354–363. Defines Whole-Language in terms of the constructivist's perspective, curriculum design, learning context, and teacher role.

Goodman, Y. M. 1980. The roots of literacy. In *Claremont Reading Conference; Forty-fourth yearbook,* edited by M. P. Douglass. Hillsdale, NJ: Lawrence Erlbaum Associates. Presents a coherent description of Whole-Language tenets and practices.

Goodman, Y. M., W. J. Hood and K. S. Goodman, 1991. *Organizing for whole language.* Portsmouth, NH: Heinemann. An edited text that provides practical ways for organizing classrooms to reflect holistic learning and teaching.

Gunkel, J. 1991. "Please Teach America": Keisuke's journey into a language community. *Language Arts* 68; 303–310. A personal account of the activities the author implemented to extend the learning of an ESL student.

Gursky, D. 1991. After the reign of Dick and Jane. *Teacher Magazine 2; 9,* 22–29. Describes and defines the art of teaching literacy development from the Whole-Language and the more traditional viewpoints.

Harlin, R., S. E. Lipa and R. Lonberger. 1991. *The Whole Language Journey.* Markham, Ont.: Pippin. Provides practical ideas, references, resources, and suggestions for teachers shifting to a Whole-Language way of teaching.

Harste, J. C., K. Short, and C. Burke, 1988. *Creating classrooms for authors.* Portsmouth, NH: Heinemann Educational Books. Represents a practical book for teachers planning Whole-Language classrooms.

Harste, J. C., V. Woodward, and C. Burke. 1984. *Language stories and literacy lessons.* Portsmouth, NH: Heinemann Educational Books. Presents a rich discussion of emergent literacy and assumptions emanating from selected findings.

Holdaway, D. 1979. *The foundations of literacy.* Gosford, N. S. W.: Ashton Scholastic. A basic source for details on teaching reading using selected Whole-Language tenets.

Hood, W. 1989. Whole language: A grass roots movement catches on. *Learning* 7:61–62. Depicts the journey two teachers took on their way to becoming Whole-Language teachers. Information is also available for TAWL support groups.

King, D. F., and D. J. Watson. 1984. Reading as meaning construction. In *Integrating the language arts in the elementary school,* edited by B. A. Busching and J. I. Schwartz. Urbana, IL: National Council of Teachers of English, pp. 70–77. Demonstrates how children learn in Whole-Language classrooms.

Koepke, M. 1991. The power to be a professional. *Teacher Magazine. 2; 9,* 35–41. An in-depth account of one teacher's growth, challenges, and changes when shifting to a Whole-Language way of teaching.

Ladestro, D. 1991. Making a change for good. *Teacher Magazine 2; 9,* 42–45. A description of the journey two middle schools made when moving toward a more holistic way of teaching.

McCauley, J. K., and D. S. McCauley. 1992. Using choral reading to promote language learning for ESL students. *The Reading Teacher* 45:526–532. Describes one reading strategy implemented with ESL students to enhance language acquisition.

McWhirter, A. M. 1990. Whole language in the middle school. *The Reading Teacher,* Vol. *4, 8,* 562–565. Describes how a middle-school teacher captured students' interest in learning through literature and writing, using dialogue journals and reading workshop.

Mills, H. and J. A. Clyde. 1990. *Portraits of whole language classrooms learning for all ages.* Portsmouth, NH: Heinemann. This resource portrays actual descriptions of how teachers immerse their students in authentic literacy activities. The classrooms are from varying educational settings and with diverse student populations.

Moore, M. A. 1991. Electronic dialoguing: An avenue to literacy. *The Reading Teacher* 45:280–286. An informative article describing how technology can enhance literacy learning.

Newman, J. and S. Church. 1990. Myths of whole language. *The Reading Teacher* 44:20–26. Identifies and examines the most commonly known myths of Whole-Language.

Newman, J. (Ed.) 1985. *Whole language—Theory into use.* Portsmouth, NH: Heinemann Educational Books. Represents a primary source for information on Whole-Language tenets and practices.

Pang, V. O., C. Colvin, M. Tran, and R. H. Barba. 1992. Beyond chopsticks and dragons: Selecting Asian-American literature for children. *The Reading Teacher* 46:216–224. Provides an in-depth discussion on criteria to use when selecting children's books for culturally diverse populations.

Purves, A. C., L. Papa, S. Jordan, eds. 1994. *Encyclopedia of English studies and language arts.* New York: National Council of Teachers of English. This encyclopedia has more than 800 annotated entries/topics that succinctly address this topic and related areas.

Quintero, E., and A. Heueta-Macias. 1992. Bilingualism and biliteracy. *The Reading Teacher* 44:306–312. Provides a description of the FIEL (Family Initiative for English Literacy) project.

Reed, L., and S. Ward. 1982. *Basic skills issues and choices,* vols. I & II. St. Louis, MO: CEMREL. Compares various holistic versus atomistic approaches to teaching in different curriculum areas, including reading and writing.

Reimer, K. M. 1992. Multiethnic literature: Holding fast to dreams. *Language Arts* 69:14–21. Identifies several important issues pertaining to the authenticity of multicultural children's literature books.

Reutzel, D. R., and R. B. Cooter. 1990. Whole language: Comparative effects on first-grade reading achievement. *Journal of Educational Research* 83:252–257. Reveals that students immersed in a Whole-Language approach score as well, or better, than those participating in a basal reader approach when given a traditional reading standardized achievement test at the end of their first-grade year.

Rich, S. 1985. Restoring power to teachers: The impact of whole-language. *Language Arts* 62:717–724. Provides a demonstration of Whole-Language at work.

Ruddell, R. B. 1992. A whole language and literature perspective: Creating a meaning making instructional environment. *Language Arts* 69:612–619. Provides an in-depth discussion on Whole-Language by focusing on how teaching facilitates learning in the classroom.

Scharer, P. L., and D. B. Detweiler. 1992. Changing as teachers: Perils and possibilities of literature-based language arts instruction. *Language Arts* 69:186, 192. Describes the challenges and successes the teacher experienced when shifting from a traditional model to an integrated model of teaching.

Schulz, E. 1991, August. Nourishing a desire to learn. *Teacher Magazine,* Vol, *2, 9,* 30–34. Describes how three elementary teachers designed their classrooms and literacy activities from the Whole-Language perspective.

Smith, F. 1971. *Psycholinguistics and reading.* New York: Holt, Rinehart & Winston. Includes selected articles that address basic tenets of Whole-Language.

———. 1981. Demonstrations, engagement, and sensitivity: A revised approach to language learning. *Language Arts* 58:103–112. Discusses key assumptions underlying Whole-Language.

———. 1992. Learning to Read: The Never ending debate. *Phi Delta Kappan* 73:432–441. Describes the reading process from the traditional language perspective

Smith, F., and K. Goodman. 1971. On the psycholinguistic method of teaching reading. *Elementary School Journal:* 177–181. Represents a seminal article on Whole-Language.

Staab, C. F. 1990. Teacher mediation in one whole literacy classroom. *The Reading Teacher,* Vol. *43, 8:* 548–552. Describes how a first grade classroom mediates the learning process in a Whole-Language classroom.

Storeygard, J., R. Cummons, M. Stumpf, and E. Pavloglou. 1993. Making computers work for students with special needs. *Teaching Exceptional Children* 26:22–24. Describes a computer and writing program utilized in a middle school to assist the needs of special-needs students and reluctant writers.

Sumara, D., and L. Walker. 1991. The teacher's role in whole language. *Language Arts* 68:276–285. Provides an account of the changing roles of two teachers when shifting toward a Whole-Language way of teaching.

Turbill, J., and B. Cambourne. 1987. Coping with chaos. Portsmouth, NH: Heinemann Educational Books. Provides a rich description of Whole-Language classrooms.

Vacca, R. T., and T. V. Rasinski. 1992. *Case studies in whole language.* Forth Worth, TX: Harcourt Brace Jovanovich. Describes how preschool and elementary teachers define their role within a Whole-Language framework.

Villaume, S. K., and T. Worden. 1993. Developing literate voices: The challenge of whole language. *Language Arts* 70:462–468. Provides an in-depth review of the issues pertaining to literature discussion groups.

Walker-Dathouse, D. 1992. Using African-American literature to increase ethnic understanding. *The Reading Teacher* 45:416–422. Provides a personal account of how the author designed and implemented a literature unit to promote deeper understanding and knowledge of the African-American culture.

Watson, D., and P. Crowley. 1988. How can we implement a Whole-Language approach? In *Reading process and practice,* edited by C. Weaver. Portsmouth, NH: Heinemann Educational Books. Represents a detailed description of Whole-Language principles and practices.

Weaver, C. 1990. *Understanding whole language from principles to practice.* Portsmouth, NH: Heinemann. An excellent reference for teachers, parents, and administrators regarding theory and practice of Whole-Language.

Wepner, S. B. 1990. Holistic computer applications in literature-based classrooms. *The Reading Teacher* 44:12–19. Provides a description of the software programs that are available to complement any literature-based or Whole-Language program.

Zucker, C. 1993. Using whole language with students who have language and learning disabilities. *The Reading Teacher* 46:660–670. Provides a description of a language arts program emphasizing the Whole-Language philosophy within an elementary language learning disabilities classroom.

Theme-Based Units

Purpose

The purpose of Thematic Units is to provide opportunities for learners to pursue integrated learning experiences wherein learners as individuals and members of different groups set goals, plan, research, compose/construct, and share ideas gleaned from their exploration of topics and issues demanding the integration of resources and tools from different subject areas.

Rationale

The concept of Interdisciplinary learning dates back to the educational philosophy and practice of Locke, Pestalozzi, Froebel, Rousseau, Spencer, and Dewey. These educators viewed learning as a process that reflected real-life experiences. Children learned to explore, experiment, and manipulate objects through sensory orientation. All child-initiated activities and observations were encouraged and reinforced.

Spencer, at the end of the nineteenth century, proposed a shift in curricular development that encompassed a "radical change in the type of curriculum and teaching methods instituted in the school." (Kazamias, 1966, 22) This educational reform, also known as the scientific movement in education, (Kazamias, 1966, 28) incorporated "natural experimental methods of science which involved manipulating objects rather than focusing on textbook learning. This procedure enabled students, with the guidance of the teacher, to proceed from simple to complex tasks (Kimball, 1932, 127) thereby promoting individuality and self-development. This process invited children to make their own investigations, to draw their own inferences, and to individually discover as much as possible" (Cavenagh, 1932).

The Progressive Educational Movement, under the guidance of John Dewey in the early 1900s, reinforced the restructuring efforts of previous educators. Dewey's efforts, however, prompted a shift in the theoretical framework that emphasized "learning by doing" in a child-oriented setting in addition to curriculum restructuring. His platform addressed meaningful and realistic activities that valued physical freedom, play, and self-discovery in accordance with an individual's realm of physical, mental, and emotional development (Caswell, 1937, 393–394). Classrooms promoted and implemented these learning situations through an Activity Curriculum program. Activities, according to Caswell and Foshay (1957), were defined as

> . . . learning situations brought about by the strong purpose of a child or group of children to achieve a worthy end desirable to themselves which draws upon a large number of different kinds of experiences and many fields of knowledge. (P. 254)

Dewey's definition, on the other hand, inferred a more individualistic and cognitive structure. He believed that a good activity

> . . . drew from many subject areas for developmentally appropriate content. It had to be purposeful so that each step or procedure opened up a new field, raised new questions,

aroused a demand or further knowledge, and suggested what to do next on the basis of what had been accomplished and the knowledge thereby gained. (Caswell, 1937, 604)

This activity program launched a new development in curriculum revitalization that emphasizes subject matter integration. This restructuring, through an integrated program approach, invites students to become collaborators in curriculum planning and social participants in the learning process. As a result, this "authentic integration takes place in the minds of the learners," thus enabling them to "explore, gather, process, refine, and present information about topics they want to investigate without the constraints imposed by traditional subject barriers." (Pigdon and Woolley, 1993, 6). Figure 1–3 compares the characteristics of an integrated approach to those of the traditional subject approach.

Integration, according to Roehler (1983), is "a strategy for intentionally combining subject matter so that students are aware of this during implementation." (P. 28) Routman (1991) defines integration as "an approach to learning and a way of thinking that respects

FIGURE 1–3. CHARACTERISTICS OF THE INTEGRATED APPROACH AND TRADITIONAL APPROACH

Possible Characteristics Typical of Traditional Approach vs. Integrated Approach

Traditional Approach	Integrated Approach
transmission	transaction
passive recipient	active-participant-negotiated learning
pre-established curriculum and materials	curriculum evolves around/emerges from issues, learner's interests, curriculum
receives meaning/independent seatwork	collaborative group sessions
teacher directed and controlled	teacher as facilitator, guide
product oriented	process and product oriented
rigid, pre-set	flexible
recitation and memorization may be emphasized	problem solving usually encouraged
survey-like	whole to part to whole
few opportunities for decision making	continuous decision-making opportunities
individual chapters and units, textbooks	thematic units, thematic cycles, literature books
passive listening, responding, correcting	discussing, predicting, reasoning, collaborating, confirming, thinking, judging, searching
singular perspective	multiple perspectives
secondary sources	primary sources
acquaints students with ideas	ownership of ideas

Permission granted by Cynthia Bertelsen, 1994.

the interrelationships of language processes—reading, writing, speaking, and listening—as integral to meaningful teaching across any area of the curriculum" (P. 276).

Busching and Lundsteen (1983), on the other hand, outline a model (see Figure 1–4) that depicts stages a teacher moves through when integrating the curriculum. Phase one "proposes that subskills be meaningfully integrated into reading, writing, listening, and speaking activities." Phase two encourages the incorporation of "various language arts to be integrated with each other," while phase three explores how "the language arts can be integrated with other subjects into the curriculum" (P. 4).

Over the years a number of educators have proclaimed the importance of curriculum integration for student learning and the availability for making connections between personal experiences and school knowledge. For instance, Dewey (1916) argued "that the great waste in school comes from the inability to utilize the experiences one gets outside of school in any complete and free way; while on the other hand, one is able to apply in daily life what one learns in school." (P. 75) In addition, Vacca and Rasinski (1992) claim that when "students are engaged in activities that genuinely meet their needs, purposes, interests, and experiences, then the curriculum is fun, relevant, and meaningful" and participation in authentic literacy events provides opportunities for them to "bring the world outside of school into the classroom" (P. 20). An avenue to incorporate students' personal experiences within the school curriculum is through the techniques of integrated curriculum units, thematic units, and thematic cycles.

Integrated curriculum units focus on the inquiry approach, which provides opportunities for learners to participate by taking control of their learning, making predictions, testing hypotheses, gathering and organizing information, synthesizing findings, and

**FIGURE 1–4. INTEGRATION MODEL DESCRIBED
BY BUSCHING AND LUNDSTEEN, 1983, 4.**

1
students actively
participate in integrated
activities that involve speaking,
listening, and reading

2
students are encouraged to interact
and incorporate personal experiences
in the reading and writing process

3
students are actively engaged in language learning
through a totally integrated curriculum by immersing
selves in authentic, self-pacing, selection and
evaluation of reading, speaking, writing, and
listening activities

building on prior knowledge. As a result, Pigdon and Woolley, among others, claim that learners reflect on their experiences, begin to value differing opinions, viewpoints, and interests, and become risk takers. (Pigdon and Woolley, 1993, 16) These units, according to Pigdon and Woolley (1993), provide opportunities for students to: (a) develop understandings through sustained interaction, conversation, or discussion about concepts, ideas, values, and modes of presenting information, (b) develop an understanding of the variety of ways in which we can present, represent, and transfer ideas about the world, (c) build on and extend their personal, out-of-school experiences, and knowledge, (d) understand the difference between real-world, factual experiences, and exploration of knowledge, and fictional imagined worlds, and (e) develop a sense of reflection about their world and their environment that leads to action, control, and conservation (p. 16). An illustration and description of the framework for designing integrated curriculum units are provided in the procedure section (See Figure 1–5).

A related and sometimes synonymous approach is thematic approaches—for example, Thematic Units and Thematic Cycles.

Thematic Units enable students to "study various subject areas through one common theme or topic which is extended into the subject areas" (Vacca and Rasinski, 1992, 259) that is "meaningful and relevant to the curriculum and student lives" (Routman, 1991, 278). Pigdon and Woolley (1993) suggest that activities within these units must be selected so that they "offer the possibility for the learners to further develop their ideas about the fields of knowledge they're studying." (P. 59) Planning for thematic units varies according to the teacher's classroom setup and curriculum orientation. For instance, within a Whole-Language classroom, teachers usually plan integrated units collaboratively with their students. Routman's (1991) guidelines for integrated unit planning are described under the procedures section (See Figure 1–6).

When developing thematic units Weaver, Chaston, and Peterson (1993) suggest five principles of learning that need to be considered when (a) teachers and students negotiate significant aspects of the curriculum, and (b) students participate in authentic language activities in and out of the classroom that relate to whole text reading and writing.

These five principles include:

1. The curriculum should not consist of work sheets and dittos but of opportunities to select and engage in a variety of natural reading, writing, discussion, experimentation, and research activities.
2. The curriculum must be negotiated between the teacher and the students. The topics and themes must be of interest to the students while providing much opportunity for language and literacy development. Decision making must encompass both long- and short-term planning.
3. Thematic units activities must be functional and purposeful. Learning must utilize authentic language and complete texts.
4. Direct and indirect teaching of skills is on an individualized basis. Focus is always on what the student currently needs in order to move forward in learning. Skills are always taught within whole texts and are not used as an isolated lesson.
5. Teaching occurs as a direct response to the student's actions, inquiry, or when the need arises.

Thematic units, according to Lukasevich (1991), focus around a central theme, selected collaboratively between teacher and students, where subject areas are integrated and explored. He recommends a seven-step process when developing thematic units. An illustration and description of these steps are provided in the procedures section (See Figure 1–7).

Edwards (1990) further develops thematic units by focusing on mathematical concepts. These units, known as *Thematic Maths,* provide opportunities for students to (1) develop creative and divergent thinking skills, (2) utilize their own knowledge of the real world while fostering new areas of inquiry and learning, and (3) explore, experiment, and expand their knowledge of mathematical and other language arts concepts rather than locating, retrieving, and computing in order to find the "right answers." (Edwards, 1990) Edwards (1990) claims that when children are presented with a challenge in the form of these units, they work for longer periods of time seeking a variety of solutions through questioning, explaining, defending, confirming, and validating their thoughts by conferencing with peers (P. 8).

Advantages for utilizing Thematic Maths include the following: (1) relevant to real-life situations, (2) activities lead to inquiry, investigation, exploration, observations, and self-discovery, (3) challenges current levels of knowledge and thinking, (4) encourages discourse and integration of language learning, (5) encourages risk taking and problem solving, (6) puts responsibility of learning onto the child, (7) students gain inner control and confidence in learning.

Thematic Cycles utilize subject areas to investigate a topic. The cycle begins with a question that becomes the focal point of the study. "The content areas are brought to bear on the topic as needed to answer the question or one of the questions that might spin-off from the original." (Vacca and Rasinski, 1992, 259) Vacca and Rasinski (1992) further denote that thematic cycles "use art, music, literature, social studies, and sciences for exploring, expanding, and answering the question that defines the central topic." Because of this, "subject areas are more closely connected" (P. 260).

Harste, Short, and Burke (1988) concurs that curriculum must be negotiated between teacher and students. He states that "the curriculum that results from the coming together of teachers and students reaches toward new potentials for knowing" (P. 366). A description and an illustration depicting the steps when developing thematic cycles are provided in the procedures section (See Figure 1–8).

Pappas, Kiefer, and Levstik (1990) emphasize the importance of integration through personal characteristics and cultural backgrounds. They state, "children bring their complex customs or styles of integration to their activities or projects. Children from different cultural backgrounds have different rules for communication. Collaboration is crucial and negotiation is the means by which participants can deal with the varying ways of participating and interacting" (P. 40).

As experienced in previous educational reforms, our schools today continue to fall short in helping students "learn tolerance and appreciation of other cultures and persons who are members of those cultures" (Rasinski and Padak, 1990, 576). It appears we have attempted to foster "tolerance, patience, appreciation, and friendship among children of different backgrounds and cultures" (Rasinski and Padak, 1990, 576) through curriculum development as denoted in Banks's (1989) four models of multicultural integration. Banks states that "these models are hierarchically arranged in terms of their sophistication in making multicultural issues a central part of the integrated program" (P. 577). Descriptions of these models and a resource list for weaving multicultural literature into the curriculum are listed in Figures 1–5 and 1–6 respectively.

FIGURE 1–5.　FOUR MODELS FOR INTEGRATING ETHNIC/MULTICULTURAL CONTENT INTO THE CURRICULUM*

Level 1: Contributions Approach	At this level, literature is used in isolated lessons to address holidays, heroes, and customs of a particular culture.
Level 2: Additive Approach	Literature depicting content, concepts, and/or themes of other cultures are added into the curriculum, but not woven through the curriculum.
Level 3: Transformation Approach	Students are encouraged to address different problems, themes, and concerns from another cultural group's perspective. This allows students to see the "interconnectiveness" of the various ethnic cultures with the dominant culture.
Level 4: Decision-Making and Social Action Approach	At this highest level, students are asked to identify social problems and concerns, problem solve, and take actions to help remedy the problem they have identified. This *empowers* them to take ownership in their own learning.

*From Rasinski, T., and N. Padak. 1990, October. Multicultural learning through children's literature. *Language Arts* 67: 576–580.

FIGURE 1–6.　WEAVING MULTICULTURAL LITERATURE INTO THE CURRICULUM

Weaving Multicultural Literature into the Curriculum

Primary Grades

Amon, Aline. *Talking Hands.* New York: Doubleday, 1968.
Baker, Jeannie. *Where the Forest Meets the Sea.* New York: Greenwillow, Scholastic, 1987.
Baker, Olaf. *Where the Buffaloes Begin.* New York: Frederick Warne, 1981.
Bang, Molly. *Willy and the Hairy Man.* New York: Macmillan, 1976.
Barnett, Joyce. *Willie's Not the Hugging Kind.* New York: Harper & Row, 1989.
Baylor, Byrd. *They Put on Masks.* Scribner, 1974.
Blue, Rose. *I Am Here.* 1971.
Bonnici, Peter. *The Festival.* Minneapolis: Carolrhoda Books, 1985.
Estes, Eleanor. *The Lost Umbrella of Kim Chu.* New York: Atheneum, 1978.

FIGURE 1–6. *(Continued)*

Friedman, Ina. *How My Parents Learned to Eat.* Boston: Houghton Mifflin, 1984.

Flournoy, Valerie. *The Patchwork Quilt.* New York: Dial Press, 1985.

Fufuka, Karama. *My Daddy is a Cool Dude.* New York: Dial Press, 1975.

Garza, Carmen Lomas. *Family Pictures: Cuadros de familia.* San Francisco: Children's Press, 1990.

Goble, Paul. *Star Boy.* New York: Bradbury Press, 1983.

Greenfield, Eloise. *Grandpa's Face.* New York: Philomel Books, 1988.

Greenfield, Eloise. *Honey, I Love.* New York: Crowell, 1978.

Greenfield, Eloise. *Nathaniel Talking.* New York: Black Butterfly Children's Books, 1988.

Haley, Gail. *A Story A Story.* New York: Atheneum, 1970.

Hamilton, Virginia. *The People Could Fly.* New York: Knopf, 1985.

Hastins, Jim. *Count Your Way Through China.* Minneapolis: Carolrhoda Books, 1987.

Howard, Elizabeth. *Aunt Flossie's Hat.* New York: Penguin, 1991.

Jameson, C. *The Clay Pot Boy.* New York: Coward, McCann, Geoghegan, 1973.

Jenkins, C. *The Little Weaver of Thai-Yen Village.* San Francisco: Children's Book Press, 1977.

Johnson, Angela. *Tell Me A Story, Mama.* New York: Orchard Books, 1989.

Kesselman, Wendy. *Angelita.* New York: Hill and Wang, 1970.

Kimmel, Eric. *Anansi and the Moss-Covered Rock.* New York: Holiday House, 1988.

Lattimore, Deborah Nourse. *The Flame of Peace.* New York: Harper & Row, 1987.

Lee, Jeanne M., *Ba-Nam.* New York: Henry Holt and Company, 1987.

Lewis, Richard. *The Moment of Wonder.* New York: Dial Press, 1964.

Louie, Ai-Ling. *Yeh-Shen: A Cinderella Story from China.* New York: Philomel Books.

Matsutani, Miyoko. *The Fisherman Under the Sea.* (English version by Alvin Tresselt.) New York: Parent's Magazine Press, 1969.

McDermott, Gerald. *Arrow to the Sun.* New York: Viking, 1974.

McDermott, Gerald. *The Stone-Cutter: A Japanese Folk Tale.* (Adapted and illustrated by Gerald McDermott.) New York: Viking, 1975.

McKissack, Patricia and Fredrick. *Martin Luther King, Jr. Man of Peace.* Hillside, NJ: Enslow, 1991.

McKissack, Patricia. *Mirandy and the Wind.* New York: Knopf, 1988.

McKissack, Patricia. *Nettie Jo's Friends.* New York: Knopf, 1989.

Meadowcroft, Enid LaMonte. *Crazy Horse Sioux Warrior.* IL: Garrard Publishing, 1965.

Mendez, Phil. *The Black Snowman.* New York: Scholastic, 1989.

Michels, Barbara & Bettye White. *Apples of a Stick: the Folklore of Black Children.* New York: Coward-McCann, 1983.

Miles, Miska. *Annie and the Old One.* Boston: Little, Brown and Co., 1971.

Miller, Montzalee. *My Grandmother's Cookie Jar.* CA: Price Stern Sloan, 1987.

Morris, Ann. *When Will the Fighting Stop? A Child's View of Jerusalem.* New York: Atheneum, 1990.

Myers, Walter Dean. *The Golden Serpent.* New York: Viking Press, 1980.

Patterson, Katherine. *The Tale of the Mandarin Duck.* New York: Lodeson Books, 1990.

Politi, Leo. *Songs of the Swallows.* New York: Scribner, 1949.

Politi, Leo. *Three Stalks of Corn.* New York: Scribner, 1976.

Ringgold, Faith. *Tar Beach.* New York: Crown Publishers, 1991.

Rogers, Jean. *Runaway Mittens.* New York: Greenwillow, Scholastic, 1988.

Sonneborn, Ruth A. *Friday Night is Papa Night.* New York: Viking Press, 1970.

FIGURE 1–6. *(Continued)*

Steptoe, John. *Mufaro's Beautiful Daughters.* New York: Lothrop, Lee, and Shepard, 1987.

Surat, Michele Maria. *Angel Child, Dragon Child.* Carnival Press, 1983.

The Coyote Rings the Wrong Bell. Chicago: Children's Press, 1991.

Tompert, Ann. *The Silver Whistle.* New York: Macmillan, 1988.

Toye, William. *The Loon's Necklace.* New York: Oxford University Press, 1977.

Tran-Khanh-Tuyet. *The Little Weaver of Thai-Yen Village.* San Francisco: Interprint, 1987.

Turner, Ann. *Nettie's Trip South.* New York: Macmillan, 1987.

Williams, M. J. *First Came the Indians.* New York: Margaret McKelderry Book, 1983.

Williams, Vera. *Cherries and Cherry Pits.* New York: Greenwillow, Scholastic, 1986.

Wolkstein, D. *The Red Lion.* New York: Crowell, 1977.

Yagawa, Sumiko. *The Crane Wife.* (Translation from the Japanese by Katherine Patterson.) New York: William Morrow, 1981.

Yep, Laurence. *Dragonwings.* New York: Harper & Row, 1975.

Yolen, Jane. *The Emperor and the Kite.* New York: Philomel Books, 1988.

Young, Ed. *Lon Po Po.* New York: Philomel Books, 1989.

Young, Margaret. *The Picture Life of Thurgood Marshall.* New York: Franklin Watts, 1971.

Upper Elementary/Middle Grades

Adoff, Arnold. *All the Colors of the Race.* NY: Lothrop, Lee & Shepard, 1982.

Amari, Saud. *Cooking the Lebanese Way.* Lerner, 1986.

Ammon, Richard. *Growing Up Amish.* New York: Atheneum, 1989.

Applegate, Frank. *Indian Stories from the Pueblos.* Rio Grande Press, 1971.

Ashabranner, Brent. *An Ancient Heritage: The Arab-American Minority.* HarperCollins, 1991.

Ashabranner, Brent. *The Vanishing Border.* Dodd, Mead and Co., 1987.

Baylor, Byrd. *When Clay Sings.* New York: Scribner, 1972.

Barrie, Barbara. *Lone Star.* New York: Delacorte Press, 1990.

Bealer, Alex. *Only the Names Remain.* Boston: Little Brown and Co., 1972.

Bethancourt, Ernesto T. *The Me Inside of Me.* Minneapolis: Lerner Publications, 1985.

Bilenko, A. *Ukranian Folk Tales.* Kiev: Dhipro Publishers, 1974.

Blume, Judy. *Starring Sally J. Freedman as Herself.* New York: Bradbury Press, 1977.

Bruchac, Joseph. *Iroquois Stories.* New York: The Crossing Press, 1985.

Bruchac, Joseph, and Michael Caduto, *Keepers of the Earth.* CO: Fulcrum.

Buck, Ray. *Jim Plunkett: The Comeback Kid.* Chicago: Children's Press, 1984.

Clark, Ann Nolan. *The Desert People.* New York: Viking Press, 1962.

Curtis, Natalie. *The Indians' Book: Authentic Native American Legends, Lore and Music.* New York: Bonanza Books, 1987.

Dawood, H. J. *Tales From the Arabian Nights.* New York: Doubleday, 1978.

Eunson, Roby. *Mao Tse-tung: The Man Who Conquered China.* New York: Franklin Watts, 1973.

Epstin, Sam and Beryl. *A Year of Japanese Festivals.* IL: Garrad Publishing, 1974.

Fisher, Sally. *The Tale of the Shining Princess. A Studia Book.* New York: Metropolitan Museum of Art and the Viking Press, 1989.

Franchere, Ruth. *Cesar Chavez.* New York: Harper & Row, 1970.

Fritz, Jean. *China Homecoming.* New York: G. P. Putnam's Sons, 1985.

Goble, Paul. *Iktomi and the Berries.* New York: Orchard Books, 1989.

Hamilton, Virginia. *The People Could Fly: American Black Folktales.* New York: Knopf, 1985.

FIGURE 1–6.   *(Continued)*

Harris, Christie. *Mouse Woman and the Vanished Princesses.* New York: Atheneum, 1976.
Homespun Tales From America's Favorite Storytellers. Jimmy Neil Smith (ed.) New
    York: Crown Publishers, 1988.
Hongo, Florence M. *Japanese American Journey: The Story of a People.* (Japanese
    American Curriculum Project, Inc.,) San Mateo, CA. 1985
Jones, Hattie. *The Trees Stand Shining.* New York: Dial Press, 1971.
Lester, Julius. *How Many Spots Does A Leopard Have? And Other Tales.* New York:
    Scholastic, 1989.
Messenger, Charles. *The Middle East.* Franklin Watts, 1987.
Mohr, Nicholasa. *Felita.* 1979.
My Heritage Series. Photographed by Chris Fairclough. London: Franklin Watts, 1985,
    1986.
Myers, Walter Dean. *The Mouse Rap.* New York: Harper & Row, 1990.
Paredes, Americo. *Folktales of Mexico.* Chicago: Chicago Press, 1970.
Patterson, Katherine. *The Master Puppeteer.* Crowell, 1975.
Paulsen, Gary. *The Crossing.* New York: Orchard Books, 1987.
Roberts, Jenny. *Samurai Warriors.* Chicago: Children's Press, 1990.
Robinson, Gail. *Raven the Trickster—Legends of the North American Indians.* New York:
    Atheneum, 1981.
Speare, Elizabeth George. *The Sign of the Beaver.* New York: Dell Publishing, 1983.
Snyder, Carol. *Ike and Mama and the Block Wedding.* New York: Coward, McCann and
    Geoghehan, 1979.
Sneve, Virginia Driving Hawk. *Dancing Teepees: Poems of American Indian Youth.* 1989.
Soto, Gary. *Baseball in April and Other Stories.* San Diego: Harcourt Brace Jovanovich,
    1980.
Steptoe, John. *The Story of Jumping Mouse.* New York: Lethrop, Lee & Shepard Books,
    1984.
Stevens, Gareth. *Children of the World: Jordan.* 1988.
Raven, B. *The Creation of the Sun and the Moon.* New York: Hill and Wang, 1968.
Taylor, Mildred. *Let the Circle Be Unbroken.* New York: Dial Press, 1981.
Taylor, Mildred. *Roll of Thunder, Hear My Cry.* New York: Dial Press, 1976.
Turner, Ann. *Nettie's Trip South.* New York: Macmillan, 1987.
Wang, Rosalind C. *The Fourth Question.* New York: Holiday House, 1991.
Weiman, Eileen. *Which Way Courage.* New York: Atheneum, 1981.
Winter, Jeanette. *Follow the Drinking Gourd.* New York: Knopf, 1988.
Yep, Laurence. *The Rainbow People.* New York: Harper & Row, 1989.

Intended Audience

Thematic units may be used with students at any level. Program planning and implementation may differ according to grade level organization and emphasis.

Description of the Procedures

Pigdon and Woolley (1993) identify the framework for designing Integrated Curriculum Units. Descriptions of components are as follows:

FIGURE 1–7. INTEGRATED CURRICULUM UNITS FRAMEWORK

A. PROGRAM LEVEL PLANNING
    1 Selection of a topic for the unit
    2 Writing specific understandings for the unit
B. ACTIVITY LEVEL PLANNING
    3 Tuning in
    4 The shared experience
    5 Sorting out the shared experience
        (a) Art activities
        (b) Drama activities
        (c) Math activities
        (d) Language activities
        (e) Generalizations
    6 Related experiences
    7 Sorting out the related experiences
    8 Values clarification
    9 Reflection and action
C. RECORD KEEPING AND EVALUATION
    10 Evaluation of the teaching strategies and materials
    11 Evaluation of the learner's development
    12 Future planning

A. Program Level Planning

  1. Selection of the topic: Topics emerge from content subjects with students involved in selecting the topic. Pigdon and Woolley clearly specify that it is vital to have a clear focus when selecting the topic while heeding the following considerations:

    (1) choose topic areas that are familiar to students,

    (2) combine curriculum with community interests with current and historical events, and

    (3) incorporate students' interests and shared experiences in topic development. (P. 20).

  2. Specific understandings for the unit: Specific understandings are general statements that give purpose and direction for the unit. These become the guiding principles when evaluating the usefulness of the unit. "These understandings help to provide the framework by which schooling can take students beyond the knowledge they gather in their own personal lives" (P. 21). Pigdon and Woolley suggest the following questions to consider when writing the understandings:

"Is this statement about the world:

-true or valid?

-worth knowing?

-appropriate to the needs of the students?

-able to expand student's current knowledge base?

-appropriate to the needs of the students?" (P. 21)

B. *Activity Level Planning*

3. Tuning In: The purpose of this component is to

"(a) provide students with opportunities to become engaged with the topic,

(b) find out what the students already know about the topic,

(c) allow students to share their personal experience of the topic,

(d) ascertain the student's initial curiosity about the topic,

(e) provide students with a focus for the forthcoming shared experience,

(f) help in the planning of further experiences and activities. This component enables the teacher to observe and gather information on what students know, what they have learned, and what they are able to do at the present time. From these observations, the teacher can pull together personal experiences, glean known and unknown information on the topic, student strengths, conceptions, and confusions.

4. Shared experiences: The purposes of shared experiences include:

"(a) further stimulate the students' curiosity,

(b) provide new information which may answer some of their early questions,

(c) raise other questions for them to explore in the future,

(d) challenge their knowledge, beliefs, and values,

(e) help students to make sense of further activities and experiences which have been planned for them." (P. 26) These planned experiences enable students to be active participants. These activities "are rich in information about the topic," and "connect the diverse background of experiences and understandings which students bring to this topic. These experiences challenge, extend, and confirm student's current thinking, as well as provide "a foundation for sustaining interest in a topic over an extended period of time, and a sense of community between students." (P. 23)

5. Sorting out the shared experiences: The activities in this component provide:

"(a) students with concrete means of sorting out and representing information and ideas arising from the shared experience,

(b) a focus for oral language exchanges which flow from the shared experience,

(c) allow students to express their ideas through visual formats, and

(d) allow for a range of diverse outcomes" (P. 26). Within this component, students are given choices of what activities they will engage in. These planned activities provide opportunities for them to talk, reflect, think, problem-solve,

experience, interpret, and organize information to arrive at new understandings.

6. Related Experiences: These experiences propose to

"(a) extend the unit in more specific directions as a result of insights gained from
the shared experience,

(b) provide more information in order to broaden the range of understandings
available to the students." (P. 30) These experiences "challenge and extend the
knowledge base of learners and take the form of information books, and videos,
or films" (P. 31).

7. Sorting out related experiences: The purpose of this "activity and the nature of the
information should determine the subject areas involved. When concluding this
section, students are encouraged to revisit the generalizations they made prior to the
shared experiences activities" (P. 32).

8. Values clarification: The purpose of this section is to encourage students to reflect,
evaluate, and share their opinions, thoughts, feelings, and perspectives. Activities
that encourage this thinking include:

"(a) group discussions,

(b) open-ended questions, such as: How did you feel about that? Why?

(c) co-operative groups which promote group discussion, dialogue, problem solving,

(d) role playing, and

(e) review of media with discussion" (P. 32).

9. Reflection and action: This component proposes to

"(a) empower students and help develop the belief that they can be effective participants in society,

(b) help students make links between their understandings and their experiences in
the real world,

(c) provide further insights into student's understandings for future unit planning"
(P. 33).

C. Record Keeping and Evaluation

10. Examples of records that students will keep include: journals, work files, lists,
charts, tables, graphs, summaries, writing samples, and self-evaluation measures
such as "What did I learn? What did I learn from working with others? What did I
learn about working with others?" (P. 34).

Teachers also need to reflect on the learning processes by answering questions such
as the following: "Did my questions encourage a range of responses and possible
alternatives? How did I allow for students to work with a range of other learners? Did
my resources demonstrate sufficient diversity, points of view, and perspectives? Did
I allow time for students to talk? Did I encourage risk taking and exploration of
ideas? Did I provide time for student reflection and self-assessment? (P. 34)

11. Teachers' collection of data, through observation and conferencing, on student learning and growth encompass the following: Did the students:

    (a) develop confidence and independence?

    (b) increase knowledge of ideas and concepts?

    (c) apply inquiry skills and processes?

    (d) develop the ability to reflect upon what has been learned?

12. Future Planning: "Evaluation is an ongoing and integral part of the planning process. It involves observation of student learning, together with a reconsideration of the specified understandings, the learning environment, and samples of student work" (P. 35).

The framework for Thematic Units as described by Routman (1991) and Lukasevich (1991) includes:

A. *Planning the Unit*

1. Select the topic that is developmentally appropriate, inviting, and that meets the academic and interest needs of students.
2. Brainstorm and web the possibilities that visually describe the connection between the topic and other subject areas, activities, literature, technology and media, community leaders and agencies.
3. Through planning, goal setting, and listing objectives the teacher and students have means to document instructional strategies and student progress.
4. An abundance and variety of materials and resources enable the students to experiment, explore, and manipulate the materials through multimodality learning.

B. *Implementation*

1. The orientation to the unit should pique student's interest. Opportunities for students to share personal experiences and knowledge is critical. Encourage students to develop questions that will lead to further inquiry, problem solving, study, and investigation.
2. Provide an environment that promotes collaboration, self-selection, discussion, approximation, decision making, and flexibility.
3. Instructional activities and experiences should be planned to incorporate whole group, small group, and individualized learning. Direct and Indirect teaching is utilized within a language-oriented context using authentic materials.
4. Culminating activities provide an opportunity for students to share their knowledge in collaborative and creative ways.

C. *Evaluation*

1. Observations, anecdotal entries, conferences, discussion groups, and student self-reflections are ongoing.
2. Opportunities for sharing, reporting, listening, and speaking are encouraged.

FIGURE 1–8. GUIDELINES FOR PLANNING AN INTEGRATED UNIT COLLABORATIVELY WITH STUDENTS (Routman, 1991, pp. 279–280).

1. Planning the Unit
   - select topic
   - brainstorm ideas
   - web possibilities
   - list questions to be explored
   - plan activities for development
   - gather resources
   - teach for genre of factual writing
   - inform, include, and invite parent participation
   - long-range planning; fieldtrips, speakers, outside assistance
   - organize and set up environment which is conducive to learning

2. Implementation
   - justification for studying the unit is shared and discussed
   - introduce and teach needed information gathering skills: note taking, research gathering, and report gathering
   - provide time for exploration, investigation, and information processing
   - group students flexibly
   - promote opportunities of collaboration, free choice-self selection
   - maintain a climate of inquiry: investigating, collecting data, gathering information, problem solving, revising, and rethinking

3. Evaluation
   - allow for student choice such as oral presentation, debate, written reports, published writing, graphs, drama, murals, dance, and song
   - provide time for sharing, speaking, and listening
   - balance teacher, peer, and self evaluation

FIGURE 1–9. THE SEVEN STEPS IN DEVELOPING A THEMATIC UNIT ACCORDING TO LUKASEVICH, 1991*

1. Selection of an interesting theme around which to study other subject areas.
2. Brainstorm/web directions to take the theme. Consider how the theme can impact on the various subject areas through learning activities.
3. Set goals and objectives for the unit.
4. Collect relevant resources and materials.
5. Plan an introduction to the unit. Focus on developing student interests and questions about the topic.
6. Plan learning activities and experiences. Include activities for whole class, small groups, and individual students. Organize activities by subject areas or teaching strategies.
7. Plan a culmination experience. The experience should help you pull together or summarize the unit of study for students.

---

*From Vacca and Rasinski, 1992: 260.

3. Students choose how they will report their investigations, findings, and reflections.
4. There must be a balance between teacher, student, and peer evaluation.

Edwards (1990) identifies the procedures for Thematic Maths below:

1. Brainstorm ideas: This component encourages students to share ideas of how to develop the theme. It is imperative at this stage for students to understand one underlying rule: "that each person is responsible for his/her own learning" (P. 9).
2. Working with the entire class: In the initial stages, students are encouraged to work on activities as an entire group. As they become familiar with these procedures, they can choose to work independently or within small groups.
3. Build a story: While students are working, it is important that the teacher stroll the room and observe students in action. Observations on what transpires through working alone or with peers, discussions, and final projects will assist in developing anecdotes on individual students.
4. Write a class story: From the observations, a classroom story can be developed that will capture the most memorable experience to be transcribed into a class story.
5. Solve a problem: "Use a real-life situation derived from theme to set a problem-solving task" (P. 13). Students are encouraged to work collaboratively to reach a solution, which will be shared with classmates.
6. Groupings: Depending on the thematic unit, students may choose to work individually or with groups. Either way, the teacher's role is to facilitate learning by providing support and feedback. Examples include: praise, questioning, sharing with the class, prompts, and modeling.

Harste et al. (1988) describe the procedures for Thematic Cycles as follows:

1. At the beginning of the school year, students are encouraged to discuss and list topics they would like to explore during the year.
2. Teacher and students then negotiate and settle on a list of potential topics for the year. One topic is chosen for study.
3. The class discusses the topic and begins webbing ideas under two sections. The teacher writes the topic in the center of the board or on butcher paper. To one side, she lists "What We Know" and students brainstorm known information. On the other side, she writes "What We Want to Know." This second section provides possible research questions and problem-solving activities for students.
4. Collaboratively, the teacher and students create, gather, and/or bring in a list of books, places, and people to whom they can go to further their knowledge on this topic.
5. Students, in groups or individually, select a question that interests them under the section "What We Want to Know."
6. Students, working in groups or individually, participate in learning activities that are developed around this theme or topic. Activities include: authentic reading and writing, hands-on materials, art, drama, music, and movement to explore and learn more about this topic.
7. As students are engaged in these activities, they informally share their insights and add them to the web.
8. At the conclusion of the theme, students share their knowledge with the class through formal or informal presentations (Pp. 366–371).

FIGURE 1–10.   GENERATIVE THEME CYCLE

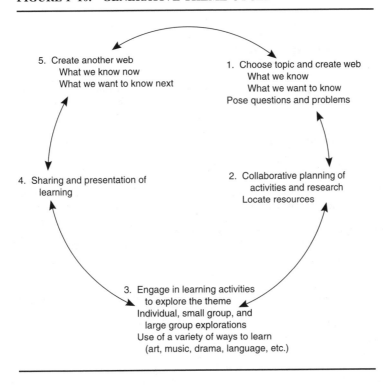

5. Create another web
   What we know now
   What we want to know next

1. Choose topic and create web
   What we know
   What we want to know
   Pose questions and problems

4. Sharing and presentation of
   learning

2. Collaborative planning of
   activities and research
   Locate resources

3. Engage in learning activities
   to explore the theme
   Individual, small group, and
   large group explorations
   Use of a variety of ways to learn
   (art, music, drama, language, etc.)

A Thematic Unit Framework Connecting Research with Practice

Tuning In: Unit Orientation

(Days 1 and 2)

- Read aloud *Just a Dream* by Chris Van Allsburg
  - Have students write about and illustrate their dream world.
  - Provide time for sharing and discussion of reflective pieces.
  - Discuss and chart what will/could happen to our world if changes are not made.
  - Have entire class brainstorm, discuss, and chart what they know about their environment and what they want to learn more about. (These lists will serve as interest group topics for small-group work.)

Investigation: Unit Implementation

(Days 2 through 20)

- Whole class activities could include
  - singing
  - poetry
  - reading aloud to students

- instructional lessons (guided by the teacher focusing on an objective, goal, or issue that is pertinent to the unit)
- Small-group activities involve interest groups gathering to discuss and research topics

Outcomes and Goal Setting: Unit Evaluation

(Days 21 through 25)

Interest groups will present and discuss their findings. Evaluations are in the form of self-, peer, and teacher evaluation. Students will collaboratively plan and identify future activities and goals. A classroom museum will be the culminating activity for this unit.

Sample List of Resources for Environmental Unit

Anderson, Madelyn K. *Oil Spills,* Watts, 1990.

Baylor, Byrd. *I'm in Charge of Celebrations.* Illustrated by Peter Parnall. Schriner, 1986.

Caduto, Michael, and Joseph Bruchac. *Keepers of the Animals: Native American Stories and Wildlife Activities for Children.* Illustrated by John K. Fadden and Carol Wood. Fulcrum Publishing, 1988.

Caduto, Michael, and Joseph Bruchac. *Keepers of the Earth: Native American Stories and Environmental Activities for Children.* Illustrated by John K. Fadden and Carol Wood. Fulcrum Publishing, 1988.

Carr, Terry. *Spill! The Story of the Exxon Valdez.* Watts, 1991.

Cherry, Lynne. *A River Ran Wild.* Harcourt, 1992.

Cherry, Lynne. *The Great Kapok Tree. A Tale of the Amazon Rain Forest.* Harcourt Brace Jovanovich, 1990.

Conserving Our World Series. Stech Vaughn Publishers.
- *Acid Rain,* by John Baines. 1990
- *Conserving the Atmosphere,* by John Baines. 1990
- *Conserving the Polar Regions,* by Barbara James. 1991
- *Conserving Rain Forests,* by Martin Banks. 1990
- *Farming and the Environment,* by Mark Lambert. 1991
- *Protecting the Oceans,* by John Baines. 1991
- *Protecting Wildlife,* by Malcolm Penny. 1990
- *The Spread of Deserts,* by Evan McLeish. 1990
- *Waste and Recycling,* by Barbara James. 1990

Cornell, Joseph. *Sharing Books with Children.* Nevada City, CA: Dawn Publications, 1979.

Cornell, Joseph. *Sharing the Joy of Nature: Nature Activities for all Ages.* Dawn Publications, 1989.

Cowcher, Helen. *Rain Forest.* Farrar, 1988.

Earth Keepers Series. Twenty-First-Century Books, 1992
- *Chico Mendes: Fight for the Forest,* by DeStefano, Susan. 1992
- *Henry David Thoreau: A Neighbor to Nature,* by Reef, Catherine. 1992
- *Jacques Cousteau: Champion of the Sea,* by Reef, Catherine. 1992
- *Rachel Carson: The Wonder of Nature,* by Reef, Catherine. 1992
- *George Washington Carver: Nature's Trailblazer,* by Rogers, Theresa. 1992
- *Gaylord Nelson: A Day for the Earth,* by Shulman, Jeffrey, and Theresa Rogers. 1992

Earthworks Group. *50 Simple Things Kids Can Do to Save the Earth,* Earthworks Press, 1991.

Ehlert, Lois. *Red Leaf, Yellow Leaf.* Harcourt, Brace, Jovanovich, 1991.

Fleischman, Paul. *Joyful Noise.* Illustrated by Eric Beddows. Harper, 1988.

Florian, Douglas. *Discovering Trees.* Scribner, 1986.

Gainer, Cindy, and Mary Ann F. Kohl. *Good Earth Art: Environmental Art for Kids.* Bright Ring Publishing.

George, Jean Craighead. *One Day in the Tropical Rain Forest.* Illustrated by Gary Allen. Harper/Crowell, 1990.

Gibbons, Gail. *Recycle!: A Handbook for Kids.* Little, 1992.

Gibbons, Gail. *The Seasons of Arnold's Apple Tree.* Harcourt Brace Jovanovich, 1984.

Going Green: A Kid's Handbook to Saving the Planet. Illustrated by Tony Ross. Puffin, 1990.

Hamilton, Virginia. *In the Beginning.* Illustrated by Barry Moser. Harcourt Brace, 1988.

Hirschi, Ron. *Fall.* Photos by Thomas Mangelsen. Dutton, 1991.

Hirschi, Ron. *Spring.* Photos by Thomas Mangelsen. Dutton, 1991.

Hirschi, Ron. *Summer.* Photos by Thomas Mangelsen. Dutton, 1991.

Lewis, Barbara A. *The Kid's Guide to Social Action: How to Solve the Social Problems You Choose–and Turn Creative Thinking into Positive Action.* Free Spirit Publishing, 1991.

Lewis, J. Patrick. *Earth Verses and Water Rhymes.* Illustrated by Robert Subuda. Atheneum, 1991.

Lingelbach, Jenepher. *Hands-on Nature: Information and Activities for Exploring the Environment with Children.* Vermont Institute of Natural Science, 1986.

Livingston, Myra Cohn. *Earth Songs,* Illustrated by Leonard Everett Fisher. Holiday, 1986.

Lowery, Linda. *Earth Day.* Illustrated by Mary Bergherr, 1990.

Luenn, Nancy. *Mother Earth.* Atheneum, 1992.

McLain, Gary. *The Indian Way: Learning to Communicate with Mother Earth.* John Muir Publications (Norton), 1990.

Raffi. "Ever Green Ever Blue." Troubadour Records, Ltd., 1990. (Manufactured and Distributed by MCA Records, Inc.)

Romanova, Natalia. *Once There Was a Tree.* Doubleday, 1985.

Rose, Debra. *The People Who Hugged the Trees: An Environmental Folktale.* Rinehart Roberts, 1990.

Schwartz, Linda. *Earth Book for Kids: Activities to Help Heal the Environment.* Illustrated by Beverly Armstrong. Learning Works, 1990.

Selsam, Millicent, and Joyce Hunt. *A First Look at the World of Plants.* Illustrated by Harriet Springs. Walker, 1978.

Suzuki, David, and Barbara Hehner. *Looking at the Environment.* Wiley, 1992.

Van Allsburg, Chris. *Just a Dream.* Houghton, 1990.

Williams, John. *The Life Cycle of a Tree.* Watts, 1988.

Yolen, Jane. *Ring of Earth: A Child's Book of Seasons.* Illustrated by John Wallner. Harcourt, 1986.

Cautions and Comments

Despite its popularity and success, critics of the Activity Curriculum concept have identified a major limitation as the "lack of a conceptual social framework" (Caswell and Foshay, 1957, 256), which is needed to revitalize and facilitate the learning process. This oversight reduced the opportunity for students "to recognize the role of culture and the function of social ideals and conditions" within that educational setting (Caswell and Foshay, 1957, 257).

Concerns regarding multicultural literature, as depicted in Rasinski's article, demonstrate the loopholes that are often present in curriculum implementation. For instance, teachers who implement multicultural literature at level one find themselves planning and implementing simple activities that more often than not inadvertently stereotype and misrepresent the culture. It is also at this level that fewer occasions arise for students to read, discuss, and study cultures other than their own. On the other hand, when implementing multiculture at the higher levels, it is apparent that more opportunities for students to "see the interconnectedness of various ethnic groups with the dominant culture" (P. 577) are available, which encourage students to "be challenged to identify,

critically analyze, and work to resolve problems related to cultural/ethnic differences" (P. 578).

The notion that *integrated learning* means that all the language must fit within or come from the content of the topic or unit is a common misunderstanding. Pigdon and Woolley contend that connections between the areas of the curriculum are made *only* when "they are natural and when they are related to the understandings on which the unit is focused" (P. 59).

Much of the research on classroom instruction depicts a conventional way of teaching and learning. This perspective portrays a teacher-controlled environment that supports learning as a part-to-whole, skill- and textbook-driven phenomenon. When examining the research results on content area reading and writing, Gee (1994) points out that research claims that "(1) all students would be reading the same text, (2) the main purpose for the reading is the acquisition of the content knowledge, and (3) acquisitions occurred will be measured at some future time by some measure under the teacher's direction and control" (P. 3).

Gee (1994), who explored various facets of student learning during and after their involvement in such units, suggested that a contextual framework occurs. When students are encouraged to participate in the learning process, instruction changes from a transmission to a transactional model; however, not all students participate in the same way. As Gee noted, individuals develop approaches that characterize the way each interprets and manages the learning tasks, and these approaches may vary in worth.

Many limitations have surfaced regarding thematic units. One drawback involves "the superficial integration of the theme and the connection between subject areas." (Vacca and Rasinski, 1992, 260) Another limitation is the "inability to link ways which maximize opportunities for students to make the connections between school and home environments and between subject areas." (Pigdon and Woolley, 1993, 13) Another limitation involves the activities within thematic units. Pigdon and Woolley (1993) claim that "all activities must provide opportunities for students to learn more about the content and not just participate in available extension tasks" (Pp. 12–13).

A fourth limitation might be the emphasis given to obtaining information. Rather than addressing one's own questions or delving into the ideas as a way of solving problems, or their application to the real world, units can be for purposes of downloading and sometimes simply copying ideas from one place to another. Sometimes the goal becomes the presentation of the unit, rather than what is gained in conjunction with the exploration, or transactions with other sets. Another limitation may emerge as a result of an emphasis upon the comprehensive treatment of a topic through textbooks, etc., hands-on experience, and the use of primary sources may be slighted. Likewise, the approach pursues an approach to subject matter learning that is comprehensive and general rather than delving, focused, or caselike. Instead of students delving into issues and subtopics, they are encouraged to develop a surveylike understanding. Many fear that the opportunity to delve may precede a survey understanding, but not vice versa. Finally, the issue of multiculturalism and achieving different perspectives is slighted in this work. (For a detailed discussion of some of these notions as they are applied in the area of social studies, the reader is referred to the Bradley Report.) With the advent of multimedia technology, teachers might be inclined to enhance their HyperCard stacks or enlist other materials. Certainly, the multimedia capabilities of CD-ROM allows information to be presented in a very lively fashion. Students pursue the exploration of topics with the aid of sound, image (both still and video), and text. They can also do so selectively or in accordance with their own interests. In addition, many of the CD-ROM versions afford students immediate access of the opportunity to crisscross from English to Spanish. These materials can be used as resources to research topics or as the basis for pulling together new units.

References

Alvermann, D. 1991. The discussion web: A graphic aid for learning across the curriculum. *The Reading Teacher,* 45:92–99. Describes the steps to follow when implementing this instructional tool to promote discussion, comprehension, and reflective responses to any reading material.

Banks, J. A. 1989. Integrating the curriculum with ethnic content: Approaches and guidelines. In *Multicultural education: Issues and perspectives* edited by J. A. Banks and C. A. McGee Banks. Boston: Allyn and Bacon, 189–207. Describes a hierarchical model for integrating multicultural literature into the curriculum.

Bertelson, C. D. (1992). A study of an integrated, personalized reading program for special needs students that reinforces the relationship between the home and school environments. Unpublished master's thesis. The Ohio State University, Columbus. This study examines how an integrated reading program impacts early literacy development and parental involvement of two primary developmentally handicapped children.

Bradley Commission on History in Schools. 1988. *Building a history curriculum: Guidelines for teaching history in schools.* Washington, DC: Educational Excellence Network. This report examines the teaching of history across the grades and the curriculum and includes major recommendations for shifting the nature of teaching and learning. References are made to notions such as multiple perspective taking, the use of primary sources, and focused study of topics vs. surveylike examinations.

Busching, B. A., and S. W. Lundsteen. 1983. Curriculum models for integrating the language arts. In *Integrating the language arts in the elementary schools,* edited by B. A. Busching and J. I. Schwartz. Urbana, IL: National Council of Teachers of English, 3–27. Provides a detailed model for integrating the language arts into existing curriculum structures.

Carraquillo, A., and C. Hedley. 1993. *Whole language and the bilingual learner.* Norwood, NJ: Ablex. Provides a framework for integrating literacy learning with language development.

Caswell, H. L., and D. S. Campbell. 1937. *Readings in curriculum development.* New York: American Book Company. Discusses the challenges of curriculum development and incorporates viewpoints of educational scholars on educational issues, problems, and concerns.

Caswell, H. L., and A. W. Foshay. 1957. *Education in the elementary school.* New York: American Book Company. Describes the major findings relating to elementary education from goals/aims to organization, policies, and practices.

Cavenagh, F. A. 1932. *Herbert Spencer on education.* London: Cambridge University Press. Describes Herbert Spencer's life and his contributions to American Education.

Crafton, L. 1994. *Challenges of holistic teachings: Answering the tough questions.* Norwood, MA: Christopher-Gordon. A resource for teachers that addresses key questions about holistic teaching.

Dewey, J. (1916). *Democracy and education: An introduction to the philosophy of education.* New York: Macmillan Company. This book described how theory is translated into practice.

Edwards, D. 1990. *Math in context. A thematic approach.* Portsmouth, NH: Heinemann. Describes how one teacher utilizes math themes with her elementary children. Sample units are included.

Exploring Nature with Jean Craighead George Web. *The WEB*, 9,* 1, 1–23. Columbus, OH: Ohio State University. Fall, 1984. (Themed issue)

Gee, J. M. 1994. *Multiple discourse use by intermediate grade students engaged in a unit approach to learn social studies content.* Unpublished dissertation. Columbus, OH: The Ohio State University.

Harste, J., K. G. Short, and C. Burke. 1988. *Creating classrooms for authors.* Portsmouth, NH: Heinemann. Provides a framework for holistic learning, including a section on Thematic Cycles.

Hydrick, J. 1990. Diskovery: Kids and technology —revelry or rivalry? *Language Arts* 67:518–524. Describes how computers can be incorporated into the curriculum as an instructional tool.

Kazamias, A. 1966. *Herbert Spencer on education.* NY: Teachers College Press. Describes Herbert Spencer's four essays on education and the implications for American education.

Keeper of the Earth Web. *The WEB*, 16,* 3, 20–27. Columbus, OH: The Ohio State University. Spring/Summer 1992. (Themed issue)

Kimball, E. P. (1932). *Sociology and education: An analysis of the theories of Spencer & Ward.* NY: Columbia University Press. Provides a framework on how Spencer's theory of education relates to other leading educational theorists.

Lukasevich, A. (1991). Organizing whole-language classrooms. In *Whole Language: Practice and Theory,* edited by V. Froese. Needham Heights, MA: Allyn & Bacon. 221–253. Provides a framework for developing Thematic Units.

Pappas, C. C., B. Z. Kiefer, and L. A. Sevstik. 1990. Planning thematic units in *An integrated language perspective in the elementary school: Theory into action.* NY: Longman. 49–70. Describes how to plan and implement thematic units.

Pidgon, K., and M. Woolley. 1993. *The big picture: Integrating children's learning.* Portsmouth, NH: Heinemann. Provides a model for integrating language learning.

Purves, A. C., L. Papa, and S. Jordan, eds. 1994. *Encyclopedia of English studies and language arts.* New York: National Council of Teachers of English. Has more than 800 annotated entries/topics that succinctly address this topic and related areas.

Rasinski, T., and N. Padak. October 1990. Multicultural learning through children's literature. *Language Arts,* 67:576–580. Defines authentic ways to integrate multicultural learning into classrooms.

Roehler, L. R. 1983. Ten ways to integrate language and subject matter. In *Integrating the Language Arts in the Elementary School,* edited by B. A. Busching and J. I. Schwartz. Urbana, IL: National Council of Teachers of English. 28–34. Describes ways to effectively integrate language and subject matter.

Routman, R. 1991. *Invitations to changing as teachers and learners K-12.* Portsmouth, NH: Heinemann. An excellent teacher resource to assist teachers when integrating the curriculum.

Short, K. G., and K. M. Pierce. 1990. *Talking about books.* Portsmouth, NH: Heinemann. Describes how educators and students can create, implement, and sustain literate communities within the school environment.

Spiegel, D. L. 1990. Materials for integrating science and social studies with the language arts. *The Reading Teacher* 44:162–165. Provides a set of six criteria to use when evaluating instructional resources. Also provides a listing of resources for teachers to utilize when implementing thematic units in the science and social studies areas.

Tierney, R. J., L. Stowell, L. Desai, and R. Keiffer. 1993. New possibilities for literature teaching and technology. In *Exploring texts: The role of discussion and writing in the teaching and learning of literature,* edited by G. E. Newell and R. K. Durst. Norwood, MA: Christopher-Gordon. pp. 175–190. Describes ways technology can aid and complement instructional practices.

Vacca, R. T., and T. V. Rasinski. 1992. *Case studies in whole language.* Fort Worth, TX: Harcourt Brace Jovanovich. Describes how preschool and elementary teachers define their role within a Whole-Language framework.

Vogt, M. E. 1991. An observation guide for supervisors and administrators: Moving toward integrated reading/language arts instruction. *The Reading Teacher* 45:206–211. Provides the guidelines and a model for supervisors and administrators to use when promoting and supporting districtwide change toward a more integrated approach to teaching.

Weaver, C., J. Chaston, and S. Peterson. 1993. *Theme exploration: A voyage of discovery.* Portsmouth, NH: Heinemann. Describes the personal journey and growth three teachers experienced when participating in a thematic research project with first and fourth graders.

Wepner, S. B. 1992. Technology and thematic units: A primary example. *The Reading Teacher* 46:260–263. Describes how software can be implemented within a thematic unit to enhance learning. A sample "technological web" is included.

Individualized Reading

Purpose

Based on the notion of seeking, self-selection, and self-pacing, Individualized Reading is designed to: (1) focus reading instruction on the individual needs of each child, and (2) aid teachers in guiding children toward assuming responsibility and initiative for their own growth in reading.

Rationale

As with any reading method, Individualized Reading is designed to develop a reader's abilities and interests. However, the basic premise in Individualized Reading differs greatly from that in other methods. Olson (1949) suggested three major principles that have become the foundation of Individualized Reading: seeking, self-selection, and self-pacing. Olson explained that students are continually exploring their own environment in search of experiences that fit with their growth and needs. Applied to reading, this means that the most conducive environment for reading growth would be one in which students are surrounded by materials to explore and select from and to read at their own pace. Such exploration is done in accordance with students' own needs and interests. In terms of actual reading instruction, the procedure that has evolved from this point of view was summarized briefly by Smith (1963) as follows:

> Each child selects a book that he wants to read. During the individual conference period, the teacher sits in some particular spot in the room as each child comes and reads to her. As he does so, she notes his individual needs and gives him appropriate help. Finally, she writes what the child is reading, his needs and strengths, on his record card. Then another individual conference is held and so on. If several children need help on the same skills, they may be called together in a group for such help. (P. 142)

One important aspect of individualized reading is that time and opportunity be afforded to students to read. It is important that students "be engaged with the print in the book while reading. If not, they are not benefiting from the reading opportunity provided by the classroom setting" (Fielding and Roller, 1992, 678). If students aren't benefiting from this instruction, then teachers must find ways to "make difficult books accessible and easy books acceptable" for students (Fielding and Roller, 1992 680). Such guidelines (Fielding and Roller, 1992, 680–681) available to teachers include:

- Modeling use and enjoyment of books
- Altering purposes for easy reading
- Utilizing books on tape
- Challenging students with easier books through book discussions, book sharing sessions
- Making nonfiction more available and familiar to student
- Preceding more difficult books with an easy book
- Providing opportunities for partner reading or read alouds

Intended Audience

Although the Individualized Reading has been more widely used in the elementary grades, the technique readily lends itself to teaching in the content areas, particularly where a multiple-textbook approach is employed to expose students to various ideas and opinions.

Description of the Procedure

An Individualized Reading program is heavily dependent on: (1) self-selection; (2) ample supply of reading material, (3) student-teacher conference, (4) extended contracts (5) flexible needs grouping, and (6) sharing books.

1. *Self-selection*   Possibly the most basic ingredient in the Individualized Reading program is that every student be taught reading with materials that the student chooses. As Veatch (1978) suggested, the student is taught to select reading material based on two criteria: (1) I like it, and (b) I can read it.

Obviously, an important teacher function is to expose students constantly to the variety of material available for reading. Through brief, enticing descriptions of these materials, the teacher can encourage the student to select the most desirable and motivating material. This, in essence, is the first responsibility of the teacher in planning—to make sure each student is given suitable material during the reading program.

2. *Ample Supply of Reading Material*   Essential to a program of self-selection is an ample supply of reading material for the student. A variety of material is needed if a student is to select a book he or she can handle with comfort. Veatch (1978) recommended that in order to maintain an adequate supply of reading material in the classroom, there should be available at least three to five titles per student.

Books are needed on many grade levels, since the range of ability in a classroom is wide. Typically, the range of difficulty should extend from one or two grade levels below the slowest reader to one or two grades above the best reader in the class. Thus, for example, in a typical first-grade class, the teacher selects books for students ranging from picture books of the earliest prereading level to those books of at least fifth-grade difficulty.

In addition, even though bright readers can effectively deal with materials of greater difficulty than average readers, their interests may be similar. Hence, a variety of books dealing with the same topic on different levels is necessary.

There are many possible sources available for a teacher who is trying to gather three to five titles for each student in the class. The school librarian can be an invaluable aid and a tremendous source of information concerning books. Public libraries and bookmobiles provide other sources of reading material for the classroom. Book fairs also can be a means of securing additional materials for the students.

Paperback books are another source for stocking the classroom library, since they are relatively inexpensive when compared to the price of hardbacks. Book clubs, such as those of Scholastic Book Services, often provide discount rates for paperbacks. Often neglected, but still excellent sources of reading materials, are magazines and newspapers. Again, they are relatively inexpensive, and a teacher can request that the students bring in old magazines or newspapers from home to maintain an adequate supply.

Finally, abandoned or old sets of basal readers can be used to supplement the book supply. Basal readers do have stories that attract children; the individual story selections can be separated into small books for distribution as "mini-books." Teachers of different grade levels can exchange a certain number of basal readers among themselves.

3. *Student-Teacher Conference*   Central to the Individualized Reading program are the individual sessions a student has with the teacher. These conferences essentially determine the character of the reading program, since during them, the student receives important personal direction in reading activity. The teacher needs to have specific purposes in mind and the ability to analyze and understand the reading performance of each student. This is essential in order to conduct a speedy, but thorough, conference and in order to ensure that each student gets the necessary amount of individual attention and instruction that will provide for optimum growth.

A teacher does not check on everything a child reads, but rather concentrates on what the child has selected and prepared for presentation. Veatch (1978) described four areas that should be explored in the conference session:

1. The mechanical aspects of the student's reading ability
2. The student's ability to read critically
3. The student's personal involvement
4. The ability to hold an audience while reading aloud

In the area of mechanical skills, the teacher might ascertain the student's ability to use word attack skills when encountering words that present difficulty. When reading critically, the student should be able to get the overall sense of the story, as well as be able to delve into the author's purposes. Knowing why a certain book is chosen is considered important for the student, not only for the student's own personal development but also for gaining the ability to recommend the book to others in the class. Personal involvement with characters in the book also should be explored. Finally, the area of oral reading with expression should be explored.

Essential to the individual conference are the records the teacher keeps on each student. It is with these annotations that the teacher can guide the student in reading and also plan for grouping activities. The following is an example of such a record:

Juan	8.5 Age	2.5 Rdg. Ach.

9/5   Horton Hatches the Egg (p. 21, oral)
       Saw value of commitment
       Group: checking organization of details
       Ind. Assign.: Vocabulary exercises

From such an annotative record, the teacher can plan the next day's reading activities for the student. For example, the student Juan might work in a group to improve his skill in reading for details. In addition, he will work on his own with vocabulary activities, or the teacher can wait until several children have the same skill need and group them together to work on that area.

4. *Extended Contracts*   In some school situations, such contracts have been extended for use in guiding students through units or projects. Figure 1–11 shows several examples of contracts that were developed to guide students' individualized and group reading and writing experiences.

5. *Flexible Needs Grouping*   Groups are formed based upon the observations and diagnoses teachers have made during individual conferences and other observations made during the school day. When the teacher sees that at least two students have the same need, a group can be formed.

It is to be emphasized that groups be formed in an individualized program when at least two students need to know something or do something that the others in class do not need to know or do. These groups are flexible in the sense that they are formed only temporarily to fill a need and then are disbanded.

This is contrary to the usual practice of grouping, which is organized on the basis of low, middle, and high reading abilities. This conventional grouping plan is usually indefinite and allows for little flexibility in instruction. In addition, such grouping allows for the negative aspects of peer pressure and labeling—the low group (e.g., "the Buzzards") become "dummies," and everyone knows it!

Groups may be formed easily when the teacher keeps good records of the individual conferences. By looking over these records, the teacher can readily see those students who are having common difficulties. For instance, the teacher can see that Juan, the student mentioned in the sample record, is only one of five students who are having difficulty with organizing their ideas. Thus, the teacher can save valuable time by grouping the five together. Instead of spending time teaching each student individually, time is efficiently used by helping all of them with the same thing at the same time.

FIGURE 1–11. AN EXAMPLE OF AN INDIVIDUALIZED THEME CONTRACT DEALING WITH VALUES AND MEDIA

Some commercials state that if you use their product, you will be more beautiful, your work will become easier, your life will be more enjoyable, and so on.

Watch 10 commercials. List the product being advertised. Check the "benefits" of using each product.

Product	Increases Beauty	Saves Time	Helps Make Friends	Lessens Work	Makes Life More Comfortable
1.					
2.					
3.					
4.					
5.					
6.					
7.					
8.					
9.					
10.					

List three "benefits" stated above that are most often mentioned in T.V. commercials.

_____

_____

_____

Can you tell what a person cares about by the bumper sticker on his or her car?

Sticker	Value
Save the Whales	_____
If you can read this you are too close	_____
Back the Farmers	_____
Add others.	_____
_____	_____
_____	_____
_____	_____

Design a bumper sticker with an important message. Make the bumper sticker and put it on your car.

FIGURE 1–11. *(Continued)*

Add a newspaper headline, story heading, or picture to the *Good News Collage.* Do the same for the *Bad News Collage.* For which collage was it easier to find pictures?

_____

Why do you think newspapers print more bad news than good news?

_____

_____

_____

Write a letter to the editor stating why you think the *Star* or *Citizen* should report more *Good News* to the people of Tucson.

Listen to the pop tunes on records or radio. Name your favorite song among the top ten hits.

Title: _____

What is the message of the song?

_____

_____

_____

Do you agree with the message? _____

_ I like the song because of its lyrics (words).

_ I like the song because of its melody (tune).

What are some of the things the following groups choose to do repeatedly and, therefore, seem to value?

1. Teenagers: _____

_____

2. Elderly People: _____

_____

3. Teachers: _____

_____

4. Musicians: _____

_____

Some people use billboards to advertise their message.

Does Kino have a message worth advertising? _____

Investigate the possibility of renting billboard space for one month to advertise our message.

Where should our billboard be located? _____

(Maybe we should ask a business with a similar message to sponsor this project.)

FIGURE 1–11.   *(Continued)*

CONTRACT COMPLETION REQUIREMENTS

State why you like or dislike a specific sculpture, painting, architecture, and so on.

Write critiques on several T.V., radio, billboard, newspaper, or magazine advertisements.

Find three examples of recorded music that generates three different feelings or emotions. Describe your feelings.

Create something of personal value in at least one of the following:

> photography
>
> music
>
> art
>
> dance

Find an object that represents these values: beauty, love, friendship, truth, peace, and equality. State your reasons for choosing each object.

Groups may also be formed for other purposes, some of which may be highly specific. Interest groups may be organized around a common concern. On the other hand, a few students can be grouped together for the specific purposes of finding more challenging reading material or for help in selecting a book at their reading level.

6. *Sharing Books*   Individualized Reading provides students with an opportunity to share their reading experiences. In common practice, the sharing of books is accomplished through written reports that, unless creatively used, become tedious. As an alternative, teachers might give students a variety of ways to share books. These sharing activities might range from simple reflection on the content of the book to a dramatic presentation of an inspiring part of the book. Role playing, pantomiming, moving scripts, advertisements, radio scripts, posters, and puppetry are suggested alternatives from which the children might select.

Cautions and Comments

Individualized Reading presents the teacher with a viable alternative to other approaches, by emphasizing personal involvement and decision making on the part of the student. However, there are some major deterrents to its use.

Since Individualized Reading is predicated upon the idea of self-selection, and self-selection from an ample supply of books, these two factors may effect the success of the program. For example, the lack of a large number of appropriate titles from which to choose may limit the self-selective process, and students may not find a title that matches both their interests and their reading abilities.

A problem that seems to arise is the pressure to complete as many individual conferences as possible in each day. Ideally, the teacher will not neglect anyone, even the brightest of readers. In reality, overly long conferences with some students will result in less available time for the other students. Thus, some students may not get the individual attention necessary to progress adequately in reading.

Similarly, the success of an Individualized Reading program is in part dependent on the vitality of the teacher-student conferences and sharing experiences. To ensure student involvement, both student conferences and sharing experiences will need to be meaningful and varied according to individual reading experiences.

A variation of individualized reading has been useful to educators in Montgomery County, Maryland. The program, Students Achieving Independent Learning (SAIL), assists low-achieving students in becoming active participants and decision makers in the learning process. The impetus of this program is to "raise students' consciousness of the strategic responses that successful readers make" (P. 20) by utilizing a four-step conceptual framework grounded within a theoretical model. Within this program, a four-step process is utilized, which consists of (a) getting ready to read, (b) before reading, (c) while reading, and (d) after reading. The purpose of the first step is to get students to set personal goals and to find a connection between the curriculum and personal aspirations. Since this program is to "convince students that constructing meaning is the core activity of reading (Bergman and Schuder, 1993, 20), the teachers must get students to delve into the reading materials as often as possible. Step 2, before reading, attempts to get students to self-select the reading material, set their own purpose for reading, and individually decide on how to process the task of reading. Step 3, while reading, requires that the students think about, select, and utilize a problem-solving and monitoring strategy that promotes individuality and responsibility for the reading task. Throughout this program, students are taught four monitoring strategies: (a) predict-verify-decide, (b) visualize-verify-decide, (c) summarize-verify-decide, (d) think aloud. In the last step, after reading, students are encouraged to choose and implement an evaluation strategy that relates to the reading task they have just completed.

Finally, Individualized Reading represents a viable alternative for the classroom teacher. Like most approaches, it demands that teachers possess an adequate understanding of the reading process and the reading curriculum. However, as an Individual Reading practice, it demands extensive teacher preparation and record keeping.

References

Bergman, J. L., and T. Schuder. 1992. Teaching at-risk students to read strategically. *Educational Leadership* 50:19–23. Provides an in-depth discussion on how the SAIL program (Students Achieving Independent Learning) impacts on low-achieving readers.

Blakely, W. P., and B. McKay. 1972. Individualized reading as part of an eclectic reading program. In *Elementary reading today: Selected articles,* edited by W. H. Miller. New York: Holt, Rinehart & Winston, 111–120. Presents the results of an investigation that lends credibility to Individualized Reading procedures.

Fader, D. N., J. Duggins, T. Finn, and E. B. McNeil. 1976. *The new hooked on books.* New York: Berkeley. Updates a discussion of a saturated book program.

Fielding, L., and C. Roller. 1992. Making difficult books accessible and easy books acceptable. *The Reading Teacher* 45:687–685. Provides guidelines for helping students become more active when participating in individual reading.

Frymier, J. November, 1992. Children who hurt, children who fail. *Phi Delta Kappa:* 257–259. Provides a brief overview of the study conducted on at-risk students and lists the instructional techniques that were successful with these students.

Greenwood, S. C. 1985. Use contracts to motivate and manage your secondary reading class. *Journal of Reading* 28:487–491. Explores how contracts, which include SSR, study skills, etc., affect student participation.

Groff, P. 1972. Helping teachers begin individualized reading. In *Elementary reading today: Selected articles,* edited by W. H. Miller. New York: Holt, Rinehart & Winston, 101–106. Reviews 12 basic questions and points of concern when planning and initiating a program of Individualized Reading.

Hunt, L. 1970. Effect of self-selection, interest, and motivation upon independent, instructional, and frustration levels. *The Reading Teacher* 24:146–151. Examines the effect of major tenets of Individualized Reading on the traditional concepts of reading levels.

Olson, W. C. 1949. *Child development.* Boston: D. C. Heath. Presents the basic principles of Individualized Reading.

Purves, A. C., L. Papa, and S. Jordan eds. 1994. *Encyclopedia of English Studies and Language Arts.* New York: National Council of Teachers of English. This encyclopedia has more than 800 annotated entries/topics that succinctly address this topic and related areas.

Sartain, H. W. 1972. Advantages and disadvantages of individualized reading. In *Individualizing reading instruction: A reader,* edited by L. A. Harris and C. B. Smith. New York: Holt, Rinehart & Winston, 86–96. Provides the pros and cons of an Individualized Reading program.

Smith, N. B. 1963. *Reading instruction for today's children.* Englewood Cliffs, NJ: Prentice-Hall, 129–162. Traces the historical development of Individualized Reading and presents examples of its use.

Veatch, J. 1978. *Reading in the elementary school,* 2d ed. New York: John Wiley and Sons. Provides the basic plans from which to establish an Individualized Reading program with particular emphasis on classroom management.

Author-Reader Cycle

Purpose

As Harste, Short, and Burke (1988) point out, authoring is a form of learning in which "the process of working with the words, paints, or gestures allows us to construct or generate meanings for ourselves as well as for others." (P. 9) The Author-Reader Cycle allows children to explore learning through print—as both readers and writers. This approach claims to give children access to authentic uses of written language for a variety of audiences in their process of learning.

Rationale

The Author-Reader Cycle is a reading and learning curricular framework that is tied to the writing process. Harste, Short, and Burke (1988) use a complex notion of authorship as it relates to learning:

Webster's Ninth New Collegiate Dictionary provides two definitions of author. The first definition is "the writer of a literary work (as a book)," but the second is more general— "one that originates or gives existence." Although the creation of written texts is certainly important, children have repeatedly shown us that authoring means much more. Authoring and literacy involve "making" meanings through any of the available communication systems (language, art, drama, etc.) to achieve personal and social goals. . . .

Current theories of cognition . . . have shown that learning is not simply a matter of transferring information from the outside world to some sort of in-head storehouse. Instead, learners must actively construct knowledge for themselves—a process that is affected by learners' current beliefs, hypotheses, interests, needs, and purposes.

In the final analysis, our interest in reading and writing is also an interest in learning. (P. 5)

Even the learning of science and mathematics is a part of authorship. The child develops or authors his or her own understandings using systems of communication. The Author-Reader Cycle takes this learning process and makes it into the basis for school curriculum:

As a curricular frame, the authoring cycle constitutes an attempt to orchestrate the how and what of teaching. By organizing curriculum around a learning cycle, participants experience, see demonstrated, and come to value how they might use literacy strategically to learn. From this perspective, authoring is a metaphor for learning, while learning is what literacy is all about. (P. 181)

While the Author-Reader Cycle resembles, in terms of the activities it includes, other literacy approaches (e.g., Whole-Language, reading/writing workshop, theme-based curriculum), this approach can be defined by what Harste, Short, and Burke (1988) would call the "deep structure" of the process:

Although [a particular teacher] handles science somewhat differently than [another teacher], the open and invitational nature of her curriculum is similar. [The teacher] understands that children do not need to engage in the same activity to have an equivalent experience. Rather than be concerned with the surface structure of lessons—whether the students are studying birds, animals, magnets, and so on—she is worried about the deep structure—whether the students are experiencing and coming to value the process of learning using the perspective of whatever discipline they are studying. (P. 188)

The Author-Reader Cycle uses literacy as an approach to learning across the content areas, based on an understanding that all knowledge is available through and represented by literacy:

A visitor to [the teacher's] room may well have difficulty knowing what phase of the authoring cycle children are in or when the reading and writing period has occurred. What they see is children reading and writing as they actively explore a topic. The authoring cycle is not perceived as something endemic to language arts, but as a general learning cycle. Children begin with what they know (life experiences), talk, sketch, read, write, listen, rethink, revise, edit, synthesize, and present. Although this is the authoring process, it is also the learning cycle. During the course of a unit of study, this cycle is engaged in over and over again. (P. 190)

While students' products may differ widely from each other, the process they use to learn is similar. Figure 1–12, from Harste, Short, and Burke (1988, 33), shows the process through which the children go even while their particular subject matters differ greatly. Finally, the authors cite several tenets on which the Author-Reader Cycle is based:

- It focuses on process, defining the language arts curriculum in terms of psycholinguistic and sociolinguistic strategies, and suggests that the content of instruction be the strategies of successful language use and learning . . .

- It views reading and writing as a disciplined creative activity that can be analyzed, described, and taught by creating supportive contexts in which the strategies of successful language use and learning can be experienced, demonstrated, and valued . . .

FIGURE 1–12.

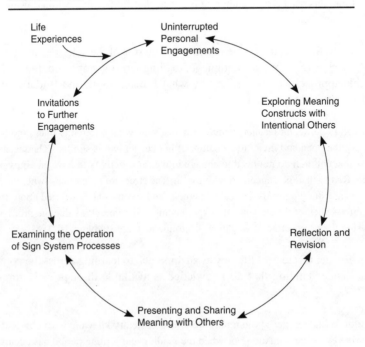

From Harste, Short, And Burke (1988, 33)

- It emphasizes that reading and writing are ways of learning and developing as well as communicating what has already been learned . . .

- It identifies cognitive universals across all language users regardless of age and posits experience rather than developmental stage as the key variable in the evolution of literacy . . .

- It suggests that in terms of what the mind does, reading and writing share much in common . . .

- It suggests that current approaches to the evaluation of a process curriculum have failed . . .

- It suggests that literacy is relative, an open potential, dependent on context of situation . . .

- It is holistic, viewing reading and writing as multimodal events and one of several systems of knowing . . .

- It highlights the functional nature of literacy both psychologically and sociologically . . .

- It teaches strategies whereby students can solve problems and learn how to learn using reading and writing as tools for learning . . .

- It stresses the inherently social nature of language and language learning . . .

- It stresses the principle that reading and writing teachers should be people who read and write with children to provide demonstrations of the strategies involved in successful written language use and learning . . .

- It sees learning as continuous and the function of curriculum as setting up the learning cycle. It suggests that teaching children the strategies involved in how to learn are the real strategies of literacy . . .

- It sees the past and future of literacy and curriculum as potentials rather than problems . . . (Harste, Short, and Burke, Pp. 208–210)

Rather than being an approach to learning literacy skills (particularly in isolation from everything else children learn), the Author-Reader Cycle is an approach to learning that employs literacy; at the same time that children use their literacies for learning, they expand their literacy strategies.

Intended Audience

The Author-Reader cycle can be used at all ages. The authors cite instances of heterogeneous groups of children with a range of interests, backgrounds, and abilities finding challenge and satisfaction with this approach to learning. In fact, the authors tend to avoid grouping children by grade or reading level.

Description of the Procedures

The Author-Reader cycle is characterized by three goals, around which all the procedures are built:

> From a language arts perspective, our first goal is to create a self-maintaining environment for authors and authorship by providing time, functional reading and writing activities, and opportunities for children to meet, learn from, and come to see themselves and their classmates as authors. A second goal is to juxtapose reading and writing so that the sense of authorship students acquire in writing is a basis for taking ownership of reading and vice versa. A third goal is to litter the environment with print so that children are provided with numerous reading and writing invitations. (P. 117)

With these goals in mind, the authors suggest certain activities that would meet these goals.

1. Environment. Both the physical classroom and the classroom schedule need to reflect the centrality of the Author-Reader Cycle. Children need to have access to plenty of good reading materials on a variety of levels; therefore it is paramount to have a good classroom library. Likewise, children need to have access to many different kinds of writing supplies—including different kinds of paper, blank books, journals, and the like. Finally, the class schedule should include regular Work Time—large blocks of time (whole mornings) on which children can depend, and during which children can work on their reading and writing.
2. Juxtaposition of Reading and Writing. The Author-Reader Cycle can be supported by numerous activities that build connections between reading and writing. Harste, Short, and Burke (1988) mention several, which appear in this book—Author's Chair, Reader's Theatre, Shared Reading, literature response activities, and so forth—as happening frequently in Author-Reader Cycle classrooms. Like the Reading-Writing workshop, the Author-Reader Cycle uses strategy lessons, tailor-made for students' current interests and concerns. Yet the Author-Reader Cycle is not limited to a particular set of activities, strategy lessons, or curriculum; to do so would be antithetical to the philosophy that undergirds this approach to literacy.
3. Invitations. "Litter the environment with print"—the basis for many of the invitations to read in the Author-Reader Cycle-based classroom. Every center—cooking, science, math—can include invitations to read. Even very young children can assist with classroom procedures that require reading. The classroom library is part of the invitation to read, as is Author's Chair—including the teacher's daily reading to children. As with reading, the writing invitations are numerous, and interconnected with reading: various kinds of journals, a classroom publishing program, pen pals, a message board for use by everyone in the class, written conversations, and theme studies across the curriculum.

Oftentimes, the work in Author-Reader Cycle classrooms takes place in the form of units of study (see theme-based curriculum), which may be initiated by the teacher or the students. Although different groups of children may study different subject matters, they tend to use a similar process. For example, students doing social studies might go through the following steps during the first four weeks of a particular theme:

FIGURE 1–13.   EXAMPLE OF READING WRITING CLASSROOM LAYOUT

Week 1: Select topic

    Interview parents
    Look for sources of information
    Read and take notes
    Keep a bibliography

Week 2: Continue reading

Interview community members
Look for other sources of information
Continue taking notes

Week 3: Continue reading and taking notes

Look through your cards
Identify central ideas
Share your central ideas with at least two other classmates
Get feedback on your ideas
Revise central ideas if needed

Week 4: Continue reading & taking notes

Look through your cards to find information that goes with your central ideas
Share the notes that go with a central idea with a classmate
Get feedback
Begin drafting this section of your report

(Harste, Short, and Burke, 1988, 189)

As can be seen in Figure 1–14, all the subject matters can be taught through the Author-Reader Cycle.

Coupled with unit-type studies the Author-Reader Cycle also includes a publishing program that emphasizes writing process. This publishing process helps children to make

FIGURE 1–14.   THE AUTHORING CYCLE

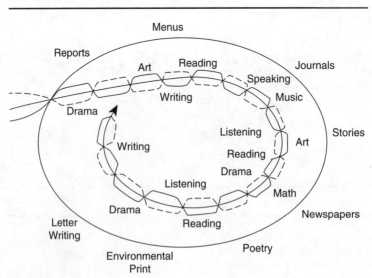

FIGURE 1–15.   THE AUTHORING CYCLE AS CURRICULAR FRAME

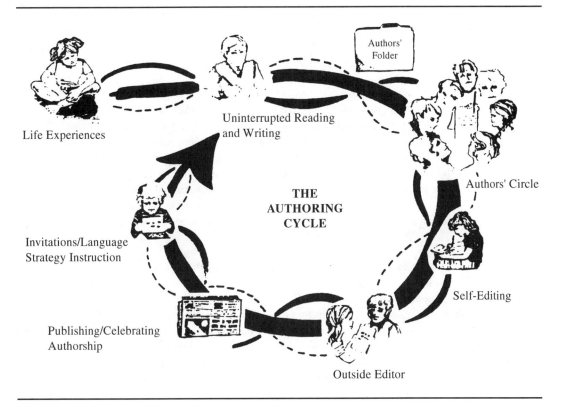

the connections between their own experiences and the experiences they have during unit study through developing their own texts.

While the publishing process of course includes written texts, the authors cite instances of a writing process-type approach being used for the creation of other materials:

> In this [Author-Reader Cycle] classroom, the teachers and children also valued texts authored in other communication systems, as demonstrated by a group of children who explored space and rockets. After looking at books and talking together, several of the children began using their knowledge of rockets to make paper rockets. All but Aaron used the same process of paper folding and gluing in their rocket constructions. While they all had used a paper cylinder for the rocket body, Aaron had devised a different way to fold and attach fins to the rocket body than the other boys. When they met together to share their "rough draft" rockets, the other boys made fun of Aaron's rocket, which looked different from theirs. Aaron, however, explained why and how he was making his rocket, and as he talked, the other boys realized that he had some good ideas. Following their Authors' Circle on the rocket constructions, the other boys made modifications in their rockets. (P. 35)

Cautions and Comments

The Author-Reader Cycle combines strategies that are well known, e.g., Author's Chair, Shared Reading, Reading-Writing Workshop, and so forth, but it does so in a way that places emphasis on the use of literacy for learning, illustrating the point that Gadamer (1976) makes about understanding:

> The understanding of a text has not begun at all as long as the text remains mute. But a text can begin to speak. . . . When it does begin to speak, however, it does not simply speak its word, always the same, in lifeless rigidity, but gives ever new answers to the person who questions it and poses ever new questions to him who answers it. To understand a text is to come to understand oneself in a kind of dialogue. This contention is confirmed by the fact that the concrete dealing with a text yields understanding only when what is said in the text begins to find expression in the interpreter's own language. Interpretation belongs to the essential unity of understanding. One must take up into himself what is said to him in such fashion that it speaks and finds an answer in the words of his own language. (P. 57)

The Author-Reader Cycle ultimately helps children to understand the texts (e.g., of the unit) through the dialogue made possible with the publishing process.

As stated above, the Author-Reader Cycle is similar to and congruent with other reading strategies mentioned in this Unit (Whole-Language, Theme-Based Units, Reading-Writing Workshop). In fact, many of the teachers mentioned in Harste, Short, and Burke (1988) began using these other strategies but then expanded to Author-Reader Cycle work as they began to approach other subject matters using literacy techniques. The main differentiation, then, between the Author-Reader Cycle and other strategies is that the emphasis in the Author-Reader Cycle is on literacy as a means for finding points of engagement between the self and the world.

Of concern to those implementing the Author-Reader Cycle is the role of the teacher. Because this framework is complex, the teacher roles become numerous and challenging, including: (1) developing a curriculum that stems from the interests of the children, (2) being an effective diagnostician, (3) responding to the individual needs of the children, and (4) being able to respond to children's diverse responses to the material.

As with other related strategies and frameworks, this framework may appear daunting to the novice. Teachers may wish to implement the Author-Reader Cycle in one part of their classroom (reading and writing are an obvious place to start) using the materials and methods for which there are many excellent resources (see the bibliographies in this book under the Theme-Based Units, Whole-Language, and Reading-Writing Workshop). As teachers become comfortable with these methods, they can expand into other subject matters as well.

It may well be difficult, as well with the Author-Reader Cycle, to ensure that students are provided with the range of opportunities for reading and writing across genres, for example, offered by more structured approaches.

One of the main strengths of the approach is that it goes beyond a statement of beliefs to a discussion of an actual practice without being overly prescriptive. Because this approach is so student-centered in philosophy, it is an ideal one to support a culturally diverse classroom. Children can be invited to read multicultural children's literature, to write about their own experiences, and to study cultures that are different from their own (see Theme Studies for further information).

Computer technology is particularly well suited to the Author-Reader Cycle. Harste, Short, and Burke (1988) mention the advantages of having a computer in the classroom for the publication process. Yet the possibilities for computers extend far beyond simple word processing capabilities. The multimedia possibilities of the computer, as pointed out by Tierney, Stowell, Desai, and Keiffer (1993), are congruent with the interconnected processes of reading and writing that comprise the Author-Reader Cycle. As computers become more prevalent in classrooms, teachers may want to invite children to explore hypertext applications, which combine image, sound, and print in innovative ways to create complex documents that can be read in different ways by different readers.

The Author-Reader Cycle uses many strategies that are familiar to teachers who run student-centered classrooms and who place a great deal of emphasis on literacy. The main difference between the Author-Reader Cycle and other approaches lies in the ideas that govern the implementation of the strategies: The Author-Reader Cycle is based on the use of literacy for learning—literacy as a means rather than as an end in itself; the literacy process as a metaphor for the learning process. Teachers who wish to implement the Author-Reader Cycle are encouraged to read Harste, Short, and Burke (1988) for the ideas on which the Author-Reader Cycle is based, and then to read the other resources mentioned below for other strategies that might be implemented in such a classroom.

References

Atwell, N. 1987. *In the middle: Writing, reading, and learning with adolescents.* Portsmouth, NH: Heinemann. Provides ways of working with adolescents; practical "mini-lessons" that might be adapted to Author-Reader Cycle.

Gadamer, H. G. 1976. *Philosophical hermeneutics.* Berkeley: University of California Press. A philosophical approach to ideas about reading.

Harste, J., K. Short, and C. Burke. 1988. *Creating classrooms for authors: The reading-writing connection.* Portsmouth, NH: Heinemann. Outlines the ideas about the Author-Reader Cycle as a learning cycle. Also contains numerous strategies for implementing the Author-Reader Cycle in the classroom.

Newman, J. (Ed.) 1985. *Whole language—Theory into use.* Portsmouth, N. H.: Heinemann. Represents a primary source for information on Whole-Language tenets and practices.

Purves, A. C., L. Papa, and S. Jordan. eds. 1994. *Encyclopedia of English Studies and Language Arts.* New York: National Council of Teachers of English. This encyclopedia has more than 800 annotated entries/topics that succinctly address this topic and related areas.

Purves, A. C., T. Rogers, and A. O. Soter. 1990. *How porcupines make love II: Teaching a response-centered literature curriculum.* New York: Longman. Response to literature activities might be adapted to the Author-Reader Cycle approach.

Tierney, R. J., L. Stowell, L. Desai, and R. Keiffer. 1993. New Possibilities for Literature Teaching and Technology. In *Exploring texts: The role of discussion and writing in the teaching and learning of literature,* edited by G. E. Newell and R. K. Durst. Discusses a multimedia approach to a social studies-type unit.

Uninterrupted Sustained Silent Reading

Purpose

Generally recognized objectives of Uninterrupted Sustained Silent Reading (USSR) are: (1) to provide students with a quiet time to practice their silent reading, (2) to provide students with models of good silent reading behavior, and (3) to increase students' abilities to sustain silent reading for longer periods of time.

Rationale

Much time is spent teaching students *how* to read; however, USSR is tied to the notion that classroom teachers should provide students with a model for reading or the opportunity to read materials for pleasure.

According to McCracken and McCracken (1978), this program provides students the following messages:

- Reading books is important
- Reading is something anyone can do
- Reading is communicating with an author
- Books are meant to be read in large sections
- Children are capable of sustained thoughts
- The teacher believes that the pupils are comprehending (because he or she doesn't bother to check)
- The teacher trusts the children to decide when something is well written, when something important has been read (because the teacher expects pupils to share after USSR). (P. 408)

In a similar vein, Sadoski (1984) suggests that USSR provides students the opportunity to practice the art of reading; to become actively involved in the reading act with materials of their own choosing, and to become better readers by reading and seeing others read.

Intended Audience

Uninterrupted Sustained Silent Reading is appropriate for students at kindergarten levels through senior high school. College and adult reading programs also could profit from the use of the technique. The technique may be used by an elementary teacher with a self-contained classroom, by a content teacher in a departmentalized program, or by a total school staff during a predetermined period of the school day (Ganz and Theofield, 1974).

Description of the Procedure

USSR contains three vital elements:

1. Preparation
2. The reading period
3. Follow-up

1. *Preparation*   Perhaps the key to the success of a USSR program is this vital first step. Students should understand what they are going to be doing during the activity, why it is important, and how it will be carried out.

The idea of USSR should be discussed with students several days in advance of the first reading session. The emphasis at this stage should be on the fact that the students will be allowed to select whatever reading material they desire to read during this period. Although students should be encouraged to bring their favorite reading material to class for USSR sessions, several students predictably will forget on occasion; therefore, the teacher should collect a variety of reading materials that will remain in the classroom and can be used during USSR sessions. The collection should be changed occasionally to provide a variety of offerings.

Teachers also should be sure to inform their administrator(s) and colleagues of what they are doing and should ask them not to interrupt unless an emergency arises.

It is essential that all students in the class understand the rules of USSR. Presentation of the rules a day or two before the start of USSR allows students and teachers to discuss why these particular regulations are necessary. It is suggested that the rules be reviewed just prior to the first USSR session. The three cardinal rules of USSR are:

a. *Everybody reads.* Both students and teacher will read something of their own choosing. Completing homework assignments, grading papers, and similar activities are discouraged. The reading should be for the pleasure of the reader.
b. *There are to be no interruptions during USSR.* The word *uninterrupted* is an essential part of the technique. Interruptions result in loss of comprehension and loss of interest by many students; therefore, questions and comments should be held until the silent reading period has concluded.
c. *No one will be asked to report what they have read.* It is essential that students feel that this is a period of free reading, with the emphasis on reading for enjoyment.

2. *The Reading Period*   The USSR period begins as soon as the students have been given a sufficient amount of time to select their reading materials and the teacher has reviewed the rules briefly. Following the first session, it may be necessary only occasionally to remind the students of the rules.

a. *Setting the time.* The time length of the very first USSR session should be such that the majority of the students within the class can easily sustain their silent reading. For the lower grades, this may mean three to five minutes; for upper elementary grades, five to ten minutes; and for secondary classrooms, ten to fifteen minutes. It is probably better initially to underestimate students' ability to sustain silent reading, since one of the goals of USSR is to increase gradually the time devoted to the activity. Depending on the ability and interest levels of the students, reasonable goals might be fifteen to twenty minutes for primary level classrooms; twenty to thirty minutes for the middle grades; and thirty minutes for high school classes. These times should be considered only as guidelines.

b. *Timing USSR.* Most teachers have found that a kitchen timer or an alarm clock works best as the timing device for USSR sessions. The timer should be set for the agreed-upon time and then placed in such a position that students are unable to see the face of the device. This procedure solves the problem of the "clock watchers" within a classroom. For this same reason, a large classroom clock should not be used as the timing device. Another advantage of the alarm clock or kitchen timer is that it provides a definite end to the USSR session. The sound of an alarm clock leaves no doubt that the reading period has come to an end, and that it is time to move on to other activities.

c. *The role of the teacher.* During the USSR period, the teacher is doing exactly what all the students in the class are doing—reading for pleasure. The teacher has the very important role of showing good, sustained silent reading behavior. For some students in the classroom, this may be the first opportunity to observe an adult who is reading for pure enjoyment.

It is important to keep this one activity in mind. There are a number of things that a teacher should not do during USSR. The class instructor should not correct papers, plan lessons, take attendance, or perform similar school-related activities. By doing this type of activity, teachers are, in effect, saying to students, "Reading is an important activity for you, but not for me." Likewise, the teacher should not move around the classroom to seek out students who are not reading or those who are potential troublemakers. Besides not serving as an adequate model, a teacher in the monitoring role becomes a potential "interrupter" of the reading process.

d. *Interruptions during USSR.* It is not unusual for interruptions to occur occasionally, especially in the initial phase of using the procedure in the classroom. Interruptions that cause the classroom teacher and a large number of students to look up from their reading should generally result in an end to the reading period for that day. However, persons guilty of interrupting should not be reprimanded; rather, the classroom teacher may simply say, "I'm sorry, but that concludes our USSR session for today. Please put your reading material away and we will proceed with our next lesson." The instructor should be prepared to move quickly to the next scheduled activity without providing the individual who interrupted with the attention that the student might be seeking. The activity immediately following the USSR also should not appear to be arranged as a means of punishment, i.e., tests and other equally unpopular activities are best scheduled at other times.

After the habit of silent reading has been firmly established, minor and unintentional interruptions may be handled smoothly without resulting in an end to the reading session. In these situations, the teacher might respond in this manner: "I hope that the interruption did not cause you to completely lose your train of thought. Do you think you can return to your reading without any problems?" If most students respond affirmatively, then the teacher provides a model by returning immediately to reading. Very minor disturbances that cause the instructors and only one or two students to look up from their reading should be ignored. After quickly evaluating the situation, the teacher should return immediately to the reading. This action has the effect of saying, "No problem. Let's continue our reading."

e. *Concluding the reading period.* USSR ends with the sound of the timer. The instructor should be prepared to move on to the next scheduled activity. Occasionally, teachers may provide students a few additional minutes of reading time. This "buffer" period allows students an opportunity to read until a more appropriate stopping point is reached.

3. *Follow-up* McCracken (1971) suggested that after the first week of USSR, the teacher may begin to think of ways to encourage sharing what has been read during the silent reading sessions. The teacher can set an example by making a brief comment about interesting ideas the students have read, by keeping a log of the books and the number of pages read, and by similar actions that show a sincere interest in the reading act. These sharing activities can result in greater student interest in reading.

It must be emphasized that such sharing activities should not begin until after the USSR activity has been firmly established. If the teacher begins to prompt students to share too early in the beginning sessions, USSR might deteriorate into something other than reading for enjoyment.

After at least six weeks of implementation, it is recommended by Halpern (1981) to administer the USSR survey to students. This survey (see Figure 1–16) is a tool that provides "teachers with information on student's reactions about USSR which can be used to remedy weaknesses and/or promote continuation of USSR" (Pp. 273–275).

Cautions and Comments

Although USSR is a simple technique and can easily be implemented in classrooms at any level, it is very difficult to evaluate. It should not be surprising that research studies, in which the influence of USSR upon achievement and attitude has been studied, have yielded quite mixed results. For instance, this program provides the following strengths

- Interest in reading
- Awareness of a variety of books
- Feelings of community within a classroom
- Awareness of the reading program and its purpose
- Information to assist in school or leisure time activities
- Appreciation of reading, which affords pleasurable experiences when engaged with books
- Improvement in writing as a result of exposure to wide reading

FIGURE 1–16. STUDENT ATTITUDE SURVEY ON UNINTERRUPTED SUSTAINED SILENT READING

This attitude survey is an attempt to determine students' feelings toward USSR. This will help your teachers decide if the USSR program should be changed and improved on in any way. On this first page you will be asked to answer a few general questions. On the other pages you will be asked to respond to statements of opinion on the different parts of the USSR program. Read the instructions carefully before responding to the statements.

General Questions

1. What grade are you in? _____

2. When did you start USSR in class?

   year _____ month _____

3. How many days a week do you do USSR? _____

4. How long is each USSR session? _____

5. How much time do you spend each day after school reading things other than school-books? _____

6. Are you male?   _____

   female?   _____

ATTITUDE SURVEY ON USSR DIRECTIONS

You are being asked to respond to a number of statements. Seven choices are given for each statement. The choices range from *disagree very strongly* to *agree very strongly.* The seven choices are:

1	2	3	4	5	6	7
	disagree				agree	
very strongly	slightly		I don't care	slightly		very strongly

Following each statement you will see a line of numbers. These seven numbers correspond to the above numbered line. Please circle the number that best describes your feelings about each of the statements. Remember that you may choose any one of the seven numbers.

Two examples are provided.

If there are any difficulties in answering this survey, please ask your teacher for help.

1	2	3	4	5	6	7
very strongly disagree	disagree strongly	disagree slightly	I don't care	agree slightly	agree strongly	agree very strongly

FIGURE 1–16. *(Continued)*

EXAMPLES

Every student should
be give free milk
at lunch time.

    1   2   3   4   5   6   7

Christmas holidays should
be longer.

    1   2   3   4   5   6   7

ATTITUDE SURVEY ON USSR

1) I think that our teacher should give us marks for reading during USSR.

    1   2   3   4   5   6   7

2) I think that students who disturb others during USSR ought to be punished by the teacher.

    1   2   3   4   5   6   7

3) I feel it is difficult to find interesting books to read during USSR.

    1   2   3   4   5   6   7

4) I would like to have a stack of comics and/or magazines in the classroom that could be used during USSR.

    1   2   3   4   5   6   7

5) I find myself reading books after school that I started during USSR.

    1   2   3   4   5   6   7

6) I used to read after school even before we started USSR.

    1   2   3   4   5   6   7

7) When our class does USSR, noise from other students in our class stops me from reading.

    1   2   3   4   5   6   7

8) I find that when we are doing USSR, noise from outside the classroom stops me from reading.

    1   2   3   4   5   6   7

9) I would read my own books after school even if we didn't have USSR during schooltime.

    1   2   3   4   5   6   7

10) I feel that USSR is a good time to try different kinds of books to see if I like them and want to finish them.

    1   2   3   4   5   6   7

10a) I think USSR is a worthwhile activity and I am pleased that our class does it.

    1   2   3   4   5   6   7

FIGURE 1–16. *(Continued)*

DIRECTIONS: Please circle either *yes* or *no* for the following statements. An example is provided. If there are any difficulties in answering this section of this survey, please ask your teacher for help.

EXAMPLE: My after-school activities are:

baby-sitting	yes	no
TV watching	yes	no
school sports	yes	no
music lessons	yes	no
homework	yes	no
kite flying	yes	no

ATTITUDE SURVEY ON USSR

11) I think that we ought to do USSR

at the time of day we now have it	yes	no
at a different time	yes	no
at different times during the day	yes	no

12) Having a book ready for USSR

is always a problem	yes	no
is sometimes a problem	yes	no
is not a problem	yes	no

13) I get my books for USSR from

a friend	yes	no
the school library	yes	no
teacher recommends	yes	no
home	yes	no
classroom library	yes	no
bookstore	yes	no
other places/people	yes	no

if yes, list _____

_____

FIGURE 1–16. *(Continued)*

(Answer *either* number 14 *or* number 15)

14) If your parents know that you do USSR, are they:

pleased that you do USSR	yes	no
of the opinion that USSR is a waste of school time	yes	no
trying to have your family do USSR together	yes	no
interested in finding out more about USSR	yes	no

15) If your parents don't know that you do USSR, should

they be told what USSR is	yes	no
they be told that you do USSR	yes	no

16) During USSR I would prefer that my teacher

read a book	yes	no
spend the time making sure that everyone in class reads	yes	no
leave the room	yes	no

17) During USSR does your teacher

stop USSR at first interruption	yes	no
mark papers, talk to others	yes	no
see that students read	yes	no
read a book	yes	no

18) I think that the amount of time that our class spends on USSR each day is:

too long	yes	no
too short	yes	no
just right	yes	no
a waste of school time	yes	no

Possible negative aspects of this procedure are:

- Lack of teacher and/or administrator modeling, due to attitudes
- Provisions not made for students lacking sufficient materials
- Classroom materials not meeting students' needs
- Disruptions within the classroom or in the hallways
- Lack of longitudinal data
- Inadequate planning and availability of materials
- Older students' attitudes differ greatly from those of younger students

Results from studies on special populations indicate that careful planning and implementation are needed in order for this procedure to be successful. Grubaugh (1986) states that, "potential poorer readers must be carefully matched with materials. If these students aren't able to engage in silent reading, adjustments should consist of small groups reading aloud" (P. 170) Allington (1975) expands this belief by stating that "remedial readers must have unlimited opportunities for reading contextual material rather than skill instruction." It is imperative that "they be given time to engage themselves with stories and books in order to become fluent readers." (P. 263) Gutkin (1990) proclaims that kindergarten children need time for book perusal and "reading." She has instituted a sustained loud reading (SLR) time, which encourages students to partner-read and share books that fascinate them. She states, "When I saw and heard the excitement from my students, I decided that, at this stage in my students' careers, silence would be more of an obstacle than a relaxing tool to enhance their relationships with books" (P. 490).

Goostree (1981) investigated elementary gifted children's attitudes toward reading. This inquiry revealed that gifted children had a higher positive reading attitude than their fellow students, but more revealing was the emergence of data on gender differences. Results indicated that "females show more positive reading attitudes than males" (P. 287). These findings are consistent with results from Parker and Paradis (1986) in which "girls at every grade level demonstrated more positive attitudes toward reading than boys in all grades but sixth. The greatest gender differences favoring females were noted in grades two, four, and five" (P. 287).

Despite the lack of consistency in data results, this program should not be overlooked. The strategy provides teachers a manageable procedure for increasing reading time. Furthermore, the teacher, by the very act of reading, is communicating the *value* of reading to the students. Conversely, any lack of interest or enthusiasm by the teacher can result in a similar reaction by the students.

Indeed, teachers are likely to be instrumental in the success of this program. They can promote positive attitudes toward and achievement in reading by: (a) planning reading activities children like, (b) providing large quantities and a variety of materials that are related to children's interests and needs; (c) promoting regular intervals of recreational and quiet reading within the school schedule; (d) demonstrating and modeling a personal valuing of reading; (e) providing a pleasant, relaxed classroom atmosphere; (f) reducing pressure to report on what was read, and (g) providing opportunities for sharing (Langford and Allen, 1983, 195). A way for teachers to promote student interest and motivation in this activity is by creating a catchy title through acronyms. Those most commonly used include

- SQUIRT (Silent, quiet, uninterrupted, individualized reading time)
- DEAR (Drop everything and read)
- DEER (Drop everything else—read)
- OTTER (Our time to enjoy reading)

USSR can be extended to the home setting by parents. Home Sustained Silent Reading (HSSR) can be used to "promote a love for reading that extends into the home while providing additional support for children and a common goal for home and school" (Demos, 1986, 263). When participating in HSSR, Demos and Fitzpatrick suggest that parents (a) "foster an interest in reading by creating an environment that places a high priority on the printed word" (Fitzpatrick, 1982, 50), (b) "support the development of attitudes and habits conducive to lifelong learning and reading for enjoyment, (c) extend reading opportunities outside the school environment, and (d) provide additional practice and application of school learning" (Demos, 1986, 263–364).

References

Allington, R. 1975. Approaches to reading and writing. *Language Arts* 52:813–815. Describes approaches to silent reading and the importance of self-selecting materials.

Benedict, G. 1982. Making reading a habit for students. *Reading Improvement* 19, 1:48–53. Reports how a school district developed student reading habits through USSR and parent program.

Berglund, R. L., and J. L. Johns. 1983. Primer on uninterrupted sustained silent reading. *The Reading Teacher* 36:534–539. Discusses in "ins" and "outs" of implementing USSR.

Clary, L. M. 1988. Helping parents help their children. *Reading Horizons* 28:172–177. Describes techniques parents can utilize at home to increase student's reading attitude and achievement.

Demos, E. S. 1986. Parents, schools, and HSSR. *Reading Horizons* 26, 4:262–265. Presents a model for parents when designing a home sustained silent reading program.

Dwyer, E. J., and V. Reed. 1989. Effects of sustained silent reading on attitudes toward reading. *Reading Horizons* 29:283–293. Describes a study that investigates students' reading achievement and attitudes.

Evans, H. M., and J. C. Towner. 1975. Sustained silent reading: Does it increase skills? *The Reading Teacher* 29:155–156. Describes a study comparing the use of USSR with the use of basal supplements.

Fitzpatrick, K. 1992. Attention parents! Your preschool child and reading. *Reading Improvement* 19:50–53. Outlines techniques parents can utilize when working with their preschooler at home.

Gambrell, L. B. 1978. Getting started with sustained silent reading and keeping it going. *The Reading Teacher* 32:328–331. Discusses preparation for and management of the USSR.

Ganz, P., and M. B. Theofield. 1974. Suggestions for starting USSR. *Journal of Reading* 17:614–616. Provides recommendations for initiating a USSR program on a schoolwide basis.

Goostree, R. C. 1981. *A study of reading interests and attitudes of 4th, 5th, and 6th grade gifted children in Missouri.* MA Thesis, Southwest Missouri State University. A study depicting the reading interests and attitudes of upper elementary gifted students.

Grubaugh, S. 1986. Initiating sustained silent reading in your school *Clearing House* 60:169–174. Summarizes the principles of a USSR program and how a school can plan and successfully implement this program.

Gutkin, R. J. 1990. Sustained —— reading. *Language Arts* 67:490–491. Recounts a kindergarten teacher's experience with USSR and its effectiveness for her learning.

Halpern, H. 1981. An attitude survey of uninterrupted sustained silent reading. *Reading Horizons* 21:272–279. An instructional tool to be used with students to "determine their attitudes toward silent reading." P. 276 The survey and description of its use are included.

Hunt, L. C. 1971. Six steps to the individualized reading program (IRP). *Elementary English* 48:27–32. Describes the intent and procedures for implementing USSR.

Kaisen, J. 1987. SSR/Booktime: Kindergarten and first grade sustained silent reading. *The Reading Teacher* 40:532–537. Modifies SSR for use in kindergarten and the first grade.

Langford, J., and E. G. Allen. 1983. The effects of U. S. S. R. on students' attitudes and achievement. *Reading Horizons* 23:194–200. A study depicting the attitudes and achievement of fifth and sixth graders participating in a USSR program.

McCracken, R. A. 1971. Initiating sustained silent reading. *Journal of Reading* 14:521–524, 582–583. Recommends six rules teachers must follow to implement USSR successfully.

McCracken, R. A., and M. J. McCracken. 1972. *Reading is only the tiger's tail.* San Rafael, CA: Leswing Press. Provides recommendations for initiating a USSR program.

——. 1978. Modeling is the key to sustained silent reading. *The Reading Teacher* 31:406–408. Describes how and what a teacher does during and after silent reading; also defines what students do.

Moore, J. C., C. J. Jones, and D.C. Miller. 1980. What we know after a decade of sustained silent reading. *The Reading Teacher* 33:455–450. Reviews the research on USSR.

Morrow, L. M., and C. S. Weinstein, 1986. Encouraging voluntary reading: The impact of a literature program on children's use of library centers. *Reading Research Quarterly* 21:330–345. Reports a study that examined whether children's voluntary use of library centers and attitudes toward reading could be enhanced by involvement in a literature program emphasizing enjoyment in books.

Parker, A., and E. Paradis. 1986. Attitude development toward reading in grades one through six. *Journal of Educational Research* 79:313–315. A study discussing reading attitudes relating to gender and grade level.

Purves, A. C., L. Papa, and S. Jordan, eds. 1994. *Encyclopedia of English studies and language arts.* New York: National Council of Teachers of English. An excellent resource that contains an extensive collection of more than 800 annotated entries/topics in English Studies and Language Arts.

Sadoski, M. C. 1984. SSR, accountability, and effective reading instruction *Reading Horizons* 24:119–123. Reviews research on USSR.

Schaudt, B. A. 1983. Another look at sustained silent reading. *The Reading Teacher* 36:934–936. Reviews research studies and guidelines suggested for implementation of USSR.

Wiesendanger, K. D., and E. D. Birlem. 1984. The effectiveness of SSR: An overview of the research. *Reading Horizons* 24:197–201. Provides an overview of USSR research.

Shared Book Experience ▪

Purpose

Shared Book Experience is an attempt to adapt the principles of early book experiences between parent and child to the classroom and to refine the procedures to be a very powerful system of learning. As described by David Doake and Donald Holdaway, Shared Book Experience is intended as a means of affording groups of students early reading experiences that are intimate and that dovetail with other language activities.

Rationale

Shared Book Experience began in New Zealand in an attempt to unite the language learning experiences of students by shifting to the center of early reading experiences "the enjoyment of a rich, open literature of favorite stories, poems and songs." (Park 1982) Holdaway (1979), who has been one of the major advocates of this approach, has suggested that the model underlying the Shared Book Experience has its roots in the same developmental tenets of learning spoken language and acquiring other learnings. He suggests, for example, that Shared Book Experience has its basis in learning experiences similar to the bedtime story situation. Just as it is important for a bedtime story to be enjoyable, interesting, and presented in relaxed circumstances, so Holdaway argues that stories should be introduced to classes in a relaxed, nonthreatening, and motivating setting. Similarly, the read-it-again phenomenon, which is a characteristic of bedtime stories, is integral to maximizing the utility of stories. In particular, stories that students look forward to rereading can be used: (1) as independent reading material, even if children role-play as readers, and (2) to focus the reader's attention on certain aspects of the text; for example, words and predictable features of language.

The major tools of the Shared Book Experience are what might be considered oversized books. These books are intended to be at the center of the reading and writing program. They serve two basic functions: They take advantage of good literature, and they capitalize upon the social dynamics of a classroom. Indeed, the initial name for Shared Book Experience was "cooperative reading." The rationale behind the enlarged text is, as the New Zealand Department of Education has suggested:

> When a teacher is working with an enlarged text . . . the right climate and the right auditory and visual conditions exist for effective skills teaching. The enlargement of print enables precise, accurate attention to be focussed on word and every letter detail. (P. 3)

As the above comments suggest, Shared Book Experience is not seen as separate from other aspects of the reading and writing program. Doake (1985) and Holdaway (1979) have viewed the use of Shared Book Experience as working hand in hand with a language experience approach and as a precursor to individualized reading. In Figure 1–17 Holdaway has depicted how the Shared Book Experience might work in conjunction with other activities. Apart from this general depiction of the interrelationships, Holdaway has discussed at length a number of reading and writing activities that might use the raw material of the books as their base.

FIGURE 1–17.   THE CYCLE OF SUCCESS IN SHARED BOOK EXPERIENCE

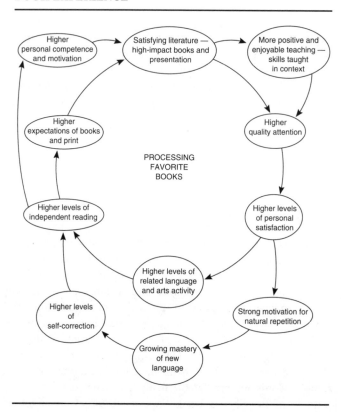

Holdaway has claimed that there are innumerable benefits that might be accrued from the use of the Shared Book Experience. His suggestion of the benefits and their cyclic nature are presented in Figure 1–18. At the heart of his advocacy of the Shared Book Experience is his belief, as he has stated, that:

> Gathered around a book as a natural, sharing community children learn more from participation than from direct instruction: they learn from the teacher's model, from their own sensible involvement, and from each other, without any sense of competition or pressure. They also learn from judicious instruction which is more intelligible because of its real and obvious purposes. (Park 1982, 819)

Slaughter (1993) suggests that the importance of this technique "is its sequencing of instruction. Children first become familiar with an entire story; teachers then use this familiarity to help students attend gradually to smaller segments of text—sentences first, then phrases and words within sentences, and finally letters within words." (P. 7)

FIGURE 1–18.　BALANCING APPROACHES AND MATERIALS

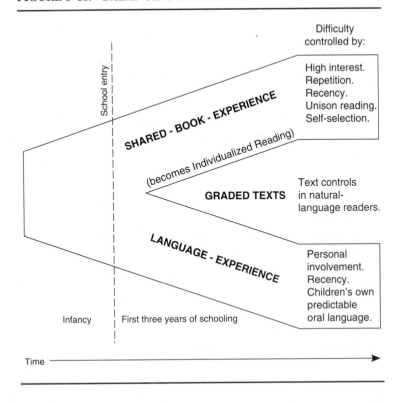

Shared Book Experiences enable children to "become readers competent in themselves and their developing abilities, enjoy predictable stories, participate in meaningful, goal-directed activities, develop a sense of belonging within the classroom community, never experience a feeling of failure since reading is encouraged—never demanded— therefore, creating an atmosphere conducive to learning" (Slaughter, 1993, 12).

Strickland and Morrow (1989) maintain that reading to young children "increases their interest in books and in learning to read. It enhances their background information and sense of story structure, and familiarizes them with differences between written and oral language." They contend that "reading to children helps them understand how print functions and how it is used. Through this social interaction, they learn early book strategies such as book handling, directionality, recognizing story structure, and the concept of authorship." (P. 322) Carger (1993) suggests that "the use of engaging and motivating children's literature can offer second language readers an exciting entrance into second language literacy by:

- Reading books portraying familiar faces and events to which children can link their own schemata makes comprehension easier and school less threatening

- Providing them with a basis for meaningful communication as they share reactions to stories

- Offering natural opportunities for generating language in reacting to and retelling stories with puppets or other props (P. 543)

- These storybook readings, retellings, and pretend readings of favorite storybooks afford second language children the opportunity to construct language creatively within a comfortable, meaning-centered activity.

- By participating in storybook activities, second language learners can "communicate their reactions and interpretation connected with the world they encountered without barriers" (P. 547).

Intended Audience

A Shared Book Experience approach can be used in almost any situation when the teacher wants to focus a group's attention on a single text. As described by Holdaway (1979), it is most suited to use in preschools or the first grade, but can be extended to language-delayed children and children with learning disabilities and effectively implemented in middle and high school classrooms.

Description of the Procedures

The Shared Book Experience centers around the use of enlarged books or overheads of good quality that are predictable stories and that can be presented to a class or group of students. These enlarged copies of different books are intended to be sufficiently interesting and predictable to engage young readers in anticipating what will happen in the story and in participating whenever selected words or phrases are repeated. As the story is read aloud to the children, the teacher will enlist the use of a pointer to ensure the children follow along. After reading, students are given language extension experiences and time to read independently either the new story or one of their previous favorites (Figure 1–19). "Little books" or small versions might be made available along with listening stations so that children who cannot handle the story or who just wanted to listen will be able to follow along.

For instance, a class that has been involved in reading a big book copy of "The Three Billy Goats Gruff" might be involved in dramatizing the story and in choral reading. Also they might choose to learn about goats or write their own story based upon this tale. The stories that the class generate might be published and used as further reading material for the class. In essence, the story serves as the stimulus for other literacy learnings. A typical Shared Book Experience involves the following activities:

1. *Tuning in*   The enjoyment of poetry and song. Here the students are given opportunities to participate in and enjoy singing or reading along with the class.

2. *Rereading of a favorite story*   If possible, students are encouraged to make predictions and read along with the story. Sometimes children can direct the reading.

**FIGURE 1–19. CHILDREN ENJOYING SHARED BOOK
EXPERIENCE DURING INDEPENDENT TIME**

3. *Learning about print and about language*   This entails what is termed functional skills teaching and innovation. Functional skills teaching includes developing comprehension skills, listening skills, learning conventions such as left to right and reference labels, prediction, confirmation and self-correction, sight vocabulary, auditory discrimination, letter-sound associations, letter names, punctuation, and intonation patterns. For this purpose, masks might be used to cover parts of words, phrases, sentences, or lines from a story as a way of focusing students' attention on elements of the print. At other times, it might entail using windows to highlight words or other activities (Figure 1–20).

Innovation is the creation of a new statement based on a familiar pattern or theme. At the simplest level, it might involve changing the name of a character in a story. At other times, it might involve changing a number of different words in the context of sentences. For example, it might involve an activity similar to the following:

FIGURE 1–20. FOLLOW-UP ACTIVITY INVOLVING WORD MASKING

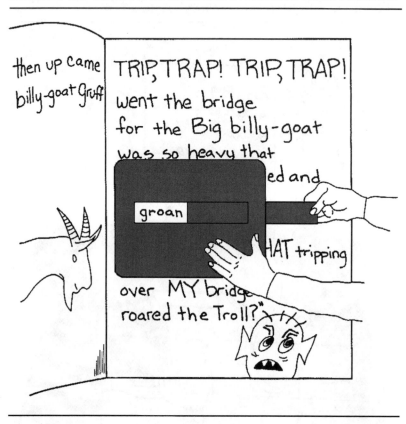

Additional activities that can be part of a shared book experience are:

1. Introduction of a new story

2. Independent reading of favorite stories

3. Expressive activities arising from the literature such as writing, dramatization, art, creative movement, etc.

As Holdaway (Park, 1982) says, the choice of material, especially the material that is enlarged, must be very carefully selected. It must be able to grip students, have a good plot, be predictable, include interesting pictures, and, if possible, have repetitive elements, patterns, and maybe rhyme.

After students develop some security with these materials, Holdaway suggests that teachers might include among the independent reading materials some of the graded readers, assuming that they are not overly stilted.

McTeague (1992), in advocating the use of shared reading activities with older learners, suggest three strategies: reading response journals, listening logs, and guiding book talks. The *Reading response journal* is "a notebook or writing folder in which students record a measure of their enjoyment of a book they have chosen for silent reading under the guidance of the teacher. They record their personal responses to the reading experience." (P. 15) *Listening logs* are used "as a response to the teacher's daily reading aloud from a literary work not otherwise available to the students." This activity enables the teacher to "deepen the authentic and personal response of every student by guiding each one to wider reading and more reflective writing" (P. 17). McTeague (1992) poses the following as potential questions while listening:

- What's going on in your mind?
- What pictures occur in your head?
- What feelings do you experience?
- What do you expect to happen?
- What questions occur to you?
- What are you thinking about? (P. 17)

Guiding student book talks, according to Chambers (1985), is a technique that enables students to explore a text as a whole class activity by listing their likes, dislikes, confusions and emerging patterns found in the text. Chambers (1985) recommends teachers to adhere to the following points when implementing this approach:

- Process can be used with whole class or small group
- The teacher's role is to guide students and to facilitate the discussion
- Students need and should feel ownership in the discussion
- Process should be a shared discovery that leads the group or class to deeper levels of understanding, interpretation, and appraisal. (P. 20)

Cautions and Comments

The Shared Book Experience has met with a great deal of success in New Zealand, Australia, Canada, and now in the United States. Holdaway warns, however, that the big books that are such an integral part of the approach are not panaceas and can be easily misused. He warns that the Shared Book Experience should not be viewed as a license to enlarge just any story. He emphasizes, as do others, that careful selection of interesting and predictable story material is essential.

Other problems that may emerge with the use of the Shared Book Experience may be inherent in the approach itself. The procedure requires a teacher who is willing to explore story readings with his or her students and a view of learning to read that is more

Whole-Language than piecemeal. It is important to realize that students learn reading not by word mastery or skill mastery.

In recent years the use of Shared Reading has become widespread. It has come to be viewed as the appropriate way to introduce reading to children and analogous in some ways to invented spelling. Just as invented spellings offer the young writer with rudimentary mechanical skills a way to write, so shared reading affords a reader involvement in reading. What seems key is the license big books offer with respect to moving away from vocabulary control and the view that children must master a set use of words prior to being able to read.

Coombs's (1987) findings revealed that average and below-average children exposed to big books were more attentive, enthusiastic, gave richer retellings of the stories, and recalled story elements more readily when Shared Book Experiences were used. She recommends that "at-risk readers should receive extended instruction with this approach . . . as they begin to develop concepts about the reading process and its purposes" (Slaughter, 7).

This approach is flexible in that it can be implemented as a comprehensive approach unto itself, or it can supplement the contemporary reading program. According to Slaughter (1993), the Shared Book Experience is "comprehensive, flexible, imaginative, stimulating, and provides teachers with an ideal basis for guiding children in their acquisition and development of literacy" (P. 14).

References

Butler, A. Not dated. *Shared book experiences.* Crystal Lake, IL: Rigby. Represents a straightforward guide to the use of big books.

Carger, C. L. 1993. Louie comes to life: Pretend reading with second language emergent readers. *Language Arts* 70:542–547. A research study describing the experiences of second language learners participating in a literature-rich environment.

Chambers, A. 1984. *Introducing books to children.* London: Heinemann. Provides a description of how to plan and implement guided book talks with students.

Coombs, M. 1987. Modeling the reading process with enlarged texts. *The Reading Teacher* 40:422–426. Describes how teachers can utilize enlarged texts to enhance children's reading development.

Doake, D. B. 1979, May. *Book experience and emergent reading behavior.* Paper presented at the International Reading Association, At-

lanta. Describes study of Shared Book Experience.

———. 1985. Reading-like behavior: Its role in learning to read. In *Observing the language learner,* edited by A. M. Jaggar and M. T. Smith-Burke. Newark, DE: International Reading Association/NCTE. Describes how Shared Book Experiences contribute to learning to read.

Handel, R. D. 1992. The partnership for family reading: Benefits for families and schools. *The Reading Teacher* 46:116–126. Describes how the family literacy projects were started in Newark, NJ, and the importance of family-school collaboration.

Harste, J., K. Short, and C. Burke. 1988. *Creating classrooms for authors.* Portsmouth, NH: Heinemann. Explores the use of shared reading in the classroom.

Heald-Taylor, B. G. 1987. Big books. In *Ideas with insights: Language arts K-6,* edited by D.

Watson. Urbana, IL: National Council of Teachers of English. Offers practical suggestions for using big books.

Holdaway, D. 1979. *Foundations of literacy.* Sydney: Ashton-Scholastic. Presents a thorough discussion of the Shared Book Experience, including theoretical rationale, examples from classrooms, and information pertaining to how the approach relates to the total school literacy program.

Lynch, P. 1986. *Using big books and predictable books.* Richmond Hill, Ontario: Scholastic-TAB. Provides practical suggestions for using big books and predictable books in the classroom.

Martinez, M. G., and W. H. Teale. Classroom storybook reading: The creation of texts and learning opportunities. *Theory into Practice* 28:126–135. An analysis of current research on storybook reading and the implications for classroom use.

McTeague, F. 1992. *Shared reading in the middle and high school years.* Portsmouth, NH: Heinemann. Provides an overview of how shared reading and collaboration between teachers and students can be implemented with older readers.

New Zealand Department of Education. 1978a. *Shared book experience procedures, Unit 6, Early reading inservice course.* Wellington: E. C. Keating, Government Printer. Provides an overview of the approach, including suggestions for activities, material, and slides demonstrating the approach.

———. 1978b. *Suggestions for making enlarged books, Early reading inservice course.* Wellington: Department of Education. Presents graphically procedures for enlarging books, including illustrations, print, choice of paper, assembling and storage.

Park, B. 1982. The big book trend—A discussion with Don Holdaway. *Language Arts* 59:815–821. Presents an interview with Donald Holdaway in which the Shared Book Experience is thoroughly discussed.

Peetoom, A. 1986. *Shared reading: Safe risks with whole books.* Richmond Hill, Ont.: Scholastic-TAB. Offers suggestions for using big books with less confident readers.

Purves, A. C., L. Papa, and S. Jordan, eds. 1994. *Encyclopedia of English studies and language arts.* New York: National Council of Teachers of English. An excellent resource that contains an extensive collection of more than 800 annotated entries/topics in English Studies and Language Arts.

Slaughter, J. P. 1993. *Beyond storybooks: Young children and the shared book experience.* Newark, DE: The International Reading Association. An excellent resource for teachers wanting to incorporate shared reading experiences into their elementary classrooms. Samples of activities, book lists, and teaching ideas are also included.

Strickland, D. S., and L. M. Morrow. 1989. Interactive experiences with storybook reading. *The Reading Teacher. 42,* 322–333. Provides an overview of the importance of reading to young children and on early reading development.

———. 1990. Storybook reading: A bridge to literary language. *The Reading Teacher* 44: 264–268. A research study focusing on the value of storybook reading with Arab kindergartners.

Trachtenburg, P., and A. Ferruggia. 1989. Big books from little voices: Reaching high risk beginning readers. *The Reading Teacher* 42:284–289. Discusses the positive aspects of utilizing big books in a primary classroom for beginning readers.

Watson, D., and P. Crowley. 1987. How can we implement a whole-language approach? In *Reading process and practice,* edited by C. Weaver, Portsmouth, NH: Heinemann. Offers an extended discussion of big books in conjunction with describing Whole-Language.

Yamada, Y. 1983. How much can children learn from a single book? *The Reading Teacher* 36:880–883. A research study describing a sixth-grade Japanese class participating in a directed group reading project.

Reading-Writing Workshop ■

Purpose

The Reading-Writing Workshop represents a comprehensive approach to reading and writing that attempts to engage students in meaningful literacy activities and to develop strategic approaches to reading and writing. The workshop approach draws from numerous sources and is compatible with other literacy approaches (e.g., Whole-Language, Author-Reader Cycle, and so forth). It has been formalized into an approach by Nancie Atwell through her work as a teacher of young adolescents and through her research.

Rationale

As Atwell (1987) points out, teachers have implicitly communicated to students certain ideas that actually impede reading, including:

- Reading is difficult, serious business.
- Reading is a performance for an audience of one: the teacher.
- "Errors" in comprehension or interpretation will not be tolerated.
- Student readers aren't smart or trustworthy enough to choose their own texts.
- Readers break whole texts into separate pieces to be read and dissected one fragment at a time.
- Re-reading a book is . . . cheating; so are skimming, skipping, and looking ahead.
- There's another kind of reading, a fun, satisfying kind you can do on your free time or outside of school.
- You can fail English yet still succeed at and love this other kind of reading. (Atwell, 152–153)

Yet good adult readers do not always finish every book they start, look up every word they don't understand, read only "great" literature, read without errors, or read according to the many expectations we have of children in reading classes. If we want children to become lifelong readers, we need to approach reading from an authentic perspective.

Likewise, traditional school practices with writing do not reflect the writing process that real writers use. As Atwell points out, for example, most writers write numerous drafts in the course of producing a finished work (she cites Hemingway's 39 drafts of the ending for *A Farewell to Arms*). Writers also write about matters that are fundamentally interesting to themselves. Finally, the traditional response to children's writing—correction after the writing has finished—does not help children become better writers.

Atwell further suggests that good readers use many of the same strategies that writers use:

Writing and Reading as Process

Writers and readers REHEARSE, planning and predicting:

■ What will I write?	■ What will I read?
■ What will it be like?	■ What will it be like?
■ How will it be shaped by my prior experiences as a writer?	■ How will it be shaped by my prior experiences as a reader?

Writers and readers DRAFT, discovering meaning:

- ■ Where will these words I am writing take me?
- ■ Where will these words I am reading take me?
    - ■ What surprises, disappointments, problems, questions, and insights will I encounter along the way?

Writers and readers REVISE, reseeing and reseeking meaning:

- ■ Is this what I expected, what I hoped for?
- ■ What do I think of the words on the page?
- ■ What new thoughts do I think because of the words on the page?
- ■ What makes sense? What needs to be changed so sense can be made?

(Atwell, 155)

The Reading-Writing Workshop, then, supports students as they acquire the same kinds of reading and writing habits that good adult readers and writers have: the ability to choose books to read and topics to write about, numerous strategies used in the context of reading and writing, ways of talking about the books they are reading and pieces they are writing, and, most important, a personal identity as a reader and writer.

Intended Audience

The Reading-Writing Workshop was developed originally for adolescents, but can be extended to children in the lower grades (see Cautions and Comments for information about using the Writing Workshop component with children in the primary grades). This approach to reading and writing has been successfully used with at-risk and learning-disabled children, as well as deaf students. An advantage of using the Reading-Writing Workshop component is that children are not limited to mainstream literature or topics. They can have opportunities to explore multicultural literature and their own experiences in writing; these opportunities may be especially helpful for children of diverse ethnic origins.

Description of the Procedures

There are two main ideas behind the Reading-Writing Workshop approach. First is that students own their own reading and writing. Students are in charge of choosing their own books to read, subject to the guidelines mentioned below, and their own subjects on which to write. Secondly, the role of the teacher is as expert reader-writer and guide rather than judge. The teacher actually reads for his or her own purposes along with the students and shares his or her reading experiences with the students. He or she writes with the students, as well, and shares that writing. Along with its guiding principles of student ownership of reading and teacher as mentor, the Reading-Writing Workshop procedure has four elements:

1. Time to read and write
2. Forums for response
3. Conferences with the teacher
4. Mini-lessons

1. *Time to Read and Write*   Various sources indicate that students in the intermediate grades read independently for only 15 minutes of their day. If students are going to become lifelong readers, they need to have the time to do it. In providing stretches of time during the school day for independent reading, the school gives the message to students that reading is important and worthwhile. Likewise, as Atwell points out, students do not take on the writer's identity based on writing a "complete" piece once a week in class. Young writers need two to three hours a week of writing time.

The bulk of Reading-Writing Workshop time is spent reading and/or writing. Because of the Maine state curriculum, Atwell's students have both reading and writing workshops at different times of the day. Some teachers might plan two days per week of Reading Workshop and three days per week of Writing Workshop. Morris (1991) gave his at-risk students choices: they could read or write, as long as they were doing one or the other of those activities.

Nancie Atwell provides some rules for the Reading Workshop aspect that help students to use this time constructively:

Rules for Using Reading Workshop Time

1. Students must read for the entire period
2. They cannot do homework or read any material for another course. Reading workshop is not a study hall.
3. They must read a book (no magazines or newspapers where text competes with pictures), preferably one that tells a story (e.g., novels, histories, and biographies rather than books of lists or facts where readers can't sustain attention, build up speed and fluency, or grow to love good stories).
4. They must have a book in their possession when the bell rings; this is the main responsibility involved in coming prepared to this class. (Students who need help finding a book or who finish a book during the workshop are obvious exceptions.)
5. They may not talk to or disturb others.
6. They may sit or recline wherever they'd like as long as feet don't go up on furniture and rule #5 is maintained . . .

7. There are no lavatory or water fountain sign-outs to disturb me or other readers. In an emergency, they may simply slip out and slip back in again as quietly as possible.
8. A student who's absent can make up time and receive points by reading at home, during study hall (with a note from a parent or study hall teacher), or after school. (Atwell, 159–160)

Likewise, Atwell has guidelines for the Writing Workshop time:

This year, we're going to have a writers' workshop every day. Every day all of you will be working in some way on your writing. And in this writers' workshop, we're going to have certain rules.

First, there's no erasing. Save that record of your thinking and how it's changed. I'm interested in how writers think and change their minds; when you change your mind, simply draw a line through.

Next, write on one side of the paper only. Writers often cut and paste—cut their writing apart and reorganize the pieces. That's hard to do when there's writing on the other side of the page.

The next rule is, save everything. You're creating a history of yourself as a writer this year, and what you decide against is as much a part of your writing as what you decide to keep. So hold on to all those false starts and ideas that don't work out and notes and doodles and preliminary drafts.

You should also date and label everything. By label I mean mark it DRAFT #1, DRAFT #2, and so on. Or NOTES, which is how I'd label the ideas for stories you just jotted down.

The next rule is, speak in quiet voices only. Beyond all else, writing is thinking. It's hard to think as a writer thinks when your thoughts are interrupted. During writing time I'll always speak softly and expect you to do the same. If you'd like to read your writing to a friend, there are places to go to quietly confer. All your writing conferences with each other will take place in the four conference corners.

And the final rule of writing workshop is, work really hard. (Atwell, 83–84)

Reading and Writing workshops provide time for students to read and write. They feature guidelines for students' behaviors that help all members of the classroom to respect the reading and writing that are taking place and to keep reading and writing central to the activities in the classroom.

2. *Forums for Response*   Along with time to read and write, students also need to have several ways to be able to respond to their reading and writing—with the teacher and with each other. Adult readers often talk to each other about books; response is an authentic reading activity. Further, a student's enthusiastic response about a book may encourage

other students to read that book next. Writers also need opportunities for response to their work. As Atwell points out, the teacher should be responding to writers during the process of writing and not after the student feels the project is finished—even if students do read "after the fact" responses from the teacher, the suggestions might not transfer to the student's next writing project. Peer responses can be helpful for writers as well; students need to have an audience for their writing that is larger than the teacher.

Responses can take verbal or written form. Verbal forms include literature response groups, peer conferencing, group sharing of writing, conferencing with the teacher (see below), and the kind of discussion that takes place in the mini-lessons (see below). Atwell discusses the importance of listening to students, particularly when responding to students' writing. Part of this listening involves recognizing the student's interest in working further on a piece and the directions in which the student wants to take the piece. Atwell also typically asks questions to find out how the students are thinking (instead of offering suggestions for how to solve problems; for example, she asks the student to list some of the options he or she might use—and then she adds a possibility to that list based on her own experiences). She cautions teachers to avoid responding like teachers (quizzing students, focusing on details of the reading and writing) and to try to respond to students as readers, writers, and mentors.

Atwell (1987) recommends using the dialogue journal (see Dialogue Journals, pp. 167–173) between teacher and student. Response journals allows the teacher individual contact on a regular basis. Students can also be encouraged to write notes to each other about their reading. Students might make their responses outside of class, or the last few minutes of class might be reserved for making responses to reading.

3. *Conference with the Teacher*   The main form of evaluation for the Reading-Writing Workshop focuses on conferences with the teacher, which can occur periodically during the school year. Reading and writing conferences provide students with chances to review their progress toward old goals and to set new ones.

Atwell discusses four kinds of writing workshop conferences. The status of the class conference occurs at the beginning of every writing workshop, in which students indicate to Atwell exactly what they plan to work on during that session. They may set deadlines and goals for themselves during this three-minute whole-class conference. This conference helps Atwell to keep track of what each individual student is working on and it helps her to help students follow through with their goals.

The second type of conference, the topic conference, helps students to come up with ideas for writing. Atwell uses open-ended questioning (e.g., "Tell me about _____" or "What kinds of writing would you like to try?") to help students come up with topics for writing:

> In this [topic conference] . . . my job isn't to tell [the writer] what he should write but to help him find out what he knows, show him I'm interested in what he knows, and then give it back to him from my perspective. (P. 101)

The third type of conference focuses on students' writing drafts. Atwell offers guidelines for these conferences, which occur throughout the writing period:

1. Keep conferences short, just a quick minute or two . . . It's important to remember that you're not asking to hear every word every student writes; if you do, you're taking control and making each of those pieces of writing your responsibility . . .

2. See as many writers as possible. If you can't get to everyone on a given day, make a note on the status-of-the-class chart of who you didn't get a chance to check in with and see them first in the next workshop.

3. Go to your students so you can control the length of the conference and see many writers . . .

4. Make eye contact with the writer. This means kneeling or sitting alongside their desks as you talk and listen . . .

5. Don't tell writers what should be in their writing, or, worse, write on their pieces. Remember the centrality of ownership to students' growth as writers. The piece of writing belongs to the writer.

6. Build on what writers know and have done, rather than bemoaning what's not on the page or what's wrong with what is there. Remember that in general students do the best they can. As you help them move forward, their best will get better.

7. Resist making judgments about the writing . . . Avoid generalized or contrived praise, too . . . Instead, praise by becoming involved in the writing, by paying and calling attention to what students know. And praise by describing the effects specific techniques have on you as reader/listener . . .

8. In questioning students, ask about something you're curious about as an inquisitive human being . . . What would you like to know more about? What didn't you understand? Then focus on just these one or two issues, taking care not to overwhelm the writer. (Pp. 94–95)

A fourth type of conference is the evaluative conference, which takes place in both reading and writing workshops. This conference consists of a meeting between teacher and student in which the teacher interviews the student and his or her reading and/or writing, they discuss the student's previous goals, and they come to agreement on new goals for the next grading period (see unit on assessment).

4. *Mini-lessons*   While mini-lessons are brief in length, they are an important contribution to the success of the Reading Workshop. Mini-lessons can include a variety of activities, from readings of poetry and literature, through short discussions of an author the students may be interested in, to the presentation of reading strategies that will benefit students. The key to mini-lessons is that they be relevant to the students' actual reading or writing. The teacher makes choices about which mini-lessons to present based on students' dialogue journals, informal and formal conferencing, and his or her own revelations about reading and writing.

While reading and writing mini-lessons may differ in terms of their subject matter, their format is essentially the same. It is important to choose a topic that can be addressed in a relatively short period of time. Larger topics can be broken up into mini-lessons that can be used successively.

One important kind of mini-lesson is one that helps students to build strategies. The following is an example of a reading lesson that gives students choices about reading strategies:

Prediction and Self-Questioning Strategies Mini-Lesson

In conjunction with a teacher's recognizing that a subset of her students do not engage as actively as they might in reading selections, especially content area material, the teacher decides to pull together the students and focus upon helping them make predictions and ask their own questions. To this end, the teacher presents a book that is new to the classroom. She shows the children the cover and asks:

What do you think this is about?

How can you tell what it might be about?

She then discusses with them the need to be actively involved in using clues as a basis for making predictions and asking themselves questions. Students discuss the types of clues that help them formulate their own questions and afford them predictions. They brainstorm a list of clues they might use:

Think about what you want to learn

Check the title, illustrations, headings, etc. as a way of suggesting questions or narrowing
    possibilities

She then brainstorms other things that help them decide upon their questions and to figure out what the book might offer.

As an extension she gets the children involved with coming up with examples of when they might use that strategy, perhaps by doing what-ifs: What if the cover was missing? What if you didn't know the name of the author? What if the book was not in English?

She then directs them to apply the strategies to their own reading and emphasizes that it's okay if the predictions don't turn out to be true. The point of making predictions is not to outguess the author but to have a starting point for reading the book. This mini-lesson could be done at least twice, once with a book that is fairly predictable and once with a surprising book—so that children can savor the surprise but still practice prediction. After reading she has the students reflect upon what they read and also talk about questions and predictions that they pursued.

Skolnick (1989) has an example of a writing mini-lesson:

> Mini-lessons are a natural time for teachers and children to explore the craft of the writer. . . . To help her second graders understand that authors choose words carefully as they write, during a mini-lesson Jane Fraser told the class: "Earlier this morning, as we shared Lilian Moore's *I'll Meet You at the Cucumbers*, I noticed that Moore used special language. Remember the way she described the truck coming down the road? 'At first he thought two small stars had tumbled out of the sky. Then he realized that what he saw were two headlights. The farmer's truck was coming down the road, home from the city.' I love the way she said that: 'two small stars had tumbled out of the sky.' Those words give me a crystal-clear image. Moore didn't say, 'He could see the lights on the truck' or just, 'He saw the truck coming down the road.' The language she chose has a special sound. As you write today, think about the words you choose. What picture do you want to give the reader? What special language will *you* try in your story today?" (P. 55)

In both of these mini-lessons, the children are invited to participate—in the first via discussion and in the second via writing. The second mini-lesson in particular exemplifies the community of readers and writers that characterizes the Reading-Writing Workshop classroom: The teacher talks about her response to a book—as a reader, and not as a teacher. She is able to articulate what in particular she likes about the writing and she offers alternatives that the writer could have chosen. Finally, she issues a single challenge—what special language will you try in your story today?

Cautions and Comments

Nancie Atwell (1987) cites numerous instances in which students have begun reading in the Reading Workshop because that was the expectation and ended up reading because they enjoyed it. Additionally, Oberlin and Shugarman (1989) have found that the Reading Workshop approach benefits learning-disabled readers—specifically contributing to a positive change in their attitudes towards reading.

Since Atwell's much-cited book, others have made suggestions about ways to implement the Reading Workshop. Reutzel and Cooter (1991) suggest that mini-lessons not only benefit the students, but they are a way that teachers can satisfy school and district curriculum demands while providing students with choice and support in authentic reading situations. The authors suggest selecting curriculum material for presentation in the form of mini-lessons as the material applies to readers' needs. Spencer (1991) provides an account of an elective Reading Workshop class set up for ninth graders. Students responded favorably to this class as an elective, and she suggests expanding the possibility to the higher grades as well. With some trepidation, Morris (1991) began to implement Reading and Writing Workshop into his class of at-risk high school students and found that the students responded—not dramatically, but there was a discernable positive response. Nower (1991) has implemented the writing workshop approach with deaf students, and Harris-Martine (1991) uses it in her classroom in an inner-city school. This approach supports the wide range of students that might be found in a culturally diverse classroom.

McAuliffe (1993) and others have pointed out children's tendencies to write strongly gendered work. In fact, boys and girls often have a hard time relating to and even understanding each other's stories. In her study of second graders, McAuliffe found that through peer feedback available in writers' workshops, children began to change their writing so that more of their classmates could engage with it. Writing workshop, then, offers children a chance to move beyond some of the narrow confines of socialization.

Other authors have challenged some of Atwell's ideas. While Ash (1990) acknowledges the importance of student ownership of reading, she also makes a case for an occasional class-read text. She found, through having her students read a James Thurber story, that her students were not engaging with the material because they weren't hearing the voices in the text. This class reading became the basis for working on an important reading strategy. Abrahamson and Carter (1991), finally, suggest that Atwell privileges fiction/narrative at the expense of great nonfiction. They suggest that despite Atwell's third rule (see above), students may find nonfiction books that don't fall into her categories to be absorbing.

Pelletier (1992) mentions several advantages of word processing across the writing process:

- Children tend to write more, and better, because of the ease with which they can edit their work.
- The computer is less fatiguing to work with than writing by hand.
- The computer is interesting to use; it is motivational.

Obviously, word processing is immediately useful in the Writer's Workshop. Other programs that allow children to create different kinds of texts (e.g., programs that combine word processing and graphics) would also be useful. Teachers may well want to consider whether Reading Workshop might include the kinds of text that are available on computer—electronic books, and multimedia materials on CD–ROM. These texts can be very engaging for students.

References

Abrahamson, R. F., and B. Carter. 1991. Nonfiction: The missing piece in the middle. *English Journal* 80:52–57. The authors argue that reading workshop should include nonfiction as well as fiction.

Ash, B. H. 1990. Reading assigned literature in a reading workshop. *English Journal* 79: 77–79.

Atwell, N. 1987. *In the middle: Writing, reading, and learning with adolescents.* Portsmouth, NH: Heinemann. A thorough and comprehensive book on reading and writing workshops.

Brent, R., and P. Anderson. 1993. Developing children's classroom listening strategies. *The Reading Teacher* 47:122–126. Uses a mini-lesson format for teaching listening strategies. Offers a good process for teaching mini-lessons.

Harris-Martine, D. 1991. Reading, writing, and literature in a Harlem second grade. In *Process reading and writing: A literature-based approach,* edited by J. T. Feeley, D. S. Strickland, and S. B. Wepner. New York: Teacher's College Press. Describes the use of reading and writing workshop-type strategies with children in Harlem.

McAuliffe, S. 1993. Toward understanding one another: Second graders' use of gendered language and story styles. *The reading teacher* 47:302–310. Describes a study of children's changing their use of language during a school year.

Morris, C. W. 1991. Giving at-risk juniors intellectual independence: An experiment. *English Journal* 80:37–41. Morris implemented reading and writing workshop with students who had repeatedly experienced failure.

Nower, B. 1991. So it doesn't disappear in air. *The Volta Review* 93:123–137. Describes a writing workshop approach with deaf students.

Oberlin, K. J., and S. L. Shugarman. 1989. Implementing the reading workshop with middle school learning-disabled readers. *Journal of Reading* 32:682–687. This study found that learning-disabled students improved in their attitudes toward and involvement with books following a reading workshop approach.

Opitz, M. F., and D. Cooper. 1993. Adapting the spelling basal for spelling workshop. *The Reading Teacher* 47:106–113. For teachers who are not ready to or cannot give up the spelling basal, here is an approach that integrates it into a workshop.

Pelletier, P. 1992. Word processing as a support to the writing process. *International Journal of Instructional Media* 19:249–257. Describes studies of word processing and children. Includes both advantages and disadvantages of word processing.

Reutzel, D. R., and R. B. Cooter, Jr. 1991. Organizing for effective instruction: The reading workshop. *The Reading Teacher* 44:548–554. Describes several strategies for organizing reading workshops.

Skolnick, D. 1989. When literature and writing meet. In *Workshop I by and for teachers: Writing and literature,* edited by N. Atwell. Describes several literary mini-lessons that connect reading and writing.

Spencer, P. S. 1991. Recovering innocence: Growing up reading. *English Journal* 80:65–69. At the behest of a student, Spencer developed an optional reading workshop that became popular with the students.

Teaching Reading as a Language Experience

UNIT OVERVIEW

For many years teachers have recognized the worth of the child's own oral language and experiences as basic ingredients in beginning reading instruction. As far back as 1908, Edmund Huey reported the use of a sentence method that drew on the child's language and experiences to describe pictures. Through the first half of this century, numerous educators cited and recommended an experience-based approach to teaching reading (e.g., Storm and Smith, 1930; Gans, 1941; Lamoreaux and Lee, 1943; Sullivan, 1986). In recent years, interest in using the language and experience of children has continued to grow. Researchers and educators in their search for the *one* best method for teaching reading have turned their attention to language acquisition and the psycholinguistic nature of the reading process. In the middle of the 1960s, the resulting approach became widely recognized and identified by its now familiar label, "the language experience approach." In the 1970s and early 1980s, the approach became widely used throughout the world. For example, Breakthrough to Literacy developed for use in Great Britain became widely used throughout the British Commonwealth (McKay, Thompson, and Schaub, 1970). Various offshoots of the approach that appeared as developments in other areas have dovetailed with the approach. For example, the procedure has been accepted for use with adolescents (e.g., McWilliams and Smith, 1981; Stratton, Grindler, and Postell, 1992) and ESL students (Dixon and Nessel, 1983), strategies have been developed for extending comprehension abilities with the procedure (Sulzby, 1980; Heller, 1988), it has been adapted for use with students with invented spellings (Coate and Castle, 1989), and adapted to the teaching of science (Tragash, 1987).

As these developments occurred with the language experience approach, researchers began exploring more intensely infant encounter with print in the environment and during shared reading experiences with parents. What emerged in conjunction with these developments were approaches that further capitalized on the language experiences of young children.

The rationale of these approaches was based on the notion that children are born with a prowess for language acquisition and that this prowess can and should be directed toward the acquisition of reading abilities. To this end, proponents of the language experience approach and the role of environmental print advocated taking advantage of the experiences that children bring to reading. By conveying these experiences through language, children can move back and forth from oral to written expression. From this foundation, children develop quite naturally the ability and interest to read widely, deeply, and fluently.

One of the key understandings that has occurred since the development of the Language Experience Approach has been the growing awareness of the nature of reading and writing development from the earliest years. Tierney (1991) discusses several longitudinal studies:

> To date, a number of researchers have offered a longitudinal perspective on the understandings children acquire as they write. Read (1971) and Chomsky (1979) have described in some detail the assumptions which tend to undergird a child's invented spellings. Harste, Burke and Woodward (1984 a & b) have offered several examples of how young children's writing develops across time. Bissex's (1980) and Baghban's (1984) case studies of their children are devoted primarily to tracing their early writing development. Graves (1982) and Calkins (1982) have offered rich descriptions of writing development across time as students begin writing and conferencing with others. . . . Taken together, the longitudinal research on early reading and writing to date has confirmed some beliefs at the same time as it has added definition and stimulated a number of issues. The view of the child as an active meaning maker constructing his or her own hypotheses in the context of daily negotiations with print and others is substantiated repeatedly. (P. 180) [Studies mentioned in this excerpt are cited in bibliography]

In conjunction with these developments, some key and interrelated understandings about the development of children's literacy have emerged:

Emergent Literacy.   Children learn to read and write in a fashion that is not unlike how they learn to talk—with opportunities to experiment, to take risks, to be engaged in meaningful interactions, and to be able to invent ways of reading and writing using their own rule systems.

Invented Spelling.   Carol Chomsky (1979) points out the role of children's use of invented spelling as they learn to read:

> Children who have been writing for months are in a very favorable position when they undertake learning to read. They have at their command considerable phonetic information about English, practice in phonemic segmentation, and experience with alphabetic representation. These are some of the technical skills that they need to get started. They have, in addition, an expectation of going ahead on their own. They are prepared to make sense, and their purpose is to derive a message from print, not just to pronounce the words. (Pp. 51–52)

Interplay of Reading, Writing, Talking, Drawing, and Peer Relationships.   Reading and writing are not isolated activities; they occur with and in relation to a number of meaning-making experiences that children have. Tierney and Shanahan (1991) demonstrate this through citing two important studies:

> . . . in conjunction with exploring the nature of literacy learning in a day-care environment for 3- and 4-year-olds, Rowe (1987) concluded that there are two general types of "intertextual" connections that are important. The first type is the *formation of shared meanings* through conversations and demonstrations so that these young literacy learners are members of a community that affords communication with others. The second type involves linking current literacy experiences to past experiences. . . . Based upon her observations of first graders, Short (1986) argues that the potential for learning and thinking are changed when the classroom environment facilitates intertextuality. A collaborative and meaning-centered learning environment engages learners more fully and actively in learning and encourages higher levels of thinking. (P. 272) [italics original]

Additionally, Dyson (1989) concludes an extensive study of children's writing by stating:

> Thus, in studying the efforts of Regina, Jake, Manuel, Mitzi, and the other young writers who shared this classroom, the focus was not on their writing alone, because writing does not evolve only from writing. Rather, the focus was on the meanings each child intended to communicate, that is, on the symbolic worlds being deliberately formed. And those worlds were revealed in the children's drawing, talking, and playing, as well as in their writing. . . . In brief, from the perspective of this book, writing development is viewed as evolving within and shaped by children's interactions with other symbolic media and other people, including their peers. Both the developmental challenges children face as writers and the resources they lean upon are found in the varied symbolic and social worlds within which they, and all authors, work. (P. 255)

Later, Dyson discusses the ramifications of her work for our understanding of literacy acquisition:

> Parents and children alike expect students to learn to read and write in school, presumably to the eventual betterment of children's social and economic futures. And, for children whose background is considered out of the "mainstream," for whatever reason (most often because the children are not middle class and/or not Anglo), becoming literate is considered a process of moving, through individual achievement, beyond present ground, beyond their families and neighborhoods.
>
> This way of thinking about school literacy needs some rethinking. Within the context of this project, children's growth as literate people was linked to the social practices that surrounded them, that is, to their discovery of literacy's rich relevance to their present interactions with friends and to their reflections on their experiences. Literacy that helps children to articulate their todays and to make ongoing connections with others may be more likely to grow with them into their tomorrows. (P. 276)

The work that has led to these three conclusions has extended and sometimes challenged past language experience approaches, especially those that may not have been developed with some of these same appreciations and understandings. As a result, some language experience approaches carry too great a focus on "correct conventions," they delay writing until after reading, and they do not work with or take advantage of the interplay of reading and writing with drawing, talking, and peer relationships.

A final major development that has affected language experience approaches has been the development of computer technology for the classroom. Reinking and Bridwell-Bowes (1986) mentions five advantages to using computers with reading and writing. They can:

1. Enhance the ability of readers and writers to interact with text.
2. Permit the external control of written language processes.
3. Lessen the drudgery associated with some aspects of reading and writing.
4. Provide individualized help and guidance during independent reading and writing activities.
5. Contribute to the development of purposeful communication in school, and thus they can bring together reading and writing activities.

As will be seen in greater detail in the discussions of individual language experience approaches, numerous different types of programs exist that enhance learning through the language experience approaches: word processing combined with speech synthesis, story development software, and desktop publishing (see Barber, 1982; Casey, 1984; Sampson, Allen, and Sampson, 1991; and Stratton, Grindler, and Postell, 1992, for specific applications of computer technology with language experience approaches).

The implementation of the language experience approach and environmental print require teacher understanding of students' experiences and abilities with language. The language experience approach involves facilitating rather than teaching children "how to learn to read" or "how to read." In other words, to teach reading as a language experience requires that the teacher respond to students as they teach themselves about reading. Teacher-directed activities should neither hinder learning nor distort appropriate reading behavior.

As Veatch (1991) points out, language experience approaches are congruent with other reading frameworks (e.g., Whole-Language frameworks, process writing approaches, and theme-based approaches to teaching). Language experience approaches have served as a basis for many student-centered literacy teaching strategies, although current uses of language experience-type activities do not differentiate so strongly between the four approaches outlined below (but are more likely to draw on Stauffer's material than Allen's curricular approach). Teachers continue to involve children in language-rich experiences and to respect and use children's language as a basis for expanding children's literacies. With these ideas in mind, teachers might review the suggestions of Allen, Ashton-Warner, and Stauffer, the research mentioned above, and then possibly generate their own strategies.

The present unit describes four strategies for teaching reading as a language experience. These strategies represent several of the major variations of this approach.

Allen's Language Experience Approach in Communication.   The Language Experiences in Communication represent an attempt by Roach Van Allen to develop a comprehensive language-based approach to reading. Most people credit Allen with nurturing the evolution of the language experience approach. Allen's intent has been to develop an approach that provides the language competencies essential to promote reading. In comparison with others, this approach provides the most comprehensive and detailed suggestions for teaching reading as a language experience.

Ashton-Warner's Organic Reading.   Organic Reading is an experience-centered approach to reading instruction based upon Sylvia Ashton-Warner's teaching experiences with Maori children in New Zealand. It is designed to bridge the gap between the language world of the child and the language world of books through the use of each child's key vocabulary.

Stauffer's Language-Experience Approach.   The Language-Experience Approach represents Russell Stauffer's conceptualization of the language experience approach for teaching beginning reading. His approach focuses on the use of individual- and group-dictated stories, the use of word banks, and the use of creative writing activities. As a beginning reading approach, it can serve either to supplement or to substitute for traditional basal reading programs.

Patterned Language Approach.   Patterned Language Approach by Bridge adopts the use of predictable story material and a structured language experience approach to provide teachers with a whole-part procedure for introducing students to reading. The procedure is intended for use with beginning readers to develop an initial vocabulary, as well as readers' use of meaning cues, syntactical cues, and graphophonic features of words.

References

Baghban, M. F. M. 1984. *Our daughter learns to read and write: A case study from birth to three.* Newark, DE: International Reading Association.

Barber, B. 1982. Creating BYTES of Language. *Language Arts* 59:472–475.

Bissex, G. 1980. *Gyns at wrk: A child learns to read and write.* Cambridge: Harvard University Press. Diary account of the emergent literacy of a child.

Calkins, L. 1983. *Lessons from a child.* Portsmouth, NH: Heinemann.

Casey, J. M. 1984. *Beginning reading instruction: Using the LEA approach with and without mi-cro-computer intervention.* ERIC Document 245-192.

Chomsky, C. 1979. Approaching reading through invented spelling. In *Theory and Practice of Early Reading, Vol. 2,* edited by L. B. Resnick and P. A. Weaver. Hillsdale, NJ: Erlbaum.

Coate, S., and M. Castle. 1989. Integrating LEA and invented spelling in kindergarten. *The Reading Teacher* 42:516–519. Explores the use of invented spelling and reading-writing connections in conjunction with the LEA.

Dixon, C. N., and D. Nessel. 1983. *Language experience approach to reading (and writing).* Hayward, CA: The Alemany Press.

Doake, D. 1985. Reading-like behavior: Its role in learning to read. *Observing the language learner,* eds. A. M. Jaggar and M. T. Smith-Burke. Newark, DE: International Reading Association/NCTE.

Dyson, A. H. 1989. *Multiple worlds of child writers: Friends learning to write.* New York: Teachers College Press.

Gans, R. 1941. *Guiding children's reading through experiences.* New York: Teachers College.

Graves, D. 1982. Patterns of child control of the writing process. In *Donald Graves in Australia,* edited by R. D. Walshe. Portsmouth, NH: Heinemann.

Harste, J. C., V. A. Woodward, & C. L. Burke. (1984a). Examining our assumptions: A transactional view of literacy and learning. *Research in the Teaching of English* 18:84–108.

———. (1984b). *Language stories and literacy lessons.* Portsmouth, NH: Heinemann.

Heller, M. F. 1988. Comprehending composing through language experience. *The Reading Teacher* 42:130–135. Discusses an adaptation of LEA intended to enhance comprehension.

Holdaway, D. 1979. *Foundations of literacy.* Gossford: Ashton, Scholastic.

Huey, E. G. 1908. *The psychology and pedagogy of reading.* New York: Macmillan.

Lamoreaux, L., and D. M. Lee. 1943. *Learning to read through experiences.* New York: Appleton-Century-Crofts.

McKay, D., B. Thompson, and P. Schaub. 1970. *Breakthrough to literacy: Programme in linguistics and English teaching.* London: Schools Council (Longman).

McWilliams, L., and D. Smith. 1981. Decision stories. *Journal of Reading* 25:142–145.

Read, C. 1971. Pre-school children's knowledge of English phonology. *Harvard Educational Review* 41:1–34.

Reinking, D., and L. Bridwell-Bowles. 1986. Computers in reading and writing. In *Handbook of reading research, vol. II.,* edited by R. Barr, M. Kamil, P. Mosenthal, and P. D. Pearson. New York: Longman, 310–340.

Rowe, D. W. 1987. Literacy learning as an intertextual process. In *Research in literacy: Merging perspectives,* edited by J. E. Readence and R. Scott Baldwin. Rochester, NY: National Reading Conference.

Sampson, M., R. V. Allen, and M. Sampson. 1991. *Pathways to literacy: A meaning-centered approach.* Fort Worth: Holt, Rinehart and Winston, Inc.

Short, K. G. 1986. *Literacy as a collaborative experience.* Unpublished doctoral dissertation. Bloomington: Indiana University.

Storm, G. E., and N. B. Smith. 1930. *Reading activities in primary grades.* Boston: Ginn.

Stratton, Beverly D., M. C. Grindler, and C. M. Postell. 1992. Discovering Oneself. *Middle School Journal* 24:42–43.

Sullivan, J. 1986. The global method: Language experience in the content areas. *The Reading Teacher* 39:664–669.

Sulzby, E. 1980. Using children's dictated stories to aid comprehension. *The Reading Teacher* 33:772–778.

Tierney, R. J. 1991. Studies of reading and writing growth: Longitudinal research on literacy development. In *Handbook of research on teaching the English language arts,* edited by J. Flood, J. M. Jensen, D. Lapp, and J. R. Squire. New York: Macmillan Publishing Co.

Tierney, R. J., and T. Shanahan. 1991. Research on the reading-writing relationship: Interactions, transactions, and outcomes. In *Handbook of Reading Research, Vol. ii,* edited by R. Barr, M. Kamil, P. Mosenthal, and P. D. Pearson. New York: Longman.

Tragash, J. R. 1987. *Teaching difficult learners science: Hands-on experiments.* Monograph #17, University of Florida Multidisciplinary Diagnostic and Training Program. ERIC Document 353-743.

Veatch, J. 1991. *Whole language and its predecessors: Commentary.* Paper presented at the Annual Meeting of the College Reading Association. ERIC Document 341-035.

Allen's Language Experience Approach in Communication ▪

Purpose

The language experience in communication represents the Language Experience Approach as advocated by Roach Van Allen (1976). It is designed to develop the language competencies essential for the promotion of reading. To this end, it provides each child with opportunities to: (1) experience communication in various situations, (2) study aspects of communication, and (3) relate the ideas of others to self.

Rationale

Historically, the writings and material of Roach Van Allen have been largely responsible for this approach's recognition and evolution. Allen's rationale for the Language Experience Approach stems largely from a project sponsored by the Department of Education, San Diego County, California, where researchers pursued the question, "Of all the language experiences available for study in the elementary school years, which ones have the greatest contribution to make to reading?" This work served to identify twenty essential language experiences and give the approach its now familiar label, *language experience.*

With the approach's evolution, these twenty experiences have been organized into a design for a total language arts/communication curriculum. Figure 2–1 shows its design (Allen, 1976, 13). Within the design, the twenty language experiences fall within a framework of three strands and occur through the development of four types of activities. The three strands are: experiencing communication, studying communication, and relating communication of others to self. The four types of activities integral to the development of these experiences are language acquisition, language prediction, language recognition, and language production.*

The implementation of Allen's curriculum design is guided by certain principles and assumptions about language and the learner, and the interactive nature of the two. The assumption is that students acquire reading and writing skills in the same way that they acquire oral language skills. It is suggested that teachers recognize that students vary in language and language acquisition in accordance with their habits, age, socioeconomic group, and geographic region; teachers should further recognize that language changes slowly, continuously, creatively, and personally. To this end, it is Allen's premise that the "one big responsibility of a teacher at any level of instruction is to help each child to habituate, and to internalize certain truths about self and language." (Allen, 1976, 52) The

---

*Language acquisition is directed toward increasing student's inventory of words, knowledge of ways to express themselves, and ability to explain the unfamiliar. Language prediction entails developing students' abilities to anticipate aspects of language and language patterns in their reading and listening. Language recognition is directed toward having students see the relationship between their language and the printed language of others. It includes developing their awareness of the characteristics of print and certain word identification skills. Language production involves having the student communicate through a variety of different media, associating most communications with speaking and writing, and realizing that ideas can be expressed, written, and read.

FIGURE 2–1. DESIGN FOR TOTAL LANGUAGE ARTS/COMMUNICATION CURRICULUM

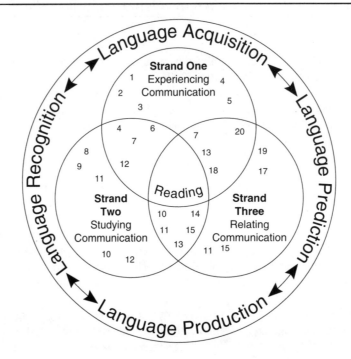

Reading in a Language Experience Approach

I. Experiencing Communication

1. Oral sharing of ideas
2. Visual portrayal of experiences
3. Dramatization of experiences
4. Responding rhythmically
5. Discussing and conversing
6. Exploring writing
7. Authoring individual books

II. Studying Communication

8. Recognizing high-frequency words
9. Exploring spelling
10. Studying style and words
11. Studying language structure
12. Extending vocabularies
13. Reading non-alphabetic symbols

III. Relating Communication of Others to Self

14. Listening to and reading language of others
15. Comprehending what is heard and read
16. Organizing ideas
17. Assimilating and integrating ideas
18. Searching out and reseaching multiple sources
19. Responding in personal ways
20. Evaluating communication of others

conceptualization of these truths became the approach's trademark. This conceptualization was:

> What I can think about, I can talk about.
>
> What I can say, I can write (or someone can write about).
>
> What I can write, I can read.
>
> I can read what others write for me to read.
>   (Allen and Allen, 1966, Level 1, 6)

In more recent years this conceptualization has evolved into the following:

> I can think about what I have experienced and imagined.
>
> I can talk about what I think about.
>
> What I can talk about I can express in some other form.
>
> Anything I can record I can tell through speaking or reading.
>
> I can read what I can write by myself and what other people write for me to read.
>
> As I talk and write, I use some words over and over and some not so often.
>
> As I talk and write, I use some words and clusters of words to express my meanings.
>
> As I write to represent the sounds I make through speech, I use the same symbols over and over.
>
> Each letter of the alphabet stands for one or more sounds that I make when I talk.
>
> As I read, I must add to what an author has written if I am to get full meaning and inherent pleasure from print.
>   (Allen 1976; reprinted by permission)

Intended Audience

Allen's Language Experience Approach can be used with students of all ages and abilities. It provides for a total language arts curriculum that can be implemented within a single group, a whole classroom, or across a whole school. The approach works with whole-class, group, or individual instruction.

Description of the Procedures

According to Allen, it is not his intention to suggest exactly how to develop a Language Experience Approach, but to suggest ways in which it might be implemented. In so doing, he assumes that teachers understand the philosophy of this approach, its curriculum rationale, learning center organization, and the use of multiple materials.

The language classroom proposed by Allen can be characterized by direct and indirect teaching activities within the framework of an instructional schedule. The direct and indirect teaching procedures entail the use of: (1) patterns of teacher-pupil interaction, (2) learning centers, and (3) planned programming. These provide the skeleton or organizational framework to which the instructional schedule clings. For purposes of discussion, the organizational framework is presented, and a presentation of specific teaching suggestions follows.

Organizational Framework

1. Patterns of Teacher-Pupil Interactions   Depending upon the nature of the activity, Allen suggests whole-class, group, or individual organizational patterns. Whole-class activities are suggested for the following:

    a. Reading aloud to or by children

    b. Oral discussion of topics of interest

    c. Oral composition of stories

    d. Films, filmstrips, and other audiovisual presentations

    e. Introduction and demonstrations of games or learning centers

    f. Seminars on various skills

    g. Singing, rhymes, choral reading, or unison reading

Group activities are suggested for the following:

    a. Teacher taking dictation for one child

    b. Children working, reading, or playing games with each other

    c. Teacher reading with individuals or groups

    d. Meeting a group's skill needs

    e. Completing work initiated with class

    f. Editing manuscripts for publication

    g. Planning and rehearsing dramatizations.

Individual activities are suggested for the following:

    a. Conferring with students about writing individual books

    b. Conferring with students concerning their progress

    c. Helping with spelling or word recognition

    d. Taking dictation from individuals for whom sharing would be inappropriate

2. Learning Centers   To meet the specific needs of the approach, Allen suggests and describes a variety of permanent and temporary learning centers for the language classroom. Several of his suggestions are described below.

    a. Strand learning centers. Once children have internalized the curriculum rationale, large centers made up of subcenters are suggested for each strand. For example, within a larger center for self-expression (Strand 1), there might be various subcenters for directing art expression, creative writing, and creative dramatics. Within a center for language study (Strand 2), there might be subcenters for editing manuscripts, review of language skills, and dictation experiences. Within a third, larger center for reflection (Strand 3), there might be subcenters for leisure reading, puppets, listening, and reading instruction.

b. The discussion center. Allen sees the discussion center as the hub of the language classroom. It is where the teacher introduces activities, stimulates interest, shares stories, establishes classroom procedures, and evaluates the program. It is where the students share and present ideas to other classmates.

c. The arts and crafts center. An arts and crafts center is suggested to provide the students a "treasure house" of creative materials and to serve as a "launching pad" for expression. This center is where children express themselves through various media within a recreational setting. Allen sees this expression as furnishing the raw materials essential for speaking, listening, reading, and writing.

d. The discovery center. A discovery center serves to highlight the language of science and encourages children to discover new things or look at familiar things with new perspectives. Toward these ends, it is equipped with microscopes, magnifying glasses, and collections of plants, insects, and minerals.

e. The dramatization center. A dramatization center serves to encourage children to discover themselves and relate to others through dramatization. The center is equipped with masks, puppets, and clothing.

f. The language study center. A language study center provides students a variety of different activities by which to acquire aspects of language, such as word study, language anticipation, grammar, and sight words.

g. Reading research center. A reading research center provides the students a place to browse, research, and read a variety of material. Intended for relaxation reading and research, it contains reference material, recreational reading materials, books written by the children, and magazines.

h. Writing/publishing center. A writing/publishing center is a place where children find both resources and motivation. Here children are stimulated to write, edit, review, and publish manuscripts. Here, newspapers, magazines, and previously published books of other children might be located.

Allen provides a number of other suggestions for learning centers that might be activated with program planning. Among his major suggestions are a music center, a cooking center, a viewing/listening center, and, for relaxation and contemplation, a quiet place.

3. Program Planning   Program planning is another essential aspect of Allen's organizational framework for teaching reading as a language experience. Program planning serves to structure learning experiences; for this purpose, Allen provides guidelines for recording, charting, and implementing the language experience program. His specific guidelines include the following suggestions:

a. Major language goals should be selected and implemented regularly and systematically. For example, language goals should be selected from each of the three strands and emphasized for no less than one week. Over a month or six weeks, each of the twenty language experience substrands should be emphasized by the teacher.

b. To serve the language concepts being emphasized, the teacher should develop learning centers to meet the students' needs and adjust the class grouping plans to afford maximum benefits.

c. Teacher-pupil interactions should be suited to the activities and needs of the students.

d. Evaluation procedures should be selected that can assess the program in terms of its objectives.

The chart in Figure 2–2 is suggested by Allen to guide program planning (Allen 1976, 88).

FIGURE 2–2. CHART TO GUIDE PROGRAM PLANNING

Name _____ Class _____ Dates _____ to _____

Theme or language emphasis: _____

Activities from the Three Strands	Classroom Organization*			Learning Centers Activated† (with materials and equipment needed)	Evaluation‡			
	TC	SG	I		In	CR	St	PC
Experiencing communication								
Studying communication								
Relating communication of others to self								
Other activities								

*TC – total class SG – small group I – individuals	†Learning centers available: Discussion, Arts and Crafts, Cooking, Dramatization, Game, Reading/Research, Viewing/Listening, Writing/Publishing, A Quiet Place	‡In – informal inventory CR – criterion reference St – standardized test PC – personal conference

Source: Allen (1976); reprinted by permission.

Specific Teaching Suggestions   In addition to the organizational framework, Allen makes several specific teaching suggestions for establishing certain learning experiences. In an effort to provide a representative and detailed examination of some essential aspects of Allen's approach, his suggestions for dictated stories are presented.

Suggestions for Dictated Stories   Dictated stories are an integral part of Allen's language experience approach. They afford students the opportunity to learn about language through experiencing, studying, and reflecting on oral communications.

Allen breaks his suggestions for dictated stories into thirteen basic steps. They are:

1. Visit with the student for the purpose of discussing a topic of interest. Have students tell the names for things and describe their color, size, shape, function, parts, feelings, taste, smell, quantity, and related actions or events.
2. Decide whether the goal is for the student to provide description or to tell a story of some kind. If telling a story is the goal, have the student tell the whole story; then decide whether to write all of the student's ideas or some of them. Allen points out that often the goals for the dictation can be served by writing only one or two of the student's ideas. As the stories or labels are written, the teacher and student should talk about the letters, their names, their formation, the sounds they represent, and their structure. As Allen (1973) suggests:

   > Talk about alphabet symbols you are using to represent the sounds the child made. (Let other children listen.) Let it be known that the letters have names, that some words begin with capital letters, that the same letters are used over and over as the first letters of words, that the same words appear over and over, that some ending sounds appear over and over, and they may tell us "how many" or "when." (P. 1)

3. After writing the story or the student's ideas, read the text back to the student and ask if the text is what the students said. The student might be asked to read along or to read some words or sentences alone.
4. Display the students' ideas or stories in the room and invite the students either to tell about their ideas or stories or to read them to the group. Some sentences might be read in unison to show the proper phrasing during reading. Have students compare their stories for word study. For example, students might study two or three characteristics of words, such as words that are the same, words that rhyme, words that begin or end the same, words with similar meanings, and words that are names. Allen suggests that teachers and students might identify these characteristics by underlining with different-colored pens.
5. Students might be invited either to read words, phrases, or sentences, or to read along in unison. Allen points out that involvement is more important at this point than correctness or the identification of poor readers.
6. The teacher or students might identify words that appear five or more times in students' stories and place them on a chart entitled "Words We All Use." Allen suggests this chart can be used as an aid for developing a reading vocabulary, as a source for word games, as a resource for the correct spelling of words, and as a way to determine if the student is ready for book reading. In terms of the latter purpose,

Allen suggests a student is ready for book reading only when the vocabulary on this chart matches the vocabulary of books.

7. The students' dictated stories are copied onto ditto masters, duplicated, bound, and distributed to each student. Eight or ten stories are suggested for each book.

8. When students become interested in writing, Allen suggests that they trace their recorded story.

9. After tracing, students might be encouraged to copy stories on spaces left between each line.

10. The students move from copying below each line to copying on a separate sheet of paper.

11. The students write their own stories on the chalkboard.

12. A group or the whole class listens to the stories and makes suggestions for editing. The edited story is written on a story strip and displayed.

13. Students involve themselves in writing and refining their own stories at the writing center. For students who cannot write, the writing center can include independent tracing, copying, and other activities.

Cautions and Comments

Allen (1976) suggests that certain features about the Language Experience Approach to teaching communication distinguish it from traditional approaches to reading and from other aspects of language experience approaches. These features include:

1. Students' oral language grows and is used to develop language acquisition, production, recognition, and prediction abilities.

2. Vocabulary control occurs naturally rather than artificially through the student's natural use and acquisition of the vocabulary they use.

3. Students' vocabulary acquisition is accelerated through developing an understanding of words and language, rather than through drills.

4. Individualization, grouping, and teaching patterns vary with students' individual and group needs and not solely with their abilities.

5. In comparison to other Language Experience Approaches, the language experience approach to teaching communication affords a comprehensive curriculum design for creating learning environments and for screening activities.

6. Word identification skills are taught directly and in relationship to writing and spelling.

7. Students initially read familiar rather than unfamiliar story material. This provides them with a basis and the confidence for reading other material.

8. Students read initially within the context of their own linguistic environment, rather than within a language environment that is unfamiliar to them.

9. Students learn about language through expression and through exposure to the various language media. These experiences afford them an understanding of language patterns and the writing system.

10. Students gain exposure to a wide variety of reading material, including newspapers, magazines, recreational reading material, reference material, and stories written by their peers.

11. The use of a variety of multimedia materials stimulates the students' interests and expression.
12. Students are afforded opportunities to become fully involved in personalized learning experiences. Their ideas are valued and used as the basis for these experiences.
13. Students internalize a pattern of thinking about reading. This pattern suggests that ideas can be spoken, written, or read.
14. Students learn to read as a result of their increased sensitivity to their environment, their language, and their discovery of how reading meets their personal needs.

The approach does distinguish itself from other traditional approaches to teaching reading and from other Language Experience Approaches. It does, as Allen suggests, provide teachers a wealth of suggestions for implementing a comprehensive language-arts-based approach to teaching reading. But certain of these suggestions might be questioned. For example, Allen states that reading, writing, speaking, and listening are closely interrelated. However, he assumes that in practice these activities can be taught concurrently and interchangeably. During the dictation of a story, the teacher would refer students to a study of how letters are formed and how they sound. As Smith (1973) suggests, reading, writing, speaking, and listening should not be taught concurrently when the interchange detracts from meaningful and purposeful communication. The emphasis on the mechanics of writing would tend to do just that. Perhaps subsequent revisions of this approach could place more stress on using "invented spellings" which, in turn, would diminish the need for dictation and require a reconsideration of the emphasis on mechanics.

Other examples of questionable practices include Allen's suggestions for direct rather than indirect word identification skills instruction, his emphasis upon words and the acquisition of a sight vocabulary, and his suggested use of choral and unison reading. Again, advocates of a psycholinguistic notion of reading (Smith, 1973) would claim this approach overemphasizes the mechanics of word-perfect reading.

Research evidence to support Allen's approach is rather limited, and what is available tends to be negative (Kendrick and Bennett, 1966). In defense of Allen, the research that has been implemented has seemed rather insensitive to the subtleties of the goals he outlined. Measurement procedures and analysis techniques have seemed inadequate to truly evaluate the effectiveness of this approach.

Allen did not invent the Language Experience Approach, but he should be given a great deal of credit for its emergence, popularity, and evolution. His Language Experience Approach to teaching communication represents his most recent efforts and his response to demands for a more comprehensive and structured language experience approach. The enigma of the approach may be that while it is not sufficiently prescriptive for some teachers, it may be too prescriptive for others.

Sampson, Allen, and Sampson (1991) bring some new issues to using Allen's Language Experience Approach. They suggest that this approach is particularly good for supporting students from diverse cultural and linguistic backgrounds:

> Meaning-centered curricula value the differences that children bring to the classroom. Many children have failed in school because . . . their language and culture were rejected as new language and new ways were imposed on them. They were considered deficient, and many failed because their self-esteem was destroyed and because the techniques used

to teach a second language of "standard English" were so different from the way they had learned their first language. (P. 358)

Difference is not only inevitable in the classroom, it is valuable. The different lives children lead allow them to bring many different experiences into the classroom to share; when the class values children's experiences, it is enriched by them as well. Further, as Dyson (1989) points out, children acquire literacy in connection with their experiences; a classroom that values children's experiences is one that gives children, as Dyson says, a literacy that "may be more likely to grow with them into their tomorrows" (P. 276).

Sampson, Allen, and Sampson (1991) also discuss the use of computer technology in relation to the Language Experience Approach. They describe several software packages that are available, software that is several steps beyond the early "skill and drill" packages that used to characterize "educational" software. Because the software arena is changing so quickly, the software packages will be discussed as types of software rather than in terms of specific packages. Other types of software that may be useful and interesting to students are being developed very rapidly; this list, then, is provisional.

- Word processing programs. These allow teachers to record children's dictated texts and to print out typed copies. Word processing programs designed for children are easy to use and allow children to edit their texts very easily. Some word processors include speech synthesizers, which allow the computer to read the text out loud. Although speech synthesis can be problematic, some speech synthesis programs allow the teacher to correct the computer's pronunciation.

- Text development software. These are more than word processors. They often have a graphics package, which allows the children to combine words and pictures in their work. For example, some packages help children to create comic books; the graphics include characters drawn in comic book style and speech balloons for the texts that children write. Story development software allows children to create their own stories and to select from graphics libraries to illustrate their stories.

- Fiction software. Story exploration software connects with children's books and allows children to extend their reading experiences through further exploration of the world of the particular story. Some of the stories currently available are not very engaging for children. Adventure games may use a story world or a new world. Children interact with that world through text and pictures. Children control the plot and often write in conjunction with using choose-your-own-adventure-type stories or open-ended adventure stories.

In his review of the use of computers in teaching language arts, Bruce (1991) mentions five possible roles for the computer:

1. *A tutor.* It can individualize instruction, provide learning material at a controlled pace, and record student progress.
2. *A tool.* It aids in reading; it allows students to produce and format texts easily; it facilitates revision of texts; it checks for spelling errors. It stores in a compact and easily ac-

cessible form all sorts of information that learners need, from style sheets to encyclopedic data.

3. *A way to explore language.* It makes the regularities, the beauties, and the difficulties of language something that students can examine and interact with in new ways.

4. *A medium.* It makes possible new modes of communication, and "hypertexts," or "hypermedia," which allow the intermixing of tables, charts, graphs, pictures, sounds, video, and text.

5. *An environment for communication.* It is a new social realm that permits new forms of meaningful communication and reconfigures the relationship among students and teachers. (P. 536) [italics original]

Computer technology can be a valued asset in classrooms in which Allen's Language Experience Approach is being used.

Finally, Allen's Language Experience Approach is congruent with and might be used in conjunction with other reading strategies, e.g., Whole-Language, Theme Studies, and the Author-Reader Cycle.

References

Allen, R. V. 1968. How a language experience program works. In *A Decade of innovations: Approaches to beginning reading,* edited by E. C. Vilscek. Newark, DE: International Reading Association. Provides a brief overview of the approach's rationale and guiding principles.

———. 1973. *Suggestions for taking dictation.* Unpublished paper, University of Arizona. Describes his suggestions for taking students' dictation.

———. 1976. *Language experiences in communication.* Boston: Houghton Mifflin. Provides a detailed discussion of the approach's rationale and methods of implementation.

Allen, R. V., and C. Allen. 1966–68. *Language experiences in reading, Levels I, II, and III.* Chicago: Encyclopedia Brittanica. Provides extensive resource material, including suggestions for lessons, teaching methods, materials, and activities, for use with elementary school students.

———. 1969. *Language experiences in early childhood.* Chicago: Encyclopedia Brittanica. Provides extensive resource material, including suggestions for lessons, teaching methods, materials, and activities for use in first-grade or early childhood programs.

———. 1976. *Language experience activities.* Boston: Houghton Mifflin. Contains more than 250 activities for use with the approach and in learning centers.

Aukerman, R. C. 1984. *Approaches to beginning reading.* 2d ed. New York: John Wiley and Sons, 331–338. Provides a detailed discussion of the approach's development, rationale, methods, and materials.

Bruce, B. 1991. Roles for computers in teaching the English language arts. In *Handbook of research on teaching the English language arts,* edited by J. Flood, J. M. Jensen, D. Lapp, and J. R. Squire. New York: Macmillan Publishing Co. Discusses five roles for computers and research related to their use in language arts programs.

Dyson, A. H. 1989. *Multiple worlds of child writers: Friends learning to write.* New York: Teachers College Press. Longitudinal study of children using reading, writing, drawing, and talking in their development of literacy.

Hoover, I. W. 1971. *Historical and theoretical development of a language experience approach to teaching reading in selected teacher education institutions.* Ed.D. thesis, College of Education, University of Arizona, Tucson. Presents a survey of the Language Experience Approach's historical development and its introduction in teacher education institutions.

Kendrick, W. M., and C. L. Bennett. 1966. A comparative study of two first-grade language arts programs. *Reading Research Quarterly* 2:83–118. Reports a research study comparing the Language Experience Approach with a traditional basal method.

Lee, D. M. and R. V. Allen. 1963. *Learning to read through experience.* New York: Appleton-Century-Crofts. Presents a 146-page overview of the Language Experience Approach.

Purves, A. C., L. Papa, S. Jordan, eds. 1994. *Encyclopedia of English studies and language arts.* New York: National Council of Teachers of English. This encyclopedia has more than 800 annotated entries/topics that succinctly address this topic and related areas.

Sampson, M., R. V. Allen, and M. Sampson. 1991. *Pathways to literacy: A meaning-centered approach.* Fort Worth: Holt, Rinehart and Winston. This is a reading textbook that is based on Allen's Language Experience Approach.

Smith, F. 1973. Twelve easy ways to make reading difficult. In *Psycholinguistics and reading,* edited by F. Smith. New York: Holt, Rinehart & Winston. 183–196. Discusses the problems associated with selected instructional principles and practices.

Ashton-Warner's Organic Reading

Purpose

Organic Reading (Ashton-Warner, 1958) is an experience-centered approach to reading instruction based upon Sylvia Ashton-Warner's twenty-four years of teaching experiences with New Zealand Maori children. It is designed to provide a bridge from the known to the unknown, a bridge that can help students move from their own experiences to sharing the written experiences of others.

Rationale

In her various books, Spinster (1958), Teacher (1963), and Spearpoint (1972), Ashton-Warner presents the rationale and details of her procedure. She states that Organic Reading is derived from the notion that learning experiences should begin with the "intrinsic" rather than with the "extrinsic"; she suggests that students should relate to their own innermost thoughts before relating to the thoughts of others. Her goal as a teacher is to "release" the native imagery and use it for working material." (Ashton-Warner, 1972, 17)

Along this line of reasoning, the student's initial exposure to reading should afford an organic, instinctive reaction to reading. As Ashton-Warner suggests:

> First words must mean something to a child. First words must have intense meaning for a child. They must be a part of his being.

> How much hangs on the love of reading, the instinctive inclination to hold a book! Instinctive. That's what it must be. The reaching out for a book needs to become an organic ac-

tion, which can happen at this yet formative age. Pleasant words won't do. Respectable words won't do. They must be words organically tied up, organically born from the dynamic life itself. They must be words that are already part of the child's being. (Ashton-Warner, 1963, 30)

Ashton-Warner claims that the longer the student's reading is organic, the stronger it will become. She suggests that teachers should reach into the minds of students to touch this key vocabulary; when a number of words are acquired, students should be given opportunities to write and read stories based upon this vocabulary. Ashton-Warner suggests that in so doing, the foundation to a lifetime of reading can be laid.

Intended Audience

Organic Reading is suited for use on either an individual, a group, or a classroom basis with any student. It was proposed as a beginning reading method with children from divergent cultures, specifically New Zealand Maori children, but has also been used in the United States.

Description of the Procedures

Sylvia Ashton-Warner describes the Organic Reading Approach as integral to the total curriculum. Organic reading would be one aspect of the organic teaching program. During a school day, students would be scheduled to do "organic work" and "standard work." Both these aspects of the school program would involve what Ashton-Warner refers to as "input" and "output" periods. As suggested by Ashton-Warner, the typical school day would entail the following activities (1963, 101):

Typical Day's Activities

Morning
    Organic Work
        Output period (approximately 1 hour, 45 minutes)
- conversation, art activities, craft activities, singing, creative dance, key vocabulary, organic vocabulary, etc.

        Input period (approximately 1 hour)
- key vocabulary (for little ones), organic vocabulary, organic discussion, stories, pictures, etc.

Afternoon
    Standard work
        Output period (approximately 1 hour)
- nature study and numbers

        Input period (approximately 50 minutes)
- standard vocabulary, standard reading, Maori book vocabulary and reading, supplementary reading, stories, songs, poems, letters (for little ones)

Organic Reading involves four movements or periods in the student's development. The first movement begins with the students' generating words they wish to learn. The latter movements involve the students in writing and reading stories.

First Movement   The first movement entails, as Ashton-Warner puts it, reaching into the child's "inner mind" to discover the child's key vocabulary. Ashton-Warner suggests that each student has a key vocabulary, which, if it is to be reached, requires a great deal of teacher sensitivity and patience. It is probed during the morning output period when the teacher holds personal conferences with each student. The teacher elicits these key words from the student and writes each on a 12 × 5-inch card as it is spoken. The student then takes the work, traces it, studies it, and, when ready to move on to other activities, places it in the teacher's word box.

Later that same morning, each student is given further experiences with these same words. Namely, a check is made to see if the words are remembered. An opportunity is given for the student to use them in organic writing and spelling activities. In the latter activities, the student will: (1) write either a sentence or a story using the key vocabulary words and (2) be presented with the words for either naming or spelling. The chalkboard rather than paper is used extensively for these activities.

Several other techniques are used to learn and check each student's key vocabulary. At the beginning of each school day, students receive their cards mixed together and emptied on the classroom floor. When the students enter, they have to scramble to find their own word cards. Ashton-Warner suggests that the recalled cards represent the student's "living" key vocabulary. Following this line of reasoning, words that are not recalled are removed and destroyed. To facilitate further learning, each student then sits with a partner, and they hear and help each other say their words.

According to Ashton-Warner, each student's key vocabulary reflects the student's inner self. The words in this key vocabulary center upon the student's primitive instincts. Specifically, they reflect ideas related to fear and sex. Among the fear words often suggested were ghost, frightened, cry, and wild. Among the sex words often suggested were kiss, love, dance, and together.

Second Movement   As the students' vocabulary develops, they progress through the other movements. By the time the second movement has been reached, the student has acquired a sizable key vocabulary and has begun suggesting words from "outside" rather than "inside," such as *happy days* and *snowy mountains*. In this movement, the use of two words replaces the use of single words; longer, yellow cards replace the white word cards. The student again traces the words written on the card, puts them in a story, and, during the morning input period, writes them on the chalkboard and spells them. Early every morning, the students will once again arrive to find their new cards piled on the floor and will begin a search for them. During this movement, the students begin to read either homemade or teacher-made books that use key vocabulary words. These are the students' stories, made from their own words by their teacher or their parents. The students read these books to themselves and each other.

Third and Fourth Movements   As the students continue to progress, they move through Ashton-Warner's third and fourth movements. During these movements, the student progresses from writing his or her own small stories with teacher assistance to writing small stories without teacher assistance to writing rather sophisticated stories.

During these movements the student's vocabulary is ever changing; Ashton-Warner suggests that words appear and disappear with their changing appeal. Whenever the student adds a new word, the teacher writes it in the back of the student's own story book. These back pages assume the role of a personal dictionary for the student.

During these movements, time is also allotted to vocabulary building, reading, sharing, and discussing stories. During vocabulary periods, students write their words on the chalkboard and spell them aloud. During organic reading and sharing, students not only read and master their own stories but also share them with others. Following organic reading and sharing, the students discuss each other's stories, then proceed to use the Maori readers. These readers contain stories collected from the work of previous children. They are intended as an introduction to reading published books.

During the afternoon input and output periods, the students are presented with standard school experiences in accordance with their level of development. These experiences purport to introduce the students to the culture at large. Experiences would include nature study, numbers, standard vocabulary, standard reading, listening experiences, songs, and poems. For students at the key vocabulary level, they would also include letter-writing activities.

Cautions and Comments

There have been a number of evaluations of Ashton-Warner's ideas (Packer, 1970; Duquette, 1972). These evaluations have yielded mixed results in terms of the carry-over of the approach to published reading programs, but they do support Ashton-Warner's claim that her approach affords a more enjoyable and meaningful approach to developing beginning readers' attitudes and abilities. As she suggests in her own evaluation of the use of the approach with American children (1972), Organic Reading may have differential success in accordance with the general attitude and desire of children for learning.

Teachers should recognize that the approach necessitates a great deal of daily preparation. Teachers would have to be aware of and record each student's developmental level and scheduled activities, and, in particular, to teach the student's key vocabulary. Teachers would need to be able to provide the mechanisms for generating stories based upon the students' vocabularies and for having students write their own stories.

It should be noted that certain aspects of Ashton-Warner's approach lack adequate development. For example, while her suggestions for using and generating key vocabulary seem reasonable, some of her proposed methods are ill-defined and poorly reasoned. In places her approach lacks sufficient definition to be understood or implemented, and some of her suggestions lack a base either in theory or in research, e.g., her procedures for spelling and writing words.

As with other Language Experience Approaches (see introduction to this unit), computer technology can be helpful in the implementation of this strategy. Desktop publishing programs and versatile word processing programs (those that allow the user a lot of flexibility in formatting) can expedite the making of books. Word processing can be used to keep track of students' vocabulary, as well.

Given that Ashton-Warner developed her reading method as she was teaching a group of minority children in New Zealand, she has a new historical presence in the current efforts to respond to the needs of children in culturally diverse classrooms. One finds congruencies between Ashton-Warner's method and the three principles that Farr (1991) suggests are important in the effective teaching of language arts to nonmainstream students:

> The most important principle of effective instruction for nonmainstream students is that of ethnosensitivity. . . . It is crucial that teachers understand that their own views of the world, or ways of using language in that world, are not necessarily shared by others. . . . A second principle involves structuring activities that comprise functional and interactive communication and allow students to feel "ownership" of their own writing. That is, writing intended as actual communication is much more effective in engaging students in literacy learning. A third principle is . . . the need for abundant experience with written texts. Such texts are replete with the linguistic responses of Western literacy. . . . The more experience students have with such texts, the more easily they will acquire the particular linguistic devices and cultural orientation that they contain. (Pp. 368–369)

Like other Language Experience Approaches, Ashton-Warner's approach does not simply create a "tolerance" in the classroom for cultural diversity, it actually uses children's own experiences as a basis from which to build learning. Cultural diversity in the classroom becomes a strength.

Finally, as Veatch (1991) points out, Ashton-Warner's work is compatible with the Whole-Language approach. It is also compatible with other reading strategies, notably, Reading-Writing Workshop, Author's Cycle, Reader and Theme-Based Units.

References

Ashton-Warner, S. 1958. *Spinster.* New York: Simon and Schuster. Describes aspects of her life as a teacher of New Zealand Maori children and refers to her organic teaching methods.

———. 1963. *Teacher.* New York: Simon and Schuster. Provides a detailed description of her organic teaching methods, their rationale, and their use with New Zealand children.

———. 1972. *Spearpoint.* New York: Alfred A. Knopf. Describes Ashton-Warner's experiences with her method while teaching in Colorado.

Aukerman, R. C. 1984. *Approaches to beginning reading.* 2d ed. New York: John Wiley and Sons, 368–371. Provides a summary description and discussion of the organic teaching methods.

Duquette, R. J. 1972. Research summary of Barnette-Duquette study. *Childhood Education* 48:438–440. Presents a summary of a research study in which Ashton-Warner's key vocabulary concept was used with students of varying reading ability in different United States cities.

Farr, M. 1991. Dialects, culture, and teaching the English language arts. In *Handbook of research on teaching the English language arts,* edited by J. Flood, J. M. Jensen, D. Lapp, and

J. R. Squire. New York: Macmillan Publishing Co. Summarizes research on cultural differences and teaching language arts.

Packer, A. B. 1970. Ashton-Warner's key vocabulary for the disadvantaged. *The Reading Teacher* 23:559–564. Presents the findings of a United States study in which words in students' key vocabulary were compared with basal word lists.

Purves, A. C., L. Papa, S. Jordan, eds. 1994. *Encyclopedia of English studies and language arts.* New York: National Council of Teachers of English. This encyclopedia has more than 800 annotated entries/topics that succinctly address this topic and related areas.

Veatch, J. 1978. *Reading in the elementary school.* 2d ed. New York: John Wiley and Sons, 343–357. Discusses key words and their relation to beginning reading.

————. 1991. *Whole language and its predecessors: Commentary.* Paper presented at the Annual Meeting of the College Reading Association. ERIC Document 341–035. Points out similarities in philosophy between several older reading strategies and Whole-Language.

Veatch, J., F. Sawicki, G. Elliot, E. Barnette, and J. Blakey. 1979. *Key words to reading: The language experience approach begins.* 2d ed. Columbus: Charles E. Merrill. Provides a description of how key vocabulary can be integrated into an individualized reading program.

Wasserman, S. 1972. Aspen mornings with Sylvia Ashton-Warner, *Childhood Education* 48:348–353. Describes a teacher's exposure to organic teaching through a workshop run by Ashton-Warner.

Stauffer's Language-Experience Approach

Purpose

The purpose of the Language-Experience Approach advocated by Russell Stauffer (1970) is to take advantage of the linguistic, intellectual, social, and cultural wealth a student brings to school so that the transfer from oral language to written language can be made.

Rationale

In the preface to his book *The Language-Experience Approach to the Teaching of Reading* (1970), Stauffer makes the following statement:

> The best label that can be applied to the Language-Experience Approach is "The Eclectic Approach to Reading Instruction." It embraces the best practices regardless of their sources and does so in a functional communication-oriented way.

He suggests that essential to the Language-Experience Approach are the relationships that exist among language, thought, and experience, and among the communicative skills of reading, writing, speaking, and listening. More specifically, he suggests:

1. Reading, writing, speaking, and listening occur within the context of purposeful communication.
2. The interests, curiosities, creativity, culture, capacity, percepts, and concepts of each individual are used.

3. The use of word recognition and word identification is developed in a meaningful context ensuring the use of meaning clues.
4. Reading skills which are taught are assimilated and used.
5. Individual interests and understandings are extended and refined.
6. An appreciation of the value and uses of reading is afforded.

To these ends, the Language-Experience Approach is a total language arts approach that relies heavily upon dictated stories, word banks, and creative writing.

Intended Audience

The Language-Experience Approach is designed for use as a beginning reading approach with students of various ages and abilities. It is appropriate for use either on a one-to-one, a group, or a whole-class basis. The Language-Experience Approach has been used with a wide variety of students, from kindergarten through middle school, and with students of varying abilities. Several variations of the Language-Experience Approach have been found to be successful with students who have language deficiencies (e.g., Franklin, 1992, and Leverett and Diefendorf, 1992). In a case study of a child with severe expressive language delay and a phonological disorder, Franklin records the importance of the Language-Experience Approach to the child's progress:

> Ryan's teacher also took dictation from the individual children in her group each week, which proved to be an important tool for Ryan's development in written language. In October of the second year, when Ryan reread his dictations during sharing time, he began to sweep his finger under the words as he had seen his teacher do when she reread language experience stories. By February, he began to add his own writing to his dictations and drawings. . . . A year later, Ryan began to prefer to do his own writing rather than dictate. (P. 47)

Additionally, Leverett and Diefendorf (1992) suggest that the Language-Experience Approach provides children who have language deficiencies with both common language to use about shared experiences and an individualized approach to reading. Finally, Dixon and Nessel (1983) have used a variation of Stauffer's approach for English as second-language learners.

Description of the Procedures

The following description of Stauffer's Language-Experience Approach is not intended to be exhaustive but instead to represent its major characteristics. The interested reader is directed to Stauffer's book *The Language-Experience Approach to the Teaching of Reading* (1970) for further details. Those aspects we will discuss include: (1) dictated experience stories, (2) word banks, and (3) creative writing.

1. Dictated Experience Stories   Dictated experience stories are the core of Stauffer's Language-Experience Approach. They provide students with the opportunity to learn to read much as they learn to talk. They also provide a means of getting started with reading and for developing, refining, and extending reading skills.

As a way of getting started, Stauffer suggests the use of whole-class dictated stories. During the first few weeks, the whole-class dictated stories provide the students an opportunity to become familiar with the procedure and to get acquainted with each other linguistically, culturally, and socially. Once familiar with the procedure, the students engage in group-dictated stories and, ideally, individual-dictated stories.

Across whole-class-, group-, and individual-dictated experience stories, the procedures used by the teacher are quite similar. For this reason, they will be discussed together.

a. Generating the dictated experience story. To generate the dictated experience story requires that the teacher locate a stimulus with which the student can associate and through which, Stauffer suggests, students can "examine more carefully the world about them, to see new horizons, to view the past and the future, and to act upon it intellectually." (Stauffer, 1970, 55) The stimulus might be an event, an idea, or a concrete object. It might involve something the students can see, touch, or feel, and, with the help of teacher questioning, discuss.

When the teacher feels the students are able and willing to generate some dictation, the stimulus is put aside and the students gather around a chart set up for dictation. For class-dictated stories, a lined chart approximately 2×3 feet is suggested; for group-dictated stories a chart approximately 12×15 inches. For individual-dictated stories, letter-size paper is suggested.

The teacher now asks the students to tell about the stimulus; as the students offer ideas, these are recorded by the teacher. In a whole-class or a group situation, only selected students would be given an opportunity to dictate sentences. Once the several sentences are recorded, the teacher might terminate the generation activity and reread the sentences to check if the recorded ideas are stated appropriately.

b. Reading the story and follow-up activities. Once the students' dictated story is completed, it is read. First the teacher reads the story; then the teacher and students read the story in unison. As the story is read and read again, the teacher points to each word. The teacher may then direct the students to draw a picture depicting their story, to identify known words in the story, or to begin other activities.

On the second day, the students are again referred to their dictated experience story. If the story is a class effort, the class is first divided into groups, with at least one child who contributes to the story in each group. Typically, the activities of the second day are sequenced in this way:

1. Each student follows along, either individually or in groups, as the teacher reads their individual, group, or class stories.
2. As the teacher points to each word, the story is read by the teacher and student in unison.
3. The whole story or portions of the story are read by selected individuals or by the author of the story.
4. The students match, name, or locate selected words.

5. The students locate and underline words they know or the whole group knows.
6. To check on known words, the teacher has the student(s) reread the dictated story orally. If the student fails to recognize a word previously underlined, the underlining is crossed, e.g., *donkey.* This marking indicates that *donkey* is no longer a known word.

On the third day, students in the class are given the opportunity to do more intense study of their stories. When stories are dictated with the whole class, the teacher reproduces the story and distributes it to each student. Individually, students read over the story and underline known words. Stories are then placed in class and personal folders. The students whose stories are generated individually or in a group are given an opportunity to reread their stories and check (after a reasonable "forgetting period") whether they still remember their words from the previous day. For the purpose of providing a schedule for group dictation, Stauffer (1970) suggests the following activities across a week:

FIGURE 2–3.   GROUP DICTATING SCHEDULE

	Group I (least mature)	Group II	Group III	Group IV (most mature)
Monday	dictating	other activities	other activities	dictating
Tuesday	re-reading and word study	dictating	dictating	re-reading and word study
Wednesday	re-reading and word study	re-reading and word study	re-reading and word study	other activities
Thursday	dictating	re-reading and word study	other activities	dictating
Friday	re-reading and word study	dictating	dictating	re-reading and word study

2. Word Banks   As Stauffer describes the word-bank file, it is "a personalized record of words a pupil has learned to read or recognize at sight." (Stauffer, 1970, 74) The file of words emanates from the dictated stories generated by the student. It includes only words that the student has identified as being known across successive days. These are words that have been underlined at least twice. As a check on the students' recognition of these words, the teacher has them identify their words. For this purpose, a small window card is suggested (see Figure 2–4). The window frame is placed over each underlined word in random order. The random ordering of presentation prevents the student's use of context.

The students' known words form the deposits and reserves of their individual word banks. Each known word is written or typed on a card (approximately 3/8 × 1 1/2 inches) and filed. As the word bank expands beyond thirty cards, an alphabetic filing system is introduced. Thus, each student gains a personalized file of known words, which acts both as a resource and as a dictionary. To use the word bank cards as a resource, Stauffer

**FIGURE 2–4. WINDOW CARD FOR THE
WORD-BANK FILE**

Window Card

Henry

Henry is my very best friend.
He is an ant that I keep in an
ant house beside my bed. He has
six legs and is brown and red.

suggests a variety of activities: composing stories, word attack activities, discrimination activities, categorization activities, and finding other occurrences of the words in print.

3. Creative Writing   Another facet of Stauffer's Language-Experience Approach grows out of the students' word banks—creative writing. Stauffer defines creative writing as "a composition that reflects a child's own choice of words, ideas, order, spelling, and punctuation" (Stauffer, 1970, 78).

The students' first encounter with writing is expected to occur with the writing of names and recognition of words. But creative word usage begins with the construction of sentences from words in the word banks. Using their word cards, students' first creative writing experiences occur when they lay out simple sentences and stories with their cards. When a word not in their card bank is required, they begin to learn to write and spell, using their new word recognition skills.

To begin creative writing experiences, Stauffer suggests the use of 12 × 18-inch paper. To provide a space for illustration, he suggests leaving the top half unlined. To guide lettering and to afford ample spacing between lines, he suggests ruling five lines with 3/4-inch spacing, and lines 3/8-inch wide between each two of these lines across the bottom of the page.

As described by Stauffer (1970, 82–83), the following guidelines may help the teacher in developing creative writing abilities from these beginnings:

a. Students should want to write rather than be coerced into writing.
b. Instructions to students should be simple and direct.
c. Creative writing topics may be suggested, but students should be encouraged to write about anything they wish.

d. Students should be encouraged to write legibly and spell accurately, but not at the expense of interfering with the flow of their ideas.

e. Students' ideas should be encouraged to flow freely through teacher assistance and questioning when needed.

f. Students' writing should be evaluated in terms of quality of expression and not purely by "adult standards."

Cautions and Comments

Stauffer's Language-Experience Approach provides the teacher with a comprehensive, well-articulated, and experience-based language-arts program for initial reading. The approach seems suitable for use with students of varying ages and capabilities. It provides for a variety of language-experience activities in all four facets of the language arts. Eventually it may be used either to supplement or to substitute for a total reading program. Stauffer's approach affords incidental instruction for the development, extension, and refinement of word identification skills, spelling skills, writing skills, concept development skills, and general comprehension.

As evidence of the approach's use and value, Stauffer provides a wealth of actual examples taken from teachers in different settings and also cites theory and research. Several related research studies are abstracted in the appendices to his book (Stauffer, 1970).

However, the approach does seem to have at least one major shortcoming. Namely, it appears that the approach places an undue emphasis on the recognition of isolated words. This emphasis occurs in the pointing to words during reading, in the identification and mastery of single words, and in the word banks composed of single, known words. Students with whom the approach is used are in danger of becoming nonfluent readers and word callers, if they give each word the power these activities suggest. If reading for meaning is our goal, the approach should place less emphasis upon word-perfect reading and the acquisition of single, known words and should give more emphasis to reading with understanding.

There are some concerns to consider in the practice of this strategy. Since the Language-Experience Approach relies on using children's own words and sentence patterns, teachers are cautioned to be sure they are using the child's own syntax and vocabulary, even if those language patterns are not shared by the teacher. This process requires careful listening to the child, since it is so easy to automatically "correct" regionalisms or ethnic dialects to "standard" English. The power of the Language-Experience Approach is that the child can read what she wrote because it is her language; if "I be six" is "corrected" to "I am six," the child will not be reading and will have to be corrected when she produces "her" sentence.

Obviously, using children's own language may be problematic in the classroom if the child uses offensive language or if the child chooses a subject matter that is not appropriate to the classroom. In these situations, the teacher may negotiate with the child about different ways to say something or the subject matter of a text. Again, this must be done in a nonjudgmental fashion (e.g., "Can you think of another word to use?"). If a story is not appropriate for general classroom consumption, you may want to encourage the child to tell that story in a different context and to choose another story for reading work (e.g., "Have you told your mom how you feel about that?").

Computer technology, as was pointed out in the introduction to this unit, can be used with Language-Experience Approaches. Casey (1984) used a computer not only in the process of working with print but also as the subject of the language experience. Certainly classroom resources such as informational texts on CD–ROM can be exciting experiences about which children may want to write. Fiction software (as described in Sampson, Allen, and Sampson, 1991) in which children interact with stories on the computer (e.g., "adventure" games) might also be good subjects for language experience stories. Stratton, Grindler, and Postell (1992) combined word processing and photography in a Language-Experience Approach with middle school students.

Word processing and desktop publishing are helpful resources for making children's language experience stories into books and for keeping track of children's vocabularies. Additionally, word processing features, such as spelling checkers and the ability to cut and paste text, help children to create quality texts with much less frustration than the texts they create in hand-writing.

Word processing may be particularly helpful in the Language-Experience Approach. Although the process of keyboarding is a concern for many teachers (should children use a computer before they know how to type correctly?) the word processor is less frustrating than hand-writing for many children, and the computer itself is intrinsically motivating. The multimedia capabilities of computers (e.g., combinations of hypertext, animation, video, written text, still images, and sound bytes) lend themselves to the Language-Experience Approach.

Finally, the Language-Experience Approach is congruent with and supportive of other reading approaches, especially Whole-Language, Theme-Based Units, and the Author-Reader Cycle.

References

Casey, J. M. 1984. *Beginning reading instruction: Using the LEA approach with and without micro-computer intervention.* ERIC Document 245-192. An account of a research project in which Language-Experience Approach was used both with and without word processing/voice synthesis. Computer technology contributed significantly to the effectiveness of the method. Includes case study of a reluctant reader.

Dixon, C., and D. Nessel. 1983. *Language experience approach to reading (and writing): Language-experience reading for second language learners.* Hayward, CA: The Alemany Press. Activities and methods for using LEA with English as a second language students.

Franklin, E. 1992. Learning to read and write the natural way. *Teaching Exceptional Children* 24:45–48. Shows how Whole-Language and Language-Experience Approaches can be used with children who have special needs.

Leverett, R. G., and A. O. Diefendorf. 1992. Students with language deficiencies. *Teaching Exceptional Children* 24:30–35. Reviews several strategies that can be used, including the Language-Experience Approach.

Purves, A. C., L. Papa, and S. Jordan, eds. 1994. *Encyclopedia of English studies and language arts.* New York: National Council of Teachers of English. This encyclopedia has more than 800 annotated entries/topics that succinctly address this topic and related areas.

Sampson, M., R. V. Allen, and M. Sampson. 1991. *Pathways to literacy: A meaning-centered approach.* Fort Worth: Holt, Rinehart and Winston, Inc. This is a reading textbook that is based on Allen's Language-Experience Approach.

Stauffer, R. G. 1965. The language-experience approach. In *First grade reading programs,* edited by J. Kerfoot. Newark, DE: International Reading Association. Provides additional information concerning Stauffer's Language-Experience Approach.

————. 1969. *Directing reading maturity as a cognitive process.* New York: Harper & Row, 186–238. Presents a detailed discussion of aspects of Stauffer's Language-Experience Approach.

————. 1970. *The language-experience approach to the teaching of reading.* New York: Harper & Row. Presents a detailed account, with examples, of the rationale and procedures of this approach.

Stauffer, R. G., and W. D. Hammond. 1967. The effectiveness of language arts and basic reader approaches to first-grade reading instruction—extended into second grade. *The Reading Teacher* 20:740–746. Presents research findings in which Stauffer's approach is compared favorably with basic reading program instruction.

Stauffer, R. G., and W. D. Hammond. 1969. The effectiveness of language arts and basic reader approach to first-grade reading instruction—extended into third grade. *Reading Research Quarterly* 4:468–499. Presents an extension of previous research findings concerning the Stauffer approach.

Stratton, B. D., M. C. Grindler, and C. M. Postell. 1992. Discovering oneself. *Middle School Journal* 24:42–43. Discusses a language experience project with middle school children.

Patterned Language Approach

Purpose

The Patterned Language Approach (Bridge, 1979; Bridge and Burton, 1982; Bridge, Winograd, and Haley, 1983) is intended to provide students success in their initial encounters with books through the use of a combination of a structured language experience approach with patterned or predictable stories. The strategy has been shown to be useful for purposes of developing an initial vocabulary, a positive attitude to reading, and the use of context.

Rationale

The Patterned Language Approach represents an adaptation of three proposals: (1) the notions of Bridge and Burton (1982) on the use of predictable stories, (2) the suggestions by Cunningham (1979) for using structured language experience stories, and (3) some of Martin and Brogan's (1971) guidelines for using patterned books. The authors of the approach claim that the approach represents a response to Frank Smith's (1978) belief that students learn to read by reading and a suggestion by K. Goodman (1976) that predictability is an essential ingredient for early reading material. The question the Patterned Language Approach addresses is: How are beginning readers to practice reading when they cannot yet read?

They respond to this question with the claim (and data supporting this claim) that patterned books, if used appropriately, are a most effective way for beginning reading. As Bridge, Winograd, and Haley stated:

Patterned books contain repetitive structures that enable readers to predict the next word or line or episode. After hearing such material read aloud, children can join in and "read" along even though at that point they are probably not able to recognize the individual words. However, repeated opportunities to recognize high frequency words in dependable contexts help them develop a sight vocabulary that can soon be recognized in other contexts. (1983, 884)

Sentence-matching activities and dictated stories are used to avoid the possibility that children just memorize the story "and are not really reading."

Intended Audience

The Patterned Language Approach is intended for use in the first grade or kindergarten. With suitable material, the approach seems suited to use with students at any age level.

Description of the Procedures

The procedure is based on the careful selection of appropriate "patterned stories," which are used in a whole-to-part fashion. Students begin with what Martin and Brogan (1971) refer to as "whole book success" in which they role-play successful readers, as well as develop a trust of print. Their attention is then focused on sentences and words for purposes of developing flexible reading strategies and an initial vocabulary.

To aid in the selection of appropriate material, Bridge (1979) and Bridge, Winograd, and Haley (1983) offer sources and guidelines for using and selecting predictable stories, as well as generating dictated stories. In terms of predictable stories, they offer several lists similar to one in Figure 2–5.

The sequence of lessons to be followed with any single book or the children's own dictated story is as follows:

1. The teacher reads the book to the group and then reads it again, inviting the students to join in when they are able to predict what is coming. The group may then be divided into subgroups for various choral readings in which they change parts. When dictated stories are used, the lesson is the same, except the first lesson is preceded with a discussion and the generation of a story is dictated by the students.
2. The teacher and students read the story from the book together. Then the story is read from a chart without the picture clues or, if a big book (see Shared Book Experience in this unit) is being used, with the pictures covered.
3. The teacher and students read the story from the chart. The students are given sentence strips containing lines of the story. They match the steps with the corresponding line in the story by placing the strip under the line.
4. The students as a group read the story from the chart. They are then given word cards to match with words on the chart.
5. The students as a group read the story from the chart. In random order, the teacher places word cards from the story at the bottom of the chart. The students locate each of these words on the story and place them in the order in which they occurred in the story. The procedure is requested for each section of the story.

FIGURE 2–5. EARLY BOOKS FOR YOUNG CHILDREN

Alphabet Books
(books that develop concepts to promote letter identification)

Anno, Mitsumasa. *Anno's Alphabet.* Crowell, 1975.

Azarian, Mary. *A Farmer's Alphabet.* Boston: Godine, 1981.

Baskin, Leonard. *Hosie's Alphabet.* New York: The Viking Press, 1972.

Bayer, Jane. *A My Name is Alice.* Illustrated by Steven Kellogg. New York: Dial, 1984.

Brown, Marcia. *All Butterflies.* New York: Scribner's, 1974.

Burningham, John. *John Burningham's ABC.* Crown, 1986.

Cleaver, Elizabeth. *ABC.* New York: Atheneum, 1985.

Crowther, Robert. *The Most Amazing Hide and Seek Alphabet Book.* New York: Viking, 1978.

Dragonwagon, Crescent. *Alligator Arrived with Apples*, illustrated by Jose Aruego and Ariane Dewey. Macmillan, 1987.

Ehlert, Lois. *Eating the Alphabet.* Harcourt, 1989.

*Feelings, Muriel. *Jambo Means Hello: Swahili Alphabet Book,* illustrated by Tom Feelings. Dial, 1974.

Gag, Wanda. *The ABC Bunny.* Coward-McCann, 1933.

Gundersheimer, Karen. *ABC Say with Me.* New York: Harper & Row, 1984.

Hague, Kathleen. *Alphabears.* Illustrated by Michael Hague. New York: Holt, 1984.

Harrison, Ted. *A Northern Alphabet.* Tundra, 1982.

Hoban, Tana. *A, B, See!* New York: Greenwillow, 1982.

Hoban, Tana. *26 Letters and 99 Cents.* New York: Greenwillow, 1987.

Hoguet, Susan Ramsay. *I Unpacked my Granmother's Trunk.* New York: Dutton, 1983.

Isadora, Rachel. *City Seen from A to Z.* New York: Greenwillow, 1983.

Kitamura, Satoshi. *What's Inside: The Alphabet Book.* New York: Farrar, Straus & Giroux, 1985.

Kitchen, Bert. *Animal Alphabet.* Dial, 1984.

Kraus, Robert. *Good Night Little ABC.* New York: Scholastic Press, 1972.

Lobel, Arnold. *On Market Street,* illustrated by Anita Lobel. New York: Greenwillow, 1981.

MacDonald, Suse. *Alphabatics.* Bradbury, 1986.

Martin, Bill, and John Archambault. *Chicka Chicka Boom Boom.* New York: Simon and Schuster, 1989.

Matthiesen, Thomas. *ABC, an Alphabet Book.* New York: Putnam, 1981.

*Musgrove, Margaret. *Ashanti to Zulu: African Traditions,* illustrated by Leo and Diane Dillon. Dial, 1976.

Neumeier, Marty and Bryon Glaser. *Action Alphabet.* New York: Greenwillow, 1985.

Owens, Mary Beth. *A Caribou Alphabet.* Brunswick, ME: Dog Ear Press, 1988.

*Provensen, Alice, and Martin Provensen. *A Peaceable Kingdom: The Shaker Abecedarius.* New York: Viking, 1978.

Rockwell, Anne. *Albert B. Cub and Zebra: An Alphabet Storybook.* Crowell, 1977.

Rubin, Cynthia (selected by). *ABC Americana from the National Gallery of Art.* Harcourt, 1989.

Stevenson, James. *Grandpa's Great City Tour: An Alphabet Book.* New York: Greenwillow, 1983.

Tudor, Tasha. *A is for Annabelle.* Walck, 1954.

Van Allsburg, Chris. *The Z was Zapped: A Play in Twenty-Six Acts.* Houghton, 1987.

Watson, Clyde. *Applebet,* illustrated by Wendy Watson. Farrar, Straus & Giroux, 1982.

FIGURE 2–5. *(Continued)*

Counting Books
(books that combine number and number language, i. e., words, cardinal and ordinal numbers)

Anno, Mitsumasa, *Anno's Counting Book.* New York: Crowell, 1977.
Anno, Mitsumasa, *Anno's Counting House.* New York: Crowell, 1982.
Aylesworth, Jim. *One Crow, A Counting Rhyme.* Illustrated by Ruth Young. Lippincott, 1988.
*Bang, Molly. *Ten, Nine, Eight.* New York: Greenwillow, Scholastic, 1983.
Becker, John. *Seven Little Rabbits.* New York: Scholastic Press, 1973.
Christelow, Eileen. *Five Little Monkeys Jumping on the Bed.* Clarion, 1989.
Ernst, Lisa Campbell. *Up to Ten and Down Again.* New York: Lothrop, Lee & Shepard, 1986.
*Feelings, Muriel. *Moja Means One: Swahili Counting Book.* Illustrated by Tom Feelings. Dial, 1971.
Gerstein, Mordicai, *Roll Over!* Crown, 1984.
Grossman, Virginia. *Ten Little Rabbits.* Illustrated by Sylvia Long. Chronicle Books, 1991.
Gundersheimer, Karen. *1,2,3, Play with Me.* New York: Harper & Row, 1984.
Hague, Kathleen. *Numbears: A Counting Book.* Illustrated by Michael Hague. New York: Holt, 1986.
Hoban, Tana. *1,2,3.* New York: Greenwillow, 1985.
Hoban, Tana. *Count and See.* New York: Macmillan, 1972.
Hoban, Tana. *More Than One.* New York: Greenwillow, 1981.
Hutchins, Pat. *1 Hunter.* New York: Greenwillow, Scholastic, 1982.
Mack, Stan. *10 Bears in My Bed.* New York: Pantheon, 1974.
McMillan, Bruce. *Counting Wildflowers.* New York: Lothrop, Lee & Shepard, 1986.
Peeke, Merle. *Roll Over! A Counting Song.* Clarion, 1981.
Quackenbush, Robert M *Poems for Counting.* New York: Holt, Rinehart & Winston, 1965.
Wadsworth, Olive A. *Over in the Meadow: A Counting-Out Rhyme.* Illustrated by Mary Maki Rae. New York: Viking, 1985.

Use of Environmental Print
(books which provide written language found in child's environment from birth)

Crewes, Donald. *Flying.* New York: Greenwillow, 1986.
Crewes, Donald. *Freight Train.* New York: Greenwillow, 1978.
Crewes, Donald. *Harbor.* New York: Greenwillow, 1982.
Crewes, Donald. *School Bus.* New York: Greenwillow, 1984.
Crewes, Donald. *Truck.* New York: Greenwillow, 1980.
Hellen, Nancy. *The Bus Stop.* Orchard, 1988.
Hoban, Tana. *Circles, Triangles, and Squares.* Macmillan, 1974.
Hoban, Tana. *I Read Signs.* New York: Greenwillow, 1983.
Hoban, Tana. *I Read Symbols.* New York: Greenwillow, 1983.
Preston, Edna Mitchell. *Where Did My Mother Go?* New York: Four Winds, 1978.

Finger Rhymes and Nursery Songs
(books that encourage and develop oral language production and responses and invite students to engage in readinglike behaviors)

Adams, Pam. *This Old Man.* New York: Grossett and Dunlap, 1974.
Aliki. *Go Tell Aunt Rhody.* New York: Macmillan, 1974.

FIGURE 2–5. *(Continued)*

Aliki. *Hush Little Baby.* Englewood Cliffs, NJ: Prentice-Hall, 1968.

Battaglia, Aurelius. *Old Mother Hubbard.* Racine, WI: Golden Press, 1972.

Bayley, Nicola. *The Nicola Bayley Book of Nursery Rhymes.* Knopf, 1975.

Briggs, Raymond. *The Mother Goose Treasury.* Coward-McCann, 1966.

Brown, Marc. *Finger Rhymes.* Dutton, 1980.

Brown, Marc. *Hand Rhymes.* Dutton, 1985.

*Declacre, Lulu, ed. *Arroz Con Leche: Popular Songs and Rhymes from Latin America.* Scholastic, 1989.

*Demi, *Dragons, and Kites and Dragonflies: A Collection of Chinese Nursery Rhymes.* Harcourt, 1986.

Glazer, Tom. *the Mother Goose Songbook.* Illustrated by David McPhail. Doubleday, 1990.

*Griego, Margot C., et al. *Tortillitas Para Mama and Other Nursery Rhymes/Spanish and English.* Illustrated by Barbara Cooney. Henry Holt, 1981.

Higgins, Doin. *Pappa's Going to Buy Me a Mocking Bird.* New York: Seabury Press, 1968.

Hill, Eric. *Nursery Rhyme Peek-a-Book.* Price, Stern, Sloan, 1982.

Keats, Ezra Jack. *Over in the Meadown.* New York: Scholastic Press, 1974.

Langstaff, John. *Oh, A-Hunting We Will Go.* New York: Atheneum, 1974.

Lobel, Arnold. *The Random House Book of Mother Goose.* Random House, 1986.

O'Neill, Mary. *Hailstones and Halibut Bones.* Garden City: Doubleday, 1961.

Oxenbury, Helen. *Helen Oxenbury's Nursery Rhyme Book.* Morrow, 1986.

Petersham, Maud, and Miska Petersham. *The Rooster Crows: A Book of American Rhymes and Jingles.* New York: Scholastic Press, 1971.

Prelutsky, Jack. *Read-Aloud Rhymes for the Very Young.* New York: Knopf, 1986.

Quackenbush, Robert. *She'll Be Coming Around the Mountain.* Philadelphia: Lippincott, 1973.

Quackenbush, Robert. *Skip To My Lou.* Philadelphia: Lippincott, 1973.

Spier, Peter. *The Fox Went Out on a Chilly Night.* Garden City: Doubleday, 1961.

Sutherland, Zena. *The Orchard Book of Nursery Rhymes.* Illustrated by Faith Jaques. Orchard, 1990.

Watson, Clyde. *Father Ox's Pennyrhymes.* New York: Scholastic Press, 1971.

Westott, Nadine Bernard. *I Know an Old Lady Who Swallowed a Fly.* Boston: Little, Brown, 1980.

*Wyndham, Robert. *Chinese Mother Goose Rhymes.* Illustrated by Ed Young. Philomel, 1968.

Zemach, Margot. *Hush Little Baby.* New York: E. P. Dutton, 1976.

Cumulative Tales

(Books which build sequentially on a connected idea)

Duff, Maggie. *Rum Pum Pum.* New York: Macmillan, 1978.

Emberly, Barbara. *Drummer Hoff.* Englewood Cliffs, NJ: Prentice-Hall, 1967.

Galdone, Paul. *Cat Goes Fiddle-i-Fee.* New York: Clarion,

Galdone, Paul. *Henny Penny.* New York: Scholastic Press, 1968.

Galdone, Paul. *The Gingerbread Boy.* Boston: Houghton Mifflin, 1975.

Hawkins, Colin, and Jacqui Hawkins, *I Know an Old Lady Who Swallowed a Fly.* Putnam, 1987.

FIGURE 2–5. *(Continued)*

Hutchins, Pat. *The Doorbell Rang.* Greenwillow, 1986.

Kent, Jack. *The Fat Cat.* New York: Scholastic Press, 1971.

McGovern, Ann. *Too Much Noise.* New York: Scholastic Press, 1967.

Nodset, Joan. *Who Took the Farmer's Hat?* New York: Scholastic Press, 1963.

Peepe, Rodney. *The House that Jack Built.* New York: Delacorte, 1970.

Rosen, Michael. *We're Going on a Bear Hunt.* Illustrated by Helen Oxenbury. Macmillan, 1989.

Tolstoy, Alexei. *The Great Big Enormous Turnip.* New York: Franklin Watts, 1968.

Wahl, Jan. *Drakestail.* New York: Greenwillow, 1978.

Williams, Linda. *The Little Old Lady Who Was Not Afraid of Anything.* Illustrated by Megan Lloyd. Harper & Row, 1986.

Wood, Audrey. *The Napping House.* Harcourt, 1984.

Repetitive Language and Story Patterns
(books with repetitive words, sentences, or phases invite the reader to learn to read naturally by responding through chanting, choral reading, or chiming in during the repetitive refrains or familiar parts)

Bennett, Jill. *Teeny Tiny.* Illustrated by Tomie de Paola. Putnam, 1986.

Barton, Byron. *Buzz, Buzz, Buzz.* New York: Scholastic Press, 1973.

Brown, Marcia. *The Three Billy Goats Gruff.* New York: William R. Scott, 1961.

Brown, Margaret Wise. *Four Fur Feet.* New York: William R. Scott, 1961.

Brown, Ruth. *A Dark Dark Tale.* Dial, 1981.

Burton, Marilee Robin. *Tail Toes Eyes Ears Nose.* Harper & Row, 1989.

Campbell, Rod. *Dear Zoo.* Four Winds, 1983.

Carle, Eric. *Do You Want to Be My Friend?* New York: Thomas Y. Crowell, 1971.

Carle, Eric. *Have You See My Cat?* Picture Book, 1987.

Galdone, Paul. *The Little Red Hen.* New York: Scholastic Press, 1973.

Galdone, Paul. *The Three Little Pigs.* New York: Seabury Press, 1970.

Ginsberg, Mirra. *The Chick and the Duckling.* New York: Macmillan, 1972.

Ginsberg, Mirra. *Good Morning, Chick.* Illustrated by Byron Barton. Greenwillow, 1980.

Hill, Eric. *Where's Spot?* Putnam, 1980.

Kraus, Robert. *Whose Mouse Are You?* New York: Collier Books, 1970.

Lillegrad, Dee. *Sitting in my Box.* Dutton, 1989.

Martin, Bill, Jr. *Brown Bear, Brown Bear, What Do You See?* New York: Holt, Rinehart and Winston, 1967.

Shaw, Nancy. *Sheep in a Jeep.* Illustrated by Margot Shaw. Houghton Mifflin, 1986.

Thomas, Patricia. Illustrated by Mordicai Gerstein. *There Are Rocks in my Socks! Said the Ox to the Fox.* New York: Lothrop, 1979.

Van Laan, Nancy. *The Big Fat Worm.* Illustrated by Jon Agee. Dutton, 1989.

Williams, Sue. *I Went Walking.* Harcourt, 1990.

Zemach, Margot. *The Teeny Tiny Woman.* New York: Scholastic Press, 1965.

Sequential Phrases and Patterns
(books that denote a numerical hierarchy or a time sequence)

Carle, Eric. *The Very Hungry Caterpillar.* Cleveland, OH: Collins, World, 1969.

Carle, Eric. *The Grouchy Ladybug.* New York: Crowell, 1977.

dePaola, Tomie. *Pancakes for Breakfast.* New York: Harcourt Brace Jovanovich, 1976.

FIGURE 2–5. *(Continued)*

Galdone, Paul. *The Three Bears.* New York: Scholastic Press, 1972.
Galdone, Paul. *The Three Billy Goats Gruff.* New York: Seabury Press, 1973.
Hutchins, Pat. *Titch.* New York: Collier Books, 1971.
Kraus, Ruth. *The Carrot Seed.* New York: Harper & Row, 1945.
Sendak, Maurice. *Chicken Soup With Rice.* New York: Scholastic Press, 1962.
Schulevitz, Uri. *One Monday Morning.* New York: Scribner's, 1967.
Ward, Cindy. *Cookie's Week.* New York: Scholastic, 1988.
Wolff, Ashley. *A Year of Beasts.* Dutton, 1986.
Wolff, Ashley. *A Year of Birds.* Putnam, 1984.

Predictable Plots
(books that provide readers with easy text, which encourages predictability and extends meaning)

Brown, Margaret Wise. *Goodnight Moon.* New York: Harper & Row, 1947.
Burningham, John. *Mr. Gumpy's Outing.* New York: Scholastic Press, 1970.
Flack, Marjorie. *Ask Mr. Bear.* New York: Macmillan, 1952.
Hutchins, Pat. *Good-Night, Owl!* New York: Macmillan, 1972.
Hutchins, Pat. *Happy Birthday, Sam.* Puffin/Penguin, 1981.
Hutchins, Pat. *Rosie's Walk.* New York: Macmillan, 1968.
Kesselman, Wendy. *There's a Train Going by My Window.* Garden City: Doubleday, 1982.
Sendak, Maurice. *Where the Wild Things Are.* New York: Harper & Row, 1964.
West, Colin. *"Pardon," Said the Giraffe.* New York: Harper & Row, 1986.
Wildsmith, Brian. *The Cat Sat on the Mat.* Oxford, 1983.

Children's Books that Encourage the Early Reading Strategies
(i.e., directionality, one-to-one matching, return sweep, and predictable and repetitive language)

Ashe, Frank. *Just Like Daddy.* New York: Simon and Schuster, 1981.
Campbell, Rod. *Dear Zoo.* New York: Four Winds Press, 1982.
Cowley, Joy. *Mrs. Wishy-Washy.* The Wright Group, 1980.
Ginsburg, Mirra. *Across the Stream.* New York: Greenwillow, Scholastic, 1984.
Jorgensen, Gail. *Crocodile Beat.* Crystal Lake, IL: Rigby Education, 1988.
Lewiston, Wendy Cheyette. *Mud.* New York: Random House, 1990.
Long, Earlene. *Gone Fishing.* Boston: Houghton Mifflin, 1984.
Melser, June and Joy Cowley. *In a Dark, Dark Wood.* The Wright Group, 1980.
Peek, Merle. *Mary Wore Her Red Dress and Henry Wore His Green Sneakers.* New York: Clarion, 1985.
*Petrie, Catherine. *Joshua James Likes Trucks.* Chicago: Children's Press, 1988.
Raffi, *Wheels on the Bus.* New York: Crown, 1988.
Shaw, Charles G. *It Looked Like Spilt Milk.* New York: Harper & Row, 1947.
Tafuri, Nancy. *Have You Seen My Mother?* New York: Greenwillow, 1984.
Titherington, Jeanett. *Pumpkin, Pumpkin.* New York: Greenwillow, Scholastic, 1986.
Wells, Rosemary. *Noisy Nora.* New York: Dial, 1977.
Wildsmith, Brian. *All Fall Down.* New York: Oxford, 1983.

Note: A * before an entry denotes multicultural literature book.

Cautions and Comments

In two studies, a Patterned Language Approach has been shown to be equal or superior to a "typical" basal approach with first graders. Bridge, Winograd, and Haley (1983) have reported that the use of a Patterned Language Approach—in contrast to a typical basal approach—spurred the acquisition of sight vocabulary, induced students to use context clues, and created more positive feelings about reading. In a second study, Bridge and Burton (1982) were not able to show significant differences, but suggested similar trends were evident in their data.

As a method for beginning formal reading instruction, the Patterned Language Approach shares a great deal in common with Holdaway's procedure for using a Shared Book Approach and R. V. Allen's Language Experience Approach for reading. What the patterned approach offers that these other approaches do not are straightforward procedures for having students simultaneously attend to meaning, the flow of a text, the syntax, and graphophonic features. What also distinguishes the approach from others is the examination of its efficacy by Bridge and others. Too few strategies are subjected to the scrutiny that systematic research examinations can provide.

What may be a limitation of the procedure is the routine itself. If followed repetitively, the specific steps suggested may become more tedious than educative. Otherwise, a great deal of care needs to go into the presentation of the material or varying the word- and sentence-matching procedures. What is also a limitation of the procedure is the failure of Bridge and her colleagues to spell out how predictable story material should be selected or produced by the teacher. When suggesting that teachers direct students' attention to words, Bridge and her colleagues never indicate which words or how many should be identified and matched.

Despite these limitations, the approach does serve the purposes for which it was intended. It represents an approach that allows students to learn to read by reading.

References

Bridge, C. 1979. Predictable materials for beginning readers. *Language Arts* 50:503–507. Describes the use of predictable or pattern stories and how they might be used by teachers.

Bridge, C., and B. Burton. 1982. Teaching sight vocabulary through patterned language materials. In *New inquiries in reading research and instruction,* edited by J. A. Niles and L. A. Harris. Washington, DC: National Reading Conference, 119–123. Presents a research study in which "patterned" stories were used.

Bridge, C., P. Winograd, and D. Haley. 1983. Using predictable materials vs. preprimers to teach beginning sight words. *The Reading Teacher* 36: 884–891. Represents the primary source for a Patterned Language Approach.

Cunningham, P. 1979. Beginning reading without readiness: Structured language experience. *Reading Horizons* 19:222–227. Describes a structured approach for using students' dictated stories.

Goodman, K. S. 1976. *Reading: A conversation with Kenneth Goodman.* Glenview, IL: Scott, Foresman. Discusses how psycholinguistic thinking applies to beginning reading.

Heald-Taylor, G. 1987. Predictable literature selections and activities for language arts instruction. *The Reading Teacher* 41:6–12. Explores the use of predictable books with suggestions for sources and a checklist to assess aspects of reading behavior (e.g., book handling).

Martin, B., and P. Brogan. 1971. *Teachers guide to the instant readers.* New York: Holt, Rinehart & Winston. Provides guidelines and suggestions for using predictable stories.

Purves, A. C., L. Papa, and S. Jordan, eds. 1994. *Encyclopedia of English studies and language arts.* New York: National Council of Teachers of English. This encyclopedia has more than 800 annotated entries/topics that succinctly address this topic and related areas.

Rhodes, L. K. 1979. Comprehension and predictability: An analysis of beginning reading materials. In *New perspectives on comprehen-sion,* edited by J. C. Hartse and R. Carey. Bloomington: Indiana University, School of Education. Presents a research study in which the worth of patterned stories was examined.

Rhodes, L. K. 1981. I can read! Predictable books as resources for reading and writing instruction. *The Reading Teacher* 34:511–518. Discusses the use of patterned or predictable stories in a classroom.

Smith, F. 1978. *Understanding reading.* 2d ed. New York: Holt, Rinehart & Winston. Presents a theoretical discussion of reading and learning to read based upon psycholinguistic thinking.

Response to Literature and Drama

3

UNIT OVERVIEW

A major goal of schooling is to afford students the opportunity to reflect on human experience. Reading can serve as a springboard for such reflections if students have access to avenues by which they can explore their reactions and insights as well as interact with others. This unit is devoted to strategies and practices that purport to offer such avenues. It includes strategies that use various modes—auditory, visual, aesthetic—for achieving and reflecting on responses.

Six strategies and practices are included in this unit. Three of the strategies enlist the use of drama; two involve a mix of writing, reading, and discussion; one involves sketching. The majority are oriented toward activating thinking and facilitating new perspectives and reexamination.

Inquest. Inquest involves readers in a combination of peer questioning and spontaneous drama as students engage in spontaneous news conferences with characters from stories they are reading.

Process Drama. Process Drama represents the use of drama in the classroom in a manner that is not theatrical, but generative, provocative, and spontaneous. Process Drama is based upon the ideas of a pioneer in education, Dorothy Heathcote.

Point, Counterpoint. Point, Counterpoint represents an attempt to empower students' interpretative repertoire by affording a forum for having them discuss various interpretations of the same story.

Response Heuristic. The Response Heuristic represents a procedure by which students are given a structured procedure for responding to text, and then interacting with others about their response.

Sketch to Stretch. Sketch to Stretch affords students the opportunity to develop a sketch of what a text meant to them and to use this text as a springboard for interacting with others about the interpretation of a text.

Readers Theater. Readers Theater involves having students develop their own adaptations and interpretations of stories, poems, and other text for presentation to peer groups.

Inquest

Purpose

The Inquest (*In*vestigative *Quest*ioning) procedure is intended to develop independent comprehension abilities by developing students' self-questioning strategies in a spontaneous drama context.

Rationale

Inquest involves readers or listeners in a combination of student questioning and spontaneous drama techniques for use with narrative. The teacher, at selected points in a story selection, interrupts the reading and has students engage in a spontaneous news conference with a character; the remainder assume the role of investigative reporters.

M. Shoop (1986), who developed the procedure, suggests that Inquest is a powerful tool for developing self-questioning at the same time that the drama context enhances critical thinking through a combination of oral language and reading. For example, she suggests that students, as investigative reporters, develop "internal dialogues, asking and answering questions, evaluating the quality of the questions in order to select the best," and that this activity develops "independent control of the comprehension process." (P. 671) Furthermore, by taking on the role of characters or investigative reporters, they draw upon their natural ability to role-play, which in turn also supports "drawing inferences" and develops "critical thinking." Shoop (1986) contends that by tying together drama and self-questioning, the two activities:

> . . . become the fabric of a strong yet flexible strategy to guide reading or listening comprehension of print. (P. 672)

Intended Audience

Inquest is intended for use with elementary to high school students. Shoop (1986) reports success with the procedure with students in grades three to six.

Description of the Procedures

Shoop (1986) suggests that Inquest may be implemented with most reading materials to be read by students or read aloud by them. Prior to initiating the procedure, Shoop suggests that students may need to be given some training in questioning/interviewing. To this end, she suggests having students view and discuss TV news reports. For example, she suggests that teachers might secure a video recording of an investigative news report and choose a short, interesting segment for demonstrating good and poor questions. Students might discuss which questions were best and why. Then, after viewing the tape, they might attempt the same interview with the teachers or students assuming the role of the interviewee. Shoop suggests that the following ideas about questions are important to elicit:

1. Questions that prompt longer responses tend to be more desirable.
2. Questions that receive short responses or yes/no responses can/should be followed by "Why?"
3. Interview questions generally are intended to elicit "information, reflection, an evaluation, or a prediction." (P. 673)
4. Effective interviews should include a variety of types of questions.

The following steps are used to implement Inquest:

1. Read the story and establish general goals. Once the teacher chooses an appropriate story (with interesting character and plot development) and decides when the story might be interrupted for purposes of the interview (usually at a "high point of action"), the students are directed to read the story up to that point, as they are expected to keep in mind questions that they might wish to ask a particular character.
2. Role-play the news conference. A volunteer is chosen to play the character to be interviewed; other class members are expected to assume the role of investigative reporters. The volunteer playing the character is expected to use the information provided in the story (up until the break in the plot) to answer questions posed by the students acting as investigative reporters. As Shoop states:

    The story is revealed to reporters through this character's eyes: information about the story events is gleaned, interpretations are drawn; "personal" reflections and evaluations are exposed; and projections about future events are obtained. (1986, 673)

    Shoop suggests that the teacher may choose to play the character or reporter in the early stages as a means of modeling responses or probes. She does emphasize, however, that these roles need eventually to be assumed by students. The first two steps can be repeated throughout the story and can include interviews with different characters.
3. Evaluate the interview. The final step involves students in evaluating the quality of the exchanges as a means of helping them plan future exchanges. For example, good and poor questioning procedures are noted for future consideration.

Cautions and Comments

Shoop claims that Inquest is a "unique student-centered" strategy that develops comprehension from the "inside-out." As she states, "comprehension is built through reader or listener interactions with characters lifted off the pages" (P. 673). Despite these claims, several questions are left unanswered as to the viability and effects of the procedure. Shoop does state that Inquest "has been successfully implemented with third and fifth graders" (1986, 671) but does not detail: (1) whether the procedure was difficult to imple-ment; (2) if there were students who had difficulty getting into role; and (3) the nature of the effects. It is easy to envision Inquest as a lively classroom activity, but the question remains: How does it contribute to ongoing comprehension development?

Recent work on Process Drama (see pp. 132–141) has created more opportunities for the use of that strategy as a specific response to literature, subsuming many features of the Inquest procedure and adding the complexity of creating a drama world in the classroom. Process Drama helps children not only comprehend the plot of a story but also the human tensions that underlie it. Yet Inquest remains a valuable strategy (with the caveats mentioned above) for teachers who might want to try out some aspects of classroom drama without creating a full-blown role-playing situation for everyone.

References

Henderson, L. C., and J. L. Shanker. 1978. The use of interpretative dramatics versus basal reader workbooks for developing comprehension. *Reading World* 17:239–243. Explores the use of interpretative dramatics for enhancing com-prehension.

Miccinati, J. L., and S. Phelps. 1980. Classroom drama from the children's reading: From the page to the stage. *The Reading Teacher* 34:269–272. Describes the use of classroom drama and role playing in conjunction with children's reading.

Purves, A. C., L. Papa, and S. Jordan, eds. 1994. *Encyclopedia of English studies and language arts.* New York: National Council of Teachers of English. This encyclopedia has more than 800 annotated entries/topics that succinctly address this topic and related areas.

Shoop, M. 1986. Inquest: A listening and reading comprehension strategy. *The Reading Teacher* 39:670–675. Describes the use of the In-quest procedure, including a delineation of the steps.

Process Drama

Purpose

The term *Process Drama* has been adopted by us to refer to educational drama practices advocated by Dorothy Heathcote and others (e.g., O'Neill, Bolton, Booth). The aim of Process Drama is to build on past experience of pupils and to facilitate a deeper under-standing of oneself and others and society in its present, past, and future.

Rationale

Use of Process Drama in the classroom has changed enormously during the last twenty-five years in England and more recently in other countries. As Johnson and O'Neill (1984) stated:

> There has been a shift in direction from an interest in personal development of the individ-ual pupil, through the acquiring of theatrical and improvisational skills to the recognition

of drama as a precise teaching instrument, which works best when it is part of the learning process. Drama is no longer considered simply as another branch of art education, but as a unique teaching tool, vital for language development and invaluable as a method in the exploration of other subject areas. (1984, 42)

Dorothy Heathcote has been to a large extent responsible for an increased interest in using drama as a tool for self-exploration and learning. Through her writings, talks, and work with children, she has done a great deal to move drama from a performance upon a stage to a dynamic means of exploring issues within the classroom. At the heart of Heathcote's drama activities is a frame or dramatic context that the teacher establishes for students to explore "in role" as they engage in a form of improvisation that requires their ongoing involvement in issues that emerge from the frame. What distinguishes Process Drama from regular improvisation is the teacher's involvement and the tensions, self-reflections, and engagements that he or she creates to move the drama. What is key is the relationship between involvement and reflection. As O'Neill has contended:

> . . . reflection is a crucial element. In drama we experience an "as if" world and at the same time create the means of reflecting on existence. A conscious and reflective attitude is likely to develop in drama because of the dynamic relationship between reality and pretense. (1985, 160)

Process Drama can be used in various ways with reading material as a stimulus for reading certain materials in a role, as a follow-up to a drama, or as a basis for the drama.

Process Drama provides a strong context for articulating a complex response to literature. The second world, created in the context of drama, takes the first world of the literary text as a starting point. Rogers and O'Neill (1993) state:

> [The parallel drama world] will share some significant features with the world of the text but may expand some and overlook others. The characters that inhabit this world may not appear in the original text, and the events and encounters that occur may have no exact parallel. But the drama world will illuminate the original and, above all, give students access to it. The keys that unlock the doors of this second [drama] world are buried in the original and can be discovered through a number of active and transferable strategies. (1993, 75)

The drama world features new characters, often characters who investigate or explain events—e.g., reporters, lawyers, or detectives—as well as characters who might have witnessed or participated in significant events—e.g., neighbors and friends. As Edmiston (1993) points out, this allows all the children in the class to take part in the experience. The drama world is based not on the external features of the text (e.g., having the same characters); instead, it brings to light the drama of the text—the motivations that drive the plot—through the students' adoption of various roles. Finally, because students may adopt several different roles in a process drama, students have an opportunity to explore the same plot events from several perspectives.

Intended Audience

Process Drama is appropriate for use with students at any level.

Description of the Procedures

Creating the Drama Context or Frame   The teacher's first task in Process Drama is to consider his/her objectives for a topic or a selection. For example, a teacher might consider what issues or themes she/he wishes to have students address or think about related to a selection. Perhaps the teacher just wants the students to consider possibilities surrounding a certain event, character, or setting more fully. With this purpose in mind, the teacher's goal is to create a drama context that has the following features: it helps students get "inside" the story; it is open-ended in that the context is not overly prescribed so that participants in this framed drama can contribute to the story or world that is created; it has certain tensions or an unpredictability associated with the drama.

To illustrate some possibilities, O'Neill, Lambert, Linnell, and Wain-Wood (1976) developed *Drama Guidelines*. One of their examples intended for use with first and second graders follows.

DETECTIVES

Preparation

At the beginning of the lesson, the teacher brings a number of objects into the drama room, such as: a necklace; a pill bottle; a large photograph of a teenage girl; an alarm clock. On the blackboard she scrawls the word 'Boathouse—'.

1. The Disappearance

Whole Group
The teacher introduces herself as coming from Scotland Yard. She has been given to understand that the pupils are all competent detectives. She needs their help. They have been called in to assist her in solving what is a rather baffling case.

On the previous night, a young girl disappeared from her home. Her name was Anne Robinson and she was 16. She was last seen when the housekeeper said goodnight to her at 10 p.m. When the housekeeper went to Anne's room at 8 a.m. the following morning, she had disappeared. Her bed had not been slept in, and there were some signs of a struggle. The alarm clock had been found on the floor, and had stopped at 11 p.m. Robbery did not appear to have been a factor in her disappearance, since a valuable necklace given to Anne by her father was still on her dressing-table. The pill bottle was open and empty. The message on the blackboard was what had been found scrawled on the dressing-table mirror in lipstick. What questions would the group like to ask?

The rest of this session consists entirely of the group questioning the teacher very closely and listening carefully to the answers which are given. In response to their questioning, it emerges that Anne's parents were recently divorced, that her father was a distinguished scientist who was attending a conference abroad at the time of her disappearance, and that she had been alone in the house with the housekeeper. The 'clues' are passed around the class and examined closely. Many searching questions are asked about the room, the possibilities of outsiders gaining entrance to the house, the various clues, particularly the pill bottle, the kind of girl Anne was, her friends, her relationship with the housekeeper, the existence of a boathouse nearby.

2. Solutions

The pupils begin to form hypotheses which include all the known clues.

The lesson ended with the class having formed a number of different opinions about the case. The teacher had succeeded in her objective of gaining the group's commitment and interest, and the pupils had listened intently throughout the lesson, both to the teacher and to each other.

In later lessons, developing this theme, the teacher's objectives were to encourage pupils to adopt different roles, and to begin to take responsibility for their own work. They interviewed various people connected with the case, with some of the pupils taking on these roles. In this case they eventually decided that the girl had been taken hostage by international terrorists. In the final sessions on this topic, they planned and carried out the rescue of the girl.

3. Further Developments

Interviews with the girl's friends, teachers, parents, neighbors.

Reenacting the possible events of the night she disappeared.

Examining the house and grounds for further evidence.

Formally presenting this evidence and its implications to the police.

An item on the girl's disappearance to be included in the 10 o'clock news.

Holding a press conference about the case.

Breaking the news of her disappearance to her parents.

Going back in time to examine the motives, plans and purposes of Anne's captors.

A list of the terrorists' demands for the press.

As her captors, explaining to Anne why she has been taken hostage.

Planning and carrying out the rescue attempt.

Helping the hostage adjust to normal life after the rescue.

In this example, the students define the mystery, including the elements and new relationship to one another. The enlistment in the drama frame ensures that they assume a vital role in the unfolding drama. It is as if the drama affords them a "safe place," allowing them to share perspectives and reactions without fear of evaluation. It is as if students can adopt what Heathcote terms "the mantle of an expert"—that is, where they can function as experts. But one should not diminish the responsibilities and commitment expected of the students. In any framed drama, students are expected: (1) to pretend; (2) to adopt/create a role; (3) to maintain and build upon the dramatic context; and (4) to cooperate/transact with others in the context of the drama.

In terms of the teacher, it is important to recognize the multifaceted nature of their responsibilities. The teacher creates the initial frame and manages the evolution of the drama, including being sensitive to the roles assumed by students and the issues being explored. Adeptly, the teacher in the previously described Process Drama: (1) moved the students quickly and economically into the drama context; (2) presented a challenge that focused the children's thinking and contributed to their being more concerned; (3) offered not only encouragement and support but also respected each student's contributions.

Two aspects of the teacher's involvement in the drama were central to the drama's success. First, the teacher assumed a role in the drama that afforded him or her the place or power to direct the drama. That is, the drama was structured from the inside. (Some dramas can be structured from the outside; others can be structured from both inside and outside.) Second, the teacher (in role) created the tension necessary to move the drama along and fuel development as well as involvement. As Heathcote (Johnson and O'Neill, 1984) has stated: "Tension of some kind must be present in the drama." (P. 95) While the task of creating tension is key, the means of doing so may not be straightforward. As Heathcote stated:

> The simple factor in making tension work is that something must be left to chance, but not more than one thing at a time. So long as there is that one factor and no one in the room knows precisely when that thing will occur (though everything has been set up so that it must occur), we have tension.
>
> Subtle tensions are useless in a class that will only respond to cruder ones. An example of such tension might be waiting in the dark for an intruder to enter a room. Or a less crude one, demanding more patience, awaiting one's turn to be interrogated, knowing that one of the group will be found guilty. The pressure must come from within the situation, not from the teacher/role insisting that it be done right. (Johnson and O'Neill, 1984, 95)

O'Neill and Lambert (1982), in their book *Drama Structures,* offer an extended discussion of Process Drama that includes guidelines for teachers. The following set of questions, guidelines, and considerations are taken from their book to illustrate some of the issues that need to be addressed in planning and orchestrating a Process Drama.

When using a role, teachers should ask themselves:

- What kind of role will be appropriate?
- Should the teacher be in a position of authority?
- Could the class cope with the teacher being in a position that is humble?
- What kinds of interactions is the role required to promote?
- What challenges can I confront the participants within my role?
- What actions can I employ (in role) to heighten surprise, contrast, or tension?
- What aids are needed that might establish the pupil's belief in the drama (a document, a photo, keys)?
- Are the tasks that are asked of pupils through the role consistent with that role?
- What steps should be taken to ensure the pupils know when the teacher is in or out of the drama or adopting a different role?
- What questions can the teacher ask that will help create, develop, focus the drama?

Examples of questions that might be useful:

- To set the scene:

  What are you doing looking in that drawer?

  How long have you been waiting?

- To seek information:

  When did this happen?

  Who was involved?

  How shall we get ready for the arrival?

- To locate group in space and time:

  I'm calling you to check if everything is okay—what's happening?

  Is this the corner where the incident occurred?

- To stimulate research:

  How long will it take us to get across country?

  What weapons can we obtain?

- To provide information:

  Are you ready to have your automobile inspected?

  How many people will be present?

- To give control:

  What can we do to make a decision?

  Are you ready to sign up?

Reflection and Discussion   Previously it was stated that the key to the drama lies in the reflection. As teachers strive to immerse students in the drama, they also must consider ways to prompt reflection. Reflection can occur in two places—inside the context of the drama or outside the Process Drama. Several drama educators contend that reflection during the drama is apt to be more powerful than after the drama. As Booth (1987) contends, drama educators want "children to stumble upon authenticity in the work" and to both experience and reflect at the same time. This kind of reflection might include having participants in the drama develop a log, discover a diary, negotiate a treaty, and so on. It might entail introducing a role (a news reporter, scientist, police officer) designed solely to engage the students in reflective thought.

While reflection within the drama may be invaluable, its role after the drama should not be ignored. After the drama, reflection affords students opportunities to revisit and rethink their thoughts and observations. By using journals, sketches, or discussion, the students might, as Booth contends:

> . . . begin to explain the motives and behavior evidenced during the drama, finding reasons and implications for assumptions and decisions they had made. . . . They reflect on the implications and consequences of their actions as the teacher questions and deepens their

ideas. The children have the opportunity to make explicit the learning that occurred. (Booth, 1987, 19)

Evaluation and Assessment   O'Neill and Lambert (1982) encourage teachers to examine the quality of the drama experience—in particular, to assess their own work and that of their pupils. As they state, "Without feedback provided by effective assessment it will be difficult for either teachers or pupils to make progress."

In assessing the drama experience, they suggest that teachers should judge the effectiveness of the strategies being used, the engagement of the pupils with the developing meaning of the work, and whether the objectives were relevant or realistic. As they stated:

> The atmosphere in the room, the level of commitment to the work, the ways in which pupils reflect on the experience, both within and outside it, their capacity to draw parallels between the dramatic situation and the real world, and their transformation of the drama experience into other expressive modes, will all be measures of the significance of the experience. (O'Neill and Lambert, 1982, 145)

Cautions and Comments

In *Drama Words,* David Booth offers an extended discussion in which he speculates about the benefits that Process Drama offers for reading and developing meaning. His summary list of the benefits is as follows:

Drama can:

- Broaden the child's experiences, both active and symbolic, before he or she reads the text
- Motivate the child's need or desire to read the text
- Prepare the child for what is to be read
- Intervene in what is being read, so that new understanding can be brought to the text
- Examine what has been read in a new light, with a view toward building new expanded meanings in a collaborative, interactive mode
- Make immediate and vital narrative that seems at first to be without contemporary application
- Help children discover the story—its challenge, its beauty, its caring, its healing, its joy, its power of revelation
- Help children develop the skills of oral interpretation. While in role, they can read aloud poems, songs, dialogue, and excerpts from novels and stories. While reflecting about the drama experience, they can share poems and journal writings
- Give children opportunities to reveal their private comprehensions in role so that through interaction these personal meanings can be expanded, adapted, clarified, and altered
- Build curriculum connections, since drama and story are the stuff of learning

- Motivate children to do both parallel reading and further reading, using other genres, reference materials, and related writings
- Stimulate children to write their own text, in role, as reflection or in appraisal. Children can do research and background writing as planning and preparation for the drama, or to find new directions as the drama develops
- Build a sense of story—words, shapes, syntax, style, structures, and author's voice
- Find or restore voice to the text

Booth (1987) is not alone in his view that Process Drama offers numerous advantages. Bolton (1985) offered the following comments about the unique learnings accrued through Process Drama. As he stated:

> Learning in drama is essentially reframing. What knowledge a pupil has is placed in a new perspective. To take on a role is to detach oneself from what is implicitly understood and to blur the edges of a given world. It invites modification, adjustment, reshaping and re-alignment of concepts already held. Through detachment from experiencing we can look at one's experiencing anew. (1985, 156)

The research examining the effects of drama upon reading tends to provide general support for drama and role-playing activities, but offers limited information on the extent to which ongoing reflection, perspective taking, and other features of Process Drama (e.g., tension) prompt the degree of generative learning suggested by the affidavits of drama educators. (For a review of the research, refer to Wagner, 1988.)

Heathcote's work, and the efforts of those who have extended it (e.g., O'Neill, Booth, Bolton), represent a major attempt to bring drama back to the classroom and redefine its nature and function. It would be a mistake to view the approach as simply improvisation or role play; Process Drama represents an attempt to thoughtfully create a learning dynamic in the classroom that engages students in first-hand experience and paces as well as adjusts the experience to afford reflection and perspective taking. Unmistakably the approach places a great deal of responsibility on the teacher. As Heathcote (1978) stated:

> The teacher must make this time slow enough for inquiry, interesting enough for loitering along the way, rigorous enough for being buffeted in the matrix of the ideas, but with suffi-cient signposts seen for respite, planning, and regathering of energy to fare forward on the way. Arrivals are those moments of being able to demonstrate our knowing, and the wan-dering is the time of learning. The teacher must delay arrivals, so that time is made for try-ing on, turning around, testing this way and that; to preserve interest and concern so that in each new examination there is chance for more understanding to take place; to press and pummel during the journey in such a way that all elements come to light, and the trav-eler feels the journey to be there; to illuminate the parts as they come clear, and guide to the next dark patch. The teacher encourages the patience to delay, curiosity to seek out, re-lationships to matter, people and ideas to be explored. We must make the task worth the doing, and as the artist pressures himself into fighting for the only creation form to bring to fruition the ideas he struggles to make clear.

Process Drama uses as its material the conflicts that drive literature—ultimately the conflicts that are of major concern to all human beings. It is interesting to note that several recent examples in the literature on drama frames involve teachers using children's literature on conflicts between groups of people—for example, the internment of the Japanese Americans during World War II (Edmiston, 1993), race relations in a Southern town (Purves, Rogers, and Soter, 1990), and relations between Native Americans and European Americans (Rogers and O'Neill, 1993). These dramatic situations offer children opportunities to consider both literary texts and the history that literature represents. They also offer children opportunities to experience multiple perspectives and to problem-solve in response to human conflict. When used with multicultural literature, Process Drama may help students learn how to negotiate with each other by having first-hand access to different perspectives.

References

Bolton, G. 1979. *Towards a theory of drama in education.* London: Longman. Discusses the learning that takes place in conjunction with Drama Frames.

———. 1985. Changes in thinking about drama. In *Theory into Practice* 24:151–157. Columbus: The Ohio State University. Traces the history of drama in schools, with special attention given to Heathcote's work.

Booth, D. 1985. Imaginary gardens with real roads. In *Theory into Practice* 24:193–198. Columbus: The Ohio State University. Explores the relationship between drama and reading.

———. 1987. *Drama words.* Toronto: Language Study Center, Toronto Board of Education. Explores the significance of his work with drama in schools.

Carroll, J. 1980. *The treatment of Dr. Lister: A language functions approach to drama in education.* Bathurst, Australia: Mitchell College of Advanced Education. Explores the language functions served when students are involved in Process Drama.

Edmiston, B. 1993. Going up the beanstalk: Discovering giant possibilities for responding to literature through drama. In *Journeying: Children responding to literature,* edited by K. E. Holland, R. A. Hungerford, and S. B. Ernst. Portsmouth, NH: Heinemann. Using examples of drama in the classroom, this article explores the ways in which drama frames extend texts,

allow children to enter the world of the story, and help children make active responses to the text.

Heathcote, D. 1978. Of these seeds becoming. In *Educational drama for today's schools,* edited by R. Shuman. Metuchen, NJ: The Scarecrow Press, pp. 1–400. Explores her notions of drama and their impact.

———. 1983. Learning, knowing and language in drama. *Language Arts,* 60:695–701. Relates drama frames to language use and learning.

Heathcote, D., and P. Herbert. 1985. A drama of learning: Mantle of the expert. *Theory into Practice* 24:151–157. Discusses the notion of mantle of the expert.

Johnson, E., and C. O'Neill. 1984. *Dorothy Heathcote: Collected writings on education and drama.* London: Heinemann. A collection of the articles, lectures, and notes of Heathcote.

O'Neill, C. 1985. Imagined worlds in theatre and drama. *Theory into Practice* 24:158–165. Discusses the role and nature of drama in the classroom.

O'Neill, C., and A. Lambert. 1982. *Drama structures.* London: Hutchinson. Perhaps the most accessible description of how to initiate Process Drama.

O'Neill, C., A. Lambert, R. Linnell, and J. Wain-Wood. 1976. *Drama guidelines.* Portsmouth, NH: Heinemann. Includes examples of drama frames with commentary.

Purves, A. C., T. Rogers, and A. O. Soter. 1990. *How porcupines make love II: Teaching a response-centered literature curriculum.* New York: Longman. Includes a section on a Process Drama response to *To Kill a Mockingbird.*

Purves, A. C., L. Papa, and S. Jordan, eds. 1994. *Encyclopedia of English studies and language arts.* New York: National Council of Teachers of English. This encyclopedia has more than 800 annotated entries/topics that succinctly address this topic and related areas.

Rogers, T., and C. O'Neill. 1993. Creating multiple worlds: Drama, language, and literary response. In *Exploring texts: The role of discussion and writing in the teaching and learning of literature,* edited by G. E. Newell and R. K. Durst. Norwood, MA: Christopher-Gordon Publishers. Discusses Process Drama as a way of responding to and extending literature.

Wagner, B. J. 1976. *Dorothy Heathcote: Drama as a learning medium.* Washington, DC: National Education Association. Discusses Heathcote within drama.

——. 1978. The use of role. *Language Arts* 55:323–327. Explores role taking and its impact on learning.

——. 1983. The expanding circle of informal classroom drama. In *Integrating the language arts in the elementary school,* edited by B. Busching. Urbana, IL: National Council of Teachers of English. Describes the nature of informal classroom drama.

——. 1985. Elevating the written word through the spoken. *Theory into Practice* 24:166–172. Describes the thinking underlying Heathcote's work.

——. 1988. Does classroom drama affect the arts of language? *Language Arts* 65:46–56. Reviews some of the research examining the effects of drama and role taking upon learning.

Point, Counterpoint

Purpose

The Point, Counterpoint response strategy was developed by Rogers (1987; 1990; 1991) as a way of helping students "build a repertoire of interpretative strategies" for dealing with complex stories.

Rationale

Rogers (1990, 1991) contends that students should be encouraged to develop their own interpretations of stories rather than acquiesce to either conventional interpretations or the imposition of a teacher's view of the selection. As she stated:

> . . . during discussions of literature there is a reliance on examining standard elements of the text (e.g., setting and plot) and building toward a conventional interpretation or "class theme" instead of building on the transactions between readers and texts. (1990, p. 278)

According to Rogers (Rogers, 1990; Rogers, Green, and Nussbaum, 1990; Rogers, 1991) students need practice in dealing with the subtleties of complex narrative, drawing upon textual and extra-textual information to derive their own interpretations rather than adopting the singular and sometimes didactic interpretation of a teacher. With this in mind, Rogers (1990; 1991) has explored the viability of carefully guided response-based discussions of literature. In particular, for purposes of alerting students to the variance that may exist across understandings of themes as well as elements (e.g., character traits) which inform various interpretations, she has developed procedures for soliciting interpretations from students, and engaging students in comparisons and contrasts of these interpretations together with interpretations offered by professional critics. As she states:

> The key to the strategy is that the students begin with their own responses and move toward more public and generalized interpretations. Interpretive authority is shared among the teacher, the students and professional critics, but final interpretations rest with individual students. (1990, p. 281)

Intended Audience

Rogers (1990; 1991) developed the strategy for use with advanced high school students engaged in interpreting literature. With some adaptation, the strategy might be suitable for use with students at various levels.

Description of the Procedures

The strategy consists of three stages:

1. Initial written responses to story
2. Discussion of class responses and themes along with the interpretations of professional critics
3. Development of final responses

Stage 1: Initial Written Responses to Story   In the first stages, Rogers (1990) suggests that the students should read the story and jot down any responses that come to mind (e.g., what the story reminds them of, personal reflections, confusions, questions, and so on). Upon completion of students' reading, Rogers (1990) has them develop a preliminary essay relating their interpretation of the story—in particular, discussing themes they feel are significant. To illustrate, Rogers (1990) acquired the following initial responses from students after reading "A Clean Well-Lighted Place" by Ernest Hemingway.

> Think of your home. Everyday you come back to it and you cook and watch T.V. and sleep in it. People are there to talk to you and understand you. This is not the case for the old man in the story. The story centered on the difference between his home and the cafe that was "a clean, well-lighted place."
>
> I think this story is about the difference between young and old. It shows that the younger waiter and the younger generation only care about themselves. The young waiter just wants the old man to go home and even says he wishes his suicide attempt had been successful, which is extremely insensitive. The older waiter sympathizes with the old man and is more sensitive to his wanting to stay in "a clean, well-lighted place."
>
> It is through the waiter's introspection that Hemingway expresses his theme that some people believe that everything is nothing and is worth nothing and how nothing really matters. However, he still believes he should try to make everything as nice as it can be. He is a realist and an idealist at the same time.

Stage 2: Discussion of Responses   The second step in the Point, Counterpoint strategy involves a discussion based on the written responses. The goal of the discussion is to have students elaborate upon their responses and then compare them. The teacher's task is to facilitate the elaboration and comparison of interpretations while maintaining the stance that a variety of interpretations are reasonable. The following is an excerpt from the class discussion of "A Clean Well-Lighted Place" that Rogers (1990) guided. Please take special note of the discussion leader's (T's) role. During the discussion, the leader points out different kinds of strategies that the readers used and contrasts the elements that informed these various interpretations.

> T: Quite a few of you wrote about the theme of young vs. old in this story in terms of the younger waiter and the older waiter. Let's see, Bob, do you want to start by telling us why you thought that was an important theme?
>
> BOB: I remember putting that as one of two themes. It was basically because of the differences in what the two waiters thought of themselves and other people. The young waiter was very concerned about himself and he just kept saying, I just want to go home and go to bed, and the older waiter feels more concern with the people and the world around him. And he showed that by opening the cafe to people who might need it.
>
> JOAN: Well, I think the light versus dark theme is more important. It kind of goes along with the young and old theme because, well, the light imagery goes with the old waiter because he liked the lighted place and that was a bright place. And also the younger waiter liked the dark place, the cafe. Well, that's what I thought.
>
> T: Karen, you mentioned the light and dark theme but you saw it a little differently. Can you tell us about that?
>
> KAREN: What I thought about the light and dark theme was that the old waiter is dark and the younger waiter is light because the older waiter and the old man had to go to light places and couldn't sleep until it was light, but the young waiter already had light in his life—a wife and comfort—so he didn't need the light.
>
> T: So he didn't have to seek it out.
>
> KAREN: Yes.
>
> T: So either way, we might say that the contrasting images or themes of lightness and darkness are central to our interpretation of the story.

Rogers (1990) suggests that sometimes the teacher may want to bring in professional critical pieces about a story as a means of illustrating the range of interpretations and interpretative strategies. For example, Rogers used the following critical pieces of "A Clean Well-Lighted Place" as a means of expanding the students' views of the range of possible interpretations viable for that story.

> Though we have reason to believe Hemingway's heart is in the waiter's prayer to nada, we also know that his heart is with the waiter in his desire to provide a clean well-lighted

place for all the solitary wanderers who must face the bitterness of nada. Unlike some other of Hemingway's stories, in which the characters are allowed to speak for his values without having earned, as it were, the right to do so, in this story the author's spokesman carries real power. Expressing a mood of bitterness against the darkness combined with a determination to fight the darkness with light—if only the clean, well-lighted place of art itself—the story can accommodate a dramatized spokesperson of a very simple, direct kind. (Booth, 1983).

[Hemingway's] style, with its avoidance of syntactical subordination—the linguistic tool with which we arrange the items of our knowledge to show priorities or relationships of cause and effect—carries a large philosophical implication: the suggestion that life is ultimately meaningless. (Lodge, 1971).

Stage 3: Development of Final Responses   The third stage of the Point, Counterpoint strategy involves the students' revising their initial interpretation. Rogers (1990) suggests directions somewhat similar to the following:

You now have an opportunity to rewrite your original essay. Feel free to incorporate any of the ideas discussed or any other reflections you may have. But, remember to back up your ideas or explain how you arrived at your ideas.

Ideally, the development of final responses takes the form of a self-assessment, including statements by students that either allude to their uncertainties or attribute a perspective to their viewpoints. Some of Roger's (1990) examples will illustrate:

Although even after the class discussion I'm not absolutely sure what the meaning of this story is, I have discovered a few themes, the theme of lightness and darkness and the theme of old versus young. It seems like the young people, such as the young waiter and the couple who walk by in the beginning of the story, somewhat seem to live more and thrive more during the daylight, while the older people, even though they needed light, were more like night people. So the light and dark theme can be incorporated into the young and old theme because the views and tastes of the older people throughout the story are contrasted to those of the young people.

My interpretation of "A Clean Well-Lighted Place" focuses on the older waiter. He desires a clean, well-lighted place because he fears darkness which symbolizes nothing. So he also fears nothing. He fears darkness and nothing because of his lack of confidence: "No, I have never had confidence." Another sentence that parallels this lack of confidence and his preference for light: "In the daytime, the street was dusty, but at night the dew settled the dust." The unsettled dust represents his lack of confidence. Because of his insecurity and fears, the older waiter prefers cleanliness and light.

The old waiter says that light and cleaner is better, while the young waiter thinks and acts as if it is not important. For instance, when he pours the old man a drink he did it very messily. The older waiter, and probably the older man, don't like the dirty bars. The older waiter thinks light is better. These things all show how the old and young theme and light and dark theme are important and intertwined.

Cautions and Comments

The Point, Counterpoint strategy proposed by Rogers (1990) represents an attempt to help students develop a more thoughtful approach to reading and interpreting complex literature. It offers teachers a framework by which they can do the following: (1) expose students to various interpretations; (2) engage students in a comparison of the elements that inform these different interpretations; and (3) encourage students to reflect on and self-assess their own interpretations. A major and worthwhile goal of Point, Counterpoint is helping students attain perspectives on their own interpretations and the procedures for doing so. The self-assessments and reflection, which are apparent in the written response Rogers has offered as illustration, suggest that the Point, Counterpoint achieves this goal. Indeed, Rogers (1991) has acquired some empirical support for this claim in a study involving a detailed analysis of selected students who were involved in using the strategy across a three-week period. Nonetheless, among several key questions remaining to be answered are: What are the characteristics of teachers, students, and curriculum that contribute to or detract from its use? Does the strategy contribute to sustained consideration of Points and Counterpoints by students?

The strategy lends itself to a number of adaptations. For example, the students might be encouraged to respond to the selection with sketches, which are then shared and revised. In this regard, some of the procedures proposed by Harste and associates for Sketch to Stretch (this unit) might be enlisted. The strategy also might be extended to require students to co-author a final essay incorporating or contrasting selected interpretations. Activities akin to televised reviews by opposing critics might be proposed. Finally, some consideration might be given to the possibility of helping students become independent users of the Point, Counterpoint strategy. Perhaps students could be encouraged to initiate dialogues with others and themselves as a means of prompting a consideration of different possible interpretations of stories.

References

Booth, W. 1983. *The rhetoric of fiction.* Chicago, IL: University of Chicago Press.

Lodge, D. 1971. Hemingway's clean, well-lighted puzzling place. *Essays in Criticism* 21(1).

Rogers, T. 1987. Exploring a socio-cognitive perspective on the interpretive processes of junior high school students. *English Quarterly* 20(3):218–230.

———. 1990. A point, counterpoint response strategy for complex short stories. *The Journal of Reading* 34:278–282. Describes the strategy including the rationale, procedures, and use.

Rogers, T. 1991. Students as literary critics: The interpretive experiences, beliefs, and processes of ninth-grade students. *Journal of Reading Behavior* 23(4):391–423.

Rogers, T., J. Green, and N. Nussbaum. 1990. Asking questions about questions. In *Perspectives on talk and learning,* edited by S. Hynds and D. Rubin. Urbana, IL: National Council of Teachers of English. Discusses the role of teacher and student talk in the development of interpretative abilities and attitudes.

Response Heuristic

Purpose

The Response Heuristic (Bleich, 1978) is designed to promote students' response to literature by helping them independently analyze and interpret literary texts.

Rationale

Answering questions after reading is the most frequently used means to get students to respond to text material, literary or otherwise. Unfortunately, questions rarely provide students with sufficient structure to enable them to evaluate ideas as they are encountered. In addition, students may become dependent on external prompts in their efforts to react to literature, i.e., they rely on teacher questions to stimulate their thinking. Thus, students do not gain a structure for their own independent analysis of text and may not be able to react beyond a mere literal parroting of it.

In order to move beyond a literal repetition of text, students need to be able to use their prior knowledge in conjunction with the text information. Thus, comprehension becomes a shared experience between reader and text or, as Petrosky (1982) stated, comprehension occurs "through some kind of structured response that leads to a dialectic which represents the interaction of readers with a text" (P. 21).

A number of reading and language educators (e.g., Tierney and Pearson, 1983) currently view reading as a composing process. In other words, comprehending text and composing text are seen as the same process—both are acts of understanding—and language use is viewed holistically rather than as a series of discrete pieces. Writing, therefore, may provide the best means to represent students' understandings of text, if reading is viewed as a composing process and not merely as an act of recall prompted by questions.

One strategy for responding to literature that provides students a structured response format as they interact with text, and that views reading, writing, and responding all as aspects of understanding, is the Response Heuristic (Bleich, 1978). Bleich stated that the only way to show understanding is for readers to become writers who express their understandings of the text in their responses. Comprehension, then, means expressing in writing a response to explain the connections that readers make between their reality (prior knowledge) and the texts they create in light of that reality. Thus, unlike recall models of comprehension, the Response Heuristic provides readers the means to discuss their thoughts and feelings while at the same time making meaning by writing an explanatory response to their reading. Bleich believes this approach to literature response represents comprehension more accurately than the use of questions.

Intended Audience

The Response Heuristic may be used with all students once they have attained the ability to express themselves in writing. Thus, it is probably most appropriate when used with upper elementary and with older students as a means of getting them to respond to literary texts.

Description of the Procedure

The Response Heuristic asks students to react in writing in the following three-part format:

1. Text perceptions
2. Reactions to the text
3. Associations with the text

1. Text Perceptions Since free response to text has a tendency to lack focus and be sketchy, the Response Heuristic is designed to get students to structure their responses in a more focused manner. The Response Heuristic begins with references to the text read. It is simply a statement of what a reader sees in the text. For instance, if the Response Heuristic were being used in conjunction with "Richard Cory" by E. A. Robinson and popularized by Simon and Garfunkel in song, some references to the text might include the following:

> Richard Cory was a gentleman admired by all. He was polite and rich, and everyone wished they were in his place.

2. Reactions to the Text Once some references to the text are given, the next step of the heuristic is for students to react to those references by writing how they felt about them. It is at this point in the response that students begin to make some links to their experiences. To continue with our example of the poem "Richard Cory," some reactions might be:

> I can understand how people look at how things appear on the outside, without bothering to look further, without bothering to find out what's going on inside. It's important to me, though, that people go beyond mere appearances.

3. Associations with the Text The last part of the Response Heuristic is where students write about the associations—their feelings and thoughts—that emanate from their perceptions of the text. It is here that the response is further explained by using examples from the students' prior knowledge and beliefs. Associations that might be formulated using our "Richard Cory" example are:

> When I was younger, I was big for my age. People, my friends, and family—especially my father—told me that I'd make a great football player because of my size. They said I was strong and fast enough to be a great back. But nobody—not a single person—bothered to ask me what I wanted. They just told me what I should do. Sure, I was big enough to play, but what good is size if the desire's not there. Besides, I hated football! People were just responding to how I looked and what I had, just as people did with Richard Cory.

Cautions and Comments

Key to the success of the Response Heuristic, or any other literature response technique, is what happens after students have responded in writing. It is essential that a sharing/discussion of students' individual responses take place. In this way, readers can see how others have interpreted a literary text and can see that a variety of thoughts, feelings, and opinions, and reasons for them, can exist about the same text or topic. Readers can begin to treat their responses as critical statements that need to be examined and discussed. In addition, they can treat their writing as drafts to be refined, revised, and edited. Following such a procedure, students gain experiences in reading, writing about what was read, discussing others' thoughts about reading, critiquing others' writing, and editing and revising.

Another concern in using the Response Heuristic is the teacher's role. If an offshoot of this literature response strategy is to create a community of readers and writers, then teachers cannot remain outside observers. They must become part of the context in which the Response Heuristic is taking place. Teachers also need to read and write and share their unique perspectives with students. If the procedure is to work, it will work best with teachers who are alert to the models that students are being provided and are either finding appropriate peer models or acting as models themselves for students.

The Response Heuristic is one way to approach response to literature. Indeed, the following frameworks for examining responses to literature strategies are recommended as possible alternatives to the Response Heuristic. They represent alternative frameworks by which teachers might structure response activities or reflect upon students' comments. They represent ways by which students might begin to analyze the actions and motives of characters, etc.

1. Transactional analysis structures (Readence and Moore, 1979) based on the experiences that describe all transactions between individuals as set forth by T. A. Harris (e.g., withdrawal, rituals, pastimes, activities, games, and intimacy).
2. Stages of moral reasoning (Readence, Moore, and Moore, 1982) based on Kohlberg's view of the sequence by which Western cultures develop moral standards, for example, in simple terms Kohlberg's stages are punishment/obedience, the marketplace, good boy/nice girl, law and order, social contract, and universal ethics.
3. Stages of confronting death (Moore, Moore, and Readence, 1983) based on individuals' reactions to death as described by E. Kübler-Ross. These stages include denial, anger, bargaining, depression, and acceptance.

References

Bleich, D. 1978. *Subjective criticism.* Baltimore: Johns Hopkins University Press. A discussion of the Response Heuristic, as well as a critical examination of responses and texts.

Moore, D. W., S. A. Moore, and J. E. Readence. 1983. Understanding characters' reactions to death. *Journal of Reading* 26:540–544. Describes how Kübler-Ross's stages of confronting death can be used as a means to help students respond to death-related literature.

Petrosky, A. R. 1982. From story to essay: Readi and writing. *College Composition and Co munication* 33:19–36. A discussion of the co nections between reading, writing, a response to literature, including some exa ples of the Response Heuristic.

Purves, A. C., L. Papa, and S. Jordan, eds. 19 *Encyclopedia of English studies and languc arts.* New York: National Council of Teach of English. This encyclopedia has more th

800 annotated entries/topics that succinctly address this topic and related areas.

Readence, J. E., and D. W. Moore. 1979. Responding to literature: An alternative to questioning. *Journal of Reading* 23:107–111. Examines the use of transactional analysis structures as a strategy for students' independently responding to literature.

Readence, J. E., D. W. Moore, and S. A. Moore. 1982. Kohlberg in the classroom: Responding to literature. *Journal of Reading* 26:104–108. Delineates the procedures for using the stages of moral development as a technique for literature response.

Tierney, R. J., and P. D. Pearson. 1983. Toward a composing model of reading. *Language Arts* 60:568–580. Discusses the notion that both reading and writing are composing processes.

Sketch to Stretch

Purpose

Sketch to Stretch is intended to help readers use sketches as a means of exploring, expressing, and sharing interpretations of selections.

Rationale

Sketch to Stretch was originally developed by Jerome Harste, Carolyn Burke, Marjorie Siegel, and Karen Feathers at Indiana University. The rationale for Sketch to Stretch is tied to the notion of transmediation—that is, taking meanings in one communication system and recasting them in terms of another system. It assumes that recasting meanings in a visual medium (sketches) allows for the generation of new meanings and the achievement of insights as a result of shifting medias. In addition, it affords the reader a means of capturing meanings in art that may not be able to be captured in verbal responses.

Sketch to Stretch also places a great deal of emphasis upon the assumption that it is important for students to realize that different readers generate different interpretations and that even the same reader may have more than one interpretation of a selection. With this in mind, integral to Sketch to Stretch are opportunities for students to have others react to the interpretations as well as share their own, and to revise their interpretations based upon these various inputs.

Intended Audience

Sketch to Stretch is appropriate for use by readers at any age level.

Description of the Procedures

In short, Sketch to Stretch involves having students generate a sketch depicting their interpretations of a text or event and then sharing it with a small group of classmates who offer their interpretations of each other's sketches.

Sketch to Stretch requires that students have a copy of a reading selection plus paper, pencil, and crayons. Harste, Short, and Burke (1988) suggest placing students in groups of four or five. In conjunction with reading a selection, the students are asked to think about the selection and draw a sketch of "what the selection meant to you or what you made of the selection. . . ." (p. 354)

Harste, Short, and Burke (1988) emphasize that it is important to do the following: (1) encourage students to experiment, (2) alert them to the fact that there are many ways of representing meanings, (3) help students focus on interpretation rather than on artistic talents, and (4) provide them ample time so that they are not rushed.

When the sketches are complete, each person in the group shares his or her sketch with other group members. Without the originator of the sketch's telling other group members of his or her interpretation, each group member says what he or she thinks the artist is attempting to say. Once everyone has been given the opportunity to suggest an interpretation, the artist presents his or her interpretation. Sharing continues in this manner until all group members have shared their sketches.

Each group selects one sketch to share with the entire class via the overhead projector if necessary. Again, class members share their interpretations prior to the artist's and the artist's group members' sharing their interpretations.

Figures 3–1, 3–2, and 3–3 represent some examples of sketches in conjunction with work with school-age children. Sometimes, it is useful for students to see examples by others or the teacher so that they have some sense of the possibilities.

FIGURE 3–1. SKETCH FOR *THE VERY HUNGRY CATERPILLAR* (CARLE 1969). FROM SIEGEL (1984).

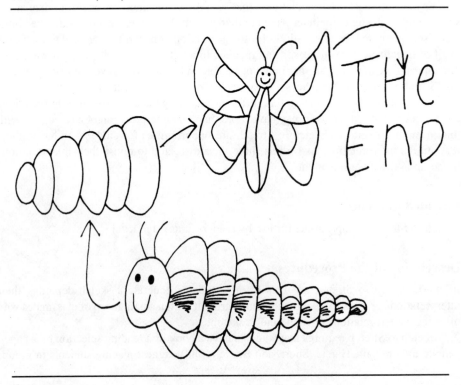

FIGURE 3–2.   SKETCH FOR *IRA SLEEPS OVER* (WABER 1972). FROM SIEGEL (1984).

Harste, Short, and Burke (1988) point out that some students may need repeated opportunities to try the activity before they begin to experiment with the meanings they are creating.

In conjunction with sharing sketches, Harste, Short, and Burke emphasize that teachers should discuss: (1) why various readers have different interpretations, and (2) that differences represent different interests and backgrounds of readers and should not be viewed as right or wrong.

Follow-up activities suggested by Harste, Short, and Burke (1988) include:

1. Developing sketches for related texts.
2. Using sketches in conjunction with doing drafts, presenting written texts, or complementing written projects.
3. Compiling sketches for class books, message boards, and the like.
4. Extending Sketch to Stretch to doing videos or animation.

Cautions and Comments

Siegel (1984) argues that the opportunity to explore interpretations through art (or dance, drama, etc.) affords the interpreter ways to access understandings, explore interpretations, and consider alternative interpretations. What is important to recognize is that meanings cast in a visual medium, such as art, are apt to afford possibilities that more verbally oriented procedures (e.g., retellings, answers to questions) might not.

In time past, both researchers and practitioners have restricted themselves to verbal displays of "correct" interpretations rather than multimedia illustrations of a variety of

FIGURE 3–3. **SKETCH FOR** *NANA UPSTAIRS, NANA DOWNSTAIRS* **(DE PAOLA 1972). FROM SIEGEL (1984).**

interpretations. The research of Siegel (1984) with fourth graders points to the power of this practice to enhance displays of understandings and motivate interest in interpretation. In her doctoral dissertation "Reading as signification," Siegel provides a theoretically rich justification for "Sketch to Stretch" and, from working with fourth graders, substantive evidence of its worth. In a similar vein, the work of Dyson (1988a, 1988b) suggests that transmediation offers learners important scaffoldings as well as vehicles for building and sharing meanings.

References

Dyson, A. H. 1988a. *Drawing, talking, and writing: Rethinking writing development.* Center for the Study of Writing, Occasional Paper No. 3, University of California—Berkeley. Discusses changes in children's imaginative texts as supported by drawing and talking with peers.

———. 1988b. Negotiations among multiple worlds. The space/time dimensions of young children's composing. *Research in the Teaching of English* 22:355–390. Discusses the interrelationships between the children's creation of written, imaginative worlds and their use of symbolic media (drawing talk).

———. 1989. *Multiple worlds of child writers: Friends learning to write.* New York: Teacher's College Press. Longitudinal study of children using reading, writing, drawing, and talk in their acquisition of literacy.

Harste, J., C. Short, and C. Burke. 1988. *Creating classrooms for authors.* Portsmouth, NH: Heinemann. Presents a brief description of the use of Sketch to Stretch.

Purves, A. C., L. Papa, and S. Jordan, eds. 1994. *Encyclopedia of English studies and language arts.* New York: National Council of Teachers of English. This encyclopedia has more than 800 annotated entries/topics that succinctly address this topic and related areas.

Purves, A. C., T. Rogers, and A. O. Soter. 1991. *How porcupines make love II: Teaching a response-centered literature curriculum.* New York: Longman. Includes visual responses to literature with adolescents.

Siegel, M. 1984. *Reading as signification.* Doctoral diss., Indiana University, Bloomington. Presents an extensive discussion of the theoretical underpinnings and describes a study with fourth graders involved in Sketch to Stretch.

Readers Theatre

Purpose

Readers Theatre is a procedure for integrating the language arts and advancing a student's motivation to read. In addition, it focuses on improving students' oral reading and interpretation, as well as their composition and comprehension abilities.

Rationale

In a recent book on Readers Theatre, Sloyer (1982) described it in these terms:

> Readers Theatre is an interpretative reading activity for all the children in the classroom. Readers bring characters to life through their voices and gestures. Listeners are captivated by the vitalized stories and complete the activity by imagining the details of scene and action. . . . Used in the classroom, Readers Theatre becomes an integrated language event centering upon oral interpretation of literature. The children adapt and present the material of their choice. A story, a poem, a scene from a play, even a song lyric, provide the ingredients for the script. As a thinking, reading, writing, speaking and listening experience, Readers Theatre makes a unique contribution to our language arts curriculum. (P. 3)

Unlike many of the strategies described in this book, Readers Theatre has emerged largely from the hands of teachers as they have crafted its use in the classroom. The rationale for using it stems largely from the enthusiasm with which students are drawn to it. Reading material that was drab and unappealing in normal classroom circumstances becomes alive, exciting, and interpretable when done in conjunction with Readers Theatre. Apart from its motivational value, what contributes to the worth of the procedure are the reading, writing, and listening skills that are refined in conjunction with the development and redevelopment of a script and its performance. What drives Readers Theatre is the performance, rather than some arbitrary determination of what is satisfactory by the teacher.

Intended Audience

Readers Theatre can be used with students at all age levels regardless of their abilities.

Description of the Procedures

Readers Theatre involves students in the process from start to finish. Students select their own material, adapt it for presentation to the class, and portray the characters in perform- ances to classmates and others. The steps that might be used in guiding the process are described below. With slight variation these steps are based upon those offered by Sloyer (1982).

1. Selecting Material   A great deal of care needs to go into the selection of materials. Certainly teachers must judge for themselves the interests of their students. But what seems desirable are tight plots with clear endings and suspense, interesting characters, lively dialogue, and appealing themes. Other than the dramatization of stories, poems, popular songs, advertisements, and other types of text lend themselves to use in Readers Theatre. For variation, sometimes the dramatization can be done in the form of a musical, a TV newscast, or a documentary.

2. Getting Started   A classroom discussion about theater or a movie is a natural spring- board for Readers Theatre. The discussion should be both open-ended and focused on what it would take to change a book into a movie.

3. A Sample to See and Read   Once students have brainstormed about play- or movie- making, they should be introduced to an example of a short story for which a script exists. The students should be given an opportunity to read both versions and discuss the types of adjustments that were made in changing the text from a story to a play and other issues that need to be considered if the play is to be performed.

4. Plan for an Adaptation   Using the story for which there already is a script as a model, the students are encouraged to choose another story from their readers or some other source for them to adapt. A short story or a single scene from a story that students will not find difficult to make into a play is recommended. Before any adaptation takes place, students should read or reread the story and discuss elements of story that are key to its dramatization. These include the characters and their attributes, the plot, the theme, and the setting.

5. Adapt the Story   For purposes of adapting the story, use larger poster paper, an overhead, or the chalkboard. Place the title as well as the time, setting, and list of characters on the poster. Then discuss the adaptation.

   a. Depending on the story, the students might discuss:

   The characters in the story and what each says

   The role of the characters and the narrator (sometimes a character can act as narrator; at other times, an observer who is not part of the action may). In order to give more students an opportunity to participate, the students may decide on two or more narrators;

The events, descriptions of feelings or observations and how they might be included in the play as action, sound effects, dialogue, or the narrator's remarks.

b. Following some discussion, write the names of the characters, including the narrator, in bold letters in the margin of the poster. Write the lines assigned to each character next to his or her name. Once the skeleton has begun to develop, encourage the students to make the language more interesting and realistic. If there are characters with no or very few lines, have them suggest revisions so that they have more to say.

c. Once the script is completed, reproduce it for performance. The fable "The Shepherd's Boy and the Wolf" and an adaptation are shown in Figures 3–4 and 3–5.

6. Preparing for Theatrical Production   In preparing for the theatrical production, students need to be introduced to some aspects of stage craft, including working out the positions and actions of the readers on the stage. For this purpose, students can be introduced to the different areas on the stages where action might occur and characters might stand or move. Props and body movements can be discussed and notes made by the students as they discuss what should occur in their play. To assist the students, time might be provided for warm-up exercises in which students experiment with expressing themselves with body actions.

Likewise, students should be given an opportunity to discuss and experiment with their lines. Again warm-up exercises might be used as a means of exploring different voices (angry, friendly, frightened), as well as appropriate pauses and pacing.

With large groups of students, the teacher may wish to organize different casts and production teams. A production team might include a director, a lighting engineer, a sound effects engineer, and a stage manager.

Once the students and teacher feel satisfied with issues of staging, students should be given an opportunity to rehearse with their cast. It should be noted that in Readers Theatre students read their lines. Memorization of a script is not pursued.

FIGURE 3–4.   THE SHEPHERD'S BOY AND THE WOLF

A Shepherd's Boy was tending his flock near a village, and thought it would be great fun to hoax the villagers by pretending that a Wolf was attacking the sheep: so he shouted out, "Wolf! Wolf!" and when the people came running up he laughed at them for their pains. He did this more than once, and every time the villagers found they had been hoaxed, for there was no Wolf at all. At last a Wolf really did come, and the Boy cried, "Wolf! Wolf!" as loud as he could. But the people were so used to hearing him call that they took no notice of his cries for help. And so the Wolf had it all his own way, and killed off sheep after sheep at his leisure.

> You cannot believe a liar
> even when he tells the truth.

FIGURE 3–5. ADAPTATION

"The Shepherd's Boy and the Wolf"

NARRATOR I: A shepherd's boy was tending his flock near a village, and thought it would be great fun to hoax the villagers by pretending that a wolf was attacking the sheep: so he shouted
BOY: Wolf!
NARRATOR II: And when the villagers came running up . . .
VILLAGERS: Wolf? Where?!
NARRATOR I: he laughed at them for their pains:
BOY: Ha ha . . . I had you fooled!
NARRATOR I: He did this more than once, and every time the villagers found they had been hoaxed, for there was no Wolf at all.
BOY: Ha ha . . .
VILLAGERS: (grumbling) That boy! He's fooled us again. Look at him laugh.
NARRATOR II: At last a wolf really did come . . .
WOLF: Yum yum! Look at those tasty lamb chops!
NARRATOR II: and the Boy cried . . .
BOY: Wolf! Wolf!
NARRATOR II: as loud as he could.
NARRATOR I: But the people were so used to hearing him call that they took no notice of his cries for help.
VILLAGERS: Ignore him. He only wants to laugh at us. He's a liar.
NARRATOR II: Meanwhile, the wolf had it his own way, and killed off sheep after sheep at his leisure.
ALL: But no one ever came to help, for you cannot believe a liar even when he tells the truth.

Source: V. S. Verson Jones, *Aesop's Fables* (New York: Avenel Books, 1912), p. 41.

7. Performing the Play and Follow-up   A language event does not end with the performance of the play. Once students perform, the teacher and class discuss how the different characters were portrayed and other aspects of how the play was staged. These discussions serve a variety of functions. Not only do they give the students feedback, they also introduce students to the possibility of revision and further refinement of a play as well as techniques and procedures that might be used in subsequent productions.

8. Preparing a Full-Length Program   Now that the students have worked through the process of adapting and performing a short story, they are ready to go on to longer productions, adapting other types of text, experimenting with different types of scripts, and trying out variations in how a play is staged. For this purpose, a number of different teams might be organized. During adaptation of the story, different segments might be parceled out to different work groups. During the planning of the performance, different groups can be involved in directing, performing, or being theater critics or reviewers.

Cautions and Comments

For over two decades, Readers Theatre has been used in classrooms by teachers who have reported the benefits of the approach with enthusiasm. In an age of musical videotapes and young moviegoers, students not only enjoy being actors and a member of an audience, they also are attracted to moviemaking and playmaking. Readers Theatre provides students an opportunity to learn about plot, characterization, and some of the less tangible features of stories such as theme, voice, and mood. Students can also explore a variety of subject matters through Readers Theatre, as Young and Vardell (1993) point out. Furthermore, this learning involves participating rather than observing, is child-centered rather than teacher-directed, and goal-directed rather than arbitrarily required. Certainly it is impossible to incorporate Readers Theatre into a classroom and not enjoy these types of capabilities.

Technology, in the form of word processing, may be beneficial to Readers Theatre activities, particularly during the process of developing the script. Additionally, there are special word processing programs just for producing drama script format.

Care should be taken not to initiate goals that surpass student capabilities. Sometimes a teacher may try to do too much or have overly high expectations for staging a play. Indeed, one of the advantages and disadvantages of Readers Theatre is the extent to which it formalizes what in many classrooms occurs rather incidentally and spontaneously. The formality of the procedure extends the use of dramatization of a story to the development of more precise reading, writing, and oral interpretation abilities. At the same time, the formality of the procedure may detract from the frequency with which teachers encourage students to project themselves, dramatize story segments, and explore different voices as they read different stories on a more frequent and incidental basis.

References

Busching, B. A. 1981. Readers theatre: An education for language and life. *Language Arts* 58:330–338. Discusses the value of Readers Theatre and offers suggestions for its implementation in the elementary school.

Coger, L. I., and M. R. White. 1982. *Readers theatre handbook: A dramatic approach to literature.* Glenview, IL: Scott, Foresman. This book presents the rationale, history, and principles underlying Readers Theatre. Several scripts and summaries of presentations are included.

Donmoyer, J., and R. Donmoyer. 1991. Readers' theater: Give us some "for instances." *Literacy Matters* 3:4–9. Provides examples of Readers Theatre and some steps for getting it started. This entire issue of *Literacy Matters* is devoted to Readers Theatre.

Hoyt, L. 1992. Many ways of knowing: Using drama, oral interactions, and the visual arts to enhance reading comprehension. *Reading Teacher* 45:580–584. Presents Readers Theatre as a strategy for improving comprehension.

Maclay, J. H. 1971. *Readers theatre: Toward a grammar of practice.* New York: Random House. Discusses the worth of Readers Theatre and makes suggestions on material selection, casting, directing, and staging.

Post, R. M. 1974. Readers theatre as a method of teaching literature. *English Journal* 64:69–72. Discusses the use of Readers Theatre in high school English classes.

Purves, A. C., L. Papa, and S. Jordan, eds. 1994. *Encyclopedia of English studies and language arts.* New York: National Council of Teachers of English. This encyclopedia has more than 800 annotated entries/topics that succinctly address this topic and related areas.

Sloyer, S. 1982. *Readers theatre: Story dramatization in the classroom.* Urbana, IL: National Council of Teachers of English. Presents a comprehensive discussion of Readers Theatre, including suggestions for planning and implementing. Represents a rich resource for locating materials appropriate for scripting.

Wertheimer, A. 1974. Story dramatization in the reading center. *English Journal* 64:85–87.

Discusses the use of Readers Theatre with reluctant readers at the elementary level.

Wolf, S. A. 1993. What's in a name? Labels and literacy in readers theatre. *Reading Teacher* 46:540–545. Yearlong study of Readers Theatre and remedial readers in a classroom.

Young, T. A., and Vardell, S. 1993. Weaving readers theatre and nonfiction into the curriculum. *Reading Teacher* 46:396–406. Discusses using Readers Theatre in content area reading.

Responding to Reading as Writers and Writing to Enhance Comprehension

UNIT OVERVIEW

Over the past decade, the results of assessments of reading achievement suggest that students generally do most poorly when they are asked questions that require careful inferential thinking and when they are asked to generate a written summary of a story. These findings are not necessarily surprising. In many classrooms, students receive very little opportunity to write; when they do, it is usually in a writing lesson, not a reading lesson. At the same time, observations or teacher-student interactions have shown consistently that teachers tend not to extend students' responses either by asking them inferential questions or by asking them to substantiate evaluative responses.

The situation, however, is changing. An upsurge of interest has occurred in teaching writing, which has included a swing toward providing students with many more opportunities to write, including writing in response to what they read and even interacting with each other about their own writing. As a result of these and other changes in practices, students are not only being encouraged to generate ideas but they are also being given feedback on the quality of their thinking. Furthermore, student responses are being developed and guided using ideas that originate with literary theorists, such as Bleich (see Response Heuristic strategy in Unit 3).

The present unit includes seven strategies to help students respond to reading as writers. Each of the strategies has emerged in recent years as a way of having students use writing in conjunction with reading and of responding to the writing.

Author's Chair/Peer Conferencing. The Author's Chair involves having students present to peers their own writing and the writing of other classroom authors or professional authors. In conjunction with peer questioning of what writers did or were trying to do, Author's Chair establishes rich linkages between reading and writing and between authors and readers.

Dialogue Journals. Dialogue Journals provide a more private forum for students to write to their teacher about what they are reading and writing, and about experiences they are having. They provide the teacher the opportunity not only to learn what students are thinking and doing but also to share thoughts and suggestions with them.

◦ *Style Study.*   Style Study involves using texts written by professional writers as a basis for comparison with or as stimuli for student writing. It is viewed as a way of enhancing critical reading and alerting students to stylistic options.

◦ *Story Impressions.*   Story Impressions is a prereading writing activity that involves students' using key concepts from a story to develop their own story or impression of how these concepts might fit together.

◦ *Probable Passages.*   Probable Passages is a writing strategy that uses students' vocabulary knowledge and knowledge of story structure to make predictions about the events of a basal selection.

Expository Reading-Writing Think-Sheets.   As students explore topics with their texts, Expository Reading-Writing Think-Sheets offer a framework for developing, refining, and revising reports.

Reading and Writing as Composing.   The Pittsburgh Reading and Writing Framework was developed by David Bartholomae and Anthony Petrosky to help students become more competent readers and writers of academic texts through a gradual process of reading and writing assignments, which begin with their own experiences and extend, over the course of a semester, into academic texts. While the approach was developed with university students, it might be implemented with success at other levels.

Author's Chair/Peer Conferencing

Purpose

The goal of Author's Chair/Peer Conferencing is to develop readers and writers who have a sense of authorship and readership that helps them in either composing process. This includes developing in students an appreciation of the following: what they read has been written by someone who has certain purposes in mind and control over what they have written; when they write they have a variety of options; and what they write can be interpreted in different ways by different readers.

Rationale

The present description of Author's Chair is taken from the work of several educators (Blackburn, 1982; Boutwell, 1983; Calkins, 1983; Graves, 1983; Graves and Hansen, 1983) and represents a composite of their ideas. To a large extent, the notion of Author's Chair was shaped in selected classrooms in which teachers had begun exploring the relationships between reading and writing. Most notable among these teachers were Ellen Blackburn and Marilyn Boutwell, whose classrooms are described in several of the articles cited in this section. The term *Author's Chair* was first applied by Graves and Hansen (1983) to activities that took place in these classrooms.

Essentially, the concept of Author's Chair grew from attempts to give writers the opportunity to hear feedback from their peers about their writing. Sometimes this feedback would be used to provide suggestions to a writer who was in the process of writing a story or report and who wanted help; or it would be a sounding board for ideas before proceeding further. Sometimes the feedback would be used to respond to a finished piece of writing or to several works written by a classmate. In time, these Peer Conferences also were used to enable students to discuss professional authors, ranging from C. S. Lewis to Judy Blume.

Researchers interested in reading-writing relationships support such experiences after examining the outcomes (Graves and Hansen, 1983; Tierney, Leys, and Rogers, 1985). They note that children who are involved in Peer Conferences acquire several abilities and sensitivities that seem desirable and are relatively unique. These include: (1) an appreciation that reading and writing involve ongoing constructive activities in which both readers and writers have many options, (2) a richer sense of what the relationship between readers and writers might be, (3) an appreciation of peer input and of the extent to which collaborations might contribute to enhancing both reading and writing skills, and (4) a better sense both of the quality of their own interpretations or written selections and of the strategies that can be used when problems are encountered during reading and writing.

Intended Audience

Although most of the descriptions of Author's Chair/Peer Conferencing emanate from the elementary school, the approaches can be used at any age level and in almost any learning situation—from a second grade reading class to writing an official business memo for a corporation.

Description of the Procedures

The use of peer conferences requires a change in the typical approach used by most teachers. In most reading lessons, teachers guide students through a reading selection with a variety of questions to ensure that they are engaged and come to understand the selection. Upon completing the selection, the teacher is likely to assign more questions or some activities, or develop some comprehension, word recognition, or study skill. Likewise in many classrooms, the teacher assigns students to write on a topic, and as the writing progresses, the teacher may help the students. Upon completing the writing assignment, the student submits the assignment to the teacher for evaluation. These scenarios represent an approach to reading and writing that is in sharp contrast to the use of Peer Conferences or Author's Chair.

The major difference is in the role of the teacher. In Peer Conferencing, the students act as advisers and evaluators along with the teacher. The teacher might orchestrate or facilitate Peer Conferences, but students are given control of many of the questions and other ideas that get introduced. At the heart of Author's Chair or Peer Conferencing is collaboration.

As classes begin to use Peer Conferences and collaboration, various permutations can emerge. For example, in a single class the range of possibilities might include coauthoring, coreading, class discussions of a peer's problem or work in progress, and small group or a paired sharing of work, ideas, or interests. To illustrate the use of Author's Chair or Peer Conferences, three variations of the group conference will be described. They include:

1. Reading and writing in progress conference
2. End of book conference
3. Peer author conference

Reading and Writing in Progress Conference At any stage during the reading or writing of a story or a report, it may be appropriate to confer. For example, as readers and writers begin to read or write a story or report, they may want to seek some input on what they are about to read or write. A writer might be unsure as to how he might begin a story, so he might meet with peers to acquire their feedback. Another child might be about to begin reading a book and he would like advice from peers who have read this same or similar books. Sometimes if groups of students are to read the same book or write on the same topic, they might share their plans or simply brainstorm together.

As readers and writers progress through a story or report, they may encounter a problem or want to share what they have done so far and what they plan to do next. Again, Peer Conferences might be organized in which students define the help they need (their reason for asking for a conference), present what they have accomplished so far, and explore reasons for being stuck, or consider what they plan to do next. The student who desired the conference is responsible for entertaining the questions and ideas of his/her peers. This might involve calling for questions from classmates as well as from the teacher. Below is a segment from a conference in which a student is wrestling with a problem in a report he is writing.

FRED: I wanted to call a conference because I'm having trouble finding information on robotics for my report. I have all these books and I started reading them. It seems that there is just too much information. I don't know what to do.

HELEN: Why did you decide upon robotics?

FRED: I'm real interested in robots and how people might use them in everyday life. Also I thought it would be interesting.

SAM: Maybe you could just do one idea of using robots. Sometimes when I do reports I get too much information, so I try to decide what I really want to say. Then I usually just take part of a big idea and use only a few books.

HELEN: You could write about just a few kinds of robots or just a few kinds of things they can do.

FRED: Umhmm. Yeah, that would help. Mr. Flores?

MR. FLORES: So what do you plan to do?

As you can imagine, similar conferences—with or without the teacher—might be held with a variety of different goals in mind. The key is providing peers an opportunity to get an issue on the floor, acquire input, and then discuss how they might use the advice.

End of Book Conference   These conferences provide students the opportunity to share their reading and writing experiences and products. When students finish the stories they have been reading or the reports they have been writing, they can set up a conference for purposes of sharing their accomplishment with their peers. This might involve providing their peers a synopsis of what they have written or read. It might involve reading the entire story or report or interesting sections of a book aloud. Also, it might include discussing what it was like to read or write this story. After sharing, the writer or reader opens the floor to peer reactions, comments, and questions. As Graves and Hansen (1983) suggest, sometimes a reader or writer might need to develop confidence, in which case peers are encouraged to give supportive comments more than interrogative questions. Hansen (1983) has illustrated two such conferences in some examples of writing conferences that took place in Ellen Blackburn's first grade classroom. As Hansen (1983) described them:

> When Scott sits on a little chair . . . and reads his published book to the whole class clustered on the floor in front of him, with their eyes glued upon him, he's scared. Scott is a fragile author. But he knows that when he has finished reading, they will clap. Then lots of hands will go up. However, Scott need not fear because no one plans to ask a question. His friends want to make comments. Regardless of whom Scott calls upon, the child will accept his writing. "My favorite part was when you rode in the ambulance." Or, "The part I liked best was when you looked in the doctor's glasses and under your skin it looked liked fish eggs." His friend didn't ask him to read that part again, but it is also Scott's favorite part and he intends to share it again. . . .

> When Jamie shared her book about her nana, a classmate asked, "Why does your Nana have a lump on her back?" Some questions are more pointed. Daniel read his book about his babysitter's cat who got stuck in the dryer, and a friend asked, "Why didn't you tell how the cat got in the dryer?" (Pp. 972–973)

Again, such conferences can be used in conjunction with stories and reports that are read by students, as well as written by them. Sometimes such conferences might involve presenting reactions to published authors similar to the following:

LISA: I loved this Judy Blume book. She tells a story about a girl who was overweight. I particularly like the way she let you know the girl's feelings. Let me read you a section. Blume is an excellent author; the only section which I thought she could have improved was her description of the eating by the girl. Also sometimes she left out some important facts. Anyhow I would recommend the book, in fact, I am planning to write a book similar to it.

FLOR: Who do you think would like this book?

LISA: Anybody who enjoys Blume or stories about people who are real and have everyday problems. I think you would like it.

PETER: How come you didn't like so much of the book and still recommend it?

LISA: No book is perfect.

ELIZABETH: In what ways will your book be similar? etc.

In contrast to reporting on professional authors, conferences about peer work might also be conducted. These are described next.

Peer Author Conferences   Unlike the conferences in which students report on professional authors or their own efforts, Peer Author Conferences refer to conferences that are given by classmates on peer writing. In this situation, the author is present and might be questioned occasionally, but somebody else—a peer reader—reports on the book and fields most of the questions and comments. The author has an opportunity to hear somebody else represent the book, including what they enjoyed, found confusing, and might use. In addition, the author along with peers has an opportunity to ask questions of the readers about their recommendations and evaluation of the book. The person who reads the book has a unique opportunity to share a book of an author whom they know and with whom they may have conferred about the book.

Cautions and Comments

As was mentioned earlier, researchers have suggested that the collaborative experiences afforded by the Author's Chair or Peer Conferencing result in improvements in a student's sense of readership and authorship, as well as an ability to evaluate and problem-solve. In fact, Leal (1993) mentions three positive outcomes of literary peer discussion groups. They are: (1) "a catalyst for learning," (2) "a platform for peer collaboration and peer tutoring," and (3) "an opportunity for exploratory talk with a real audience." She also found that the use of the genre "informational storybook" (books that combine factual information in a fictional narrative framework) was associated with longer discussions by the children, more predictions about the text, and more connections outside the text, such as prior knowledge.

In conjunction with using Author's Chair and other group activities, Brent and Anderson (1993) suggest that teachers help children to develop good listening skills. Specifically, they suggest not only that teachers themselves model good listening skills, but also that they provide instruction in the form of minilessons:]

> Children can be taught to predict what they might hear, follow directions, appreciate language, identify main ideas and supporting details, draw justifiable inferences, differentiate fact from fiction, and analyze critically. Strategies such as watching the speaker, focusing to block distractions, visualizing, formulating questions, making mental associations, pre-

dicting while listening, summarizing, and taking notes are all useful to children as they work to improve their listening abilities. In addition, children should be taught how to select strategies to match the listening situation. (P. 124)

Apart from the benefits of author's chair-type discussions, the opportunity to confer provides students with a rich resource that often goes untapped in classrooms—namely, one's own peers. Furthermore, if conferencing opportunities extend to works in progress, teachers can move away from just assigning and assessing reading and writing to developing strategies for use as reading and writing actually occurs. By providing a forum for making public any difficulties and strategies, as Graves and Hansen (1983) and Tierney, Leys, and Rogers (1985) have argued, readers and writers are likely to become both better self-monitors and more flexible strategy users.

Finally, providing children with an opportunity to respond to each other's work challenges narrow gender roles, which children may take on in their writing, as McAuliffe's work indicates. Sheila McAuliffe (1993) found that children were very likely to use strongly gendered language and story subjects, such that boys and girls had a hard time understanding each other's stories when sharing them in an author's chair-type forum. She found that stories written later in the school year were more likely to feature both male and female story characteristics, stories to which both boys and girls made positive responses. She concludes:

> This yearlong study of a whole language classroom pointed out the importance of *intent* in the process of communication. When understanding broke down, it seemed the students' intent or desire to share meanings caused them to continue to try to understand and be understood. . . . By creating this kind of writers' workshop, a teacher can set up social structures that encourage learners to try to understand one another. When writers ask their audience for response, they want the responders' views of their written messages. These views, including those of the other gender, are then available to use for clarifying original drafts.

Author's Chair may also help children to respond in less ethnocentric ways, provided that children who are outside the dominant culture of the class feel supported in and respected for their readings of and responses to their peers' work.

Three obstacles appear likely to stand in the way of successful conferencing in many classrooms. First, most teachers place themselves on center stage; a conferencing approach requires them to establish quite a different social setting for reading and writing. Second, a teacher may find that children do not automatically take to the approach. Their comments may seem off-base, too general, or too tentative. Some students need encouragement, support, and repeated opportunities before the conferences seem worthwhile. In a recent study, Hittleman had a great deal of success establishing more effective Peer Conferences, using a combination of peer and teacher modeling (Hittleman, 1983). Third, many of the conferences that were described are based on two tenets: (1) students should have the opportunity to write for longer than 30 minutes twice a week (they should be given enough time to write extended stories and reports of their own choosing); and (2) writing experiences contribute to reading. Unless these two tenets are observed in a classroom, some of the conferences described could not take place.

References

Atwell, N. 1987. *In the middle: Writing, reading and learning with adolescents.* Portsmouth, NH: Boynton/Cook-Heinemann. Describes her use of Peer Conferencing and Author's Chair in the middle grades.

Blackburn, E. 1982. The rhythm of writing development. In *Understanding writing,* edited by T. Newkirk and N. Atwell. Chelmsford, MA: Northeast Regional Exchange. Describes several of her experiences in the first grade as she observed her students writing and interacted with them.

Boutwell, M. 1983. Reading and writing: A reciprocal agreement. *Language Arts* 60:6, 723–730. Describes the features of her classroom that supported a reciprocal agreement between reading and writing, including the conferences that were initiated.

Brent, R., and P. Anderson. 1993. Developing children's classroom listening strategies. *The Reading Teacher* 47:122–126. This article identifies important listening strategies and components of lessons for helping children to acquire these strategies.

Calkins, L. M. 1983. *Lessons from a child.* Portsmouth, NH: Heinemann. In this story of one child's growth in writing, Calkins illustrates what influences and classroom procedures are woven into the child's development.

———. 1986. *The art of teaching writing.* Portsmouth, NH: Heinemann. Describes the rationale and procedures for Peer Conferencing.

Graves, D. 1983. *Writing: Teachers and children at work.* Exeter, NH: Heinemann. Provides a full description of how teachers might teach writing in conjunction with the use of a conference approach. Graves provides extensive guidelines for how teachers might confer with students, which can be applied to Peer Conferencing.

Graves, D., and J. Hansen. 1983. The author's chair. *Language Arts* 60:176–183. Describes the nature and benefits derived in a first-grade classroom that initiated the use of Author's Chair.

Hansen, J. 1983. Authors respond to authors. *Language Arts* 60:970–976. Describes several different types of conferences with examples from her observations in classrooms.

———. 1987. *When Writers Read.* Portsmouth, NH: Heinemann. Describes Author's Chair in the context of many other strategies that support children's reading and writing.

Harste, J. C., K. G. Short, and C. B. Burke. 1989. *Creating classrooms for authors.* Portsmouth, NH: Heinemann. Presents several activities and suggestions for implementing sharing by authors and readers.

Hawkins, T. 1977. *Group inquiry techniques for teaching writing.* Urbana, IL: ERIC Clearinghouse on Reading and Communication Skills/NCTE. Describes several procedures for organizing and developing discussion of writing by peers.

Healy, M. K. 1980. *Using student writing response groups in the classroom.* Berkeley: University of California, Bay Area Writing Project. Describes the use of peer response groups in classrooms.

Hittleman, C. G. 1983. *Peer conference groups and teacher written comments as influences on revisions during the composing processes of fourth grade students.* Unpublished doctoral diss., Hofstra University. Presents a thorough study of the use of Peer Conferencing in the fourth grade.

Karelitz, E. B. 1993. *The author's chair and beyond: Language and literacy in a primary classroom.* Portsmouth, NH: Heinemann. Describes several reading and writing strategies, including Author's Chair.

Leal, D. J. 1993. The power of literary peer-group discussions: How children collaboratively negotiate meaning. *The Reading Teacher* 47:114–120. Analyzes examples of children's discussions and shows the kinds of meanings children engage with and derive from them.

McAuliffe, S. 1993. Toward understanding one another: Second graders' use of gendered language and story styles. *The Reading Teacher*

47:302–310. Describes a study of children's gender use in their stories and how this changed through peer response in a Whole-Language classroom.

Newell, G. E., and R. K. Durst, eds. 1993. *Exploring texts: The role of discussion and writing in the teaching and learning of literature.* Norwood, MA: Christopher-Gordon Publishers, Inc. Collection of articles, many of which discuss Author's Chair-type techniques.

Purves, A. C., L. Papa, and S. Jordan, eds. 1994. *Encyclopedia of English studies and language arts.* New York: National Council of Teachers of English. This encyclopedia has more than 800 annotated entries/topics that succinctly address this topic and related areas.

Purves, A. C., T. Rogers, and A. Soter. 1990. *How porcupines make love II: Teaching a response-centered literature curriculum.* New York: Longman. Discusses many ways of helping students respond to literature, including Author's Chair-type techniques. Focuses on older students.

Tierney, R. J., M. Leys, and T. Rogers. 1985. Composition, comprehension, and collaboration: An analysis of two classrooms. In *Contexts of literacy,* edited by T. Raphael and R. Reynolds. New York: Random House. Describes the classroom parameters for a conferencing approach for both reading and writing and the comments and responses of some fourth-grade students.

Dialogue Journals

Purpose

Dialogue Journals, as described by Staton (1980), are intended to provide students an opportunity to share privately in writing their reactions, questions, and concerns about school experiences (and sometimes personal matters) with the teacher without any threat of reprisal or evaluation. It affords the teacher an opportunity to learn what each individual child is doing and thinking, and then to offer counsel.

Rationale

Although the term *Dialogue Journal* has a rather recent history, the use of journals per se has a long history dating back to when individuals began using writing as a means of record keeping and of reflecting upon their lot in life. In school situations, journal writing has often assumed a life of its own as English teachers, and sometimes science teachers, have introduced it into the daily or weekly life of their students. Often journals were used to encourage diarylike entries of what took place in the way of progress on a project; sometimes they were used to give students the opportunity to respond freely to what took place at school or home, or to respond to a book or some other form of literature. The negative side of journals is that they can become tedious or, with some students, never take hold. Some students don't enjoy the experience and find the task boring; some may be very withdrawn or are not sufficiently introspective to talk "to themselves." Also, if journal writing becomes a preoccupation, then both the students and the teacher will likely find the experience a chore. On the positive side, and what accounts for the widespread advocacy of journal writing, are testimonies of the benefits. As Kirby and Liner (1981) suggest:

Simply stated, the journal is the most consistently effective tool for establishing fluency that I have found. True believers swear that the journal works on some mystical principle because some nonfluent, nontalking, and apparent nonthinking students have blossomed so dramatically through journal writing. (P. 45)

Other testimonies attest to further advantages: (1) the opportunity that journal writing provides for more open responses to classroom assignments; (2) the vehicle that it provides for teacher feedback, counseling, and response; and (3) the chance that it gives for dealing with each student individually.

The notion of Dialogue Journals is a partial refinement of journal writing. The major characteristic that distinguishes Dialogue Journals from other forms is the importance given to communications between the student and the teacher. Dialogue Journals are more like a daily letter or memo to the teacher. While the teacher might not respond to every entry, the intent of Dialogue Journals is to have students write to the teacher and to have the teacher write a genuine response to the student. Often the Dialogue Journal is quite open-ended and the student includes letters on all sorts of matters, from diets to schoolwork to sporting events. Sometimes students have journals that are intended to record reactions and concerns to specific experiences, such as reading and writing. If the latter is the case, the teacher might ask the students to include, either occasionally or on a regular basis, specific types of information in their journals. In all of these situations, the child writes and the teacher responds. The advantage is that the teacher and student can share, on a one-to-one basis, matters for which most classroom situations do not allow sufficient time in the course of the day.

Intended Audience

Dialogue Journals can be used with students at any age level.

Description of the Procedures

To illustrate the procedures for Dialogue Journals, the following examples (Figures 4–1 and 4–2) are taken from a third-grade classroom in which the teacher provided time every day for students to write entries in two journals: a reading journal and a writing journal. The original entries have been rewritten, and the names of the student and teacher changed to ensure their privacy. Otherwise they are reproduced exactly.

The four journal entries represent some of the different types of comments that students might be prompted to make in their journals. They include examples of comments by the students about what they have been reading and writing and their experiences in doing so. They include reflections about peer relationships, and responses to and inquiries directed at the teacher.

The teacher's entry represents a rich assortment of reflections in response to what the student has shared and an attempt to extend the child's thinking. One of the comments offered by the teacher discusses how the student's experiences were similar to her own (I also picture in my head as I read); at the same time the teacher's comments reflect an attempt to extend these ideas (it is a sign of good writing) and offer some advice (tell the

FIGURE 4–1. EXAMPLES OF DIALOGUE JOURNAL ENTRIES

FIGURE 4–2. EXAMPLES OF DIALOGUE JOURNAL ENTRIES

OCT. 20, Sailing
I could really see
and hear and feel
the waves That
really was neat. I
like the part when
Billy and the kids race
and the boat tips
over! The picturs
were neat to! They
did a excellent job.

Sara,
I sometimes can see, hear, and feel things that I am reading about too. It's usually when the writing is good, when the author makes every thing come alive!
You describe their writing and congratulate thomas one author would to another. I think that's neat!
Thank You,
L. Rietveld

April 13
Today I am writing
on Indian Art with
Brenda. We done a lot
so far but we are kind
of having trouble
because we have to
interview Mrs. Johnson
and she wasn't there
when we went. Any
way we'll try again.

Sara,
I must congratulate you on your Carnival story. You included so many interesting details!
As for interviewing Mrs. Johnson perhaps you could put a note asking for an appointment in her box. Have you and Brenda written down the questions you wish to ask her? Would you like to borrow a tape recorder?
L. Rietveld

Dear Miss Rietveld
Do We
have to
Do It.
! ! ! !

Feb, 10
Today I will write
about Kara . SHE A
JERK !!! She writes
on my desk and she
wrote me a note and
asked me If I liked
Sam . I didn't think
she is funny.
Kara Stinks !!!
The End

Angie,
You sound very angry. Maybe, you, Kara, and I could meet to discuss this problem. Or maybe you could show her this part of your journal?
What do you think you should do?
L. Rietveld

author). It is interesting to note the teacher's written comments following one student's lengthy discussion of a classmate with whom there is some enmity. The teacher does not evaluate the student's comments as either right or wrong. The student's feelings are accepted as legitimate, and the teacher offers a couple of suggestions as to how she might deal with her feelings. What is important to note is the teacher's respect for the privacy of the journal as well as the nonjudgmental and nonprescriptive nature of the teacher's reaction. Decisions to be made are left up to the student.

Getting Started   Nancy Atwell has discussed beginning Dialogue Journals in her eighth grade classroom (Atwell 1984). She described how she initiated the journals:

> This folder is a place for you and me to talk about books, reading, authors, and writing. You're to write letters to me, and I'll write letters back to you.
>
> In your letters to me, talk with me about what you've read. Tell me what you thought and felt and why. Tell me what you liked and didn't like and why. Tell me what these

books meant to you and said to you. Ask me questions or for help, and write back to me about my ideas, feelings, and questions.

While there are other ways to begin Dialogue Journals and other types of journals, Atwell's comments describe for students the purpose of the journal and give a very open-ended sense of what might be included. Once initiated, it is important that the journal writing not be shortchanged in terms of time allocation. Unless uninterrupted time is put aside during the school day for everybody to write in his/her journal, the possibility of obtaining meaningful journal entries diminishes.

Responding to Journals   In many ways suggestions for responding to journals should be rather obvious, yet there are guidelines to keep in mind when responding. Apart from recommending that journal responses by a teacher be sincere, thoughtful, and regular, the following represents a compilation of commonsense suggestions based upon Kirby and Liner (1981).

1. Protect the privacy of the journal. Don't ever read aloud journal entries or share journal entries without the permission of the author.
2. Be an active reader and sincere respondent. Write general remarks, share your ideas, make specific suggestions, and react rather than correct.
3. Be honest with students. In those situations where students tell you more than what you want to know or include language you would not care to read, tell them to cut it out.
4. Look for something good. Don't give up on students; rather, encourage them and avoid sarcasm.
5. Make journal writing special and interesting. Don't let it become a chore; respond eagerly and with interest. Take a break from journal writing if necessary.
6. Be aware that you cannot be expected to respond every day to each student's journal entry. Don't make promises to the students about the frequency with which you might respond.

Staton (1987) also provides some guidelines for the content of teachers' responses:

- acknowledge the students' topics and encourage them to elaborate on their interests;
- affirm and support each student: the private dialogue is a great place for compliments about appearance, behavior;
- add new, relevant information about topics, so that *your* response is interesting to read;
- don't write (much) more than the students do;
- avoid glib comments like "good idea" or "very interesting." These cut off rather than promote dialogue.
- ask very few questions. The goal is to get students to ask *you* questions, and make your writing so interesting that they will want to know more. (P. 62) [italics original]

Hallberg (1987) points out some possible ethical problems in teachers' responses to students' journals. Although he is discussing journals in the college classroom, his concerns may be equally important for younger students. Further, while he discusses intensive journal writing, the issues he raises may be of concern in Dialogue Journals as well:

> There are some ethical problems involved in using such intensely personal and emotional materials in a college classroom. There may be some psychological hazards as well. Does the assignment of "Intensive Journal" work invade a student's right to privacy? And does the emotional intensity of the work involve classroom instructors in activities best left in the hands of trained psychotherapists? (P. 296)

Finally, Lewis (1993) describes a moment in her own teaching in which she failed to recognize the legitimacy of a child's interpretation of a story; her own economic class values prevented her from seeing that the child had found a way of understanding a text that was based on his experience and the text itself but which was different from the "standard" reading of the text. Although this moment occurred during a "think-aloud" interaction between teacher and student, the point may be well taken for Dialogue Journals. The advantage of the Dialogue Journal is that it provides individualized contact between teacher and student. The disadvantage may be the same—if the teacher cannot engage with the multiple possibilities for reading that result from ethnic and economic diversity in the classroom.

Cautions and Comments

The description of journal writing that has been offered is quite condensed. The present discussion is restricted to Dialogue Journals that were used by elementary students for purposes of responding to reading and writing. Journals can easily be used in other ways—with projects, such as a group investigation of a problem or topic, with field trips, or with any special activity. For example, Gordon and Macinnis (1993) report on the use of Dialogue Journals in mathematics; the journals helped teachers to understand children's mathematical misconceptions and to address their instruction accordingly. Beach and Anson (1993) describe a variation of the Dialogue Journal in which peers respond to each other and Funkhouser (1991) reports on having parents respond in a Dialogue Journal to their children's writing. Taylor (1991) uses a variation of the Dialogue Journal, "literature letters," to have children respond to each other about their own writing—as a form of peer feedback. There are no age restrictions on the use of journals; some educators have even successfully used them with preschoolers. For example, Elliott, Nowasad, and Samuels (1981) have reported involving parents in helping their preschoolers with the transcription.

Finally, Bruce (1991) points out that one function of computers is as a form of communication. With networks between classroom computers, across schools, and via electronic mail across the world, the Dialogue Journal can begin to provide students with a chance to enter written book discussions with other readers from all over.

What is the value of journal writing? There have been very few research studies in which the worth of any type of journal writing has been explored. In terms of evidence of their worth, most of the support comes in statements from educators who have been involved in the experience. Staton (1980), for example, has commented on the value that was derived from using Dialogue Journals by a teacher, Leslee Reed:

> . . . the openness of the journal as a forum for personal problems as well as for academic ones captures the natural function of language as intentional communication about what matters most to the person. An attitude of trust and interest in everything the writer says characterizes Leslee Reed's attitude toward her students and what they write in their journals. "I learn something new everyday about each one of them. They are fascinating and exciting to get to know." It is no wonder that their willingness to express their own ideas, feelings and experiences in written language improves and creates in them a confidence about writing in general that too few people their age or any age enjoy." (P. 518)

Or, as Nancy Atwell (1984) commented when describing how Dialogue Journals and other factors worked together in her classrooms, "It's a dining room table with seventy chairs around it." (P. 251)

References

Atwell, N. 1984. Writing and reading literature from the inside out. *Language Arts* 61:240–252. Describes the use of Dialogue Journals for reading and writing in an eighth grade classroom.

Beach, R., and C. M. Anson. 1993. Using peer-dialogue journals to foster response. In *Exploring Texts: The role of discussion and writing in the teaching and learning of literature,* edited by G. E. Newell and R. K. Durst. Norwood, MA: Christopher-Gordon Publishers, Inc.

Bruce, B. 1991. Roles for computers in teaching the English language arts. In *Handbook of research on teaching the English language arts,* edited by J. Flood, J. M. Jensen, D. Lapp, and J. R. Squire. New York: Macmillan Publishing Company. Describes roles for the computer in the language arts classroom and related research.

Davis, F. A. 1984. "Why you call me Emigrant?": Dialogue journal writing with migrant youth. *Childhood Education* (November-December). Describes the use of Dialogue Journals in a migrant education project by New Jersey teachers.

Elliott, S., J. Nowasad, and P. Samuels. 1981. "Me at School," "Me at Home": Using journals with preschoolers. *Language Arts* 58:688–691. Describes the use of journal writing in a preschool where the teacher and the parents were involved in transcribing entries.

Funkhouser, L. L. 1991. Gifted students respond to their reading. In *Process reading and writing: A literature-based approach,* edited by J. T. Feeley, D. S. Strickland, and S. B. Wepner. New York: Teacher's College Press. Describes using Dialogue Journals (between teacher and child and between parent and child) in a classroom for gifted students.

Gordon, J. C., and D. Macinnis. 1993. Using journals as a window on students' thinking in mathematics. *Language Arts* 70:37–43. Dialogue Journals can help teachers understand how their students are thinking about mathematical concepts.

Hallberg, F. 1987. Journal writing as person making. In *The Journal Book,* edited by T. Fulwiler. Portsmouth, NH: Heinemann. Discusses personal journals in the classroom and ways of keeping these from becoming problematic experiences for students.

Harste, J. C., K. G. Short, and C. Burke. 1988. *Creating classrooms for authors*. Portsmouth, NH: Heinemann. Provides suggestions for using Dialogue Journals as well as related activities such as written conversations.

Kirby, D., and T. Liner. 1981. *Inside out*. New York: Boynton-Cook. Presents an overview, guidelines, and suggestions for journal writing.

———. 1988. *Inside out*. 2d ed. Portsmouth, NH: Heinemann. Updates the previous edition with a fuller discussion of practices and their theoretical underpinnings.

Kreeft, J. 1984. Dialogue writing—Bridge from talk to essay writing. *Language Arts* 61:141–150. Addresses the question of how Dialogue Journals help students' writing skills, with examples to highlight teacher strategies and student growth.

Lewis, C. 1993. "Give people a chance": Acknowledging social differences in reading. *Language Arts* 70:454–461. Analysis of a think-aloud in which a child offered a reading of a text that was significantly different from that of the teacher.

Markman, M. 1985. *Teacher-student dialogue writing in a college composition course: Effects upon writing performance and attitude*. Unpublished doctoral diss., University of Missouri. Researches the effectiveness of Dialogue Journals with college students.

Newkirk, T. 1982. Young writers as critical readers. In *Understanding writing*, edited by T. Newkirk and N. Atwell. Chelmsford, MA: Northeast Regional Exchange. Describes the notion of bringing students inside written language as critics, enthusiasts, and participants.

Purves, A. C., L. Papa, and S. Jordan, eds. 1994. *Encyclopedia of English studies and language arts*. New York: National Council of Teachers of English. This encyclopedia has more than 800 annotated entries/topics that succinctly address this topic and related areas.

Staton, J. 1980. Writing and counseling: Using a dialogue journal. *Language Arts* 57:514–518. Describes the use of Dialogue Journals and their value.

———. 1984a. Thinking together: The role of language interaction in children's reasoning. In *Speaking and Writing, K–12*, edited by C. Thaiss and C. Suhor. Describes the rationale, purposes, and benefits of Dialogue Journals.

———. 1984b. *The interactional acquisition of practical reasoning in early adolescence: A study of dialogue journals*. Unpublished doctoral diss., University of California at Los Angeles. A research study of the use of Dialogue Journals.

———. 1987. The power of responding in dialogue journals. In *The Journal Book*, edited by T. Fulwiler. Portsmouth, NH: Heinemann. Describes several aspects of Dialogue Journals (as reading events, communication, and place for response) and provides guidelines for their implementation.

Staton, J., J. Kreeft, and L. Gutstein, eds. *Dialogue*, Washington, DC: Center for Applied Linguistics. *Dialogue* is a newsletter about the uses, benefits, and theory of Dialogue Journals. It is available through the Center for Applied Linguistics, 3520 Prospect Street, N.W., Washington, DC 20007.

Staton, J., R. Shuy, and J. Kreeft. 1982. *Analysis of dialogue journal writing as a communicative event*. Washington, DC: National Institute of Education Grant No. G-80-0122, Center for Applied Linguistics. (ERIC Document No.: vol. 1, ED 214-196; vol. 2, ED 214-197). A two-volume description of the use of Dialogue Journals, including purposes, structure, and benefits.

Staton, J., R. W. Shuy, J. K. Peyton, and L. Reed. 1988. *Dialogue journal communication: Classroom, linguistic, social and cognitive views*. Norwood, NJ: Ablex. Represents the original extended study of Dialogue Journals.

Taylor, D. F. 1991. Literature letters and narrative response: Seventh and eighth graders write about their reading. In *Process reading and writing: A literature-based approach*, edited by J. T. Feeley, D. S. Strickland, and S. B. Wepner. New York: Teacher's College Press. Describes using a Dialogue Journal approach in which students write about each others' writings.

Style Study

Purpose

Style Study has two purposes: (1) to engage students in critically reading their own writing and the writings of others (classmates as well as professional authors); and (2) to enhance students' appreciation of stylistic options, including their sensitivity to the styles of different authors.

Rationale

Caplan developed Style Study in conjunction with her teaching experiences in high school literature classrooms. All of the activities involved in Style Study revolve around using student writing as a springboard for developing an appreciation of rhetorical options. Students write paragraphs and essays on selected themes, share these texts with each other, and compare their renditions with those developed by professional authors. One of the goals is to have the students consider what makes different paragraphs effective. As Caplan (1987) states, "Students learn new composing strategies from each other as they notice how different writers tackle the same idea with varying approaches." (Pp. 10–11) Caplan suggests that such comparisons are not intended to establish that the novelist's version is better than the students' or that the students should be writing like the novelist, but to help the students notice alternatives while preparing them for an author's style. It is Caplan's claim that when students parallel and later evaluate distinguishing styles of major authors, not only may they come to appreciate the talent and craft of the writer— develop "a feel" for a writer that enables them to appreciate how style contributes to the story—but they may also learn new rhetorical devices for delivering ideas. It should be noted that Caplan's activities extend beyond writing that is so directly tied to reading; many of her activities center upon having students pull together their own ideas in response to a story.

Intended Audience

Although Caplan's activities were developed for use with high school students in literature classrooms, they can be adapted for use with students at the elementary level.

Description of the Procedures

Style Study activities tend to fall into the following categories: (1) "showing" and "telling" writing activities; (2) parallel writing; and (3) extended writing activities using reading selections as resources.

1. Showing and Telling Writing Exercises   Showing writing involves having students elaborate on a general statement using specifics. The goal of showing writing is to challenge a writer to convince a reader of an idea without directly "telling" the idea. To this end, Caplan suggests steering students away from topic sentences toward developing an idea in much the same way that one pursues the game of charades: that is, dramatizing an idea without giving the whole thing away. In order to demonstrate what a showing paragraph is, she begins by presenting students with the following two paragraphs and discussing their differences.

A Telling Paragraph

Each morning I ride the bus to school. I wait along with the other people who ride my bus. Sometimes the bus is late and we get angry. Some guys start fights and stuff just to have something to do. I'm always glad when the bus finally comes.

A Showing Paragraph

A bus arrived. It discharged its passengers, closed its doors with a hiss and disappeared over the crest of a hill. Not one of the people waiting at the bus stop had attempted to board. One woman wore a sweater that was too small, a long skirt, white sweater socks, and house slippers. One man was in his undershirt. Another man wore shoes with the toes cut out, a soiled blue serge jacket and brown pants. There was something wrong with these people. They made faces. A mouth smiled at nothing and unsmiled, smiled and unsmiled. A head shook in vehement denial. Most of them carried brown paper bags rolled tight against their stomaches.

(E. L. Doctorow, *The Book of Daniel,*
New York: Random House, Signet Edition, 1971, 15)

Then she presents them a thesis statement for which they are expected to develop a paragraph. Examples of these statements are presented in Figure 4–3.

What is crucial is that once these writings are developed, they are shared and critiqued. Caplan emphasizes that it is important to have students go beyond saying, "It was really good!" to "What was good about it? How did he show . . . ?"

These exercises are often tied directly to reading selections. After the first chapter of *Call of the Wild,* for example, students might be assigned the sentence "Buck is an intelligent dog" or, after reading the first two chapters of Hemingway's *The Sun Also Rises,* students might be assigned the sentence "Jake disapproves of Robert Cohn." The students' task is to prove the claims using evidence from the chapters. Sometimes the writing activity may precede the reading of a selection. For example, prior to reading a segment from *The Great Gatsby,* students might develop paragraphs from the statement "The living room was romantic." As students share and compare their paragraphs, they consider features of style and various rhetorical options. Then, as they move on to reading the Fitzgerald excerpt from *The Great Gatsby,* they have the opportunity to discuss this work in the same spirit as they discussed each other's. At the same time that they can look back to appreciate their style, they become attuned to the subtleties of Fitzgerald.

A final variation of these writing exercises involves the reverse—moving from showing paragraphs to telling sentences. For example, students might be given the task of generating a statement that provides meaning to or explains the significance of all the collected facts for a paragraph from Mark Twain.

The house was a double log one, with a spacious floor (roofed in) connecting it with the kitchen. In the summer the table was set in the middle of that shady and breezy floor, and

FIGURE 4–3.   THESIS STATEMENTS

The room was vacant.

She has a fantastic personality.

The party was great.

I was very embarrassed.

My room is a mess.

The concert was disappointing.

My mother bugs me.

The math test was a killer.

The food at the party was incredible.

Those girls are snobs.

The jocks think they're cool.

He looked guilty.

He eats like a pig.

The weather made me nostalgic.

The relationship changed.

The drive in the car was uncomfortable.

School is boring.

Teenagers should not have curfews.

My friend was steaming mad.

This school has great school spirit.

The pizza tasted good.

The loss was devastating.

The living room was a warm, inviting place.

She acted older than her age.

People make or break a party.

Advertisements can be misleading.

The F grade should be abolished.

Camping is a rewarding experience.

My parents are great people.

Reality set in.

She changed.

The weather was perfect.

A student's life is hard.

The streets were crowded.

The puppy was a terror.

He is artistic.

She is creative.

The afternoon was a romantic one.

The principal was effective.

The game was a close one.

The book was intriguing.

Haste makes waste.

They lived happily ever after.

The climb was exhausting.

The roller coaster was the scariest ride at the fair.

The crossword puzzle was tricky.

The new student was lonely.

The fire drill went miserably.

The substitute teacher was strange.

The speaker got everyone's attention.

---

the sumptuous meals—well, it makes me cry to think of them. Fried chicken, roast pig; wild and tame turkeys, ducks and geese; venison just killed; squirrels, rabbits, pheasants, partridges, prairie chickens; biscuits, hot batter cakes, hot buckwheat cakes, hot "wheat bread," hot rolls, hot corn pone; fresh corn boiled on the ear, succotash, butter-beans, string-beans, tomatoes, peas, Irish potatoes, sweet potatoes, buttermilk, sweet milk, "clab-ber"; watermelons, muskmelons, cantaloupes—all fresh from the garden; apple pie, peach pie, pumpkin pie, apple dumplings, peach cobbler—I can't remember the rest. The way that the things were cooked was perhaps the main splendor—particularly a certain few of the dishes. For instance the corn bread, the hot biscuits and wheat bread and the fried chicken.

> (Samuel Langhorne Clemens, *The Autobiography of Mark Twain*, ed. by
> Charles Neider, 1959. New York: Harper and Row Publishers, Inc., 4)

2. Parallel Writing   Caplan also advocates having students try to parallel the writer's style. As she states, "If possible, I want them to match his structures part-of-speech for part-of-speech, supplying their own fictional scenes for narration." She suggests begin-ning with a simple sentence. "The men paraded by the stand," which might become "The leaves fluttered by the monument," then graduating to inventing parallel versions of several paragraphs. After they have practiced paralleling a number of author's passages, she then suggests going one step further and experimenting with versions of simple stories (e.g., Cinderella) in the style of Hemingway, Fitzgerald, or others.

For example, Caplan's students took simple stories and mimicked Fitzgerald and Salinger.

Peter Peter Pumpkin-Eater
by Jennifer
Peter Peter Pumpkin-Eater
Had a wife and couldn't keep her
He put her in a pumpkin shell
 And there he kept her very well.

The Great Pumpkin-Eater: F. Scott Fitzgerald
About halfway between Peter's cottage and his barn was a mammoth pumpkin. This was where Peter kept his wife—in a giant hollowed out squash, with a door and a window carved out of the thick orange skin, and a chimney where the prickly stem should be, a thin wisp of smoke always trailing its way to the crystal-blue sky.

The fact that he kept his wife in a pumpkin was known by virtually everyone. His neighbors resented having such an eyesore on their street, ruining the appearance of the other glittering, fashionable houses; they were shocked that his wife actually resided there, amid slimy walls and large seeds that peppered the squishy floor.

Though I was curious to see the girl who allowed her husband to keep her in a pumpkin I had no desire to actually set foot in an overgrown vegetable—but I did. I met Peter on his way home from work one day, and when we stopped by his gate he stared hard at me and, taking hold of my elbow, literally forced me up the graveled path.

"Come along," he insisted. "I want you to meet my wife."

I followed him to the door of the pumpkin, aware that a pair of eyes watched our approach through filmy white curtains.

It was then that I realized that I could never go inside that pumpkin. I mumbled an apology and, wheeling around, I hurried back out onto the street, thoughts massing like turbulent clouds in my head.

I went to the park and sat there brooding on Peter's odd habit of keeping his wife in the shell of a pumpkin. Peter believed in it, though, and if his wife was content to reside in a squash, then maybe one morning we would come to understand them.

The Wife in the Pumpkin: J. D. Salinger
I had nothing to do in my damn crummy hotel room except think. I remembered a story a friend had told me once. Well, not really a friend. I had only met him once, at a party. I remember. Anyway, this guy told me about some bastard named Peter. Peter Pumpkin-Eater is what all his neighbors called him. They really did. That killed me. At first, I thought it

meant he actually ate pumpkins. Raw or something. But damn if he doesn't keep his wife in this great big hollowed out one. A pumpkin, I mean. I wonder how they got all that crap out of it. You know, the damn pumpkin guts and all. And what did they do with all the seeds? Did they just throw them away or did they plant them? Maybe there's a farm full of overgrown pumpkins somewhere.

Well, old Peter, he keeps his wife in there because he can't pay the lousy mortgage on his house. So he doesn't own the house anymore and they've got nowhere to stay. Then old Peter, he comes up with this swell idea of living in a squash. I guess his wife didn't mind. She could have left the bastard. I wonder what her name was. I forgot to ask. Anyway, my friend says that Peter keeps her very well. He must or else he has a very dumb wife. I don't know why he got the name "Pumpkin-Eater" though. I would have called him old "Peter Peter Pumpkin-Dweller" or something. But that damn story kills me every time I think of it anyway.

3. Extended Writing Activities Using Reading Selections as Resources   Caplan's suggestions for activities extends beyond preparing students to deal with an author's stylistic idiosyncrasies to having students pull together their own ideas. For example, when students have read *The Great Gatsby,* Caplan suggests that they might be asked to compare Gatsby's quest for Daisy Buchanan with the quest for the American Dream. In conjunction with being introduced to investigative reporting (including the use of field notes, interviews, and other research techniques), students were asked to examine certain books (e.g., Tom Wolfe's *The Right Stuff*) and articles for purposes of seeing examples of reporting style.

In addition to these activities, Caplan has developed procedures for introducing students to research reports, compare-contrast papers, and persuasive essays. These are reported at length in *Writers in Training* (1984).

Cautions and Comments

Caplan's suggestions for developing writing in conjunction with teaching literature distinguish themselves from other strategies in that her approach is quite structured. In particular, for most activities, all of the students are expected to respond to the same topic in a similar fashion either showing, telling, or developing parallel versions. Furthermore, most of the suggestions tie writing to reading in a rather deliberate fashion. Students are expected to fine-tune their ability to read their own texts evaluatively at the same time that a great deal of emphasis is placed upon fine-tuning their appreciation of stylistic alternatives.

Although detailed research studies of this approach are lacking, Caplan and Keech (1980) and Caplan (1987) have pursued analyses of students' writings, and have interviewed graduates in hopes of attaining an understanding of the strengths and weaknesses of the approach. The outcomes of their analyses of these data support Caplan's claims at the same time that they highlight some of the potential limitations. For example, one of the students who had been involved in the program made the following comment: "It's a way of growing, expanding oneself through voicing one's thoughts (writing) and listening to other's thoughts (reading)." (Caplan, 1987, 29). In contrast, other students were reported to be less favorably inclined. As Caplan (1987) commented:

> When I asked my students what they considered to be the value of parallel writing, one student commented: "It gives you a little confidence to think, hey man, I can do that; I can sound like F. Scott Fitzgerald." Another student confessed that she really didn't like doing the writing but that "It worked out after awhile. You just kept working at it, and your writing sounded neat—definitely neat. It didn't sound as though a high school student had written it." (P. 29)

In accordance with this student's comments, several questions remain regarding the effects of the activities: Do students feel empowered or overwhelmed by the styles of others? Do they lose their own voice as they parallel the style of others? In what ways do comparisons of their responses with those of professional authors fuel their own stylistic development?

Caplan is the first to admit to the possible limitations of her approach. As she stated:

> For some students I expect the practices related to Style Study might have been burdensome, and the question remains whether or not some students might have felt deflated—even disempowered—by having to do the parallel writings and mimickings. (1987, 31)

What she is quite adamant about is that examining stylistic alternatives should be used with the view of celebrating achievements. She endorses neither the lock-step use of these activities nor a predetermined set of stylistic preferences.

References

Caplan, R. 1984. *Writers in training: A guide to developing a composition program for language arts teachers.* Palo Alto, CA: Dale Seymour. A comprehensive explanation of the activities, rationale, and outcomes of Style Study.

———. 1987. Style study. *The Quarterly* 9:10–14, 29, 31. Describes those aspects of Style Study involving the integration of reading and writing with reflections on interview comments of poor students.

Caplan, R., and P. Keech. 1980. *Show-writing: A training program to help students be specific.* Berkeley, CA: Bay Area Writing Project. Discusses the use of showing writing and earlier thinking of Caplan. Includes analyses of the effects upon student writing.

Purves, A. C., L. Papa, and S. Jordan, eds. 1994. *Encyclopedia of English studies and language arts.* New York: National Council of Teachers of English. This encyclopedia has more than 800 annotated entries/topics that succinctly address this topic and related areas.

Tierney, R. J., R. Caplan, L. Ehri, M. K. Healy, and M. Hurdlow. 1989. Writing and reading working together. In *Writing and reading: Collaboration in the classroom?* edited by A. H. Dyson. Urbana, IL: National Council of Teachers of English. Describes Caplan's Style Study in the context of research on and practical applications of the writing and reading relationship.

Story Impressions

Purpose

Story Impressions was developed by McGinley and Denner (1987) as a way to help students realize that reading involves actively thinking about ideas. The developers of the procedure consider the use of Story Impressions akin to doing the first draft of a composition.

Rationale

Story Impressions is a prereading writing activity that differs from most kinds of prereading activities in that it involves students' using key concepts from a story to develop their own story or impression of how these key concepts might fit together. McGinley and Denner (1987) developed the procedure based upon the belief that a major goal of a prereading activity should be to have the reader build anticipatory models or blueprints that are confirmed or modified as the reader encounters the actual text. They claim that the technique is "wholly consistent with and directly derivable from current model based views of the reading process" (1987, 239), which they suggest supports the following view of readers:

> To comprehend, the reader must use the clues supplied by the author to activate appropriate prior knowledge structures, usually called schemata. Once active, the schemata can serve as a basis for making predictions.
>
> The proficient reader then tests his or her schema based predictions by evaluating them for goodness of fit with the subsequent information (clues) supplied by the author. (1987, 248)

They point out that the technique varies in two important ways from the directed reading-thinking activity (DR-TA). First, clues are systematically sampled from the top-level structure of the story. Second, with Story Impressions the students develop a story based on the clues they are provided.

Intended Audience

McGinley and Denner (1987) suggest that the approach can be used with students of all ages. They claim that they have had teachers use the approach successfully with grades two and above.

Description of the Procedure

Story Impressions are key concepts in the form of clue words and phrases that the student is expected to fit together into an impression or draft of a story. Figure 4–4, for example, lists key concepts selected from Edgar Allen Poe's "The Tell-Tale Heart" and a story developed by an eighth grader.

FIGURE 4–4.   STORY IMPRESSIONS (PREREADING) ACTIVITY BASED ON POE'S "THE TELL-TALE HEART"

Story impressions given to a class	An eighth grader's story written from the story impressions

house
↓
old man
↓
young man
↓
hatred
↓
ugly eye
↓
death
↓
tub, blood, knife
↓
buried
↓
floor
↓
police
↓
heartbeat
↓
guilt
↓
crazy
↓
confession
	There was a young man and his father, an old man. They lived in a house on a hill out in the bouniey's. The old man hated his son because he had an ugly eye.
	    The young man was asleep in his bedroom when he was awakened by screaming. He went to the bedroom and saw his father laying in the tub. There was blood everywhere and a knife through him.
	    The young man found a tape recording hidden behind the door on the floor. He turned it on there was screaming on the tape. The young man started to call the police, but then he stopped and remembered what his mother had told him. She had told him that he had a split personality. So he called the police and confessed to being crazy and killing his father. His heartbeat was heavy as he called.

Introduction of Story Impressions   To introduce Story Impressions to students, McGinley and Denner suggest the following steps:

Step 1. Provide a general introduction, e.g., "Today we're going to make up what we think this story could be about."

Step 2. Direct students to the list of key concepts by saying, "Here are some clues about the story we're going to read. We're going to use these clues to write our own version of the story. After that, we'll read the story together to see if the author had ideas similar to ours."

Step 3. After students read through the list of clues, they are encouraged to brainstorm how the ideas might connect. The teacher might jot down possibilities on an overhead or the chalkboard.

Step 4. Using the brainstormed ideas, a class story is developed (on the board or transparency) that ties together the clues.

Step 5. The students read the author's actual story and discuss how their story compares. McGinley and Denner stress that a match with the author's story is not important. Instead, what is important is to compare how the clues were woven together similarly or differently.

Step 6. Either in small groups or as individuals, the students develop their own stories based upon clues from another story.

Guidelines for Developing a Set of Story Impressions   McGinley and Denner have established guidelines for developing a set of Story Impressions:

1. Include key words and phrases (preferably from the text with a maximum of three words per clue) that represent the character, setting, and key elements from the plot.
2. Restrict the number of key words or phrases to ten or fifteen for a short story or fifteen to twenty for a young adult novel.
3. Arrange the clues vertically with arrows or lines to indicate their order.

Suggestions for Variations on the Use of Story Impressions   McGinley and Denner (1987) offer various suggestions of ways that Story Impression clues can be used for other purposes. For example, they suggest that Story Impressions might also be used as guideposts from which students offer their own questions prior to reading or as aids to having students develop reports, as well as make notes. In addition, they suggest that Story Impressions could be used to develop or reinforce selected skills, (e.g., how ideas interrelate and are sequenced).

Cautions and Comments

The authors have reported the results of several studies that substantiate the positive contribution that Story Impressions makes to comprehension with students in grades two and eight (McGinley and Denner, 1985; Denner, 1989). What seems to be missing from their studies, however, is a comparison with other prereading activities and an examination of on-line measures to assess the impact of Story Impressions on the thought processes of students as they read. Also, it would be interesting to learn how students compare their renditions with those of the author (e.g., what features they note in common or at variance).

As a vehicle for integrating reading and writing, Story Impressions seems to have definite potential. The technique affords the students the opportunity to relate their experiences to key concepts. In other words, it allows the students to establish their frameworks and themselves as authors prior to being introduced to a text developed by a professional author. The procedure, as presently described by McGinley and Denner, tends to fall short in offering suggestions for how the students' versions might be shared, discussed, and compared en route to validating the students' drafts. Likewise, their research needs to consider the impact upon the students' view of themselves as authors, their appreciation of their craft and the craft of others, and their development as writers.

References

Denner, P. R. 1989. *The effects of providing story impressions as prereading/writing activity on the story comprehension and oral reading miscues of second grade readers.* Research report, Idaho State University. Presents a study exploring the use of Story Impressions with second graders.

Denner, P. R., and W. J. McGinley. 1986. The effects of story-impressions as a prereading/writing activity on story comprehension. *Journal of Educational Research* 82:6, 320–326. Presents a study of the effects of Story Impressions upon eighth graders' comprehension.

McGinley, W. J., and P. R. Denner. 1985. *The use of semantic impressions as a previewing activity for providing clues to a story's episodic struc-ture.* Paper presented at the Northern Rocky Mountains Educational Research Association Annual Meeting, Jackson, WY. Describes the use of Story Impressions as a previewing activity.

————. 1987. Story impressions: A prereading/writing activity. *Journal of Reading* 31:248–253. Presents a detailed description of the use of Story Impressions.

Purves, A. C., L. Papa, and S. Jordan, eds. 1994. *Encyclopedia of English studies and language arts.* New York: National Council of Teachers of English. This encyclopedia has more than 800 annotated entries/topics that succinctly address this topic and related areas.

Probable Passages

Purpose

Probable Passages (Wood 1984) is designed to: (1) use writing as a vehicle to learn basal selections; and (2) employ the important vocabulary words of a selection to enhance comprehension.

Rationale

Probable Passages is an attempt to incorporate the use of writing in a traditional basal lesson. Instead of setting time aside in the already busy schedule of the school day to do a writing lesson, Wood recommends that it simply be used in a typical lesson as a major means of learning. In addition, like Possible Sentences (see Unit 8 in this book) and Story Impressions (this unit), Probable Passages uses the key vocabulary of the basal selection to capitalize on students' prior knowledge of the topic and stimulate their comprehension.

Probable Passages also relies on students' intrinsic knowledge of story grammar (see Unit 9 of this book), or the common elements of how a story is structured and how a person forms a mental image of it. In essence, students use their knowledge of a story (setting, problem, plan, solution, etc.) and their knowledge of the relevant vocabulary in a selection to make predictions about what the story will be about. These predictions become the "Probable Passage," and students are directed to read or listen to the story to see what the actual events of it are. Thus, Probable Passages enables teachers to develop and use an integrated reading/writing lesson with basal stories.

Intended Audience

Probable Passages was originally intended to be used in reading/language arts periods with basal stories in the elementary grades. However, it can be adapted for use with expository material in content classrooms.

Description of the Procedure

Wood states that Probable Passages involves a series of four stages that will span two to three days of instruction, depending on story length. The four stages are

1. Preparation
2. Prereading
3. Reading
4. Postreading

1. Preparation Stage   Begin by analyzing the basal selection for key terms or for words that will require extra emphasis. These vocabulary words should be placed on the board or on an overhead projector. The words listed below and the sample lesson to follow are from a basal story entitled "The Case of the Whistling Ghost" by Donald Sobol.*

Next, develop the categories that correspond to the structure of the story. These categories will change from story to story depending on what type it is. In the case of our sample, the following will be used: setting, characters, problem, solution, and ending.

To finish the preparation of the lesson, develop an incomplete Probable Passage to be used by students both before and after reading. The incomplete Probable Passage should correspond to the categories listed in the previous step. For the sample lesson, it would look like this:

2. Prereading Stage   First, the teacher reads the list of words to the students to make sure they know how the words are pronounced. In this way words that are in students' listening vocabulary, but not in their reading vocabulary, may become known. Then students are asked to examine the words to see if they might be able to make a story out of them.

Next, provide students with the story categories and have them place the words into their appropriate slots. In doing so, point out to students that some words may fit more than one category and that other words may be filled in (those from their prior knowledge) to help them construct a good story. Ask students to justify their categorizations to demonstrate their own thinking and to share their version of what the Probable Passage might be. A possible listing of the words in the categories for our sample lesson would be:

Setting	Characters	*Problem*	*Solution*	*Ending*
deserted house	Encyclopedia Brown	whistling ghost	spider web	made up story
	Rocky Smith	stolen camera	detective	
	Fabius		clues	

*In "Full Circle," *Series r: Macmillan Reading,* edited by C. B. Smith and V. A. Arnold. New York: Macmillan, 1983.

Finally, ask students to use the words in the categories to write a logical Probable Passage using the incomplete passage you developed. The teacher acts as a facilitator by asking appropriate questions such as "How can we make that idea fit in this part of the passage?" or "How can the sentence be reworded to make it more meaningful?" In doing so, lengthy responses can be reduced. The students work and make predictions until they can reach a consensus regarding the content of the Probable Passage. The Probable Passage from our sample lesson might look like this:

Probable Passage

The story mainly takes place *in a deserted house. Encyclopedia Brown* is a character who *lives near the house.* A problem occurs when *he and Rocky Smith see a whistling ghost in the house and have their camera stolen.* After that, *they go to a detective for help.* Next, *they search for clues.* The problem is solved when *a spider web gives them an important clue.* The story ends *when Fabius gives them a made up story and is caught lying.*

3. Reading Stage   The students are directed to read the story or to listen to it being read by the teacher. In either case, the purpose is to verify the accuracy of their Probable Passage as compared to the actual passage.

4. Postreading Stage   During this final stage of the lesson, students engage in a discussion of what changes need to occur in their categorization of the vocabulary and their Probable Passage to reflect the actual events of the story. In this case, students would have to change the word *detective* to the character listing, since it is associated with Encyclopedia Brown, and move *Rocky Smith* to the ending. This will clear up the confusion of the characters in the Probable Passage. The revision of the passage to reflect more accurately the story's actual events might look like this:

Revised Passage

The story mainly takes place *in a deserted house. Encyclopedia Brown* is a character who *is a boy detective.* A problem occurs when *Fabius is scared by a whistling ghost and has his camera stolen.* After that, *they go to search for clues.* The problem is solved when *a spider web gives them an important clue.* The story ends *when Rocky Smith gives them a made up story and is caught lying.*

Cautions and Comments

Probable Passages is a strategy that uses a team approach in emphasizing vocabulary, writing, and comprehension in a single lesson. Students are given the opportunity to use their knowledge of story structure and prior knowledge of the vocabulary to make predictions about a story to be read, i.e., to make connections between what they know and what they are about to learn.

As such, students who may lack a large backlog of prior experiences and/or intuitive knowledge of story structure may find this lesson structure to be quite difficult and will need direction. At the same time, the collaborative approach may compensate for this problem in that students can rely on one another for help. Furthermore, some modeling of the thinking processes involved in Probable Passages may be in order for this lesson to be successful with some students.

Wood suggests that students can eventually work in small groups to write their own Probable Passages and to revise them after reading. Working in small groups or individually also will enable students to share their predicted passages and see the range of possibilities that exist for a good story. To this end, students might be reminded that the way the author wrote the story is not the only way it can be done and that their versions of the story have merit, too.

Readence, Bean, and Baldwin (1989) also suggest that Probable Passages can be adapted for use in the content areas with expository text. In this case, the vocabulary selected for use in the lesson is categorized under the labels of the text structure that the selection uses: e.g., problems and solutions, causes and effects. Students then are given an incomplete Probable Passage for only the "problems" part of a particular text structure, in this case the problem-solution structure. They are asked to fill in the passage with the words categorized as "problems" and then to write a second paragraph for the "solutions" using the words categorized as such. The lesson concludes with the evaluation/comparison step as with basal stories. This adaptation may provide a useful alternative for teachers to help students cope with the learning of new text material as well as to incorporate the use of writing as a means of learning in subject matter areas. Unfortunately, this adaptation, like the original version of the strategy, lacks empirical validation at this time.

References

Purves, A. C., L. Papa, and S. Jordan, eds. 1994. *Encyclopedia of English studies and language arts*. New York: National Council of Teachers of English. This encyclopedia has more than 800 annotated entries/topics that succinctly address this topic and related areas.

Readence, J. E., T. W. Bean, and R. S. Baldwin. 1989. *Content area reading: An integrated approach*. 3rd ed. Dubuque, IA: Kendall/Hunt. Describes the use of Probable Passages with expository text.

Wood, K. 1984. Probable passages: A writing strategy. *The Reading Teacher* 37:496–499. The original version of Probable Passages for use with basal stories.

Expository Reading-Writing Think-Sheets

Purpose

Expository Reading-Writing Think-Sheets is the label we have given to the expository writing program and, more recently, the cognitive strategy instruction in writing developed by Raphael and others. Expository Reading-Writing Think-Sheets are intended to guide the development of expository reading and writing skills in conjunction with teacher-student, student-student, student-self interactions through the various phases (planning, drafting, and revising) of writing.

Rationale

Raphael, Englert, and Kirschner (e.g. Raphael, Englert, and Kirschner 1986, 1989; Raphael and Kirschner, 1985) developed Expository Reading-Writing guides in an attempt to teach upper elementary students expository reading and writing skills. As they argue:

> . . . when children reach the upper grades of elementary school, where there is a greater emphasis on learning content, their progress in writing often declines. . . . One reason for this decline may be that children are not being taught how to read and learn from informational or content area texts. (1989, 262)

With this in mind, Raphael, Englert, and Kirschner have pursued a program of research exploring the viability of guiding the development of expository reading/writing skills. Several areas of research serve as the basis for their approach: studies of the influence of text structure (especially mapping) on comprehension and composition; the role of different social contexts (especially peer response groups) upon student learning; and tenets emerging from teacher-researcher collaborations and explicit teaching. Essentially the approach of these authors involves extensive use of what they refer to as Think-Sheets:

> . . . to prompt teachers to model and think aloud as they teach writing, to encourage teacher-student dialogue about strategies appropriate to each phase, to prompt appropriate student-student dialogue during peer editing and to encourage useful student-self dialogue as students write independently. (Raphael, Englert, and Kirschner, 1989, 774)

Over time, Raphael, Englert, and Kirschner hope that the Think-Sheets serve more as reminders (rather than guides) as students internalize the hints.

Intended Audience

The strategy was intended for use with upper elementary students but also seems appropriate for use with older students.

Description of the Procedures

Raphael, Englert, and Kirschner (1989) have emphasized that their approach has been subjected to a great deal of refinement and will likely be subjected to further refinement in conjunction with additional research and development. In its current form, the use of Think-Sheets and the changing teacher role is central to the approach.

Seven Think-Sheets constitute their current approach. They are Think-Sheets intended as guides for:

Planning

Organizing

First draft

Thinking about first draft

Editing

Revision

Final draft

The Planning Think-Sheet is intended to guide a consideration of the topic, purposes, and audience. The Think-Sheet for planning (Figure 4–5) merely prompts the reader to consider these items.

FIGURE 4–5.   THINK-SHEET FOR PLANNING

Author's name _____ Date _____

TOPIC: _____

WHO: Who am I writing for?

WHY: Why am I writing this?

WHAT: What do I already know about my topic? (Brainstorm)

1. _____

2. _____

3. _____

4. _____

HOW: How do I group my ideas?

The Organizing Think-Sheet involves the selection and use of a mapped pattern guide (See Unit 9 for a description of mapping). The pattern guides offer students a way of framing their ideas in accordance with whether the predominant text structure is compare/contrast, problem solution, explanation, or narrative. Figure 4–6 is an example of a Think-Sheet for a compare/contrast guide.

The First Draft Think-Sheet is merely a blank sheet of lined colored paper. The use of color is to denote that the paper is a first draft—that is, a work in progress.

In hopes of prompting students to reflect upon their first draft, a Think-Sheet is directed to thinking about the first draft. The questions on this sheet represent a self-check directed at having students consider how interesting, clear, and organized their first draft is. In addition, it is intended to prepare students for the possibility of an editing conference. Figure 4–7 includes a copy of a thinking about the First Draft Think-Sheet.

FIGURE 4–6. THINK-SHEET FOR ORGANIZING: COMPARISON/CONTRAST

What is being compared/contrasted?

On what?

| Alike? | Different? |

On what?

| Alike? | Different? |

On what?

| Alike? | Different? |

FIGURE 4–7.   THINK-SHEET FOR THINKING ABOUT THE FIRST DRAFT: COMPARISON/CONTRAST

Author's Name _____

Read to check information.

What is my paper mainly about?

What do I like best? Put a * next to the best part and explain why.

What parts are not clear? Put a ? next to the unclear parts, and tell why they are not clear.

Is the paper interesting? Tell why or why not here:

Question yourself to check organization.

Did I:

Tell what two things are compared and contrasted?	Yes	Sort of	No
Tell things they are being compared and contrasted on?	Yes	Sort of	No
Tell how they are alike?	Yes	Sort of	No
Tell how they are different?	Yes	Sort of	No
Use keywords clearly?	Yes	Sort of	No

Plan for editing conference.

What parts do I want to change? (For anything marked "Sort of" or "No," add to, take out, reorder?)

1. _____

2. _____

What questions do I want to ask my editor?

_____

_____

The fifth Think-Sheet is for editing. To this end, Raphael and associates have developed five versions—one for each of the four text structures taught as well as a generic version. They state that the generic version "is used when students begin to combine the different structures as they write more complex papers." (Raphael et al. 1989, 277) The Editing Think-Sheet is intended for use in conjunction with having a student author share his or her piece with a peer editor. The author reads the piece to the editor and then asks him/her to respond to several questions ranging from what the piece is about, its clarity, its interestingness, how well the piece is organized, and, for purposes of revision, suggestions for change. A copy of the Editing Think-Sheet for compare/contrast texts is shown in Figure 4–8.

FIGURE 4–8.   THINK-SHEET FOR EDITING: COMPARISON-CONTRAST

Author's Name _____ Editor's Name _____

Read to check information. (Authors: Read your paper aloud to your editor.)

What is the paper mainly about?

What do you like best? Put a * next to the part you liked best and tell why you like it here:

What parts are not clear? Put a ? next to the unclear parts, and tell what made the part unclear to you:

Is the paper interesting? Tell why or why not here:

Question yourself to check organization.

Did I:

Tell what two things are compared and contrasted?	Yes	Sort of	No
Tell things they are being compared and contrasted on?	Yes	Sort of	No
Tell how they are alike?	Yes	Sort of	No
Tell how they are different?	Yes	Sort of	No
Use keywords clearly?	Yes	Sort of	No

Plan revision.

What two parts do you think should be changed or revised? (For anything marked "Sort of" or "No," should the author add to, take out, reorder?)

1. _____

_____

2. _____

_____

What could help make the paper more interesting?

Talk.

Talk to the author of the paper. Talk about your comments on this editing think-sheet. Share ideas for revising the paper.

The Revision Think-Sheet is then used to help the student author decide what suggestions will be heeded. As they state, "The Revision Think-Sheet . . . is designed to promote author's consideration of their editor's comments but still give them control of their papers." (Raphael et al. 1989, 278) To this end, students are expected to list all of the suggestions and then decide on those they plan to address. A copy of the Revision Think-Sheet is shown in Figure 4–9.

FIGURE 4–9. THINK-SHEET FOR REVISION

Author's Name _____

List suggestions from your Editor.

List all the suggestions your editor has given you:

a. _____

b. _____

c. _____

d. _____

e. _____

Decide on the suggestions to use.

Put a * next to all suggestions that you will use in revising your paper.

Think about making your paper more interesting.

List ideas for making your paper more interesting to your reader.

_____

_____

_____

Return to your first draft.

On your first draft, make all changes that you think will improve your paper.
Use ideas from the list you have made on this think-sheet.

After revising their draft, the students then move to the Final Think-Sheet, which is their final draft. The format of this Think-Sheet is simply blank, white, lined paper.

Teacher's Role   Raphael and associates emphasize that the Think-Sheets are intended to provide a structure to guide and model different aspects of writing at the same time that students acquire shared understandings and vocabulary for discussing what they are doing. They hope that the students will become more self-initiating and self-regulating as they internalize the strategies and notions about writing made explicit via the Think-Sheet. As they state:

> As students gradually internalize the questions on the Think-Sheets and take ownership of the writing process themselves, they begin to work independently of the teacher. When

they reach the level of self-regulation, they will no longer need external support, either from the Think-Sheets or the teacher. (Raphael et al. 1989, 281)

Cautions and Comments

Expository Reading-Writing Think-Sheets represent one of a number of different strategies for guiding the development of an expository report. For example, Cunningham and Cunningham (1987) have suggested the use of a feature matrix to show teachers how to help students extract and organize ideas in conjunction with reading and writing. Holston and Santa (1985) have developed the procedure RAFT for helping students think through a topic prior to writing a report.

Several features distinguish Raphael and associates' Think-Sheets. The set of Think-Sheets is tied to a program of research and development, and, as a result, has been subjected to a great deal of refinement and revision. The Think-Sheets are relatively comprehensive. As guides to writing different texts, they represent an amalgamation of procedures intended to help students generate, organize, reflect upon, frame (using different text structures), share, enlist feedback on, and revise ideas. Finally, suggestions for using the Think-Sheets are tied to an attempt to support self-regulated learning.

In terms of shortcomings, Raphael and associates (1988) have discussed the possibility that Think-Sheets may become an end unto themselves rather than a springboard for students' self-regulated and flexible thinking. They have reported, for example, that some students may treat the Think-Sheets as distinct from one another and pay "little attention to the purpose of the Think-Sheet or to the general goal of sharing information on a given topic, making the paper as interesting and informative as possible." (Raphael et al. 1988, 794)

References

Cudd, E. T., and L. Roberts. 1989. Using writing to enhance content area learning in the primary grades. *The Reading Teacher* 42:392–405. Uses paragraph frames as a means of guiding expository writing and reading.

Cunningham, P. M., and J. W. Cunningham. 1987. Content area reading-writing lessons. *The Reading Teacher* 40:506–512. Explores the use of feature matrix and other devices to show teachers how to help students extract and organize critical information.

Purves, A. C., L. Papa, and S. Jordan, eds. 1994. *Encyclopedia of English studies and language arts.* New York: National Council of Teachers of English. This encyclopedia has more than 800 annotated entries/topics that succinctly address this topic and related areas.

Raphael, T. E., and B. W. Kirschner. 1985. *The effects of instruction in comparison/contrast text structure on sixth-grade students' reading comprehension and writing products* (Research Series No. 161). East Lansing: Michigan State University, Institute for Research on Teaching. Discusses research related to the use of Think-Sheets.

Raphael, T. E., C. S. Englert, and B. W. Kirschner. 1986. *The impact of text structure instruction and social context on students' comprehension and production of expository text* (Research Series No. 177). East Lansing: Michigan State

University, Institute for Research on Teaching. Reports research related to the use of Think-Sheets.

————. 1986, in press. *Students' metacognitive knowledge about writing* (Research Series No. 176). East Lansing: Michigan State University, Institute for Research on Teaching. Also *Research in the teaching of English* (in press). Discusses the students' awareness of the writing process and structures.

Raphael, T. E., B. W. Kirschner, and C. S. Englert. 1986. *Text structure instruction within process-writing classrooms: A manual for instruction* (Occasional Paper No. 104). East

Lansing: Michigan State University, Institute for Research on Teaching. Provides samples of materials and lessons for implementing the Expository Writing Program.

————. 1988. Expository writing program: Making connections between reading and writing. *The Reading Teacher* 41:790–795. Discusses the use of Expository Reading-Writing Think-Sheets with less able students.

————. 1989. Acquisition of expository writing skills. In *Reading and writing connections,* edited by J. Mason. Boston: Allyn and Bacon. Represents a comprehensive description of the strategy and research program.

Reading and Writing as Composing

Purpose

Reading and Writing as Composing is the name we have assigned the seminar approach to reading and writing developed by D. Bartholomae and A. Petrosky (1986) at the University of Pittsburgh. The approach helps students to become more competent readers and writers of academic texts through a gradual process of reading and writing assignments that begin with their own experiences and extend, over the course of a semester, into academic texts.

Rationale

One of the cornerstones of the Reading and Writing as Composing program is an understanding of reading that allows for the possibility of multiple interpretations of a text rather than the "main idea" approach to text, which assumes that there is one "right" reading. Inherent to multiple possibilities in reading texts is the idea that readers "compose" their readings as much as they compose when writing. Therefore, reading and writing are necessarily interconnected processes.

Further, the university asks students to do a particular kind of reading and writing; students must learn to operate within a specific discourse in order to succeed in college-level reading and writing. There are students who are not successful users of this discourse. They are able to handle the mechanics of reading, but they are hesitant composers of readings—and writings. Bartholomae and Petrosky designed a program that helps these students take on reading and writing within academic discourse.

The program begins with students' experiences, provides them with opportunities to recast these experiences in several different ways, and helps them to consider their experiences in relation to experiences of others—the authors they read and their own classmates. Over the course of the program, students develop their own theories related to their experiences and later compare their theories with those of established academics. Pittsburgh's Reading and Writing as Composing introduces students to academic discourse and conventions, using the kinds of reading and writing methods and thinking processes that established academics use in the actual development of and response to theory.

Intended Audience

Bartholomae and Petrosky designed this method for college students who were not able to handle the reading and writing demands of college classes. The method lends itself for use across students of various ages, including elementary and high school students.

Description of the Procedures

The Reading and Writing as Composing program reflects Bartholomae and Petrosky's attempt to design a seminar-type course in which students not only respond to the knowledge of others, but also create their own knowledge. Salvatori (1986) uses concepts from Gadamer's work on hermeneutics to describe the workings of the program:

> The basic design of each assignment retains throughout (though less overtly in the first
> four assignments) a tripartite scheme which guides students through what Gadamer names
> as the three fundamental phases of the hermeneutic process: (1) *to understand* first of all,
> (2) *to interpret* that understanding, and finally (3) to apply the knowledge gained in the act
> of reflexivity (i.e., the ways in which one thinks and the reasons for thinking that way) to
> the subject matter under investigation and to life experiences. (P. 139) [italics original]

The authors describe two versions of the program, one for younger students (using adolescence as its subject matter) and one for nontraditional students (using work for its subject matter). Each of these programs draws on students' own experiences and provides students with an opportunity to engage with issues that are important to them.

Along with the recognition of the interconnections between reading and writing and the use of a subject matter that brings in students' experiences, the Basic Reading and Writing course places responsibilities for learning on the students, as Bartholomae demonstrates in his description of a teaching event:

> I walk into my class, ask my students to turn to a passage I've chosen the night before,
> and I read it to them aloud. It's a difficult passage because it pushes against the available
> language of daily life—it talks about a moment when [Richard] Rodriguez [author of *Hun-
> ger of Memory*] read Hoggart's *The Uses of Literacy,* cites a passage from that book, and
> talks about how that reading (Rodriguez's reading of Hoggart) gave a "shape to desire." I
> read the passage aloud and ask my students, "What does this say?" Not, "What does this
> mean?" but "What does this say?" And there is silence. I wait, as I have learned to do,
> since this is not a silence, I think, that a teacher should fill, not if he wants to teach compo-
> sition. (Bartholomae, 1986, p. 90)

Bartholomae avoids reading for a single meaning (by refusing to ask, "What does this mean?"). He also refuses to provide (his) answers for students; instead, he challenges them to find their own and he gives them the time to do so.

The Reading and Writing as Composing program requires students to do a significant amount of interconnected reading and writing, using various strategies to help students learn to cope with the kind of reading and writing required by the university. The box below shows the reading and writing assignments and a sample week's schedule:

Summary of Assignments (adapted from Bartholomae and Petrosky, 1986)

Writing Assignment 1: In-class diagnostic exam.
Written response to a chapter from Margaret Mead's *Blackberry Winter*

Writing Assignment 2: Significant event from own life
Rough draft

Reading Assignment A: *I Know Why the Caged Bird Sings*
Journal entry in response to reading

Writing Assignment 3: Significant event from own life
Revision and extension

Reading Assignment B: Drafts and revisions of significant event writing
Response to other students' writings

Reading Assignment C: *The Catcher in the Rye* (alternate: *Ordinary People*)
Journal entry in response to reading

Writing Assignment 4: Event that was not a turning point
Rough draft

Writing Assignment 5: Event that was not a turning point
Revision and extension

Writing Assignment 6: Self as representative case
Rough draft

Reading Assignment D: *Hunger of Memory* (alternate: *A Separate Peace*)
Journal entry in response to reading

Writing Assignment 7: Self as representative case
Revision and extension

Writing Assignment 8: In-class writing
Response to *Hunger of Memory*

Writing Assignment 9: Editing
Edit assignment #6

Reading Assignment E: Reflection
Journal entry that reflects on the books read so far

Writing Assignment 10: In-class essay exam
Compare two characters' experiences of adolescence

Writing Assignment 11: Deliberately making changes in life
Rough draft in preparation for autobiography

Writing Assignment 12: Writing about self
Review papers and write about the person who emerges from those papers

Writing Assignment 13: Autobiography
First draft

Writing Assignment 14: Autobiography
Revision and extension

Writing Assignment 15: Autobiography
Second revision and extension as necessary

Writing Assignment 16: Autobiography
Final version, typed, ready to distribute to rest of class

Reading Assignment F: Collection of autobiographies
Journal entry in response to autobiographies

Reading Assignment G: *Passages*
Journal entry in response to reading

Writing Assignment 17: Identify crises from section of *Passages*
In-depth analysis of one part of book, write as psychologist

Writing Assignment 18: In-class assignment
Identify significant terms in a chapter of *Passages* and apply to case study

Writing Assignment 19: Autobiographies as case studies
Identify patterns, report findings, begin to explain these findings

Reading Assignment H: *Vanishing Adolescent*
Journal entry in response to reading

Writing Assignment 20: In-class essay exam
Agreeing or disagreeing with a point from *Vanishing Adolescent*

Writing Assignment 21: Response to *Vanishing Adolescent*
Connect own analysis of autobiographies with *Vanishing Adolescent*

Reading Assignment I: *Coming of Age in Samoa*
Journal entry in response to reading

Writing Assignment 22: In-class essay exam
Key factors in *Coming of Age in Samoa*

Writing Assignment 23: Conflict
Use *Vanishing Adolescent* and *Coming of Age in Samoa* plus own ideas

Writing Assignment 24: Becoming an adult
Use own study of autobiographies plus other readings

Final Exam: *Blackberry Winter*
Write about the main ideas in the reading.

Sample one-week schedule (adapted from Demario, 1986)

Week of September 17

Monday 17	Wednesday 19	Friday 21
Collect Reading Assignment A	Return A	Return #4
Assign Reading Assignment B	Collect Writing Assignment #4	Discuss at least one student paper (writing assignment)
Prediscussion exercises for *Caged Bird* (worksheet completed by small groups in class)	Discuss *Caged Bird*	Discuss *Caged Bird*
Discuss *Caged Bird*—whole class		Assign #6
		1 hr. Sustained Silent Reading
		Journal entry based on SSR

Reading   Students read several assigned texts, a collection of autobiographies written by their classmates, and a few books chosen by themselves over the course of fourteen weeks. Reading assignments are accompanied by specific instructions:

> We'd like you to read the whole book, *I Know Why the Caged Bird Sings,* by next Friday. This gives you a full week. Plan to sit and read for periods of time that are longer and longer, rather than for many short sittings. When you bring the book to class on Friday, we'll want to know how you went about reading it. Be prepared, that is, to point to passages or sections of the book (if there are any) where you got bogged down or lost. Would you also keep track of the time you spend reading? . . . As you read, keep a pencil or pen in your hand or nearby; do not underline or take notes, but if you come across something that seems significant or puzzling or something that you'd like to bring up in class discussion, put a mark in the margin or through the page number so that you can find it later. (Bartholomae and Petrosky, 53)

These instructions help students to read more fluently through suggesting that they read for longer and longer periods of time and by giving them a way of remembering important things in the text without notetaking or other disruptive activities. The course also includes an hour per week for in-class Sustained Silent Reading. Students can read books for the Basic Reading and Writing Course or other books that they have always wanted to read but have never gotten around to. They cannot do reading for other courses during SSR.

Following the completion of reading assignments, students participate in class discussions. They often work in small groups, answering questions about the text that help with comprehension, e.g., who are the characters in the text and what are the events that take place. The small-group members then decide which of the events are the most important. Passionate whole group discussion is often engendered as students argue about which events are the most significant in the book.

The first texts read in the class are largely autobiographical. Students focus on the adolescents featured in these texts and connect the experiences represented in the text with their own experiences. Salvatori (in Bartholomae and Petrosky, 1986) describes the dialogue the program sets up between students and texts, and between reading and writing as the students come to grips with understanding and making meaning. The program helps students to make connections between their own experiences and the reading they do. During this process of making connections, students find ways of articulating their own theories of adolescent development—the important issues to adolescence and the ways in which adolescents cope with the challenges presented to them. Later texts present academic theories of adolescents. The students can then compare their own work with those of the academy. Because students have come up with their own ideas during the first half of the program, they are in a much stronger position to respond to the academic ideas presented in the last half.

Writing   Students accomplish several kinds of writing during the program: journals, essays, an autobiography, and essay exams.

1. Journals: Part of the reading instructions include instructions on making written responses to reading in journals:

   > After you finish reading the book, you'll write in the part of your journal in which you record responses to the assigned reading. Here's how we want you to write. As soon as you can after you have read the book, sit down for one hour and write your response. We want you to write the first things that come to your mind when you think back on what you have read. We're not interested in summary, because we have read the book, too. Tell us, instead, what stands out for you. Then, tell us what things in your own life you can associate with what has stood out for you. These associations may be ideas of yours, feelings, experiences, memories of other books, of other courses, or things people have said to you. You want to move away from recording what stands out for you as significant to a way of accounting for why these passages or sections are significant. It's very important that you write this two-fold response and that you write for an hour, an hour of straight, uninterrupted writing. (Bartholomae and Petrosky, 53–54)

   Journal entries are not graded for correct form in writing. They are a place for students to put down their thoughts—to record their reading of the book. Students also write for the last ten minutes of the SSR, in response to their reading.

2. Essays and autobiography. The first writing assignments for the class are autobiographical, in conjunction with the autobiographies that are being read. Many of the assignments dovetail with one another. For example, the autobiography that students write mid-semester (and which becomes a "class publication"—a collection of autobiographies that form one of the assigned texts—see Figure 4–1) is actually the result of three different assignments. Later in the program, students read theoretical texts and incorporate these ideas in their writing.

3. Essay exams. Students receive practice in an academic genre, the essay exam, a few times during the semester. They read a text and write a response during a two-hour class period. Students are instructed to make nonpersonal responses to the readings when they write in this genre. The essay exams provide the teachers with a measure of how students' readings and responses change over the course of the semester.

The final significant aspect of the course is the writing process the students use. Teachers duplicate students' writing assignments (the writer can choose to remain anonymous) and discuss these in the class. Students quickly discover an audience for their writing—their fellow students—and they begin to care about their audience's reaction to their work. This feedback is purported to help students go through the revision process, which the class supports and uses.

Toward the end of the program, after students have begun to be interested in using written language successfully, the teachers introduce the concept of editing. Once again, though, the teachers are careful to put students in charge of their own work; rather than editing for the students, teachers place checkmarks at the end of lines in which there are mistakes. It is up to the students to find out what the mistakes are and how to correct them. Students begin to learn the mistakes they make the most often and ways to correct those mistakes.

Of special note in this strategy is the role of teacher response to students' works. Perhaps because they are working with college students and academic discourse, Bartholomae and Petrosky bring very sophisticated analyses to their students' work. For example, the authors cite a student's response to an assignment to "recall an experience from the last two years or so that strikes you as particularly significant, one that has changed the way you are or the way you think about things" (P. 32). They then analyze the response:

> This essay has a clearly discernible structure, but the structure does not represent an act of inquiry as inquiry is defined by the conventions of classroom discourse. The writer can turn his experience with wrestling and Brother Lawrence into a subject and he can provide commentary on that subject, but neither subject nor commentary stand within the language and methods of the university. The subject is consumed by the conventional Boy's Life narrative of struggle and success. And Brother Lawrence, who comes forward as a key figure in the narrative, disappears in the concluding commentary. The student's discussion of how and why the experience was significant, a discussion that provides a "reading" of the narrative, offers a reading that turns most of what he has said into insignificant detail. Friere would say that the student has not learned to "problematize" his "existential situation." (P. 33)

The authors (and the others who teach in the same program) bring to their students a complex array of responses to text: an analysis of text structure, an analysis of different discourses (Boy's Life vs. university), and a connection, through Friere, with critical pedagogy.* Bartholomae and Petrosky can articulate the ways in which the text fails within academic discourse. While they don't introduce Friere into their classrooms per se, the authors use their understandings of students' texts to generate questions, which in turn get the students thinking—and ultimately revising their texts.

Cautions and Comments

Several writers have extended Bartholomae and Petrosky's approach.

Rubin (1991) criticizes Bartholomae's assignments as being too general and provides examples of two writing assignments that are more specific. Although Rubin's point is well taken, Bartholomae might argue that part of the students' responsibilities might be to problem-solve in order to complete the assignments. In fact, Bartholomae and Petrosky (1986) mention that the response to the first assignment is simply occasionally copying the text that is to be commented on. The authors mention that this response is a desperate move by students who are in over their heads. Rather than making the first assignment even simpler, the authors allow this response. As students learn more about how to engage with text and how to represent that engagement, they can see their own growth and change from initial failure to some sort of success. In other words, the initial difficulty with assignments may be valuable in the long run for students.

*Critical pedagogy (including the work of Paolo Friere and others) analyzes social and economic conditions and their relationships to teaching and learning.

While this strategy has been developed for college students who need remedial work, it is possible that a variant of this strategy might form the basis for advanced work for high school students (or even elementary school students). It is interesting that Bartholomae and Petrosky took a very advanced teaching methodology (the graduate seminar) and adapted it for use with beginning college students. The graduate seminar assumes that students are competent to make contributions to knowledge as well as receive information from others. It is possible that this method could be adapted to younger students as well.

Teachers of younger students might want to use some of Bartholomae and Petrosky's approaches to reading students' texts. These approaches help teachers get beyond surface features of writing and begin to engage with types of discourse, genre issues, and critical connections between literacy and ideology. Ultimately, the understandings made possible by these forms of analysis help teachers to become more thoughtful respondents to students' writing.

Ostrom (1992) points out that there are two conflicting pedagogies for first-year college students at work: the work of Elbow and others, which focuses on finding one's own voice, and the work of Bartholomae, which has students learn to write within the realm of academic discourse. The Course in Basic Reading and Writing is designed to provide students with access to academic discourse—ways of reading and writing that help students succeed in college. Since the course has this goal, it is much more structured than most writing process classes in which students find their own directions in discourse.

The students for whom this course is designed are already marginal to the university. Hindman (1992) and McClure (1992) question the ideology/value of putting marginal students in the position of having to use academic discourse—of being limited to this particular form of discourse. The question raised here is a difficult one to answer. On the one hand, Bartholomae and Petrosky's curriculum allows a group of students to have access to a particular discourse from which they have been traditionally excluded (e.g., because of class or ethnic origin). Besides, many of the texts that Bartholomae and Petrosky use are multicultural in nature, e.g., Angelou's *I Know Why the Caged Bird Sings* and Rodriguez's *Hunger of Memory,* and Frisk (1992) extends these possibilities by suggesting the use of rap music as a text. On the other hand, it is precisely this particular discourse that has contributed to the racism and classism that have excluded these people in the first place. Do the students need to be changed—or should we change the discourse? How does discourse get changed—by people who are comfortable with it from the beginning, or by people who struggle to engage with it? Who decides if a discourse is worthy of access by an individual?

References

Bartholomae, D., and A. Petrosky. 1986. *Facts, artifacts and counterfacts: Theory and method for a reading and writing course.* Upper Montclair, NJ: Boynton/Cook Publishers. Describes the curriculum of the Basic Reading and Writing Course. Includes articles written by several teachers in the course that illuminate various aspects of the course (e.g., the editing sequence) and case studies of individual students.

Bartholomae, D. 1986. Wandering: misreadings, miswritings, misunderstandings. In *Only connect: Uniting reading and writing,* edited by T. Newkirk. Upper Montclair, NJ: Boynton/Cook Publishers. Discusses and analyzes college students' reading of several texts. Bartholomae accesses students' reading through their writing.

Frisk, P. J. 1992. *Rap music and the first-year writing curriculum.* Paper presented at the Annual Meeting of the Conference on College Composition and Communication (43rd, Cincinnati, OH, March 19–21, 1992) ERIC Document 343-151. Suggests using rap as a text for Reading and Writing as Composing classes.

Hindman, J. E. 1992. *Gestures? We don't need your stinking gestures!: Empowerment through radical teachers and cultural action for freedom.* Paper presented at the Annual Meeting of the Conference on College Composition and Communication (43rd, Cincinnati, OH, March 19–21, 1992) ERIC Document 343-151. Critique of the politics of Bartholomae and Petrosky's methods.

McClure, M. F. 1992. *Valuing student texts/students valuing texts.* Paper presented at the Annual Meeting of the Conference on College Composition and Communication (43rd, Cincinnati, OH, March 19–21, 1992) ERIC Document 345-250. Critique of the politics of Bartholomae and Petrosky's methods.

Ostrom, H. 1992. *Surviving to write and writing to survive: The complex case of Langston Hughes.* Paper presented at the Annual Meeting of the Conference on College Composition and Communication (43rd, Cincinnati, OH, March 19–21, 1992) ERIC Document 344-215. Suggests using Langston Hughes in freshman composition classes, since many of Hughes's struggles were similar to those of freshmen attempting to learn to deal with academic discourse.

Purves, A. C., L. Papa, and S. Jordan, eds. 1994. *Encyclopedia of English studies and language arts.* New York: National Council of Teachers of English. This encyclopedia has more than 800 annotated entries/topics that succinctly address this topic and related areas.

Rubin, L. 1991. *Combining the personal and analytical: Assignments for basic writing.* Paper presented at the Annual Meeting of the Conference on College Composition and Communication (42nd, Boston, MA, March 21–23, 1991) ERIC Document 335-685. Provides alternative assignments for this method.

General Frameworks

UNIT OVERVIEW

In most classrooms, teachers approach reading instruction and content area learning (e.g., social studies and science) with a general framework within which students are guided through a range of activities. The present unit describes three frameworks that have been labeled *general frameworks*. Two of the strategies are used primarily with short selections included in anthologies. The third strategy, the instructional framework, is used with content area textbook material. The three frameworks exemplify the type of guidance used to develop teacher's guides that accompany textbook and traditional basals.

Directed Reading Activity (DRA).   Over the years, the Directed Reading Activity has probably been the most widely used framework for a "total" reading lesson. In many ways, it has served as the basis for many of the lessons that have been developed to accompany basal reading selections. Five basic steps constitute a DRA. These steps purport to provide the structure for the improvement of a wide spectrum of reading skills—the most important of which is comprehension. This strategy, which may be applied to reading selections that vary in both length and readability, is suggested for use with students at all grade levels.

Directed Reading-Thinking Activity (DR-TA).   Assuming that critical reading performance requires the reader to become skilled at determining purposes for reading, the Directed Reading-Thinking Activity emphasizes that the reader declares his or her own purposes for reading. Like the DRA, the Directed Reading-Thinking Activity may be applied to reading selections that vary in both length and readability, and it is suggested for use with students at all grade levels.

Instructional Framework.   The three major phases of the Instructional Framework—preparation, guidance, and independence—provide the content teacher with a viable design for presenting a unit of study. The framework provides a means for teaching both the important reading skills (process) the students need and the important concepts (product) of the unit. Thus, process and product merge in hopes of developing independent learners. The strategy is most commonly used to accompany content area textbook material, but can be used with both fictional and expository materials with students in grades four and above.

Directed Reading Activity

Purpose

The purpose of the Directed Reading Activity (DRA) (Betts, 1946) is to: (1) give teachers a basic format from which to provide systematic instruction on a group basis; (2) improve students' word recognition and comprehension skills; (3) successfully guide students through a reading selection; and (4) engage students in reading text (Blanton and Moorman, 1990).

Rationale

DRA is a structured strategy used by classroom teachers as a comprehensive means to provide reading instruction to children through a reading selection and was once used as the basis for developing teaching guidelines for basal reader selections. Indeed, Betts (1946) compiled the guidelines that various authors of basal readers generally recommended for teaching reading. Betts described a plan to follow when there was general agreement among the authors:

> First, the group should be prepared, oriented, or made ready, for the reading of a story or selection. Second, the first reading should be guided silent reading. Third, word-recognition skills and comprehension should be developed during the silent reading. Fourth, the reading—silent or oral, depending upon the needs of the pupil—should be done for purposes different from those served by the first, or silent, reading. Fifth, the follow-up on the "reading lesson" should be differentiated in terms of pupil needs. (P. 492)

Intended Audience

The DRA is normally associated with basal reader instruction in the elementary grades, but the teacher may adapt it for any reading selection. For example, Shepherd (1973) has illustrated the use of DRA with content area textbooks from the middle school level through high school.

Description of the Procedures

Although there may be minor differences as to what constitutes the DRA, it usually contains the following components, all of which the teacher may modify to fit a student's needs:

1. Readiness
2. Directed silent reading

3. Comprehension check and discussion
4. Oral rereading
5. Follow-up activities

Stage 1: Readiness   The readiness, or preparation, stage of the DRA involves getting students ready to enter the story by relating the story selection to their past experiences, developing their interest in reading it, and setting their purposes for reading. Four components comprise the readiness stage of the DRA.

a. *Develop concept background*   Here it is suggested that the teacher connect the new concepts that the students will be exposed to in the reading selection with their previous experiences or readings. Any misconceptions or hazy understandings by the students are expected to be clarified before they read the story.

   The teacher may build background through various means, including discussions centering around the story title and illustrations in the selection, personal experiences of the students related to the story content, films, pictures, maps, or other audiovisual displays.

b. *Create interest*   Starting with the notion that children must be interested or motivated to read a selection in order to maximize their comprehension and enjoyment of its contents, the teacher attempts also to create interest in the early stages. The mechanical side of the selection alone, its title and the various illustrations, many times may serve to arouse students' interest; however, the teacher may also have to keep creating enthusiasm for students to read the story effectively. In some cases developing conceptual background (the previously discussed section) may suffice. If not, the teacher may choose to read a short, introductory portion of the selection in hopes of inspiring the students to want to read the rest. At other times, the teacher may wish to use multimedia material and/or experiences to stimulate interest.

c. *Introduce new vocabulary*   Here the teacher's task is to prepare students for any words they will encounter that are outside the students' reading vocabularies and word recognition abilities. To emphasize word meanings and not just word pronunciations, the teacher may introduce new vocabulary in context, both orally and visually. For example, the teacher might first use the word *orally* in a sentence, followed by a visual presentation on the chalkboard using meaningful phrases or sentences. The introduction of new vocabulary is not a time for drill or for emphasizing word attack skills. Instead, it is the time to give students oral familiarity with selected words. Typically, a teacher introduces no more than five words at once.

d. *Establish purpose*   Based upon the notion that the establishment of clear, concise purpose for reading a selection determines the quality of the readers' comprehension, the teacher poses questions for the students to answer in their silent reading. The overall question the teacher should consider is, "What are the students reading for?" For example, the teacher must decide whether to set a general purpose for the entire selection, such as "Read to find out the series of events that led to the downfall of the dictator," *or,* if the teacher decides to set more specific purposes for each part of a selection, another example is "Read to find out how the dictator came to power before you go on to other parts of the selection."

The presentation of the readiness stage of the DRA should take approximately five to fifteen minutes but will vary in length and emphasis according to the ability of the students and the complexity of the selections. For less advanced students, it may be necessary to spend a longer time preparing them to read the selection than when preparing more advanced students. Depending upon how the teacher approaches the readiness stage, one component may encompass other aspects of this step. For instance, introducing new vocabulary may create interest and develop concept background simultaneously. With the exception of establishing purpose, which should conclude the readiness stage, the teacher need not present the other components in any established order.

Stage 2: Directed Silent Reading   Following the readiness stage of the DRA, the students should read the selection silently to seek answers to the purpose-questions that the teacher has set. It is emphasized that the teacher have students read the selection silently, and not orally. This way is more rapid, it is more characteristic of everyday reading needs, and it gives the students an opportunity to use their work attack skills without expressed effort.

If readiness activities have been thorough, many students will work efficiently with very little, if any, teacher help. The teacher should encourage students to work out word recognition problems independently; however, he or she might also be available in the event a student requests help with confirmation or analysis. Since silent reading is not a time for word attack drills, it is suggested that teachers guide students who require help to clues that will aid them in unlocking the meaning of unknown words. If students seem unable to decode certain words, the teacher usually will provide these words so that reading may proceed. The teacher can make note of those words that give students particular difficulty and/or those specific skill needs of students as they attempt to decode words. Later, teachers can plan appropriate individual and/or group activities to counteract those difficulties.

Stage 3: Comprehension Check and Discussion   Discussion activities follow each silent reading segment that is assigned. An obvious start of the discussion can be answering the purpose-questions set during the readiness stage, although discussion may begin naturally on the other aspects of the selection. During the discussion it is appropriate to stress and develop comprehension abilities. For example, teachers might formulate discussion questions to extend and challenge the ideas students glean from their reading.

Stage 4: Oral Rereading   This stage of the DRA may occur in conjunction with the previous stage (comprehension check and discussion) or the teacher may use it to set new purposes for reading. The teacher may set these purposes independently, new purposes may develop out of the discussion, or they may serve as a preparation for a follow-up activity. Rereading may also occur if students are confused about one of the discussion questions. If such is the case, the new purpose is for students to read to solve problems that have resulted from the discussion. Students reread rapidly to locate information under question and then orally reread to the group to alleviate the confusion or to verify a point.

Stage 5: Follow-up Activities Follow-up activities include experiences that build and extend skill development and activities that add to, or enrich, students' understanding of the concepts in the story. This is also an appropriate time for the teacher to review any skills that were noted to have produced difficulties during the silent reading. Such activities are suitable on an individual basis, in a small group, or in a whole class situation.

The rationale behind this type of follow-up activity is that practice with, and opportunities to use, skills that present difficulty to students will provide them with the reinforcement necessary to learn those skills. As such, the use of basal reader workbooks, teacher-made worksheets, or commercially available material is often suggested to strengthen those specific skills that the DRA showed to be of concern.

Activities that can enrich or extend students' understanding of the story's concepts start with the premise that the application of newly learned concepts to other types of activities will further enhance and broaden new learning. Such extension activities may involve creative work, study activities, or extended reading. Creative work may include writing about personal experiences related to the story, preparing dramatization, and making illustrations for the story. Study activities may include workbook exercises and teacher-made practice material. Students may also do research into the information they gain from the selection in order to organize it into a chart or table format. Examples of extended reading might include selected readings in other texts or library books on related topics, or reading to find answers to questions that arise in the discussion of the story.

Cautions and Comments

The effective use of the DRA requires the teacher to be sensitive to the students' needs, to the differential demands of text, and to the adequacy of the DRA as a lesson framework. In this respect, the DRA seems to have one shortcoming; namely, it seems to be too teacher-dominated, which reduces the opportunities for students to "develop active, inquiring minds" (Nessel, 1989, 55). Interactions occurring between teachers and pupils flow mainly from the questions and activities that the teacher prescribes.

Nessel (1989) believes that "the type of instruction that is implemented in today's schools is one identifiable factor contributing to passive reading." (P. 55) As a result, the procedures followed in DRA could develop in students a dependence on teacher direction rather than on their own self-initiated reading-thinking processes. Results gleaned from Blanton and Moorman's (1990) study on reading instruction using the DRA framework convey that:

- an inordinate amount of DRA time was consumed by activity unrelated to the lesson
- teacher behavior reflected more time in questioning, telling, and defining rather than utilizing meaningful higher order thinking skills and processing
- teachers provided few explanations, rarely modeled, or demonstrated skills for students
- inconsistencies between teacher focus and instructional outcomes were evident

In addition, studies by Davidson (1970) and Petre (1970) compared the DRA with the Directed Reading-Thinking Activity (DR-TA) and found results favoring the DR-TA. Nessel (1989) identifies the following as advantages favoring DR-TA:

- students are actively involved at the higher levels of thinking
- teachers ask students to speculate rather than telling them what they will read about
- students anticipate what will happen based on knowledge gleaned from the discussion
- teachers recognize and praise student thinking and predictions (P. 57)

Another concern about the use of the DRA involves skill development (including oral reading, word recognition, comprehension, and study skills). If implemented properly, and related to the actual reading assignment, skill instruction has the potential to be purposeful and relevant. However, if skills instruction is rote or isolated from a selection, as worksheet exercises often are, then it is often meaningless, as argued by Sachs (1981), Osborn (1984), and Blanton, Moorman, and Wood (1988).

Despite these limitations, the DRA has adaptive potential to teach almost any reading selection. Aspects of other strategies described in this book may serve as supplements to the DRA. For example, teachers can effectively utilize ReQuest (see Unit 7) as a replacement for the readiness stage of the DRA. DRA's potential can serve other subject areas as well.

Part of the DRA's adaptive potential has to do with classroom management and ability grouping. For example, when basal reading programs are used, teachers can use the DRA for a week with various ability groups. An example of such a schedule follows:

A Week-Long Schedule for a Directed Reading Activity

Day One

Minutes	Group I	Group II	Group III
3–5	Teacher briefs students whom he or she does not work with directly. Students working directly with teacher organize themselves.		
25–30	*Stage I—Introducing the Selection* (Teacher present) Teacher introduces new story. *Stage II—Directed Silent Reading* (Teacher present) Students read story silently. *Stages III & IV— Comprehension Check and Oral Rereading* (Teacher present) *Stage V—Follow-up* Students reread and write an alternative ending.	*Independent Reading* (Students independently) or *Bookmaking*	*Stage V—Follow-up* (Students independently) Students work through activities reviewing outline. Students check own work. *Independent Work* (Students independently) Students begin work on a research problem.

Day One, *Continued*

Minutes	Group I	Group II	Group III
5–10	Teacher checks those students working independently, giving individuals help if needed.		
20–25	*Stage V——Follow up* (Students independently) Workbook activities. *Independent Reading* (Students independently)	Stage I—Introducing *the Selection* (Teacher present) *Stage II—Directed Silent Reading* (Teacher present) *Stage III—Comprehension Check* (Teacher present) *Stage IV—Oral Rereading* (Teacher present)	*Stage V—Follow-up* Students skim story to locate answers to questions. They create questions and ask them of each other. *Independent Reading*

Day Two

Minutes	Group I	Group II	Group III
3–5	Teacher organizes for instruction and briefs students.		
	Stage V—Follow-up (Teacher present) Teacher goes over work exercises. *Stage IV—Oral Rereading* (Teacher present) Oral rereading of selected conversations in story. *Stage V—Follow-up* (Teacher present) Word identification instruction.	Independent Reading (Students independently)	*Independent Reading* (Students independently)
3–5	Teacher organizes for instruction and briefing.		
15–20	*Stage V—Follow-up* (Students independently) Workbook activities. *Independent Reading* (Students independently)	Stage V—Follow-up (Students independently) Students complete dealing with context clues. *Independent Work* Research project.	*Stage V—Follow-up* (Teacher present) Review work from previous day. Students classify information from story and summarize.
5–10	Teacher checks work of groups, organizes for instruction, and briefs students.		
15–20	*Independent Reading* (Students independently)	Stage V—Follow-up (Teacher present) Teacher reviews use of context and other word identification skills.	*Skills V—Follow-up* (Students independently) Students continue work. *Independent Reading of Work*

Day Three

Minutes	Group I	Group II	Group III
3–5	Teacher organizes for instruction and briefs students.		
15–20	*Independent Reading* or *Independent Work* (Students independently) Dictated story; Bookmaking.	Stage V—Follow-up (Students independently) Students reread story silently to answer thought questions. Students prepare dramatization.	*Stage V—Follow-up* (Teacher present) Review classifying and summarizing. Reread parts of story for a radio show.
5–10	Group III shares reading experiences with Groups I and II (radio play).		
20–25	*Stage V—Follow-up* (Teacher present) Teacher checks workbook exercises. *Stage I–Introduces the Story* (Teacher present) *Stage II—Directed Silent Reading* *Stages III & IV—Compre- hension Check & Oral Rereading* (Teacher present)	Stage V—Follow-up (Students independently) Continue on previous activities. *Independent Reading* or *Independent Work* (Students independently) Research project.	*Stage V—Follow-up* (Students independently) Read related stories. Students use reference books to look for answers to questions related to stories.
3–5	Teacher checks with other two groups and organizes class.		
10–15	Group II presents dramatization of story.		

Day Four

Minutes	Group I	Group II	Group III
3–5	Teacher organizes for instruction and briefs students.		
20–25	*Stage V—Follow-up* (Students independently) Students skim story to locate answers to specific questions. Students organize events from story into the correct sequence. *Independent Reading* (Students independently)	*Independent Reading* (Students independently) *Independent Work* (Students independently) Research project.	*Stage V—Follow-up* (Teacher present) Discussion of previous work. *Stage I—Introduces the Selection* (Teacher present) *Stage II—Directed Silent Reading* (Teacher present) *Stage III— Comprehension Check & Stage IV—Oral Rereading* (Teacher present)

Day Four *(Continued)*

Minutes	Group I	Group II	Group III
3–5	Teacher checks work of groups, organizes for instruction, and briefs groups.		
20–25	*Independent Reading* (Students independently) *Independent Work* Students move to learning center for research work.	*Stage V—Follow-up* (Teacher present) Teacher discusses students' answers to thought questions from previous day. *Stage I—Introduces Selection* (Teacher present) *Stage II—Directed Silent Reading* (Teacher present) *Stage III—Comprehension Check* *Stage IV—Oral Rereading* (Teacher present)	*Stage V—Follow-up* (Students independently) Students organize information they recall from story into an outline. *Independent Reading* (Students independently)
3–5	Teacher introduces several new books for independent reading. Children share books they have read and enjoyed.		

Day Five

Minutes	Group I	Group II	Group III
3–5	Teacher briefs class and organizes for instruction.		
15–20	All three groups participate in independent reading. This may be through the use of U.S.S.R. (see Unit 1)		
3–5	Children terminate reading. Organize for class activity.		
15–20	Selected students may elect to continue reading for a few minutes. Remainder of class shares personal reading through book reports, posters, dramatizations, or displays. Teacher and children list five favorite magazine or newspaper articles.		
15–20	*Stage V—Follow-up Activities* (Teacher present) Students discuss and develop a mural based upon story.	*Independent Reading or Work* (Students independently)	*Independent Reading or Work* (Students independently)
Note:	The above pattern is suggestive rather than prescriptive. For each group the sequence would vary from week to week. Depending upon the nature of activities and the students' needs, the teacher might alter group structure in terms of size, membership, and number.		

References

Betts, E. A. 1946. *Foundations of reading instruction.* New York: American Book. Presents one of the original descriptions of the general principles and assumptions behind the DRA.

Blanton, W. E., and G. B. Moorman. 1990. The presentation of reading lessons. *Reading Research and Instruction* 29:35–55. A research study in which the effectiveness of DRA with skill instruction was explored.

Blanton, W. E., G. B. Moorman, and R. G. Wood. 1986. A model of direct instruction applied to the basal skills lesson. *The Reading Teacher* 40:299–304. Proposes a direct instruction model that extends the DRA framework.

Davidson, J. L. 1970. *The relationship between teachers' questions and pupils' responses during a directed reading activity and a directed reading-thinking activity.* Unpublished doctoral diss., University of Michigan. Presents a research study in which the efficacy of DRA is questioned.

Donlan, D. 1985. Using the DRA to teach literary comprehension at three response levels. *Journal of Reading* 28:408–415. Explores the use of the DRA as a means of aiding interpretation.

Greabell, L. C., and N. A. Anderson. 1992. Applying strategies from the directed reading activity to a directed mathematics activity. *School Sciences and Mathematics* 92:142–144. Presents a math lesson on problem-solving utilizing the DRA framework.

Karlin, R. 1975. *Teaching elementary reading: Principles and strategies.* 2d ed. New York: Harcourt, Brace, Jovanovich, 146–151. Describes the steps involved in the DRA when used with a basal reader.

Miller, W. H. 1977. *The first R: Elementary reading today.* 2d ed. New York: Holt, Rinehart & Winston, 59–78. Provides general guidelines for using the DRA in the guise of a basal reader lesson.

Nessel, D. 1989. Do your students think when they read? *Learning, 18,* 55–57. Compares the DRA model with the DR-TA model of direct instruction.

Osborn, J. 1984. The purposes, uses, and contents of workbooks and some guidelines for publishers. In *Learning to read in American schools: Basal readers and content texts,* edited by R. C. Anderson, J. Osborn, and R. J. Tierney. Hillsdale, NJ: Erlbaum. Discusses the strengths, weaknesses, and use of workbooks accompanying basal reading lessons.

Petre, R. M. 1970. *Quantity, quality and variety of pupil responses during an open-communication group directed reading-thinking activity and a closed-communication structured group directed reading activity.* Unpublished doctoral diss., University of Delaware. Presents a research study in which the efficacy of DRA is questioned.

Purves, A. C., L. Papa, and S. Jordan. 1994. *Encyclopedia of English studies and language arts.* New York: National Council of Teachers of English. An excellent resource that contains an extensive collection of more than 800 annotated entries/topics in English Studies and Language Arts.

Sachs, A. W. 1981. *The effects of three prereading activities on learning disabled children's short-term reading comprehension.* Unpublished doctoral diss., George Peabody University. Presents a research study in which the effectiveness of the DRA was examined.

Shepherd, D. L. 1973. *Comprehensive high school reading methods.* Columbus, Ohio: Charles E. Merrill, 132–138. Outlines steps to adapt the DRA for use in the content fields.

Spache, G. D., and E. B. Spache. 1977. *Reading in the elementary school.* 4th ed. Boston: Allyn and Bacon, 46–53. Provides an outlined procedure for teaching a typical basal reader lesson.

Stauffer, R. G. 1969. *Directing reading maturity as a cognitive process.* New York: Harper & Row, 35–86. Describes an alternative procedure to the DRA—The Directed Reading-Thinking Activity. Using the same fundamental steps as the DRA, this strategy promotes more student involvement.

Directed Reading-Thinking Activity

Purpose

The Directed Reading-Thinking Activity (DR-TA) is intended to develop students' ability to read critically and reflectively. Broadly speaking, it attempts to equip readers with: (1) the ability to determine purposes for reading; (2) the ability to extract, comprehend, and assimilate information; (3) the ability to examine reading material based upon purposes for reading; (4) the ability to suspend judgments; and (5) the ability to make decisions based upon information gleaned from reading.

Rationale

Russell Stauffer (1969) developed the DR-TA to provide conditions that would produce readers who could think, learn, and test. Stauffer suggests that these readers

> . . . will learn to have the strength of their convictions and the courage to deal with ideas. They will not be fearful but courageous; not blind, but discerning; not hasty, but deliberate; not deceitful, but honest; not muddled, but articulate; not acquiescent, but militant; not conceited, but modest; not imitative, but original. (P. 84)

Stauffer based his notions upon the belief that reading is a thinking process that involves the reader in using his or her own experiences to reconstruct the author's ideas. The reconstruction begins with the generation of hypotheses based upon the reader's doubts and desires. It continues with the reader's acquisition of information and the generation of further hypotheses during reading. The reconstruction terminates with the resolution of the reader's doubts and desires. Stauffer puts this into practice with the DR-TA as follows:

> . . . either the reader declares his own purposes or if he adopts the purposes of others, he makes certain how and why he is doing so. He also speculates about the nature and complexity of the answers he is seeking by using to the fullest his experience and knowledge relevant to the circumstances. Then he reads to test his purposes and his assumptions. As a result, he may: one, find the answer he is seeking literally and completely stated; two, find only partial answers or implied answers and face the need to either restate his purposes in light of the new information gained or to suspend judgment until more reading has been done; three, need to declare completely new purposes. (P. 40)

Intended Audience

As with the Directed Reading Activity, the teacher can easily adapt the DR-TA for any selection at any level of difficulty. Toward a balanced reading program, Stauffer suggests the extension and differentiation of the DR-TA for both group and individual use. With groups, he suggests using it with from eight to twelve students. Shepherd (1978) has also suggested using the DR-TA with content fields.

Description of the Procedures

The DR-TA has two parts—a process cycle and a product. The process cycle involves the reader in the following: setting purposes for reading, adjusting the rate and the material for these purposes, reading to verify purposes, pausing to evaluate understanding, then proceeding to read with the same or with different purposes. The product of the DR-TA is the extension and refinement of students' ideas and thinking.

Stauffer suggests procedures for a group DR-TA, which the teacher can extend and adapt into an individualized version.

1. *Group DR-TA*   There are certain essential phases in the implementation of a group DR-TA. The first phase involves directing reading-thinking processes. The second phase involves fundamental skill training.

   a. *Phase 1: Directing the reading-thinking process.* Directing the reading-thinking process involves the reader in three steps: predicting, reading, and proving. As students proceed through a selection, they predict or define purposes for reading; they read and select relevant data; and they evaluate and revise predictions, using the information they acquire.

Maria (1989) argues that since background knowledge is an important factor in reading, it is imperative that the teacher develop an appropriate introduction to the reading selection that incorporates student diversity and experiences. It is possible that some students come to school with "limited experiences with regard to reading comprehension which are more common for middle class children, and are thus taken for granted by authors of children's texts" (Maria, 1989, 296). Because of this fact, the teacher must "bridge the gap by finding an anchor point in what all children know and what they need to know to understand the text." (Maria, 1989, 298) In doing so, "the teacher shifts the focus from the text to the children and estimates what kind of background knowledge they have for these central concepts" (Maria, 1989, 298). Maria (1989) provides the following guidelines to assist teachers in bridging this gap: (a) implement a variety of prereading strategies that will maintain student motivation and interest, (b) utilize the prereading strategy that will be the most effective and suitable for the particular text, (c) teacher scaffolding and visual props may be needed to build background experiences, (d) utilize activities that merge prior knowledge with active participation, such as group discussions and brainstorming, partner or small-group interactions, and visual props to integrate and display knowledge (Pp. 297–299).

The teacher, the material, and the group are all essential to the success of this activity. The teacher has to create an environment that will arouse students' curiosities and meet their reading needs. The group serves to audit and extend the thinking of its members. The material provides, Stauffer states, "the substance for cognition" (1969, 46). To this end, he suggests the material should be well written, appealing in content, and of an appropriate difficulty level. For the purpose of directing the reading-thinking processes, the teacher may treat the selection in segments. Here is an example of how teachers might implement this phase with a selection divided into segments.

1. Each student either receives or locates a copy of the selection; the teacher directs the student to study either the title or the pictures on the first page.

    a. What do you think a story with this title might be about?

    b. What do you think might happen in this story?

    c. Which of these predictions do you agree with?

    The teacher encourages students to make several different suggestions and to discuss agreement or disagreement with one another's suggestions. The teacher promotes this interaction. Richek (1987) argues that an important element to the success of the DR-TA is positive dynamics and interactions. Richek (1987) proclaims that it "builds anticipation and sharpens the thinking process. In addition, students often serve as effective models for each other" (P. 635).

2. When the teacher introduces the DR-TA, he or she first familiarizes students with the strategy for dealing with unknown words. That is, if students encounter unknown words, the teacher would expect the students to implement the following steps in the specified order:

    a. Read to the end of the sentence

    b. Use picture clues, if available

    c. Sound out the word

    d. Ask the teacher for help

    Before asking for teacher assistance, the student should try to figure out the word and, according to Stauffer, the teacher should give the student the opportunity to do so.

3. The teacher directs the students to read a segment of the story silently to check their predictions. The teacher is responsible for ensuring that students read for meaning, observing reading performance, and helping students who request help with words. When the latter occurs, the teacher might have the student suggest a word it might be, explain what the student did to figure out the word, and, if the word is still unknown, the teacher provides it. Note that the teacher introduced no vocabulary prior to reading the story. Stauffer suggests this is unnecessary, given the vocabulary controls and systematic word identification programs found in basal readers.

4. After students have read the first segment, the teacher asks them to close their books and the comprehension check begins.

    Questions serve to guide the students' examination of the evidence, their evaluation of their previous predictions, and their generation of new predictions.

    "*Were you correct?*" or "*What do you think now?*" force students to examine the proof of their predictions. Oral reading of a particular sentence directs students to share their evidence with other group members.

    "*What do you think now?*" or "*What do you think will happen?*" encourage students to screen their ideas and to make predictions about events to come.

5. The students read the next segment of text and with each new segment of reading material, continue the predicting-reading-proving cycle. As students proceed, they

come upon more and more information; divergent conjectures begin to converge. At the beginning of the selection, predictions usually tend to be divergent. Toward the end of the reading, predictions should tend to converge.

b. *Phase 2: Fundamental skill training.* After the students have read the selection, the teacher has completed the first phase of the DR-TA—directing the reading-thinking of the selection. Now the second phase begins. Stauffer refers to this phase as the phase when "skill training of a different kind is accomplished" (1969, 64). The second phase entails reexamining the story, reexamining selected words or phrases, and pictures or diagrams, for the purpose of developing systematically and concurrently the students' reading-thinking abilities and other reading-related skills. These might include word attack, the use of semantic analysis, concept clarification and development, power of observation, and reflective abilities. The format of these activities varies but, in many cases, is also similar to the suggested exercises in the teacher's edition, the workbooks, or the skillbooks that accompany most basal reading systems.

2. *Individualized DR-TA*   Individualized DR-TAs apply, extend, and refine the skills and abilities that students acquire in group DR-TAs. Stauffer claims that individualized DR-TAs afford a systematic method by which students can learn about themselves in terms of their own interests, tasks, judgments, and thinking abilities.

Teachers can introduce individualized DR-TAs after group DR-TAs or in conjunction with them. Familiarity with group DR-TA procedures is a prerequisite for introducing an individualized DR-TA.

There are several features that distinguish an individualized DR-TA:

1. It does not use traditional grouping; instead, each student is free to work with a minimum of interruption, in pursuit of his or her interests. If interests coincide, students may occasionally work together.

2. The teacher expects students to know why they are to select materials, what materials they might select, and how they should select them. To this end, the teacher schedules time for selection of material and for discussion of selection techniques. The teacher may help students either individually or in groups to formulate interests, needs, and methods for selection.

3. Students should generate their own reading purposes and be familiar with the predicting-reading-proving cycle of the DR-TA. Either worksheet or student record cards might direct these processes.

4. At scheduled times, students should share their work or what they have read with others. This process might involve the use of posters, bulletin boards, dramatizations, reports, and the like.

5. As the need arises, students receive incidental or systematic skills instruction, individually or in groups.

6. Students should abide by class rules that are established to ensure individual rights and efficient learning.

7. Students should keep meaningful records on a daily or weekly basis. These records might track students' activities, the stories they read, or their skill needs.

8. Students can develop other language-related skills (oral expression, written expression, listening) through presentations, reports, verbal sharing, and other activities.

9. Throughout the individualized DR-TAs, the teacher should serve various functions, including the following:

   a. Organizing groups for projects and skill training

   b. Organizing the schedule to ensure flexibility and efficiency

   c. Pacing the various activities to afford maximum success and a minimum of frustration

   d. Establishing operating rules to facilitate learning and thinking

   e. Maintaining meaningful records to map individual progress and planning future activities

   f. Guiding, directing, and assisting students

Richek (1987) provides four variations of DR-TA that can assist teachers in meeting the needs of students at various stages of their development (P. 635). These include:

- Eliciting Predictions Without Justification

  This format can be utilized when students are unable or unwilling to support their predictions. Once students experience success and gain confidence, the teacher can prompt for justifications.

- Directed Listening-Thinking Activity (DL-TA)(Stauffer, 1980)

  This procedure can be implemented with students who speak English as a second language. "Students listen to the text rather than read it." Through active listening, students "learn what to expect from difficult narratives, yet, are freed from reading text that is above their instructional level. This also increases their facility with language which transfers to reading. The key is to provide challenging listening selections" (P. 635).

- Silent Directed Reading-Thinking Activity (Silent DR-TA)

  This variation "encourages independence in reading and has the added benefit of requiring a written response. It eliminates potential public embarrassment and intimidation and allows students to pace their own reading" (P. 635).

- Directed Reading-Thinking Activity Source (DR-TA Source)

  "This form helps students reflect upon the role that they play as readers in the reading process. When making predictions, students specify which part of the prediction was engendered by the text and by background knowledge" (P. 636)

Cautions and Comments

As lesson frameworks, the Directed Reading Activity and the DR-TA are suitable for use with almost any reading selection. But the DR-TA has certain features that distinguish it from the directed reading activity. First, the DR-TA places a heavy emphasis upon the relationship between reading and thinking. It encourages students to be aware of and to develop their own reading-thinking processes through initiating their own purposes for reading and making predictions. DR-TA invites "free participation by all students regardless of reading abilities. The only possible response is one made by the child, utilizing both information gleaned from the text in conjunction with existing knowledge. As the reader is required to prove his/her prediction, s/he must actively interact with the text's message" (Widomski, 1983, 308). Second, the role of the teacher is different. Stauffer (1968) describes the teacher's role "as one of an intellectual agitator facilitating discussion among and between students about a particular text" (Widomski, 1983, 308). Unlike the DRA, the DR-TA materials govern teacher-pupil interactions and students' purposes for reading; the teacher's questioning does not prescribe this interaction. The teacher does not assume the role of either questioner or judge. Instead, the teacher becomes a moderator and a facilitator. Third, vocabulary is treated differently; the student does not meet words prior to reading but as they occur in context. In those studies in which comparisons have been made of the two procedures, the DR-TA has fared better (Davidson 1970; Petre 1970). To see some of these differences more clearly, consider the use of both the DRA and DR-TA with a single selection (see the sample lesson plan in this section).

Widomski (1983) suggests incorporating DR-TA with semantic webbing, which "enables students to construct a visual display emphasizing ways for readers to organize and integrate concepts of a story in aiding comprehension of text" (P. 309). She argues that using "information gained in semantic webbing to test predictions for DR-TA will produce the following benefits:

- builds story schema and story grammar
- establishes insights into varying author styles
- strengthens inferential and evaluative skills
- builds generalizations and deductive reasoning (P. 312)

Davidson (1982) believes the DR-TA is a sophisticated procedure when used appropriately. In order for this to occur, teacher in-service and training must be provided. Davidson provides suggestions for teachers to "help them refine and develop the needed skills" (P. 58). Stieglitz and Oehlkers' (1989) findings reveal that teachers respond positively to innovative teaching procedures when provided appropriate in-service training and materials. For teachers familiar with traditional reading materials, the DR-TA affords a useful alternative, but one that they should not use repeatedly. For example, teachers might wish to vary both the treatment of the reading-thinking phase and the format of activities within the fundamental skill phase, since with repeated use, children become "programmed" to the strategy rather than becoming involved in reading-thinking interactions. If teachers find their students unable or unwilling to make predictions, they may supplement the approach with games and activities that encourage predictive behaviors. Teachers may find the presentation of either incomplete pictures, jigsaw pieces, or cartoons useful devices for generating predictions. And teachers may sometimes read a story to students for the purpose of either introducing or supplementing the predicting-reading-proving cycle.

Sample Lesson Plan for a Directed Reading Activity and a Directed Reading-Thinking Activity

To compare the use of a Directed Reading Activity and a Directed Reading-Thinking Activity, here are two lesson plans for the same selection. One lesson plan represents what a teacher might typically do using a Directed Reading Activity approach. The other lesson plan represents what a user might typically do with a Directed Reading-Thinking Activity.

The Selection

The selection we chose for this purpose is a story entitled "The Surprise," suitable for use in a second grade classroom. "The Surprise" tells what happened to a child's box of cookies. The child had made the cookies for his or her teacher. The teacher inadvertently sits on the box, crumbling the child's cookies. The story ends happily, with the children and the teacher having a party.

Directed Reading Activity

I. *Introducing the Selection*
In the Directed Reading Activity, the teacher introduces the selection by attempting to do four things: build an interest in the story, build concept background, introduce new vocabulary, set purposes.
Show children a white box. Ask them what they think the box is (create interest). Explain to students that what you have is a surprise. Have them tell about surprises they have received (concept background). Write the words *surprise* and *children* on the chalkboard. Have the students say the words and use them in a sentence (introduce vocabulary). Direct children to the story entitled "The Surprise" and have them read the first page to learn who is getting the surprise (setting purpose).

II. *Directed Silent Reading*
As the students silently read the designated section, the teacher stands by to help. If the student has difficulty with a word, the authors suggest the teacher provide it immediately. Once the students have located the answer to the question, the teacher directs them either to mark with their finger, or to remember the word, sentence, or section that told them the answer.

Directed Reading-Thinking Activity

I. *Introducing the Selection*
In the Directed Reading-Thinking Activity, the teacher encourages the students to make their own predictions concerning what they are about to read. The teacher neither introduces vocabulary nor sets purpose.
Show children a white box. Ask them what they think the box is. Explain to students that what you have is a surprise. Have them turn to the story entitled "The Surprise" and have them make predictions about the surprise. Ask questions like: *What do you think will happen in this story?* (The teacher might refer them to the picture clues.) Direct students to read the first page to learn about their predictions.

II. *Directed Silent Reading*
As the students silently read the designated section, the teacher stands by to help. If the student has difficulty with a word, there is a set procedure to follow. This procedure involves:

1. Reading to the end of the sentence;
2. Using picture clues, if available;
3. Sounding out the word; and
4. (If the students still do not recognize the word) asking the teacher.

Once the students have finished the designated page, they turn over their books and await the teacher.

III. *Comprehension Check and Skill Building*

IV. *Oral Rereading*
The teacher asks the students to answer this previous question: *Who was the surprise for?* The students share their answers and verify them by orally rereading the sentences or sentence that yielded the answer. The teacher asks other related questions: *Who is Miss Day? Who is Jay?*

Repetition of Phases I, II, III, & IV

As the students progress through the rest of the selection in segments, the teacher sets further purposes for their reading, the teacher checks their comprehension, and the students orally reread to verify answers.

III. *Comprehension Check and Skill Building*

IV. *Oral Reading*
The Teacher asks the students how accurate their predictions were. The students produce the proof they used to verify their predictions by orally rereading the sentences or sentence that yielded the answer. The teacher asks students to share what else they now know.

Repetition of Phases I, II, III, & IV

As students progress through the rest of the selection in segments, the teacher asks them to make further predictions, to silently read to verify them, to revise, and to evaluate these predictions. Students refine predictions with more information, as in the phase described under *Introducing the Selection*. Students repeat Directed Silent Reading, Comprehension Check, Skill Building, and Oral Rereading.

A teacher may use the patterns exemplified here for teaching a story or article at any level; however, there may be some differences. The teacher may or may not break the selection into segments. What the teacher actually does within each phase will vary, depending on the selection, the students themselves, and their purposes for reading.

Follow-up Activities

In the Directed Reading Activity, various and sundry follow-up activities usually occur. In the main, they center upon developing the following skills:

1. Comprehension
2. Word identification
3. Study skills
4. Literary appreciation and understanding
5. Vocabulary
6. Oral reading

In addition, typical follow-up activities afford opportunities for enrichment.

Here are some examples:

1. *Oral rereading.* Explain to students that the story they have read has plenty of conversation; have them take parts and reread the story.
2. *Comprehension.* Write several sentences that describe events that either did or did not happen in the story. Have the students decide which events did happen and then arrange the order.

Follow-up Activities

In the Directed Reading-Thinking Activities, the follow-up activities are virtually the same as those we propose for a directed reading activity. Indeed, a teacher might use the examples here across both strategies. To follow-up the Directed Reading-Thinking Activity, Stauffer suggests Fundamental Skill Activities that would be similar to the follow-up activities suggested in most basal programs.

The children did not like the cookies.
The children had a party.
Jay made little cookies.
Jay dropped the box.
They went to the zoo.

3. *Word identification.* Have students locate these words in the story: looked, carried, hurried, parties. Have students locate the endings and root words.

4. *Enrichment.*
   a. Present the students with a recipe they might follow to make cookies. Make some as a group project.
   b. Have students make a surprise for a friend.
   c. Dramatize the story.

References

Bear, D. R., and M. Invernizzi. 1984. Student directed reading groups. *Journal of Reading* 28:248–252. Explores the benefits of group DR-TAs.

Davidson, J. L. 1982. The DR-TA: Avoiding common pitfalls. *Reading Horizons* 23:54–58. Provides solutions to the common misconceptions of DR-TA.

———. 1970. *The relationship between teachers' questions and pupils' responses during a directed reading activity and a directed reading-thinking activity.* Unpublished doctoral diss., University of Michigan. Presents a research study in which the efficacy of DRA is questioned.

Dixon, C. N., and D. D. Nessel. 1992. *Meaning making: Directed reading and thinking activities for second-language students.* Englewood Cliffs, NJ: Prentice-Hall. A good source for use with ESL students.

Gill, J. T., and D. R. Bear. 1988. No book, whole book, and chapter DR-TAs. *Journal of Reading* 31:444–451. Explores the use of the DR-TA without books, with entire books, or chapters.

Haggard, M. R. 1988. Developing critical thinking with the directed reading-thinking activity. *The Reading Teacher* 41:526–535. Provides an extended discussion of the DR-TA, its rationale and use.

Maria, K. 1989. Developing disadvantaged children's background knowledge interactively. *The Reading Teacher* 42:296–300. Describes knowledge to increase children's reading comprehension.

Nessel, D. 1987. The new face of comprehension instruction: A closer look at questions. *The Reading Teacher.* 40:604–606. Provides sample questions for teachers to ask during a reading lesson.

Petre, R. M. 1970. *Quantity, quality and variety of pupil responses during an open-communication group directed reading-thinking activity and a closed-communication structured group directed reading activity.* Unpublished doctoral diss., University of Delaware. Presents a research study in which the efficacy of DRA is questioned.

Purves, A. C., L. Papa, and S. Jordan, eds. 1994. *Encyclopedia of English studies and language arts.* New York: National Council of Teachers of English. An excellent resource that contains an extensive collection of more than 800 annotated entries/topics in English studies and language arts.

Richek, M. A. 1987. DRTA: 5 variations that facilitate independence in reading narratives. *Journal of Reading* 30:632–636. Describes the variations of DR-TA that a teacher can implement in order to meet individual student needs and development.

Shepherd, D. L. 1978. *Comprehensive high school reading methods.* 2d ed. Columbus, OH: Charles Merrill. Presents a discussion of how the Directed Reading-Thinking Activities might be used in the content areas.

Stauffer, R. G. 1960. Productive reading-thinking at the first grade level. *The Reading Teacher* 13:183–187. Presents a brief description of the use of reading-thinking strategies with first graders.

————. 1969. *Directing reading maturity as a cognitive process.* New York: Harper & Row. Intended for the graduate or advanced student, this text presents a detailed description of the procedure and its rationale.

————. 1970. *The language-experience approach to the teaching of reading.* New York: Harper & Row, 132–176. A readable description of the strategy and its use.

————. 1976. *Teaching reading as a thinking process.* New York: Harper & Row. Intended for the less advanced student, this text presents the procedure in detail, but with less theory.

Stauffer, R. G., and M. M. Harrel. 1975. Individualized reading-thinking activities. *The Reading Teacher* 28:765–769. Describes a program for individualizing Directed Reading-Thinking Activities.

Stieglitz, E. L., and W. J. Oehlkers. 1989. Improving teacher discourse in a reading lesson. *The Reading Teacher* 42:374–379. A research study depicting the effects of teacher in-service on behaviors and DR-TA procedures.

Valeri-Gold, M. 1987. Previewing: A directed reading-thinking activity. *Reading Horizons* 27:123–126. Provides sample questions for teachers to ask when engaged in a DR-TA lesson.

Widomski, C. L. 1983. Building foundations for reading comprehension. *Reading World.* 22:306–313. Provides an overview of the effectiveness of combining two techniques, DR-TA with semantic webbing, to increase reading comprehension.

Instructional Framework

Purpose

The purpose of the Instructional Framework (Herber 1970, 1978) is to: (1) provide content area teachers with a structure for presenting a content lesson; and (2) teach not only the content (product) of the unit but also the skills (process) necessary to understand the content.

Rationale

Most content reading materials are written at a relatively high level of sophistication. The introduction of new concepts can be confounded by technical vocabulary and complex explanations.

It would seem that students need a structure that helps them cope with the process of learning so that they can meet the product expectancies of learning. Herber's Instructional Framework is designed to provide just that structure. Specifically, the Instructional Framework provides a structure for lessons that is intended to guide students' reading processes and products. The eventual aim is to enable students to apply these structures independently in their own reading.

Intended Audience

The technique may be used at all levels with students whose learning requires them to understand content reading material. The study guide component allows for individual instruction or for instruction with the entire class.

Description of the Procedures

Before the classroom teacher can implement the Instructional Framework, decisions are necessary regarding: (1) the major concepts to be emphasized within a given selection; (2) each concept's relative importance to the unit and to the subject as a whole; (3) the major technical vocabulary terms that appear to be important in understanding and communicating the major concepts; and (4) the specific skills the students need in order to learn the concepts. After the teacher has made these decisions (Herber, 1970, 1978), the content instructor is ready to prepare the content lesson.

The basic structure of the Instructional Framework has three major components: (1) preparation, (2) guidance, and (3) independence. A sample lesson plan for an Instructional Framework follows the description of these three components.

1. *Preparation*   Before students are assigned to read the new chapter, the teacher should "prepare" them for the assignment. The amount of time spent on the preparation stage of the lesson depends upon the students' reading and study skills and their background experiences with the topic. The order may vary from one unit to the next, but the specific stages of the preparation phase are:

   a. Motivation. Although sometimes difficult to attain, the goal should be to complete the preparation stage of the lesson with each student's wanting to learn more about the topic. This can be accomplished by involving the students as much as possible in the learning act itself. Field trips, films, filmstrips, records, tapes, study prints, and demonstrations are just a few of the motivational techniques the classroom teacher might use. The remaining steps within the preparation phase of the Instructional Framework are designed to provide the students with further motivation.

   b. Background information and review. Authors of content material assume that students have a certain amount of knowledge related to the particular content unit. If this background information is not present, it is the responsibility of the content teacher to "fill the gaps." Otherwise, a review of information already known by the students also is suggested. This segment of the strategy provides the important "mind set" for learning the new information.

   c. Anticipation and purpose. At the conclusion of the preparation stage, students should anticipate certain new understandings to be gained. Establishing purposes in two very specific areas—the product (ideas to be discovered) and the process (skills to be applied in order to gain that information)—can heighten students' anticipation.

   d. Direction. After students understand what skills are necessary to learn the new information, the instructor gives the students specific assistance in ways to use these identified skills. If the students are already accomplished in the specific skill, a brief review may be all that is necessary; however, if the teacher is aware of student skill deficiencies, this would be the time when skills teaching takes place. For example, suppose that the author of the unit under consideration has consistently used the organizational pattern of cause-effect. An understanding of cause-effect patterns might then be appropriate for students, as it will aid their text understanding.

e. Vocabulary development. A major hurdle for students in content material is the technical language of the particular subject under study. To assist the student in the acquisition of the important concepts, the major vocabulary in any given unit is pretaught. A variety of strategies for preteaching vocabulary can be found in Unit 8 of this text.

2. *Guidance*   As a logical follow-up to this purpose setting and direction, the teacher then provides guidance in two important areas—the development of skills (the process) and the development of concepts (the product). This structured form of support is determined by the nature of the material and the abilities of the students. The two components of the guidance phase of the Instructional Framework are:

a. Development of skills. Here, Herber (1970) suggests the use of reading guides, a special type of study guide "designed to show students how to apply skills as they read" (P. 36). A detailed explanation of the development and use of reading guides, including numerous examples, is available in Herber's *Teaching Reading in Content Areas* (1978).

Using the example mentioned above, during the direction portion of the preparation stage, the instructor teaches the students how to recognize and glean information from the organizational pattern of cause-effect. A reading guide could then be used to develop that new skill further while, at the same time, the teacher guides the student to the important information within the unit. For example, the teacher might list in a study guide some possible causes and require the students to supply the effects they gleaned from the selection.

b. Development of concepts. Another type of study guide, designed to improve students' understanding of the major concepts of the unit, is the reasoning guide (Herber, 1970). The reasoning guide involves the development and use of a study guide for postreading extensions. This form of guidance allows the content instructor to lead the student to the major concepts within the selection and to extend the student's understanding both critically and creatively.

3. *Independence*   Finally, the teacher must provide opportunities for students in the (1) application of skills and (2) application of concepts. In both instances, it is important that students have occasions to use these newly acquired skills and concepts in other settings. As Herber (1978) suggests, this approach may entail coaching by the teacher. For example, indirect questioning by the teacher may implicitly alert the student to the use of the framework in the student's own reading, which may entail recalling prior uses of the framework and a discussion of its possible use with other material.

Sample Lesson Plan For an Instructional Framework*

Example of Instructional Framework

I. PREPARATION
    A. Motivation
        1. Could discuss possible results of "suburban sprawl." What happens each time a new subdivision is built in our community?
        2. Refer to picture on page 232 of a portion of a marketplace in Guadalajara, Mexico. "What do you see?" What basic need of man could be filled by the items pictured?" (Kimble, Teachers Edition, 233)
    B. Background Information and Review
        1. If available, show film "Foods around the World." (Coronet Instructional Films, 11 min., color)
        2. Following specific discussion of film, ask, "What is needed in order to use land for growing crops or raising animals?" (Kimble, T. E., 233) List these points on board. List might include: sunlight, soil, water, proper temperature, seed, methods of planting, methods for insuring proper growth, methods for harvesting, food for animals, shelter for animals.
        3. "Can we raise crops or animals in an area that does not have all these things? If so, what is needed to do so?" (Kimble, T. E., 233)
        4. "Can you see how we can relate what we learned in the last chapter on the haves and the have-nots to this chapter on food?"
    C. Anticipation and Purpose
        1. As a result of the above discussion, students should have some notion of the type of information we will be learning in this chapter.
        2. Set purposes in terms of
            a. Content. Example: "In our study of this chapter, we will want to note
                (1) How increased population affects the available land and the actual food supply
                (2) Ways in which dependence on other nations is good and bad
                (3) How improved technology might overcome some of our problems."
            b. Process. Example: "You will learn much of this information if you can
                (1) Accurately interpret the wealth of information displayed on the six maps in this short chapter
                (2) Recognize the two writing patterns that the author uses throughout this chapter—cause-effect and comparison-contrast."
    D. Direction
        If students do not possess sufficient map-reading skills or if they have not been taught the two organizational patterns mentioned above, provide appropriate instruction for one or both of these skills. This teaching can be done by using the material within this chapter or by using supplemental material. If students already possess these skills, such instruction will not be necessary.
    E. Language Development
        This particular chapter is divided into three segments by the text author. The following terms may be pretaught as an introduction to each lesson:
        Lesson 1. Arable land, cultivation, tillage, polder
        Lesson 2. Strains, steppes, plant breeder, animal breeding, mixed farming
        Lesson 3. Custom, tradition, agricultural specialists.

---

*Developed for "Trailblazers in the Search for Food," in G. H. T. Kimble, 1972, *Man and His World.* Morristown, NJ: Silver Burdett, Chap. 12, 232–251.

II. GUIDANCE

Guide(s) may be developed to provide students with an opportunity to use the newly acquired skill(s) taught in the Direction phase mentioned above and, at the same time, to learn the important chapter content.

The guide below could be used with the first portion of this chapter.

Cause-Effect Relationships

Cause	*Effect*
1. "In England and Wales, . . . more than 100,000 acres of land are needed yearly for new homes, factories, airfields, highways, parking lots, and playing fields. Nearly all of this land is first-rate farming land." (Kimble, 233)	1.

The following actions resulted in specific changes to land previously thought of as nonproductive (Kimble, 235):

2. In the Netherlands, they turned the Zuider Zee into land called *polders*.	2.
3. The Egyptians built the High Dam across the Nile at Aswan.	3.
4. The Soviet Union built dams and irrigation canals.	4.

III. INDEPENDENCE

The teacher should provide opportunities in which students might use their newly learned skills and concepts in new settings. Here are some of the possibilities with this chapter:

1. Establish research groups to explore more specifically the Netherlands *polder* plan, the Aswan Dam, and other land-reclamation projects.
2. Invite a local agricultural specialist to class ". . . to discuss new strains of plants or animals that are being developed in your own area." (Kimble, T. E., 242)
3. "Divide the class into groups and assign each one a vegetable—rutabaga, broccoli, brussels sprouts, etc. Each group is to plan a campaign that will 'sell' the vegetable to the rest of the class." (Kimble, T. E., 250)

Cautions and Comments

The Instructional Framework provides teachers with a structure for presenting a content lesson; it provides students with a procedure for acquiring understandings from content reading. But the strategy is teacher-dominated rather than student-centered. Because it is labor-intensive for the teacher and teacher-centered, it might be more difficult to adapt this strategy to a heterogeneous classroom—with children of differing abilities and with children who have differing perspectives in their approach to material. Indeed, the constant use of the lesson plan format along with study guides and graphic organizers may impose on rather than develop students' own reading-learning abilities and strategies. Toward the goals of increasing student independence, and responding to individuals in the classroom, the teacher needs to vary the Instructional Framework with the differential needs of students across texts.

Arguably, the Instructional Framework has some other major shortcomings. Whereas current approaches to subject matter learning emphasize "hands-on" experience, the use of primary sources, the Instructional Framework is oriented toward the use of secondary sources or textbook companies for the secondhand treatment of topics. Likewise, the framework encourages an approach to subject matter learning that is comprehensive and general rather than delving, focused, or caselike. Instead of students delving into issues and subtopics, they are encouraged to develop a surveylike understanding. Many fear that the opportunity to delve may precede a survey understanding, but not vice versa. Finally, the issue of multiculturalism and achieving different perspectives is slighted in this work. For a detailed discussion of some of these notions as they are applied in the area of social studies, the reader is referred to the Bradley Report.

The constant use of this lesson plan format along with the teacher-developed study guides may result in less-than-exciting lessons. The creative teacher should seek ways to vary the strategy in order to ensure total student involvement and eventual student independence. Some teachers might be inclined to create their hypercard stacks or enlist other materials (e.g., see Tierney, Stowell, Desai, and Keiffer, 1993). The use of informational sources on computers, such as CD–ROM disks, might help to make the Instructional Framework more interesting to students, because students find the computer to be intrinsically interesting. Further, the multimedia capabilities of CD–ROM allow information to be presented in a very lively fashion; students can pursue the exploration of topics with the aid of sound, image (both still and video), and text. They can also do so selectively or in accordance with their own interests. In addition, many of the CD–ROM versions afford students immediate access or the opportunity to crisscross from English to Spanish, and so forth.

An individual content teacher may find it extremely difficult and time-consuming to develop a program centered around the concept of the Instructional Framework. For that reason, teacher teams might be formed to develop such a program. Personnel involved in pre- and in-service training sessions could set aside sufficient amounts of time so that teachers could take part in meaningful activities designed to "pay off" in the classroom. Finally, an increasingly large number of school districts are reassigning their more experienced reading teachers to positions as resource teachers. One of the major functions of these individuals could well be to assist the content teachers in the development and use of the Instructional Framework.

For an extended discussion of this strategy, the reader is directed to the description of study guides found in Unit 9 of this text.

References

Bradley Commission on History in the Schools. 1988. *Building a history curriculum: Guidelines for teaching history in the schools.* Washington, DC: Educational Excellence Network. This report examines the teaching of history across the grades and the curriculum and includes major recommendations for shifting the nature of teaching and learning. References are made to notions such as multiple perspective taking, the use of primary sources, and focused study of topics vs. surveylike examinations.

Herber, H. L. 1970. *Teaching reading in content areas.* Englewood Cliffs, NJ: Prentice-Hall. The original source of information on the Instructional Framework.

———. 1978. *Teaching reading in content areas.* 2d ed. Englewood Cliffs, NJ: Prentice-Hall. The primary and updated source of information on the Instructional Framework.

————. (1993). *Teaching in content areas with reading, writing, and reasoning.* Needham Heights, MA: Allyn & Bacon. Chapter 5 provides an updated discussion of the Instructional Framework.

Tierney, R. J., L. Stowell, L. Desai, and R. Keiffer. 1993. New possibilities for literature teaching and technology. In *Exploring texts: The role of discussion and writing in the teaching and learning of literature,* edited by G. E. Newell, and R. K. Durst. Discusses a multimedia approach to a social studies-type unit.

Purves, A. C., L. Papa, and S. Jordan, eds. 1994. *Encyclopedia of English studies and language arts.* New York: National Council of Teachers of English. This encyclopedia has more than 800 annotated entries/topics that succinctly address this topic and related areas.

Vacca, R. T., and J. L. Vacca. 1993. *Content area reading.* 4th ed. New York: HarperCollins. Discusses Herber's Instructional Framework using the components of prereading, reader-text interactions, and postreading.

Discussion and Cooperative Learning

UNIT OVERVIEW

It should come as no surprise that a number of educators argue for reading instruction that allows students the opportunity to interact with one another about what they read. They lament what appears to be the status quo—namely, teacher control of the floor, limited extended interchanges between students and teachers or among the students themselves, and students' view that the end goal is achieving a single correct response to a text.

In the late eighties, discussion and cooperative learning received an increased amount of attention as educators became interested in the aforementioned issues and adopted a view of reading that was tied to social considerations. The present unit includes a description of a few representative strategies. However, it should be noted that other units include procedures that could be considered cooperative and could involve discussion. The unit on Response to Literature and Drama, as well as the unit on Responding to Reading as Writers and Writing to Enhance Comprehension, includes several strategies incorporating the use of peer interaction and discussion.

The present unit includes five discussion and cooperative learning techniques.

Great Books' Shared Inquiry.   Shared Inquiry is the discussion procedure suggested by the Great Books Foundation. The discussion procedure features interpretative reading and group discussion of selected works using a rather structured approach to ensure that responses are text-based and that respondents are fully involved.

Conversational Discussion Groups.   Conversational Discussion Groups involves creating an environment using a selected stimulus and ground rules for discussion that mimic an "outdoor cafe" conversation in hopes of motivating and enhancing student involvement and comprehension.

ECOLA (Extending Concepts Through Language Activities).   ECOLA represents an attempt to provide teachers with guidelines for having students generate a written response to what they read and pursue peer input en route to developing an appreciation of different possible interpretations, and considering possibilities for revising their responses.

Discussion Web.   The Discussion Web employs a think-pair-share discussion cycle and a graphic aid to give students an opportunity to share their own thoughts as they interact with others in paired, small-group, and whole-group settings.

Jigsaw.   Jigsaw is considered a cooperative learning technique directed at having students develop expertise in certain topic areas and then using this expertise to inform group members.

Great Books' Shared Inquiry

Purpose

Shared Inquiry is the discussion procedure suggested by the Great Books Foundation. The Great Books Foundation claims that the procedure achieves a number of goals, including flexibility, critical analysis skills, reading comprehension, a deeper understanding of self and others, as well as the motivation and desire to be lifelong learners.

Rationale

Founded in 1947, the Great Books Foundation (GBF) aims to foster the education of children and adults through reading and group discussion of books carefully selected for their richness, complexity, literary merit, meaningfulness, appeal, and length. The book selection includes a set of paperbound Great Books, Junior Great Books, as well as reader aids and a handbook on reading and discussion.

   The discussion procedure features interpretative reading and group discussion based upon what might be considered a rather text-based view of literary interpretation. As the Foundation has stated:

> Reading serious literature is a collaboration—a meeting of minds—between author and reader. The author provides the complete work, but doesn't tell the reader what to think about it: the reader must strive to understand, to interpret, what the author is saying. It is this interpretative process that is the focus of shared inquiry. (Great Books Foundation 1987, v)

   The Great Books Foundation suggests that questions addressing "specific problems about the meaning of a work" are at the heart of Shared Inquiry. At the start of the discussion, the group leader poses an interpretative issue derived from his/her own reading of the work and for which he/she has not yet developed a satisfactory answer. The group leader probes the responses of participants with follow-up questions to guide their scrutiny of the text, to tie together ideas from the group, and eventually to derive a resolution. The leader may challenge and probe but must not provide answers. Although the goal is helping readers understand the work, a number of secondary purposes are supposedly achieved. As has been stated:

By trying out ideas and exchanging and examining opinions, they (participants) build their own answers to the interpretive question under discussion, and they develop their own ways of understanding the work . . . participants gain experience in communicating complex ideas, and in supporting, testing, and expanding their own thoughts . . . participants develop the habit of reflective thinking . . . participants learn to give full consideration to the ideas of others, to weigh the merits of opposing arguments, and to modify their initial opinions if the evidence demands it. (Great Books Foundation 1987, v–vi)

A key assumption underlying their approach to integrating a work is tied to an assumption verging upon the belief that comprehension proceeds from literal to interpretive to evaluative and that the reader's task is to unravel the author's meaning. As the GBF states:

Comprehension and appreciation of the facts of a work lay the foundation for the next level of reading: interpretation.
To interpret a story or essay is to construct explanations of what the author wants us to think about. (1987, 2)

The Great Books Foundation recognizes that both leaders and participants may need time and practice to achieve much in the way of success with Shared Inquiry. It also should be noted that the Great Books Foundation requires group leaders to make a commitment to the Great Books program by using their materials and being trained to lead discussion groups.

Intended Audience

Shared Inquiry is designed for students from the second through the twelfth grade. With adaptation, it could be used with younger students.

Description of the Procedures

The following description of Shared Inquiry includes:

1. Guidelines for leaders preparing for discussion
2. Guidelines for leading a discussion
3. Other features

1. Guidelines for Leaders Preparing for Discussion   The Great Books Foundation suggests that group leaders follow a number of steps prior to initiating Shared Inquiry. They include:

1. Reading the selection twice and taking notes addressing insights, questions, interesting issues, and important points.
2. Identifying genuine issues of meaning: issues that are puzzling and that lend themselves to alternative interpretations, and from these issues, writing just as many interpretative questions. Suggestions are offered regarding possible sources for

interpretive questions. They include: character motives, striking or unusual use of language, prominent details, words, phrases, or sentences that can be understood in more than one way or connections between parts of the text.

3. Sorting questions by issue and for each issue trying to identify the basic questions and cluster of questions.

4. If possible, prediscussing the issue with a colleague to ensure that your questions are clear, interesting, and truly interpretive.

5. Selecting one of your clusters to discuss first, reserving others for use after your initial interpretive issue is addressed.

2. *Guidelines for Leading a Discussion*

a. *Rules governing discussion.* There are four rules that govern Shared Inquiry. They are:

- Only those who have read the selection may take part in discussion.
- Discussion is restricted to the selection that everyone has read.
- All opinions should be supportable with evidence from the selection.
- Leaders may only ask questions—they may not answer them.

b. *Opening the discussion.* Participants are expected to prepare as the group leader did. That is, they are expected to read the selection twice and take notes. In the case of initiating Shared Inquiry for the first time, Great Books Foundation suggests that the group leader might emphasize the following:

- Selections have been chosen for their literary merit.
- Shared Inquiry involves participants learning from one another.
- Discussion will focus on a question that seems key to understanding the story.
- Four rules (previously mentioned) apply for various reasons (which the leader should explain).

In introducing notetaking, the Foundation suggests that the leader should: (1) encourage the participants to mark anything that interests them or puzzles them, or anything they want to remember for discussion; (2) share their own notes and/or have participants show their notes.

For the discussion to begin the teacher poses a question (e.g., Why does Jack climb the beanstalk the third time?). The participants write down the question and record their initial answers. Then, after every question is read, the teacher asks one of the participants, by name, to give his or her response. The teacher uses a seat chart to keep track of the participants' ideas, and to note contributors' names and what they said.

c. *Conducting discussion.* The Great Books Foundation offers several guidelines for leading discussions. They include:

- Lead slowly so that answers can be clarified and explored.
- Listen carefully to participants' ideas, looking for subtle differences or ways to relate comments.

- Use seating charts (see Figure 6–1) to keep track of ideas, who said what, and as a way to follow-up on discussion. (Also, charts might be shared with participants.)
- Encourage participants to talk with one another, asking each other questions, and answering each other directly.
- Strive for clarification of ideas.
- Help participants relate ideas to each other and to the basic questions.
- Have participants turn to the text frequently to support and check ideas.
- Encourage participants to challenge any assumptions in the leader's questions.
- Make sure everyone has an opportunity to contribute.
- Ask follow-up questions often (to clarify comments, to substantiate opinions, to solicit additional opinions, to develop an idea by pursuing its implications, to test whether an idea is consistent with the facts, to select a line of inquiry).

d. *Reaching a resolution.* Once the leader considers that the interpretative issue has been thoroughly discussed and that further discussion is not likely to be productive (e.g., ideas are being repeated, digressions are occurring), the leader is expected to: (1) repeat the basic question; (2) give the opportunity for input to anyone who did

FIGURE 6–1. EXAMPLE OF A SEATING CHART

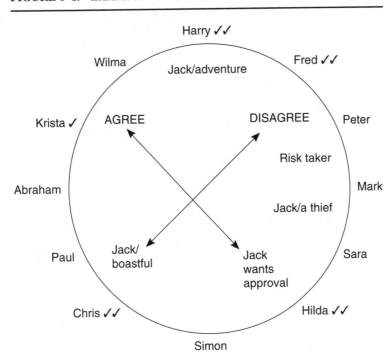

not have an answer addressed; and (3) compose a final answer taking into account the ideas offered by the group. After participants have had a chance to formulate their response, the leader asks if anyone arrived at a response that differs substantially from his/her previous response and has those students share how their ideas were influenced.

e. *Post-discussion activities/new line of inquiry.* Following the resolution phase, a line of inquiry might be launched with a different basic question. Or postdiscussion activities such as writing projects can also be suggested.

3. Other Features   The Great Books Foundation offers guidelines for helping leaders deal with difficulties that might emerge (e.g., digressions, inattentiveness, failure to respond to the question, nervousness, vocabulary), and proposes a text analysis procedure for looking at a passage in a story or essay closely en route to achieving a foothold. "In textual analysis, a group discusses a single passage line by line and sometimes word by word, raising questions about its meaning." (Great Books Foundation 1987, 48)

Cautions and Comments

Shared Inquiry has been well received. In 1987, the Great Books Foundation claimed to be training over 18,000 leaders every year.

As a procedure for guiding discussion, Shared Inquiry offers discussion leaders a systematic approach for preparing for discussion, mobilizing student interactions, and reading resolutions. At the same time, the procedure includes carefully developed guidelines by which group leaders might monitor the success of discussions and initial strategies to improve them. In this regard, some of the guidelines are worth reviewing for purposes of any type of discussion—that is, whether a Shared Inquiry approach is adopted or Great Books are used.

Some assumptions upon which the Shared Inquiry is based may be questionable. First, the mandate to use a selected list of books may appear to be somewhat suggestive of having a canon. Second, the approach places a great deal of emphasis on the text and appears to discount a reader's background of experience and any connections that a reader might make from that to other works. This seems rather problematic, given what we know about how the reader's active involvement, including intertextual ties, is crucial to comprehension. Third, there is the stated assumption that reading proceeds from literal to interpretive to evaluative. Current views of reading comprehension suggest a more dynamic view in which comprehension is never purely literal and is apt to proceed from the evaluative to interpretive to literal as in reverse. Fourth, the approach is teacher-directed in that basic questions stem from the teacher rather than the child. While the approach sponsors participant input and interrogation of one another, it seems that a worthwhile next step would be to have participants develop their own basic questions and clusters.

The claims offered by the Great Books Foundation pertaining to the benefit accrued from such an approach warrant careful study. Although several studies report that the approach has a generally positive impact, the precise claims suggested in their handbook have not been studied.

References

Davis, J. A. 1961. *Great books and small groups.* New York: Gephard Press. Describes the use of the Great Books discussion procedures.

Feiertag, J., and L. Chernoff. 1987. Inferential thinking and self-esteem: Through the junior great books program. *Childhood Education* 63(4):252–254. Explores the development of thinking abilities and self-esteem with the use of the Great Books program, including discussion procedure.

Fitzpatrick, E. A. 1952. *Great books: Panacea or what?* Milwaukee: Bruce Publishing Co. Discusses some of the strengths and weaknesses of the Great Books program.

Great Books Foundation. 1987. *An introduction to shared inquiry.* Chicago: Great Books Foundation. The primary source for information on how to plan and implement Shared Inquiry.

Conversational Discussion Groups

Purpose

The purpose of Conversational Discussion Groups is to create an environment for the discussion of reading selections that facilitates sharing and a balance between peer interaction and expert guidance—and enhances exploration, transmission, and construction of meanings.

Rationale

Conversational Discussion Groups was developed by O'Flahavan (O'Flahavan and Huxtable, 1987; O'Flahavan, 1989) in response to the question "What if classroom discussions were more like conversations, more like the sorts of discussion people have over coffee, after seeing a movie—a common text—together?" As O'Flahavan stated:

> The goal as we conceived it was fashioned after an "outdoor cafe" metaphor, where a group of people come together after seeing a movie and discuss what it meant to them. The group process . . . was relinquished to the students, as was the on-line negotiation of meaning during discussion.

O'Flahavan (1989) sees the procedure as a first step toward openness and student participation in classroom situations where the teacher's control of the floor and lines of thinking predominate. While the approach spells out a specific procedure, it is intended to be more of an abstract way of thinking rather than formulaic. Instructionally, the approach aspires to build upon the Vygotskian notion of the role of social learning, principles drawn from studies examining parent-child interactions, and metacognitive notions associated with attempts to prime student independence. Accordingly, O'Flahavan claims the approach has the following characteristics: immersion in meaningful problem; equal access to monitoring, and regulation of relevant group processes for all participants; group as scaffold for the individual; and reflection about group and individual process.

Intended Audience

The strategy can be used with students at any level.

Description of the Procedures

There are three stages to Conversational Discussion Groups:

1. Introduce/review rules
2. Lines of thought
3. Debriefing

O'Flahavan (1989) suggests that, prior to initiating how a Conversational Discussion Group might be orchestrated for use in a classroom, consideration should be given to the students' ability to participate in groups. To this end, he suggests that a teacher might try out a story discussion. Specifically, he suggests the following:

- Establish a heterogeneous group (six to eight students) who can work together.
- Direct the students to read a thought-provoking story.
- Construct a thematic question (e.g., with *Stone Soup,* "Is it okay to use tricks to get what you want?") that is presented to the students. Begin the discussion, but leave for a few minutes and observe from a distance how the group participates. Note group processes and how the students use the text to support their ideas. Return and finish the discussion.

Based on such tryouts, O'Flahavan proposes that the teacher can develop the group process rules and problem-solving heuristics to help the students develop their interpretations as they are involved in the Conversational Discussion Groups. With this as a basis, the teacher moves to introduce students to the rules for the subsequent discussion.

1. Introduce/Review Rules   The teacher introduces/reviews the rules and strategies with the group and discusses with the group others that might be added or might substitute for those on the list. Examples of rules for the discussion and heuristic strategies for negotiating are presented in Table 6–1.

O'Flahavan suggests that the rules should be visible to the group members as reminders of strategies they might use. With this in mind, he suggests that they be placed on large cards and attached to a wall, and so on, so that group members can evoke them from time to time.

2. Lines of Thought   After reading the story selection, the teacher presents to the group the first of three questions. Each question is presented on a sheet of paper large enough for all members of the group to review. The teacher does not return to the group until asked to do so by the group or when they perceive an opportune moment. O'Flahavan

TABLE 6–1.   EXAMPLES OF DISCUSSION RULES AND HEURISTIC STRATEGIES FOR NEGOTIATING MEANINGS

Discussion Rules

One at a time
If you say yes/no, state why
Stay on the subject
Ask each other questions when someone is quiet
Don't hog the floor
Let other people talk
When you are ready, ask me (the teacher) to return

Heuristic Strategies

Back up your ideas with the story
Back up your ideas with your own experience

(1989) proposes that teachers adhere to the following code of conduct as the students discuss:

I begin the discussion with one of my predetermined questions, and do not ask another until the students let me know it is time;

I monitor their discussions from afar;

I look for possible opportunities for intervention, and make plans to address them later;

I am a resource to the students when they need me;

I speak only when spoken to.

Upon returning to the group, the teacher has the freedom to initiate, instruct, monitor, give feedback or praise, and the like. For instance, when the teacher returns (usually upon the request of the group), the group's response or responses are presented, and, at this point, the teacher might model a key strategy, comment, provide feedback, challenge, and so on, prior to presenting the next question.

The three question types that O'Flahavan suggests might be left with the group are:

a. *Background knowledge question.* The intent of this question is to have the students discuss how their experiences relate to the selection. For example, the first question in a line of thought for the story "The Hare and the Tortoise" might be "How do you feel about someone who is always bragging?"

b. *Transition to the text question.* The intent of this question is to have the students consider the ideas gleaned from the text. For example, the second question in a line of thought for the story "The Hare and the Tortoise" might be "Did the hare's bragging affect the tortoise and did the tortoise's attitude affect the hare?"

c. *Beyond the text question.* The intent of the third question is to have the students pull together an interpretation based on the text and their personal reactions. A question that might serve this purpose is "What can we learn from this story?"

3. Debriefing   A debriefing serves the purpose of having students reflect on what they have achieved and learned, which might help them next time. To this end, O'Flahavan (1989) suggests that the teacher should return to the group and have them discuss three questions:

- How did we go about getting our answers today?
- How did we do?
- What can we do to improve next time?

Another device for helping students reflect on their contribution is the use of pieces of a pie as a means of getting students to talk about their contribution to the discussion. For example, O'Flahavan suggests presenting students with a model of a pie with different-colored wedges representing different shares of the whole pie. As he stated: "If discussion were like a pie and each person could carve out a slice for him/herself, how big would the shares of pie be?"

Cautions and Comments

O'Flahavan (1989) has stressed that the Conversational Discussion Group should be viewed as a framework for enabling students to achieve equal participation with teachers as they put forth "theories, conjectures, queries, conclusions, challenges, and rebuttals while talking about texts." Recognizing that different groups of students and teachers may be more or less capable of taking control of elicitation right away, O'Flahavan suggests that the teacher may want to initiate the Conversational Discussions with varying degrees of teacher responsibility. Teachers, O'Flahavan suggests, should begin with the question "What can we do to get better talking about literature?"

To date, a limited amount of research on the procedure has been pursued. In one study, second graders were involved in Conversational Discussion Groups for sixteen weeks (O'Flahavan, 1988). Their responses were compared to students in regular teacher-directed discussions of stories. The data collected consisted of student observations as well as student perceptions of the group, themselves, and measures of reading compre-hension. The procedure tended to have the most effect on the students' perception of the group itself and the worth of the process; the impact on comprehension seemed negligible. What remains unanswered are the following questions: Will involvement in Conversa-tional Discussion Groups enhance student's consideration of different possible interpreta-tions of a selection? Do this and other forms of discussion prompt students to consider more ideas (text-based and reader-based) and connect as well as evaluate these ideas? To what extent do students need some support in developing interpretations that compare each other's responses and build on such analyses? To what extent do teachers need some support in understanding the nature of interpretation and ways to expand the repertoire of their students' skills and strategies?

References

Goldenberg, C. 1992–1993. Instructional conversations: Promoting comprehension through discussion. *The Reading Teacher* 46:316–326. Describes another strategy on which the premise is that discussion should be more like a conversation.

O'Flahavan, J. 1988, December. *Conversational discussion groups: A study of second graders leading their own discussions.* Paper presented at the National Reading Conference, Tucson, Arizona. An examination of the effects of Conversational Discussion Groups on student perceptions and other variables.

————. 1989. *An exploration of the effects of participant structure upon literacy development in reading group discussion.* Doctoral diss., University of Illinois-Champaign. Extended study comparing the effects of Conversational Discussion Groups (teacher-led and student-led) with traditional practice.

O'Flahavan, J., and J. Huxtable. 1987, December. *A case for teacher/researcher collaboration: Commitment to change.* Paper presented at the National Reading Conference, St. Petersberg, FL. Describes the evolution of the strategy along with a discussion of teacher change.

ECOLA (Extending Concepts Through Language Activities)

Purpose

ECOLA (Extending COncepts through Language Activities), which was developed by Smith-Burke (1982), represents an attempt to integrate reading, writing, speaking, and listening for purposes of developing a reader's ability to interpret and monitor his or her own comprehension.

Rationale

As Smith-Burke states, ECOLA is intended to focus "students on the constructive nature of reading and the need to monitor to be sure the interpretation one constructs makes sense" (P. 177). For this purpose, the ECOLA lesson framework places a great deal of importance on the following learning experiences:

1. *Purposeful reading of text.* Goals for reading a text are thoughtfully developed based upon an understanding of the author's intent and any reason the teacher might have for using the text. Eventually these goals are initiated solely by students.
2. *Written responses.* To crystalize a reader's understanding, students are expected to commit themselves to an interpretation in writing, which they may revise, however, after discussion.
3. *Discussion.* Discussion is viewed as a basis for generating ideas, examining purposes, evaluating interpretations, and considering the efficacy of strategies.
4. *Self-monitoring.* Students are encouraged to verbalize their confusions, commit themselves to an interpretation, and discuss their strategies for understanding text.

Intended Audience

The ECOLA strategy is intended for use with students in upper elementary school through high school. It seems appropriate to use with a variety of texts.

Description of the Procedures

Five steps constitute the procedure. The steps are: (1) setting a communicative purpose for reading; (2) silent reading for a purpose and criterion task; (3) crystalizing an interpretation through writing; (4) discussing and clarifying interpretations; and (5) writing and comparing.

Step 1: *Setting a communicative purpose.* To set a purpose that is communicative requires first a determination of the purposes for which the text might be read. This requires a teacher to determine what he or she would like the students to glean from the text, based upon a consideration of the author's purpose.

Once a determination has been made of the purposes for which the text might be read, two further decisions need to be made. A teacher must decide what type of support the students need; for example, a teacher should examine the text and determine what type of additional preparation for reading a selection (e.g., discussion of key ideas) might be needed. Also, a teacher should determine the actual task to which students are expected to respond. For example, several questions for reading a selection might be subsumed under a general purpose for the assignment.

Step 2: Silent reading for a purpose and a criterion task. Students are reminded of their purpose(s) for reading and made aware that they should be able to support their interpretations with ideas from the text, their background knowledge, or reasoning. Smith-Burke suggests that it is reasonable for different students to read with different goals in mind.

Step 3: Crystalizing comprehension through writing. The purpose of this step is to develop in students the ability to self-monitor and to begin to learn how to verbalize what they don't understand. During this step, each student and the teacher write a response to the overall question or purpose for reading. In writing a response, students are assured that answers will be kept confidential. They are encouraged both to commit themselves to an interpretation and to write about anything that they find confusing. To clarify these problems, they are urged to ask other students. It is then the responsibility of others to explain how they dealt with the same problems.

Step 4: *Discussing the lesson.* Students are organized into groups no larger than four in size and given a time limit in which they are expected to discuss interpretations, compare responses, and challenge conclusions. Each student is expected to share and explain the basis for his or her conclusion.

Step 5: Writing and comparing. The final step is to have students, in small groups or individually, generate a second interpretation. If done as a group, then a consensus must be reached by discussion and resolution. After the revised interpretation has been completed, the students are encouraged to discuss the changes that were made and to talk about the strategies they found helpful in understanding the text.

An example of the ECOLA strategy, applied to a familiar fable, is given in Figure 6–2.

Cautions and Comments

Smith-Burke (1982) has offered some guidelines for the use of ECOLA. Since ECOLA is a very intensive process, she has suggested that the approach not be used constantly. Instead, certain steps might be omitted and other approaches occasionally substituted. Also, she has emphasized that the teacher is responsible for leading discussion, giving the

FIGURE 6–2. EXAMPLE OF ECOLA APPLIED TO A FAMILIAR FABLE

Story: The Hare and the Tortoise (from *Aesop's Fables*)

The familiar fable describes a foot race between a hare and a tortoise. The hare, thinking he could win the race easily because of his speed, lies down to rest and soon falls to sleep. While the hare is sleeping, the tortoise crosses the finish line and the hare wakes to find he has lost.

1. Setting a communicative purpose

The teacher briefly summarizes the fable and then sets a clear purpose for reading through a discussion with the class.

> Why were fables written?
> Were fable authors trying to communicate a message?
> Has anyone read a fable? Was there a message in that fable for the reader's own life?
> How did you feel about the character(s) in the fable?
> What could a reader (or hearer) of a fable gain from a story of animals?

2. Silent reading for a purpose and a criterial task

> What is the message of this fable?
> Will everyone agree or could there be many messages?
> Why might someone see (hear?) a different message?

3. Crystalizing comprehension through writing

Students write about the fable particularly in relation to the purpose stated in Step 2 (above).

4. Discussing the lesson

As students share their ideas and interpretations, their reactions to the fable may change.

5. Writing and comparing

The teacher reviews purposes for reading and writing.

> Was your second interpretation different from your first?
> What led you to reconsider?
> How did you decide what to change and what not to change?
> Do you think there can ever be one definitive interpretation of a fable or story?

students feedback, and modeling; students are responsible for deciding how to read and for monitoring what they read.

Although Smith-Burke's guidelines are not elaborated and the approach lacks substantiation, the procedure represents a welcome addition to the field. It is among very few strategies that respond to the alarming finding from the National Assessment of Educational Progress that readers have difficulty formulating a written response to text. The procedure distinguishes itself further in terms of meeting obvious needs in its pursuit of argumentation over piecemeal or partial interpretations and its commitment to the refinement and redevelopment of a reader's interpretation following discussion. What distinguishes the strategy even further is the utilization of a child-centered, rather than teacher-directed, consideration of strategies and their efficacy. Self-monitoring is nurtured rather than demanded.

References

Bartholomae, D., and A. Petrosky. 1985. *Facts, artifacts and counterfacts: A basic reading and writing course for the college curriculum.* New York: Ablex. Presents the reading-writing program developed at the University of Pittsburgh. The approach involves more extensive use of writing prior to reading and responding to texts.

Brown, A. L. 1980. Metacognitive development and reading. In *Theoretical issues in reading comprehension,* edited by R. J. Spiro, B. Bruce, and W. F. Brewer. Hillsdale, NJ: Erlbaum,

pp. 453–481. Presents a thorough discussion of self-monitoring and its role and development.

Smith-Burke, M. T. 1982. Extending concepts through language activities. In *Reader meets author/bridging the gap,* edited by J. Langer and M. Smith-Burke. Newark, DE: International Reading Association, pp. 163–179. Presents a description of the steps involved in ECOLA with examples of teacher-student dialogue.

Discussion Web

Purpose

The purpose of the Discussion Web (Alvermann, 1991) is to provide students with a graphic aid to help them clarify their thinking by eliminating inconsistencies and contradictions in their thought processes. By employing a think-pair-share discussion cycle, students are given an opportunity to use their own voices as they interact with others in paired, small-group, and large-group situations.

Rationale

Discussion can play a valuable part in helping students interpret their reading selections, particularly when multiple points of view are examined (Alvermann, Dillon, and O'Brien, 1987). In such selections, students are able to enrich their understanding of what they read as they are given the opportunity to view their own interpretation of a text in light of how others may interpret the same text. Thus, students may reexamine their own thinking as they develop a tolerance for differing points of view.

Alvermann (1991) rightfully points out, though, that a problem inherent in most discussions is the tendency of the teacher and/or a few students to dominate the flow of classroom talk. When this occurs, other students can become inhibited and are unwilling to share their opinions. Alvermann believes the Discussion Web provides the appropriate vehicle to overcome this problem by giving all students the opportunity to assume their own voices in classroom discussions. Using a think-pair-share discussion paradigm, the Discussion Web first has students *think* individually about the ideas they wish to contribute to the discussion and interact with a partner about these ideas. Next, the partners work with a second pair to try to achieve a consensus by eliminating inconsistencies and clarifying their thinking. Finally, the group of four decides which remaining ideas a spokesperson from the group will share with everyone in the whole-group discussion that follows. In this way students have multiple opportunities to assume their own voices in a variety of cooperative settings.

The Discussion Web evolved from a graphic aid originally developed by Duthie (1986) to help social studies students describe *why* something happens rather than just *what* happens when they are asked to write analytical essays of readings previously assigned. Alvermann says that her version of the Web differs from Duthie's in three ways: (1) the Discussion Web involves all four language processes, not just reading and writing; (2) the Web functions as either a prereading or prewriting strategy, not just a postreading lesson; and, (3) it requires cooperative learning, not just individual work.

Intended Audience

The Discussion Web can be used across the curriculum with a variety of grade levels. Perhaps its most appropriate use, however, is with narrative material where differing points of view can be examined.

Description of the Procedures

Alvermann discussed five steps that typically are used with the Discussion Web:

1. Preparation for reading
2. Introducing the Discussion Web
3. Small-group discussion
4. Whole-class discussion
5. Follow-up activities

1. Preparation for Reading   Similar to the preparation stage of the Directed Reading Activity (Unit 5: General Frameworks), the Discussion Web begins by activating prior knowledge, introducing new vocabulary, and helping set purposes for reading. For instance, if students were about to read "The Necklace" by Guy De Maupassant, they might be introduced to the main character, Mathilde, her dreams about life, and the concept of *pretense.* The students might be helped in setting their own purposes for reading by asking them to generate what they think the story might be about. Some may read to find out more about Mathilde and her life; others might read to find the importance of the necklace.

In this story Mathilde, who dreams of a life of riches and splendor, and her husband, who does not have the income to support such a life, are invited to an important party. Instead of making do with the clothing she owns, Mathilde decides she must have a new dress, regardless of the expense. However, she is still not satisfied with the new dress, since she has no appropriate jewelry. Mathilde's husband suggests she borrow some jewelry from her friend so that she will feel that she has dressed accordingly for the party. Mathilde borrows a diamond necklace and has a delightful time at the party, basking in her own admiration and others' attention. When she returns home, Mathilde discovers that the necklace is missing. Unable to find it, she and her husband decide to replace it. This costs them their entire savings, and they mortgage the rest of their lives. After ten years of unaccustomed hard work, leading the grim life of the poor and losing her youth and beauty, Mathilde and her husband finally pay off their debt for the necklace. It is then, upon a chance meeting with her friend from whom she borrowed the jewelry, that Mathilde discovers the necklace was an imitation and was not worth very much money at all.

2. Introducing the Discussion Web   After students have read the selection and satisfied their own purposes for reading, Alvermann suggests that the Discussion Web be introduced. Continuing with our example using "The Necklace," the Discussion Web could be introduced with questions such as "Did Mathilde deserve the life she was forced to lead?" or simply "Did Mathilde deserve her life?" The students would be provided with a Web that might look like Figure 6–3.

FIGURE 6–3.   DISCUSSION WEB FOR THE NECKLACE

Students are placed in *workable* partnerships and are asked to discuss the pros and cons of Mathilde having to lead the life she did because of the loss of the necklace. Alvermann suggests that the partners work on the same Web but take turns writing down in the Yes and No columns the reasons they believe Mathilde did or did not deserve her life. Students are asked to write down only key words or phrases in the columns and do not have to fill each line of the Discussion Web. However, they are encouraged to have an equal number of reasons in the Yes and No columns; in this way they will be looking at both sides of the issue and, therefore, will be engaged in some form of critical thinking.

3. Small-Group Discussion   After students have had sufficient time to discuss some reasons for their thinking, the teacher then pairs one set of partners with another. This small group of four students is given the task of comparing their reasons for Mathilde's deserving or not deserving her life. Alvermann states that the goal of the group is to work toward a consensus. Students are told that it is acceptable for individual members to disagree with a group conclusion in working toward a consensus as: (1) the discussion process will be more effective if each member of the group keeps an open mind concerning the reasons that others may give, and (2) dissenting views can be heard at the time of the whole-group discussion. Alvermann feels that knowing beforehand that they will have an opportunity to be heard should encourage students to work toward consensus, particularly the older and more mature students.

4. Whole-Class Discussion   Once each small group has reached consensus, a spokesperson is selected (by the teacher or the group members themselves). Each group is then given three minutes to decide which of the reasons discussed best supports the group's conclusion. Alvermann suggests that this reason be written down by the spokesperson at the bottom of the Discussion Web. Since only one reason will be cited by each group, the possibility is reduced that the last groups to report will have nothing new to say. The different spokespersons report for their group as part of the whole-class discussion, also providing any dissenting opinions that may have emerged.

5. Follow-up Activities   Alvermann states that to provide closure on the lesson after the whole-class discussion, have students respond in writing to the same Web question just discussed, in this case "Did Mathilde deserve her life?" Students should include in their response not only their own ideas but also those expressed by other class members. These writings should be posted prominently in the classroom so that they can be shared and give everyone an opportunity to reflect on the contributions of others.

Cautions and Comments

Alvermann (1991) has illustrated, with the teachers' own examples from kindergarten, second- and fourth-grade levels, that the Discussion Web can be used at the elementary level with narrative material. She also discusses how it might be used for social studies, science, or mathematics classes with adaptations. Perhaps therein lies the strength of the Discussion Web—its versatility. It seems the Discussion Web can be adapted and modified to fit particular instructional situations. For instance, with mathematical story problems the Yes/No classification of the Web could be changed to Relevant/Irrelevant to examine critically the relevance of certain information included in story problems toward their solutions. In science experiments the scheme could be changed to Hypothesis 1/Hypothesis 2 to examine probable answers to questions posed. In social studies the stances of famous historical figures on important issues can be looked into. Substituting the word *Slavery* for the question in the Discussion Web and the words *Lincoln* and *Douglas* for *Yes* and *No* would give students an opportunity to examine this critical historical issue. Finally, with basal stories the Web might be used with reading groups rather than whole classes, which results in fewer steps in the lesson and more direct reporting by the students.

Although the Discussion Web does intuitively sound like a useful instructional strategy to aid reading and learning across the curriculum, it must be remembered that the only evidence reported on its effectiveness is anecdotal in nature. Additionally, there are other concerns that should be kept in mind when using a strategy of this type. First, as with any discussion strategy, the type of classroom interaction differs from the typical teacher-to-student-to-teacher pattern found in traditional instructional situations. Therefore, both the teacher and the students will have to deal with management and control issues as they attempt this strategy. Second, teachers will have to be knowledgeable in how their students work with one another. For instance, Alvermann suggests that students be placed in "workable partnerships" (P. 94) when using the Web. Workable groupings, be it a pair or a small group, are sometimes difficult to formulate. Third, students who are reticent to volunteer may still have problems with this even when using a *safe* strategy such as the Web. Finally, though the strategy calls for giving an equal number of reasons in each of the yes and no columns, this is not always the reality of each instructional situation. For example, students might find more reasons to say that Mathilde deserved her life because of her pretentiousness, than to say she did not deserve her life.

References

Alvermann, D. E. 1991. The Discussion Web: A graphic aid for learning across the curriculum. *The Reading Teacher* 45:92–99. Describes the use of the Discussion Web in the classroom.

Alvermann, D. E., D. R. Dillon, and D. G. O'Brien. 1987. *Using discussion to promote reading comprehension*. Newark, DE: International Reading Association. A handbook of various instructional techniques that can be used in the content areas, with accompanying illustrative examples.

Alvermann, D. E., and D. A. Hayes. 1989. Classroom discussion of content area reading assignments: An intervention study. *Reading Research Quarterly* 24:305–335. Describes a 6-month intervention study examining the discussions of assigned readings in high school classrooms.

Duthie, J. 1986. The web: A powerful tool for the teaching and evaluation of the expository essay. *The History and Social Science Teacher* 21:232–236. The article from which the Discussion Web was adapted.

Jigsaw

Purpose

The purpose of Jigsaw (Aronson, Stephan, Sikes, Blaney, and Snapp, 1978; Slavin, 1986) is to help students cooperatively learn new material using a team learning approach. Students are responsible for becoming an "expert" on one part of a lesson and then teaching it to other members of their team.

Rationale

Jigsaw was originally developed as a means to promote positive race relations in public school classrooms (Aronson et al., 1978), but was also found to have beneficial effects on learning. The basic premise behind the strategy is that giving students the opportunity to share what they have learned, to hear what others have to say, and to teach and be taught by their peers is essential in the lifelong process of learning and socialization. Johnson, Maruyama, Johnson, Nelson, and Skon (1981) have found that instruction that was based on cooperation and collaboration resulted in significant gains in achievement, social development, and self-esteem.

As such, Jigsaw embodies the concept of peer tutoring in its efforts to help students read and learn from text. It is designed to increase students' sense of responsibility for their own learning and that of others. Not only must students learn their assigned material but they must also be prepared to share and teach that material to other members of their team. Thus, students are dependent on one another and must cooperatively work together in order to learn the material.

Intended Audience

Jigsaw seems most appropriate for middle and secondary students in subjects such as social studies, literature, and some parts of science, and in other areas where concepts rather than rote learning are the goal of instruction. Radebaugh and Kazemak (1989) also recommend the use of cooperative learning in college and study skills classes.

Description of the Procedures

Slavin (1986) discussed the use of Jigsaw in two parts: teacher preparation and classroom use. Teacher preparation consists of materials development and preparation, and assignment of students to teams. Classroom use consists of introducing the strategy to the class, facilitating the use of teams and expert groups, and giving the quiz.

1. Teacher Preparation   Select a unit of study that you would like to cover in a two-day to three-day period and that can be broken down into four sections. If students are to read the material in class, the sections should not require more than 30 minutes to read; if the material is to be assigned for homework, sections may be longer. For instance, if the unit of study is Andrew Jackson, the material might be broken down into his early life, his war exploits, the Presidency, and his later life.

a. *Expert sheet.* For each section of the material, design an "expert sheet" that tells students what material they are to read, gives them purpose-setting questions, and tells them which expert group they will work with. Thus, students will be provided the pages to be read and what they must gain expertise in and teach to their team members.

b. *Quiz.* Make a two-question quiz for each section of the unit. Quiz questions should be challenging since students will have the time necessary to read and discuss the material. Multiple-choice questions should be used for ease of scoring. There will be ten possible points for the quiz, as students will get double credit for the questions for which they become an expert.

c. *Team assignment.* Students should be assigned to teams to represent a cross-section of the class. In other words, students should be assigned by achievement, sex, and if appropriate, race. In this way, all teams will be heterogeneously balanced, and no team will have an advantage over another. In addition, students will not be able to self-select themselves into teams with their friends.

2. Classroom Use   Plan to introduce Jigsaw and have the students begin reading on Day 1. On Day 2 they can finish reading and work in their expert groups. Finally, on Day 3 students report to their assigned teams and take the quiz. This schedule can be adjusted depending on the difficulty of the material and whether the reading assignment is given for homework.

Day 1. Introduce the idea of Jigsaw in the following manner:

> You are going to work in learning teams to study the unit on _____ . Each of you will have a special topic to learn about. You will read the material and discuss it with members of other teams. Then you will return to your team as an expert to teach your teammates about your topic. Finally, everyone will be quizzed on all topics. You must work with one another so that the whole team can do well on the quiz. Your team's score will be totaled and compared with other teams' scores.

Next, students are grouped into their preselected teams, and the expert sheets are handed out randomly to individual team members. Students are directed to read their sheets so that they know the topic about which they will be learning and what questions they need to answer. Finally, tell students to begin reading their assignments. Teachers will need to decide if students will read only their assigned pages or will read the whole assignment and concentrate on the assigned pages. Even more of a premium is placed on cooperative learning if students each possess a unique set of learnings.

Day 2. Have students finish their reading and introduce the expert groups as follows:

> Now you will have a chance to discuss your topic with others who have the same topic. In these groups you will decide what are the most important ideas about your topic. You will each share your information with one another. Take notes on important ideas. Try to think of what questions will be asked on the quiz. You will then go back to your team to report your findings.

Students should work in their expert groups for approximately 20 minutes.

Day 3. Have students return to their respective teams and report on what they have learned from their expert groups. Main points should be emphasized, and attention should be paid to what they think might be on the quiz. Team reports should take approximately 20 minutes. If deemed necessary, a class discussion may follow the team reports that should focus on input from the "experts." At the conclusion of the reports and discussion, the quiz should be given. Once the quizzes are scored, team members can add their point totals together to get their team score.

Cautions and Comments

A tremendous amount of research has been conducted concerning cooperative learning (see Johnson et al., 1981; Slavin, 1983 for reviews), the basis of Jigsaw. The research consistently indicates that students engaged in such learning achieve more, have better attitudes toward learning, and feel more positive about themselves. In particular, Slavin (1983, 1986) indicated that cooperative learning works best when groups are given a goal that can be attained only through cooperation and are held individually accountable for achieving the group goal.

However, it is still not surprising that Jigsaw and other cooperative learning techniques are used infrequently. The lecture method is still the predominant means of instruction in the classroom, and teachers, by and large, feel uncomfortable using small groups. As such, teachers who feel that chaos will result if small groups are used will probably not use this strategy.

Other concerns about Jigsaw need to be mentioned. Absences can cause problems, since teams rely on their members to learn and score well on quizzes. Sometimes, no matter how well teams are planned, team members may not get along. Indeed, Battistich, Solomon, and Delucchi (1993) found that the quality of the group interaction was directly related to the friendliness of the group members and their desire to work collaboratively. Constant reassignments of team members will cause problems. A predominance of slow learners in one classroom may cause problems with the student balance teachers are trying to achieve across teams. It may be that a slow learner has to be paired with a higher achiever so that individual and team learning can be more effective. Finally, existing materials sometimes do not easily lend themselves to be divided into four sections. Sections of text may not always stand by themselves.

References

Aronson, E., C. Stephan, J. Sikes, N. Blaney, and M. Snapp. 1978. *The jigsaw classroom.* Beverly Hills, CA: Sage. Describes the use of Jigsaw as a means to deal with integration.

Battistich, V., D. Solomon, and K. Delucchi. 1993. Interaction processes and student outcomes in cooperative learning groups. *The Elementary School Journal* 94:19–32. A study that examined cooperative learning in relation to various academic and social outcomes in elementary schools.

Johnson, D. W., G. Maruyama, R. T. Johnson, D. Nelson, and L. Skon. 1981. Effects of cooperative, competitive, and individualistic goal structures on achievement: A meta-analysis. *Psychological Bulletin* 89:47–62. A synthesis of research on cooperative learning attesting to its effectiveness in increasing student achievement and self-esteem.

Mattingly, R. M., and R. L. Vansickle. 1991. Cooperative learning and achievement in social studies: Jigsaw II. *Social Education* 55:392–395. Research showing the effectiveness of a version of Jigsaw with ninth-grade students in geography.

Radebaugh, M. R., and F. E. Kazemak. 1989. Cooperative learning in college reading and study skills classes. *Journal of Reading* 32:414–418. Description of the use of cooperative learning in college developmental reading/study classes.

Slavin, R. E. 1983. *Cooperative learning.* New York: Longman. Another review of research on cooperative learning.

———. 1986. *Using student team learning.* 3rd ed. Baltimore, MD: Johns Hopkins University, Center for Research on Elementary and Middle Schools. Instruction manual for using Jigsaw and other team learning strategies.

Comprehension Development and Thinking Critically

UNIT OVERVIEW

The basic goals of reading are to enable children to gain an understanding of the world and of themselves, to develop appreciations and interests, to find solutions to their personal and group problems, and to develop strategies by which they can become independent comprehenders. Logically, comprehension should be considered the heart of reading instruction, and the major goal of that instruction should be the provision of learning activities that will enable students to think about and react to what they read—in short, to read for meaning.

The present unit describes 11 strategies for the improvement of reading comprehension and critical thinking. Reviews of the research are included in two chapters, Tierney and Cunningham (1984) and Pearson and Fielding (1991). The strategies are designed to help teachers in one or more of the following ways:

1. Activate students' prior knowledge
2. Guide students' reading of a text
3. Foster active and engaged reading
4. Reinforce concepts gleaned from the text reading
5. Encourage careful/critical thinking when reading a text

Many of these strategies may substitute or augment parts of the lesson frameworks described in Unit 5. A brief summary of each strategy follows:

PReP Technique.   The PReP technique provides a teacher with a means to prepare students to read a text selection and, at the same time, analyze their responses so as to tailor subsequent instruction to student needs.

Anticipation Guide.   An Anticipation Guide is designed to activate students' prior knowledge about a topic by having them react to a series of statements related to the major concepts to be encountered in their text reading. Thus, it also provides students a guide for their reading.

Text Preview.   A Text Preview is a teacher-devised introductory passage used before reading a selection. It is designed to build background knowledge by providing a detailed framework for comprehending a complex narrative or expository text.

ReQuest Procedure.   The ReQuest procedure uses a reciprocal questioning technique in an attempt to encourage students to formulate their own questions about material and thereby learn purposeful, thoughtful reading. The ReQuest procedure can be applied to either a reading passage or a picture, and it is suggested for use with students at all levels.

Question-Answer Relationships.   Question-Answer Relationships are designed to help students answer comprehension questions by providing them a format for analyzing the task demands of questions. This strategy seems to be appropriate for middle-school students.

GIST.   The GIST procedure provides students with a format for generating gist, or summary, statements of paragraphs and short passages. It progresses from a teacher-directed small-group strategy to one in which students independently generate their own summary statements.

Explicit Teaching of Reading Comprehension.   The Explicit Teaching of Reading Comprehension is a framework for the direct instruction of reading comprehension. Its intent is to get students to independently apply comprehension skills learned through explicit teaching to other reading situations. The strategy is useful for students at all grade levels.

Think-Alouds.   Think-Alouds is a modeling procedure based upon explicit teaching intended to make students aware of the comprehension processes enlisted as reading is pursued.

Induced Imagery.   Induced Imagery are procedures that teachers model explicitly in hopes of helping students visualize as they read.

Dialogical-Thinking Reading Lesson.   The Dialogical-Thinking Reading Lesson is designed to promote critical thinking when elementary students are engaged in reading basal stories and must decide what they believe about a story-specific issue.

Inquiry Chart.   The Inquiry Chart is an instructional procedure that uses a data chart of information from multiple sources so that students may critically evaluate a topic under study.

References

Pearson, P. D., and L. Fielding. 1991. Comprehension instruction. In *Handbook of reading research: Volume II,* edited by R. Barr, M. L. Kamil, P. B. Mosenthal, and P. D. Pearson. New York: Longman.

Tierney, R. J., and J. Cunningham. 1984. Research on teaching reading comprehension. In *Handbook of reading research,* edited by P. D. Pearson. New York: Longman.

PReP Technique

Purpose

The PreReading Plan (PReP) was developed by Langer (1981) with the following goals: (1) to give students an opportunity to generate what they know about a topic and to extend these ideas and evaluate them; and (2) to provide teachers with a procedure for assessing the adequacy of the students' prior knowledge about a specific topic, and for determining the language that students use to express their ideas.

Rationale

The PReP technique represents an extension of the research of the late 1970s on the relation between prior knowledge and reading comprehension (e.g., Anderson and Freebody, 1981; Anderson, Pichert, and Shirey, 1979; Anderson, Reynolds, Schallert, and Goetz, 1977; Anderson, Spiro, and Anderson, 1978). By providing students opportunities for their brainstorming (listing on a chart or the chalkboard the students' ideas), developing associations for and reflecting and reformulating these ideas, Langer (1980, 1981, 1982) claims, the technique can be used to help students access what they know about a topic prior to reading. For those students who know a lot about a topic, it can be used to help them determine what is relevant and what is irrelevant. For those students who may be unaware that they know something about a topic, the technique helps them access relevant knowledge. For those students who know very little about a topic, the technique helps extend their understandings sufficiently to prepare them for learning from their texts. Alternatively, the technique might be used as a flag for determining the readiness and needs of different students. As Langer (1981) stated:

> When preparing students for a reading activity, we can help them become aware of relevant prior knowledge, while we judge whether or not that knowledge is sufficient for comprehension of the text. And that point we will be able to make knowledgeable decisions about reading assignments and instruction and related concepts. (P. 153)

To guide teachers in their assessment of the response of students, Langer (1982) lists characteristics of the type of associations that students with either a lot or very little prior knowledge will likely generate. Her own research, in collaboration with Nicholich (Langer and Nicholich, 1981), suggests that her analyses of prior knowledge are better than IQ or standardized reading test scores in predicting student recall of a specific passage.

Intended Audience

Langer does not specify any particular audience for the technique. It would seem reasonable to use the procedure with groups of students at almost any grade level, either as preparation for reading or in conjunction with other learning experiences such as excursions, films, and the like.

Description of the Procedure

Use of the PReP technique has two facets:

1. Engaging students in group discussion around key concepts
2. Analyzing the nature of student responses

1. Engaging Students in Group Discussion   A group discussion directed at key concepts from a topic that students are to explore represents the heart of the PReP technique. Prior to initiating the discussion, the teacher is expected to determine what the key concepts are that he or she wishes the students to address, and in which ways they might stimulate discussion or associations with those key concepts. For example, a teacher about to embark upon a unit on, or have the students read a text about, underwater exploration might isolate selected key concepts (e.g., geography of the oceans and problems with deep-water exploration) and introduce the students to the topic with a photo or an artist's depiction of deep-water sea life. The ensuing discussion involves a three-step process:

Step 1: Initial Associations with the Concept (What comes to mind when . . . ?)
   Using the picture or some other stimulus, the teacher encourages brainstorming (What comes to mind when . . . ? What do you think of . . . ? What might you see, hear, feel . . . ? What might be going on . . . ?). As students generate ideas, the teacher jots them down on the chalkboard.

Step 2: Reflections on Initial Associations (What made you think of . . . ?)
   During the second step, students are expected to explain the free associations they generated in Step One. This is intended to encourage students to become aware of the bases of their own individual associations, as well as those generated by their peers, and to evaluate the usefulness of these ideas.

Step 3: Reformulation of Knowledge (Have you any new ideas about . . . ?)
   In this step the teacher asks the students if they have any new ideas or ideas they wish to change or refine. While Step Two often results in triggering new ideas, Step Three serves to probe if there are any changes, deletions, revisions, or additions. The teacher's role in this and other steps is accepting and inquisitive rather than evaluative and critical.

2. Analyzing Student Responses   To provide teachers with the diagnostic information necessary to determine the instructional needs of students, Langer proposes that teachers pursue an analysis of the free associations generated by the students. She offers guidelines by which they might determine if students have well-formed, partly formed, or ill-formed knowledge structures:

a. Students with very little knowledge about a concept will generally focus on low-level associations with morphemes (prefixes, suffixes, or root words); words that sound like the stimulus word, or first but not quite relevant experiences.
b. Students with some prior information will generally mention examples, attributes, or defining characteristics.

c. Students with much prior information about a concept will generally offer information that suggests evidence of integration with high-level concepts. Their responses might take the form of analogies, definitions, linkages, and superordinate concepts.

As Langer points out, a reader's responses may vary across the three steps of the technique, so any analysis should not be restricted to one of the steps but should use all three. To assist teachers in the use of the technique and in a determination of the level of students' prior knowledge, Langer offers several examples of student responses and discusses how these responses might be analyzed and what they might suggest for teaching. Students with some or much knowledge may need some teacher guidance but are probably quite capable of reading the selection. Langer suggests that students with little knowledge will need direct instruction in concepts. An example of such an analysis is presented in Figure 7–1.

FIGURE 7–1.   DIAGNOSTIC ANALYSES OF STUDENT RESPONSES TO PReP

General Topic: Underwater Exploration

Key Topic: Geography of the oceans (picture of cross-sectioned ocean topography)

Student	*Responses*	*Level*
Robin	1. sandy, dark, and cold on bottom	some—attribute
	2. only a few plants or animals can live there	
	3. not many plants or fish there	
Kim	1. drifting sand and rocks	some—attribute
	2. ocean floor changes	
	3. ocean geography is different from land geography because ocean geography changes more	much—analogies
Terry	1. depth of water varies	some—attribute
	2. plants and fish vary with depth of water	
	3. depth of water must affect the marine life	much—superordinate
Jay	1. plants, fish, and water	little—association
	2. different fish in different places	
	3. fish live where they like, how deep the water is	some—attribute
Casey	1. bacteria, shells, lots of fish and whales	little—association
	2. oceans have lots in them	
	3. oceans have more life in them	much—superordinate

Cautions and Comments

Langer's PReP technique offers the teacher much that is worthwhile. First, PReP provides teachers with a straightforward framework for preparing students for a selection while, at the same time, it encourages teachers to study the responses of readers and adjust their instruction accordingly. Second, Langer's suggestions are offered as guidelines and include enough exceptions, examples, and interpretations to prompt intelligent use of the technique. Third, Langer's steps go beyond simply allowing students to free-associate to having them think about their ideas and revise them. Fourth, Langer provides the teacher with procedures that can be used to apply the strategy to classroom situations, including the suggestions of a grid upon which teachers could map out the responses of a whole class. In addition, the steps involved in the procedure are broad enough to be applied to almost any textbook or instructional activity involving concept development.

Langer's technique has one other feature that distinguishes it. Namely, Langer has studied carefully the guidelines for analyzing levels of prior information. In a study with Nicholich (Langer and Nicholich, 1981), Langer was able to show that her method for analyzing prior information was a better predictor of reading comprehension of a particular passage than were IQ or a standardized reading achievement measure.

The technique, however, has its limitations. Despite the research data on the procedure, it is questionable whether students' prior knowledge can be so accurately assessed by using the three steps Langer proposes or the guidelines she advocates for analyzing responses. She alludes to exceptions but we are never sure how many students might be misclassified. Some students may be as unwilling to free-associate as some readers are tentative about inferencing. Possibly the procedure would be better applied after reading a paragraph or two, a synopsis, or a related passage. Ideally, Langer should have determined her classes of response *after* she had determined which students had adequate comprehension and which students had inadequate comprehension. An a priori determination seems less than desirable. Potential users of the technique should realize that, apart from some claims from selected users, the instructional worth of the procedure has yet to be determined. Whether the strategy improves comprehension of a passage, concept development, or awareness of what readers know has yet to be determined. Likewise, whether the technique improves teacher decision making in this realm is an issue awaiting research validation. In the meanwhile, the technique may serve to point teachers and students in the right direction, and the effects of this technique are unlikely to be detrimental.

References

Anderson, R. C., and P. Freebody. 1981. Vocabulary knowledge. In *Comprehension and teaching: Research reviews,* edited by J. T. Guthrie. Newark, DE: International Reading Association. Discusses the role of vocabulary in reading comprehension based upon an extensive review of the literature.

Anderson, R. C., J. W. Pichert, and L. L. Shirey. 1979. *Effects of the reader's schemata at different points in time* (Tech. Rep. No. 119). Urbana: University of Illinois, Center for the Study of Reading, April. (ED 169 523) Provides research support for the influence of prior knowledge upon reading comprehension.

Anderson, R. C., R. D. Reynolds, D. L. Schallert, and E. T. Goetz. 1977. Framework for comprehending discourse. *American Education Research Journal* 14:367–381. Presents research support for a schema-theoretical point of view of reading comprehension.

Anderson, R. C., R. J. Spiro, and M. C. Anderson. 1978. Schemata as scaffolding for the representation of information in connected discourse. *American Educational Research Journal* 15:433–440.

Langer, J. A. 1980. Relation between levels of prior knowledge and the organization of recall. In *Perspectives in reading research and instruction,* edited by M. L. Kamil and A. J. Moe. Washington, DC: National Reading Conference, 23–33. Provides the research bases for using PReP to assess levels of prior knowledge.

———. 1981. From theory to practice: A prereading plan. *Journal of Reading* 25:152–156. Represents a very practical description of how PReP can be used.

———. 1982. Facilitating text processing: The elaboration of prior knowledge. In *Reader meets author/bridging the gap,* edited by J.

Langer and M. Smith-Burke. Newark, DE: International Reading Association. Discusses the use of PReP, including examples of responses by students.

Langer, J. A., and M. Nicholich. 1981. Prior knowledge and its effect on comprehension. *Journal of Reading Behavior* 13:375–378. Represents a research study in which the validity of using PReP as a means of assessing background knowledge was addressed.

Molner, L. A. 1989, November. *Developing background for expository text: PReP revisited.* Paper presented at the annual meeting of the National Reading Conference, Austin, TX. (ED 316 843) Study that revealed positive effects using PReP for high school social studies students on a measure of delayed topic knowledge. Additionally, students with large amounts of prior knowledge appeared to benefit most from PReP.

Pearson, P. D., and D. Johnson. 1978. *Teaching reading comprehension.* New York: Macmillan. Represents a practical introduction to the theory and practice of teaching reading comprehension.

Anticipation Guide

Purpose

The Anticipation Guide (Readence, Bean, and Baldwin, 1995) is designed to: (1) activate students' knowledge about a topic before reading and (2) provide purpose by serving as a guide for subsequent reading.

Rationale

The Anticipation Guide attempts to enhance students' comprehension by having them react to a series of statements about a topic before they begin to read or to engage in any other form of information acquisition. It utilizes prediction by activating students' prior knowledge, and it capitalizes on controversy as a motivational device to get students involved in the material to be read.

Numerous studies (e.g., Pearson, Hansen, and Gordon, 1979) have pointed out the efficacy of activating students' knowledge about a topic before they read in order to enhance comprehension. Other ways to promote better comprehension have also been suggested. Herber and Nelson (1986) have recommended that statements be used in lieu of questions as an initial means to get students more involved in their learning because statements require students only to *recognize* and respond, while questions require students to *produce* a response. Production of their own questions and statements, which is a more sophisticated learning behavior than recognition alone, becomes the end goal of such instruction. In addition, Lunstrum (1981) suggested that controversy could be used as a motivational technique for reading by arousing students' curiosity about a topic and getting them to use the text to corroborate their stance on an issue.

The Anticipation Guide incorporates all of these comprehension-enhancing strategies by asking students to react to statements that focus their attention on the topic to be learned. Students' previous thoughts and opinions about that topic are activated by using statements that are carefully worded so as to challenge students' knowledge bases and to arouse their curiosity. Students then become motivated to read to resolve the conceptual conflict. In this way, misconceptions about a topic can be brought out and inaccuracies dealt with. Furthermore, the Anticipation Guide can also be used as the basis for postreading discussion wherein students react a second time to the statements, this time dealing with the text information as well.

Intended Audience

The Anticipation Guide can be adapted for use at any grade level and can be used with a variety of print and nonprint media. Statements used in the guide can be modified and read to younger or slower students, who may be unable to read them on their own. In addition, the Anticipation Guide can be used to introduce a film, filmstrip, lecture, audiotape, or field trip, as well as to introduce a text reading assignment. Thus, the guide can be realistically applied in most learning situations.

Description of the Procedures

Readence, Bean, and Baldwin (1995) recommend the following steps to implement an anticipation guide:

1. Identify major concepts
2. Determine students' knowledge of these concepts
3. Create statements
4. Decide statement order and presentation mode
5. Present guide
6. Discuss each statement briefly
7. Direct students to read the text
8. Conduct follow-up discussion

1. Identify Major Concepts   The ideas to be learned by reading the text should be determined by a careful perusal of the material and of the teacher's manual, if one is available. The step is analogous to what normally happens in good lesson planning. The following example of constructing and using an Anticipation Guide is adapted from one provided by Head and Readence (1992). Using a text entitled "Food and Health," the following concepts were identified:

a. Food contains nutrients that your body needs for energy, growth, and repair.

b. Carbohydrates and fats supply energy.

c. A balanced diet includes the correct amount of all the nutrients needed by your body.

d. Every food contains some calories of food energy.

2. Determine Students' Knowledge of These Concepts In order to determine how the main concepts support or challenge what the students already know, the teacher must consider the students' experiential background. The whole class, as well as individual students, will have to be considered in this step. In our nutrition example, socioeconomic level is one, but only one, factor that may have a bearing on the kinds of statements that eventually result.

3. Create Statements The number of statements to be created varies with the amount of text to be read and, particularly, the number of concepts that have been identified. In addition, the ability and maturity levels of the students influence statement making. Three to five statements are usually a good number to aim for. The most effective statements are generally those in which the students have sufficient knowledge to understand what the statements say, but not enough to make any of them a totally known entity.

4. Decide Statement Order and Presentation Mode An appropriate order must be determined to present the guide. Usually, the order follows the sequence in which the concepts are encountered in the text, but that is subject to each teacher's judgment.

The guide may be presented using the chalkboard, an overhead transparency, or a ditto sheet that is handed out individually. A set of directions and blanks for students' responses should be included. The directions must be worded appropriately for the age and maturity levels of the students.

5. Present Guide Continuing with our Anticipation Guide example on nutrition, the following guide is given the students:

Anticipation Guide: Food and Health

Directions: Below are some statements about food and nutrition. Read each statement carefully and place a checkmark next to each statement with which you agree. Be prepared to defend your thinking as we discuss the statements.

_____   1. An apple a day keeps the doctor away.

_____   2. If you wish to live a long life, be a vegetarian.

_____   3. Three square meals a day will satisfy all your body's nutritional needs.

_____   4. Calories make you fat.

When presenting the guide to students, it is advisable to read the directions and statements orally. You should emphasize that students will share their thoughts and opinions about each statement, defending their agreement or disagreement with the statement. Students can work individually or in small groups to formulate a response.

6. Discuss Each Statement Briefly   A discussion ensues, with the teacher first asking for a show of hands from students to indicate their agreement or disagreement. The teacher tallies the responses. The discussion should include at least one opinion on each side of the issue per statement. As other students listen to the opinions offered, they can evaluate their own view in terms of the others.

7. Direct Students to Read the Text   Students are now told to read the text assignment with the purpose of deciding what the author would say about each statement. As they read, students should keep two things in mind: their own thoughts and opinions as well as those voiced by others, and the way in which what they are reading relates to what was discussed.

8. Conduct Follow-up Discussion   After reading, the students may respond once again to the statements. This time they should react in the light of the actual text. Thus, the guide now serves as the basis for a postreading discussion in which students can share the new information gained from reading and how their previous thoughts may have been modified by what they understand the reading to say. It should be made clear to the students that agreement with the author is not mandatory.

Cautions and Comments

The Anticipation Guide presents a versatile format for use by teachers to activate students' prior knowledge about a topic to be learned and to motivate them to pursue that information. In essence, the guide provides for the following: (1) active involvement by students in their own learning; (2) the use of prediction as a means to stimulate comprehension; and (3) guidance in the form of purpose-setting behaviors as students interact with the text in their effort to verify their predictions.

In addition, the Anticipation Guide has some diagnostic value for teachers in formulating and executing their instructional plan. As students discuss the statements before reading, teachers can assess the depth and breadth of students' knowledge about a topic. This allows teachers to make tentative instructional decisions about the time required for learning, the kind of materials that may be most appropriate, and what alternative strategies would be beneficial to the students. Lipson (1984) has expressed some concern about the negative effects of inaccurate prior knowledge on learning. Because of this diagnostic character of the Anticipation Guide, teachers can readily take appropriate steps to rectify students' misconceptions when inaccurate or incomplete knowledge is discovered.

Perhaps the most difficult aspect of constructing an Anticipation Guide is selecting appropriate statements to be used. Guide statements must be within students' previous knowledge and, therefore, must be on the experience-based level of comprehension. But the statements must also be on a higher level of generality in order to be an effective teaching and learning strategy. Using statements that are merely fact-based is ineffective. Students should discuss reasons for holding or forming opinions, not simply recite easily found facts.

For instance, if we used a statement in our example guide on nutrition such as "the recommended minimum daily allowance of vitamin A is 1.5 mg," the statement would be virtually useless as a tool to enhance learning. That type of statement is based on fact, not experience. Either students would know it or they wouldn't; in essence, it becomes a true-false statement. If the student does know it, then it has no value as an instructional tool. Conversely, if the student doesn't know it, then it will not serve as a knowledge-activation device. Students must be allowed to use their prior experiences in order to benefit from the use of prereading statements. Teachers are cautioned that, though such statements are more difficult to construct, experience-based statements are crucial to the success of Anticipation Guides or any other guide based on prediction.

References

Alvermann, D. E., and J. Swafford. 1989. Do content area strategies have a research base? *Journal of Reading* 32:388–390. Discusses the research base associated with various strategies and practices.

Ericson, B., M. Hubler, T. W. Bean, C. C. Smith, and J. V. McKenzie. 1987. Increasing critical reading in junior high classrooms. *Journal of Reading* 30:430–439. Discusses the use of Anticipation Guides as a means to promote critical thinking.

Head, M. H., and J. E. Readence. 1992. Anticipation guides: Enhancing meaning through prediction. In *Reading in the content areas: Improving classroom instruction,* 3d ed., edited by E. K. Dishner, T. W. Bean, J. E. Readence, and D. W. Moore. Dubuque, IA: Kendall/Hunt, 227–233. Provides a detailed description of the construction and use of Anticipation Guides.

Herber, H. L., and J. B. Nelson. 1986. Questioning is not the answer. In *Reading in the content areas: Improving classroom instruction,* 2d ed., edited by E. K. Dishner, T. W. Bean, J. E. Readence, and D. W. Moore. Dubuque, IA: Kendall/Hunt, 210–215. Discusses the role of statements in learning from text.

Lipson, M. Y. 1984. Some unexpected issues in prior knowledge and comprehension. *The Reading Teacher* 37:760–764. Describes the problematic effects of inaccurate prior knowledge on comprehension.

Lunstrum, J. P. 1981. Building motivation through the use of controversy. *Journal of Reading* 24:687–691. Offers controversy as a means to arouse curiosity and enhance comprehension.

Pearson, P. D., J. Hansen, and C. Gordon. 1979. The effect of background knowledge on young children's comprehension of explicit and implicit information. *Journal of Reading Behavior* 11:201–219. Presents a research study exploring the facilitative effects of prior knowledge on learning from text.

Readence, J. E., T. W. Bean, and R. S. Baldwin. 1995. *Content area reading: An integrated approach,* 5th ed. Dubuque, IA: Kendall/Hunt. Delineates the steps involved in using an Anticipation Guide and provides numerous examples.

Text Preview

Purpose

The Text Preview (Graves, Cooke, and LaBerge, 1983) is designed to: (1) build students' background knowledge about a topic before reading; (2) motivate students to read; and (3) provide an organizational framework for comprehending a text.

Rationale

The major premises behind the use of the Text Preview are similar to that of the Antici-pation Guide, namely, that comprehension is enhanced when readers draw upon their prior knowledge and are interested in the topic. However, this prereading strategy goes beyond simply drawing upon students' prior knowledge; it actually attempts to build their knowl-edge about a text selection before students read.

When faced with a novel selection, students may have a difficult time with unfamiliar vocabulary, syntax, and/or text structure. This could be further complicated by a narrative where characters, setting, or events are not made explicit and must be inferred. A Text Preview can give readers this information so that when they begin reading the selection they have a framework to understand the characters and events at the text-explicit level and beyond. Text Previews also serve to motivate student interest because explicit con-nections are made between topics to be read and students' experiences. In addition, students can be further stimulated because the text preview is designed to speak directly to them.

Research support for Text Previews (e.g., Graves, Cooke, and LaBerge, 1983; Graves and Prenn, 1984) have demonstrated the efficacy of using them with students of middle school through high school age who have varying ability levels. Text Previews also have been shown to be effective with both narrative and expository texts. Finally, they have been shown to not only help students understand text selections but also to improve their attitude about reading the texts.

Intended Audience

Text Previews seem most useful for upper elementary through high school students who encounter a variety of text situations, some of which may be novel and/or difficult. They may be especially useful for low ability students who lack sufficient prior knowledge or the necessary motivation to read and understand a potentially difficult text selection.

Description of the Procedures

Graves, Prenn, and Cooke (1985) described the use of previews for narrative selections in two parts: (1) preparation and construction, and (2) presentation.

1. Preparation and Construction of Text Previews   A text preview is a detailed script written in such a way as to provide an organizational framework to enhance students' comprehension of a text selection. Specifically, it consists of three parts: (a) an interest-building section, (b) a synopsis of the selection, which includes a description of characters and setting, and (c) a section that includes a purpose-setting question or directions for reading.

The interest-building section is designed to pique students' interest by asking a few rhetorical questions and making a connection between a familiar topic and the topic of the selection. The synopsis consists of a brief discussion of the story's theme, along with an introduction to the characters and, if appropriate, the setting and point of view. Finally, students are given questions or directions to guide their reading. Included here is a sample text preview written for *"The Sniper"* (O'Flaherty, 1926).

Text Preview: *"The Sniper"**

Trying to get along with other people is very important to most of us. Just imagine what the world would be like if that were the case! Yet, try as we may, we know that is not how people are. Do you remember the last time you got into an argument or fight with someone? What were its consequences? What is even worse is getting into a fight or argument only to find out that it resulted in hurting some other person you really cared for! Has that happened to you? What were your thoughts and feelings when you found out?

In the story you are about to read entitled "The Sniper," the main character is found on a rooftop at night with the sounds of guns in the background. It is wartime. Suddenly, a shot rings out, barely missing the sniper. It is the enemy trying to kill him.

Just then, an enemy car approaches. The sniper performs his duty and kills two of the enemy. Just as he does, another shot rings out, this time wounding the sniper so he can't hold his rifle any longer. Yet, he must do something as daybreak is approaching. The sniper can't be caught on the rooftop in daylight, and his escape is covered by the enemy who wounded him. Then the sniper thinks of an escape plan. After all, this is war and he must survive the enemy, no matter who it may be.

What is the sniper's plan? Will it be successful? And, who is the enemy? You will have to read to find out.

The first step in the construction of a Text Preview is to become thoroughly familiar with the selection. This may mean reading it more than one time. When this is done, it must be decided how to build an analogical bridge between what the students know and the theme or topic of the story. Thus, it is important to think of real-life, day-to-day events that touch the lives of the students. It is this bridge that will become the first part of the Text Preview.

Next, write the synopsis of the story. This should be a brief description of the characters, setting, point of view, and plot up to the point of the climax. This should give students the gist of the story and how it is organized. The last section of the Text Preview suggests the outcome for which the students should be looking as they read the story. It might suggest a general approach or directions for reading. It might also alert them to a special twist they might encounter as they read.

---

*From L. O'Flaherty. 1926. *Spring sowing*. New York: Alfred A. Knopf.

2. Presentation of Text Previews The use of Text Previews is fairly straight-forward. Graves and associates (1985) recommend the following steps:

- Tell students that you're going to introduce a new story.
- Read the interest-building section of the preview to the students. It is best to read the preview rather than paraphrase it since a casual presentation of it belies the care and time involved in its construction.
- Give students a few minutes to relate the information to their prior knowledge and discuss it.
- Read the remainder of the Text Preview.
- Direct students to read the selection.

Previewing a story should take five to ten minutes, including the discussion. The discussion should be focused and is not designed to promote a lengthy dialogue.

Cautions and Comments

Perhaps the greatest concern in using Text Previews is the amount of time it takes to develop one. Thus, it is recommended that they only be used for particularly challenging and important stories. Teachers must weigh the benefits gained by students with their use versus the amount of time and energy they expend in their creation. However, research on Text Previews seems to show that the effort is well worth it; students report that previews help them to understand the text selections better. Graves and associates (1985) also suggest that (1) Text Previews may only be used with students who are likely to have trouble with a particular text; or (2) briefer previews, using lists of characters or only the interest-building section, might be used.

Readence, Bean, and Baldwin (1995) provide additional guidelines for developing Text Previews when using them with expository material. The preview might contain a review of important points along with a definition of key vocabulary terms and focusing questions that move students from text-explicit thinking to more implicit and experience-based thinking. Such changes are necessary to consider because of the nature of expository text.

Finally, as an alternative to the regular use of Text Previews, teachers are encouraged to consider them as potential writing assignments. Once students become familiar with previews, they can be asked to read a story and write a Text Preview for students in other classes. The process of writing a preview will cause students to consider thoroughly the ideas offered in the selection and to think critically about them.

References

Ericson, B., M. Hubler, T. W. Bean, C. C. Smith, and J. V. MacKenzie. 1987. Increasing critical reading in junior high classrooms. *Journal of Reading* 30:430–439. Discusses the use of Text Previews as a means to promote critical thinking in English classrooms.

Graves, M. F., C. L. Cooke, and M. J. LaBerge. 1983. Effects of previewing difficult short stories on low ability junior high school students' comprehension, recall, and attitudes. *Reading Research Quarterly* 18:262–276. Original study that validated the use of Text Previews.

Graves, M. F. and M. C. Prenn. 1984. Effects of previewing expository passages on junior high school students' comprehension and attitudes. In *Changing perspectives on research in reading/language processing and instruction,* Thirty-third Yearbook of the National Reading Conference, edited by J. A. Niles and L. A. Harris. Rochester, NY: National Reading Conference, 173–177. Research study using eighth grade social studies students showing that Text Previews can improve comprehension and attitudes, even with expository text.

Graves, M. F., M. C. Prenn, and C. L. Cooke. 1985. The coming attraction: Previewing short stories. *Journal of Reading* 28:594–598. Review of theoretical and research support on Text Previews and a discussion of their practical applications.

Readence, J. E., T. W. Bean, and R. S. Baldwin. 1995. *Content area reading: An integrated approach,* 5th ed. Dubuque, IA: Kendall/Hunt. Discusses the use of Text Previews as a pre-reading strategy with examples from both narrative and expository texts.

ReQuest Procedure

Purpose

The ReQuest procedure (Manzo, 1968) is designed to encourage students to: (1) formulate their own questions about the material they are reading and develop questioning behavior; (2) adopt an active, inquiring attitude to reading; (3) acquire reasonable purposes for reading; and (4) improve their independent reading comprehension skills.

Rationale

Manzo, the originator of the ReQuest procedure, suggests that while teacher questioning and purpose setting are important to reading comprehension, of greater importance is the development of the students' abilities to ask their own questions and to set their own purposes for reading. He suggests that these skills facilitate the students' acquisition of an active, inquiring attitude and their ability to examine alternatives and to originate information. These things he considers essential if students are to transfer problem-solving involvement to different contexts.

Intended Audience

ReQuest is suitable for use with students at levels ranging from kindergarten to college. Although it was originally devised for use on a one-to-one basis, it can also work with groups of up to approximately eight persons.

Description of the Procedures

In the ReQuest procedure, an individual student and teacher silently read sections of a selection and then take turns asking and answering each other's questions about that selection. The teacher's function is to model good questioning behavior, to provide feedback to the student about his or her questions, and to assess whether the student has established reasonable purposes for independently completing the passage.

There are six steps teachers should follow in using the ReQuest procedure:

1. Preparation of material
2. Development of readiness for the strategy
3. Development of student questioning behaviors
4. Development of student predictive behaviors
5. Silent reading activity
6. Follow-up activities

1. Preparation of Material   Preparation of the material entails previewing the selection for the purpose of:

a. Selecting material at an appropriate level for the student

b. Selecting material appropriate for making predictions

c. Identifying appropriate points within the selection where the student could plausibly make predictions

2. Development of Readiness for the Strategy   Manzo (1969) suggests the following protocol and guidelines as those appropriate for beginning a ReQuest session.

> The purpose of this lesson is to improve your understanding of what you read. We will each read silently the first sentence. Then we will take turns asking questions about the sentence and what it means. You will ask questions first, then I will ask questions. Try to ask the kinds of questions a teacher might ask in the way a teacher might ask them.
>
> You may ask me as many questions as you wish. When you are asking me questions, I will close my book (or pass the book to you if there is only one between us). When I ask questions, you close your book. (P. 124)

The teacher might also explain these points during or prior to the session: each question deserves to be answered fully: "I don't know" as an answer is unacceptable; unclear questions are to be rephrased; and uncertain answers should be justified by reference to the text. In addition, it may be necessary at times to introduce some of the vocabulary contained in the selection and/or develop some background for understanding the passage. For example, the teacher may need to give the student oral familiarity with some of the more difficult words in the selection. Also, in order to develop some background for understanding the passage, the teacher might alert the student to the basic concepts involved by a brief and general discussion of the title.

Therefore, in introducing the ReQuest procedure, the teacher should be aware of the need to:

a. Build student interest in the procedure

b. Introduce selected vocabulary

c. Develop some background for understanding the passage

d. Provide the student with an understanding of the rules of ReQuest

3. Development of Student Questioning Behaviors At this point, both the teacher and the student participate in the reciprocal questioning procedure. As Manzo's protocol suggests, this procedure entails:

a. *Joint silent reading.* Both the student and teacher read the first sentence of the selection.

b. *Student questioning.* The teacher closes his or her book, and the student questions the teacher. The teacher responds with an answer, reinforces appropriate questioning behavior, and, if necessary, requests rephrasing of unclear questions.

c. *Exchange of roles.* The student finishes questioning and removes his or her copy of the material. Then the teacher questions the student.

Throughout this phase, the teacher exhibits good questioning behavior and provides feedback to the student about the student's questions. When taking the role of questioner, the teacher should endeavor to extend the student's thinking. To this end, the teacher might use various types of questions, including questions that build upon prior questions and require the student to integrate information. When responding to the student's questions, the teacher could use both verbal and nonverbal reinforcement. For example, a student's question might be reinforced with a statement such as "That's a great question. I really have to . . . " or "I hope I can ask questions that tough that will make you. . . . "

4. Development of Student Predictive Behaviors At an appropriate point in the procedure (i.e., when the student has read enough to make a prediction about the rest of the material), the exchange of questions is terminated. Assuming the role of agitator, the teacher attempts to elicit predictions and validations from the student. At this point, the teacher might ask, "What do you think will happen? . . . Why do you think so? . . . Read the line that proves it." It may prove helpful to develop a list of suggested predictions and a ranking from most likely to least likely.

If the prediction and verifications are reasonable, the teacher and student can move to the next step—silent reading activity. If the predictions are unreasonable, the teacher and student may continue reading and exchanging questions until another opportunity to elicit predictions arises. However, if the student is unable to make a reasonable prediction after having read three paragraphs, the teacher should terminate this activity. As Manzo suggests, "It may be self-defeating to continue beyond this point" (1969, 125).

5. Silent Reading Activity The teacher now directs the student to read the remainder of the selection. At this point, the teacher might say, "Read to the end of the selection to see what actually did happen." During this period, the teacher can either read along with the student or stand by to assist. Manzo suggests that it is important to give aid in a manner that does not disrupt the student's comprehension, that is, does not destroy the student's train of thought.

6. Follow-up Activities Numerous worthwhile tasks are suitable for follow-up activities. Manzo suggests that readers might engage in activities that verify or apply the information gained from reading. Other useful activities may emanate from a reconsideration and discussion of student predictions. For example, the teacher could encourage the student to consider variations or adaptations of the story.

Cautions and Comments

For those teachers using ReQuest for the first time, Manzo offers a number of suggestions. He advises working with individuals rather than with groups, and for the first encounter, he suggests the use of specific question types: immediate reference, common knowledge, related information, open-ended discussion, personalized discussion, further reference, and translation. Dishner and Searfoss (1974) have also offered an evaluation form that can be used in conjunction with a teacher's use of the procedure.

With children for whom ReQuest is a new experience, a questioning game or activity may be useful as a starter. Students may wish to underline those ideas about which they want to ask questions; students' confidence in their ability to formulate questions can be vital to their successful involvement in the ReQuest procedure.

At certain times, modifications of the ReQuest procedures may be desirable. For example, in order to provide more varied interactions between questioner and respondent, it may be desirable to alternate the role of questioner after each question. Also, greater flexibility seems desirable in the selection of sections of the passage to be read at one time. Rather than proceed sentence by sentence, one might look for natural breaks within the passage. In a group situation, there are numerous possibilities. One example is where the roles of questioner and respondent either alternate around a circle or proceed at random within the circle. Often a group, as a whole, enjoys challenging the teacher. With kindergarten children, Legenza (1974) has successfully applied a modification of ReQuest using pictures. The suggested protocol in this situation runs as follows:

> Let's ask each other questions about this picture to see if we can learn all the things we can about it. In order to help us to learn all we can, let's both look at the picture first and ask me any questions you can think of about this picture and I'll see if I can answer them—then I'll ask you some questions and you see if you can answer them. (Manzo and Legenza 1975, 482)

Another possible modification is an incomplete questioning technique. This technique requires the student or teacher to initiate an incomplete question: for example, "Why did John . . . ?" The other party completes the question and directs it at the initiator.

With or without these modifications, the ReQuest procedure appears to be a very effective strategy. The various permutations of the ReQuest procedure provide a viable tool for exploring, extending, and encouraging student hypothesizing. ReQuest facilitates student involvement in problem solving and necessitates teacher awareness of the student's level of involvement.

Over the last ten years, Palincsar (e.g., Palincsar and Brown, 1984) has done several studies using a modification of the ReQuest procedure that she has termed Reciprocal Teaching. These studies suggest that reciprocal questioning training, in conjunction with training in summarizing, clarifying, and predicting, may be beneficial in improving students' comprehension. Studies by Manzo, the originator of ReQuest, and Legenza also provide empirical support for its use.

References

Alvermann, D. E. and J. Swafford. 1989. Do content area strategies have a research base? *Journal of Reading* 32:388–390. Discusses the research base associated with various strategies and practices.

Dishner, E. K., and L. W. Searfoss. 1977. Improving comprehension through the ReQuest procedure. *Reading Education: A Journal for Australian Teachers* 2 (Autumn):22–25. Presents an expanded and more specific set of directions for the ReQuest procedure.

———. 1974. *ReQuest evaluation form.* Unpublished paper, Arizona State University. Evaluation form that provides step-by-step implementation.

Helfeldt, J. P., and W. A. Henk. 1990. Reciprocal question-answer relationships: An instructional technique for at-risk readers. *Journal of Reading* 33:509–514. Describes an instructional strategy that integrates ReQuest with Question-Answer Relationships.

Helfeldt, J. P., and R. Lalik. 1979. Reciprocal student-teacher questioning. In *Reading comprehension at four linguistic levels,* edited by C. Pennock. Newark, DE: International Reading Association, 74–99. Reports a study in which ReQuest was shown to be more effective than teacher questioning.

Kay, L., J. L. Young, and R. R. Mottley. 1986. Using Manzo's ReQuest model with delinquent adolescents. *Journal of Reading* 29:506–510. ReQuest is shown to work with incarcerated youths, improving their self-esteem.

Legenza, A. 1974. *Questioning behavior of kindergarten children.* Paper presented at Nineteenth Annual Convention, International Reading Association. Describes the use and effectiveness of the ReQuest Picture Treatment with kindergarten children.

Manzo, A. V. 1968. *Improving reading comprehension through reciprocal questioning.* Unpublished doctoral diss., Syracuse University. Primary reference. Describes the original development of the ReQuest procedure, rationale, piloting, and empirical support of its effectiveness.

———. 1969. The ReQuest procedure. *Journal of Reading* 12:123–126. Manzo's first article based upon the ReQuest procedure. Describes the rationale, procedures, and suggestions for use.

———. 1985. Expansion modules for the ReQuest, CAT, GRP and REAP reading/study procedures. *Journal of Reading* 28:498–503. Updates the use of these study techniques in hopes of increasing student independence.

Manzo, A. V., and A. Legenza. 1975. Inquiry training for kindergarten children. *Educational Leadership* 32:479–483. Presents the procedures and empirical support for use of ReQuest with kindergarten children.

Palincsar, A. S., and A. L. Brown. 1984. Reciprocal teaching of comprehension-fostering and comprehension-monitoring activities. *Cognition and Instruction* 2:117–175. Research that found positive results for using reciprocal questioning and other metacognitive strategies for promoting comprehension.

Question-Answer Relationships

Purpose

Question-Answer Relationships (QARs) was developed by Raphael (1982b) as a procedure for enhancing students' ability to answer comprehension questions by giving them a systematic means for analyzing task demands of different question probes.

Rationale

Stemming from her concern that students are frequently asked questions in school but receive little or no guidance in knowing how to answer them, Raphael generated a strategy whereby readers are encouraged to analyze the task demands of questions prior to answering them. The system she devised for students to use involves having students identify three types of questions: text explicit or "right there," text implicit or "think and search," and scriptal or "on my own." This system was based upon a taxonomy suggested by Pearson and Johnson (1978) in which comprehension responses were described as follows: text explicit if the information to be used for the most appropriate response is stated explicitly in the text; text implicit if the response information is located in the text but requires the integration of textual material; and script implicit if the response information is located in the reader's knowledge base.

The system itself is presented to teachers and students in a carefully crafted fashion. Using the research on developing independent comprehenders as a basis (see Tierney and Cunningham, 1984), Raphael applies four principles of instruction to help readers analyze the task demands of questions: (1) give immediate feedback; (2) progress from shorter to longer texts; (3) begin with questions for which the task demand is more straightforward and go on to questions that require the use of multiple sources; and (4) develop independence by beginning with group learning experiences and progressing to individual and independent activities.

Raphael's claims about the efficacy of the strategy has been substantiated by research. Raphael and Pearson (1982) found that students in the fourth, sixth, and eighth grades who had been taught the strategy by a university researcher were more successful in answering questions than students who had not received the instruction. In a follow-up to this study, Raphael, Wonnacott, and Pearson (1983) taught fourth grade teachers how to use the strategy and obtained similar results. They found that the trained teachers were pleased with the strategy and that students outperformed comparable groups of students who received no such directed learning experiences. In a third study Raphael and McKinney (1983) examined developmental differences in children's performance and training requirements. With older students (eighth graders compared with fifth graders), orientation was as effective as training, and the performance of students improved by training, but not by simply being reminded to apply QARs at the time of testing.

Intended Audience

Raphael has used the procedure successfully with students of varying ability levels from grades four through eight. With some modification the procedure could be used with students at earlier grade levels. The strategy has worked most effectively with younger students (fifth and fourth graders), especially with those that are less able.

Description of the Procedure

At the heart of QARs is having the student identify the response demands of various questions (either "right there," "think and search," or "on my own"), then using a knowledge of the response demands to generate an answer. For this purpose, Raphael (1982b) offers the following guidelines and student response format as a way of accustoming readers to the strategy. Once the reader has learned the strategy, Raphael suggests that the focus should be on the best possible response to the question.

Initial use of the format entails having students circle the QAR strategy they will use. During this initial period, a student's response to a question is less important than the student's assessment of the task demands. In other words, it would be okay if the reader generated a wrong answer, but correctly identified the task demands. Later, when students move to determining and writing in the answer, the actual answer the reader generates becomes important.

To introduce most students to the strategy, Raphael suggests a week of intensive training followed by maintenance activities. Adaptations are recommended if a teacher deems them necessary. Four lessons make up the first week's intensive training.

Lesson 1. The first lesson is intended to introduce students to the task demands of different questions and to provide some initial practice at identifying task demands in conjunction with answering questions. For this purpose, Raphael recommends that instruction similar to the following be given in groups.

Using the previously suggested guidelines and response format (see Figures 7–2 and 7–3), the teacher would explain:

> We are going to talk about different types of questions and the best way to answer them. Sometimes your workbook or I give questions that ask for information you can find quite easily in the book. Other time you won't find the answer there. I will describe three kinds of questions: "Right There," "Think and Search," and "On My Own." Each type can be figured out by deciding where you get the information for the answer. We call this a Question-Answer Relationship, or QAR for short." (Raphael 1984, 189)

Raphael (1984) recommends that initially the teacher discuss the difference between text-based and knowledge-based responses, prior to discriminating between the two text-based strategies. Following the introduction, she suggests that three practice stages can be used with short passages of two or three sentences. In the first stage, she suggests giving students passages to read with questions for which the answer as well as the QARs are identified. During this stage, she suggests discussing the type of QAR each question represents. In the second stage, she suggests giving students passages, questions, and responses to these questions, and having students generate as a group the QAR for each. Finally, in the third stage, she suggests having students determine the QARs and respond with answers.

Lesson 2. The purpose of the second lesson is to provide the students with review and further guided practice as they read slightly longer passages (75 to 150 words). Specifically, Raphael recommends that the teacher begin the lesson with a review of each QAR category and then some guided practice with five questions that require different responses with a passage of approximately 75 to 150 words. She suggests the students do the first passage as a group

FIGURE 7–2.   ILLUSTRATIONS TO EXPLAIN QARs TO STUDENTS

In the Book QARs

In My Head QARs

Right There

The answer is in the text, usually easy to find. The words used to make up the question and words used to answer the question are **Right There** in the same sentence.

Author and You

The answer is *not* in the story. You need to think about what you already know, what the author tells you in the text, and how it fits together.

**Think and Search
(Putting It Together)**

The answer is in the story, but you need to put together different story parts to find it. Words for the question and words for the answer are not found in the same sentence. They come from different parts of the text.

On My Own

The answer is not in the story. You can even answer the question without reading the story. You need to use your own experience.

and then, as a group, that they be given feedback after they finish the second passage independently. As the students proceed with subsequent passages, Raphael emphasizes the importance of giving the students feedback, as well as having them justify their answer to the question and their choice of a QAR. Also she suggests that the teacher explain why an answer is acceptable on the grounds of both accuracy and strategy.

FIGURE 7–3.   PASSAGE—"LIGHTING A MATCH"

When lighting a match, it is important to follow these steps carefully. First, tear one match out of the matchbook. Second, close the matchbook cover. Third, strike the match against the rough strip on the outside of the matchbook. Finally, after the match has been used, blow it out carefully, and be sure it is cool before you throw it away.

1. What are the first two steps to correctly light and use a match?

   Right There _____

   Think and Search ____

   On My Own _____

2. Why should you be sure the match is cool before you throw it away?

   Right There _____

   Think and Search ____

   On My Own _____

3. What should you do after a match has been used and is still burning?

   Right There _____

   Think and Search ____

   On My Own _____

4. Why should you close the cover before striking the match?

   Right There _____

   Think and Search ____

   On My Own _____

5. What do you strike the match against to light it?

   Right There _____

   Think and Search ____

   On My Own _____

Lesson 3. In the third lesson, Raphael suggests extending the QAR task to a passage approximately the length of a short story selection. She suggests dividing the selection into four sections and generating two questions of each of the three types (a total of six questions) for each section. The first section would be completed in conjunction with reviewing the strategy; students would complete the remaining three sections independently, prior to acquiring feedback.

Lesson 4. For the fourth lesson, Raphael suggests using material typically found in the classroom—a basal story or a social studies or science chapter. She suggests giving the students the passage as a single unit with six questions from each QAR category. The student would be expected to read the passage, determine the QAR for each question, and answer it.

Maintaining QARs. To maintain the use of QARs, Raphael recommends a weekly review lesson and suggests some fun activities (e.g., a courtroom game that requires readers to respond to questions from students who role-play lawyers with the source of answers) that might be reinforcing. To supplement the use of QAR, she suggests that the training program might be extended to more systematic use with content material.

Cautions and Comments

The QAR represents one of the more thoroughly researched instructional strategies that have been developed in recent years. Raphael has gone to great lengths to explore its utility thoroughly at different grade levels with students of varying ability. She reports having most success with students of average and below average ability in grades four through eight. She also claims that the strategy can be easily learned by teachers, and she has explored the worth of different in-service training experiences with the technique (see Raphael, 1984). What is lacking from her research data are the long-term benefits or detriments that might arise from using the strategy. We do not know whether students who have been trained to do QARs are better at answering questions after some time has elapsed after training. Nor do we know if the students are better monitors of their own ability to read or answer questions. Furthermore, we have no descriptive data of how QARs influence the reasoning processes that readers use to answer questions and continue reading. Raphael (1984) suggests that with older students there may be interference that arises as a result of considering the task demands.

Two concerns that seem worth mentioning about QAR relate to problems with using the taxonomy. First, the taxonomy was intended to describe question-answer types rather than to facilitate a determination of correct responses. As readers consider answering a question, they might be better advised to consider the goal of the question and the point of the passage rather than whether the answer is forthcoming from such discrete categories as a text or reader. Second, QAR may not enhance comprehension in as straight-forward a fashion. To determine the nature of the relationship between a question and answer would seem to follow from rather than precede answering the question. If this be the case, QAR might be best viewed as helping readers achieve feedback on their responses rather than answers to questions.

References

Pearson, P. D., and D. D. Johnson. 1978. *Teaching reading comprehension.* New York: Holt, Rinehart & Winston. Presents an overview of the nature of reading comprehension and instructional issues. The taxonomy used by Raphael is described in this book.

Raphael, T. E. 1982a. *Improving question-answering performance through instruction* (Reading Education Report No. 32). Urbana: University of Illinois, Center for the Study of Reading, March. Provides an extensive discussion of the procedure, including pages teachers could use as transparencies or duplicating masters.

————. 1982b. Question-answering strategies for children. *The Reading Teacher* 36:186–190. Presents a clear description of how students might be taught to use QARs, including lesson plans and guidelines for teachers.

————. 1984. Teaching learners about sources of information for answering comprehension questions. *Journal of Reading* 27:303–311. Presents an overview of the results of several studies that have explored the utility of QAR.

———. 1986. Teaching question-answer relationships, revisited. *The Reading Teacher* 39:516–523. Modifies and updates QAR.

Raphael, T. E., and P. D. Pearson. 1982. *The effect of metacognitive awareness training on children's question-answering behavior* (Tech. Rep. No. 238). Urbana: University of Illinois, Center for the Study of Reading, March. Reports the first of three research studies in which QARs were taught to students in grades four, six, and eight.

Raphael, T. E., C. A. Wonnacott, and P. D. Pearson. 1983. *Increasing students' sensitivity to sources of information: An instructional study in question-answer relationships* (Tech. Rep. No. 284). Urbana: University of Illinois, Center for the Study of Reading, July. Reports an attempt to have selected fourth grade teachers trained to teach their students to use QARs.

Raphael, T. E., and J. McKinney. 1983. An examination of fifth and eighth grade students' question answering behavior: An instructional study in metacognition. *Journal of Reading Behavior* 15:67–86. Reports an exploration of developmental trends in the use of QARs by students.

Simmonds, E. P. M. 1992. The effects of teacher training and implementation of two methods for improving the comprehension skills of students with learning disabilities. *Learning Disabilities Research and Practice* 7:194–198. Study that demonstrated the superiority of using QARs versus traditional comprehension instruction with learning-disabled students in grades one to nine.

Tierney, R. J., and J. W. Cunningham. 1984. Research on teaching reading comprehension. In *Handbook of reading research,* edited by P. D. Pearson, R. Barr, M. L. Kamil, and P. Mosenthal. New York: Longman. Reviews the research on teaching reading comprehension, including QAR and related approaches.

GIST

Purpose

The GIST procedure (Generating Interactions between Schemata and Text) was developed by Cunningham to improve students' abilities to comprehend the gist of paragraphs by providing "a prescription for reading from group sentence-by-sentence gist production to individual whole-paragraph gist production" (1982, 42).

Rationale

Cunningham (1982) claims that the GIST procedure is an effective instructional tool for guiding student summary writing, which, in turn, improves their learning from text. The procedure has its roots in three sets of studies. First based upon the work of Kintsch (1977), Dooling and Christiansen (1977), and Anderson (1978), Cunningham argues for a strategy that engages a reader's background knowledge while using cues from the text in the order in which they were presented. The GIST procedure, Cunningham claims, is such a strategy. Second, justification for the value of summary or GIST generation comes from his own research (Cunningham, 1982) as well as the research of Doctorow, Marks and Wittrock (1978) and Taylor and Berkowitz (1980) in which students who wrote summaries following each paragraph increased their learning from text. Third, Cunningham used the work of Day (1980), Brown, Campione, and Day (1981) and, more directly, Doctorow, Marks, and Wittrock (1978) to generate the instructional procedures for guiding students' use of the procedure. The technique represents a teacher-directed, small-group strategy that takes students from writing summary statements for sentences to generating GIST statements for paragraphs.

Intended Audience

Although Cunningham has only investigated the use of the strategy in the fourth grade, the technique might be used with students at higher levels who need guidance in summary writing.

Procedure

There are two versions of the procedure: a paragraph version and short passage version. The steps involved in each are outlined below.

1. Paragraph Version   In the paragraph version, students are asked to generate summary statements of no longer than 15 words as they read a paragraph sentence by sentence. After reading the first sentence they are expected to summarize what the text stated. Then as each additional sentence of a paragraph is exposed, students are expected to incorporate the additional information into a new statement of no more than 15 words. The following illustrates the steps a teacher would follow with a paragraph.

Step 1: *Selecting appropriate paragraphs.* The first step in using the procedure is to elect several paragraphs, each with three to five sentences, that have a gist. The following paragraph is representative of the type of text Cunningham has used.

> The theory of how planets were formed differs from the one generally accepted a couple of decades ago. At that time, it was thought by most astronomers that the planets formed as the result of a wandering star passing too close to the sun and sucking chunks of matter out of its fiery mass. The decline of this theory occurred on the basis of new evidence and new calculation which suggested that the planets developed from random particles which grew larger as they attracted others by their gravity.

Step 2: *Students read the first sentence.* Step 2 involves having students read the first sentence of the paragraph for purposes of retelling it in their own words. Cunningham (1982) recommends that the sentence be displayed on an overhead, chart, or chalkboard with 15 blanks underneath. The blanks are the spaces in which students are expected to fit their summaries.

Step 3: *Students generate summaries.* In this step, students are asked to retell in a statement of 15 or fewer words what they read in the sentence. Writing one word in every blank, students as a group dictate and revise the statement until they are satisfied with it. The sentence is uncovered if a student wishes to reread the sentence; otherwise, the text is put aside and the students are expected to generate their summary based upon memory. Only after generating their summary are the students encouraged to reread the text. At that time, by comparing their summary statement with the text, students are expected to decide for themselves whether they wish to revise their GIST further. Once satisfied, the students proceed with step 4.

Cunningham (1982) emphasizes that teachers should be careful not to interfere with the students' decision making. He discourages teachers from evaluating the summary or interfering, even if the students' statement represents an exact duplication of the text.

Step 4: Reading the first two sentences. The fourth step involves having students read the first and second sentence and retell them in the same number of words used for the first sentence alone.

Step 5: Generating a summary for sentence one and two. The fifth step involves having students generate a single sentence (no longer than 15 words) that summarizes both sentences one and two. Again students are encouraged to revise their statement until they are satisfied with it. As a final check on the adequacy of the sentence, students are given an opportunity to compare what they generated with the text prior to proceeding with the next step.

Step 6: Continue with the procedure for the remainder of the paragraph. In step 6, the procedure outlined above is continued with the addition of each new sentence until the students have produced a single statement of 15 words or less that they feel best summarizes the paragraph.

Step 7: Moving beyond a sentence-by-sentence approach to a paragraphs approach. As students develop in their ability to generate such statements across a variety of different paragraphs, Cunningham suggests moving toward the presentation of paragraphs. In addition, as students develop in their ability to generate summaries, teachers are urged to give students opportunities to produce their own GIST statements individually rather than as a group.

2. *Short Passage Version*   The short passage version parallels the paragraph version.

Step 1: Selecting appropriate passages. The teacher selects short passages of an appropriate difficulty level, each with a GIST, and three to five paragraphs in length. The passage is placed on an overhead.

Step 2: Reading the paragraph. All the paragraphs are covered over but the first one. Twenty blank spaces are placed on a chalkboard, and the students are directed to read the paragraph so they can retell it in their own words in one statement of 20 or fewer words.

Step 3: Students generate summaries. When students have finished reading the paragraph, the overhead transparency is removed and students are asked as a group to start writing their summaries. Writing one word per blank, students dictate and edit the statement until it is complete. Students may review the paragraph at any time, but they are expected to dictate and edit form memory. When students feel that their statement is an accurate summary of the paragraph, the step is complete. The teacher is expected to enforce the 20-word rule; the students are expected to determine how satisfied they are with the final statement.

Step 4: *Students read and summarize subsequent paragraphs.* The chalkboard is erased, and the students proceed to read and summarize the first two paragraphs in no more than 20 words. The same procedures are used for leading them through the entire passage.

Step 5: *Generating summaries for whole passages and developing independence.* Cunningham recommends using the strategy with as many different short passages as necessary until the students become adept at efficiently producing GIST statements. Thereafter, he suggests that the teacher might have the students respond to the whole passage rather than paragraph-by-paragraph. Furthermore, when the students as a group become quite capable of producing gist statements, he suggests that students might be encouraged individually to produce GIST statements.

Cautions and Comments

There are positive features and some possible limitations to the procedure. On the positive side, Cunningham has carefully developed a step-by-step procedure for helping students write brief summaries of GISTs that are accountable to the text. If teachers follow Cunningham's steps, students are expected to move from group summaries to generating their own individual summaries. Furthermore, students are given procedures and encouragement so that they should be able to evaluate for themselves the adequacy of their summaries. In this regard, an important and worthwhile feature of the technique is the discussion and revisions that emerge in conjunction with the group's refinement of their statement. Another positive feature, which should not be overlooked, is Cunningham's (1982) scrutiny of the technique in a research study that involved fourth graders. His findings suggest that, if having students generate summaries is your goal, then the GIST technique is possibly better than nothing or other writing experiences.

In terms of limitations, there are a number of problems that might arise as teachers implement the technique. Can it be assumed that students will be able to readily transfer summarization skills acquired with a sentence to a paragraph to a whole text? Will students be able to judge the adequacy of their summaries without some criteria for so doing? Of overall importance, is summary writing always worthwhile? Even Cunningham alludes to the possibility that some texts do not lend themselves to summarization. Even if it is worthwhile, are there other procedures that expedite the generation of summaries? We tend to think that the procedure is likely to become tedious if used repeatedly. Furthermore, the procedure seems to assume that summaries can be readily developed by reading in a linear, sentence-by-sentence fashion. This assumption seems questionable.

References

Anderson, R. C. 1978. Schema-directed processes in language comprehension. In *Cognitive psychology and instruction,* edited by A. M. Lesgold, J. W. Pellegrino, S. D. Fakkema, and R. Glaser. New York: Plenum Press. Presents a theoretically oriented discussion of the nature of reader-text interactions during reading comprehension. The ideas presented in this article serve as some of the basis for the GIST technique.

Bean, T. W., and F. Steenwyk. 1984. The effect of three forms of summarization on sixth graders' summary writing and comprehension. *Journal of Reading Behavior* 16:297–306. Study that demonstrated that GIST could improve students' comprehension and summary writing.

Brown, A. L., J. C. Campione, and J. D. Day. 1981. Learning to learn: On training students to learn from texts. *Educational Researcher* 10:14–21. Presents a discussion of how past research suggests reading comprehension abilities might be developed.

Cunningham, J. W. 1982. Generating interactions between schemata and text. In *New inquiries in reading research and instruction,* edited by J. A. Niles and L. A. Harris. Thirty-first Yearbook of the National Reading Conference. Washington, DC: National Reading Conference, 42–47. Describes a research study and represents the major source for information on the GIST procedures.

Day, J. D. 1980. *Teaching summarization skills: A comparison of training methods.* Unpublished doctoral diss., University of Illinois. This thesis has proved seminal to other studies of summarization and for purposes of guidelines for teaching reading comprehension.

Doctorow, M., C. Marks, and M. Wittrock. 1978. Generative processes in reading comprehen-sion. *Journal of Educational Psychology* 70:109–118. Represents an earlier study of summarization that served partly as justification for the procedure.

Dooling, D. J., and R. E. Christiansen. 1977. Levels of encoding and retention of prose. In *The psychology of learning and motivation,* edited by G. H. Bower. New York: Academic Press. Presents a theoretically oriented discussion of reading comprehension. Cited by Cunningham as influential in guiding the basis for developing the GIST technique.

Kintsch, W. 1977. On comprehending stories. In *Cognitive processes in comprehension,* edited by M. A. Just and P. A. Carpenter, Hillsdale, NJ: Erlbaum. Provides a discussion of the nature and role of summarization in reading comprehension.

Taylor, B., and S. Berkowitz. 1980. Facilitating children's comprehension of content material. In *Perspectives on reading research and instruction,* edited by M. L. Kamil and A. J. Moe. Twenty-ninth Yearbook of the National Reading Conference. Washington, DC: National Reading Conference. Represents an earlier study of summarization that Cunningham (1982) cites as contributing to the justification of his procedure.

Explicit Teaching of Reading Comprehension

Purpose

The Explicit Teaching of Reading Comprehension is intended as a framework for developing reading comprehension skills and strategies that can be applied to other reading situations without teacher support.

Rationale

In the late 1960s and early 1970s, developmental psychologists began to explore the possibility that reading comprehension and other problem-solving abilities were amenable to change with appropriate intervention. Subsequently, throughout the 1970s and early 1980s, several research studies were pursued in which deliberate and carefully planned attempts were made to explore the instructional characteristics of effective reading comprehension instruction. The question governing these pursuits was: Can students be made aware of reading comprehension strategies or be taught skills that will transfer to independent reading situations? What emerged as a response to this question and from these research pursuits was Explicit Teaching of Reading Comprehension. In other words, as researchers explored different procedures for teaching selected reading comprehension strategies and skills (e.g., summarizing, inferencing, self-questioning, relating background knowledge, finding the main idea and relevant details), several recommendations for instructions seemed forthcoming (Brown, Campione, and Day, 1981; Day, 1980; Gordon and Pearson, 1983; Hansen and Pearson, 1983; Palincsar and Brown, 1983). These have been pulled together and now are labeled by some educators "Explicit Teaching" (Pearson and Leys, 1984). The features that constitute Explicit teaching have been discussed in several papers (Brown, Campione, and Day, 1981; Tierney and Cunningham, 1984; Pearson and Gallagher, 1983; Pearson, 1984; Roehler and Duffy, 1984; and Tierney, 1982). The features include:

1. *Relevance:* students are made aware of the purpose of the skill or strategy—the why, when, how, and where of the strategy.
2. *Definition:* students are informed as to how to apply the skills by making public the skill or strategy, modeling its use, discussing its range of utility, and illustrating what it is not.
3. *Guided practice:* students are given feedback on their own use of the strategy or skill.
4. *Self-regulation:* students are given opportunities to try out the strategy for themselves and develop ways to monitor their own use of the strategy or skill.
5. *Gradual release of responsibility:* the teacher initially models and directs the students' learning; as the lesson progresses, the teacher gradually gives more responsibility to the student.
6. *Application:* students are given the opportunity to try their skills and strategies in independent learning situations, including nonschool tasks.

Intended Audience

Explicit Teaching is a generic plan for developing a wide range of strategies. It seems to be an appropriate framework for teaching students at all ages.

Description of the Procedure

During any Explicit Teaching lesson certain key elements will be present; others may be optional. For example, the following is based on those suggested by Pearson and Leys (1984) as an integral part of Explicit Teaching:

Step 1: Introduction to the skill or strategy through examples and review. Refer or expose the students to examples of the skill in the "real world," including the purpose for using the strategy.

Discuss how, when, where, and why the strategy or skills are used. If possible, contrast them with other skills; for example, contrast main idea with details, fact with opinion, good summaries with poor summaries. If the skill has been treated previously, review what they know about the skill.

Step 2 (optional): Have the children volunteer additional examples and discuss them.

Step 3: Label, define, model, and explain the skill or strategy. In this step, the skill or strategy is given a specific label and its application demonstrated with teacher modeling. As the teacher models, students are given guidelines by which they might use the skill or strategy and also examples of faulty strategy usage or skill application.

Step 4: Guided practice. In this step, examples are done together in order to prepare the students for independent practice and to determine who is incurring difficulty with the skill or strategy.

Step 5: Independent practice. The students work through the same type of exercise, but do so independently.

Step 6: Application. Students are given a variety of situations in which they are encouraged to apply the skill and discuss its application. This might entail applying the skill or strategy to other text or to situations outside of school.

What follows is an example of applying this lesson framework to comprehension skills. Specifically, it illustrates the Explicit Teaching of a main idea.

An Example of Explicit Teaching Applied to Main Idea

1. Introduction to the skill or strategy

In the first part of the lesson, examples are provided and the relevance of the strategy established. This can be done by relating what you are going to do to something with which the child has had experience. At the same time, the purpose for teaching the strategy is established.

Ask: "Have you ever had to give a brief description of something? Have you ever wondered what it would be like to give the news on the radio or television? Imagine it was your turn to give the news. Usually you have a few minutes to present in a nutshell the main idea and a few key facts. Now suppose you have been given lots of stories by your classmates. Your task is to present them, but before you do so, you need to isolate the main idea and most relevant details. What would you do?"

2. Labeling, modeling, defining, and explaining

In the next phase the teacher labels, models, defines, and explains the skill. Through teacher modeling and student discussion, the how, when, and where of the strategy is presented. Negative instances (i.e., demonstrations of faulty applications) are given, as well as clear examples of appropriate strategy or skill usage.

The teacher explains that they are going to learn more about how to find the main idea. Students read one of the stories for which the main idea needs to be established.

My name is Sally. I have four gerbils. One is pure white and two have brown spots. The fourth one is all black with a pink nose.

The teacher explains: "The story tells how many different and colorful gerbils Sally has. The reason I know this is the second sentence tells how many gerbils Sally has. The other sentences talk about not the size nor what they eat, but about the color of the gerbils. What is

3. Guided practice

In this step the teacher and students walk through an example together.

4. Independent practice

Students should be given the equivalent of a checklist by which they can not only guide their own use of the strategy but can also check whether they have succeeded.

5. Application

The next essential step is application. Your goal should be for the self-initiated and successful use of the strategy or skill without the teacher.

key in finding the main idea is finding out the most important ideas or facts stated about the topic. The main idea is: Sally has four colorful gerbils. Let's look at another story."

"Let's do the next story together. This is Juan's story. . . . "

The teacher directs the children to a third story. The teacher says: "Try one by yourself this time. Remember the main idea is what is important about the topic. Decide whether the main idea of Pam's story is about:

    Adela's home run
    Adela's best friend
    Adela's favorite sport

Before you make a final decision, ask yourself:

    Did you find the important ideas or facts?
    Did you decide what they were all about?
    Does your main idea cover all the ideas or facts? If not . . . choose another."

The teacher has children share their choice and explain. Other examples follow.

The teacher suggests: "Now try to do some on your own. Remember to use the self-help questions."

After checking these exercises, the teacher says: "Today we have learned about main idea. Can anybody think of where else one might use this skill? Let's see if it could help us with our social studies."

Children are encouraged to discuss how it might help in social studies and take out their social studies books to try it out. Other applications are discussed.

Cautions and Comments

As an approach to developing independent reading comprehension abilities, Explicit Teaching has a large number of advocates. In support of this approach are a number of research studies in which considerable success was achieved in teaching students selected skills and strategies. At a time when we were well aware of the shortcomings in our methods of teaching reading comprehension, Explicit Teaching seemed a timely solution for upgrading our practices. Furthermore, it was a commonsense approach. It represents what some educators who had looked at effective instruction had specified as key elements (e.g., Rosenshine, 1983).

Despite these qualities, Explicit Teaching should not be accepted without question. The results of experiments in which Explicit Teaching was used were not very well sustained beyond the course of the experiment; and evidence of the application of skills or strategies, either spontaneously or planned, was lacking. Unfortunately, no comparisons exist of Explicit Teaching with learning that is less teacher-centered and more collaborative or discovery-oriented. No data exist by which a determination can be made as to whether an Explicit Teaching procedure might take away from the tendency of some students to self-initiate their own learning strategies. For example, if the approach were more collaborative and less teacher-dependent, perhaps students would be more open to define and use a great many more strategies for themselves at times other than those tied to a teacher's plans.

Apart from these limitations, there are some other issues that stand in the way of the use of the Explicit Teaching model of teaching reading comprehension. Such a model assumes that there are well-defined strategies to teach. Unfortunately, a detailed description of comprehension strategies and skills that are worth teaching—that is, are likely to lead to improvements in comprehension performance—does not exist. The problems facing explicit teaching are compounded by problems in describing how readers actually do use some of the skills that might be taught.

References

Baumann, J. F. 1983. A generic comprehensive instructional strategy. *Reading World* 23:284–294. Presents a reading comprehension instruction based on Explicit Teaching notions.

———. 1988. Direct instruction reconsidered. *Journal of Reading* 31:712–729. Discusses when direct/explicit teaching is and is not appropriate.

Baumann, J. F., and M. C. Schmitt. 1986. The what, why, how and when of comprehension instruction. *The Reading Teacher* 39: 640–647. Discusses features integral to the use of Explicit Teaching.

Brown, A. L., J. D. Campione, and J. D. Day. 1981. Learning to learn: On training students to learn from texts. *Educational Researcher* 10:14–21. Discusses the research related to developing independent comprehension including ramifications for instruction.

Campione, J. 1981. *Learning academic achievement and instruction.* Paper delivered at the Second Annual Conference on Reading Research, New Orleans. Discussed the notion of gradual release of responsibility and other key notions of relevance to Explicit Teaching.

Day, J. D. 1980. *Teaching summarization skills: A comparison of training methods.* Unpublished doctoral diss., University of Illinois at Urbana-Champaign. Represents a research study in which Explicit Teaching practices were explored.

Durkin, D. 1978–79. What classroom observations reveal about reading comprehension instruction. *Reading Research Quarterly* 14:481–533. Presents a dismal picture of the teaching of reading comprehension in schools.

———. 1984. Do basal manuals teach reading comprehension? In *Learning to read in American schools,* edited by R. C. Anderson, J. Osborn, and R. J. Tierney. Hillsdale, NJ: Erlbaum. Discusses how basals have approached the teaching of reading comprehension.

Gordon, C., and P. D. Pearson. 1983. *The effects of instruction in metacomprehension and inferencing on children's comprehension abilities* (Tech. Rep. No. 277). Urbana: University of Illinois, Center for the Study of Reading. Presents a research study involving Explicit Teaching of reading comprehension.

Hansen, J., and P. D. Pearson. 1983. An instructional study: Improving the inferential comprehension of fourth grade good and poor readers. *Journal of Educational Psychology* 75:821–829. Describes the use of Explicit Teaching in conjunction with research on the influence of attempting to teach students to develop inferential comprehension strategies.

Kameenui, E. J., and P. Shannon. 1988. Point counterpoint: Direct instruction reconsidered. In *Dialogues in literacy research,* edited by J. E. Readence and R. S. Baldwin. Thirty-seventh Yearbook of the National Reading Conference. Chicago, IL: National Reading Conference. Debates the pros and cons of direct instruction.

Palincsar, A., and A. Brown. 1983. *Reciprocal teaching of comprehension monitoring activities* (Tech. Rep. No. 269). Urbana: University of Illinois, Center for the Study of Reading. Describes the use of Explicit Teaching in conjunction with having students take the teacher's role in their own learning.

Palincsar, A. S., Y. M. David, J. A. Winn, and D. D. Stevens. 1991. Examining the context of strategy instruction. *Remedial and Special Education* 12:43–53. A discussion of six models of strategy instruction, including Explicit Teaching.

Pearson, P. D. 1984. Direct explicit teaching of reading comprehension. In *Comprehension instruction,* edited by G. G. Duffy, L. R. Roehler, and J. Mason. New York: Longman. Discusses research and theory related to Explicit Teaching.

Pearson, P. D., and M. C. Gallagher. 1983. The instruction of reading comprehension. *Contemporary Educational Psychology* 8:317–344. Reviews the research on reading comprehension instruction and presents a model for teaching based upon the gradual release of responsibility.

Pearson, P. D., and M. Leys. 1984. Teaching comprehension. In *Reading, thinking and concept development: Strategies for the classroom,* edited by T. L. Harris and E. J. Cooper. New York: The College Board. Describes Explicit Teaching with examples.

Roehler, L. R., and G. G. Duffy. 1984. Direct explanation of comprehension processes. In *Comprehension instruction,* edited by G. Duffy, L. Roehler, and J. Mason. New York: Longman. Describes research attempting to make processes explicit.

Rosenshine, B. 1983. Functions of teaching. *Elementary School Journal* 83:355–351. Presents a framework for teaching based upon the research on effective schools.

Tierney, R. J. 1982. Learning from text. In *Secondary school reading,* edited by A. Berger and H. Alan Robinson. Newark, DE: International Reading Association. Presents an extended discussion (both pro and con) of Explicit Teaching.

Tierney, R. J., and J. Cunningham. 1984. Research on teaching reading comprehension. In *Handbook of reading research,* edited by P. D. Pearson. New York: Longman. Presents a comprehensive review of the research on teaching reading comprehension, including studies using Explicit Teaching.

Think-Alouds

Purpose

Think-Alouds are intended to help readers examine and develop reading behaviors and strategies.

Rationale

Think-Alouds have been used as a means of studying the cognitive processes that readers and writers use as they develop meanings (e.g., Olshavsky, 1976–77; Flower and Hayes,

1980). As an instructional procedure, however, Think-Alouds have rarely been used. Davey (1983) proposes that they might be used as a means of helping poor readers adopt a meaning orientation to print, monitor their comprehension, and apply self-correction strategies. With this in mind, Davey identifies five aspects of a skilled reader's thinking that studies have shown are frequently lacking among poor comprehenders (making predictions, visualizing, linking with prior knowledge, monitoring, and self-correction). Furthermore, she contends that recent work on self-monitoring and problem solving suggests that teachers can help students acquire theses skills through modeling by the teacher followed up by ample practice by the students. As she stated:

> The modeling process is founded on the belief that if teachers describe their own thoughts about a text (so that students can see a mind responding to a specific passage) the students will realize how and when to do the same. (1983, 45)

Such modeling is followed by practice, which includes the use of checklists "to stimulate student involvement and verify that readers were using this procedure" (P. 46).

Intended Audience

Think-Alouds can be used with school-age students at any level.

Description of the Procedures

Davey offers only broad guidelines for the use of Think-Alouds. She suggests four basic steps:

1. Teacher modeling
2. Student partnerships for practice
3. Independent student practice using checklists
4. Integrated use with other materials

1. Teacher Modeling   Initially, Davey suggests that teachers should select passages that "contain points of difficulty, contradictions, ambiguities, or unknown words" (P. 45). These materials are read aloud together with the use of Think-Alouds by the teacher (with students following along silently). As a guide for teachers she offers a number of examples of Think-Alouds:

a. *Making predictions or showing students how to develop hypotheses.*

"From the title I predict that this section will tell how airplane pilots adjust for winds."

"In this next part I think we'll find out what caused these plane crashes."

"I think this is a description of flight simulators."

b. *Describing your visual images.*

> "I have a picture of this man in my mind. He looks like a mild mannered, well-dressed business man."

> "I can see the horse kicking down the stable door as the flames come closer . . . I can feel the heat of the fire and pressure of the moment."

c. *Sharing an analogy or showing how prior knowledge applies.* Davey refers to this as the "like-a" step.

> "This is like a time when I was late for school and it began to thunderstorm."

d. *Verbalizing a confusing point or showing how you monitor developing under-standings.*

> "This seems to be confusing."

> "I am not sure how this fits in."

> "This is not what I expected."

e. *Demonstrating fix-up strategies.*

> "I need to check this out. I'll read ahead for a moment."

> "I need to think about this. Let me rethink what was happening."

> "Maybe I'll reread this."

> "Perhaps I better change my picture of what is happening."

In conjunction with teacher modeling, Davey suggests that teachers might encourage their students to add their own thoughts.

2. Student Partnerships for Practice After several modeling experiences, Davey suggests that students might work together with partners to practice Think-Alouds. Each student takes a turn reading and thinking aloud with short passages. The partner listens and offers his or her thoughts. Davey stresses that carefully developed materials should be used initially prior to moving to school materials of various types of lengths.

3. Independent Student Practice with Checklists After working with partners, Davey suggests that students should practice independently with the use of checklists to ensure student involvement and verify the use of procedures. (See the example in Figure 7–4.)

4. Integrated Use with Other Materials After initial experiences with modeling and Think-Alouds, Davey suggests that teachers need to give ample practice with school materials and integrate the use of Think-Alouds with other lessons and content reading. To this end, she suggests occasional demonstrations of how to read, and why and when to use certain strategies. For example, she suggests that the teacher might illustrate his or her thinking prior to reading a content book: "Before I read this, let me think about what this is like and try to get a feel for what this will be about. I'll look over the headings."

FIGURE 7–4. EXAMPLE OF A CHECKLIST

While I was reading, how did I do?

(Put an X in the appropriate column.)

	Not very much	*A little bit*	*Much of the time*	*All of the time*
Predicting				
Picturing				
"Like-a"				
Identifying problems				
Using fix-up				

Cautions and Comments

The use of think-alouds in conjunction with attempting to help students approach their reading strategically with a meaning orientation is long overdue, and Davey's proposal is worthwhile for offering a feasible framework. Her suggestions for guiding students to read more strategically are thoughtful and systematic. In particular, her list of five possible strategies may not be exhaustive, but it offers a starting point for both teachers and students. Furthermore, her suggestions for teaching modeling, student partnerships, the use of checklists, and help for students in integrating the use of Think-Alouds offer some structure to the approach.

Some limitations to the approach should be mentioned. First, apart from Davey's affidavits regarding the effectiveness of their use, little data exist on the long-term benefits of Think-Alouds. Davey, for example, stated that learners, with whom she used the strategy, became quite strategic and more positive about reading after three weeks of practicing Think-Alouds. Left unanswered is the extent to which any student gains are sustained and whether the Think-Alouds work with different students and texts. Second, Davey has assumed that students become more strategically oriented if teachers model and guide the use of Think-Alouds. Perhaps a different approach would work as well, if not better. For example, students might become more strategic if they discussed what they did and did not do before, during, and after reading. Perhaps they would gain from being viewed as a co-investigator rather than being expected to aspire to achieve a teacher's Think-Aloud behaviors. In addition, some students may need more concrete or supplemental guidelines to implement strategies effectively. Saying you will do or are doing something may or may not reflect the efficacy with which said strategy is used or the thinking underlying the use of a strategy.

A number of other educators have proposed similar procedures for making thinking explicit. Gordon (1985) has developed a Think-Aloud procedure that encourages students to integrate what they know with ideas they glean from the text. Duffy and Roehler (1987) have suggested a procedure (responsive elaboration) that reflects a more student-based approach. Smith and Dauer (1984) have developed procedures for using Think-Alouds in content reading situations. Paris, Cross and Lipson (1984) have emphasized group discussions about cognitive strategies that can improve reading using metaphors such as "Be a reading detective."

References

Baumann, J. F., L. A. Jones, and N. Seifert-Kessell. 1993. Using think alouds to enhance children's comprehension monitoring abilities. *The Reading Teacher* 47:184–193. Describes an instructional program using Think-Alouds to help fourth-graders monitor their comprehension.

Davey, B. 1983. Think-aloud—modelling the cognitive processes of reading comprehension. *Journal of Reading* 27:44–47. Presents a thorough description of the use of Think-Alouds.

Davey B., and S. M. Porter. 1982. Comprehension rating: A procedure to assist poor comprehenders. *Journal of Reading* 26:197–202. Describes attempts to have students rate their comprehension.

Duffy, G. G., and L. R. Roehler. 1987. Improving reading instruction through responsive elaboration. *The Reading Teacher* 40:514–515. Offers a detailed description of how teachers can guide students to make their thinking more explicit.

Flower, L., and J. Hayes. 1980. The dynamics of composing: Making plans and juggling constraints. In *Cognitive processes in writing,* edited by L. W. Gregg and E. R. Steinberg. Hillsdale, NJ: Erlbaum, 1–50. One of several articles describing the use of Think-Alouds as a research technique for studying writing processes.

Gordon, C. J. 1985. Modeling inference awareness across the curriculum. *Journal of Reading* 28:444–447. Discusses strategy that encourages students to integrate what they already know with text information in order to make inferences.

Olshavsky, J. 1976–77. Reading as problem-solving: An investigation of strategies. *Reading Research Quarterly* 12:654–674. Describes various Think-Aloud and introspective techniques to study reading processes.

Paris, S., D. R. Cross, and M. Y. Lipson. 1984. Informed strategies for learning: A program to improve children's reading awareness and comprehension. *Journal of Educational Psychology* 76:1239–1252. Reports a study directed at one use of metaphors to facilitate thinking about reading.

Smith, R. J., and V. L. Dauer. 1984. A comprehension-monitoring strategy for reading content area materials. *Journal of Reading* 28:144–147. Explores the use of Think-Alouds with content reading materials.

Induced Imagery   ■

Purpose

Induced Imagery is a procedure for guiding students to generate mental images (about what is read) as a means of enhancing comprehension.

Rationale

In 1984, Tierney and Cunningham concluded from their review of research on reading comprehension that there were "sufficient data for educators to be optimistic that imaging activity is effective" (P. 622). Since their review of the research, additional studies have provided still further support for the positive effects that either training in imaging or spontaneous imaging has upon comprehension (Gambrell and Bales 1984; Sadoski 1983, 1985).

Based upon Gambrell's own research and that of colleagues, Gambrell, Kapinus, and Wilson (1987) developed guidelines for how teachers might enhance the comprehension of readers through training in inducing images. Gambrell et al. cite two values for students' imaging or developing mental pictures. As they state:

> Mental images have two great values: they provide a framework for organizing and remembering information from text, and when students induce images, they expand more energy for integrating information across text. Benefits occur in both comprehension and recall. (1987, 639)

Gambrell's approach to teaching students to develop mental images is based upon teacher modeling followed by student practice. Her argument is that the progression from teacher-directed to student-directed learning is "essential for independence in comprehension" (Gambrell et al., 1987, 638).

Intended Audience

The strategy is appropriate for use with students of school age. It was especially developed for poorer students who may not spontaneously develop mental pictures.

Description of the Procedures

Gambrell et al. (1987) offer broad guidelines for helping students develop mental pictures. They suggest three basic steps:

1. Teacher modeling
2. Guided practice
3. Independent practice

1. Teacher Modeling   Teacher modeling is directed at what, why, and how. Gambrell et al. (1987) suggest this statement for introducing students to what mental imagery is: "Today we will concentrate on making mental images. Mental imagery is a reading strategy that helps you comprehend what you're reading." This is followed by an explanation of *why* mental imagery is useful. "Sometimes when we read we can make pictures in our minds about what we're reading. Making mental images—picturing the characters, picturing what is happening—can help us understand what we read, and it can also help us remember what we read" (P. 639–640).

To introduce students to how readers might evoke mental imagery, Gambrell et al. suggest that teachers offer demonstrations in response to passages that include descriptive detail, and be brief. For example, they suggest that teachers might distribute or place on an overhead a passage such as "The Collision."

> **The Collision**
> High Street was relatively busy on this dark and cool winter's night. There were a few pe-
> destrians out and a steady stream of cars. Suddenly, every pedestrian's attention turned to
> the road. A Pinto slammed on his brakes—its bright lights shining suddenly as the driver
> of the next car (a Maverick) hit its brakes. At first, nobody noticed that the brake lights of
> the Maverick did not shine. Instead they watched as an old BMW went slamming into the
> back of the Maverick which then slid into the Pinto.

The teacher might say, "I have a short passage called 'The Collision' that I'm going to read aloud to you. I'll try to make images in my head as I read. I'll describe how I use mental imagery to understand and remember what I read." The teacher would then read the selection and model his or her thinking.

> "The selection is entitled 'The Collision.' I can imagine a number of collisions; cars, peo-
> ple. As I read on about 'High Street,' 'pedestrians,' and 'a steady stream of cars' on this
> 'dark night,' I can picture a busy street with car lights and traffic. As I read on I can pic-
> ture the Pinto slamming its brakes followed by the Maverick. I can picture the 'brake
> lights' of the Pinto, followed by the 'dimness' of the Maverick. Then I can picture 'the old
> BMW' crashing into the rear of the Maverick. My picture now includes the drivers being
> jerked in their seat belts as glass shatters over the pavement."

The process of teaching the thinking-aloud, Gambrell et al. suggest, should conclude with a comment such as, "The images I make in my mind will help me understand what I've read about the collision."

2. Guided Practice   Gambrell et al. (1987) suggest that the teacher initiate guided practice with short passages, perhaps some teacher modeling of the first part of the passage(s), and discussion among the students of the nature of their images. The discussion of the nature of their images and the similarities and differences is intended to help students clarify and refine their use of imagery. With additional brief passages, the students are given "more responsibility for using mental imagery independently" (Gambrell et al., 1987, 640).

3. Independent Practice   In conjunction with helping students develop independence, Gambrell et al. (1987) offer three suggestions: (1) practice with additional texts that lend themselves to mental imagery; (2) encourage imagery use in other reading situations (for example, they suggest reminding students to use imagery while reading content area texts and during leisure reading); and (3) direct/guide students to use additional strategies (e.g., predicting, summarizing, self-questioning) to complement imaging or in those situations that do not lend themselves as readily to imaging.

Cautions and Comments

Inducing students to create mental images as they read represents an important goal. The images students create as they read help them tie together the ideas, contribute to the joy of reading, and mobilize predictions and understandings.

The proposal by Gambrell et al. includes several key features that are worthy of note. First, they emphasize that students should share and compare their images. It should be stressed that there may not be a single correct image, but students should expect to have some details that overlap. Second, Gambrell et al. stress helping students develop independence, including the ability to use images flexibly in various situations. They do not assume that students will transfer the ability to conjure up images without encouragement.

On the negative side, this proposal suffers from a few limitations. The authors' approach to having students develop images is very teacher-centered. Perhaps students could discuss images that they conjure spontaneously, rather than be overwhelmed by the teacher's mental pictures. Second, Gambrell et al. seem to assume that students can conjure up images if they hear about others doing so. Perhaps they need to be encouraged to do some other things en route to conjuring up images. It may be that predictions, identification with characters, and so on could help those students who do not generate images so spontaneously.

References

Alvermann, D. E., and J. Swafford. 1989. Do content area strategies have a research base? *Journal of Reading* 32:388–390. Discusses the research base associated with various strategies and practices.

Gambrell, L., and R. J. Bales. 1984. Mental imagery and the comprehension monitoring performance of fourth and fifth grade poor readers. *Reading Research Quarterly* 21:454–464. Reports a study in which fourth and fifth graders were trained to induce images.

Gambrell, L. B., and P. B. Jawitz. 1993. Mental imagery, text illustrations, and children's story comprehension and recall. *Reading Research Quarterly* 28:264–273. Study demonstrating that induced imagery, attention to illustrations, and the combination of the two improved children's comprehension and recall of stories.

Gambrell, L., B. A. Kapinus, and R. M. Wilson. 1987. Using mental imagery and summarization to achieve independence in comprehen-

sion. *Journal of Reading* 30:638–642. Describes guidelines for helping students become independent at using mental imagery.

Sadoski, M. 1983. An exploratory study of the relationships between reported imagery and the comprehension and recall of a story. *Reading Research Quarterly* 19:110–123. Reports a study in which students self-report images that are related to their comprehension.

———. 1985. The natural use of imagery in story comprehension and recall: Replication and extension. *Reading Research Quarterly* 20:858–867. Reports a study that replicates an earlier study looking at the relationship between student self-reports of images and comprehension.

Tierney, R. J., and J. Cunningham. 1984. Research on teaching reading comprehension. In *Handbook of Reading Research,* edited by P. D. Pearson. New York: Longman. Includes a discussion of research on inducing imagery.

Dialogical-Thinking Reading Lesson

Purpose

The Dialogical-Thinking Reading Lesson (D-TRL) was designed by Commeyras (1990, 1991, 1993) to promote critical thinking for elementary students during their reading instruction. The goal of the D-TRL is to engage students in reflection and critical thinking in order to get them to decide what they believe about a story-specific issue during basal reading instruction.

Rationale

Critical thinking plays a key role in developing a responsible citizenry. Commeyras (1993) believes that in order to cope with the information age and its complexity, including a deluge of conflicting, misleading, or erroneous information, students need to be prepared from an early age to think critically. The more emphasis that can be placed on thinking and reflection in reading instruction, the better prepared will be the next generation of citizens to think critically about moral, social, and political issues that may arise. Therefore, Commeyras developed the D-TRL as one means to promote careful thinking and "encourage students to (a) return to the text to verify or clarify information; (b) consider multiple interpretations; (c) identify reasons to support interpretations; and (d) evaluate the acceptability and relevance of competing or alternative interpretations." (P. 487)

In developing the D-TRL, Commeyras drew insight from work in dialogical thinking, the use of discussion in teaching, and social cognition. Citing Paul (1987), Commeyras defines dialogical thinking as the serious consideration of competing or alternative points of view for issues of significance. The D-TRL asks students to engage in dialogical thinking in trying to identify reasons to support alternative conclusions regarding a central story issue. In order to engage in dialogical thinking, Commeyras continues, discussion is required. In the D-TRL, discussion becomes the means for students to offer more than one point of view, react to other points of view, develop their understanding of the alternatives provided, and make judgments that are well informed. Finally, since dialogical thinking and discussion involve collaboration with others, aspects of social cognition come into play with the D-TRL as students' efforts to think critically are developed and guided by their interactions with their peers and the teacher.

Intended Audience

Commeyras (1990) developed the D-TRL for use in teaching sixth graders to critically think about basal stories. Further modification of the procedure occurred in 1991 in a research study with fifth-grade students who were labeled learning disabled. Thus, the D-TRL seems appropriate for most elementary students regardless of their learning capabilities.

Description of the Procedure

There are two basic phases for each D-TRL: (1) the reading phase, and (2) the discussion phase.

1. Reading Phase   Commeyras states that it is particularly important to select basal stories that lend themselves to a discussion of an issue that can be approached from more than one viewpoint and that students will find interesting or significant. Commeyras (1993) provides a listing of story titles and discussion questions appropriate for use with the D-TRL. To illustrate the use of the D-TRL the story entitled "Making Room for Uncle Joe," by A. B. Litchfield, was drawn from this listing.

"Making Room for Uncle Joe" is about a family, with three children, who must open their home to Joe, a Down's syndrome adult. Joe's special school has to close so the family, with some misgivings, has to take Joe in until new accommodations can be found. The story describes how the family tries to adjust to Joe and vice versa and the trials and tribulations involved. When a new apartment finally has been located for Joe to live in, everyone is sad that he has to leave. The family decides to invite Joe to stay permanently, and he happily accepts.

Commeyras recommends that the entire selection be read by the students on their own. With less able students who need help reading the story, she suggests a more guided approach wherein each page of the story is read and then shared. Follow-up discussions during this phase are informal, with the goal being simply to reconstruct the story line. Commeyras mentions that regardless of students' ability levels the reading phase should be conducted in such a way as to ensure that all students comprehend the story well enough to participate in the discussion phase that follows.

2. Discussion Phase   This phase of the lesson consumes the most time, as Commeyras considers it conceptually the most important part of the D-TRL. The components involved in the discussion phase are: (a) central question, (b) identifying reasons, (c) evaluating reasons, and (d) drawing conclusions. It is suggested that the chalkboard be organized according to these basic components before the discussion phase of the D-TRL begins. Thus, the board might look like the following:

CENTRAL QUESTION

Support	Truth	Side A	Side B	Truth	Support

a. *Central question.* The discussion phase begins with the teacher introducing the central question and the two hypothesized conclusions. In the case of our example story, Commeyras recommends that the central question be: "What should Uncle Joe do?" The conclusions to be discussed would be: (A) "Uncle Joe should stay with the family," and (B) "Uncle Joe should move to the apartment." These are written on the board for students to see.

Based upon their understanding of the story, students are asked if they have a preference for either conclusion. Commeyras contends that multiple purposes are served by asking students to take a position before identifying reasons of support for either conclusion. First, it creates initial involvement for students, as they must consider whether or not they actually have a position on the issue. Additionally, it allows the teacher to assess the initial positions of the students for later comparison to their conclusions at the end of the lesson. It also allows the teacher to judge the extent to which individual students might be willing to alter their position in the face of new evidence or to hold back their consideration when there is insufficient evidence. Commeyras views these as two important critical thinking dispositions.

b. *Identifying reasons.* In this step of the procedure students are asked to explore in depth each hypothesized conclusion by identifying reasons of support for each. Thus, in our example students would be asked to identify reasons to support why Uncle Joe should stay with the family as well as reasons to support why Uncle Joe should move to the apartment. The following are some reasons students might identify:

Side A: Uncle Joe should stay with the family.

1. The family loves Uncle Joe.
2. Uncle Joe cannot take care of himself.
3. It would be best to be around normal people.

Side B: Uncle Joe should move to the apartment.

1. Uncle Joe can take care of himself.
2. It is best that Uncle Joe be with people like himself.
3. He will always be considered to be different from anyone else because he is retarded.

The students' reasons are written on the board regardless of whether they seem wrong, do not make sense, or may be contradictory. Since students will be asked at a later time to evaluate the truth and relevance of each reason, it is important to accept all reasons at this time. Having the teacher make judgments at this point will deny students the opportunity to examine their own thinking as well as stifle discussion. Commeyras also cautions that the teacher may need to engage in rephrasings and questions with students who need help in identifying and/or articulating their reasons. Additionally, as the discussion leader, the teacher must be judicious and ready to relinquish control over the discussion when it becomes lively and students demonstrate the ability to keep interacting with one another. In the case of our example this could easily happen as students discuss the pros and cons of having Down's syndrome and one's ability to function in the real world or the stereotypes people hold about mental retardation.

c. *Evaluating reasons.* After reasons are identified for each position and listed on the board, the students need to evaluate them in terms of their truth and their relevance. Commeyras advises that a code be used to indicate on the board the students' decision about whether a reason could be true (T), false (F), or depends (D). Since a reason must also be relevant as well as true, students should indicate this, using a (Y) to indicate the reason is relevant or (N) if it is not.

Applying the criteria of truth and relevance to each reason will not always lead to clear-cut answers and consensus, but teachers are advised that what matters in doing this is that only verifiable information be used as the basis for a decision. Some reasons can be verified with the text information while others may be done with prior knowledge or logic. Once a reason has been verified as true, then the students need to judge how strong the support is for a particular conclusion. In this way students are engaged in critically thinking about what is important in making informed decisions about what they believe.

With our example, each reason might not be considered to be true. For instance, in the case of whether or not Uncle Joe can take care of himself, it depends—with some things he might be able to; with others he might not. Further, that Uncle Joe is different due to his retardation might be true, but it may not necessarily be relevant to concluding that he should move to an apartment.

d. *Drawing conclusions.* Commeyras recommends that to culminate this lesson every student be given an opportunity to state what she or he believes about the central question, given all the thinking and discussion that preceded it. At the same point, some students may still withhold judgment because they have not made up their minds. This is an appropriate option for those students not ready to draw a final conclusion. She suggests that a viable alternative to discussing final conclusions would be to write about them and share them at a later time.

Cautions and Comments

There is no doubt that the Dialogical-Thinking Reading Lesson is teacher-dominated and teacher-controlled. Commeyras acknowledges this but offers alternatives once students understand the structure and intent of the lesson. To shift more responsibility to the students for their own learning, students could become involved in selecting stories, questions, and/or conclusions. As an interim step, teachers might have students work in small groups to evaluate the reasons for one side of a central question and present these to the whole class. Once they are able to do this, then they might be given a story and asked to generate the conclusions that could be drawn from it. On the other hand, it can also be argued that even if the agenda has been previously set, the astute teacher will probably accept alternative conclusions introduced by students as long as they are viable.

Other suggestions for using the D-TRL include using it with younger students by simplifying the task. For instance, Commeyras suggests that with first or second graders the teacher might concentrate on just identifying reasons rather than evaluating them, until such time that the students are able to generate alternative reasons on their own. The D-TRL might also be coupled with other instructional strategies. It would seem that other strategies in this unit like ReQuest and the Anticipation Guide would be appropriate lead-ins to the discussion phase of this lesson. Likewise, the discussion strategies of the previous unit are useful with the D-TRL. From a topical standpoint, it can also be pointed out that stories dealing with a multicultural emphasis would be most appropriate for use with this technique, as the D-TRL allows for an in-depth discussion of varying viewpoints.

References

Commeryas, M. 1990. Analyzing a critical-thinking reading lesson. *Teaching and Teacher Education* 6:201–214. Description of a critical-thinking reading lesson that provided the foundation for the D-TRL.

———. 1991. *Dialogical-thinking reading lessons: Promoting critical thinking among "learning-disabled" students.* Unpublished doctoral diss., University of Illinois, Champaign. Research that formed the basis for the D-TRL.

———. 1993. Promoting critical thinking through dialogical-thinking reading lessons. *The Reading Teacher* 46:486–494. The description of the steps involved in the D-TRL.

Paul, R. W. 1987. Dialogical thinking: Critical thought essential to the acquisition of rational knowledge and passions. In *Teaching Thinking Skills: Theory and Practice,* edited by J. B. Baron and R. J. Sternberg. New York: W. H. Freeman. Discussion of the role of dialogical thinking in teaching.

Inquiry Chart

Purpose

The purpose of the Inquiry Chart, also known as the I-Chart (Hoffman, 1992), is to provide a systematic procedure for nurturing critical thinking in the classroom. By using a chart of guiding questions and information gained from multiple sources of information, the I-Chart gives students the opportunity to study a topic in depth and from potentially differing points of view.

Rationale

Critical thinking has received considerable attention in recent years, probably due in large share to a backlash on teaching the *basics.* Hoffman states that "the results of tests [are] showing that students can do the basics but they are woefully inadequate when asked to think" (P. 122). Hoffman believes that critical thinking skills are learned and that, with good instruction, these skills can be acquired successfully by all students.

Feeling that a reading of any single text to students, regardless of its point of view, only encourages those students to accept arguments in print without question, Hoffman developed the I-Chart as a means for students to examine multiple sources of information for points of consistency/inconsistency and, therefore, provide a rich context for nurturing the skills of critical thinking. Hoffman credits the development of the I-Chart to previous work by Ogle (1986) on K-W-L (see Unit 10: Studying) and McKenzie (1979) on helping students organize reports.

The I-Chart uses a data chart that has students record what they already know about a topic, what they want to learn about it, and a summary of what they did learn from their readings. The I-Chart allows students to gather this information from multiple text sources and organize it on the chart for summarization, comparison, and evaluation.

Intended Audience

Although Hoffman specified no grade level for which the I-Chart was to be used, it seems that this strategy would be appropriate for older students in the upper elementary grades and higher. I-Charts seem to be best used with expository-type material (e.g., history, science) where alternative points of view could be explored.

Description of the Procedure

Hoffman describes the I-Chart strategy as being organized around three phases: (1) planning, (2) interacting, and (3) integrating and evaluating.

1. Planning Phase   The planning phase consists of those activities that teachers engage in before working with the students. Typically these activities involve topic identification, question formation, I-Chart construction, and materials collection.

    a. *Topic identification.* The topic to be used with the I-Chart procedure is identified by the teacher and may be based on the curriculum, the textbook, and/or student interests. For purposes of illustration, our I-Chart topic will be mammals. As Hoffman has indicated, the topic might be almost anything, such as Christopher Columbus, dinosaurs, the Civil War, rocks and fossils, American Presidents, or Adolf Hitler.

    b. *Question formation.* In this step of the procedure the teacher identifies two to four questions of significance that will drive the inquiry process using the I-Chart. Hoffman suggests that for the initial uses of the I-Chart, teachers might use the class textbook and identify the most important ideas that are presented and cast them in the form of questions. To continue with our example topic, the following questions might be identified: (1) What defines a mammal as distinct from other animals? (2) In what ways are mammals alike? (3) In what ways are mammals different? (4) How are mammals grouped?

    c. *I-Chart construction.* The I-Chart is constructed and displayed with the name of the topic and the guiding questions recorded in the top row. It should be large enough (e.g., newsprint, butcher paper) for everyone to see. The structure of the I-Chart is given in Figure 7–5. As the study of the topic progresses, the remaining parts of the I-Chart are filled in.

    d. *Materials collection.* The final part of the planning phase is the collection of the materials dealing with the topic. The sources should include the class textbook as

FIGURE 7–5. STRUCTURE OF THE I-CHART

GUIDING QUESTIONS

	TOPIC	1.	2.	3.	4.	Interesting Facts and Figures	New Questions
SOURCES	WHAT WE KNOW						
	1.						
	2.						
	3.						
	SUMMARY						

well as other texts, trade books, encyclopedias, and CD–ROM, among others. When the particular source is used in instruction, Hoffman suggests that the bibliographic information be recorded in the left column of the I-Chart, under Sources.

2. Interacting Phase   The interacting phase of the I-Chart procedure involves those activities in which the teacher and the students work directly, using the students' prior knowledge and the source materials to begin filling out the I-Chart. This phase consists of the exploration of prior knowledge and beliefs, the sharing of interesting facts and new questions, and reading and recording.

    a. *Exploration of prior knowledge and beliefs.* In the initial part of this phase the teacher interacts with the students to probe what prior knowledge they may have related to how the students might respond to each of the guiding questions. The information is recorded on the I-Chart in the row labeled "What We Know" under the appropriate question. This information is recorded regardless of whether it is accurate or is contradictory. In our example of mammals, students might list defining characteristics as "having hair" and "can't fly." Mammals might be alike because "they all have skeletons." They might be different because "only man has hands and legs." Finally, mammals might be grouped by "size."

    b. *Sharing of interesting facts and new questions.* In the last two columns of the "What We Know" row, the teacher should record other information, unrelated to the guiding questions, volunteered by the students. Under the "Interesting Facts" column other information from students' prior knowledge should be written. For instance, students might offer that "both men and kangaroos are mammals." Under the "New Questions" column the teacher should record any question the students may have that is different from the listed questions.

    c. *Reading and recording.* The final step of the interacting phase involves the reading of the various sources collected previously by the teacher and the recording of students' responses from these sources to the questions listed. The amount of time taken in this step will vary from days to weeks depending on many factors including the number of sources and guiding questions. With multiple copies of a source, the teacher could have the students do either independent or guided reading; with single copies of a source, the teacher might choose to read it aloud. Following the reading and discussion of each source, the teacher records any information from each that will answer the questions posed on the I-Chart. Hoffman points out that the recording should be as accurate as possible, even to the point of quoting the material. Any interesting facts and new questions derived from the reading should also be added at this time; with subsequent readings the teacher asks the students to look back at the new questions listed to see if any answers or important insights are forthcoming. It is to be remembered that the eventual size of the I-Chart will be based on the number of sources as well as the number of questions; therefore, the structure given in Figure 7–5 will vary with the I-Chart topic.

3. Interacting and Evaluating Phase This final phase entails the completion of the I-Chart and sharing of the findings. The steps consist of summarizing, comparing, researching, and reporting.

    a. *Summarizing.* The students are asked to generate summary statements for each of the guiding questions as well as the interesting facts column. They are asked to use all of the information recorded on the I-Chart and synthesize it into a cohesive answer to each question. This will require students to move beyond the facts stated and to account for converging as well as conflicting information in making their summaries. The summaries are recorded in the bottom row of the I-Chart.

b. *Comparing.* In this step students are asked to compare the information gained from individual sources and their summaries with their prior knowledge and beliefs. Students should examine new information gained as well as reconcile any misconceptions. In examining the prior knowledge recorded from our example of mammals, students would need to correct their beliefs regarding the characteristics of mammals, how they are different, and how they are grouped.

c. *Researching.* As students continue their research process, new questions accumulate on the I-Chart. It is here that questions that are still unanswered are identified and become the basis for individual or small group research. Students are directed to continue the research process to find answers to these questions.

d. *Reporting.* In this final step of the procedure students report back to the whole class their findings concerning the unanswered questions identified in the previous step.

Cautions and Comments

Hoffman concedes that his description of the I-Chart procedure is one in which the teacher assumes "a fairly directive/controlling role" (P. 125). However, he states that this must be the case in introducing the procedure to students. Once students are familiar with how to be flexible in using text to support their learning, the goal is to gradually yield responsibility for controlling the inquiry process to the students. In fact, he mentions a number of procedural variations to encourage independent learning by students that teachers might consider once the basic steps of the strategy are known. These include letting the students: (1) identify the topic; (2) generate the questions to be researched; (3) identify the sources to be investigated; and, (4) decide the information to be recorded on the I-Chart.

Other suggestions include the use of cooperative learning strategies (see Unit 6: Discussion and Cooperative Learning) in lieu of whole-group procedures. Eventually, the I-Chart could become the basis for independent inquiry. Once students have been successful using the strategy on a whole-group and small-group basis, they might be given a blank I-Chart and asked to work through the inquiry process themselves from beginning to end. Finally, Hoffman feels that the summary statements at the bottom of the I-Chart can become the basic structure for students to expand them into paragraphs and, in turn, for the paragraphs to become the basis for complete written reports. Thus, he sees value in the strategy as a tool for helping students learn to prepare formal reports.

One caution to keep in mind when using the I-Chart procedure is that some students may experience difficulty in synthesizing information into summaries. This is a complex process akin to developing main ideas from supporting details, a process many students will find arduous. Teachers may need to move slowly with this part of the procedure, as it is central to its overall success.

Finally, teachers may find that the I-Chart can be useful in dealing with multicultural issues in the classroom. The in-depth study and its use of multiple sources seem to make this strategy ideal for exploring such topics.

References

Hoffman, J. V. 1992. Critical reading/thinking across the curriculum: Using I-Charts to support learning. *Language Arts* 69:121–127. Describes the rationale and steps for developing and using the I-Chart.

McKenzie, G. 1979. Data charts: A crutch for helping pupils organize reports. *Language Arts* 56:784–788. Article on helping students organize reports, the basis of part of the I-Chart procedure.

Ogle, D. M. 1986. K-W-L: A teaching model that develops active reading of expository text. *The Reading Teacher* 39:564–570. Another article that formed part of the basis for I-Charts.

Meaning
Vocabulary
Strategies

UNIT OVERVIEW

Without a doubt there exists a strong relationship between vocabulary knowledge and reading comprehension. Anderson and Freebody (1985) hypothesized in conjunction with an extensive review of research: "Word knowledge is a requisite for reading comprehension: people who do not know the meanings of words are most probably poor readers" (P. 367). Conversely, it is often presumed that if students are introduced to relevant vocabulary as they encounter it in text, their ability to construct meaning from text will be enhanced.

Though there is no doubt that much experience with natural language will enhance vocabulary development (Anderson & Nagy, 1991), our rationale is that teachers who have access to a repertoire of strategies that will introduce and reinforce relevant vocabulary words are in a better position to help students learn and retain words. Thus, seven strategies are described in this unit that teachers can use in various aspects of the instructional lesson to promote students' vocabulary development.

Possible Sentences.   Possible Sentences is designed to help students determine the meanings of unknown words by pairing them with known words in sentences they think might "possibly" be found in a text. Thus, the strategy enables students to predict word meanings and verify their accuracy as they read.

List-Group-Label.   Based upon a strategy originally developed by Taba, List-Group-Label asks students to free-associate terms related to a stimulus topic, and then to group and label these terms. Thus, the strategy serves as a means to activate students' prior knowledge about related concepts or to review concepts gleaned from reading.

Contextual Redefinition.   Contextual Redefinition is designed to enable students to use context to make an informed guess about a word's meaning. In addition, it attempts to provide students with a strategy for using context in independent reading situations.

Feature Analysis.   Feature Analysis is an attempt to expand and refine students' vocabulary and related concepts after they read. In essence, it uses categorization as a systematic means to reinforce word meaning.

℮   *Word Map.*   The Word Map provides a framework for developing students' understanding of concepts, including the hierarchical structure of these concepts and their attributes.

Vocabulary Self-Collection Strategy.   The Vocabulary Self-Collection Strategy is designed to promote growth in either students' general or content area word knowledge. It is based on their prior experiences and encourages independent vocabulary development.

Levin's Keyword Method.   The Keyword Method is a mnemonic strategy in which the student devises a keyword, which looks or sounds like the original word to be learned, to associate new information with a mental image to aid in later recall of the target word.

References

Anderson, R. C., and P. Freebody. 1985. Vocabulary knowledge. In *Theoretical models and processes of reading,* 3rd ed., edited by H. Singer and R. B. Ruddell. Newark, DE: International Reading Association, 343–371.

Barr, R., M. L. Kamil, P. Mosenthal, and P. D. Pearson, eds. 1991. *Handbook of reading research: Volume II.* New York: Longman. Chapters by Anderson and Nagy (690–724) and Beck and McKeown (789–814) explore the research literature on word meanings and vocabulary acquisition.

Flood, J., J. M. Jensen, D. Lapp, and J. R. Squire, eds. 1991. *Handbook of research on teaching the English language arts.* New York: Macmillan. The chapter by Mason, Herman, and Au (721–731) explores children's developing knowledge of words.

Possible Sentences

Purpose

Possible Sentences (Moore and Moore, 1986) is designed to help students to (1) learn new vocabulary to be encountered in a reading assignment; (2) make predictions about sentences to be found in their reading; (3) provide purpose for reading; and (4) arouse their curiosity concerning the text to be read.

Rationale

Possible Sentences was designed as a means to enable students to determine independently the meanings and relationships of unfamiliar words in text reading assignments. Students make predictions about the relationships between the unknown words, read to verify the accuracy of the predicted relationships, and use the text to evaluate and refine their predictions. Thus, prediction is used to create interest and to focus students' attention on the meanings and concepts to be acquired.

Intended Audience

Moore and Moore (1986) specified that Possible Sentences could be used whenever students encounter unfamiliar vocabulary during reading assignments in subject matter classrooms. Therefore, it is implied that Possible Sentences can be used with middle and secondary students in content areas. However, the strategy is probably appropriate for all levels of students reading and learning from expository text.

Description of the Procedures

Possible Sentences is a five-part lesson and consists of the following steps:

1. List key vocabulary
2. Elicit sentences
3. Read and verify sentences
4. Evaluate sentences
5. Generate new sentences

1. *List Key Vocabulary*   To begin a Possible Sentences lesson, the teacher lists the essential vocabulary of a text selection on the board and pronounces the words for the students. The teacher has determined beforehand that the words are central to the major concepts to be encountered in the text and that they can be adequately defined by their content. For instance, from a text on skin disorders, the following terms might be listed:

Skin Disorders	
moles	warts
acne	freckles
boils	athlete's foot
virus	infection
fungus	congenital

2. *Elicit Sentences*   Students are then asked to use at least two words from the list and make a sentence, one they think might possibly be in the text. The sentences are recorded, one at a time, on the board, and the words used from the list should be underlined. It is important that the sentences be recorded exactly as given, even if students provide incorrect information. This is necessary for the evaluation phase that follows. Students may use words already in previous sentences as long as a new context is created. Continue eliciting sentences until students can produce no more or until a specified length of time has elapsed. However, encourage students to use every word from the list at least once.

   Below are some possible sentences students might offer with the list of words related to skin disorders:

1. Warts are caused by an infection.
2. Moles can be a congenital infection.

3. You shouldn't squeeze boils or acne.

4. Moles and freckles are harmless.

5. Either fungus or a virus causes athlete's foot.

3. *Read and Verify Sentences*   Students are asked to read the text to check the accuracy of the sentences generated.

4. *Evaluate Sentences*   With the text available for reference, a discussion ensues as each sentence is evaluated. Sentences that are not accurate are either omitted or refined, according to what the text states. The discussion of the sentences calls for careful reading, since judgments as to the accuracy of sentences must be defined by students.

Examining the possible sentences related to skin disorders, sentence 3 is accurate as it stands. Sentence 1 will have to be redefined. Warts are not caused by infections; they are viral in nature. Sentence 2 also needs refinement. Moles can be congenital, but they are not infections. Sentence 4 is technically correct; however, it is more accurate to state that "Moles and freckles are harmless unless irritated." Finally, sentence 5 needs to be modified to state that athlete's foot is caused by a fungal infection.

5. *Generate New Sentences*   After the original sentences have been evaluated, the teacher asks for additional sentences. This step is taken to further extend students' understanding of the meanings and relationships of the vocabulary terms. As new sentences are generated, they are checked against the text for accuracy. All final sentences should be recorded in their notebooks by the students.

Cautions and Comments

Possible Sentences is a structured language activity that requires students both to recognize the contextual setting of words and to produce their own contextual settings. However, there are some concerns that teachers need to be aware of before implementing a Possible Sentences lesson. Care needs to be taken to ensure that vocabulary can be defined by the context. Authors do not always provide explicit contexts in their writing, and this strategy requires that the context be one in which the meaning of a word is at least directly implied. In addition, the choice of vocabulary terms needs to be considered to conduct a successful lesson. If only unfamiliar words are chosen from a text, students will have difficulty generating sentences. Particularly with passages of a highly technical nature, it is essential also to list some words that will be familiar to students. Otherwise, students will not be able to use their prior knowledge to make connections between what they know and the unfamiliar words they are to learn. Finally, if too many technical words are found in a text or if an absence of defining contexts is noted, then it may behoove the teacher to choose a different strategy or, even more appropriately, a different text.

Possible Sentences provides students an opportunity to use all language processes as they learn new word meanings. Using their prior knowledge, students are asked to make connections between new and known vocabulary words and evaluate them. Students use speaking to express these connections; they use listening to hear other students' ideas and connections. They read to verify the possible sentences generated, and the refined versions are written in their notebooks. Thus, students become actively involved in their new learning.

There is an additional benefit in using Possible Sentences. Teachers are able to assess what knowledge students bring to the learning task, how they rectify their misconceptions about a topic, and whether or not students have actually learned the word meanings and their related concepts.

References

Moore, D. W., and S. A. Moore. 1986. Possible sentences. In *Reading in the content areas: Improving classroom instruction,* 2nd ed., edited by E. K. Dishner, T. W. Bean, J. E. Readence, and D. W. Moore. Dubuque, IA: Kendall/Hunt, 174–179. Describes the rationale, procedures, and suggestions for using Possible Sentences.

Moore, D. W., and S. A. Moore. 1992. Possible sentences: An update. In *Reading in the content areas: Improving classroom instruction,* 3rd ed., edited by E. K. Dishner, T. W. Bean, J. E. Readence, and D. W. Moore. Dubuque, IA: Kendall/Hunt, 196–202. A refinement and update of the Possible Sentences strategy.

Stahl, S. A., and B. A. Kapinus. 1991. Possible sentences: Predicting word meanings to teach content area vocabulary. *The Reading Teacher* 45:36–43. Research study validating Possible Sentences as an effective means to teach vocabulary and foster recall.

List-Group-Label

Purpose

List-Group-Label (Taba 1967), also called semantic mapping (Johnson and Pearson, 1978, 1984), is designed to encourage students to (1) improve their vocabulary and categorization skills; (2) organize their verbal concepts; and (3) aid them in remembering and reinforcing new vocabulary.

Rationale

The List-Group-Label (LGL) lesson was originally conceived by Taba as a means to help students deal with the technical vocabulary in science and social studies classes. It is based on the notion that categorizing words can help students organize new concepts and experiences in relation to previously learned concepts. In essence, LGL attempts to improve upon the way in which students learn and remember new concepts.

Intended Audience

List-Group-Label was originally used by Taba with elementary school students. However, the strategy seems appropriate for students at all grade levels.

Description of the Procedures

List-Group-Label is an easy-to-implement three-part strategy that uses (1) listing, (2) grouping/labeling, and (3) follow-up.

1. *Listing* The teacher begins the LGL lesson by selecting a one- or two-word topic to serve as a stimulus for listing words. Using a chalkboard, an overhead transparency, or any other means appropriate for recording students' responses, the stimulus topic is written at the top of the board or paper. Topics should be drawn from the materials that students are reading and from which they are learning. For example, if students are about to start a unit on volcanoes, volcanoes might be used as the topic to begin an LGL lesson. On the other hand, almost any topic of which the students have some prior knowledge might be suitable.

Students are asked to brainstorm related to the topic, i.e., to think of any word or expression related to the topic. Using our volcano example, the teacher might say, "Think of any word or words that reminds you of the topic 'volcano.' " Responses are recorded, and the teacher should accept all word associations given by the students, unless the response cannot be justified by the student.

The list of words should be kept manageable. Depending on the topic itself and the grade level of the students, approximately 25 responses should be adequate. When most children have had an opportunity to offer a response, the listing portion of the lesson can be terminated by stating, "I'll take only two more words." Below is a list of responses students might generate using volcano as a stimulus topic:

	Volcano	
lava	Mt. St. Helens	eruption
explosion	ash	rocks
destruction	magma	Pompeii
fire	death	earthquake
dust	smoke	heat
Krakatoa	cinders	molten

2. *Grouping/Labeling* To begin this portion of the lesson, the teacher should read the list orally, pointing to each word as it is pronounced. For older students this step may not be necessary, but it is cautioned that even older readers, particularly those of lesser ability, may benefit from it. The students are then instructed to make smaller lists of words related to (in this case) the topic of volcanoes, using only words from the large list that the class generated. These smaller groupings should consist of words that have something in common with one another; and each grouping should have at least three words in them. Words from the large list may be used in more than one smaller group, as long as the groupings are different. Students are also told they must give their group of words a label or title that indicates the shared relationship they possess.

3. *Follow-up* Using another part of the chalkboard or piece of paper, the teacher solicits and records categories of words and their labels from the students, one grouping at a time. After a category is recorded, the student offering the group must state verbally why the words have been categorized in the particular way stated. In this way, all students can see category possibilities that may not have occurred to them.

The following are possible groupings that may be generated from the large list of volcano words:

1. lava, ash, rocks, dust, smoke = things emitted from a volcano
2. Mt. St. Helens, Krakatoa, Pompeii = famous volcanoes
3. explosion, destruction, death, earthquake = results of a volcanic eruption
4. lava, fire, cinders, molten, magma = hot volcanic parts

Cautions and Comments

Perhaps the most beneficial aspects of List-Group-Label are the modeling and sharing that are built into the strategy. It is through this sharing that students are exposed to ideas and concepts that may be beyond their experiential background and, thus, enable learning to occur. Therefore, it is most important that modeling and sharing be emphasized as part of the lesson.

Modeling may also occur as part of the instruction that the teacher provides. For younger or poorer students for whom categorization might prove to be a problem, the teacher should "walk" students through the "how" and "why" of LGL. This might include: (1) constructing the first category and providing a title for it to show students the process of categorization; (2) providing an initial list of words for students to group and label; (3) making the categories yourself and having students label them; and (4) providing the labels and having students find words to fit the category.

Other suggestions for using List-Group-Label include the use of small groups of students to categorize and label rather than just having individual students accomplish this task on their own. This increases the interaction and sharing among individuals, as well as streamlining the whole group discussion that follows groupings and labeling; i.e., instead of individuals reporting their groupings, only a spokesperson for each small group does the talking. For younger students or groups of students, LGL may also be personalized by recording the individual's or group's name by the category that has been offered.

It must also be mentioned that LGL is based on the notion that some prior knowledge is essential for the lesson to be successful. If a teacher assumes prior knowledge on the part of students where little or none exists, LGL stands little chance for success. For instance, using volcano as a stimulus topic for students who are too young will probably result in very few word associations being given. Similarly, using an unfamiliar topic such as "parts of the brain," even with older students, will usually result in failure, too.

Obviously, prior knowledge plays much less of a role in LGL if the strategy is used as a means of reinforcement in the postreading portion of an instructional lesson. In such a case, knowledge gained from the text is going to take precedence over prior knowledge.

Therefore, LGL can be an excellent strategy for review purposes, even if the topic was originally unfamiliar. Indeed, Bean, Inabinette, and Ryan (1983) found that high school subjects produced significantly higher vocabulary retention scores when LGL was used as a postreading review strategy.

Other problems that may occur with LGL involve aspects of categorization. It is cautioned that semantic, meaning-oriented groupings be emphasized rather than those that focus on surface commonalities of words chosen for a grouping. For example, the following category is perfectly legitimate, though not what is called for in LGL.

explosion, destruction, eruption = three syllable words

If such a category should occur, teachers are cautioned that they must accept the category but point out that meaningful, rather than surface, associations are desired. Another categorization problem that might occur is the propensity of some students to try to make the largest grouping they possibly can. This can be dealt with by simply limiting the number of words that may be used in one group to five or, at the most, to seven words. Finally, some words defy classification. To deal with this, Readence and Searfoss (1986) suggested creating a "misfit" list of all those words that do not fit a category. Exploring why certain words do not fit a category can also prove instructionally beneficial for students.

As a closing note, the diagnostic value of LGL should be mentioned. In a prereading situation, teachers can find out what it is that students know and what it is that will require teacher instruction. In a postreading situation, teachers can find out what students have learned and what will require reteaching. Finally, as a straight vocabulary development lesson, teachers can find a source of words from students' experiences that might require clarification.

References

Bean, T. W., N. B. Inabinette, and R. Ryan. 1983. The effect of a categorization strategy on secondary students' retention of literacy vocabulary. *Reading Psychology* 4:247–252. Research study that reports positive effects for the use of List-Group-Label as a postreading strategy.

Heimlich, J. E., and S. D. Pittelman. 1986. *Semantic mapping: Classroom applications.* Newark, DE: International Reading Association. A monograph devoted exclusively to the use of List-Group-Label in the classroom.

Johnson, D. D., and P. D. Pearson. 1978, 1984. *Teaching reading vocabulary.* New York: Holt, Rinehart and Winston. A text that explores vocabulary development in general and List-Group-Label in particular.

Readence, J. E., and L. W. Searfoss. 1986. Teaching strategies for vocabulary development. In *Reading in the content areas: Improving classroom instruction.* 2nd ed., edited by E. K. Dishner, T. W. Bean, J. E. Readence, and D. W. Moore. Dubuque, IA: Kendall/Hunt, 183–188. Discusses the use of categorization in general and List-Group-Label in particular as a means to develop vocabulary.

Taba, H. 1967. *Teacher's handbook for elementary social studies.* Reading, MA: Addison-Wesley. Describes the original uses of the List-Group-Label strategy.

Contextual Redefinition

Purpose

Contextual redefinition (Readence, Bean, and Baldwin 1995) is designed to help students: (1) use context to unlock the meaning of unknown words, and (2) make informed, rather than haphazard, guesses about word meanings using context.

Rationale

Contextual Redefinition is a strategy that stresses the importance of context in predicting and verifying word meanings. Context enables students to make more informed guesses about the meaning of words in print and to monitor those predictions by checking them for syntactic/semantic appropriateness as reading progresses. Since authors frequently provide clues to the meanings of words in sentences, it is essential that students be able to use those clues as an aid in deriving meaning from print. Contextual Redefinition provides a format for deriving the meaning of unknown words that capitalizes on the use of context and endeavors to give students a strategy that can be used in their own independent reading.

Intended Audience

Contextual Redefinition is appropriate for students of all grade levels who may encounter in their reading a few difficult words that may be defined in the context in which they occur.

Description of the Procedures

Contextual Redefinition may be implemented using a five-step procedure: (1) select unfamiliar words, (2) write a sentence, (3) present the words in isolation, (4) present the words in context, and (5) use a dictionary for verification.

1. *Select Unfamiliar Words* Words to be used with this strategy are not randomly chosen; rather, they are identified in conjunction with the reading assignment at hand. Teachers should examine the text to be read to select those words (a) whose meaning may be necessary to understand the important ideas of the text and (b) whose meaning or use may present trouble to students as they read. For the sake of demonstrating this strategy, the following words will be used: hippophagy, carapace, and arachibutyrophobia.

2. *Write a Sentence* At least a sentence context needs to be provided so that students have appropriate clues to each word's meaning. If the text already has such a context, use it; otherwise, one will have to be created. If a context is created, it is recommended that various types of clues (e.g., synonyms, comparison/contrast, definition, etc.) should be

used. In this way students are able to experience the variety of ways authors may provide help in conveying meaning.

With our example the following sentences might be used:

(a) The drought had been so long and severe that the cattle had died. Only the horses had survived. Yet, the natives were so hungry that they had to resort to *hippophagy* to avoid starvation.

(b) Without its *carapace,* a turtle is subject to certain death from its enemies or the elements.

(c) Because Waldo was born with a cleft palate, he would never eat peanut butter. Though he was told by the doctors that he was totally healed, Waldo had developed *arachibutyrophobia.* Because of that, peanut butter was out of the question.

3. Present the Words in Isolation   Using an overhead transparency or a chalkboard, ask students to provide definitions for each word. It is suggested that the teacher pronounce each word as it is introduced so students at least know how the word sounds. When offering their individual guesses, students must provide a rationale for them. As a group, students should try to come to some consensus as to what they believe the best meaning is. Obviously, some predictions may be "off-the-wall" or even humorous. However, this is part of the process of learning; focusing on associations with recognizable parts of the word when it is in isolation robs the reader of the clues provided by a surrounding context. In other words, guesses offered when a word is presented in isolation are usually haphazard and uninformed.

With our example words, it is easy to see that some students could say that *hippophagy* has something to do with hippos, that *carapace* has something to do with a pace car at a race, and that *arachibutyrophobia* has something to do with a fear of spiders.

4. Present the Words in Context   At this point in the lesson, students are presented each word in its appropriate context, using the sentence or sentences from the text or those developed by the teacher. Again, students are asked to offer guesses about the meaning of each word and provide a rationale for each definition. In doing this, less able students are able to experience the thinking processes involved in using context to derive a meaning. In other words, students are able to act as models of appropriate reading behavior for one another. As before, students should try to come to some consensus as to the best meaning of the word offered.

In this part of the strategy, students should learn that context provides much information about the meaning of words and allows for quite informed predictions. In addition, students should learn that simply guessing at a word in isolation to get its meaning is not very accurate and can be frustrating.

5. Use a Dictionary for Verification   In this step, a student or students are asked to consult a dictionary to verify the guesses offered. The dictionary definition is shared with the rest of the class, and a discussion ensues concerning the quality of the predictions given when the words are presented (a) in isolation and (b) in context. It is now that teachers should point out or, even better, have students discover, the differences involved in guessing during these two steps of contextual redefinition.

Cautions and Comments

Contextual Redefinition provides teachers with a format to help students learn the use of context in ascertaining the meanings of unfamiliar words. It is easy to implement, requires little extra teacher preparation to use, and does have the potential for transfer to students' other reading situations. Furthermore, the strategy allows students to become actively involved in the discovery of new word meanings rather than just passive receivers of teacher-provided meanings.

It must be remembered, however, that Contextual Redefinition is a strategy to introduce new vocabulary words, not a strategy to teach and reinforce vocabulary words. Therefore, teachers must provide the necessary extension activities for students in order to ensure that the words are retained. In addition, another concern about this strategy is one that Gipe (1978–79) stated in her research on teaching word meanings. Teachers should try to ensure that the words used in explaining a new word are familiar; one cannot expect a student to learn a new word when it is first introduced in a sentence that has other unknown entities in it.

A final mention must be made of the importance of modeling behavior. Built into the strategy is the reading behavior of fluent readers; fluent readers use all available clues (graphophonic, syntactic, semantic) to derive the meaning of an unknown word. Contextual Redefinition tries to demonstrate to students that this is the proper way to cope with unknown words in text reading assignments. Modeling behavior is also used when students explain their thought processes to others in the class. It must not be assumed that all students will deal equally well with the various contexts that can be encountered. As students share their thoughts and ideas with one another, this presents an opportunity for others to pick up on and understand what happens in deriving meaning from print. Finally, it should be stressed that very little research on the use of Contextual Redefinition exists to date.

References

Cunningham, J. W., P. M. Cunningham, and S. V. Arthur. 1981. *Middle and secondary school reading.* New York: Longman. Presents Contextual Redefinition as a strategy to help middle/secondary students deal with new vocabulary.

Gipe, J. P. 1978–79. Investigating techniques for teaching word meanings. *Reading Research Quarterly* 14:624–644. Research study that found that a vocabulary teaching method emphasizing context proved effective.

Readence, J. E., T. W. Bean, and R. S. Baldwin. 1995. *Content area reading: An integrated ap-proach.* 5th ed. Dubuque, IA: Kendall/Hunt. Presents the steps involved in conducting a Contextual Redefinition lesson in the content areas.

Tierney, R. J., J. E. Readence, and E. K. Dishner. 1990. *Reading strategies and practices: A compendium.* 3rd ed. Boston: Allyn and Bacon. Chapter 6 presents Preview in Context, a vocabulary strategy useful when an existing context provides clues to the meaning of an unknown word and students can be talked through the discovery of its meaning.

Feature Analysis

Purpose

Feature Analysis (also called semantic feature analysis by Johnson and Pearson 1978, 1984) is designed to help students to:

1. improve their vocabulary and categorization skills;
2. understand the similarities and differences in related words; and
3. expand and retain content area vocabulary and concepts.

Rationale

Feature Analysis is a categorization strategy derived from the theoretical construct of the cognitive structure as the way in which individuals organize knowledge. Briefly, as human beings process information, categories are established in the cognitive structure based largely on cultural and experiential patterns. Rules (Feature Analysis) are formulated to allocate objects (words or concepts) into these categories. In this way, category interrelationships are established in the cognitive structure so that individuals can search their category systems (knowledge) efficiently to make sense of their experiences. Of practical relevance, Feature Analysis is intended to provide a systematic procedure for exploring and reinforcing vocabulary concepts through the use of categorization.

Intended Audience

Johnson and Pearson (1978) described Feature Analysis as a strategy that could be used with elementary students to develop their vocabulary. However, it can also be used to refine and reinforce vocabulary and related concepts in a postreading situation in content area classrooms.

Description of the Procedures

Feature Analysis may be implemented using the following six steps:

1. Select category
2. List words in category
3. List features
4. Indicate feature possession
5. Add words/features
6. Complete and explore matrix

1. *Select category*   The key to Feature Analysis is to start slowly and to begin with something familiar to students. A category topic (e.g., pets) is selected by the teacher. Once students are familiar with the strategy, the kinds and the abstractness of the category topics (e.g., freedom, climate) may increase. For illustration purposes, we use a rather simplistic example with the category of pets.

2. *List Words in Category*   Once the category topic has been introduced, the teacher provides words that name concepts or objects related to the category. As students become

accustomed to the strategy, they should provide these words. In the case of our example of pets, the following words might be introduced initially: (a) dog, (b) fish, (c) hamster, (d) frog, and (e) duck.

3. *List Features*   The teacher must now decide what features (traits, characteristics) are to be explored in the category *pets*. As before, students should provide these features once they become familiar with the strategy. Since some category topics would have many features that could be explored, as is the case with our example, start with only a few features and build on them later in the lesson. For our example, features to be examined are whether the pet (a) lives on land, (b) lives in the water, (c) has wings, (d) has fins, (e) has legs, and (f) has fur.

   After the first three steps of the strategy have been completed, we should have a feature matrix that looks like the following:

CATEGORY: PETS						
	land	water	wings	fins	legs	fur
dog						
fish						
hamster						
frog						
duck						

4. *Indicate Feature Possession*   Students are guided through the feature matrix for the purpose of deciding whether a particular pet possesses each of the features. When beginning Feature Analysis, it is recommended that a simple plus/minus (+/-) system be used to indicate feature possession. A more sophisticated system, such as a form of the Likert scale (1 = never; 2 = some; 3 = always), may be substituted once students are familiar with the strategy, and a system that explores the relative degree of feature possession is desired. Feature possession should be based on typical patterns, i.e., though some dogs may not have fur, this is not typical of them. The feature matrix for pets should look as follows using a +/- system:

CATEGORY: PETS						
	land	water	wings	fins	legs	fur
dog	+	−	−	−	+	+
fish	−	+	−	+	−	−
hamster	+	−	−	−	+	+
frog	+	+	−	−	+	−
duck	+	−	+	−	+	−

5. *Add Words/Features*   At this point in the strategy, it is time to expand the matrix. The teacher, or preferably the students, should generate new words to be added, followed by new features to be analyzed. Depending on the familiarity of the category or time limitations, the teacher may wish to set a limit on the number of words or features that can be added. This will typically be done automatically as categories become more abstract and begin to rely less on the prior knowledge that students may possess.

In our example, words such as (a) turtle, (b) rabbit, and (c) snake might be added. Features to be added might include (a) has feathers, (b) swims, and (c) flies. Adding words and features to the matrix is an attempt to further expand students' vocabulary and to develop concepts through categorization. The next and final step completes the strategy.

6. *Complete and Explore Matrix*   Students proceed now to complete the feature matrix by using the identical feature possession system as before with the added words and features. Our final example matrix might look like this:

	land	water	wings	fins	legs	fur	feathers	swims	flies
				CATEGORY: PETS					
dog	+	−	−	−	+	+	−	−	−
fish	−	+	−	+	−	−	−	+	−
hamster	+	−	−	−	+	+	−	−	−
frog	+	+	−	−	+	−	−	+	−
duck	+	−	+	−	+	−	+	+	+
turtle	+	+	−	−	+	−	−	+	−
rabbit	+	−	−	−	+	+	−	−	−
snake	+	−	−	−	−	−	−	+	−

The final part of this step is the exploration of the feature matrix. Students are asked to examine how words in the matrix relate, yet how they are still unique. For instance, it can be noted that even though the dog, the hamster, and the rabbit are different pets, they still have many similar traits. At the same time, they are also different from all the other pets listed and compared. In addition, it can be seen that only certain pets have wings or typically swim.

Exploring the feature matrix is best accomplished when the students, rather than the teacher, note these similarities and differences. Further expansion of the matrix may continue at this point, if the students so desire or the teacher assigns it.

Cautions and Comments

On the positive side, Feature Analysis has been shown to be effective with selected students (Bos and Anders, 1990; Johnson, Toms-Bronowski, and Pittelman, 1983), is relatively easy to implement, and can be fun. On the negative side, it does present some concerns of which teachers need to be aware. Categorization, as espoused in this strategy, is more sophisticated than it normally is. Some students may find Feature Analysis to be difficult at first. If such is the case, Readence and Searfoss (1980) suggest that simple categorization exercises and strategies such as List-Group-Label (this unit) be used as a means to introduce the concept of categorization and to act as a way into Feature Analysis. A second concern revolves around the plus/minus feature possession system. The strategy looks at typical patterns related to feature possessions, yet there are many exceptions to what is typical. Looking at our example, it can be argued that there are flying fish and that ducks "live," at least part of the time, in the water. It is recommended that if Feature Analysis is to be used frequently in the classroom, then teaching students to use a more sophisticated analysis system is warranted. This may lessen the amount of haggling that students do in the analysis process. Finally, as with any strategy, the more actively involved the students become in category selection and in the selection of words and features to be explored, the better the strategy will work.

Categorizing Feature Analysis as strictly a vocabulary development technique for elementary students presents a very narrow view of this strategy. It has great potential in other aspects of vocabulary development, as well as in becoming an integral part of both elementary and secondary reading and content area lessons. Baldwin, Ford, and Readence (1981) have shown how Feature Analysis can be used as an alternative approach to teaching students word connotations. Perhaps the best use, however, of this strategy is when it is used as a means to reinforce the vocabulary and related concepts of text in a content area reading lesson (Readence and Searfoss, 1980; Stieglitz and Stieglitz, 1981). For example, if students were involved in a health unit on drugs, Feature Analysis would be an excellent means to reinforce and review the likenesses and differences of the various drugs. After all, not all drugs are habit forming, create physical dependence, or are hallucinogens! Feature Analysis provides an effective means for examining these characteristics.

References

Anders, P. L., and C. S. Bos. 1986. Semantic feature analysis: An interactive strategy for vocabulary development and text comprehension. *Journal of Reading* 29:610–616. Discusses the theoretical and research bases for Feature Analysis as well as providing a practical example.

Baldwin, R. S., J. C. Ford, and J. E. Readence. 1981. Teaching word connotations: An alternative strategy. *Reading World* 21:103–108. Describes and provides examples of Feature Analysis as a means to help students learn word connotations.

Bos, C. S., and P. L. Anders. 1990. Effects of interactive vocabulary instruction on the vocabulary learning and reading comprehension of junior-

high learning disabled students. *Learning Disability Quarterly* 13: 31–42. Research study that found that feature analysis was an effective means of learning new vocabulary for learning disabled students.

Johnson, D. D., and P. D. Pearson. 1978. *Teaching reading vocabulary.* New York: Holt, Rinehart & Winston. A text that explores vocabulary development in general and Feature Analysis in particular.

———. 1984. *Teaching reading vocabulary.* 2d ed. New York: Holt, Rinehart & Winston. An updated version of the aforementioned text.

Johnson, D. D., S. Toms-Bronowski, and S. D. Pittelman. 1983. *An investigation of the effective-*

*ness of semantic mapping and semantic fea-
ture analysis with intermediate grade level
children.* Program Report 83–3. Madison:
Wisconsin Center for Education Research,
University of Wisconsin. Presents the findings
of a carefully conducted study of the use of the
technique.

Readence, J. E., and L. W. Searfoss. 1980. Teaching
strategies for vocabulary development. *English Journal* 69:43–46. Discusses the use of
Feature Analysis as a means to extend vocabulary concepts in the postreading portion of an
instruction lesson.

Stieglitz, E. L., and V. S. Stieglitz. 1981. SAVOR the
word to reinforce vocabulary in the content
areas. *Journal of Reading* 25:46–51. Discusses Feature Analysis as a means to reinforce vocabulary in the content areas.

Word Map

Purpose

The Word Map (Schwartz and Raphael, 1985), also known as the Frayer model (Frayer, Frederick, and Klausmeier, 1969), is designed to (1) develop students' conceptual knowledge about a topic, and (2) show hierarchical relationships of associated concepts.

Rationale

The Word Map is a systematic teaching technique that attempts to develop students' to-be-learned concepts based upon existing conceptual background. As a result, word concepts are taught by the notion of associating the new to the known.

Thelen (1982) has stated that showing students how concepts are hierarchically related is an important step in helping them learn new concepts, but it might not go far enough. It may be that certain concepts to be learned might need more in-depth processing and that they are better understood when students can generalize the concepts to new situations. Thus, it may be that with certain concepts, just providing a graphic organizer (see Unit 9) may be insufficient for students to fully grasp a concept. Thelen suggested that the Word Map was a useful alternative for attaining concepts.

The Word Map also attempts to clarify concepts by showing how they are hierarchically related. However, it suggests that if examples and nonexamples of new concepts, as well as their relevant and irrelevant attributes, are also provided, the students' learning will be even better. Therefore, the strategy examines superordinate, coordinate, and subordinate aspects of concepts, and also stresses those characteristics common to examples of that concept.

Intended Audience

Because of the sophistication involved in the hierarchical arrangement of the Word Map, the strategy is appropriate only for middle and secondary students. Even then, less able middle school students might have difficulty coping with the strategy.

Description of the Procedures

Thelen (1982) recommended that the Word Map be implemented using the following seven steps:

1. Develop the target concept
2. Define the concept
3. Present the concept
4. Finish constructing the hierarchy
5. Guide students to relevant attributes
6. Guide students to irrelevant attributes
7. Complete teaching the concept

1. *Develop the Target Concept* A hierarchy should be constructed that incorporates the supraordinate, coordinate, and subordinate aspects of the target concept. A supraordinate aspect of a concept is a term that refers to a common, more general concept of which the target concept is a member. Therefore, if our target concept is *reptiles,* the supraordinate concept might be *vertebrate.* An even more general term would be *animal.*

   A coordinate aspect of the target concept is a term that denotes other members of the same general, or supraordinate, concept. For instance, a coordinate concept for reptiles is *amphibians.* Finally, a subordinate aspect of the target concept is a term that possesses specific features of the target concept and is of a lower classification. In the case of reptiles, subordinate terms might be *alligators, snakes,* and *lizards.* Thus, the following hierarchy (Searfoss and Readence, 1994) might be constructed for the target concept *reptiles.*

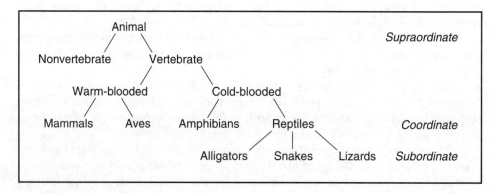

2. *Define the Concept* Before presenting the concept, be sure to delineate the relevant attributes for later discussion. Relevant attributes may be defined as characteristics that describe the target concept. Relevant attributes of reptiles, then, might be (a) a vertebrate, (b) breathes air, (c) has scales or bony plates, (d) lays eggs, (e) lacks hair, and (f) is cold-blooded. The examination of relevant attributes of a concept leads students to see not only what an example of it is but also what is not an example of the concept. For instance, a human would not be an example of a reptile, since human beings do not have scales or bony plates, do not lay eggs, are hairy, and are warm-blooded. This provides students the opportunity to see the likenesses and differences involved in attempting to define a concept.

3. *Present the Concept* At this time students are provided the target concept to be learned and are asked to contribute examples of it. This can be done either individually or in small groups. The examples can be listed on the board as they are offered. Students may challenge one another's examples as to whether it is an appropriate example. Thus, *gila monsters, chameleons, snakes, alligators, lizards,* and *iguanas* can be categorized as appropriate examples of reptiles. On the other hand, if *toads* or *eagles* were offered, they could be challenged as nonexamples and should be properly classified as amphibians and aves, respectively.

4. *Finish Constructing the Hierarchy* Provide students the concept hierarchy that was originally constructed in Step 1. It is essential that the teacher explain why the terms are arranged as they are. The teacher should use questioning techniques to involve the students as much as possible in offering terms that might fit in the resulting diagram to promote fuller understanding.

5. *Guide Students to Relevant Attributes* Once all possible examples are given, have students decide what characteristics they have in common (from Step 2). Any misconceptions may be cleared up with regard to what the target concept—in this case, reptiles—is.

6. *Guide Students to Irrelevant Attributes* Now have students find differences among the examples offered that do not change the example into a nonexample. In other words, what differences may exist among reptiles that are inconsequential and do not change the example's inclusion as a reptile? Again, this will lead to fuller understanding of the concept. With regard to reptiles, irrelevant attributes might include *whether they walk or slither, what they eat,* or *the size of their eggs.*

7. *Complete Teaching the Concept* To complete the Word Map, provide students with other examples and nonexamples they may not have thought of. These could be concepts they may encounter in their reading; doing so will provide additional reinforcement. When this is completed, students will have offered or been supplied the hierarchy from Step 1 and a list of examples, nonexamples, relevant attributes, and irrelevant attributes. With our reptile example, this list might look like this:

1. *Examples*	2. *Nonexamples*
gila monsters	toads
chameleons	eagles
snakes	human beings
alligators	birds
lizards	frogs
iguanas	aardvarks
3 *Relevant Attributes*	4. *Irrelevant Attributes*
vertebrate	walk or slither
cold-blooded	what they eat
lay eggs	size of eggs
lacks hair	color
breathes air	number of eggs
scales or bony plates	where they live

Cautions and Comments

The Word Map provides students with a number of different ways to think about the meaning of word concepts. It allows students to discover how new concepts are related to known concepts and to see what a concept represents as well as what it does not represent. As a consequence, it should help students generalize the newly learned concept to other learning situations. In past research, the Word Map has been used as a basis for developing texts. In studies by Peters (1979) and by Moes, Foertsch, Stewart, Dunning, Rogers, Seda-Santana, Benjamin, and Pearson (1983), such texts were found to be more understandable than texts lacking such a framework.

Key to the success of the Word Map is student involvement and discovery learning. It is essential that students be involved as much as possible in the creation of the concept hierarchy and in the provision of examples, nonexamples, relevant attributes, and irrelevant attributes. It is a fact that a teacher-created hierarchy and teacher-provided examples and attributes will not be as effective a learning environment as one in which students actively participate.

A final problem with the Word Map may be the terminology used in conducting the lesson. The terms *supraordinate, coordinate,* and *subordinate* may be too complex for some students, particularly those who are less able. Teachers may do well to use another set of terminology, such as *more general, equal,* and *more specific* to ensure that the strategy will be effective.

References

Frayer, D. A., W. C. Frederick, and H. J. Klausmeier. 1969. *A science for testing the level of concept mastery* (Working paper No. 16). Madison, WI: University of Wisconsin Research and Development Center for Cognitive Learning. Presents some of the original thinking about the Word Map.

Moes, M. A., D. J. Foertsch, J. Stewart, D. Dunning, T. Rogers, I. Seda-Santana, L. Benjamin, and P. D. Pearson. 1983. *Effects of text structure on children's comprehension of expository text.* Paper presented at the National Reading Conference, Austin, Texas. Using the Frayer model as a guide to developing text, these researchers compared the effects upon comprehension of the same information presented using different structures.

Peters, C. 1979. The effect of systematic restructuring of material upon the comprehension process. *Reading Research Quarterly* 11:87–110.

Studied the effects of using the Frayer model to structure texts.

Schwartz, R. M. 1988. Learning to learn vocabulary in content area textbooks. *Journal of Reading* 32: 108–118. Use of the Word Map strategy in the content areas.

Schwartz, R. M., and T. E. Raphael. 1985. Concept of definition: A key to improving students' vocabulary. *The Reading Teacher* 39:198–205. Describes the use of the Word Map strategy.

Searfoss, L. W., and J. E. Readence. 1994. *Helping children learn to read.* 3rd ed. Boston: Allyn and Bacon. Provides a discussion and examples of the Word Map.

Thelen, J. 1982. Preparing students for content reading assignments. *Journal of Reading* 25:544–549. Delineates the steps involved in implementing the Word Map.

Vocabulary Self-Collection Strategy ▪

Purpose

The Vocabulary Self-Collection Strategy (Haggard 1986a, 1986b) is designed to help students to: (1) generate vocabulary words to be explored and learned, and (2) use their own interest and prior knowledge to enhance vocabulary growth.

Rationale

The Vocabulary Self-Collection Strategy (VSS) is a versatile vocabulary development procedure that can be used to stimulate growth in word knowledge. Haggard based her claims for the utility of VSS on the following premises: "(1) Internal motivation exerts a strong influence on vocabulary acquisition and development, (2) Written text is a major source for new words and terms, (3) Adults develop systematic, personalized strategies for word learning, (4) Words which label or define experience are learned more quickly and easily than those which do not, and (5) The art of collecting words increases sensitivity to new words and enjoyment in word learning." (1986b, 640) In other words, students are asked to use their own interests and prior experiences as the basis for learning words that they will encounter in their reading assignments.

Intended Audience

The Vocabulary Self-Collection Strategy may be used with students at all grade levels, either as an adjunct to class reading assignments or in lieu of regular vocabulary instruction.

Description of the Procedures

The Vocabulary Self-Collection Strategy consists of the following four steps:

1. Selecting the words
2. Defining the words
3. Finalizing the word lists
4. Extending word knowledge

1. *Selecting the Words*   Students are asked to go through their assigned reading to identify one word they think should be studied further. For instance, in a content lesson students should select words that seem important to understanding the content. Sometimes the class may break up into two- or three-member teams and discuss the words and their meanings before the class as a whole considers them.

If VSS is being used as a spelling lesson, students are asked to "collect" a word that has meaning to their daily lives. These words that students believe the whole class should learn are brought in and presented to the class. No matter what the design of the VSS lesson, the teacher should also select a word. This can become the means by which the teacher ensures that a particularly important word becomes part of the lesson.

2. *Defining the Words*   Students or teams of students are asked to nominate one word or term they believe should be learned. The teacher does likewise. As the words are recorded on the chalkboard or an overhead, each of them is defined from its original context and reasons for nominating the words are offered. The teacher leads a discussion for clarification and expansion of each word's meaning, adding whatever information the students and teacher have from prior knowledge or gained from the reading selection necessary to come up with the appropriate definition. If necessary or desirable, the dictionary may be checked to verify definitions.

3. *Finalizing the Word Lists*   Once the discussion is completed, the list of words must be narrowed down by eliminating duplications, words already known, and words that the students do not wish to learn. The words that comprise the final list are redefined so students can record the words and their definitions in their vocabulary journals. Students may decide to record words that were discarded in their personal vocabulary lists.

4. *Extending Word Knowledge*   Follow-up activities are used to enable students to refine and expand the meanings of the words on the final list. As part of a lesson for general vocabulary development, words can be tested as is normally done if they pertain to the lesson selected. Other activities may need to be redesigned if existing activities do not deal with all the words. With a content selection, the words should be incorporated into the materials for the unit being studied and can be tested as to how they apply to the text.

Cautions and Comments

The Vocabulary Self-Collection Strategy seems easy to implement because the burden of work falls on students. It does seem to provide students with an anchor for new learning as it capitalizes on their experience and word knowledge. In addition, they become actively involved in the lesson through the selection and discussion of words to be learned.

Just as VSS seems versatile in dealing with vocabulary development of various kinds, it can be adapted to be used as a prereading strategy with content material. Though described here as a postreading strategy, VSS can be used with text materials before students actually read them. Students are asked to preview the text before they read it for the purpose of identifying one or two words they feel are important to understanding the text. The words would be defined and recorded as before, except that students would have the opportunity to learn something about the word before they actually read the assignment.

While VSS sounds intuitively appealing as a vocabulary development technique, some concerns about the strategy must be mentioned. First, the strength of the strategy—student self-selection of words—may also be perceived as limiting. The words students may choose as important in a reading assignment may exclude important words. Some teachers would view this as creating a problem if the goal is to have students understand certain text concepts. Second, though not limited to this particular strategy, the necessity of follow-up activities is crucial. Relying on students to develop useful understandings of key concepts should not be left to only a discussion of the words and their recording in a journal. Finally, though Haggard (1986b) has done some research on the variable of self-collection with university level students, no empirical validation of this strategy exists to date with either elementary or secondary level students.

References

Haggard, M. R. 1986a. The vocabulary self-collection strategy: An active approach to word learning. In *Reading in the content areas: Improving classroom instruction,* 2d ed., edited by E. K. Dishner, T. W. Bean, J. E. Readence, and D. W. Moore. Dubuque, IA: Kendall/Hunt, 179–183. The original discussion of the strategy.

———. 1986b. The vocabulary self-collection strategy: Using student interest and world knowledge to enhance vocabulary growth. *Journal of Reading* 29:634–642. Discusses the use of VSS with a variety of materials and expands upon the theoretical rationale for the strategy.

Ruddell, M. R. 1992. Integrated content and long term vocabulary learning with the vocabulary self-collection strategy. In *Reading in the content areas: Improving classroom instruction,* 3rd ed., edited by E. K. Dishner, T. W. Bean, J. E. Readence, and D. W. Moore, 190–196. Dubuque, IA: Kendall/Hunt. An update of the strategy with particular application to content areas.

Levin's Keyword Method

Purpose

The Keyword Method (Levin, 1983) is a mnemonic strategy that helps students to learn new information by associating it with interactive visual images for later recall.

Rationale

Levin (1983) states that learning new information using the Keyword Method is based on a process of recoding, relating, and retrieving. First, students must recode, or transform, the unknown word to be learned into a more meaningful keyword that looks or sounds like the original. An example might be the word *potable,* which means suitable for drinking. *Potable* is recoded to the familiar word, *pot,* which is then related to the original word by the use of an actual picture or a mental image of a pot of cool spring water sitting in front of you after you have crossed a hot desert. With recoding and relating established, students are now able to use the keyword to retrieve the correct meaning when they encounter the new word. In other words, on seeing the word *potable,* students are reminded of the keyword *pot.* This, in turn, leads them to think of the picture or an appropriate visual image that then leads them to the correct response of "suitable for drinking."

The effectiveness of Levin's Keyword Method is also based upon adherence to three assumptions about picture strategies for learning. First, pictures or images can facilitate learning because they provide a means by which to learn difficult material. Second, the more directly related the pictures or images are to the content to be learned, the more effective the learning will be.

Finally, even given the previous two assumptions, research suggests that the pictures will not be helpful if they are not familiar enough to provide an organizational framework for understanding and retrieving the new information. Levin's Keyword Method meets this assumption and the two aforementioned assumptions by enabling students to recode the new material to be learned into a concrete keyword and relate it within a visual image so that it can be easily retrieved.

Intended Audience

Levin's Keyword Method was originally used to improve college students' ability to learn a foreign language (Atkinson, 1975). Since then, the use of this strategy has expanded to help students, elementary through college, to learn vocabulary and content facts.

Description of the Procedures

Konopak and Williams (1988) described how to use Levin's Keyword Method in the classroom employing the following steps: (1) teacher preparation, (2) modeling, (3) guided practice, (4) independent practice, and (5) transfer.

The strategy will be considered using an example adapted from Konopak and Williams (1988, 685–687). It involves a fifth grade science unit on minerals in which students are asked to recall the names and primary use of various minerals.

1. *Teacher Preparation*   Using the text passage, the teacher must decide what particular minerals are to be learned and where each of them is used. Next, a keyword must be assigned to each mineral. Then, the visual image of the keyword interacting with its primary use is developed. It is recommended that an actual illustration be used to demonstrate this image; however, an elaborate statement may be used if it can easily create a mental image for the students. The following are example items:

Mineral	Keyword	Primary Use	Image
rhodonite	road	home	a road going through a living room
fluorite	flower	industry	a vase of flowers sitting on a workbench in a factory
corundum	car	home	a car driving through a living room

2. *Modeling*   Tell students that they will be using a study strategy to help them remember the names of minerals they need to learn and their use. To demonstrate Levin's Keyword Method, use the example of amber. Provide a short description of it and tell them it is used

primarily in the home. Explain to them that a keyword, which either looks or sounds like *amber,* will help them learn the information they need to know. Since *hamburger* sounds like the target word, it becomes the keyword for that mineral. Next, students are shown a picture of a hamburger sitting on a chair in a living room. They are informed that by thinking of the picture they will remember that amber (hamburger) is a mineral used primarily in the home (living room). Other demonstrative examples should follow until students understand the concepts of the strategy.

3. *Guided Practice* Distribute to the students a short passage about the first target mineral, rhodonite, which is used in the home, and an illustration showing a road going through a living room. The target word, *rhodonite,* and the keyword, *road,* should be used as captions for the illustration. The students are directed to read the passage and examine the accompanying picture for the purpose of recalling the mineral and its use. The picture should be discussed as to how it helps them recall the information.

4. *Independent Practice* Break students into small groups of three or four members and have them read the rest of the text information about minerals. Provide them with keywords and have them develop their own mnemonic images, given the examples you previously prepared. These should be shared with the whole class.

5. *Transfer* To initiate the successful transfer of this strategy from teacher-provided keywords and illustrations to student-oriented mnemonics, provide additional text information about minerals without supplying a keyword. Students will then need to read the material and develop their own mnemonics to aid in the recall of the material. They will need to be reminded of the study technique and how effective they may have found it. Students will also need encouragement and feedback as they develop their own visual images. Again, these should be shared with the whole class for purposes of feedback.

To further promote transfer, watch for other opportunities for students to use the strategy in their other subject matter areas. They may need to be prompted by the teacher or other students until it is fully learned.

Cautions and Comments

Levin's Keyword Method provides students with the means to recall new content material by employing a workable study strategy that includes familiar, concrete images to facilitate their learning. Unlike most of the strategies described in this unit, Levin's Keyword Method is well documented as a means to help students remember new vocabulary (for reviews, see Pressley, Levin, and Delaney, 1982; Pressley, Levin, and McDaniel, 1987). The strategy has proved to be an effective learning technique for both good and poor readers at all levels on a variety of learning tasks.

Nonetheless, there are a number of disadvantages to the strategy. First, it can be very time-consuming for the teacher to generate keywords and their accompanying images. Second, the visual images initially used are teacher-provided, not student-provided, resulting in potentially less personal involvement by students in their own learning. Third, the extent to which students can transfer the keyword technique to other areas of study is relatively unknown at this time.

References

Atkinson, R. C. 1975. Mnemotechnics in second-language learning. *American Psychologist* 30:821–828. Examines the use of the Keyword Method with second-language learners.

Konopak, B. C., and N. L. Williams. 1988. Using the keyword method to help young readers learn content material. *The Reading Teacher* 41:682–687. A practical discussion on the background and use of the Keyword Method.

Konopak, B. C., N. L. Williams, and E. S. Jampole. 1991. Use of mnemonic imagery for content learning. *Reading, Writing, and Learning Disabilities* 7: 309–319. Study showing that Levin's Keyword Method was useful with middle level students with learning disabilities in science.

Levin, J. R. 1983. Pictorial strategies for school learning. In *Cognitive strategy research: Educational applications,* edited by M. Pressley and J. R. Levin. New York: Springer-Verlag. An examination of the role of pictures in learning.

Levin, J. R., M. E. Levin, L. D. Glasman, and M. B. Nordwell. 1992. Mnemonic vocabulary instruction: Additional effectiveness evidence. *Contemporary Educational Psychology* 17: 156–174. Studies citing the effectiveness of the Keyword Method with elementary and middle school students in individual, paired, and small-group instructional formats.

Pressley, M., J. R. Levin, and H. D. Delaney. 1982. The mnemonic keyword method. *Review of Educational Research* 52:61–91. A review of research on the strategy.

Pressley, M., J. R. Levin, and M. A. McDaniel. 1987. Remembering versus inferring what a word means: Mnemonic and contextual approaches. In *The nature of vocabulary acquisition,* edited by M. G. McKeown and M. E. Curtis. Hillsdale, NJ: Erlbaum, 107–127. An updated review of research on the Keyword Method.

Reading and Writing Across the Curriculum: Content Area Literacy

UNIT OVERVIEW

In recent years a great deal of attention has been given to how information is presented in narrative and expository text (Barr, Kamil, Mosenthal, and Pearson, 1991). Researchers have invested considerable effort and devised elaborate systems for analyzing how different texts are structured and whether there are certain text features that regularly cause students difficulty. As these characteristics of text have been described, educators have devised strategies and lesson frameworks to prepare students to deal with text features.

The present unit describes ten strategies, which range from procedures for preparing students to read a selection by presenting key concepts to training students in techniques of connecting sentences (for purposes of highlighting complex syntactic structures) to teaching students about complex text structures (for purposes of dealing with content area textbooks).

Graphic Organizers   The Graphic Organizer can be used as a preteaching or postteaching strategy for purposes of introducing or reinforcing the key concepts in a text and how they might be structured.

Study Guides   The backbone of the Instructional Framework is the Study Guide, which students use in dealing with the content. Study Guides can guide students through their content area textbook reading by focusing their attention on the major ideas presented.

Selective Reading Guide   The Selective Reading Guide provides the content teacher with an opportunity to guide the students to the relevant information within the content unit.

Guided Reading Procedure   Incorporating the techniques of unaided recall of facts, self-correction, recognition of implicit questions, organization of ideas, and brief quizzes, the Guided Reading Procedure attempts to improve attitudinal and skill aspects of reading comprehension. Although the Guided Reading Procedure can be used with children at various levels, it seems best suited for grades three and above.

° *Idea Mapping*   Idea Mapping is a method of spatially representing the overall structure of expository text. It provides students with a framework for carefully reading expository text, and it provides teachers a tool for examining the nature of text prior to classroom use.

° *Text Structure Strategy*   The Text Structure Strategy is based on the premise that if students are taught different prototypical expository structures, they can use an understanding of these structures as an aid in comprehending texts that have similar structures.

° *Story Grammars and Story Maps*   Story Grammars and Story Maps include a description of two different strategies that are based on the theoretical notions of the structure of stories. Story Maps present guidelines to generate questions that accompany short narratives found in basal readers. Story Grammars provide students with a framework for identifying the plot structure and other key elements of a story.

° *Sentence Combining*   Sentence Combining is aimed at increasing the syntactic knowledge of students. This knowledge serves as a basis for improving writing fluency and reading comprehension.

° *Guided Writing Procedure*   The Guided Writing Procedure is designed to facilitate the synthesis of text material through the use of free association and writing.

° *I-Search Paper*   The I-Search Paper is a technique designed to help students research a topic by capitalizing on their need to investigate that topic. It incorporates a discussion of what is known about a topic, a story of the investigation of the topic, and what was learned about it.

References

Barr, R., M. L. Kamil, P. B. Mosenthal, and P. D. Pearson, eds. *Handbook of reading research: Volume II*. New York: Longman. Chapters by Pearson and Fielding (pp. 815–860), Tierney & Shanahan (pp. 246–280), and Alvermann and Moore (pp. 951–983) discuss research on reading and writing in the content areas.

Graphic Organizers

Purpose

The Graphic Organizer (Barron, 1969), originally called the Structured Overview, is designed to: (1) provide a logical means of preteaching the technical vocabulary of a content chapter, (2) present the students an idea framework designed to show important conceptual relationships between content vocabulary, and (3) help content teachers clarify teaching goals.

Rationale

The technical vocabulary of a content subject often proves quite difficult for students. It is Barron's argument that content teachers must be ever mindful of this fact and should seek ways of making the task less complicated for the students. The Graphic Organizer provides a systematic approach for doing just that. The subject matter instructor presents a picture, or schematic diagram, of the important words in the chapter and discusses with the students how these words relate one to another. Barron (1969) stated that "words assume the form of 'advance organizers' and provide the students with the cues to the 'structure' of subjects" (P. 29). Thus, the organizer serves as a point of reference as the students begin reading and studying the chapter in more detail.

Intended Audience

Earle (1969) reports the use of the Graphic Organizer with students in grades seven and above. It is further suggested that teachers in grades four, five, and six could profit from the use of the technique. On occasion, the procedure might be used by the teacher alone in the preparation of a particularly difficult unit.

Description of the Procedures

In order to describe the use of the Graphic Organizer by the content teacher, the following three stages will be discussed:

1. Preparation
2. Presentation
3. Follow-up

1. *Preparation* Perhaps the most critical stage in the development and use of Graphic Organizer is this first step. It is at this point that the instructor, by working through this rather simple process, makes some key decisions regarding the major ideas to be stressed during the unit. Four components of the preparation stage summarize the desired sequence.

 a. *Select words.* Rather than moving through the chapter in search of difficult words, the teacher proceeds in a more systematic manner (Herber, 1978). The first step in this preparation stage, then, is for the instructor to select the major concepts or understandings that are important for the students to know at the conclusion of their study of the topic. By working through the chapter in this manner, the teacher is actually establishing instructional objectives for that particular chapter.

Word selection logically follows selection of major concepts. The teacher can now deal with one major idea at a time and ask the question "What important words in this chapter help to describe, explain, or communicate this idea?" By asking this question for each of the major concepts, the content teacher has identified those technical terms that the student will need to know. Often a number of difficult words within the chapter are eliminated because they do not tie in directly to the major concepts.

To give an example, a social studies teacher may be introducing a chapter on organization of the United States government. The concepts chosen for instruction are: (1) the United States government consists of three governing branches; and (2) a system of checks and balances maintains the powers of each branch of government. The words that might be selected by the teacher as important for understanding these concepts are *checks and balances, Senate, legislative, United States government, executive, judicial, House of Representatives, President, veto and override,* and *judicial review.*

b. *Arrange words.* The task now is to arrange these words into a diagram form that helps students see the terms and how they interrelate. There is not necessarily a right or a wrong diagram for a given set of terms, but it would appear that some arrangements are better than others. With several pieces of scratch paper available, the teacher might try out several possibilities, then select the one that appears to be the most appropriate.

Continuing the example of the words chosen by the social studies teacher, the words might be arranged in numerous ways. Figure 9–1 gives one example.

FIGURE 9–1. AN EXAMPLE GRAPHIC ORGANIZER

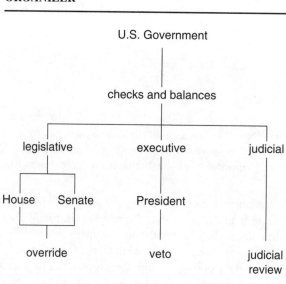

Graphic Organizers may be designed for the total chapter. For longer, more complicated chapters, the subject matter instructor may design several organizers, each tied to a major concept. Whatever the decision, the overriding question to be answered is "Will this organizer assist students to better understand the major concepts and major words of the chapter?" If the answer is "yes," then the teacher has developed a valuable teaching tool.

c. *Add previously learned key words and ideas.* Learning new information is generally easier for students if they can relate the new ideas to previously learned information; therefore, the content instructor is advised to select several important words that the students mastered in previous units and insert them in this new organizer. By completing this step, the teacher is saying to the students that the subject is more than a set of isolated units with little or no relationship to each other. In the example of the words dealing with the United States government, the teacher may decide to add previously learned vocabulary, if that would enhance understanding of the Graphic Organizer.

d. *Evaluate organizer.* Content instructors, by their very training, interest, and experience, are experts in their chosen fields; therefore, they may have forgotten what it was like when they first began to pursue information in their major subject. A Graphic Organizer may be easily interpretable by the content specialist but still be too difficult for a group of high school juniors. This final step in the preparation stage, therefore, is critical. It is advisable to try out the organizer on someone who is not an expert in the field. One could do this with a student or with a fellow teacher in another discipline. Explain the organizer and then ask appropriate questions that tell you whether the person grasps the relationships among the terms used in it. Often people will answer questions in such a manner that they provide the kind of information necessary to suggest some minor revisions that result in a more appropriately constructed design. Once satisfied with the appropriateness of the organizer, the teacher should use it in the context of a total lesson in a regular classroom.

2. *Presentation*   As a preteaching tool, the organizer is presented on the chalkboard or with an overhead transparency. The instructor actually talks the students through the organizer and adds new pieces to it. Students are encouraged to participate. They may add information with which they are already familiar or ask questions regarding the organizer. The teacher may pose questions to check the students' understanding of it. The important thing is that the teacher and the students use the language of the subject matter and simultaneously explore the relationships of these words to each other. It is important to remember that one should not anticipate mastery of terms and relationships at this time.

The entire procedure may take from five to ten minutes, depending on the ability and achievement level of the students and on the complexity of the organizer. At the conclusion of this segment of the preparation stage, the students should have an idea framework that should make more detailed learning easier.

3. *Follow-up*   The Graphic Organizer may also be used as the students move further into the chapter itself. A student's reaction to an especially difficult idea encountered in the

reading might result in the teacher's responding, "Do you remember how this idea tied to . . . ?" as a portion of the organizer is created on the chalkboard. Thus, the organizer becomes a major point of reference throughout the teaching of a particular chapter. New information may be added when the instructor suggests, "Let's see how this new information fits into the organizer that we have been using." For some classes, the organizer might be placed on a large piece of poster paper and put on the bulletin board. In this way, students may refer to it at any time.

Cautions and Comments

The Graphic Organizer alone may not teach the technical vocabulary of a chapter as thoroughly as the content instructor may desire. A support system designed to teach the language of the subject more thoroughly is suggested. Earle and Barron (1973) outline a strategy that includes three components: (1) Graphic Organizer, (2) skills teaching, and (3) extension activities. Graphic Organizers are designed and utilized in the manner just described. The skills teaching phase of the strategy occurs in the preparation stage of the Instructional Framework (see discussion of the Instructional Framework in Unit 5) and involves the detailed teaching of several of the more important terms used in the organizer. Extension activities give students opportunities to use the words during or following the reading of the chapter. Extension activities are generally paper-and-pencil exercises designed to reinforce the students' understandings of the terms. Matching exercises, word puzzles, and categorizing activities may be used for this purpose. Small-group and whole-class discussion may follow the completion of the activities.

Several studies cited in the reference section indicate the value of this procedure. However, one wonders whether a strategy that imposes upon students a structure for thinking and reading would be as beneficial as a strategy that might activate students' own ideas. To this end, an organizer might be developed from the student's own ideas prior to, during, or after reading. In this way, the organizer may become more personalized and less abstract.

Barron (1979) has suggested that Graphic Organizers can be used as a means of postreading reinforcement and review if students are given the task of constructing their own organizers. Multiple copies of each word to be used in the organizer are made, using index cards, and passed out to students in small groups. Students are given the task of arranging the words in a diagram to show how they are related. Blank index cards are also provided if students wish to add their own vocabulary terms. The teacher's responsibility in this postreading Graphic Organizer strategy is to circulate among the groups, providing support and feedback. The culminating activity is for the class to develop a single Graphic Organizer under the teacher's direction. By using organizers in this manner, students become more actively involved in their learning.

For students who may have trouble initially in constructing their own Graphic Organizers, Readence and Moore (1979) have suggested an interim step between teacher-constructed and student-generated organizers that may serve as an effective transition. The same diagram that was presented to students in the prereading portion of a lesson can be used to help students recall the assigned reading material after reading. Words are deleted from the original organizer and replaced with blanks. Deleted words are listed below the incomplete Graphic Organizer in random order. The students' task is to complete the diagram using the deleted words, either from recall or by using the text. Individual ditto sheets would be advantageous in this activity.

Finally, in a quantitative and qualitative review of Graphic Organizer research, Moore and Readence (1984) found that students exposed to postreading Graphic Organizers learned more than those students exposed to prereading Graphic Organizers, particularly when vocabulary was the criterion variable. They also found that one of the advantages for using prereading organizers was that the teachers involved in the studies felt that they were better prepared to teach their lessons after having constructed a Graphic Organizer.

References

Alvermann, D. E., and P. R. Boothby. 1986. Children's transfer of graphic organizer instruction. *Reading Psychology* 7:87–100. Research study finding that postreading Graphic Organizers enabled fourth graders to transfer the effects of that instruction to their ability to recall novel text.

Barron, R. F. 1969. The use of vocabulary as an advance organizer. In *Research in reading in the content areas: First year report,* edited by H. L. Herber and P. L. Sanders. Syracuse, NY. Reading and Language Arts Center, Syracuse University, 29–39. Presents the basis for the use of Graphic Organizers within the content classroom. Describes how Graphic Organizers may be used in relation to a total vocabulary teaching strategy utilizing preteaching and extension activities.

———. 1979. Research for classroom teachers: Recent developments on the use of the structured overview as an advance organizer. In *Research in reading in the content areas: Fourth report,* edited by H. L. Herber and J. D. Riley. Syracuse, NY: Syracuse University Reading and Language Arts Center, 171–176. Describes the evolution of the Graphic Organizer strategy and its application in postreading.

Dunston, P. J. 1992. A critique of graphic organizer research. *Reading Research and Instruction* 31:57–65. Updated review on the effectiveness of Graphic Organizers.

Earle, R. A. 1969. Use of the structured overview in mathematics classes. In *Research in reading in the content areas: First year report,* edited by H. L. Herber and P. L. Sanders, Syracuse, NY: Reading and Language Arts Center, Syracuse University, 49–58. Describes a study in which Graphic Organizers were used in both seventh and ninth grade mathematics classes. Significant differences in favor of the use of Graphic Organizers versus no preteaching were observed when a delayed-relationship test was administered.

Earle, R. A., and R. F. Barron. 1973. An approach for testing vocabulary in content subjects. In *Research in reading in the content areas: Second year report,* edited by H. L. Herber and R. F. Barron. Syracuse, NY: Reading and Language Arts Center, Syracuse University, 84–100. Describes a total vocabulary teaching strategy designed for content teachers. Strategy components include (1) Graphic Organizers, (2) skills teaching, and (3) extension activities.

Herber, H. L. 1978. *Teaching reading in content areas.* 2d ed. Englewood Cliffs, NJ: Prentice-Hall, 47–158. Discusses the use of the Graphic Organizer with examples.

Moore, D. W., and J. E. Readence. 1984. A quantitative and qualitative review of graphic organizer research. *Journal of Educational Research* 78:11–17. A synthesis of the research examining the effectiveness of the Graphic Organizer as a classroom strategy.

Readence, J. E., and D. W. Moore. 1979. Strategies for enhancing readiness and recall in content areas: The encoding specificity principle. *Reading Psychology* 1:47–54. Examines the use of the Graphic Organizer as both a prereading and postreading activity.

Study Guides

Purpose

Study Guides (Earle, 1969; Herber, 1978) are designed to (1) guide a student through reading assignments in content area textbooks, and (2) focus a reader's attention on the major ideas presented in a textbook.

Rationale

Reading in a content area textbook may demand a relatively high level of skill development. As Herber argues, this kind of reading entails the student's acquiring an awareness of levels of comprehension and of how to function at each level. Then, once secure in these levels, the student should acquire the ability to consider and deal with the organizational patterns of the different reading materials. Toward this end, Study Guides can be useful in developing the ability of students to learn how to read. Specifically, Study Guides purport to develop the student's understanding of, and ability to deal with, levels of comprehension, the organizational patterns of different texts, and the specific skills these might require. Study Guides do this by structuring and guiding the reading of textbook material or students' postreading reasoning.

Intended Audience

Study Guides are used mainly in conjunction with content area subjects. They may be used in both individual and group instructional situations and can be adapted to aid students regardless of the students' ability level in reading.

Description of the Procedures

Discussion of Study Guides as an integral part of a well-planned lesson will include the following three components: (1) development of Study Guides, (2) construction of Study Guides, and (3) use of Study Guides.

1. *Development of Study Guides* Before they can construct a Study Guide for use with their students, teachers must analyze the content material to be read by the students for both content and process (Earle, 1969). By analyzing the materials, teachers are assured that the Study Guide material used by students will be in keeping with the content objectives teachers have in mind.

In analyzing the material for both content and process, teachers themselves should first thoroughly read the material they plan to assign to students. Teachers are then better able to select the content to be emphasized during the lesson. In this way, portions of the assigned material that fit the overall objectives of the subject will be emphasized, and those portions not doing so can be deleted, thus leaving students the opportunity to concentrate on the portions deemed important.

For example, with a reading assignment from a social studies course involving "the Black Revolution," a teacher might decide that the concepts *black nationalism, nonviolence, black power, separatism,* and the advocates of these courses of action, are important for students to master.

Once the content to be emphasized has been decided, teachers must then decide the processes (skills) that students must use in acquiring that content. Earle (1969) and Herber (1978) suggested that the decisions made regarding the skills to be used in mastering the material concern an understanding of levels of comprehension and patterns of organization.

Herber (1978) described three levels of comprehension: literal, interpretive, and applied. Literal understanding involves identifying factual material and knowing what the author said. Interpretive understanding involves inferring relationships among the details and knowing what the author meant. Finally, applied understanding involves developing generalizations that extend beyond the assigned material. With the content to be emphasized, the teacher must decide what levels of understanding students will need.

Earle (1969) described four patterns of organization in which textual information is frequently found: cause and effect, comparison and contrast, sequence or time order, and simple listing. Dealing with the particular way in which information is organized in a text aids students in mastering the content. Therefore, the teacher must ascertain the pattern of organization for the information in a given text. Together with levels of comprehension, the identification of patterns of organization provides students with the necessary structure to study the assigned material.

Continuing with our example of the Black Revolution, the teacher might determine that all three levels of understanding are necessary to deal successfully with the portions of the text to be emphasized. In addition, the comparison-and-contrast pattern of organization may be found to be used by the text authors in organizing their information.

One last step must be accomplished before the Study Guide is constructed. The teacher must consider the students' abilities in relation to the content and processes to be emphasized. By doing this, the teacher can provide differing amounts of assistance to ensure that all students complete the assignment successfully.

In this step the teacher must consider two points: the students' competencies and the difficulty of the material itself (Earle, 1969). Keeping these two factors in mind, the teacher decides how much structure should be provided for each student to address the content. For instance, the teacher can provide aids to locate the desired material in the form of page and/or paragraph numbers. Also, the teacher must decide whether guides should be constructed for only a single level of comprehension or for differential levels, so particular students may be assigned only to deal with those levels commensurate with their abilities. Teachers, knowing the individual needs and abilities of their students, will have to make these kinds of judgments and vary the structure of Study Guides to ensure the success of their students.

2. *Construction of Study Guides*   Once decisions have been made regarding the content and process and the types of assistance to be provided, teachers are ready to construct their Study Guides. Although there is no standard form that a Study Guide must take, Earle (1969) recommends the following guidelines:

a. Avoid overcrowding print on the Study Guide, as overcrowding may overwhelm some students.

b. Make the guide interesting enough so students will be motivated to deal with the information.

c. Be sure the guide reflects the instructional decisions made with regard to content and process.

Continuing with our previous example, Study Guides can be constructed to aid students in mastering the concepts and in acquiring the skills needed to do so. Here are two examples of Study Guides, one concerning levels of comprehension and the other involving the comparison-and-contrast pattern of organization.*

READING GUIDE #1:
LEVELS OF COMPREHENSION

* Literal level

** Interpretive level

*** Applied level

* 1. What are the basic steps of a nonviolent campaign? (p. 634, par. 4)

*** 2. Why did the political leaders of Birmingham refuse to engage in good faith?

** 3. Why does Stokely Carmichael think "integration is a joke"? (p. 636)

*** 4. Why do you think the authors say that the SNCC has become more militant since the early 1960s?

** 5. Why did SNCC choose the black panther as its symbol? (p. 637)

* 6. What is black nationalism? (p. 639, par. 1)

** 7. Why did the man in the tavern say the extremists would end up in concentration camps? (p. 640)

*** 8. Why do so many people think the racial problem has to be solved in our generation? (p. 640)

* 9. What does the term "black Jim Crow" mean? (p. 641, par. 4)

* 10. Who is Thurgood Marshall (p. 642, par. 3)

** 11. Why does Thurgood Marshall fear the black militants? (p. 643, par. 2)

*** 12. Why do black people think black studies programs are essential?

---

*From Dishner and Readence (1977). Copyright © 1977 by the College Reading Association. Reprinted by permission of the College Reading Association, J. E. Readence, and E. K. Dishner. Based on material from M. Sandler, E. Rozwenc, and E. Martin. "Strategies of the 'Black' Revolution," in *The People Make a Nation*. Boston: Allyn and Bacon, 1971, 634–644.

READING GUIDE #2:
PATTERNS OF ORGANIZATION

Directions: 1. Match the name of a black leader in Column A with his strategy in Column B. Put the number of that name in the blank provided in Column B.

2. Match the name of a black leader in Column A with the ideas in Column C. Put the number in the blank provided in Column C.

A. Names

1. Martin Luther King
2. Stokely Carmichael
3. Roy Innes
4. Roy Wilkins
5. Thurgood Marshall

B. Strategies

_____ black nationalism

_____ anti-separatism

_____ nonviolence

_____ leadership through education

_____ black power

C. Ideas

_____ Our philosophy is one of self-determination.

_____ White power has been scaring black people for 400 years.

_____ Direct action is the only way to force the issue. (p. 635)

_____ You can't use color for an excuse for not doing what you should be doing. (p. 643)

_____ Current black studies programs represent another form of segregated education. (p. 641)

_____ Nothing will be settled with guns or rocks.

_____ You must be able to accept blows without retaliation.

_____ We must rehabilitate blacks as people. (p. 639)

_____ Black history is significant only if taught in the context of world history.

_____ Our idea is to put people in office who will work for the people they represent. (p. 638)

It should be noted that these sample guides have been constructed with varying amounts of assistance (page and paragraph numbers) and level of comprehension designated. Teachers may decide to use only one or all of the levels, depending on what decisions have been made with regard to individual students.

3. *Use of Study Guides*   Study Guides should be used in the context of a well-planned lesson. Students should be prepared for the reading assignment through background development and a purpose-setting discussion. A follow-up discussion also might be provided after the guides have been used. The Instructional Framework or the Directed Reading Activity (both described in Unit 5) may provide the lesson framework needed to incorporate the Study Guides as one element in that lesson.

When first using Study Guides, teachers may need to walk students through a portion of a guide so that they will become acquainted with the procedure and will be better able to use the guides. Specifically, this step may aid students in seeing how the relationship between content and process can be fostered.

Groups of students can work on Study Guides cooperatively in lieu of using them individually. In this way, students can collaboratively arrive at responses to the guide. The activity promotes students' active involvement in the reading/learning process.

Finally, as students develop sensitivity to Study Guides and begin to transfer their new learning to other situations, the varying structure included in the initial guides may be progressively withdrawn. In this way, students are encouraged toward independence in their reading.

Cautions and Comments

Study Guides can provide a means of encouraging students to become active participants in the learning process rather than passive observers. In addition, Study Guides aid teachers in ensuring that the important concepts present in text material are communicated to students. Particularly in group situations, Study Guides represent a unique opportunity to explore ideas; they do not tie students directly to recall-type learning.

Study Guides are versatile, and their judicious use may provide the kind of instructional environment necessary to develop students' independence in reading and thinking. As such, various studies have provided substantial support for the efficacy of Study Guides (see Herber and Barron, 1973; Herber and Vacca, 1977; Herber and Riley, 1979).

However, two cautions should be mentioned concerning Study Guides. First, it does take time and effort on the part of the teacher to develop, construct, and use them effectively. This caution, however, should be put into perspective alongside the benefits to students' understanding and the possibility that teachers might work cooperatively on their development.

Second, although Study Guides are designed to move readers toward eventual independence, they are essentially teacher-directed activities. Teachers, not readers, decide what is important in reading the texts.

Decision making, therefore, in this learning situation rests almost entirely with teachers. Those educators concerned with creating a learning environment that involves students as much as possible must bear this factor in mind when using Study Guides. In partial response to this point, Herber (1970) remarked:

> How much better for students to expend energy using skills to explore content rather that discovering the skills by which the content will eventually be explored. Although we should fear too much structure, we should also fear the lack of it. (P. 131)

References

Armstrong, D. P., J. Patberg, and P. Dewitz. 1988. Reading guides—Helping students understand. *Journal of Reading* 31:532–541. Reports the successful use of Study Guides with narrative material in high school.

Bean, T. W., D. Searles, H. Singer, and S. Cowen. 1990. Learning concepts from biology text through pictorial analogies and an analogical study guide. *Journal of Educational Research* 83:233–237. Study demonstrating the effectiveness of Study Guides when coupled with pictorial analogies for high school biology students.

Dishner, E. K., and J. E. Readence. 1977. Getting started: Using the textbook diagnostically. *Reading World* 17:36–49. Recommends the use of Study Guides as diagnostic tools for the content area teacher.

Earle, R. A. 1969. Developing and using Study Guides. In *Research in reading in the content areas: First year report,* edited by H. L. Herber and P. L. Sanders. Syracuse, NY: Reading and Language Arts Center, Syracuse University, 71–92. Provides directions for the content area teacher in how to develop and use Study Guides as an instructional tool.

Herber, H. L. 1970, 1978. *Teaching reading in content areas.* Englewood Cliffs, NJ: Prentice-Hall. Discusses the use of Study Guides in conjunction with the Instructional Framework, a teaching strategy for content area teachers.

Herber, H. L., and R. F. Barron, eds. 1973. *Research in reading in the content areas: Second year report.* Syracuse, NY: Syracuse University, Reading and Language Arts Center. Includes studies exploring the effectiveness of Study Guides.

Herber, H. L., and R. Vacca, eds. 1977. *Research in reading in the content areas: The third report.* Syracuse, NY: Syracuse University, Reading and Language Arts Center. Includes studies that examined the use of Study Guides.

Herber, H. L., and J. D. Riley, eds. 1979. *Research in reading in the content areas: The fourth report.* Syracuse, NY: Syracuse University, Reading and Language Arts Center. Features additional studies that examined the use of Study Guides.

Miller, K. K., and J. E. George. 1992. Expository passage organizers: Models for reading and writing. *Journal of Reading* 35:372–377. Study that revealed positive effects in reading and writing for sixth graders using Study Guides highlighting the structure of textbooks.

Wood, K. D., D. Lapp, and J. Flood. 1992. *Guiding readers through text: A review of study guides.* Newark, DE: International Reading Association. A practical guide to the use of Study Guides, with numerous examples.

Selective Reading Guide

Purpose

The major objectives of the Selective Reading Guide (also called Selective Reading Guide-O-Rama) (Cunningham and Shablak, 1975) are: (1) to lead students to the major ideas and supporting details within a content text chapter, and (2) to teach students flexibility in their reading.

Rationale

The Selective Reading Guide assumes that since most students are not experts in the subject, they are not able to select with ease the important textual information. That is, it assumes most students read the material as if everything within the chapter were of equal importance. The subject matter instructor is in a position to guide students through the reading assignment by providing them with clues as to which information is important and which can be skimmed lightly.

Intended Audience

The Selective Reading Guide can be used with students in grades six and above. It would appear to be better suited for use with those students who need additional guidance in their reading.

Description of the Procedures

Before an instructor can design any type of guidance tool for students, several important decisions must be made during the planning stage of the lesson. Of primary importance is the identification of the major concepts and understanding to be derived from the chapter. Subject matter instructors should ask themselves the following questions:

1. What should students know when they finish this chapter?

   a. What are the major concepts that the students should understand?

   b. What supporting information or details should they remember on a long-term basis?

2. What should students be able *to do* when they finish the chapter?

   a. What background information is essential to perform the required tasks?

By making a brief list of the answers to the above questions, content teachers can identify the essential information within the text chapter that they want their students to understand. The next step is to move through the book chapter and identify portions of the text that provide students with the previously identified important information. After lightly noting in the margins of their teacher's edition the letters *M* for main ideas and *D* for important details, content instructors are ready to design the Selective Reading Guide.

Perhaps the easiest way to approach this task is to imagine a group of three or four students. It is assumed that content teachers have already completed the preparation stage of the lesson (see description of the Instructional Framework in Unit 5). Students will have their texts open to the first page of the chapter to be studied and are now ready to read the chapter. What information should the teacher provide so that the students will key in on the important ideas that have been identified? The response to this question is the type of information that will be written down in guide form.

Several examples might be in order to illustrate the preceding discussion. The teacher might note important information in the following manner:

- P. 93, paragraphs 3–6. Pay special attention to this section. Why do you think Hunter acted in this manner? We will discuss your ideas later in class.

- P. 94, subtopic in boldface print at top of page. See if you can rewrite the topic to form a question. Now read the information under the subtopic just to answer the question. You should pick up the five ideas very quickly. Jot down your answers in the space provided below.

- P. 94, picture. What appears to be the reaction of the crowd? Now read the fifth paragraph on this page to find out why they are reacting as they are.

- P. 95, paragraphs 5–8. Read this section very carefully. The order of the events is very important and you will want to remember this information for our quiz.

The same approach is used when noting information within the chapter that, based upon the content teacher's analysis, is of little or no importance. The following example illustrates this situation:

- P. 179, all of column 1. The author has provided us with some interesting information here, but it is not important for us to remember. You may want just to skim over it and move on to the second column.

- Pp. 180–181. These pages describe a fictitious family who lived during the Civil War. You may skip this section because we will learn about the lifestyles of the time through films, other readings, and class discussions.

- Pp. 221–222. Recent discoveries in science have improved the information contained on these pages. I will discuss this information with you in class. Now move on to page 223.

By pointing out unimportant information as well as important ideas in the text, content teachers are purported to be effectively communicating to their students that they must be flexible in their reading. Teachers may even wish to communicate literally to their students the notion that all words in print are not necessarily of equal value for the reader who is attempting to ascertain the author's important ideas.

The completed guide should appear in a logical order and should move the student from the beginning of the chapter through the end of the unit. Thus, through the use of the Selective Reading Guide, content teachers are saying to the youngsters: (1) pay close attention to this, (2) skim over this material, (3) read this section carefully, and (4) you can read this section rather quickly, but see if you can find out why, and so on.

Cautions and Comments

As with most guidance tools, this strategy should be used sensitively. The Selective Reading Guide might work best with those students who need the assistance and who could profit from structured approaches to developing selected skills. A conscious effort should be made by the teacher to remove this assistance as the students learn the mechanics of reading and studying text material. This weaning process might begin following the use of the Selective Reading Guide for a two- or three-month period. The students should be told when this is taking place and occasionally reminded that, for example, they should continue to pay particular attention to the pictorial information within the unit.

For those students who have difficulty handling the written version of a Selective Reading Guide, the instructor can just as easily design a cassette tape version. Oral direction will now lead the students through the selection. The instructor might advise the student to " . . . turn off the recorder now and read very carefully these first two paragraphs on page 96. When you have finished, turn the recorder on again and I will discuss the material you read." By providing approximately five seconds of dead space on the tape, the student is allowed sufficient time to handle the mechanics of turning off and on a cassette tape recorder. Of course, the student will have all the time necessary to read and study once the recorder is off.

References ▌

Cunningham, D., and S. L. Shablak. 1975. Selective reading guide-o-rama: The content teacher's best friend. *Journal of Reading* 18:380–382. Introduces the concept of the Selective Reading Guide and provides examples for its construction.

Davey, B. 1986. Using textbook activity guides to help students learn from textbooks. *Journal of Reading* 29:489–494. Discusses the advantages of using a form of the Selective Reading Guide and suggests how it can be implemented in content classrooms.

Guided Reading Procedure ▌

Purpose

As developed by Manzo (1975), the Guided Reading Procedure is designed to: (1) assist students' unaided recall of specific information read; (2) improve the students' abilities to generate their own (implicit) questions as they read; (3) develop the students' understanding of the importance of self-correction; and (4) improve the students' abilities to organize information.

Rationale

Many teachers expect their students to remember the facts in a story or in a chapter from a content textbook. The Guided Reading Procedure (GRP) is intended to provide the teacher with a logical series of instructional steps that can lead to the majority of the students in a given classroom addressing the content. The group or whole class recalls orally the information they have just read silently. The teacher then asks them to confirm, organize, and note relationships. These, Manzo argues, are essential factors in advancing an attitude of comprehension accuracy and, ultimately, reading comprehension ability. As Manzo (1975) contends:

... the GRP enriches skills by having the teacher allow students to see implicit questions, by strengthening determination to concentrate during reading, and by encouraging self-correction and organization of information within minimal teacher direction. (P. 288)

Intended Audience

Teachers can use the Guided Reading Procedure at the primary level, although it appears most appropriate for students in the middle grades through college level. It also is important to note that GRP is a group activity and may not be effective as a one-on-one strategy.

Description of the Procedure

The Guided Reading Procedure may use narrative selections or informational material. The selection should be short enough so that the majority of the students can complete the reading comfortably in one sitting. Manzo (1975) provides a rule of thumb to use in deciding appropriate length. His suggestions on number of words and amount of reading time for average readers follow. For primary students, allow three minutes or approximately 90 words; for intermediate students, three minutes or approximately 500 words; for junior high students, seven minutes or approximately 900 words; for senior high students, ten minutes or approximately 2,000 words; and for college students, twelve minutes or approximately 2,500 words.

Manzo (1975) outlines six basic steps to be followed for the GRP:

1. Prepare the student for the reading assignment.
2. Students read and recall information.
3. Return to article for additional facts and corrections.
4. Organize the remembered material.
5. Provide students with thought-provoking questions.
6. Test students on their knowledge of the information.

1. *Prepare the Student for the Reading Assignment* As with any good teaching lesson, students should work through some form of readiness task before they plunge into the actual reading assignment. This preparation may take the form described under the Directed Reading Activity (Unit 5), the Instructional Framework (Unit 5), the Survey Technique (Unit 10), or the ReQuest procedure (Unit 7), among others. Regardless of which strategy the teacher employs, it is vitally important that the students understand why they are reading the printed material before them. The general purpose, at least for this particular lesson, is for them to remember as many of the details as possible. Teacher/student agreement on this purpose is of critical importance to the strategy's success.

2. *Students Read and Recall Information* With their purpose clearly in mind, the students read the material silently while the teacher stands by to assist students who may have difficulty with the reading. Students are advised that, upon completion of their

reading, they are to turn the material facedown on their desks and wait until their classmates have finished the assignment.

When the large majority of the students have finished the reading, the instructor asks the students to tell what they remember. The emphasis at this point is on unaided recall of the material read. The teacher serves as the recorder and notes on the chalkboard each bit of information suggested by the students. In order to speed the process and avoid extensive writing, an abbreviated form of recording is suggested.

3. *Return to Article for Additional Facts and Corrections*   When the students are no longer able to recall information from memory, the teacher allows them to return to the selection in order to add additional information and to correct inaccurately recalled details. The teacher adds the new information to the board and corrects inaccuracies noted by the students.

4. *Organize the Remembered Material*   The teacher now asks the students to organize the material into a modified outline form. Sometimes the instructor may ask questions to lead the students to an outline highlighting the main ideas and supporting details through the location of more general statements and their supporting details. Sometimes the teacher may have students organize the information and the sequence in which the information was presented. Questions such as the following may be useful: "What happened first in this section?" "What came next?" "Where does this information appear to fit best?" At other times, the teacher or the student may suggest alternative outline forms.

5. *Provide Students with Thought-provoking Questions*   The teacher should direct his or her efforts at this point toward helping the students understand how this new information relates to material they previously learned. Initially, the questions may need to be fairly specific. For example, "How does this new information about Jackson support what we learned about him last week?" As the students become more familiar with this segment of the technique, the teacher may turn to less specific questions that place more responsibility upon the students during this transfer-of-learning stage. Questions of a more general type might include: "Do you see any relation between this information and the material we studied last week?" or "Give me some examples of how this material supports last week's unit." During this step, the teacher serves as a model by asking thoughtful questions that require students to synthesize new information with previously learned information.

6. *Test Students on their Knowledge of the Information*   Following this rather intense reading/reacting activity, the teacher should take time to check the students' short-term memory of the ideas they presented. A short quiz will provide the students an opportunity to reveal how much information they have learned as a result of the procedure. Although Manzo suggests no specific test format, the teacher could use either matching, multiple-choice, short answer, essay items, or some appropriate combination of question types.

The teacher may provide students additional opportunities to " . . . manipulate and deliberate" (Manzo 1975, 291) over the material read. The teacher may also wish to check recall over longer periods of time.

Cautions and Comments

The GRP strategy is a rather intense activity, which may prove beneficial when used selectively. For example, with selected "meaty" reading material (i.e., material containing much important information), the GRP affords students an opportunity to read that information, to interact with others' interpretations of the material in the classroom, and to organize the material. The GRP is a teacher-directed but student-dominated activity that can lead to improvements in readers' understandings. Cunningham, Moore, Cunningham, and Moore (1983) describe an interesting variation of the Guided Reading Procedure. They label it simply the *guided listening procedure.* After sufficiently preparing them for the listening activity, the teacher asks the students to remember as much as they can from the selection. The teacher then reads a short selection orally, taping it at the same time. The remaining steps are similar to those we described earlier, with one obvious exception. Rather than returning to the printed material to confirm student recall, the teacher plays the tape recording and asks the students to raise their hands to stop the tape when they wish to discuss specific pieces of information.

Due to the nature of this particular strategy, Manzo (1975) recommends that the teacher use the Guided Reading Procedure no more than once every two weeks. With appropriate reading selections, a logical variation might be to use the GRP every other week, with the guided listening procedure employed on the off-week.

Finally, the efficacy of the GRP was investigated by Ankney and McClurg (1981) and Bean and Pardi (1979). Ankney and McClurg found the GRP to be useful in helping fifth and sixth graders learn social studies. Bean and Pardi found that the GRP, used in combination with a prereading survey technique, was effective in enhancing the learning from text of poor seventh-grade readers.

References

Ankney, P., and P. McClurg. 1981. Testing Manzo's guided reading procedure. *The Reading Teacher* 34:681–685. Validates the use of the GRP with social studies classes and offers suggestions for its use.

Bean, T. W., and R. Pardi. 1979. A field test of a guided reading strategy. *Journal of Reading* 23:144–147. Study that found that the GRP used in combination with a prereading strategy was effective in improving comprehension and retention.

Cunningham, P. M., S. A. Moore, J. W. Cunningham, and D. W. Moore. 1983. *Reading in elementary classrooms: Strategies and observations.* New York: Longman. Presents a brief description of a variation of the GRP—the guided listening procedure.

Hayes, D. A. 1989. Helping students GRASP the knack of writing summaries. *Journal of Reading* 33:96–101. Combines the use of the GRP with summarization.

Manzo, A. V. 1975. Guided reading procedure. *Journal of Reading* 18:287–291. Provides the rationale and specific steps that make up the GRP strategy.

Spiegel, D. L. 1980. Adaptations of Manzo's guided reading procedure. *Reading Horizons* 20:188–192. Presents various modifications of the GRP.

Idea Mapping

Purpose

Idea Mapping (Armbruster and Anderson, 1982) was developed for purposes of spatially representing the overall structure of expository text. It is purported to have several instructional uses: (1) to afford teachers a tool for examining the nature of a text prior to classroom use; (2) to direct students to appreciate the structure characteristics of different text; and (3) to provide teachers and students with a framework for carefully reading expository text.

Rationale

Based upon the work of Hanf (1971), Merritt, Prior, and Grugeon (1977), and, most notably, Armbruster and Anderson (1982), mapping has emerged as one of the more popular tools for analyzing text. The mapping technique incorporates the visual-spatial conventions for diagramming ideas and the nature of relationships between ideas: concept and example, concept and properties, concept and definition, temporal succession, cause and effect, conditional, and comparison. These relationships and their mapping scheme are depicted in Figure 9–2. If extended to a whole text, as depicted in Figure 9–3, the overall pattern provides a spatial representation across the whole text. Armbruster and Anderson (1982) suggest that a variety of basic text structures are forthcoming from these overall analyses of text. If the question is asked, "Why or how was the text written?" then the following description of text types usually emerges: (1) description—a listing of properties, characteristics, or attributes; (2) compare/contrast—a description of similarities and differences between two or more things; (3) temporal sequence—relationship between ideas that is largely sequential; (4) explanation—an interaction between at least two ideas or events that is causal or conditional; and (5) definitional/examples—a definition of a concept and examples of the concept. In conjunction with these overall text patterns, Armbruster and Anderson (1982) suggest that there are two types of frameworks or frames of text: static and dynamic. Static refers to text that is largely descriptive or definitional in character; dynamic refers to text that is more explanatory in nature.

Instructionally, Armbruster and Anderson (1982) argue that mapping is a tool by which teachers and students can build a coherent model of the meaning of the text. It serves to involve students with the meaning of the text; it focuses their attention on text structure; and it provides for the transformation of prose into a diagrammatic or visual representation. However, in one research study in which the worth of mapping was examined, training in the use of mapping did not sustain long-term gains in comprehension (Armbruster and Anderson, 1980).

Intended Audience

Mapping has been used extensively with high school students and college-level students as an aid to improving their comprehension of expository text. Simplifications of the procedure (see Cautions and Comments) might be appropriate to use with students at the elementary level.

FIGURE 9–2. TYPES OF MAPPED RELATIONSHIPS

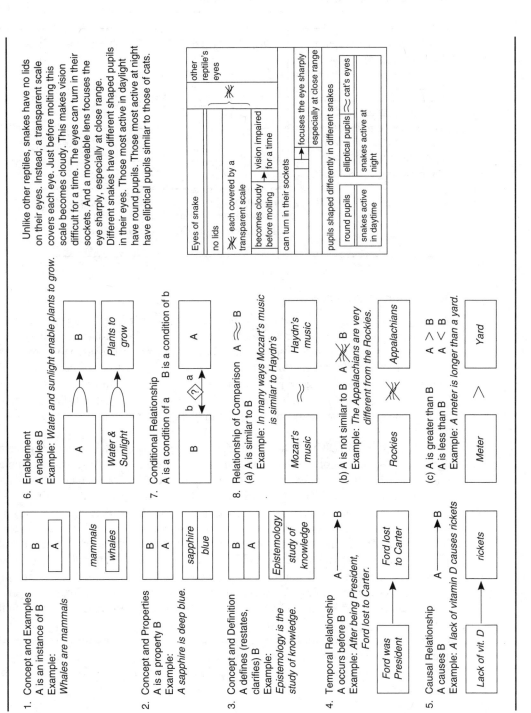

FIGURE 9–2. TYPES OF MAPPED RELATIONSHIPS

FIGURE 9–3.   SAMPLE OF TOP-DOWN EXERCISE

FDR's New Deal Program had three general aims.

This exercise requires students to supply the three general aims of the New Deal.

FDR's New Deal Program had three general aims.

relief   recovery   reform

This exercise requires students to supply more detailed information—definitions and examples of FDR's general aims.

Description of the Procedure

Mapping can have countless uses, ranging from simply revealing the map of a text to students prior to having them read the text, to having students (or the teacher) create detailed analyses of a text. The present description of mapping is restricted to proposals by Armbruster and Anderson (1982) in which students respond to maps generated by the teacher. In particular, they have pursued the use of maps in two different ways: (1) top-down, or starting with the overall framework for a text and refining it or filling in the text, and (2) generalizing from some given details to higher order structures.

Using Maps Top-down   The goal for top-down use of maps is to have students generate higher order structures or the main idea and to use this top-level structure to complete written map exercises. For example, a teacher about to assign a chapter on the establishment and growth of cities might begin by giving students a map similar to Figure 9–3.

This frame or map represents the higher order ideas that readers could use to guide their reading of the text. As a written exercise and as a form of evaluation, students could fill out the details of the map. To constrain the task further, the teacher could use the specialized mapping symbols to indicate the exact type of information the reader would be expected to insert. For example, in the map given in Figure 9–4, the form of the map tells the students whether they are to provide definitions, examples, attributes, and so on.

Sometimes a text is especially difficult to understand. Say the purpose for which the text was written or for which you wish to have your students read it is not congruent with the structure of the text. In these types of situations, it might be useful to introduce the students to the general principle that is overriding. This might be done in the form of introducing students to an additional map that complements, but does not match, the texts assigned to be read.

FIGURE 9–4. SAMPLE OF TOP-DOWN MAP

Using Maps Bottom-up   Using maps bottom-up involves helping students derive higher order structures by guiding the students to generate principles, supraordinate concepts, or main ideas. For example, a bottom-up exercise might have students infer the label for slots from a definition for some attributes. In Figure 9–5, several examples of this type of activity are given. As Armbruster and Anderson (1982) indicate, in many respects these activities represent merely "the converse of the top-down" (P. 16).

Other variations of a bottom-up approach might entail presenting the students with a listing of the ideas from a text that they are to organize into a map based on a reading of the text. Figure 9–6 includes such an exercise.

Obviously there are a variety of different ways in which students can be involved in moving from the details of a map or text to representing that text coherently. Of course, teachers need to have examined the text carefully prior to being able to develop such activities. They need to have developed their own map of the text and considered what they deem as desirable learning outcomes for their students. In choosing mapping as a tool, whether mapping be used in a bottom-up or top-down fashion, they need to consider just what content they want their students to address, as well as how they would like them to approach the texts. Mapping is not just a vehicle for examining ideas from a text; it is intended to alert students to text features. Indeed, in order to engage in the different activities that have been suggested, students need to be familiar with mapping procedures. They need to know the symbols used to represent different relationships in text, the basic text structures, and the fact that information is presented in different variations of these standard forms.

Cautions and Comments

Mapping is not the only form of text analysis, nor is it the only one that provides for the diagrammatic representation of texts and that has been applied to classrooms. Two other such approaches have been developed and adapted for use as instructional tools: networking (Dansereau, 1979) and flowcharting (Geva, 1983). Networking and flowcharting, like

FIGURE 9–5.   SAMPLES OF BOTTOM-UP EXERICSES

This exercise requires students to find the supraordinate heading.

This exercise requires two levels of generalization: (a) supraordinate terms for the definitions in the three categories, and (b) a supraordinate heading for the terms generated in a.

FIGURE 9–6. SAMPLE OF BOTTOM-UP MAPS (SEE MODEL)

Directions to students:
Make an i-map using the following terms from the chapter on muscle structure.

     striations
     muscle fibers
     striated muscles
     elongated cells
     sarcolemna
     40% of body weight
     highly specialized cells

Possible Student Response:

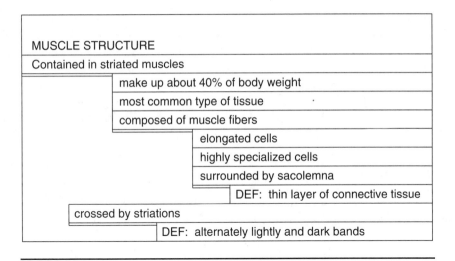

mapping, involve having students diagram or use diagrams to chart the ideas and relationships represented within the text. Studies by Bartlett (1978), Dansereau, Holley, and Collins (1980), Geva (1983), Margolis (1982), and Armbruster and Anderson (1980) tend to offer rather mixed results about the benefits of using such techniques. These studies have suggested that most students find that the procedures offer very little, and have no obvious or immediate payoff for the investment in time and effort to learn such systems. In all cases, the researchers appear to have been forced to streamline their presentation of the system to students, have gone to great pains to make it interesting, and have tended to avoid making students repeatedly do detailed analyses of texts. As is the case with mapping, most researchers tend to support the use of text analytic procedures by teachers for purposes of creating instructional activities based upon diagrammatic depictions of text and to appreciate the information represented by a text.

Instead of detailed analyses of text, some educators have proposed simplified procedures for interconnecting ideas (see Davidson, 1982). Apart from mentioning these developments, there are some other issues. One of the major drawbacks to mapping and these other text analysis procedures is the extent to which they make readers accountable to another author's text. As students read, they should be pursuing their own goals and composing their own text. As presently used, text analysis, specifically mapping, ties the readers to the text they are assigned to read when perhaps it would be more worthwhile to have students generate maps of what they glean from a text and what they might write for themselves. A second drawback to mapping and other text analytic procedures is the extent to which learning how to use a system requires learning the terminology and symbols of that system. Perhaps it would be more appropriate to let students develop their own systems initially and leave the adoption of standardized procedures to later and more extensive uses of the procedure.

References

Armbruster, B. B., and T. H. Anderson. 1980. *The effect of mapping on the free recall of expository text* (Tech. Rep. No. 160). Urbana: University of Illinois, Center for the Study of Reading. Presents a research study in which college-age students were trained in the use of mapping.

———. 1982. *Idea mapping: The technique and its use in the classroom* (Reading Education Report No. 36). Urbana: University of Illinois, Center for the Study of Reading. Presents various guidelines and examples of how Idea Mapping might be used in the classroom.

Bartlett, B. J. 1978. *Top-level structure as an organizational strategy for recall of classroom text.* Unpublished doctoral diss., Arizona State University, Tempe. Presents a thorough research study that examines the benefits of teaching rhetorical structures.

Dansereau, D. F. 1979. Development and evaluation of a learning strategy training program. *Journal of Educational Psychology* 71:64–73. Discusses the use of networking with college-level structures.

Dansereau, D. F., C. D. Holley, and K. W. Collins. 1980, April. *Effects of learning strategy training on text processing.* Paper presented at the annual meeting of the American Educational Research Association, Boston. Presents the findings of a research study in which networking was taught to college-level students.

Davidson, J. L. 1982. The group mapping activity for instruction in reading and thinking. *Journal of Reading* 26:52–56. Describes a simplified version of Idea Mapping.

Geva, E. 1983. Facilitating reading comprehension through flow-charting. *Reading Research Quarterly* 18:384–405. Presents the findings of a research study in which flowcharting was used to help students deal with expository text.

Hanf, M. B. 1971. Mapping: A technique for translating reading into thinking. *Journal of Reading* 14:225–230. Presents a simplified version of mapping for use by high school students.

Holley, C. D., and D. F. Dansereau, eds. *Spatial learning strategies: Techniques, applications, and other issues.* Orlando, FL: Academic Press. Includes several articles describing the use of mapping and other spatial learning strategies.

Lambiotte, J. G. 1992. Effects of knowledge maps and prior knowledge on recall of science lecture content. *Journal of Experimental Education* 60:181–201. Study demonstrating positive effects for maps when used with students who have lower prior knowledge in biology.

Margolis, K. 1982. *An instructional study of helping readers identify the gist in expository text.* Unpublished diss., University of Illinois, Urbana-Champaign. Presents a research study in which high school students were involved in topically defining expository text.

Merritt, J., D. Prior, and D. Grugeon. 1977. *Developing independence in reading.* Milton Keynes, England: Open University Press. Describes the use of mapping and how it might be applied to text.

Miccinati, J. L. 1988. Mapping the terrain: Connecting reading and academic writing. *Journal of Reading* 31:542–551. Explores the use of maps and their influence on reading and writing.

Piccolo, J. A. 1987. Expository text structure: Teaching and learning strategies. *The Reading Teacher* 40:838–847. Explores the uses of mapping with reading and writing of selected topics.

Tierney, R. J., and J. Mosenthal. 1982. Discourse comprehension and production: Analyzing text structure and cohesion. In *Reader meets author/bridging the gap,* edited by J. Langer and M. Smith-Burke. Newark, DE: International Reading Association. Presents an overview of six different text analysis sentences, including mapping, together with implications for classroom use.

Text Structure Strategy

Purpose

The Text Structure Strategy is designed to help students recognize and use expository text structures in order to better understand and recall informational-type texts.

Rationale

The ability to perceive the organization of text material has long been viewed as a valuable reading strategy (Niles, 1974). For example, it has been suggested that knowledge of how the ideas in a text can be bound together to form a logical whole enables students to understand, and later recall, that material better than if the text is perceived as a series of discrete entities. Indeed, research (e.g., McGee, 1982) has shown that readers who are knowledgeable about text structure have an advantage in comprehension and recall over readers who aren't aware of the organization of text.

There are roughly two types of text material encountered by students in schools: (1) narrative, or story-type, texts such as those found in much of the content of basal readers and literature anthologies; and (2) expository, or informational-type, texts such as those found in science or social studies books. Not surprisingly, students are more familiar with narrative text than expository text. One of the reasons for this is simply that students have more exposure to story-type material both before they start school and in the primary grades, where it predominates instruction.

A second reason is that narrative texts have a consistent structure (setting, initiating event, internal response, attempt, consequence, and reaction), while expository texts may take a variety of structures. Meyer and Freedle (1984) list five different types of expository text structures: (1) description, (2) collection, (3) causation, (4) problem/solution, and (5) comparison. In addition, they found that text structures that are better organized (causation, problem/solution, comparison) are more easily recalled than text structures that display less organization (description, collection). The following teaching strategy focuses primarily on the first three types of expository text structures.

Intended Audience

Expository text structure is mainly encountered in content area textbooks that are usually associated with middle and secondary schools. However, content area texts are frequently used in the primary grades, and samples of expository passages are increasingly finding their way into basal readers. Therefore, teaching students to use expository text structure is appropriate for students at all grade levels.

Description of the Procedures

Prerequisite to any strategy to teach text structure successfully are three factors suggested by McGee and Richgels (1986). First, teachers must be knowledgeable about structure, i.e., they have thoroughly analyzed text so they can focus students' attention on the specific aspects that let one recognize and use text structure. Second, the passages used for instruction are well organized and consist of a predominant structure. Third, the students must become actively involved in using the strategy while they read and afterward.

Before we present a teaching strategy for expository text structure, the three main text structures mentioned earlier will be defined. A causative text structure is one in which a relationship is specified between reasons and results in a time sequence. A problem/solution structure is similar to a causative structure except that solution is added to the structure that is designed to break the causative link. Finally, a comparative structure organizes elements on the basis of their similarities and differences and implies no causality or time sequence. (For an in-depth examination of text structure in general, see Pearson and Camperell, 1985.)

The following general strategy for teaching expository structure is recommended by Readence, Bean, and Baldwin (1995) and consists of (1) modeling, (2) recognition, and (3) production.

1. *Modeling*   Before expecting students to use text structure, it is necessary to demonstrate what it is. This can be done by having teachers model their thought processes for students as they (the teachers) use text structure. In essence, teachers think aloud for students. Passages that students will encounter in their reading should be used, since those are most relevant for students. During modeling, it is essential to show students a particular text structure and point out *why* it is a certain type and *how* that structure type is organized. Furthermore it is necessary to point out any words that signal, or cue, the reader into what the text structure is. It has been found that signal words such as *however, because,* and *therefore* assist students in becoming aware of text structure and improving their recall (Meyer, Brandt, and Bluth, 1980).

2. *Recognition*   This part of the teaching sequence amounts to walking students through a particular text structure. This can be accomplished by asking judicious questions that focus students' attention on selected aspects of the structure. Teachers may wish to start the recognition step on a listening level first. By listening, students can attend directly to the structure, particularly when a difficult text might cause students to divide their attention between reading the text and perceiving the structure. In addition, teachers may also choose to begin with sentences or paragraphs before moving on to lengthier passages. The essential part of this step, however, is that the students verbalize the why and how of the text structure. In this way teachers begin to shift responsibility for learning text structure from themselves to the students. As a guide to helping students recognize text structure, Bartlett (1978) offers the accompanying checklist.

CHECKLIST FOR TEACHING
TEXT PATTERNS

1. Did you pick out the organization as *problem-solution?*

   If so, _____ great!

   In not, _____ did you ask the two questions before reading?

   or,

   _____ did you find the main idea? ("The problem is . . . sugar and starch?")

   _____ did you find how this main idea was organized? (one part about a *problem,* another part about a *solution*)

2. Did you write the name of the top-level organization at the top of the recall page?

   If so, _____ so far, so good!

   If not, _____ mmmmm!

3. Did you write down the main idea as the first sentence?

   If so, _____ keep it up!

   If not, _____ oh no!

4. Did you have *two* parts in arranging your sentences?

   If so, _____ not far to go now!

   If not, _____ tut tut!

5. Were the *two* parts: one for the problem, one for the solution?

   If so, _____ I bet you remembered a lot!

   If not, _____ oh cripes!

6. Did you check?

   If so, _____ double halo!

   If not, _____ don't be overconfident!

---

3. *Production*   Once students have gained some facility in perceiving text structure, they should now be ready to produce a text structure on their own. Just as recognition precedes production, a logical extension of perceiving text structure through reading is producing it through writing. Using a Graphic Organizer or some other form of skeletal outline based upon a text passage, students are directed to compose their own version of the passage. They are told to write using a particular text structure and whatever signal words are appropriate to cue that structure. Writing is thus used as a means to reinforce students' knowledge of text structure; and writing with a particular structure in mind should also reinforce the logical organization necessary in effectively communicating through writing.

Cautions and Comments

Attempts to teach text structure have yielded mixed results. Taylor and Beach (1984) were able to be successful at improving the reading comprehension abilities of middle graders by instruction in certain text structures. Other studies have yielded fewer gains. We would question whether text structure can or should be taught isolated from content and purpose. Teaching text structure by itself, without any emphasis on what is being written and why, would seem likely to detract from meaningful negotiations between authors and readers.

Another problem relates to reality. It is cautioned that not all text that students encounter will be well organized. In reality, often text is not organized in a straightforward manner. To cope with this dilemma, Alvermann (1981) has suggested that the text be reorganized into more useful relationships by employing a Graphic Organizer, which places the important ideas in a format that depicts a well-organized text structure. By doing so, she found that both the quantity and quality of recall by students was facilitated.

McGee and Richgels (1986) go one step further in their suggestions for dealing with poorly formed text. They recommend that, instead of Graphic Organizers, a discussion should take place of the text in comparison to what an idealized, or well-organized, text on that topic would look like. Following that, the text should be revised, creating a well-formed piece with an apparent structure and explicit links. Thus, writing is again used as a means to reinforce students' knowledge of text structure. Along this line of reasoning, Harrison (1982) has had a great deal of success in having high school students rewrite their textbook material for each other.

References

Alvermann, D. E. 1981. The compensatory effect of graphic organizers on descriptive text. *Journal of Educational Research* 75:44–48. Research study showing positive effects on comprehension for the use of Graphic Organizers with poorly organized text.

Armbruster, B. B., T. H. Anderson, and J. Ostertag. 1989. Teaching text structure to improve reading and writing. *The Reading Teacher* 43:130–137. Describes a strategy for teaching text structure to fifth graders that enhances reading comprehension and summary writing.

Bartlett, B. J. 1978. *Top-level structure as an organizational strategy for recall of classroom text.* Unpublished doctoral diss., Arizona State University, Tempe. A study that yielded very positive results due to the teaching of four commonly found structures to ninth graders.

Harrison, C. 1982. *The nature and effect of children's rewriting school textbook prose.* Paper presented at the Ninth World Congress of Reading, Dublin. Describes a study in which high school students rewrote texts and their rewritten versions were compared with the original texts for comprehensibility.

McGee, L. M. 1982. Awareness of text structure: Effects on children's recall of expository text. *Reading Research Quarterly* 17:581–590. Study that found that those students who were aware of text structure comprehended better than those who were not aware of structure.

McGee, L. M., and D. J. Richgels. 1986. Attending to text structure: A comprehension strategy. In *Reading in the content areas: Improving classroom instruction,* 2d ed., edited by E. K. Dishner, T. W. Bean, J. E. Readence, and D. W. Moore. Dubuque, IA: Kendall/Hunt. Discusses the use of writing as a means to teach text structure.

———. 1992. Text structure strategies. In *Reading in the content areas: Improving classroom instruction,* 3d ed., edited by E. K. Dishner, T. W. Bean, J. E. Readence, and D. W. Moore, 234–247. Dubuque, IA: Kendall/Hunt. An update of their 1986 discussion.

Meyer, B. J. F., and R. O. Freedle. 1984. Effects of discourse type on recall. *American Educational Research Journal* 21:121–143. Study that found that certain types of expository text were comprehended better than others.

Meyer, B. J. F., D. Brandt, and G. J. Bluth. 1980. Use of top-level structure in text: Key for reading comprehension of ninth-grade students. *Reading Research Quarterly* 16:72–103. Study that found an advantage for using signal words to assist students in perceiving text structure and improving recall.

Niles, O. S. 1974. Organization perceived. In *Perspectives in reading: Developing study skills in secondary schools,* edited by H. L. Herber, Newark, DE: International Reading Association. Emphasizes the practical aspects of teaching text structure.

Pearson, P. D., and K. Camperell. 1985. Comprehension of text structures. In *Theoretical models and processes of reading,* 3d ed., edited by H. Singer and R. B. Ruddell. Newark, DE: International Reading Association, 323–342. Review of research on text structure with recommendations for research and instruction.

Readence, J. E., T. W. Bean, and R. S. Baldwin. 1995. *Content area reading: An integrated approach,* 5th ed. Dubuque, IA: Kendall/Hunt. Describes a variety of strategies for teaching text structure.

Slater, W. H. 1985. Teaching expository text structure with structural organizers. *Journal of Reading* 28:712–718. Study in which ninth grade students were taught to use text structure through highly structured practice and application.

Taylor, B., and R. W. Beach. 1984. The effects of text structure instruction on middle grade students' comprehension and production of expository text. *Reading Research Quarterly* 19:134–146. Describes a research study in which the authors evaluated the effects on comprehension of writing texts with structures.

Story Grammars and Story Maps

Purpose

Story Grammars and Story Maps aid readers in their development and use of a sense of story. During reading comprehension, they direct the questions that teachers use in conjunction with the guided reading of a story.

Rationale

In 1947, Gates advocated the importance of a sense of story in the reader's comprehension of narrative. Now several decades later, a number of educators are proponents of procedures for developing in readers a sense of story and ensuring that the guidance they receive is true to the story line. What has spurred this recent interest in stories is the propagation of a number of different procedures for analyzing stories—for defining what some researchers have labeled as a grammar for stories. In this vein, the efforts of Kintsch (1977), Mandler and Johnson (1977), Rumelhart (1975), Stein and Glenn (1979), Thorndyke (1977), and Warren, Nicholas, and Trabasso (1979) are most notable. One of the major theses in this work is that stories have a somewhat predictable grammar that readers can sense and use in comprehending them. Consider the following story and its depiction in Figure 9–7.

Although there are various ways a story might be depicted graphically, this figure illustrates some features of attempts to define what constitutes a story in terms of these grammars. As the figure suggests, a story can be organized into several categories of events, such as setting and event sequences, which in turn can be broken down into subseries of initiating events, reactions (internal and external responses), and resolutions.

FIGURE 9–7.   EXAMPLE OF A STORY GRAMMAR ANALYSIS OF A SIMPLE TEXT

Text:

1. Dick lived on a farm in Vermont.

2. One night we heard a fox in the chicken coop.

3. He knew he had to kill it.

4. Dick got his rifle.

5. and went to the chicken coop.

6. He surprised the fox with a chicken in its mouth.

7. Dick shot the fox where it stood.

8. Dick buried the fox.

With these methods, educators have generated two types of strategies for improving readers' comprehension of stories. Beck and McKeown (1981) developed the notion of a Story Map for use in preparing the questions to guide a reader through a narrative selection. Cunningham and Foster (1978) and Dreher and Singer (1980) generated guidelines for developing in students a sense of story, which the students themselves can apply to narratives.

Intended Audience

For purposes of generating questions for a story, the Story Map procedures can be applied to any story—whether it be a narrative intended for adults or for very young children. If developing a sense of stories by using a Story Grammar framework is your goal, most students beyond the sixth grade have such a sense. Some researchers have suggested that even at the fourth grade level, most children have a sense of story.

Description of the Procedures

Both the use of a Story Grammar (Cunningham and Foster, 1978; Dreher and Singer, 1980) and the use of Story Maps (Beck and McKeown, 1981; Pearson, 1982) will be described.

Story Grammars   Apart from their use in text analysis research, Story Grammars have been used in instructional settings for purposes of heightening student awareness of the structure of stories. Cunningham and Foster (1978) describe procedures they developed and used with sixth-grade students. Their intent was to generate a study guide framework that they might be able to use with not just one but most of the stories the students are assigned. The framework that was developed is presented in Figure 9–8.

What follows is a description of what occurred as the procedure was introduced to the class:

> Ms. Foster noted the group's resistance to something new, then told them that it would be clearer once she gave them an example. She proceeded to tell them a story of the knight rescuing the lady and filled in the diagram on the board as she went along. Several students commented that they understood a little better, and Ms. Foster proceeded to do the first story in the short story book. All of the students read along silently as Ms. Foster read the story aloud. As she read a page, she filled in the diagram on the board.
>
> By the time she reached the third page of the first story, some students were joining her in choosing answers. She then shifted the procedure by saying, "Okay, who are the characters in this part of the story? . . . "Has the location changed?" (P. 368)

The lesson continued in this fashion throughout the remainder of the story. Once the story was complete the teacher explained that the diagram, when completed, included the important parts of the story.

FIGURE 9–8. SIMPLIFIED DIAGRAM OF A STORY'S STRUCTURE

Story

Setting

A. 1. Location
   2. Time
   3. Characters
B. 1.
   2.
   3.
C. 1.
   2.
   3.
D. etc.

Theme

A. Main goal of the
   main character

Plot

A. 1. Subgoal
   2. Attempt to
      accomplish
      subgoal
   3. Outcome of
      attempt
B. 1.
   2.
   3.
C. 1.
   2.
   3.
D. etc.

Resolution

A. Does the main
   character
   accomplish
   his/her goal?
   Explain.

Taken from Cunningham and Foster (1978).

In a similar attempt, Dreher and Singer (1980) had students fill out the chart given in Figure 9–9. The first step in their procedure was to explain the chart and its components, and then distribute a story and copies of the chart for the students to complete with the help of the teacher. After discussing the chart with students and the reasons for responding as they did, a second story and chart were distributed for them to complete in groups of three. This was followed with a third story and chart, which were to be completed independently by each student.

Story Maps   Story Maps are used to generate questions for the guided reading of any narrative. The design of questions around a Story Map involves a rather simple procedure. Based upon an intuitive sense of what the premise or starting point of a story is, the teacher lists major events and ideas that make up the story. This list includes explicit and implicit events, as well as any links between these events. This framework serves as the basis for generating questions for the story. It ensures questions that, as Beck and McKeown (1981, 915) point out, "match the progression of ideas and events in the story." They feel it is more appropriate to keep to addressing a story's progression in terms of events and ideas, before dealing with ideas out of sequence or extending the reader's

FIGURE 9–9.   STORY STRUCTURE CHART

Fill in the sentences from the story that fit each part of this chart.

1. Setting

Where does the story take place?

Who are the main characters of the story?

When does the story take place?

_____

_____

Is there any other information that helps us get the picture of what things are like at the beginning of the story?

_____

_____

2. Goal

What is the main *goal* or purpose of the main character?

_____

_____

Is there any other information about the main character's goal? Maybe the story explains the reason the main character wants the goal.

_____

_____

3. Plot

How does the main character try to get the goal?

A. First try

Something happens.

_____

What does the main character do?

_____

How did it turn out?

_____

Is there any other information about the *first try?*

_____

B. Second try

Main character makes a new plan to get the goal.

_____

Main charcter tries new plan.

_____

How did it turn out?

_____

Is there any other information about the *second try?*

_____

4. Ending

Did the main character get the goal?

_____

Is there any other information about the way the story ended?

_____

_____

Taken from Dreher and Singer (1980).

FIGURE 9–10.   STORY AND STORY MAP

Ring Story (By Julia De Voss)

   "You'd better not lose this ring, Pam" Pam's sister advised as Pam slid the shining ring onto her middle finger. "It's my favorite ring and I'm letting you wear it only because of the dance."

   Pam looked at the golden ring glittering in the sun. The tiny red stone shone like a light and sent an oblong red shadow across Pam's hands. Tonight was the dance and now everything was perfect—her dress, her shoes, and the ring.

   Putting the finishing touches on her dress, Pam heard her father's voice. "Let's go, Pam," he called, "it's time go to the dance!" Pam ran excitedly down the stairs, glancing at her image reflected in the hall mirror. All was in place . . . everything except the ring. Pam stared at her empty finger in disbelief. Where had it gone?

   Quickly Pam raced back upstairs. In a panic she looked everywhere she had been since she placed the precious ring on her finger. She tore through her dresser drawers, through her closet, back through the hallway. Her eyes scanned every inch of the floor. There was no ring.

   "Daddy!" Pam yelled downstairs, "Wait a minute more, I'm coming!" Pam ran into the bathroom. She had just washed her hands. Perhaps the ring had slipped off her finger and had fallen into the sink. Pam stared down into the empty bowl. The ring was gone. Slowly she raised her eyes to her face now streaked with tears.

   "I'll tell Daddy I can't go to the dance until I find the ring," she said to herself.

   Sadly Pam raised her hands to wipe her eyes—and there on her finger twinkled the golden ring. It had been there all the time, on her other hand.

   "Next time," Pam said as she smiled at her reflection, "I'll stop and think before I look so hard for something that isn't lost!"

STORY MAP
THE SETTING
Character(s): Pam, Pam's sister and father
Place: Pam's home

   ↓

THE PROBLEM
Pam cannot find her sister's ring.

   ↓

THE GOAL
Pam must find the ring.

 EVENT 1 Pam looks everywhere she had been in her bedroom.

→ EVENT 2 Pam looks in the bathroom sink.

→ EVENT 3 Pam looks at her hands.

   ↓

THE RESOLUTION
Pam finds the ring on her own hand.

FIGURE 9–10. *(Continued)*

Question 1.   Where and when did the story occur? (The first question always deals with the setting. Leave the question out only if it does not seem important to the story.)

Question 2.   Who is the hero or heroine? (Usually a question about the protagonists will follow.)

Question 3.   What is Pam's problem? What did Pam need? Why is Pam in trouble? (This question can take various forms, but it deals with the protagonist's problem and leads into the next question, which is a goal question.)

Question 4.   What does Pam need to do? (This is the first of a series of questions that follow the events of the story.)

Question 5.   What was the first thing Pam tried to do to get out of her predicament?

Question 6.   What did she do when that didn't work?

Question 7.   Why did she become depressed?

Question 8.   How did Pam finally solve her problem?

Question 9.   What lesson did she learn?

---

interpretation of the story. As they stated, "The extension of text ideas can enhance comprehension if a map of the story has already been developed" (P. 915).

Figure 9–10 is an example of a Story Map generated for a story and the questions derived from the map. The last few questions deal with the resolution and, although there is no fixed number of questions that might be asked, the key is to have addressed the main story elements based on the story map. Other questions that might be more provocative (If you were. . . . ?) or allow for more interpretive responses (What might the ring symbolize. . . . ?) might be introduced at this time.

Cautions and Comments

The use of Story Grammars as a tool to sensitize students to stories, and the application of Story Maps for the purpose of developing questions to guide the treatment of story selections, represent sincere attempts to apply research to practice. What is debatable is whether they have taken all factors into consideration. For instance, Cunningham and Foster (1978) reported that the bottom students liked reading stories using Story Grammar frameworks, and they believed these students improved in their ability to comprehend stories. In contrast, in a similar study Dreher and Singer (1980) were not as impressed with the results they got with fourth graders. Subsequently, they criticized Cunningham and Foster (1978) for their claims and argued that students did not appear to need Story Grammar instruction because they already have a well-developed sense of story. A later study by Fitzgerald and Spiegel (1983) seems to have, at least, temporarily put an end to the disagreement. In their study, 20 fourth graders who were identified as lacking a keen sense of story profited from instruction directed at developing their sense of stories. The fact that they were able to identify such students and that these students showed gains due to instruction supports the use of such frameworks with selected students.

What about Story Maps? Are Beck and McKeown's claims reasonable? Beck and McKeown (1981) claim that an integrated and sequential line of questioning will lead to better story understanding than either a random barrage of questions or a mix of provocative questions, opportunities for interpretative response, and story line questions. Unfortunately, we do not have the data to substantiate their claims. Intuitively, a well-ordered set of questions would seem to be better than a random set, but less intuitively reasonable is the suggestion that provocative questions and interpretative probes may detract from story understanding. Often such probes may be what engages the reader; indeed, they may fuel the reader's interest to read more thoughtfully and diligently.

There are some issues that cut across the use of both Story Maps and Grammars. As Brewer and Lichtenstein (1982) argued, a Story Grammar framework does not make a story a story. In fact, their research points to the fact that what distinguishes a story are more aesthetic aspects of a reader's response, such as suspense. Perhaps an argument can be made for facilitating emotional response to a story over or in conjunction with dealing with the story elements. Maybe readers should be encouraged to enjoy rather than dissect a story. These are questions that, owing to lack of data, have to be answered subjectively.

References

Beck, J., and M. G. McKeown. 1981. Developing questions that promote comprehension: The story map. *Language Arts* 58:913–918. Provides an overview of the Story Map and reasons for its use.

Beck, J., M. G. McKeown, E. S. McCaslin, and A. M. Burke. 1979. *Instructional dimensions that may affect comprehension.* University of Pittsburgh: Learning, Research and Development Center. Presents the notion of Story Map and compares it with strengths and weaknesses of the guided reading in basals.

Brewer, W. F., and E. H. Lichtenstein. 1982. *Stories are to entertain: A structural-affect theory of stories* (Tech. Rep. No. 265). Urbana-Champaign, IL: University of Illinois, Center for the Study of Reading. Presents an argument against the value of Story Grammars and for the role of suspense in story understanding.

Cudd, E. T., and L. L. Robert. 1987. Using story frame to develop reading comprehension in a first grade classroom. *The Reading Teacher* 41: 74–81. Offers suggestions for having students respond in writing to story frames for selections.

Cunningham, J., and E. O. Foster. 1978. The ivory tower connection: A case study. *The Reading Teacher* 31:365–369. Discusses a teacher's attempt to use Story Grammars as a way of sensitizing sixth graders to story structures.

Davis, Z. T., and M. D. McPherson. 1989. Story map instruction: A road map for reading comprehension. *The Reading Teacher* 43:232–240. A practical discussion of the use of Story Maps to promote elementary students' comprehension.

Dreher, M. J., and H. Singer. 1980. Story grammar instruction is unnecessary for intermediate grade students. *The Reading Teacher* 34:261–268. In conjunction with a partial replication of the Cunningham and Foster (1978) study, this article questions whether Story Grammar instruction is necessary.

Fitzgerald, J., and D. L. Spiegel. 1983. Enhancing children's reading comprehension through instruction in narrative structure. *Journal of Reading Behavior* 15:1–17. Reports a research study involving training 20 students who were found lacking in story structure awareness.

Gates, A. I. 1947. *The improvement of reading,* 3d ed. New York: Macmillan. A classic among college texts with some discussion of the importance of developing a sense of story.

Gurney, D., R. Gersten, J. Dimino, and D. Carnine. 1990. Story grammar: Effective literature instruction for high school students with learning disabilities. *Journal of Learning Disabilities* 23:335–342. Study showing the effectiveness of story grammar with learning disabled students in high school literature classes.

Kintsch, W. 1977. On comprehending stories. In *Cognitive processes in comprehension,* edited by M. Just and P. Carpenter. Hillsdale, NJ: Erlbaum. Offers a description of the processes involved in story comprehension.

Mandler, J. M., and N. S. Johnson. 1977. Remembrance of things parsed: Story structure and recall. *Cognitive Psychology* 9:111–151. Presents justification for the use of Story Grammars.

Pearson, P. D. 1982. *Asking questions about stories.* Boston: Ginn. Discusses and demonstrates the use of Story Maps with basal story selections.

Pincus, A. R. H., E. B. Geller, and E. M. Stover. 1986. A technique for using the story schema as a transition to understanding and event based magazine articles. *Journal of Reading* 30:152–159. Explores the use of story analysis together with cloze and summary writing to guide the reading of expository text.

Rumelhart, D. E. 1975. Notes on a schema for stories. In *Representation and understanding: Studies in cognitive science,* edited by D. G. Bobrow and A. M. Collins. New York: Academic Press. Presents one of the seminal theoretical discussions of Story Grammars.

Spiegel, D. L., and J. Fitzgerald. 1986. Improving reading comprehension through instruction about story parts. *The Reading Teacher* 39:676–685. Discusses the impact on comprehension of teaching story elements.

Stein, N. L., and C. G. Glenn. 1979. An analysis of story comprehension in elementary school children. In *New directions in discourse processing,* edited by R. O. Freedle. Norwood, NJ: Ablex. Discusses Story Grammars and the research pertaining to children's story understanding.

Thorndyke, P. W. 1977. Cognitive structures in comprehension and memory of narrative discourse. *Cognitive Psychology* 9:77–110. Presents research and theory related to Story Grammars.

Warren, W. H., D. W. Nicholas, and T. Trabasso. 1979. Event chains and inferences in understanding narratives. In *New directions in discourse processing,* edited by R. O. Freedle. Norwood, NJ: Ablex. Presents a method for analyzing stories based upon event chains that can be applied to all stories and used as a basis for generating questions.

Sentence Combining

Purpose

Sentence Combining is an instructional procedure aimed at increasing syntactic knowledge and thereby increasing both writing performance and reading achievement.

Rationale

Disenchanted with the methodology associated with teaching writing using analytic procedures and formal grammar, but at the same time encouraged by the interrelationships shown to exist between syntax and language processing, many have come to acclaim Sentence Combining as a means of improving both writing fluency and reading comprehension (Combs, 1975; Mellon, 1967; Stotsky, 1975; Straw and Schreiner, 1982). Sentence-Combining instruction teaches students to read two or more short, simple sentences and combine them into one sentence. The thinking underlying Sentence Combining and its more recent counterpart, sentence reduction (Ney, 1976), is based on the assumption that sensitizing students to the method by which ideas are expressed and related in text will develop their ability to compose and comprehend.

In past research, Sentence Combining has been found to have a positive effect on writing fluency with elementary students (Green, 1972; Perron, 1974), with secondary students (Combs, 1975; O'Hare, 1973), and with college-level students. In reading research, attempts to validate the claims regarding Sentence Combining are less substantial. A study by Crews (1971) showed that Sentence Combining did not improve the reading comprehension abilities of fourth graders. In a study with ninth graders by Howie (1979), Sentence Combining and sentence reduction had no impact upon either a cloze test or the Gray Oral Reading Test. On the other hand, Machie (1982), as well as Straw and Schreiner (1982) and Obenchain (1971), reported positive results for Sentence Combining.

In recent years, Sentence-Combining activities have extended beyond small sets of sentence pairs to what has been termed "rhetorical sentence combining," in which students must combine several sentences from a text.

Intended Audience

Sentence-Combining activities in their simplest form can be used with students in the primary grades. Most frequently, the activities have been applied to students in the upper elementary school through college.

Description of the Procedure

Sentence Combining can be traced back to textbook activities in which students were expected to join together sentences with coordinating conjunctions (*and, at the same time, as well as*), conditionals (*if, since, although*), relative pronouns (*which, that*), and causal temporal connectives (*when, because, as, before, during*). The most widely used method stems from the work of O'Hare (1973), who replicated an earlier curriculum by Mellon (1967). What made O'Hare's approach distinctive was the elimination of grammatical terminology. O'Hare devised a method of providing written cue words for each Sentence-

Combining transformation that disposed of the need for technical terminology to complete the operation.

Introducing Students to Sentence Combining   Initially students are introduced to the notion of Sentence Combining through examples offered by the teacher of sentences that demonstrate the use of a connective or another method of combining sentences. During these demonstrations, students are directed to notice how sentences are combined, based on the meaning they imply and how they sound rather than on any set rule. In an attempt to direct students to determine the worth of a certain combination (based upon meaning and not a rule), students are asked to share their combinations and to judge as a group which combinations of the same sentences are acceptable and which should be rejected. From those that are acceptable, they determine (by consensus) the sentence combination they prefer. Throughout these deliberations, students are encouraged to discuss the bases for their rejections, acceptances, and preferences.

Sentence Combining Activities: Sequencing   Sentence Combining is usually done by units dealing with separate and somewhat distinct skills. A unit might address the use of *and* between clauses; another unit might deal with appositives. For each unit there are examples that are modeled and application activities that are discussed and evaluated. Most teachers usually adopt Sentence Combining as an approach in which these various skills are sequenced across one or more semesters. Some teachers prefer to use Sentence Combining for selected skills only. In the latter cases, the Sentence-Combining activities often are integrated into the writing or reading program, based on the curriculum in place or on diagnosis by the teacher.

As students develop confidence in combining groups of sentences, theoretical Sentence-Combining activities may be used to extend, supplement, or apply these skills. Examples of selected Sentence-Combining activities are given in Figures 9–11 and 9–12.

Cautions and Comments

In the rationale section, selected research studies offer mixed support for the influence of Sentence-Combining instruction on reading comprehension. Unfortunately, there are problems with interpreting such results, since each study included different subjects, different tests, and a different approach to Sentence Combining. In Obenchain's study, for example, Sentence-Combining instruction was extended to having students respond to essay questions in the literature units; in other studies, Sentence-Combining instruction was more isolated. Intuitively, Obenchain's approach seems more reasonable.

It would seem that if we are to understand and use Sentence Combining, we need more information about what students are deriving from instruction. As Stotsky (1975) argued, any gains due to Sentence Combining are more indirect than direct. It is possible that Sentence Combining forces students to attend to sentences; and this attention, rather than increasing syntactic knowledge, accounts for any changes in writing fluency or reading comprehension.

Since its inception, Sentence Combining has become differentiated as different advocates have developed their own approaches. For example, not all methods include the

FIGURE 9–11. GRAMMATICAL SENTENCES COMBINING (APPOSITIVES)

Combine each sequence of sentences below into a single sentence with at least one appositive.

Example:

1. One of the most controversial public school issues is "mainstreaming."
2. "Mainstreaming" is the growing practice of integrating physically and mentally handicapped children into regular classes.

One of the most controversial public school issues is "mainstreaming," *the growing practice of integrating physically and mentally handicapped children into regular classes.*

OR

"Mainstreaming," *one of the most controversial public school issues,* is the growing practice of integrating physically and mentally handicapped children into regular classes.

A. 1. Pet owners upset by soaring veterinary costs can now register for Medipet.
   2. Medipet is a prepaid insurance plan for dogs and cats.
B. 1. The Parthenon is an ancient temple in Athens.
   2. The Parthenon was dedicated to the goddess Pallas Athena.
   3. Pallas Athena was the special patroness of the city.
C. 1. Murphy's Law is that if anything can go wrong, it will.
   2. Murphy's Law is known to schoolchildren the world over as "Jellybread always falls jelly-side down."
D. 1. When a victim suffers a major burn, damage usually extends far beyond the burn site.
   2. A major burn is one in which at least 20 percent of the skin is lost.
E. 1. Herbert Hoover was a civil engineer before becoming President.
   2. Herbert Hoover helped to precipitate the Great Depression.
   3. The Great Depression was the most serious economic upheaval in United States history.

same sequence of skills. Some methods teach Sentence Combining as an isolated curriculum strand; others support a more integrated approach; other Sentence-Combining approaches have students apply these skills to their reading and writing of essays. The basis for selecting O'Hare's Sentence-Combining approach for description in this book was based on its widespread use and on some of its features. Specifically, among the features that seem impressive are the avoidance of grammatical terminology and the emphasis O'Hare gives to having students develop criteria for judging the acceptability and preference of some combinations over others. Such judgments by students would seem to have benefits that extend to developing an attitude that texts are never perfect.

FIGURE 9–12.   RHETORICAL—SENTENCE-COMBINING APPOSITIVES

Combine the following sentences into an effective essay that includes several appositives.

Example:

1. The Pentagon is our nation's military headquarters.
2. The Pentagon is a maze of corridors and offices.
3. The Pentagon is a labyrinth, confusing and intimidating to outsiders.

   The Pentagon, our nation's military headquarters, is a maze of corridors and offices, a labyrinth confusing and intimidating to outsiders.

THE LIFE AND DEATH OF A CELL

1. The bacteria cell is like a fortress.
2. The fortress is self-contained.
3. The cell is an organism.
4. The organism has parts.
5. The parts function for protection.
6. The parts function for nourishment and waste disposal.
7. The parts function for reproduction.
8. Outside the wall of the bacteria cell is a capsule.
9. The capsule is a layer.
10. The layer is slimy.
11. The layer is jellylike.
12. The layer helps protect the cell from chemicals.
13. The chemicals are in its surroundings.
14. The cell wall is another layer.
15. The layer is protective.
16. The layer encloses the organism.
17. The layer keeps food molecules out.
18. The food molecules are large.
19. A bacteria cell secretes enzymes.
20. Enzymes are chemicals.
21. The chemicals break down the molecules so that they can enter the cell.
22. The molecules are large.
23. The molecules are of starches.
24. The molecules are of proteins.

Examples for both figures taken from D. Dikaer, A. Kerek, and M. Morenburg, *The writer's action: Sentence combining activities.* New York: Harper & Row, 1979.

Regardless of the method that a teacher might use, what seems problematic is the possibility for Sentence Combining to become an end in itself. Sentence-Combining activities that are done mindlessly seem to offer very little that is worthwhile.

References

Combs, W. E. 1975. *Some further effects and implications of sentence-combining exercises for the secondary language arts curriculum.* Unpublished doctoral diss., University of Minnesota. Presents research that examines carefully the worth of Sentence Combining.

Crews, R. 1971. A linguistic versus a traditional grammar program—the effects on written sentence structure and comprehension. *Educational Leadership* 29:145–149. Presents research in which the effects of Sentence Combining on reading and writing are explored.

Green, E. 1972. *An experimental study of sentence-combining to improve written syntactic fluency in fifth grade children.* Unpublished doctoral diss., Northern Illinois University, DeKalb. Presents research on the effects of Sentence Combining.

Howie, S. M. 1979. *A study of the effects of sentence combining and writing ability and reading level on ninth grade students.* Unpublished doctoral diss., University of Colorado, Boulder. Presents research on the effects of Sentence Combining.

Machie, B. C. 1982. *The effects of a sentence-combining program on the reading comprehension and written composition of fourth grade students.* Unpublished doctoral diss., Hofstra University. Presents research on the effects of Sentence Combining.

Mellon, J. C. 1967. *Transformational sentence-combining: A method for enhancing the development of syntactic fluency in English composition.* Washington, DC: U. S. Office of Education Cooperative Research Project 5–8418. Provides an extended report of the rationale and uses of Sentence Combining, including research data.

Neville, D. D., and E. F. Searls. 1991. A meta-analytic review of the effect of sentence-combining on reading comprehension. *Reading Research and Instruction* 31:63–76. Greatest effects for Sentence Combining are found for elementary students.

Ney, J. W. 1976. The hazards of the course: Sentence combining in freshman English. *English Record* 27:70–77. Presents a research-based discussion of the use of Sentence Combining.

Obenchain, A. 1971. *Effectiveness of the precise essay question in programming the sequential development of written composition skills and the simultaneous development of critical reading skills.* Unpublished master's thesis. George Washington University. Presents research on the influence of Sentence Combining on reading and writing improvement.

O'Hare, F. 1973. *Sentence combining: Improving student writing without formal grammar instruction.* Urbana, IL: National Council of Teachers of English. Presents a primary source for the use of Sentence Combining.

Perron, J. D. 1974. *An explanatory approach to extending the syntactic development of fourth grade students through the use of sentence-combining methods.* Unpublished doctoral diss., Indiana University, Bloomington. Presents research on the use of Sentence Combining.

Stotsky, S. L. 1975. Sentence-combining as a curricular activity: Its effect on written language development and reading comprehension. *Research in the Teaching of English* 9:30–71. Represents a substantial review of Sentence-Combining methods, research, and its utility.

Straw, S. B., and R. Schreiner. 1982. The effect of sentence manipulation on subsequent measures of reading and listening. *Reading Research Quarterly* 17:339–352. Presents research on the influence of Sentence Combining on reading performance.

Guided Writing Procedure ▪

Purpose

The Guided Writing Procedure (Smith and Bean, 1980) is designed to: (1) activate and assess students' prior knowledge of a text topic before reading occurs; (2) evaluate students' written expression in a content area; (3) improve students' written expression through guided instruction; and (4) facilitate the synthesis and retention of text material.

Rationale

The Guided Writing Procedure (GWP) attempts to use the process of writing as a means to help students learn from text. As a perusal of the present book attests, a number of strategies are offered using the language processes of reading and listening as a means of helping students learn from text. In addition, a number of these strategies advocate the notion that the processes needed to learn content material can be taught concurrently with the content itself. It is precisely this notion that Smith and Bean state also holds true for the development of writing fluency, i.e., the processes of writing can be taught concurrently with the content itself.

Writing takes its own form and style in each content area; it is with this in mind that GWP was developed. Since relatively few specific procedures have been offered by which writing might be integrated with the learning of content, the GWP has been suggested as a means of implementing such an approach.

Intended Audience

The GWP was originally intended to be used with students at the middle and secondary levels as an aid to developing writing fluency and enhancing learning from text. In addition, it can be used with elementary students using short selections with factual, rather than story-type, content.

Description of the Procedure

Smith and Bean state that using the GWP involves a series of specific procedures spanning several days of content instruction. Two general steps are involved:

1. Informal diagnosis of prior content knowledge and written expression
2. Teaching content and written expression

1. *Informal Diagnosis of Prior Content Knowledge and Written Expression* Begin the GWP by asking students to brainstorm any thoughts they have related to the topic to be learned: for example, "the Solar System." Record everything students say verbatim on the board or overhead projector. The following ideas related to the solar system might be offered by students:

nine planets	Earth
sun is center	revolution around sun
Milky Way	Venus and Mars closest
Jupiter largest	Saturn has rings

Next, have students vote on which ideas seem to be the major ones and which are details. These ideas are organized into an outline or Graphic Organizer on the board or overhead. The design of the outline is to get students to cluster their ideas. Now, students are ready to write one or two short paragraphs, using the outline or Graphic Organizer as a guide. Students are told that this will constitute their "first draft." These drafts are collected, and students are assigned to read the text.

At this point, teachers should examine the students' paragraphs rapidly and analyze them for organization of ideas, style, and mechanics. It is suggested that rather than writing any edits on these first drafts, a "Concept and Writing Checklist" be used to record this information for each individual student. Below is an example of a student's paragraph on the solar system and a representative checklist that may be used for record-keeping purposes.

FRED'S DRAFT

The solar system consists of nine planets and the sun is the center and the earth is one of them. Jupiter is the largest and Saturn has rings while Venus and Mars are the closest.

Concept and Writing Checklist

(√ = OK; 0 = Needs improvement; ? = Can't tell)

Student

Fred

Criteria

Organization of ideas
  Clear topic   ?
  Supporting details/examples   ?
  Logical flow   ?
  Comments: _____ *What do you want the reader to know?* _____

Style
  Shows variety in:
  Word choice   √
  Sentence length   ?
  Comments: _____ *Too many "ands"* _____

Mechanics
  Complete sentences   √
  Capitalization   0
  Punctuation   0
  Spelling   √
  Comments: _____

In this example Fred has shown that he can organize his ideas well. His problems arise in word choice (too many *ands*), sentence length, punctuation (he needs to use commas and periods), and capitalization.

2. *Teaching Content and Written Expression*   At this point, one or more days have lapsed since the initial draft. The teacher now displays an illustrative draft on the board or overhead along with the checklist as a guide. This draft may be an actual student's or a composite of several first drafts. Perhaps the best example to use is one that contains inaccurate text information as well as inappropriate writing criteria. Using the checklist and text information, the class as a whole should contribute ideas to edit the illustrative paragraph.

Students' papers are now returned, and they are asked to use the checklist to help them edit their own drafts. At this point students edit for both content and writing inaccuracies.

This second draft is collected, and a follow-up quiz is given on the material read. As an alternative, a postreading activity for vocabulary and/or concept reinforcement may be used. As soon as possible, teachers should examine the second drafts and compare them to the initial checklist results. Individual conferences may be used to provide help for students whose writing has not shown growth. Smith and Bean suggest that a positive trend should be noted in students' ability to use ideas and express themselves in writing.

Cautions and Comments

The Guided Writing Procedure presents teachers with a way to introduce and teach text material. On the positive side, research conducted by Konopak, Martin, and Martin (1987, 1990) and Martin, Konopak, and Martin (1986) and designed to investigate the impact of the GWP on students' writing and content learning has shown that it significantly improves the quality of their writing. Students also become more adept at integrating text information and prior knowledge and, further, produce writing that is more carefully edited.

On the negative side, some concerns about the procedures need to be mentioned. Smith and Bean fail to extend their suggestions to preparing students for writing; for instance, they fail to suggest that students might examine examples of text written by professional authors. Also, they fail to go far enough in how they suggest a teacher might help students deal with their own ideas. Apart from organizing ideas, students should perhaps select those ideas upon which they wish to focus and, prior to writing, they might consider how their ideas could be arranged. In conjunction with helping students develop and refine ideas, Smith and Bean confound revision (i.e., the reexamination and redevelopment of ideas) with editing. Furthermore, their checklists seem more cumbersome than helpful. Nor have the authors discussed the possibility of having students write reports that are more ongoing or that are coauthored.

Another major problem lies with their suggestions for teacher evaluation. In their failure to consider procedures by which peers might offer and obtain feedback, they put the teacher in the unenviable position of being the only source of feedback and of spending a great deal of time grading.

References

Konopak, B. C., S. H. Martin, and M. A. Martin. 1987. An integrated communication arts approach for enhancing students' learning in the content areas. *Reading Research and Instruction* 26:275–289. Research study demonstrating the effectiveness of the GWP for improving the quality of students' ideas and aiding them in synthesizing text information with prior knowledge.

———. 1990. Using a writing strategy to enhance sixth-grade students' comprehension of content material. *Journal of Reading Behavior* 22:19–37. Demonstrates the effectiveness of the GWP with middle school students in world history.

Martin, M. A., B. C. Konopak, and S. H. Martin. 1986. Use of the guided writing procedure to facilitate reading comprehension of high school text materials. In *Solving problems in literacy: Learners, teachers, and researchers,* Thirty-fifth Yearbook of the National Reading Conference, edited by J. A. Niles and R. V. Lalik. Rochester, NY: National Reading Conference, pp. 66–72. Another study validating the use of the GWP as a strategy to enhance content learning.

Readence, J. E., T. W. Bean, and R. S. Baldwin. 1995. *Content area reading: An integrated approach,* 5th ed. Dubuque, IA: Kendall/Hunt. Describes the GWP and other writing to learn alternatives.

Searfoss, L. W., C. Smith, and T. W. Bean. 1981. An integrated strategy for second language learners in content area subjects. *TESOL Quarterly* 15:383–389. Research study that shows the efficacy of the GWP with second-language learners in content areas.

Smith, C., and T. W. Bean. 1980. The guided writing procedure: Integrating content reading and writing improvement. *Reading World* 19:290–298. The original discussion of the GWP.

I-Search Paper

Purpose

The purpose of the I-Search Paper (Macrorie, 1980; 1988) is to provide an alternative to the traditional research, or term, paper that is frequently used as a class assignment. With the I-Search Paper students are asked to investigate a topic of their choosing, interview people and visit places associated with the topic, and tell the story of their search.

Rationale

Macrorie conceives of the traditional term paper assignment as dull and unimaginative. It forces students to report on a topic, possibly not of their choosing, by reading, synthesizing, and rewriting the works of others. Although the intent of the assignment is to help students learn to use the library and to write research reports, in the process Macrorie fears the term paper might actually destroy students' natural curiosity for books, for reading, and for writing.

The I-Search Paper, on the other hand, is designed to inspire students to capitalize on their innate curiosity and experience in a hands-on fashion the topic of their investigation. Students choose their own topic and interview people who have something to do with it. They visit places to observe people engaged in activities related to the topic. They read outside sources to give them the information to enhance their knowledge of the topic and help them to interpret what they observe. Students' papers become the story of their search and of what they learned, or didn't learn. Because they have chosen topics of interest they care about and devised their own means of investigation, Macrorie believes students will want to write their papers.

Intended Audience

The I-Search Paper can be used in any classroom where term papers might regularly be given as assignments to students. With modification for age or ability levels, the I-Search Paper could be used across the curriculum with a variety of grade levels.

Description of the Procedures

Although there seems to be no set procedure for doing the I-Search Paper, students become engaged in the following stages in formulating the paper:

1. Choosing a topic
2. The search
3. Writing the paper

1. *Choosing a Topic*   For the I-Search assignment to be effective, students must select a topic that will engage them, or sustain their interest over a period of time. The topic must be something students truly want to know about. It should be something that will fulfill a need in the student's life rather than a teacher's idea of what would be good for the student to pursue. In other words, the topic must be something to satisfy the student and not just something that seems appropriate for school. Macrorie suggests, therefore, that there is no limit to what the topic for the I-Search Paper becomes.

2. *The Search*   Once the topic is decided upon, the experience of the investigation begins. Macrorie provides the following suggestions:

   a. The topic should be shared with the class, or an assigned small group of students, for feedback. Reasons for pursuing the topic should be shared, and any offers of help should be given. This might include leads to follow, names, addresses, phone numbers, and so forth. If the chosen topic were "hot-air ballooning," the name of someone who's taken a hot-air balloon ride would be useful, as would the phone number of a local company.

   b. Students should consult with experts or authorities about where to find pertinent information about their topic. Students need to know what are the most important books, magazines, newspapers, and other sources on the topic. In our example, telephoning an experienced balloon rider might turn up all kinds of useful information. This information should be tracked down, and notes made of what might be useful.

   c. Before students interview an expert on a topic, they should discuss how best to approach that individual. They need to decide if they can approach the individual directly, through someone who knows the person, or by telephone, and when the best time to do it would be. In our hot-air balloon example, it would not be wise to approach an expert when that person is getting ready to take off in a balloon; making an appointment at the person's convenience would probably be most appropriate.

d. Students should know something about their topic before they interview an expert. People who are experts are busy because they are experts; but, they usually enjoy helping others because it gives them a chance to talk about what they know best. On the other hand, they usually don't like to waste time. Therefore, it is best to be informed before the interview. In our example it would be best to read about hot-air balloons, the chase crews, and the kinds of competition that a balloonist might enter before encountering the expert.

e. Once an interview is completed, students should test the information gained from the expert against that of other experts. Students need to find out how the expert's peers rate the information. Does it hold up against other people's comments? How do the peers rate the reputation of the expert?

f. Students need to be sure to consult with both primary as well as secondary sources. Primary sources are those individuals who can talk to you about what they're doing, or events or objects you can observe on your own; secondary sources are the people, newspapers, or books that can tell you what others have done.

3. *Writing the Paper*   Macrorie points out that a good way to organize the I-Search Paper is for the student to write the story of what was done in the search, in the order in which the events occurred. Not everything that was said or done needs to be reported; however, anything important in the search or that caused the student to make a decision during the search should be reported. He suggests that the paper be written in four parts:

a. What the student knew—or didn't know when the topic was selected.

b. Why the student is writing the paper. The need for pursuing the topic should be made evident; students should discuss the potential difference the search may make in their lives.

c. The search.

d. What the student learned—or didn't learn, and what was gained from the experience.

Macrorie suggests that the I-Search Paper conclude with documentation in the form of a list of sources and experts that were consulted during the search. In this way the reader is provided an overview of the information sources and can also assess the reliability of the search itself.

Cautions and Comments

The I-Search Paper seems to be a strategy that teachers can use with students of any age or ability level. Because of the experiential basis of the strategy, it seems particularly appropriate for at-risk students in multicultural settings where the relevancy of what is being taught can take on greater meaning. In fact, Alejandro (1989) describes a unit on cultural values and behavior with which students could use the concept of the I-Search. Arnold (1989) also shows how I-Search could be adapted for remedial students.

I-Search lends itself to cooperative learning (see Unit 6). Instead of individual I-Search topics, a small group of students might decide to collaborate to investigate a mutually agreed-upon topic. In this way, the reading of secondary source material, the interviewing and/or observation of primary sources, and the writing of the paper all could be done cooperatively.

Finally, Caplan (1984) suggests that students might need to engage in some preparatory exercises which would help them rehearse for the writing of the paper before it actually has to be written. For instance, he suggests that students should read an effective piece of personal journalism from a known author before attempting such writing on their own, or participate in an exercise that teaches them how to describe an environment before they initiate a search in which such a task is required.

References

Alejandro, A. 1989. Cars: A culturally integrated "I-Search" module. *English Journal* 78:41–44. Describes a unit on culture using I-Search techniques.

Arnold, L. K. 1989. A new approach to I-Search for remedial students. *English Journal* 78:44–45. Describes a means to adapt the I-Search procedures to remedial students.

Caplan, R. 1984. *Writers in training: A guide to developing a composition program for language arts teachers.* Palo Alto, CA: Dale Seymour. Chapter 8 of this text discusses the I-Search Paper.

Dellinger, D. G. 1989. Alternatives to clip and stitch: Real research and writing in the classroom. *English Journal* 78:31–38. Discusses the I-Search Paper as an alternative to the traditional research paper.

Macrorie, K. 1980. *Searching writing.* Rochelle Park, NJ: Hayden. Original source of the I-Search Paper.

———. 1988. *The I-Search paper.* Portsmouth, NH: Heinemann. Revised and updated edition of the original text.

Studying

10

UNIT OVERVIEW

Some view studying as a special form of reading. Study-type reading is an attempt to enlist and organize material from texts in such a way as to enhance thinking as well as later attempts to review and retain it. Thus, students need to have access to strategies that will develop their thinking as they focus their attention on selected aspects of text. Such strategies should include techniques that enable students to deal with information gleaned from various sources: textbooks, oral presentations, media, and so on.

Additionally, studying involves the awareness of and the ability to control one's own learning, or metacognition. Metacognition is knowing what you know and knowing how you know what to do. Individuals with good metacognitive abilities can actively control their learning from text.

The eight strategies discussed in this unit present various ways to help students study and retain text and text-related information. They range from a strategy that incorporates the use of annotations, to one that helps students independently set their purpose for reading, to one that enables students systematically to interpret graphic aids.

K-W-L. K-W-L (What I *K*now, What I *W*ant to Learn, What I *L*earned) is a teaching model designed to help students learn from nonfiction text in any content area. It consists of brainstorming, purpose-setting through questioning, and then examining answers to those questions.

REAP Technique. Designed to help students analyze reading material in different ways, REAP offers alternative formats for annotating text. The strategy consists of four basic steps: *R*ead, *E*ncode, *A*nnotate, *P*onder; thus, the resulting acronym—REAP.

Survey Technique. Designed as a spinoff of the SQ3R method of study, the Survey Technique offers the teacher and students an opportunity to walk through the chapter together. Most useful with students who might find the material especially difficult, the Survey Technique also furnishes the teacher an opportunity to show the students a model of good study behavior.

PORPE.   Based on the use of writing and a model of what effective readers do when reading text, PORPE (*P*redict, *O*rganize, *R*ehearse, *P*ractice, *E*valuate) is a study strategy designed to help students prepare for essay exams.

Notetaking System for Learning.   Much of what students learn in secondary and college classrooms comes from the instructor via the lecture method. Effective notetaking procedures can do much to aid students in learning and retaining a vast amount of information. The Notetaking System for Learning provides a systematic means to organize and review class notes.

Guided Lecture Procedure.   A strategy described as not only a notetaking technique but also a teaching and studying technique, the Guided Lecture Procedure uses active listening and small groups to aid students in learning from text.

Graphic Information Lesson.   The Graphic Information Lesson is designed to help students discover how graphic aids can enhance comprehension while it simultaneously helps them in reviewing and interpreting important text information.

PLAE.   PLAE (*P*replan, *L*ist, *A*ctivate, *E*valuate) involves students in planning activities before undertaking studying, monitoring those strategies as they learn, and checking and evaluating their effectiveness after learning.

K-W-L

Purpose

K-W-L represents a three-step procedure intended to help teachers become more responsive to helping students access appropriate knowledge when reading expository text.

Rationale

Growing out of the research findings that have highlighted the importance of a reader's background knowledge, and concern that teachers have tended to neglect the active engagement of a reader's background knowledge and interest, Ogle (1986a) developed K-W-L to ensure that teachers had a framework to elicit children's background knowledge and engage student interest.

The framework involves well-developed procedures for brainstorming, generating categories for organizing ideas, specifying questions, checking what they have learned, and guiding further reading. The rationale behind these procedures is tied to Ogle's belief in the need for a mix of group and individual activities and procedures that help scaffold students' own ideas and interests. As Ogle stated, the teacher

. . . helps students keep the control of their own inquiry, extending the pursuit of knowledge beyond just the one article. The teacher is making clear that learning shouldn't be framed around just what an author chooses to include, but that it involves the identification of the learner's questions and the search for authors or articles dealing with those questions. (Ogle 1986a, 569)

Intended Audience

The framework is intended for use with expository text. Although it is apt to be more widely used with older students, it could be enlisted with students at any age level.

Description of the Procedure

K-W-L involves three basic steps: accessing what I know, determining what I want to learn, and recalling what I did learn as a result of reading. In hopes of making the steps concrete, Ogle suggests the use of a worksheet (see Figure 10–1). For the first two steps of the process the teacher and student engage in oral discussion followed by personal responses; in the third step the sequence reverses.

Step K—What I Know   Step K involves two steps: brainstorming and generating categories for ideas. Prior to reading the selection students are intended to brainstorm in response to a concept that the teacher puts forth. Guidelines for selecting the concept to be presented for brainstorming are quite detailed and well thought out. Rather than present students with overly general concepts, Ogle suggests beginning with something specific. To illustrate, as Ogle states:

> . . . when the class will read about sea turtles, use the words sea turtles as the stimulus, not "What do you know about animals in the sea?" or "Have you ever been to the ocean?" A general discussion of enjoyable experiences on the beach may never elicit the pertinent schemata. . . . If there appears to be little knowledge of sea turtles in your students' experiences, then ask the next more general question, "What do you know about turtles?" (Ogle 1986a, 565)

FIGURE 10–1.   K-W-L STRATEGY SHEET

1. K—What we know	W—What we want to find out	L— What we learned and still need to learn
2. Categories of information we expect to use		
A.	E.	
B.	F.	
C.	G.	
D.		

As students offer ideas, Ogle suggests that the teacher might jot down ideas on the board, a chart, or an overhead, and then use them as a basis for encouraging discussion. In terms of the sea turtle example, the students might consider whether facts pertain to all sea turtles. Furthermore, in hopes of deepening thinking and provoking uncertainties to be confirmed by reading, Ogle suggests asking volunteers to indicate: "Where did you learn that?" and "How might you prove it?"

The second part of Step K involves generating categories of information likely to be encountered when students read. For example, prior to reading an article on sea turtles, the teacher might follow the brainstorming with a discussion of possible categories of information. The teacher might say: "Before we read this article on sea turtles, let's think awhile about what kinds of information are most likely to be included. Look at this list of things we already know: Do some of them fit together to form a general category or information (i.e. habitat, enemies)?"

Ogle recognizes that students may initially find this approach difficult and proposes that some teacher modeling might be needed. Sometimes it might only be necessary for the teacher to suggest one or two categories before the students will suggest others. At other times, the teacher might find it worthwhile to relate what they will read to other topics that they have learned and the types of categories of information they acquired.

Step W—What Do I Want to Learn?   In conjunction with brainstorming and developing categories, students begin to develop interests and curiosities. Sometimes these interests and curiosities are associated with uncertainties; at other times they reflect a drive to learn more about some aspect of the topic. The teacher's goal with Step W is to turn these uncertainties, interests, and so on, into reasons to read. By highlighting gaps in ideas, disagreements, and intriguing ideas, the teacher attempts to provoke questions. After discussing various possible questions for the group, the teacher encourages each student to specify his or her own questions—that is, the questions that he/she is interested in having answered.

Once each student has developed his/her questions, students read the selections. With some selections there may be some teacher preview so that students have some expectations and feel for the article. Again, depending upon length, this selection may be read in sections or in its entirety.

Step L—What I Learned   As students complete the article, the students write down what they have learned and check what questions they still need answered. Ogle stresses the importance of going beyond the single selection so that the "clear priority of their personal desire to learn" ensures precedence over "what the author has chosen to include." (Ogle 1986a, 567). Here is an example transcript taken from Ogle (1986a, 567–569).

> TEACHER: Today we're going to read another article about animals. This one is about a special kind of spider—the Black Widow. Before we begin the article, let's think about what we already know about Black Widows. Or if you aren't familiar with this kind of spider, think about some things you know about spiders in general, and we can then see if those are also true for the Black Widow. [Teacher writes Black Widow spider on the board

and waits while students think about their knowledge of spiders. Next she elicits ideas from children and writes their contributions on the board.]

TONY: Spiders have six legs.

SUSAN: They eat other insects.

EDDIE: I think they're big and dangerous spiders.

TEACHER: Can you add more about what you mean when you say they're big and dangerous?

EDDIE: They, they, I think they eat other spiders. I think people are afraid of them, too.

STEPH: They spin nests or webs to catch other insects in.

TOM: My cousin got stung by one once and almost died.

TEACHER: You mean they can be dangerous to people?

TOM: Yah, my cousin had to go to the hospital.

TEACHER: Does anyone else know more about the Black Widow? Tammy?

TAMMY: I don't think they live around here. I've never heard of anyone being stung by one.

TEACHER: Where do Black Widows live? Does anyone know? [She waits.] What else do we know about spiders?

JOHN: I think I saw a TV show about them once. They have a special mark on their back. I think it's a blue triangle or circle, or something like that. If people look, they can tell if the spider's a Black Widow or not.

TEACHER: Does anyone else recall anything more about the way they look? [She waits.] Look at what we've already said about these spiders. Can you think of other information we should add?

JOHN: I think they kill their babies or men spiders. I'm not sure which.

TEACHER: Do you remember where you learned that?

JOHN: I think I read an article once.

TEACHER: OK, let's add that to our list. Remember, everything on the list we aren't sure of we can double check when we read.

TEACHER: Anything more you think we should know about these spiders? [She waits.] OK, before we read this article let's think awhile about the kinds or categories of information that are likely to be included. Look at the list of things we already know or have questions about. Which of the categories of information have we already mentioned?

PETER: We mentioned how they look.

TEACHER: Yes, we said they're big and have six legs. And someone said they think Black Widows have a colored mark on them. Good, description is one of the main categories of information we want to learn about when we read about animals or insects. What other categories of information have we mentioned that should be included?

ANNA: Where they live; but we aren't sure.

TEACHER: Good, we should find out where they live. What other kinds of information should we expect to learn from the article? Think about what kinds of information we've learned from other articles about animals.

DIANE: We want to know what kind of homes they make.

RAUL: What do they eat?

ANDY: How they protect themselves.

CARA: How do they have babies? How many do they have?

TEACHER: Good thinking. Are there other categories of information we expect to learn about. [She waits.] We've thought about what we already know and what kinds of information we're likely to learn from an article on Black Widow spiders. Now what are some of the questions we want to have answered? I know we had some things we weren't sure about, like where these spiders live. What are some of the things you'd like to find out when we read?

CARA: I want to know how many baby spiders get born.

RICO: Do Black Widows really hurt people? I never heard of that, and my dad knows a lot about spiders.

ANDY: Why are they called Black Widows? What's a widow?

TEACHER: Good question! Does anyone know what a widow is? Why would this spider be called a "Black Widow"? [After eliciting questions from several students, the teacher asks each child to write their own questions on their worksheet.] What are the questions you are most interested in having answered? Write them down now. As you read, look for the answers and jot them down on your worksheet as you go, or other information you don't want to forget. [The students read the article.]

TEACHER: How did you like this article? What did you learn?

RAUL: The Black Widow eats her husband and sometimes her babies. Yuck! I don't think I like that kind of spider!

STEPH: They can live here—it says they live in all parts of the United States.

ANDY: They can be recognized by an hourglass that is red or yellow on the abdomen.

TEACHER: What is another word for abdomen? [She waits.] Sara, please look up the word abdomen. Let's find out where the hourglass shape is located. While Sara is looking the word up, let's check what we learned against the questions we wanted answered. Are there some questions that didn't get answered? What more do we want to know?

Cautions and Comments

K-W-L represents a thoughtfully developed framework that appears to support student-initiated learning which is text-based but not by a single text or rigid teacher guidance. Ogle claims that the strategy has helped students become better readers of expository text at the same time as it has helped teachers develop a more interactive teaching style—a style that supports student involvement and initiation before, during, and after reading. In her various articles detailing the use of the procedures (including comparison with selections with which the procedure was not used), Ogle indicates that students taught using K-W-L remember what they have pursued and over time become more actively involved in reading. The extent to which they elicit their own background knowledge increases as does their ability to generate categories. Ogle also suggests that teachers have reported to her that students ask if they can use K-W-L, and when they do they read "noisily" with "ahs" and "ohs." At the same time as students seem responsive to the strategy, Ogle claims that teachers seem amenable to its use and aware of the extent to which it facilitates a more interactive approach. Despite these affidavits, the approach should be more rigorously evaluated for purposes of refining its use as well as examining some of the claims.

Since its inception, variations of K-W-L have emerged. For example, Carr and Ogle (1987) suggested K-W-L Plus, which incorporated the use of mapping (Hanf, 1971) and summarization procedures (Brown and Day, 1983).

References

Brown, A., and J. Day. 1983. Macrorules for summarizing texts: The development of expertise. *Journal of Verbal Learning and Verbal Behavior* 22:1–14. Presents guidelines for helping students summarize.

Carr, E., and D. Ogle. 1987. K-W-L plus: A strategy for comprehension and summarization. *Journal of Reading* 30:626–631. Presents a variation on K-W-L and describes its use with ninth graders.

Hanf, M. 1971. Mapping: A technique for translating reading into thinking. *Journal of Reading* 14:225–230, 270. Presents guidelines for mapping, which has been used as an aid to categorization.

Jennings, J. H. 1991. A comparison of summary and journal writing as components of an interactive comprehension model. In *Learner factors/teacher factors: Issues in literacy research and instruction,* edited by J. Zutell and S. McCormick. Fortieth Yearbook of the National Reading Conference, 67–82. Chicago: National Reading Conference.

Ogle, D. 1986a. K-W-L: A teaching model that develops active reading of expository text. *The Reading Teacher* 39:564–570. Represents the primary source detailing the use of K-W-L.

———. 1986b. K-W-L group instruction strategy. In *Teaching reading as thinking,* edited by A. S. Palincsar, D. S. Ogle, B. F. Jones, and E. G. Carr. Alexandria, VA: Association for Supervision and Curriculum Development. Describes the use of K-W-L in conjunction with developing thinking skills.

———. 1992. KWL in action: Secondary teachers find applications that work. In *Reading in the content areas: Improving classroom instruction,* 3d ed., edited by E. K. Dishner, T. W. Bean, J. E. Readence, and D. W. Moore, 270–282. Dubuque, IA: Kendall/Hunt. Describes the use of K-W-L in the content areas.

REAP Technique

Purpose

The REAP technique (Eanet and Manzo, 1976) is designed to: (1) improve the comprehension abilities of readers by helping them synthesize an author's ideas into their own words, and (2) develop students' writing ability as an aid for future study and recall of ideas they acquire through reading.

Rationale

The REAP (*R*ead, *E*ncode, *A*nnotate, *P*onder) technique starts from the premise that readers comprehend best when asked to communicate the ideas gleaned from a passage they have read. REAP is conceived as an alternative to the Directed Reading Activity and the Guided Reading Procedure, described earlier in this text.

Specifically, the REAP technique actively involves readers in processing the ideas an author has set down in print. The purpose is for readers to communicate in their own words an understanding of the text and discuss those ideas with others. In this way the readers internalize a text-based understanding. It is perceived that this internalization enhances the meaningful processing of those ideas, thus crystallizing the readers' own thinking concerning the author's message.

REAP uses writing as a vehicle to translate an author's ideas into the readers' own words, so this strategy also serves to enhance the writing skills of students. In addition, these written translations may serve as the basis for continued study or for review of an author's ideas. Thus REAP, requiring active involvement with print, can encourage students' maturity and independence in reading.

Intended Audience

The REAP technique is intended for use from junior high through college. It may provide the basis for group instruction or may be adapted for individual use as a study method.

Description of the Procedure

The REAP technique consists of four stages:

> R—Reading to discover the author's ideas
> E—Encoding the author's ideas into one's own language
> A—Annotating those ideas in writing for oneself or for sharing with others
> P—Pondering the significance of the annotation

Central to the REAP technique is developing students' ability to write annotations. Therefore, the discussion of the REAP strategy follows these steps: (1) writing annotations, (2) teaching students to write annotations, and (3) pondering the annotations.

1. Writing Annotations   Writing annotations requires readers to interact with the ideas of the author, to synthesize them into their own language, and to set them down in writing. Eanet and Manzo (1976) and Manzo (1973) described several different types of annotations that students might use. Types include the heuristic annotation, summary annotation, thesis annotation, question annotation, intention annotation, motivation annotation, and critical annotation.

To serve as examples, annotations have been constructed for the following selection:

> We encourage children to act stupidly, not only by scaring and confusing them, but by boring them, by filling up their days with dull, repetitive tasks that make little or no claim on their attention or demands on their intelligence. Our hearts leap for joy at the sight of a roomful of children all slogging away at some imposed task, and we are all the more pleased and satisfied if someone tells us that the children don't really like what they are doing. We tell ourselves that this drudgery is good preparation for life, and we fear that without it children would be hard to "control." But why must this busywork be so dull? Why not give tasks that are interesting and demanding? Because, in schools where every task must be completed and every answer must be right, if we give children more demanding tasks they will be fearful and will instantly insist that we show them how to do the job. When you have acres of paper to fill up with pencil marks, you have no time to waste on the luxury of thinking. By such means children are firmly established in the habit of using only a small part of their thinking capacity. They feel that school is a place where they must spend most of their time doing dull tasks in a dull way.*

a. Heuristic annotation

>   We encourage children to act stupidly, not only by scaring and confusing them, but by boring them . . .

The heuristic annotation depicts the essence of the author's message through the selection of the author's words. Like the above quotation, it should stimulate a reaction.

b. Summary annotation

>   Schools may become more interesting places for children if they are provided with meaningful activities designed to promote thinking rather than dull, repetitive busywork.

The above annotation provides a summary of the selection by condensing the author's ideas on the type of activities children should face in school. The summary annotation omits examples, descriptions of presently used activities, and explanations of recommended school tasks. It presents only a synopsis of the author's main ideas.

c. Thesis annotation

>   If schools became places to think, they would challenge and threaten the status quo.

A thesis annotation is a precise statement of the selection's theme, the author's point of view. Use of this type entails dealing with what the author is saying. The above statement attempts to do this briefly and incisively.

*J. Holt, *How Children Fail* (New York: Pitman, 1964), 210–211.

d. Question annotation

What do teachers consider good preparation for life? Why is there no time to work on "the luxury of thinking?" How do students react to school?

A question annotation involves addressing the germane ideas of a selection in question form. In the above annotation, the questions address the points in the passage by Holt.

e. Intention annotation

As Holt tries to do in his other writing, he attempts to convince his reader of his thesis by painting a negative picture of the status quo.

An intention annotation entails specifying the author's reasons for writing. The annotator considers what is given by the author and what is known of the author. It is obvious that the annotator has read other material by Holt.

f. Motivation annotation

Holt is trying to suggest what is wrong with schools and give a solution to the problem. It is his argument that schools are monotonous when they should be challenging students to think.

A motivation annotation is a statement in which the author's motives, biases, and perceptions are addressed. The above annotation speculates as to Holt's motives for writing the selection.

g. Critical annotation

Holt is right. Schools may become more interesting places for children if they provide experiences which challenge them to think. Clearly, school is more learning the system than learning to solve problems. Clearly, schooling is largely irrelevant.

The critical annotation details the author's point of view, the annotator's reaction to this position, and the basis for the annotator's reaction. In the above annotation, the annotator reacts positively to Holt and defines some reasons.

The different annotations may or may not be suitable for different selections. As Eanet and Manzo suggested, ". . . some annotations are more suitable to some types of writing than are others" (P. 648). The teacher or annotator needs to address this possibility prior to proceeding with annotations.

2. Teaching Students to Write Annotations   It is suggested that students cannot be expected to write annotations cogently without prior exposure to the process. That is, students must learn this skill and practice it before a teacher can expect them to use it successfully.

Eanet and Manzo (1976) recommended the following paradigm in teaching students to write annotations:

Step 1: Recognizing and defining

Step 2: Discriminating

Step 3: Modeling the process

Step 4: Practicing.

A summary annotation illustrates the paradigm.

a. Step 1: *Recognizing and defining.* The teacher asks students to read a short selection and then furnishes them with a summary annotation. Using questioning techniques and discussion, the teacher should elicit from the students how the furnished annotation relates to the selection read. In lieu of whole-group instruction, the teacher may choose to have small groups of students attempt to work jointly at this task. In either case, the goal of the teacher is to aid students in formulating the concept of the summary annotation.

b. Step 2: *Discriminating.* As in the previous step, the teacher asks the students to read another short selection. However, the teacher now presents them with multiple annotations. The recommended number is three annotations, one of which constitutes a good summary annotation. The other two should be erroneous in some fashion—either too broad, too narrow, or too divergent from the ideas in the selection. Again through class discussion, students should choose the best annotation. They should justify their choice and explain why the other choices are unsatisfactory. Small groups are also a recommended alternative to the whole-group instructional situation. The task of discriminating between good and poor annotations will further refine students' skill with annotations.

c. Step 3: *Modeling the process.* Students now read a third selection. The teacher demonstrates to the students how to write the summary annotation effectively. It is most crucial that the teacher walk the students through this step by telling them the thought processes undertaken in writing the annotation. The teacher should demonstrate to the students the relationships between the major ideas so that students will be able to write a cogent annotation, or rewrite it as necessary. This modeling process is essential in communicating what a good summary annotation is, and what students should do to arrive at it.

d. Step 4: *Practicing.* The practicing step has two parts. First, the students read a new passage and individually write an annotation. Then, after forming groups of three or four, students develop the best summary annotation possible, using their individual attempts as the basis for this interaction. Students also may refer to the passage if necessary. The total group then compares, discusses, and evaluates the final group products.

3. Pondering the Annotations   This part of the annotation process corresponds to the ponder stage of the REAP strategy. The students ponder, or process, it for personal study or for classroom activities. The annotation has now become a powerful tool for comprehension and study, limited only by teachers' imagination and students' needs.

Specifically, Eanet and Manzo (1976) recommend four uses of annotations. First, this technique may be useful in a reading class, either developmental or remedial, that uses individualized instruction. As the teacher works with individuals, the other students read individually from materials of their choice. Before the end of class, each student writes a summary annotation on the material read that day. This process serves the students as a short review when they begin reading the next day. It also provides the basis for both an individual conference with the teacher and a progress check. When the students have read the whole book, they write a new, more comprehensive annotation that includes a critical evaluation and attach it to the book. This annotation will serve as an aid for other readers who choose to read the book.

Second, the instructor may adapt this annotation procedure for the school library. As students finish reading a book, they write an annotation, and the library keeps it on file. When new readers select a book, they can consult the annotations file in making their decision. The annotations can provide other students with information about a book before they read it.

Third, annotations may be used to prepare secondary or college English students in classes for writing projects. The annotations can serve as a foundation for more extensive critique writing. For example, students may read and annotate two or three articles that offer varied opinions on a topic of interest. Next, students would write a comparative essay or research paper on the topic, using the annotations as the basis.

Finally, the teacher may use the annotations as required readings to enhance students' study efforts on materials of importance in the curricula. This assignment promotes in-depth study and provides the basis for classroom discussion and review. These required annotations may also serve to improve the writing skills of students.

Cautions and Comments

Too often students approach their textbook reading and notetaking with a vague overall purpose such as "pull out main ideas." The REAP technique affords a systematic procedure by which teachers can guide their students' interactions with author's ideas. Specifically, this technique can serve to direct and record purposeful interactions between a reader and a text. REAP can guide the reader to use alternative annotations as a way to select appropriate procedures for gleaning, recording, and using textual information.

The strategy appears to have some major shortcomings. Specifically, many students may find the task of writing annotations both difficult and painstaking. Students may lack the necessary background knowledge to actively pursue annotations. In addition, they may not be sufficiently issue-driven to interrogate the texts with their questions as basis for response. Some may find it difficult to the point of distraction to put their ideas into words. Obviously, the teacher should use the strategy selectively, with students for whom it is appropriate and with text for which it is relevant. If teachers use REAP in a lock-step fashion with all students, they may find the strategy either inappropriate or more difficult than the task they intended to teach.

References

Eanet, M. 1978. An investigation of the REAP reading/study procedure: Its rationale and efficacy. In *Reading: Discipline inquiry in process and practice,* edited by P. D. Pearson and J. Hansen. Twenty-seventh Yearbook of the National Reading Conference. Clemson: National Reading Conference, 229–232. Reports a study in which the efficacy of REAP is explored.

Eanet, M. G., and A. V. Manzo. 1976. REAP—A strategy for improving reading/writing study skills. *Journal of Reading* 19:647–652. Presents a detailed discussion of how to use the REAP technique in the classroom.

Manzo, A. V. 1973. CONPASS: English—A demonstration project. *Journal of Reading* 6:539–

545. Describes the use of annotations as an aid to improving reading comprehension.

———. 1985. Expansion modules for the ReQuest, CAT, GRP and REAP reading/study procedures. *Journal of Reading* 28:498–503. Updates the use of these study techniques in hopes of increasing student independence.

Survey Technique

Purpose

The Survey Technique (Aukerman 1972) is intended to: (1) provide the students with a systematic approach for previewing a content chapter and (2) provide the classroom teacher with an additional approach to use in preparing students to read the text.

Rationale

The acquisition of effective study skills is recognized as one of the major goals of upper-level reading instruction. The Survey Technique described by Aukerman (1972) provides the content teacher with a systematic means of walking the students through the first step of Robinson's (1961) SQ3R method of study. Specifically, the Survey Technique is designed to prepare the students for the reading of a text by arranging a whole-class overview of the text material. By using the technique on numerous occasions throughout the school year, the teacher attempts to lead the student to understand the importance of previewing prior to reading.

Intended Audience

Although probably more useful at the secondary level, the Survey Technique may also be used at the upper elementary level. It could certainly be useful at this level when the students are scheduled to tackle an especially difficult chapter. As with most highly structured procedures, the technique would appear most valuable for students who have difficulty with the text material.

Description of the Procedures

The Survey Technique serves as a substitute for the readiness stage of the Directed Reading Activity or the preparation stage of the Instructional Framework (both Unit 5). The objective is to prepare the students for the actual reading of the text by arranging a whole-class overview procedure that results in an understanding of the total chapter content.

As with other instructional strategies discussed in this book, decisions must be made by the teacher as to what particular information to emphasize. By identifying the major understandings the students are to acquire in a given chapter, the content instructor becomes aware of portions of the chapter that need to be emphasized during the class survey.

Aukerman (1972) outlined a six-step procedure that can be used with any traditionally designed content textbook. The technique follows easily when the text chapter contains the following format: chapter title, introduction, main headings with subtopics, summary, review questions, and exercises.

With that format in mind, the teacher can adapt Aukerman's six-step procedure in this way.

1. Analysis of Chapter Title   After reading the title with the students, the instructor might ask questions such as, "What do you think this chapter is going to be about?" "What do you already know about this topic?" "How do you see this chapter relating to the unit we just completed?" Regardless of reading ability, all students can participate in this type of activity.

2. Analysis of Subtitles   The teacher will note each of the subtitles so that each student will understand the overall outline for the chapter topic. This preview may also involve the second step in Robinson's (1961) SQ3R method—the question step. Students could be asked to turn each of the headings into a question. The resulting questions provide the students with specific purposes for reading the text under each of the headings. For example, the subtitle "Advantages of Cotton Production" results in the question "What were the advantages of cotton production?"

Questions can be developed by the class as a whole and placed on the chalkboard or on an overhead projector. After using the Survey Technique on several occasions, the content instructor might request that each student develop his or her own set of questions. Whether as a whole-class or as an individual activity, the development of questions results in a student-produced guide that should be extremely valuable when students are later asked to read and study the chapter in more detail.

3. Analysis of Visuals   Often some of the most important information in a chapter can be found in the visuals of the chapter. Many students ignore these aids, while others may not possess the necessary skills to interpret the pictorial information. This third step in the Survey Technique gives the content teacher an opportunity to stress the importance of these visual aids and, if necessary, to teach the students how to obtain information from them. The following bar graph example, Figure 10–2, might appear in a seventh-grade geography book.

The teacher would ask questions to determine if the students were able to glean information from the bar graph. Two questions might be: "What is the major cotton producing state in the United States?" "What do you suppose the authors of our text meant by the term 'Expressed in 1,000-Bale Units?' " If the students have difficulty with these two questions, the teacher could take a brief period of time to describe the major features of a bar graph and to show students how much information can be obtained from such a simple figure. With the graph shown in the particular example, it would probably be necessary to explain the numerical system so that students would understand that they

FIGURE 10–2.   EXAMPLE OF A BAR GRAPH

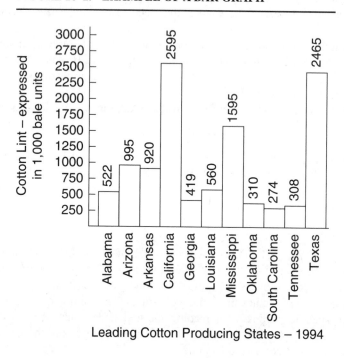

would need to multiply the number of units depicted on the graph times 1,000 to determine the actual number of bales produced by each state; i.e., in 1994, California actually produced 1,000 × 2,595 = 2,595,000 bales of cotton. Other questions might include the following: "Where are the majority of the leading cotton-producing states located?" "Why do you think Kentucky is not one of the major cotton-producing states?"

4. Introductory Paragraph(s)   Many textbook authors use one or more introductory paragraphs to set forth the important ideas within the chapter. Students might be asked to read this information silently. The discussion that follows should concentrate on how the information in the introduction fits with the information discovered in the first three steps of the procedure. A question like the following might be used: "Now that we have read this introductory material, can you see how this information supports some of the things we discovered as we surveyed the chapter?"

5. Concluding Paragraph(s)   Generally, the final paragraphs of a content text chapter provide a summary of the chapter content. By reading the summary before reading the total chapter in detail, students receive additional confirmation of what they discovered in all the previous steps of their survey.

6. Deriving the Main Idea   Aukerman suggests that out of Steps 4 and 5, reading and discussing the introductory and concluding paragraphs, the class as a whole should develop a concise statement that could stand as the main idea of the chapter. The statement should be written out on the board or put on a transparency for all to see. Students should now be ready to pursue a more detailed study of the chapter content.

Cautions and Comments

The Survey Technique appears to be worthwhile in its own right as well as serving as an excellent means of introducing students to the initial phases of the SQ3R method of study and of demonstrating the value of this technique for studying content material. In addition, as instructors observe students using the Survey Technique more effectively, instructors could gradually withdraw this structure, thus allowing the students to take more responsibility for their own learning.

A minor shortcoming of the procedure is the exclusion of review questions at the end of a chapter. Assuming they are worthwhile, they could be used as a check of the efficacy of surveying other facets of a chapter prior to reading the text. For example, one effective way of using end-of-chapter questions within Aukerman's Survey Technique would be to deal with these questions immediately after a discussion of the chapter title. The teacher or a student could read aloud each question to the class and ask the students to note briefly what they think the answer to that question might be. If students have no idea of the answer to a particular question, they are advised to leave it blank. After each question has been considered individually by each student, and possibly after a small group discussion, the instructor can deal with the questions in a whole-class discussion. By using the chapter questions in this manner, the teacher is saying to the students, "Let's find out what the author thinks is important in this chapter and let's see how much of this information we already know." Thus, students have an opportunity to review their previous knowledge of the topic before they move on to more detailed study of the unit.

Following this procedure, the remaining five steps of the Survey Technique could be used to gain further information on the topic. After the main idea has been derived, the class could return to the questions at the end of the chapter to discover how many new answers resulted from the survey procedure. It is not unusual for students to answer correctly 20 to 30 percent of the questions during their initial attempt at them and answer another 20 to 30 percent after surveying the chapter.

References

Aukerman, R. C. 1972. *Reading in the secondary school classroom.* New York: McGraw-Hill, 47–62. Presents a detailed discussion of how the Survey Technique might be used by the content teacher.

Robinson, F. P. 1961. *Effective study,* rev. ed. New York: Harper & Row. Provides a detailed description of the SQ3R method of study.

PORPE

Purpose

PORPE (*P*redict, *O*rganize, *R*ehearse, *P*ractice, *E*valuate) is a study strategy developed by Simpson (1986, 1992) designed to help students in: (1) actively planning, monitoring, and evaluating their learning of content; (2) learning the processes involved in preparing for essay examinations; and (3) using the process of writing as a means for learning content area material.

Rationale

Simpson has stated that PORPE evolved in response to: (1) her desire to see if writing could be used as an independent learning strategy for any content area and (2) students' anxieties and lack of knowledge about preparing for and taking essay examinations.

PORPE is based upon the work of Baker and Brown (1984), Emig (1977), and Palincsar and Brown (1984). Baker and Brown (1984) described effective readers as individuals who possess the following metacognitive skills:

1. Clarify their purposes for reading by understanding the explicit and implicit demands of the task
2. Identify the important aspects of a message
3. Focus attention on the major content and not the trivia
4. Monitor their ongoing activities to ascertain whether comprehension is occurring
5. Engage in self-questioning to determine if their purpose is being achieved
6. Take corrective action when failures in comprehension are identified

Emig (1977) advocated that students be required to put into writing the concepts they are reading about to be able to more fully understand and evaluate their learning. Finally, Palincsar and Brown (1984) found that when students are given the specific steps in performing a comprehension task, receive extensive teacher modeling and repeated practice in relevant contexts, and are told why the steps are important in their learning, they can learn to behave as effective readers.

Intended Audience

PORPE was developed for use with college students who lacked a comprehensive study system. As such, it probably could be used with high school students for the same purpose.

Description of the Procedures

PORPE consists of the following five steps: (1) predict, (2) organize, (3) rehearse, (4) practice, and (5) evaluate.

1. Predict   This first step is designed to have students predict potential essay questions to guide their subsequent study after they have finished an initial reading of the text. In doing so, students are expected to clarify their purposes for future reading, identify crucial aspects of the text, and focus on the major content. In addition, the predicted essay questions must cause the students to synthesize and evaluate the material, since lower-level, text-explicit thinking would not be helpful to them.

Because of the difficulty of this step and its importance to the rest of the strategy, Simpson has broken it down into four phases. In the first phase students should be introduced to the language used in essay construction. Words such as *explain, compare, contrast,* and *criticize* should be defined and discussed for them. In the second phase the teacher should model for students the processes involved in predicting essay questions from a text assignment. These should be recorded and discussed so that students understand how and why the questions were formed. In this way students can be made to see that such questions originate from important aspects of the reading.

Once many sessions of modeling are completed, the third phase begins: provide students stems for potential essay questions on a specific topic. Ask them to complete the questions, cueing the students into the use of the words used for constructing essays introduced earlier. For instance, the words *compare* and *contrast* should be used in writing an essay question about causes of the War Between the States from the perspectives of the North and the South. After much practice in a variety of content areas, students can enter the fourth phase in which they will independently develop their own questions. These predicted questions should be shared with the class, working in small groups. The questions should be discussed and evaluated to identify the most plausible ones.

2. Organize   In this step students organize the key information that will answer the predicted essay questions. They summarize and synthesize the material in an effort to sense the overall structure of the unit. Then, for each predicted question, students are to outline their answers in their own words or create a map, chart, or graphic organizer depicting the answer.

Simpson suggests that teachers can facilitate this process in a number of ways. Initially, teachers should share their own outlines or maps of the predicted essay questions and explain their construction. Students can then use these as models and rehearse and practice for the test. However, since it is the intent of PORPE to have students work through this process independently, teachers should quickly move them into small groups where they can generate their own organization. The results of each small group should be shared with the class and discussed.

Teachers may also find it useful to provide the students with examples of several different student maps or outlines for their critique. It would be profitable to include a bad example—one in which the question is ignored, key examples are overlooked, and/or the organization is lacking or completely missing. The final part of this step occurs when students work on their own organization with written teacher feedback. Although the actual format is left up to each student, the teacher needs to check for accuracy, completeness, and use of examples. The importance of the selective rereading and thinking that precedes the construction of a map or outline also should be stressed at this point.

3. Rehearsal   During this step of PORPE, students are to place key ideas, examples, and overall organization into their long-term memory for later recall during the essay examination. The notion of recall versus recognition should be discussed as well as the processes of memorization, in particular the ideas of recitation and self-testing. The following guidelines might prove helpful:

a. Have students begin rehearsal by reciting aloud the organization they have generated. They are expected to test themselves by repeating the structure orally or in writing from memory.

b. Once this is mastered, students are expected to gradually add key ideas and examples from the outline, a section at a time. They should test themselves and, if correct, add a new section.

c. Once the overall structure, ideas, and examples are committed to memory, students are expected to test themselves several times over a period of days to ensure that the information stays in long-term memory. It should be emphasized that rehearsal is a slow, continual process, not one that is conducted overnight.

4. Practice   In the practice step, students validate their learning by writing out in detail what they recited in the rehearsal step. Simpson suggests that many students may need the teacher to model the processes involved in writing effective essay answers. In doing so, the teacher should stress the following to the students:

a. Sketch an outline of the answer to the question before writing actually begins.

b. Make sure the opening statement of the answer rephrases the question or takes a position.

c. Use transitional words such as *first* or *on the other hand* to ensure that the structure of the answer is obvious.

d. Include examples for each major point made.

e. When the writing is finished, check the outline to see if it matches the written answer. Finally, read the written answer to be sure it makes sense.

5. Evaluate   The final step of PORPE requires that students evaluate the quality of their practice essay answers. Students are expected to learn to evaluate their answers as a teacher would; in this way they will learn to monitor whether they need to return to the organizing or rehearsal step of the strategy or are really ready for the actual examination. To facilitate this evaluation, it is suggested that students might rate themselves on their answers to the following questions:

a. Is the question answered directly?

b. Is there an introductory sentence that rephrased the question or took a position on the question?

c. Is the essay organized with major points made obvious to the reader?

d. Were examples used to prove and clarify each point?

e. Were transitions used to cue the reader?

f. Did the content make sense?

The guiding questions can be used in several ways. The teacher may collect the practice essays and judge the quality of the essays themselves. The teacher can also provide sample essays and ask students to rank order them from best to worst. Students should be prepared to justify their decisions in a group discussion. Because of the difficulty of the step, teachers may need to organize several sessions where students read, discuss, and evaluate the quality of various essays. Once they become accustomed to judging the merits of essay answers, they can begin to work independently at this task.

Cautions and Comments

PORPE capitalizes on an integrated language arts approach to content area learning as well as the principles behind the Explicit Teaching of Reading Comprehension (see Unit 7) in the development and use of the strategy. According to Simpson, it has been tried successfully for a number of years with college developmental students. Furthermore, Simpson (Simpson, Hayes, Stahl, Connor, and Weaver, 1988; Simpson, Stahl, and Hayes, 1989) conducted research validations of the strategy in which she found that students trained in using PORPE outperformed students using traditional methods on recognition and recall measures. In addition, PORPE students wrote better essays.

By the author's own admission, PORPE "not only takes a while to master, but also takes a lot of study time" (Simpson 1986, 412). Moreover, she points to the fact that steps one and five are difficult for students; therefore, teachers will need to organize their time and instruction and plan accordingly. Thus, it seems that students will have to persevere in order to see positive effects with the strategy; students needing more immediate feedback may give up on the strategy. The length of time that students persevere may also be dependent on the amount of time teachers give to the strategy and the quality of instruction they provide. This criticism may not be unique to PORPE; it may be true of any study system that students are taught.

References

Baker, L., and A. L. Brown. 1984. Metacognitive skills and reading. In *Handbook of reading research,* edited by P. D. Pearson, R. Barr, M. L. Kamil, and P. Mosenthal. New York: Longman. Review of the research on metacognition as it relates to comprehension and study.

Emig, J. 1977. Writing as a mode of learning. *College Composition and Communication* 28:122–129. Examines the role of writing in the process of learning.

Palincsar, A., and A. L. Brown. 1984. Reciprocal teaching of comprehension-fostering and comprehension-monitoring activities. *Cognition and Instruction* 1:117–175. Research showing that poor readers can become effective readers with proper comprehension training.

Simpson, M. L. 1986. PORPE: A writing strategy for studying and learning in the content areas. *Journal of Reading* 29:407–414. The introduction and description of the strategy.

———. 1992. PORPE: A study strategy for learning in the content areas. In *Reading in the content areas: Improving classroom instruction,* 3d ed., edited by E. K. Dishner, T. W. Bean, J. E. Readence, and D. W. Moore, 340–348. Dubuque, IA: Kendall/Hunt. Updated discussion of the strategy.

Simpson, M. L., C. G. Hayes, N. Stahl, R. T. Connor, and D. Weaver. 1988. An initial validation of a study strategy system. *Journal of Reading Behavior* 20:149–180. Research study pointing to the effectiveness of PORPE.

Simpson, M. L., N.A. Stahl, and C. G. Hayes. 1989. PORPE: A research validation. *Journal of Reading* 33: 22–28. Research studies that substantiated the claims for the effectiveness of PORPE.

Notetaking System for Learning

Purpose

The Notetaking System for Learning (Palmatier 1973) is designed to: (1) provide students with a systematic means of organizing class notes, and (2) provide a sound means for reviewing content information.

Rationale

Although there are certainly exceptions, many content classrooms at the secondary and college levels are structured around class lectures, supplemented by textbook assignments. Most traditional notetaking techniques consider only one portion of the class at a time; i.e., they deal with taking notes in lectures or with notetaking procedures for specific reading assignments. Palmatier's Notetaking System for Learning (NSL) is a flexible system that encourages the student to combine the two approaches.

Intended Audience

Although it is believed that some simplified notetaking procedures should be taught at an earlier point, the Notetaking System for Learning appears best suited for students in the ninth grade through college. It also would seem appropriate for above-average students in grades seven and eight.

Description of the Procedures

Obviously, in order for students to use any type of notetaking procedure, they need to have available the basic notetaking materials—paper and pencils. As many classroom teachers know, this is the point at which many notetaking strategies can and do break down.

It is suggested that students use only one side of 8 1/2 x 11-inch loose-leaf notebook paper with a three-inch margin on the left side of the page. If this legal-line paper cannot be purchased, students can add their own margins to standard notebook paper. The following discussion of the procedure will focus on these three major components of the system: (1) recording, (2) organizing, and (3) studying.

1. Recording   Notes generally are first recorded from the lecture, with reading notes added at a later time. The lecture notes are placed to the right of the three-inch marginal line. The specific format is best left to the individual student, but Palmatier (1973) does suggest the use of a format that utilizes both: (a) subordination—a modified outlining procedure—and (b) space. Space will vary depending upon the degree of change between items presented. If the lecture information appears to flow easily from one idea to another, then little space is left between the noted ideas; however, at the point when the topic obviously changes course or when there is some confusion as to how the ideas tie together, the student would be advised to leave a larger space so that more information may be added later.

Again, the student should not use the back of the notebook paper. This will only cause confusion when the student later tries to organize or study the notes. The completed notetaking procedure should result in a format similar to the one shown in Figure 10–3. Note that each page should be numbered as the notes are recorded. This will avoid some confusion during the study portion of the procedure.

2. Organizing If time is available, immediately following the lecture session the student should organize his or her notes while the ideas and details are fresh. The student has two tasks during this portion of the NSL procedure:

    a. *Labeling.* By examining separately each informational unit within the recorded notes, the student should be able to provide labels that briefly describe the information presented. Labels should be placed to the left side of the marginal line and directly in line with the appropriate recorded notes.

    b. *Adding.* Following the labeling process, Palmatier (1973) suggests that the student now insert important information from the text directly into the lecture notes. If adequate space has been provided between important ideas, the reading notes may be easily added to the lecture note page; if more space is needed, the back of the notebook paper can now be used in this integration process.

Following the above procedure, a page of notes now could resemble the example in Figure 10–4.

3. Studying The Notetaking System for Learning provides not only a simple means for recording ideas but also a systematic approach to the study of the notes. Since both lecture and reading notes are recorded within the system, the student will have no need to return to the text material or to shuffle back and forth between two sets of notes.

For study purposes, the notes are removed from the loose-leaf binder and spread out so that only the left-hand margin of each page is visible. The labels now become the focal point for the study session.

FIGURE 10–3.

FIGURE 10–4.

The type of exam for which the student is studying can dictate the manner in which the notes are approached. For an objective test, the student might approach the labels at random, thus approximating the multiple choice, true-false, and matching questions on this type of exam. For an essay test, the student might approach the study task in a more organized manner, usually starting at the beginning of the notes and moving through them in the order in which they were presented. The labels in the left hand margin become the question stems for the purpose of study. A label is transformed into a question, which the student proceeds to answer. Verification is obtained by lifting the next page of notes and reading the information written to the right of the label. This procedure is followed throughout the study period. As the information on a page is learned, it can be returned to the loose-leaf notebook. Study concludes when all the pages are back in their proper place in the notebook.

Cautions and Comments

Secondary teachers and college professors often complain about the inability of their students to take adequate notes. Yet it is rare indeed to find the word notetaking in a secondary text or in a school district's curriculum guide. Very simply, the skill is not taught; rather it is assumed the student will develop it.

Teachers at the secondary level who rely heavily upon the lecture method may want to spend a portion of their instructional time teaching the students how to take notes efficiently. The time investment should pay off in students' more complete understanding of the subject. Teachers will also be developing an important survival skill that their students will be sure to need in other course work.

In teaching a strategy such as the Notetaking System for Learning, it is important that it be presented early in the school year. To determine if the class as a whole needs such instruction, the teacher might conclude a presentation near the beginning of the first unit by asking the students to turn in their day's notes for the purpose of an informal evaluation.

As Anderson and Armbruster (1984) have cautioned, for any notetaking strategy to be viewed as effective, attention focusing and purposeful information processing should be apparent.

References

Anderson, T. H., and B. B. Armbruster. 1984. Studying. In *Handbook of reading research,* edited by P. D. Pearson. New York: Longman. Discusses the efficacy of notetaking as a study strategy.

Palmatier, R. A. 1971. Comparison of four notetaking procedures. *Journal of Reading* 14:235–240, 258. Compares four notetaking procedures for relative effectiveness and efficiency.

———. 1973. A notetaking system for learning. *Journal of Reading* 17:36–39. Presents a detailed explanation for a notetaking procedure that has proved useful to secondary and college students.

Tierney, R. J., J. E. Readence, and E. K. Dishner. 1990. *Reading strategies and practices: A compendium,* 3d ed. Boston: Allyn and Bacon. Discusses the Herringbone Technique (312–316), another notetaking technique that capitalizes on asking six basic questions of text: Who? What? When? Where? How? and Why?

Guided Lecture Procedure

Purpose

The Guided Lecture Procedure (Kelly and Holmes, 1979) is designed to provide students with a systematic technique for listening and taking notes.

Rationale

The Guided Lecture Procedure (GLP) was developed as a means of overcoming many of the problems college students have in listening and thinking about a lecture, synthesizing what was stated, and recording accurate notes. Essentially, students are asked to refrain from notetaking during a lecture and engage in intensive listening and thinking for the purpose of retaining the information presented. It is based upon the principles and lesson structure of the Guided Reading Procedure developed in 1975 by Manzo (see Unit 9) and, as such, the authors describe the GLP as not only a notetaking procedure but also a teaching and studying technique.

Intended Audience

Although it was developed for college level students, the GLP seems suitable for all students who are in classes in which much information is given through the lecture format.

Description of the Procedure

The GLP consists of the following steps: (1) prepare, (2) listen and recall information, (3) organize notes, and (4) reflect and rewrite notes.

1. Prepare   Prior to beginning the lecture, students should be provided the purpose for listening by reading and copying the lecture objectives. These should be given in brief form on an overhead projector or the chalkboard, stated as terminal objectives, and limited to three or four in number. Younger students should probably get even fewer objectives. In addition, any new vocabulary should also be listed alongside the objectives. Thus, this step is designed to give students a framework for what to expect from the lecture.

2. Listen and Recall Information   At this time students are to engage in active listening and not take notes for the purpose(s) specified as the lecture begins. The amount of time the teacher will lecture will depend on the number of objectives to be met as well as the age and ability level of the students. However, at no time should the lecture extend beyond thirty minutes.

When the lecture has terminated, students are directed to write down in short form all they can recall. They are encouraged to engage in a form of visual thinking by mentally perusing the information presented to see what interconnections can be formed with the material recalled. Students are given a maximum of five minutes to perform this task, depending on the amount of information presented. It is the intent of this activity to highlight for students what they did not understand or could not connect.

3. Organize Notes   The students are now assigned to work in small groups to use a collaborative process to recapitulate the lecture. It is discussed in terms of the objectives and vocabulary previously specified by: (a) putting the notes in sequential order, (b) recognizing the major concepts and pertinent details, and (c) drawing appropriate conclusions. It is during this time that students actually prepare their lecture notes by working collaboratively to recognize concepts they may have missed independently. The teacher acts as a guide during this time by circulating among the small groups to answer questions and clarify their task.

4. Reflect and Rewrite Notes   At the conclusion of the lesson, or as soon as possible thereafter, students are asked to reflect on what they have learned through the lecture and the GLP activities themselves. This is done in order to conceptualize and organize the new knowledge and, subsequently, build long-term memory and motivate students to participate in active study. Upon reflection, students are asked to write, without the use of their notes, the major concepts, pertinent details, and conclusions of the lecture. The final GLP activity allows students to retain the most important information and provides an opportunity for them to appraise their knowledge of the material in their notes.

Cautions and Comments

The Guided Lecture Procedure is based on the principles of: (1) purposeful listening to recall information; (2) collaborative self-questioning and self-correction to fill in missing information and correct inconsistencies in recalled information; and (3) organization and reflection to facilitate long-term retrieval of information. As such, the GLP uses all four language processes and offers students the opportunity to interact with others to analyze lecture material until it is comprehended thoroughly and accurately.

On the other hand, the GLP purports to be a notetaking, studying, and teaching procedure. While there is no doubt about its former two purposes, teaching only takes place in the sense that the teacher can provide information through the lecture and by answering questions that may arise when students are in small groups. Absent from the GLP are modeling with regard to how to take notes, how to distinguish main ideas from details, and what differentiates good notes from bad notes. In addition, there is no provision for student independence; i.e., the GLP offers no suggestions for moving students from collaborative small-group work to independent application.

References

Kelly, B. W., and J. Holmes. 1979. The Guided Lecture Procedure. *Journal of Reading* 22:602–604. Provides the rationale and steps for the GLP.

Manzo, A. V. 1975. Guided reading procedure. *Journal of Reading* 18:287–291. Describes the strategy on which the GLP is based.

Tierney, R. J., J. E. Readence, and E. K. Dishner. 1990. *Reading strategies and practices: A compendium,* 3d ed. Boston: Allyn and Bacon. Describes the Listening Guide (326–328), another strategy to help students listen and take notes.

Graphic Information Lesson

Purpose

The Graphic Information Lesson (Reinking, 1992) helps students to: (1) discover how graphic aids can promote reading comprehension, and (2) review and interpret important text information.

Rationale

Graphic comprehension, or graphic literacy, refers to the ability to interpret charts, maps, graphs, and other pictorial presentations that are commonly used to supplement the prose in textbooks, nonfiction tradebooks, and newspapers. For students to use graphic aids effectively, they must be able to integrate the information found in them with that of the text and their own prior knowledge.

Unfortunately, pictorial presentations of text concepts in nonverbal or semiverbal form tend to be difficult for students and are seemingly ignored as specific instructional objectives in basals and content area texts. Since graphs are prevalent in text material of all types and quite diverse in their construction [see Fry (1981) for an examination of a Taxonomy of Graphs], the need for instructional activities that help students develop skills in graphic comprehension seems clear. The Graphic Information Lesson (GIL) is designed to enable students to interpret and to think divergently about graphic presentations and their relationship to text information.

Intended Audience

Reinking (1992) stated that GIL has been used successfully with middle school students in their regular content area classes. It also seems appropriate for secondary developmental/remedial reading teachers to use with students who encounter graphic information in their reading assignments or for any student who encounters trouble in their interpretation.

Description of the Procedure

The Graphic Information Lesson was developed for use as an occasional postreading activity with text that contains one or more graphic aids that are pertinent to students' understanding of important text concepts, particularly at higher levels of comprehension. The GIL is divided into three stages: (1) determining graphic information, (2) integrating and synthesizing new information, and (3) reinforcing and applying graphic information.

1. Determining Graphic Information   After reading the text, the teacher leads a discussion to determine what information is found in particular graphic aids and how it relates to the text information. Although the students will probably initially focus on text explicit information, the teacher should ask questions at the text implicit and experience-based levels of comprehension that focus on the relationship between the graphic aid and the text. The teacher may also model these higher level thought processes for students, if necessary. In addition, the teacher helps students learn to judge if the information in the graph is supplemental, redundant, or complementary to the text. This stage of the GIL serves as a diagnostic step for teachers in that they can determine how well students can or cannot interpret graphic displays. If necessary, teachers can then teach the appropriate skills students need for graphic comprehension.

2. Integrating and Synthesizing New Information   The purpose of this stage of the GIL is to have students synthesize information derived from the text and use it to judge the validity of the graphic aids. The teacher presents several examples of pseudographs, graphic displays related to but not included in the text. They are invented by the teacher and may or may not be accurate or believable when compared with the text information. It is the students' task, individually or in small groups, to decide the accuracy and/or believability of these pseudographs, based on text information or their prior knowledge. If they base their decisions on text information, students must document them by furnishing page numbers.

This stage of the lesson is important because it allows students to review and integrate the text information. It also attempts to provide students with the appropriate context for demonstrating how good readers evaluate and process graphic information.

3. Reinforcing and Applying Graphic Information   In this stage activities are designed that require students to apply what they have learned in the previous two stages of the GIL to make decisions about graphic aids in relationship to the text. It also gives students an opportunity to work independently.

The kinds of activity used in this stage must extend students' awareness and use of graphic aids and are only limited by teachers' creativity. Some activities will need to be more straightforward and focus on text explicit information, but eventually the repeated use of the GIL would allow all students to engage in more sophisticated exercises. Reinking provided the following examples:

a. Students can create their own pseudographs to be shared and/or critiqued with the class.

b. When multiple graphics exist, have students defend their choice of the most important graphic aid in the text.

c. Students could be asked to elaborate on the relationship between two or more graphic aids found in the text.

d. Have students critique the author's use of graphic aids by making suggestions about eliminating redundant or confusing graphs and adding other, more useful ones.

Cautions and Comments

The Graphic Information Lesson seems to be a unique and viable strategy for helping students acquire and synthesize concepts found in graphic aids with those found in the text. It attempts to get students to think about the ideas represented in graphic material.

Two other features of this approach are worth noting. First, it follows the principles of the Explicit Teaching of Reading Comprehension. Teachers model for students the desired comprehension behavior, and students are given guided practice with feedback and opportunities for independent application. Some of the cautions and comments discussed for Explicit Teaching (see Unit 7) apply. Second, it directs teachers to integrate the teaching of process with the learning of content, i.e., students are not taught comprehension skills devoid of content.

The second stage of this lesson seems to be a key to the entire strategy. The evaluation of the pseudographs allows students to become involved in a gamelike atmosphere; thus, the learning is lively and enjoyable. Should the teacher not create effective pseudographs, the lesson ultimately may not be motivating and, therefore, beneficial. It is noteworthy that the strategy includes the possibility of having students do their own pseudographs. Perhaps more emphasis could have been placed upon student-generated graphics, especially in classroom situations that have the technologies to facilitate the use of graphics. To date, research examining the use of the procedure is limited. Indeed, only observational data currently support the use of the graphic information lesson.

References

Fry, E. 1981. Graphical literacy. *Journal of Reading* 24:383–390. Discusses the need for graphic comprehension and presents a taxonomy of graphs.

Gillespie, C. S. 1993. Reading graphic displays: What teachers should know. *Journal of Reading* 36:350–354. Discussion of graphic aids and the use of the GIL.

Reinking, D. 1992. Integrating graphic aids into content area instruction: The graphic information lesson. In *Reading in the content areas: Improving classroom instruction,* 3d ed., edited by E. K. Dishner, T. W. Bean, J. E. Readence, and D. W. Moore. Dubuque, IA: Kendall/Hunt, 364–370. A description of the GIL.

PLAE

Purpose

The purpose of PLAE (*Preplan, List, Activate,* and *Evaluate*) is to provide students with a study system to monitor and control their learning. Simpson and Nist (1984) conceptualized PLAE as a means to help students become independent learners through developing their metacognitive awareness during studying.

Rationale

Success in studying seems to revolve around both the awareness and knowledge about strategies to use and the ability to regulate them. Strategy regulation amounts to planning activities prior to undertaking a task, monitoring those activities during learning, and evaluating their effectiveness after task completion. Because many students lack the metacognitive ability to regulate their study strategies, their chances of academic success are limited.

As a consequence, Simpson and Nist developed PLAE based upon a model of learning developed by Bransford (1979). In this model Bransford stated that, if learning is to occur, the following factors must be considered: 1) the nature of the materials, e.g., how they are structured, the difficulty level; 2) learner characteristics, e.g., skills, attitudes, knowledge; 3) the learning activities, e.g., attention, rehearsal, elaboration; and, 4) the evaluative tasks, e.g., recognition, recall, problem solving. Using this framework, PLAE takes into consideration five operations necessary for student-directed strategy control and regulation (Nist and Simpson, 1989):

1. Students must learn how to establish goals, allocate resources, and make a plan of action that will incorporate the appropriate strategies and distribute practice over time.
2. Students must have a repertoire of strategies for the many tasks and texts they will encounter, since there is no one superior or generic method of study.
3. Students must learn how to select the most appropriate strategies based upon the characteristics of the text, the task, and their own learning preferences.
4. Students must learn how to activate and monitor a plan of action and make appropriate changes, when necessary.
5. Students must learn how to evaluate their plan's success or failure in terms of goals and the task in order to plan for future situations. (P. 183)

Intended Audience

PLAE was originally developed with at-risk college students in mind. However, it seems logical that the strategy could also be used with high school as well as upper-level junior high students.

Description of the Procedure

Four stages describe the implementation of PLAE: 1) Preplanning, 2) Listing, 3) Activating, and 4) Evaluating.

1. Preplanning In this stage of the strategy students are asked to define the study task assigned. Simpson and Nist (1984) suggest that students ask themselves a series of questions to get a clear idea of the task and complete this initial stage of PLAE:

a. When will the test be? What other tasks need I complete during the time before the test?

b. What will the test cover? Will it cover just the assigned reading? Class lectures? Outside reading?

c. How many questions will be on the test? What kind of questions will they be? What kind of thinking will be required?

d. What will the format of the test be?

e. How much will this test count in the total grade?

f. What kind of grade do I want on this test?

g. How much time will I need to spend in studying and reviewing for the test?

h. How will studying for this test change my regular schedule?

2. Listing In this stage of PLAE students must decide how to deal with the task outlined in preplanning and develop a plan for studying. In essence, they must decide which of the study strategies that they have at their disposal is most appropriate for the demands of the studying task. Then they must decide how to implement the selected strategies. Simpson and Nist suggest that students record the strategies, why they think the strategies are appropriate, and how they will complete their study plan.

For instance, if students decide that PORPE (described earlier in this unit) is an appropriate study strategy for the assignment they have been given, they should record that strategy and why they decided to use it. In this case it might be to give themselves preparation for an essay test. In completing their plan of study they will record that they plan to predict some essay questions and write answers to them. Further, they should record when and where they will do their studying and how long it will take them. In this case they might say, "Tomorrow at home in my room for 90 minutes."

3. Activating Here students implement their plan of study and monitor its effectiveness in accomplishing the task. They should question whether the selected strategies are getting them ready for the test to come or whether they should decide to change their plan. Simpson and Nist suggest students use the following questions as a guide during plan activation:

a. Am I following my proposed plan?

b. If not, why? What seems to be causing me trouble? Did I schedule something else I didn't take into account?

c. Can I make changes without sacrificing the goals I set in preplanning?

d. Am I comprehending and retaining the ideas I want to? If not, why?

e. Should I choose another study strategy or reallocate my study time?

4. Evaluating   In the final stage of PLAE students check what they gained from this studying session against their performance on the test. If they followed carefully the previous stages of the strategy, students should feel confident about what they know and how well they are prepared for the test. In evaluating their test performance, they are giving themselves feedback on how well PLAE worked. Simpson and Nist argue that students should do a question-by-question evaluation for each item missed so that modifications can be made before the next cycle of PLAE occurs. Since the PLAE procedure is cyclical rather than linear, this step is important for success in future tests. Simpson and Nist offer the following questions for students to ask in guiding the evaluation of their test performance:

a. Why did I miss this question? Did I misunderstand it? Did I not read it correctly? Or did I just not know the answer?

b. If I didn't know the answer, from where did the question originate? Assigned reading? Class lectures?

c. What type of question was it?

d. Is there any pattern to my mistakes?

e. Did I select the most appropriate strategies for the assigned task? If not, what strategies should I use next time a similar task occurs?

Cautions and Comments

PLAE attempts to get students to experience the metacognitive processes necessary for independent learning by guiding them in how to define their learning tasks, select the most appropriate study strategies, and activate/evaluate the effectiveness of their plan of action. Indeed, in empirical studies by Nist and Simpson (1989, 1990) and Nist, Simpson, Olejnik, and Mealey (1991), students who used PLAE not only improved their test performance but also their metacognitive abilities.

These research studies do make PLAE unique among most instructional strategies in that there is evidence of its effectiveness in multiple experiments. However, further exploration of the long-term effects of PLAE is needed as well as investigating qualitatively what is going on when students apply PLAE techniques in studying situations. Most importantly, however, would be to investigate the applicability of PLAE with other than college-level subjects. Studies using younger students would be most appropriate.

References

Bransford, J. D. 1979. *Human cognition: Learning, understanding, and remembering.* Belmont, CA: Wadsworth. A very readable text on cognitive psychology.

Nist, S. L., and M. L. Simpson. 1989. PLAE, a validated strategy. *Journal of Reading* 33:182–186. The initial empirical validation of the strategy.

———. 1990. The effects of PLAE upon students' test performance and metacognitive awareness. In *Literacy theory and research: Analyses from multiple paradigms,* edited by J. Zutell and S. McCormick. Thirty-ninth Yearbook of the National Reading Conference, 321–327. Chicago: National Reading Conference. The second of three studies on PLAE that found that the strategy was successful in improving test performance and metacognitive abilities.

Nist, S. L., M. L. Simpson, S. Olejnik, and D. L. Mealey. 1991. The relation between self-selected study processes and test performance. *American Educational Research Journal* 28:849–874. Results of this study corroborate those previously conducted on PLAE.

Simpson, M. L., and S. L. Nist. 1984. PLAE: A model for planning successful independent learning. *Journal of Reading* 28:218–223. The original source of PLAE.

Intervention Programs for "At Risk" Readers

UNIT OVERVIEW

The term *at risk* became widely used as schools, legislatures, and industry became increasingly concerned that: (1) students were failing to achieve the basic literacy skills to participate fully and productively in society; (2) most attempts to address the needs of this population have not been successful; (3) the costs of students failing were immense, especially when measured over time; and (4) remedial programs seemed to offer little in the way of long-term benefits.

No longer is it satisfactory to have the child show growth in the remedial setting; it is now essential that the transition back to a regular classroom be achieved—that is, the student should have the skills and strategies to maintain the ability to read and to grow as a reader. This unit describes several of the more notable attempts to meet the needs of at-risk readers. They include strategies dating back over 50 years as well as some more current ones.

In the first two editions of this book, several of the programs described in this unit were included in the unit entitled "Multisensory Strategies for Teaching Reading." The current unit represents a mix of those programs along with two notable additions—namely, the Reading Recovery and Success for All programs.

Reading Recovery.   The Reading Recovery program is a one-to-one intervention program for the poorest readers in the first grade and an intensive training program for teachers. These students receive reading recovery interventions for 30 minutes every day with a trained teacher until they develop the self-improvement system needed to return to the regular classroom.

Success for All.   The Success for All program is a schoolwide tutoring program for readers in grades one to three who are experiencing difficulties. The program emphasizes early, intensive intervention and prevention and focuses much of its thrust on disadvantaged schools.

Monroe Methods.   The Monroe methods represent an approach in which sound blending is merged with kinesthetic responses. For teachers of disabled readers, it purports to provide various methods to overcome the difficulties that these readers incur in beginning reading.

Gillingham-Stillman Method. The Gillingham-Stillman method represents an approach that emphasizes students' auditory abilities in learning to read. Based on the theories of Samuel Orton, the Gillingham-Stillman procedure provides an alphabetic method by which words are built through associations involving students' visual, auditory, and kinesthetic processes. It purports to provide teachers of disabled readers a systematic approach to teach reading in a progression from letters to words, from words to sentences, and from sentences to stories.

Fernald Technique. The Fernald technique has been perhaps the most widely used practice for teaching remedial reading. It represents a comprehensive approach to developing reading abilities from low to normal ability based initially on multisensory learning.

Reading Recovery

Purpose

The major goals of Reading Recovery are to reduce reading failure through early intervention and to help students develop a "self-improving system" for continued growth in reading.

Rationale

The Reading Recovery program is a one-to-one intervention program for the poorest readers in first-grade classrooms (i.e., the lowest 20 percent). These students, deemed at risk, are placed in a program that provides 30 minutes daily (in addition to their regular classroom teaching) with a trained Reading Recovery teacher who uses a specific lesson framework. The students continue receiving this instruction until they are brought up to the average of their class and have developed the necessary self-improvement strategies to maintain that level. The power of Reading Recovery is purported to be "in the framework of the lesson itself and in the development of teacher knowledge and problem-solving ability." (Pinnell, DeFord, and Lyons, 1988, 2)

A number of principles guide the Reading Recovery teachers. They are:

1. Reading is a strategic process that takes place in the reader's mind. A goal of Reading Recovery is to help readers develop a meaning orientation to print that includes the ability to enlist effective strategies in a flexible and integrated way.
2. Reading and writing work together to enhance basic understandings of both processes. Throughout the Reading Recovery program, reading and writing are used flexibly to help children make connections between the two.

3. Children learn to read by reading. A basic tenet of Reading Recovery is the notion that for children to make accelerated growth they must actively engage in reading. As Pinnell, DeFord, and Lyons (1988) state:

> Almost every minute during the lesson, children actively engage in reading or writing messages and stories. Familiar material helps children build fluency and experience success; new materials challenge children to do independent problem solving. (1988, 13).

4. Children need to develop fruitful concepts of what reading is. Reading Recovery assumes that children need to develop both a reader-based view and a text-based view of meaning making. They need experiences that focus on integrating reader-based and text-based processes.
5. It is expedient and productive to help children early. Reading Recovery claims that difficulties in learning to read emerge early and should be dealt with as soon as possible.
6. Children who have difficulty can and do make accelerated progress. A goal of Reading Recovery is to engage in fast pacing as the student and teacher work together en route to accelerating growth and student development of independent learning strategies.

The Reading Recovery approach is an early intervention program designed for at-risk first graders having difficulty learning to read. Daily individual lessons, explicit teaching for strategies, and following the child rather than a prescribed curriculum are three features that distinguish this program.

Clay's observational findings on low and high progress readers is the cornerstone of the program. She differentiates these types of readers by saying,

> . . . low progress readers tend to operate on a narrow range of strategies. They rely on what can be invented from memory for the text by paying little or no attention at all to visual details. . . . Whereas high progress readers operate on print in an integrated way in search for meaning, which results in high accuracy and high self-correction rates. . . . The ability to shift to higher and lower strategies, also known as "toing and froing" enables the high progress readers to monitor their reading, integrate knowledge about directional rules of printed language, space formats, and punctuation cues (Clay, 1988). This increases the likelihood for reading to become automatic. (p. 7)

Reading Recovery was originated by M. Clay in New Zealand. According to Clay, the program emerged in response to a request by readers to initiate a research and development effort aimed at helping young children with reading difficulties. As a result, Clay "spent two years observing children and teachers in tutoring situations and then a year in field trials of the procedures that we considered had worked well" (Clay 1982a, 173). In particular, Clay's research team constructed a framework for teachers working one-to-one with at-risk students. In 1979, Reading Recovery became a nationwide program in New Zealand; in 1984 it was introduced in the United States and Australia.

Intended Audience

Reading Recovery is a program for at-risk students who are in the first grade.

Description of the Procedures

For a fuller description of Reading Recovery, books and articles on the reference list should be consulted. What follows is only a partial description of the program. The description includes an overview of the following: (1) diagnostic procedures and roaming around the known, (2) lesson frameworks, (3) exiting principles, (4) teacher training procedure.

Diagnostic Procedures and Roaming Around the Known   Several principles undergird Reading Recovery diagnostic practices. First, Reading Recovery relies on a battery of diagnostic procedures for input on a student's reading behavior. As Clay emphasized, "Teachers are advised to apply as many as possible to the children. . . . Reducing the scope of our observations increases the risk that we will make erroneous interpretations" (Clay, 1979b, 10). Second, the use of an initial screening procedure should not diminish the fact that Reading Recovery is involved in ongoing diagnosis of students throughout their involvement in the program as well as in conjunction with their transition back to the classroom. Third, the diagnostic procedures are not intended to displace teacher observation. Reading Recovery teachers are expected to notice significant behaviors apart from what is tested.

The initial screening done of students in American schools involves using a combination of the classroom teacher's ranking, kindergarten teacher's opinion (if available), scores and observed responses on the six tasks of the Observation Survey, and a qualitative synthesis of these responses written on the Observation Summary. The six tasks include:

1. Letter identification (upper and lowercase letters)
2. Word test (high frequency words)
3. Concepts about print (Clays's assessment of child's knowledge of print and book handling)
4. Writing vocabulary (exhaustive list of child's known words, beginning with own name, ability to write high frequency words, writing samples from class)
5. Hearing and recording sounds in words (Dictation test) (assessing knowledge of 37 phonemes presented in a sentence)
6. Text reading (running record for purposes of determining the nature of the reader's errors and highest level at which 90 percent accuracy is attained)

The summary of the Observation Survey "brings together what the teacher has observed. She describes what the child can do, what is partially known at the boundaries of his knowledge as it were" (Clay, 1993a, 71). The goal of this initial assessment is threefold: to justify special help or involvement in the Reading Recovery program; to acquire some baseline data for use in documenting growth; and to acquire a sense of where and how to start.

"Roaming around the known" represents the student's introduction to the program. "The most important reason for roaming is that it requires the teacher to stop teaching from her preconceived ideas. She has to work from the child's responses. This will be her focus throughout the programme" (Clay, 1993b, 13). These ten days of exploration are intended to serve a variety of purposes:

- Provides the teacher and child the opportunity to develop a relationship of trust
- Enables the teacher to see what the child initiates as well as what the child can and cannot do outside the constraints of the testing situation and away from the classroom
- Provides opportunities for systematic observation
- Gives the child a feeling he is "really reading and writing"
- Provides a foundation for further learning on which the teacher can build the individualized program (Clay, 1993b, 13)

Lesson Framework   A Reading Recovery lesson has 7 components that emphasize reading, writing, problem-solving strategies, and much student-teacher interaction. Within this model, students are taught to be strategic learners, which leads to the development of a "self-extending system." Within this framework, the teacher becomes the focal point rather than the curriculum. The teacher is perceived as the instructional decision maker and the researcher. She constantly observes the child's behavior, quickly reflecting on why the child reacted as she or he did, and responds with appropriate praise or prompts to extend this child's learning.

The components of the daily 30-minute lesson follows:

1. Familiar rereading of two or more books

    Students self-select at least 2 books that are known stories to read aloud. "A familiar book is not a memorized book," says Clay. This rereading encourages "confidence and fluency, and provides practice in orchestrating reading behaviors while also allowing the reader to discover new things about print" (Clay, 1993b, 38). During the reading of these books the focus is on the meaning of the text and the student's use of strategies as he or she reads fluently. With this in mind, the teacher talks to the child about the story rather than correcting him/her.

    The teacher's goal is to find the hardest book (natural language rather than controlled vocabulary) that the child can handle with 90 percent accuracy. The intent is to find books that are easy enough for the child to use effective strategies, and difficult enough for independent problem solving.

2. Running Record on the previous day's new story

    This book reading enables the teacher to become an observer of the child reading the story and engaging with the text using problem-solving strategies, and is also one way to attain an ongoing record of the child's progress—especially strategy development. The teacher records student's reading behaviors and will select one or two to use as teaching points. (For a discussion of the Running Record, see Unit 14.)

3. Letter identification and/or word making and breaking

This component provides opportunities for students who know few letters and words to learn how to look at print as a cuing source when reading and writing. "For consistency, always do a little letter work after taking the Running Record in the lesson. When most of the letters are known, shift to some speedy work on making and breaking words (using magnetic letters) and giving attention to generating new words from known words" (Clay, 1993b, 25).

4. Writing a story and hearing sounds in words

The child-generated written story helps the child "think about the order of sounds in spoken words and to help analyze a new word he wants to write into its sequence of sounds" (Clay, 1979a, 1988, 64). This child is asked to repeat the story so that this model can be used as a framework on which to monitor his own writing. (Clay, 1993)

When the child comes to a problem word, the sounds (at least the initial sound) are predicted/isolated. Sometimes phonic segmentation is used, based upon Elkonin (1975). These procedures break the sounds represented by the letters into boxes, e.g.,

Clay has stressed that it is important that children become aware of sound sequences in words.

As she stated:

> We have worked with some children who find it extraordinarily difficult to hear the sounds that go to make up words. For example, some children consistently focus on the final sounds of a word, and for them, this completely masks the initial sounds.

> The teacher has to work with such children individually and act as an analyzer of words into sounds. This is analogous to acting as his scribe at first when he cannot write. The teacher articulates the words very slowly and gradually develops the same skill in her pupil (Clay, 1979b, 5).

As Clay suggests, an essential feature of Reading Recovery is helping students to segment words. Initially, this is pursued with counters, not letters. This approach ensures that children learn that there may be more than one letter for every sound. When the child has a good grasp of segments, he or she is then moved into associating the letters with the segments. As with the early segmentation activities (for counting syllables and so on), Elkonin boxes are used. As the students develop competence, the emphasis on sound segmentation is more incidental and may not entail using the boxes.

5. Cut up story

Just as children are encouraged to segment words into sounds so, too, are they involved in cutting up stories into a descending order of language units (phrases, words, structural segments, clusters of letters, single letters). . . . The cut-up sentence provides practice with "assembling sentences, one-to-one correspondence of words spoken and written, directional, checking, and monitoring behaviors, breaking oral language into segments, and word study (from occasionally cut up words)" (Clay, 1993b, 35).

A cutting up activity, for example, might begin by having the child choose a portion of the story that was liked. The teacher and/or child would write that portion of the story twice and the child, with or without the teacher's help, would read the text pointing to each word. The teacher would then cut up the text, starting with the first word, emphasizing its word components. The child would then be expected to reassemble the text, initially with the story model present and later without it. Depending upon the child's familiarity with the names of letters, plastic letters on a magnetic board might also be used to assemble known words.

It should be noted that the procedures for helping students link sounds to letters, acquiring word analysis procedures, developing fluency, and so on, extend beyond these activities. Clay's *Reading Recovery: A Guidebook for Teachers in Training* (1993b) should be consulted for details.

6. New book introduction

Book selections are seen as vital to the success of the lesson. The book selected must be "within the child's control, uses words and letters he knows or can get to using his present strategies, and should be a minimum of new things to learn if the teaching goal is the integration of skills" (Clay, 1979a, 1988, 68).

During the new-book orientation, Clay (1993b) contends that "the child must know what the story is about before he reads it." (p. 37) In order to do this, the teacher makes the child familiar with the story, by discussing pictures, new words, and story language. The goal is to ensure that the child has the ideas and language he/she needs to read the story in his or her head.

7. New book attempted

This component enables the student to read the book with help. The overall aim is to provide opportunities for students to orchestrate and monitor their use of strategies and for teachers to confirm and reinforce these behaviors. To this end, Clay has developed quite elaborate procedures to ensure that teachers know how to help students develop ways of effectively initiating appropriate reading behaviors and monitor their use. The second reading of this book is to get fluency. On subsequent days, the book is reread and placed in a box with other books the child has read. As Clay (1979b) has suggested, "A child on the way to independence needs as many books as possible at his level" (p. 54).

The basic framework of the Reading Recovery lesson should be viewed as a partial guide. Within this framework, every child's program will differ as he or she reads and writes different materials and as various skills and strategies are developed. The teachers who work in Reading Recovery undergo intensive training in the use of various procedures to help them plan each child's program and develop each one's reading abilities. For example, each teacher receives extensive training in an elaborate array of teaching strategies intended to help students acquire and be able to orchestrate a repertoire of strategies, including directional movement, self-monitoring, cross-checking, use of multiple cue sources, and self-correction. In other words, teachers are trained to have enormous skills at helping students based on a repertoire of teaching strategies they themselves are expected to acquire and be able to enlist thoughtfully with different students. For example, the teacher is encouraged to enlist a variety of probes and encouragements to have the child think aloud as he or she enlists meaning cues, visual cues, structure cues, sound cues (both together and separately), cross-checking to ensure accuracy. Comments such as: Does it make sense? Does that look right? What would you expect to see? You made a mistake; can you find it? How did you know? Will you check to see if what you read looks right? and so on, pervade the teacher's responses to the child as the teacher aims to help students develop the self-improving strategies necessary to be independent.

Clay has pointed out that the goal is to develop readers who improve whenever they read. They have strategies by which to monitor, search for cues, discover new things for themselves, cross-check cues, confirm by repeating or reviewing, self-correct, and solve new problems as they develop fluency with longer and less predictable texts that have less familiar language.

Exiting Principles   There is no set time for exiting the program. The program continues for the child until he or she is reading at about the average level for his/her school or class and when the child has acquired the strategies needed to continue without extra help. Typically, the program lasts 12 to 16 weeks. As Clay states:

> There is no fixed set of strategies nor any required levels of text nor any test score that must be attained to warrant discontinuing. It is essential that the child has a system of strategies which work in such a way that a child learns from his own attempts to read. (1979a, 1988, 87).

Some of the things a child ready for discontinuing will be able to do will include (Clay, 1993b, 58–59):

- Directional movement
- One-to-one matching
- Self-monitor reading
- Cross-checking
- Use of multiple cue sources
- Self-correction

It should be noted that although Reading Recovery lessons may cease, extensive follow-up is carried out to ensure that students receive continued support in the classroom context.

Teacher Training Procedure   It is claimed that the key to successfully implementing Reading Recovery does not lie with a set of procedures but in the staff development that enables teachers to work with students insightfully and adeptly. Reading Recovery teachers are certified teachers who volunteer for the program, have had at least three years' experience in teaching young children, possess proven ability to establish rapport with children, and undergo one year of intensive Reading Recovery training, as well as annual follow-ups. The demanding one-year program involves a full-time commitment to learn-ing Reading Recovery procedures through working with four students (individually), demonstrations, seminars, analyses of lessons, close monitoring of their own teaching, observing and interpreting reading behaviors, and so on. After the initial training year, they are expected to continue to pursue active contact with Reading Recovery procedures as they meet with fellow Reading Recovery teachers, view demonstration lessons, and refine organization skills.

When implementing Reading Recovery instruction in a school, several organizational models are suggested. (Teachers work with at least four children each day for half a day.) Sometimes a Reading Recovery teacher will work with a regular class for half the day and then work with four children for the other half. Other models involve having a separate Reading Recovery teacher who works with the teacher.

Apart from training teachers, an integral feature of Reading Recovery is the prepara-tion of Reading Recovery teacher leaders. These teacher leaders undergo a very rigorous training that goes beyond the regular teacher training to learning how to assume a leadership role. In many ways the experience is akin to an internship program. The teacher leaders work with other teacher leaders as they work with children and with Reading Recovery teachers also working with children. At the same time, they learn how to initiate, operate, and direct the preparation of Reading Recovery teachers.

To be a Reading Recovery teacher requires training by authorized teacher leaders who themselves have been trained to serve in those roles. It should be emphasized that the aforementioned description provides some information about Reading Recovery, but should not be viewed as comprehensive or as a substitute for the necessary training.

Cautions and Comments

Reading Recovery has been acclaimed as one of the most successful early innovative programs for at-risk students. Whereas attempts to pull out at-risk students have a long history of failure—especially when the students return to the regular classroom—Reading Recovery boasts a very high success rate. In 1986–87, the Ohio Reading Recovery Sites reported an average of 82 percent success rate with discontinued students; in 1987–88 they had a success rate with discontinued students of 86 percent.

At the end of first grade, more than two-thirds of the discontinued students were reading equal to or above the first graders. While such results are heartening, the short-comings of these data should not be overlooked. The aforementioned data are based on students who were discontinued and not the total population of students receiving Reading Recovery training. Across some of the tests, the effects of a low ceiling may inflate the success of selected students. Indeed, the students' responses to text reading—a test with no ceiling—seem less impressive than some of the other tests. Furthermore, the data emerging from New Zealand suggest that the effects may wane after the students reenter the regular classroom.

The Concepts About Print (CAP), an observational instrument, has been well re-ceived by educators as a tool to identify "individual differences in children" by capturing "what children are visually attending to, identifying if reading progress in an appropriate direction is occurring, and what action teachers should take to try to change the child's responses" (Clay, 1989, 268, 270).

Attempts in making this tool more valid for individuals within the USA and abroad include modifications for the visually impaired by Tompkins and McGee (as cited in Clay, 1989) with the development of a Concepts About Braille test and the importance of translating the test to meet the dialect and language differences of individuals.

Research results with these modifications reveal the role culture and language play in the learning process. For instance, results from Griffin's (as cited in Clay, 1989) two-year longitudinal study with preschoolers in USA Headstart Programs found that children in parallel cultures were developing concepts about print, and that their print awareness was similar to that of mainstream groups (Clay, 1989, 270–271). In Rodriguez's (as cited in Clay, 1989) study on Mexican-American preschoolers, results "showed the importance of stating instructions in the language children understood best." She found that "children with the lowest English language scores scored higher on CAP when the instructions were in Spanish, whether the text was in English or Spanish, and lower when the tasks were given with English instructions" (p. 272).

There are some other reasons why one might quibble with some of the features of Reading Recovery. Some educators would argue that Reading Recovery may be identifying students too early. For example, they would suggest that the first month of the first grade may be a time of massive adjustment for the child and might not indicate how well the child might perform thereafter. Educators, sensitive to the differences in the social situation of Reading Recovery and the regular classroom, may question the extent to which discontinued students have acquired the self-improving social skills necessary to succeed in the regular classroom. Advocates of a more whole-language orientation might argue that the approach has a tendency to place more stress on mediating skills such as letter-sound correspondence, sound blending, accurate word recognition, and so on, than might be justified. Educators interested in reading comprehension might consider the approach more text-based than reader-based. For example, strategies such as brainstorming, visualizing, self-questioning, engagement, and so on, appear to receive only indirect emphasis. Teacher educators might argue that the teacher training procedures appear somewhat formulaic as teachers are expected to commit themselves to the principles and practices advocated by Clay (1979a, 1988).

Apart from these concerns, few educators can argue that Reading Recovery has amassed a distinguished record of success and a rather unique commitment to accountability in terms of expectations for students, training teachers, training teacher leaders, and, above all, research that scrutinizes these enterprises and their impact.

References

Allington, R. 1992. How to get information on several proven programs for accelerating the progress of low-achieving children. *The Reading Teacher* 46:246–248. An overview of three programming efforts, extended to at-risk students, to help accelerate learning.

Clay, M. M. 1975. *What did I write?* Portsmouth, NH: Heinemann. Illustrates authentic writing samples of emergent writers as they develop written language.

———. 1979a, 1988. *The early detection of reading difficulties.* Auckland, New Zealand: Heinemann. Represents the primary source for information on Reading Recovery, including diagnostic and instructional procedures.

————. 1979b. *Reading: The patterning of complex behavior.* Auckland, New Zealand: Heinemann. Presents a detailed account of Clay's views on reading and reading instruction.

————. 1982a. *Observing young readers: Selected papers.* Portsmouth, NH: Heinemann. A compilation of research reports that depict early learners' growth and progress over time.

————. 1982b. Reading Recovery: A follow-up study. In *Observing young readers: Selected papers,* edited by M. M. Clay. Exeter, NH: Heinemann. Reports the findings of a follow-up study along with implications.

————. 1989. Concepts about Print in English and other languages. *The Reading Teacher* 42:268–276. Describes the purpose for this observational instrument and the modifications made to be statistically effective with emergent learners of other languages.

————. 1991. *Becoming literate: The construction of inner control.* Portmouth, NH: Heinemann. Describes the patterns of change that emergent learners experience when engaged in authentic literacy activities.

————. 1991. Developmental learning puzzles me. *Australian Journal of Reading* 14:263–275. Provides a discussion on the definition of developmental learning.

————. 1991. Why is an in-service programme for Reading Recovery teachers necessary? *Reading Horizons* 31:355–372. This article provides a rationale for utilizing an intensive in-service model for training teachers, teacher leaders, and teacher leader trainers.

————. 1993a. *An observation survey of early literacy achievement.* Portsmouth, NH: Heinemann. This text was written for teachers and researchers who work with young readers and writers and describes the procedures to follow when administering and scoring the six assessment tasks in the Observation Survey and when utilizing a Running Record.

————. 1993b. *Reading Recovery: A guidebook for teachers in training.* Portsmouth, NH: Heinemann. This text is used by teachers in training. It describes the components and procedures of a Recovery lesson.

Deford, D. E., C. A. Lyons, and G. S. Pinnell. 1991. *Bridges to literacy learning from Reading Recovery.* Discusses how teachers and students can work within a collaborative setting while focusing on literacy learning.

DeFord, D. E., G. S. Pinnell, C. A. Lyons, and P. Young. 1987. *Report of the follow-up studies—Columbus, Ohio—Reading Recovery project 1985–1986, 1986–1987.* (Technical Report). Columbus: Ohio State University. One of several reports on the impact of Reading Recovery on at-risk students.

————. 1987. *Report of the follow-up study, Reading Recovery project, Vol. IX.* Columbus: Ohio State University. One of several reports on the impact of Reading Recovery on at-risk students.

Elkonin, D. B. 1975. USSR. In *Comparative reading: Cross-national studies of behavior and processes in reading and writing,* edited by J. Downing. New York: Macmillan. Provides a description of the phonic segmentation that served as a basis for Clay's phonic practices.

Geeke, P. 1988. *Evaluation report on the Reading Recovery field trial in Central Victoria, 1984.* Australia: Centre for Studies in Literacy, University of Wollongong. Represents a critical evaluation of Reading Recovery in Australia.

Holland, K. 1987. *The impact of Reading Recovery program on parents and home literacy contexts.* Unpublished doctoral diss., Ohio State University, Columbus. Examines the effects of Reading Recovery on home literacy and parents.

Huck, D., and G. Pinnell. 1985. *The Reading Recovery project in Columbus, Ohio: Pilot year 1984–1985* (Technical Report). Columbus: Ohio State University. Describes the Reading Recovery project during its initiation in Columbus, Ohio.

Jones, N. K. 1991. Helping to learn: Components and principles of Reading Recovery training. *Reading Horizons* 31:422–438. Provides an in-depth overview of the components within the Reading Recovery teacher training program.

Lyons, C. A., G. Pinnell, K. Short, and P. Young. 1986. *The Ohio Reading Recovery project: Volume IV pilot year. 1985–1986.* (Technical Report). Columbus: Ohio State University. One of several reports of the impact of Reading Recovery.

Lyons, C., G. Pinnell, P. Young, and D. E. DeFord. 1987. *Report of the Ohio Reading Recovery project, State of Ohio, Year One 1986–1987.* Volume VIII (Technical Report). Columbus: Ohio State University. One of several reports on the impact of Reading Recovery.

Lyons, C. A., G. S. Pinnell, A. McCarrier, P. Young, and D. DeFord. 1988. *The Ohio Reading Recovery project: Volume X and State of Ohio Year 1987–1988.* Columbus: Ohio State University. One of several reports on the impact of Reading Recovery.

Peterson, B. 1987. *The characteristics of text which support beginning readers.* Unpublished doctoral diss., Ohio State University, Columbus. Explores the features of text that work best with young students.

Pinnell, G. S. 1986. Helping teachers help children at risk: Insights from the Reading Recovery program. *Peabody Journal* 62:70–85. Explores issues pertaining to helping teachers help children who are at risk.

———. 1987. Helping teachers see how readers read: Staff development through observation. *Theory Into Practice* 26:51–58. Discusses staff development issues as they pertain to Reading Recovery.

Pinnell, G. S., D. E. DeFord, and C. A. Lyons. 1988. *Reading Recovery: Early intervention for at risk first graders.* Arlington, VA: Educational Research Service. Presents an overview of Reading Recovery, including results of studies of its effects.

Pinnell, G. S., M. D. Fried, and R. M. Estice. 1990. Reading Recovery: Learning how to make a difference. *The Reading Teacher* 43:282–295. Provides an in-depth discussion on Reading Recovery lessons and procedures, the teacher training model, and research findings within the USA.

Pinnell, G., K. Short, C. A. Lyons, and P. Young. 1986a. *The Reading Recovery project in Columbus, Ohio: Volume II. Year One 1985–1986.* (Technical Report). Columbus: Ohio State University. One of several reports on the impact of Reading Recovery.

———. 1986b. *The Reading Recovery project in Columbus, Ohio: Volume III. Year One 1985–1986* (Technical Report). Columbus: Ohio State University. One of several reports on the impact of Reading Recovery.

Pinnell, G. S., C. A. Lyons, D. E. DeFord, A. S. Bryk, and M. Seltzer. 1994. Comparing instructional models for the literacy education of high-risk first graders. *Reading Research Quarterly, 29,* (1) 9–39. This study investigated the effectiveness of reading recovery as determined by comparison with three other instructional models.

Purves, A. C., L. Papa, and S. Jordan. 1994. *Encyclopedia of English studies and language arts.* New York: National Council of Teachers of English. An excellent resource that contains an extensive collection of more than 800 annotated entries/topics in English studies and language arts.

Success For All

Purpose

Success for All (Slavin, Madden, Karweit, Livermon, and Dolan, 1990) is a schoolwide tutoring program that emphasizes prevention and early, intensive intervention. It is designed for schools that have large disadvantaged populations, and its intention is to make sure that all children are successful in basic skills, especially reading, the first time they are taught. Success for All uses certified teachers acting as one-on-one tutors for students who are experiencing difficulty in reading in grades one to three.

Rationale

Wasik and Slavin (1993) suggest that four theoretical tenets provide the background for Success for All. First, children do not learn to read through isolated exercises about print; reading and learning to read should be done through interaction with meaningful text. Second, as a strategy for cracking the code, phonics should be taught systematically. Although children engage in reading meaningful and interesting text, the stories should use a vocabulary that is phonetically controlled. Third, emphasis should be placed on meaning as children are taught to see the relationship between the words they read and the understanding that they gain from them. Merely recognizing the words is not enough. Finally, children should be directly taught strategies that will make them successful readers. Those children with problems in reading do not possess the effective metacognitive strategies that will help them read. Children should be taught the when, how, and why of using reading strategies.

Therefore, the following instructional components of reading are emphasized in practice: decoding, prior knowledge, reading strategies, inference making, metcognition and error detection, and error correction. Success for All emphasizes that reading occurs in the reader's mind, it is a strategic process, and direct teaching of strategies is crucial.

Intended Audience

Success for All is a preventive tutoring program in reading intended for low-achieving children in the early grades.

Description of the Procedure

Success for All will be described using its seven programmatic components:

1. Reading tutors
2. The program
3. Assessments at eight weeks
4. Preschool and kindergarten
5. Family support team
6. Program facilitator
7. Teachers and teacher training

1. *Reading Tutors*   A major component of Success for All are the reading tutors, certified teachers with experience in teaching primary reading, Chapter I, and/or special

education. They tutor in one-on-one situations with children who are not successful in their reading groups. Twenty-minute sessions drawn from an hour-long social studies period are used to support what is being taught in the regular reading groups. However, the tutors also identify learning problems and seek to use different strategies to make reading progress.

During daily reading/language arts periods, tutors reduce class size to 15 to 20 by serving as additional reading teachers. To coordinate the instructional approaches with individual children, teachers and tutors record children's specific problems and needs on communication forms and meet at regular intervals.

Tutors also give informal reading inventories to each child. From the information gained, decisions are made about reading-group placements and the need for tutoring. Additional assessments, which include teacher judgment and more formal assessments, are given at eight-week intervals and are used to make revised decisions about group placement and tutoring. Priority for tutoring is given to first graders because of the major function of Success for All, to help all readers become successful from the beginning and avoid becoming remedial readers.

2. *The Program*　During most of the day, students are assigned to age-grouped, heterogeneous classes of 25, but during the 90-minute reading period the students are regrouped by reading ability into homogeneous classes of 15 to 20 students. For example, the one to two reading class might contain students from grades one to three, as they are all reading at that level. Regrouping allows the teacher/tutor to teach the whole class simultaneously, without the need to put them into smaller groups; this organization becomes more efficient as it reduces the time spent in seat work and increases time for direct instruction. In turn, this eliminates the need for workbooks and other follow-up activities that would be found in normal, multigrouped classrooms.

At all levels teachers begin the reading class by reading children's literature to the students and discussing it to improve their comprehension, oral vocabulary, and story structure knowledge. In grades kindergarten to one, Success for All emphasizes the development of basic language skills through the use of storytelling, retelling, and dramatizing with literature. Big books, language development kits, and oral/written composing activities serve to develop children's print concepts, knowledge of story structure, and receptive/expressive language.

In the second semester of kindergarten beginning reading is introduced. Letters and sounds are introduced through oral language activities and moved to written symbols. Learned letter sounds are reinforced by reading stories using those same sounds. The reading program uses phonetically regular but meaningful minibooks and emphasizes the following: repeated oral reading to partners and the teacher, instruction in story structure and comprehension skills, and integrated reading and writing lessons.

When kindergartners reach the primer reading level, they are introduced to reading and composition activities based on cooperative learning using the school's basal series. These activities emphasize prediction, story structure, story-related writing and summarization, vocabulary, and decoding practice. Working in teams the students share their writing, engage in structured discussions and partner reading, and work on their vocabulary from an understanding of the story. In addition to basal instruction, teachers provide teams direct instruction in comprehension skills. Teachers are also provided classroom libraries of trade books at students' reading levels, and students are asked to read at home for 20 minutes each night. These independent readings are shared in class through presentations, summaries, and puppet shows twice weekly.

In the second year of Success for All, programs for writing/language arts based on cooperative learning are introduced. These programs use a structured writing process approach and focus on teaching students to respond to and facilitate each other's writing.

3. *Assessments at Eight Weeks*   Each eight weeks teachers assess the progress of each student. These results determine the need to receive tutoring, change group assignment, modify instruction, and identify other forms of assistance such as vision screening or family intervention.

4. *Preschool and Kindergarten*   Success for All schools attempt to provide a half-day preschool and/or a full-day kindergarten for eligible children. These programs focus on giving students developmentally appropriate learning experiences and emphasize language development and use. Additionally, nonacademic art, music, and movement activities are provided in a series of thematic units.

5. *Family Support Team*   Parents are considered to be essential to the success of the program. At each school site a support team works to make families comfortable with the school and provides specific services. Depending on the resources of the school, this team might consist of social workers, attendance monitors, assistant principals, counselors, and any other appropriate person already in the school. The team works to get parents to support what the children are doing in school, and it contacts parents to see what help can be provided to get children who are frequently absent to school. Parenting education is also provided for interested families. Finally, family support assistance is provided when students are having academic difficulties due to problems at home.

6. *Program Facilitator*   At each school an experienced teacher works as a program facilitator to oversee the operation of Success for All. This individual helps plan the overall program, works on scheduling, and visits classes and tutoring sessions to provide help as individual problems arise. The facilitator works directly with teachers on matters of curriculum and classroom management and coordinates any activities that concern the instructional staff and the family support team.

7. *Teachers and Teacher Training*   The staff development model used in Success for All provides brief initial training for teachers mixed with extensive classroom follow-up and group discussion. Teachers and tutors receive two days in-service at the year's beginning and a detailed teacher's manual. The in-service sessions focus on implementing the reading program; the teacher's manual provides general teaching strategies and specific lessons. Tutors receive an additional day of in-service training for tutoring strategies and assessment. Throughout the year the facilitator organizes other in-service sessions on

topics such as classroom management or cooperative learning, as needed. Facilitators also organize informal sessions with groups of teachers for sharing, problem solving, and discussion of changes for individual children.

Cautions and Comments

Success for All seems to present a highly structured, intensive, and well-thought-out program of reading-problem prevention. Students are challenged and kept moving forward. The tutor acts as a model of strategies that the student should be using for effective reading. While one might argue with various components of the program, such as the extent to which phonics instruction plays a part in the whole process, research has indicated that Success for All is just that—a success!

A summary of the results for various studies on Success for All presented by Wasik and Slavin (1993) indicates that students made substantial increases in achievement when compared to their matched counterparts not participating in the program. Additionally, assignments to special education because of learning problems were greatly reduced, and retentions were virtually eliminated. These findings are particularly impressive when one considers the fact that these programs took place in high-at-risk, disadvantaged schools. Still, further research needs to look qualitatively at the program for consistency across school sites as well as across tutoring sessions.

References

Madden, N. A., R. E. Slavin, N. L. Karweit, L. J. Dolan, and B. A. Wasik. 1993. Success for All: Longitudinal effects of a restructuring program for inner-city elementary schools. *American Educational Research Journal* 30:123–148. Presents a longitudinal study documenting the positive effects of the program.

Slavin, R. E., N. A. Madden, N. L. Karweit, L. J. Dolan, and B. A. Wasik. 1991. Research directions: Success for All: Ending reading failure from the beginning. *Language Arts* 68:404–409. A description of the program.

Slavin, R. E., N. A. Madden, N. L. Karweit, B. J. Livermon, and L. J. Dolan. 1990. Success for All: First-year outcomes of a comprehensive plan for reforming urban education. *American Educational Research Journal* 27:255–278. Report of the first-year results of the program.

Wasik, B. A., and R. E. Slavin. 1993. Preventing early reading failure with one-to-one tutoring: A review of five programs. *Reading Research Quarterly* 28:179–200. A review of the positive effects of Success for All.

Monroe Methods

Purpose

The purpose of the Monroe methods (1932) is to overcome a student's impediments to reading by providing drills and devices that involve motor responses to synthetic word recognition instruction.

Rationale

Monroe proposed drills and devices to reduce the student's errors in reading, to build up discriminations not being made, and to utilize to the fullest discriminations that are being made. She claimed that just as two individuals may think of the same object differently, so different individuals learn to read differently. From this standpoint, she suggested the use of "the possible secondary or vicarious steps in word recognition that are not usually presented in ordinary instruction" (Monroe, 1932, 111). In accordance with an individual's abilities and needs, methods would be selected requiring motor responses whenever possible. As reasons for stressing motor responses, she suggested that:

1. Motor responses are more easily observed by the teacher and student.
2. Motor responses are probably a part of the normal reading process, and movement serves to intensify this process.
3. Motor responses reinforce and develop precise discriminations of the auditory and visual features of words.
4. Motor responses assist in directing attention to learning.

Furthermore, as Monroe (1932) noted:

> To the usual child, the emphasis on motor response as outlined here, and the placement of the secondary links in the learning process, may be an unnecessary procedure, detracting from the enjoyment through the mechanical devices for recognition of words. The child who has not learned to read, however, and who for the first time finds that he can succeed in reading simple words and sentences, even if by somewhat laborious methods, finds a new interest and enthusiasm for reading, and a new respect for his own capacities.

Intended Audience

The Monroe methods are intended for those students who deviate to the extent that they have failed or are failing to read by ordinary procedures. Ideally, the methods are intended for use on a one-to-one basis, but they can and have been used with small groups.

Description of the Procedures

Monroe's methods have as their ultimate goal the development of the ability to read fluently, "comprehendingly, accurately, pleasurably, and with as little effort as possible" (Monroe 1932, 136). The methods described herein are seen as a means to this end for disabled readers. These methods are intended to be modified to meet the errors or difficulties they attempt to overcome. They address:

1. Faulty vowels and consonants
2. Reversals
3. Addition of sounds
4. Omission of sounds

5. Substitution of words
6. Repetition of words, and
7. Omission of words

1. *Faulty Vowels and Consonants*   Monroe suggested that there are many sources for the type of difficulty in which students need help in discriminating speech sounds, in establishing association with letters, and in sequencing these sounds into words. Monroe suggested three steps to this end.

a. The first step is to develop the student's ability to discriminate speech sounds. In this step, students are presented with cards containing pictures of several objects beginning with the same consonant or containing the same vowel. These pictures may be obtained from magazines. Examples of the objects used are:

> *b,* as in *boy; book*
> *e,* as in *pen; hen*

To develop discrimination, the student is presented with cards containing unlike sounds, for example, *m* compared with *s.* The student is instructed to articulate clearly the sound represented by either the letter *s* or *m,* then name the pictured object. If the name of the object begins with the sound the student is asked to articulate, then the student retains the card. As the student proceeds, more difficult discriminations are presented. For example, *s* compared with *sh.* Where the student appears confused, an attempt is made to develop discrimination by articulated movements. To provide variety in the activity, the student is asked to generate words for beginning sounds.

b. The second step involves establishing associations between letters and their most frequent sounds. The suggested procedure involves a sounding-tracing technique. The student traces over a letter written by the teacher, while simultaneously articulating the sound. The procedure is repeated until the student can look at the letter and articulate the sound it represents on sight. Monroe suggested that usually five or six consonant sounds can be learned at one sitting. After the student has retained the associations for five or six consonant sounds, a short vowel sound is presented. The student then is taught to blend the consonants and vowels to form words. From this point, the words learned are listed systematically, traced manually, and reviewed frequently. The student begins to proceed through word family drills. The method was illustrated by Monroe (1932) with the following example:

> The teacher wrote the word to be learned in large handwriting on a piece of paper. She said to the child, "See this word? This word is man. Say man. Now let me see how slowly you can say man, like this, m-a-n. Now I want you to do two things at the same time. Take your pencil and trace over this word while you say m-a-n slowly. Be sure to speak quickly enough and write slowly enough that you will come out just even."

Monroe gave a series of word lists to be learned in this manner. These lists begin with words composed of three sounds, including one short vowel, and end with words containing several syllables. Recall is checked by presenting the students with the words printed on cards. The student is instructed to articulate the separate sounds and to blend them.

As a variation of the tracing method, Monroe proposed substitution or a "sound-dictation" method. The sound-dictation method entails the student's writing the words as the teacher dictates the sounds, then rereading the list.

  c. As soon as the student has acquired a vocabulary of a number of words, the next step can be introduced. This step can be implemented concurrently with step *b.* The step entails having the students read stories with a controlled phonetic language. "Phonetically irregular" words would be avoided, but if added to the stories, these words would be taught by tracing and by whole-word methods.

2. *Reversals*   To overcome difficulties incurred as a result of reversals, Monroe made various suggestions for providing cues to direction. The tracing-sounding method described for vowels and consonants were suggested for dealing with many of the more discrete reversals of letters and words. To develop a consistent direction for reading words, it was suggested that the student be instructed to follow, using the sliding motion of a pencil or a finger, the letters within words, then to follow the words within lines and to follow lines on a page. If the student's motor control proves too inaccurate for this approach, then retyping of the selection leaving more space between the lines was suggested. In some cases, Monroe suggested having the students underline, or write the words under each line. In extreme cases, she suggested presenting the students with words on cards, printed in large and raised type. With eyes closed, the student traces the word until it can be differentiated.

3. *Addition of Sounds*   Monroe claimed that sounds are added to words, such as tack and track, either due to student confusion of one word with another or as a result of a previous error. To cope with the former case, she suggested auditory and visual drilling to eradicate the confusion. To cope with the latter, no special drill was suggested. Monroe claimed that the correction of the previous error was sufficient to eliminate these errors.

4. *Omission of Sounds*   Monroe suggested that the omission of sounds occurred as a result either of speech defects and discrimination difficulties, or of an overstress on speed of reading. To correct these difficulties, she suggested either speech training, sound tracing, training in dividing words into syllables, or encouraging a slower reading rate.

5. *Substitution of Words*   Monroe expressed differentiated concern for the substitution of words. She suggested that instances of meaningful substitution of words, such as *father* for *dad,* should be overlooked, but meaningless substitutions, such as *day* for *dad,* should be corrected. To cope with the latter, she suggested either moving the student to easier material or increasing the student's reading vocabulary.

6. *Repetition of Words*   Monroe suggested several methods for dealing with occurrences of repetition of words. In cases where other errors cause the repetition, no specific drill

was suggested. She claimed that these types of repetition decrease with the treatment of other errors. In cases of habitual repetition, she suggested that the habit be made obvious to the student, by both the teacher and the student reading in unison. In cases where reversals accompany repetitions, manual guidance in the direction of reading was suggested. In cases of repetition that occur as a result of students stalling for time, she suggested no specific method but claimed that this kind of repetition would be eliminated with the acquisition of word analysis skills.

7. *Omission of Words* Monroe associated word omission with excessive reading speed. To cope with this type of error, she suggested slowing the reader's rate, either through the use of unison reading or by retyping the stories, leaving increased spacing between the lines of print.

Cautions and Comments

Monroe (1932) claimed that for 27 disabled readers whose reading ability placed them halfway through the first grade, the average gain was 1.3 grades after approximately 26 hours of instruction (over an eight-month period) with her methods. In comparison, a control group gained only 0.14 grades. Monroe suggested that her methods were means to an end and not ends in themselves. As she stated:

> Although our methods stressed the mechanics of word-recognition, we utilized the recognition of words, not as an end in itself, but as a means to accomplish the final goal of reading, i.e., the comprehension of meaning. (P. 136)

The question arises: Do the students reach these ends by these means? Monroe claimed they do. As she suggested:

> Re-examinations of children taught by these methods show that after the initial start in reading is made, the children become more and more like normal readers. The secondary links, while utilized extensively by the children at first, become less in evidence and seem to disappear. Speed of reading develops gradually without specific pressure. Words are grouped into phrases and larger thought units. After remedial training, reading takes on the characteristics of normal performance until the child meets a strange, unfamiliar, or forgotten word. The mechanical links thereupon immediately become evident as the child attacks the word. Incipient tracing or articulary movements appear until the word is recognized and the child proceeds with the reading. Thus, it appears that the child ultimately builds up an organization of responses which is very similar to the usual reading performance of unselected children, although the underlying steps in building the organization are somewhat different. (P. 114)

Although the procedures suggested by Monroe are less insensitive to individual differences and do not divorce word recognition from comprehension, these procedures do seem to place undue emphasis upon a synthetic-letter and word-by-word type of reading. For a further discussion of these points, the reader should refer to the Cautions and Comments sections of the various strategies presented in Unit 12: Word Identification.

References

Bond, G. L., and M. A. Tinker. 1973. *Reading difficulties: Their diagnosis and correction.* 3d ed. Englewood Cliffs, NJ: Prentice-Hall, 501–504. Presents a discussion and evaluation of Monroe's methods.

Chall, J. 1967. *Learning to read: The great debate.* New York: McGraw-Hill, 166–168. Presents a discussion of Monroe's methods and research on the disabled reader.

Monroe, M. 1932. *Children who cannot read.* Chicago: University of Chicago Press. Describes the methods, their rationale, their utility, and potential use.

Gillingham-Stillman Method

Purpose

The purpose of the Gillingham-Stillman method (Gillingham and Stillman, 1973) is to provide the reader, "disabled" or "potentially disabled," who has a specific language difficulty, with a method for learning to read that is consistent with the evolution of language functions.

Rationale

Gillingham and Stillman (1973) argue that students with specific language disabilities will learn to read successfully only with methods that are consistent with the evolution of language functions. The system they have suggested is based upon the theoretical position and work of Samuel Orton. As suggested in the foreword to Gillingham and Stillman's 1965 text, *Remedial Training for Children with Specific Disabilities in Reading, Spelling, and Penmanship,* their goal was to organize remedial techniques to make them consistent with Orton's (1937) working hypothesis.

According to Gillingham and Stillman, Orton hypothesized that specific language disabilities he observed may have been due to hemispherical dominance in specific areas of the brain. He related certain instances of reading disability to the difficulty students might potentially have when dealing with inconsistencies that result from mixed dominance. Mirror writing and reversals seemed to be evidence of these difficulties.

The method, as it was developed by Gillingham and Stillman, purports to be new, different, and exclusive. It purports to be new and different in that it provides a "phonetic method" consistent with the evolution of language functions. It purports to be exclusive in that students using it engage in this and only this method. Gillingham and Stillman have claimed that the best teachers for this method are those familiar with traditional reading and spelling instruction. These teachers, it is argued, are cognizant of the need for and utility of Gillingham and Stillman's method.

Intended Audience

The Gillingham-Stillman method is intended for use with students who, due to specific language disabilities, have had or may have difficulty learning to read or spell. These disabled readers or potentially disabled readers should not include students who show either low mental abilities or sensory deficiencies. The method is intended for use with third graders through sixth graders, but has been adapted for use with older and younger students.

Description of the Procedure

To introduce students to the system, Gillingham and Stillman suggest a narrative entitled "The Growth of Written Language." The narrative is intended to provide a positive mind-set; it traces, with examples, the evolution of communications from spoken language to picture writing to alphabetic writing. The narrative ends with a description of the Gillingham-Stillman method and an explanation to the students that the difficulty they have incurred with reading it is not unique. As Gillingham and Stillman (1973) suggest, the latter message might be handled as follows:

> Now I am going to begin with you in an entirely different way. We are going to use the Alphabetic Method. You are going to learn the sounds of the letters, then build them into words. You will find it real fun and it will be nice for you to be attempting something which you can do.
>
> There are a great many children, more than you have any idea of, who have had the same kind of trouble that you have. Some of them have grown to be famous men and women. Boys and girls now doing well in college and business were taught to read and write as I am going to teach you. (P. 37)

Thereafter, a sequence of exercises beginning with the learning of letters and letter sounds, then blending sound to words, and finally to sentence and story reading is suggested. Within this framework, the technique will be described in this sequence:

1. Letters
2. Words
3. Sentences and stories
4. Other

1. *Letters*   The first principle of the technique is to teach the sounds represented by letters and then build these into words. To this end, each word family is taught by associations involving visual, auditory, and kinesthetic processes.

There are three associative processes involved. The first associative process involves two parts:

a. The teacher shows the student a letter and says it. It is then repeated by the student.
b. The same procedure is followed for the sound represented by the letter. The teacher says it. The student repeats it.

The second associative process involves responding with the name of a letter to the sound represented by the letter. That is, the teacher makes the sound represented by the letter and the student names the letter represented.

The third associative process involves learning the letter form. Learning of letter forms takes place in the following manner:

a. The teacher writes and explains the letter form.

b. The student traces the teacher's lines, copies them, writes the word from memory, and then writes the word without looking at what is being written.

There are several guidelines for the teacher to follow across these associative processes:

a. Letters are always introduced by a key word, such as *b,* and would be presented in the context of boy; when the *b* card is shown, the pupil would be expected to respond with *boy.*

b. Drill cards are used to introduce each letter, provide repetition, and improve the accuracy of sound production.

c. Students learn to differentiate vowels and consonants by the manner of their production and through the use of different-colored cards, e.g., white for consonants, salmon for vowels.

d. The first letters presented to the student should represent clear sounds and nonreversible letter forms.

e. An "echo" speech procedure in which the teacher drills the student in reproducing sounds is suggested for students incurring pronunciation difficulties.

f. For reinforcement purposes, students who know the name and sound represented by a letter are asked to respond to the names of letters with the sounds they represent.

g. In instances where writing takes place, cursive writing is preferred and suggested over manuscript writing.

2. *Words*   After ten letters are well known, blending them into words begins. Drill cards forming a word are placed in front of the student, and the student is required to blend the sounds represented by these letters, such as *h-i-m, t-a-p, a-t, i-f, h-i-p.* It is the teacher's responsibility to devise ways of drilling words effectively. These words, printed on colored cards, are placed in what has been termed the student's "Jewel Case." Time drills are imposed; in some instances, students' growth in accuracy is graphed.

After a few days of sound blending, the student is required to reverse the procedure and analyze words into the component sounds. For example, the teacher might say the word *m-a-p* slowly and have students name and find the cards for each sound. As further reinforcement, the student might write the word. As the student writes the word, each letter is named and then the word is spoken.

Typically, not more than one or two additional sounds are introduced each day. When a letter might represent more than one sound, only one of the sounds would be introduced. As word families are introduced, the drill card and Jewel Case card files are expanded. On a single day, the various activities might be organized as follows:

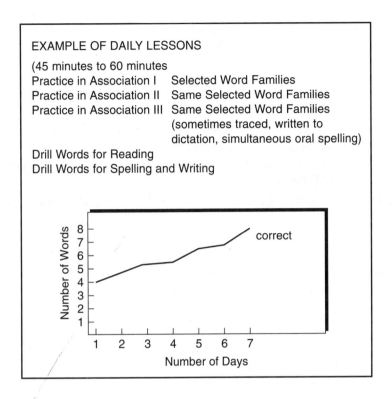

EXAMPLE OF DAILY LESSONS

(45 minutes to 60 minutes
Practice in Association I   Selected Word Families
Practice in Association II   Same Selected Word Families
Practice in Association III   Same Selected Word Families
                                    (sometimes traced, written to
                                    dictation, simultaneous oral spelling)

Drill Words for Reading
Drill Words for Spelling and Writing

3. *Sentences and Stories* After students can read and write any three-letter "perfectly phonetic" word, sentence and story reading is begun. It begins with simple, highly structured stories, referred to as "Little Stories," which are presented to the student to read and write.

Several of these Little Stories are available from Gillingham and Stillman. The following is an example:

Pat sat on the mat.

She had a hat.

The hat was on Pat.

A rat sat on the mat.

Pat ran.

The rat ran.

For both sentence and story reading, students are required to prepare silently. Their task is to read the story or sentence silently until they can read it perfectly. Any words with which the students may have difficulty are either sounded out, or, in cases where words may be unfamiliar, such as "phonetically irregular words," pronunciation is provided. The students are encouraged to be accurate and to avoid guessing. For sentence and story writing, Little Stories are dictated by the teacher. As the teacher dictates the story, avoiding unnecessary repetitions, the students write the words.

4. *Other*   As the students' reading skills develop, the teacher may want to use further guidance provided by Gillingham and Stillman:

   a. Students learn that polysyllabic words are formed by syllables in the same way monosyllabic words are formed by letters. To this end, students are presented with and asked to combine detached syllables, and are taught to identify the appropriate accent by trying the accent on each syllable.

   b. Dictionary use is taught for the purpose of identifying the pronunciation of words.

   c. To deal with a few selected words which are phonetically irregular, whole-word drill is suggested.

   d. Finally, until the student completes a major portion of the phonics program, he or she is discouraged from reading independently.

Gillingham and Stillman suggested that the technique would yield substantial benefits, assuming that sufficient time is provided. At a minimum, they suggest the technique requires a commitment of five lessons per week for no less than two years. Eventually, they suggest, the student will be able to return to a regular class; but unless returning students can read their texts and assignments fluently, they should be assisted in reading them.

Cautions and Comments

There appear to be several important similarities and differences between the Gillingham-Stillman technique and other multisensory approaches—for example, the Fernald technique. Both the Gillingham-Stillman and Fernald techniques emphasize constant reinforcement and repetition through the use of visual, auditory, and kinesthetic modalities; both prefer cursive writing to manuscript; and both attempt to develop a positive mind-set in the reader prior to the commencement of remediation. In terms of differences, Gillingham and Stillman insist upon a letter-by-letter, structured, synthetic phonics approach, in contrast to Fernald's concern that students not proceed letter by letter but select their own words to learn, and initially learn through all modalities.

Although the Gillingham-Stillman technique purports to yield positive results, there are reasons to caution potential users. First, very few contemporary authorities still accept the theoretical position of Orton as tenable. Second, students who learn by these methods may have a tendency to emphasize pronunciation over meaning. This synthetic letter-by-letter approach, with its emphasis upon word-perfect reading, places an undue emphasis on the mechanics rather than reading for meaning. For a further discussion of these points, the reader should refer to the Cautions and Comments sections of the various strategies presented in Unit 12: Word Identification.

References

Chall, J. 1967. *Learning to read: The great debate.* New York: McGraw-Hill, 169–170. Presents an evaluation and discussion of Orton's notions of reading disability and Orton's suggestions for remedial reading methods.

Gearhart, B. R. 1973. *Learning disabilities: Educational strategies.* St. Louis: C. V. Mosby, 103–107. Presents a detailed discussion of the major aspects of the technique.

Gillingham, A., and B. W. Stillman. 1965, 1973. *Remedial training for children with specific disability in reading, spelling and penmanship.* Cambridge, MA: Educators Publishing Service. Provides the rationale and history, and serves as the manual, for the Gillingham-Stillman technique.

Harris, A. J., and E. R. Sipay. 1975. *How to increase reading ability.* 6th ed. New York: David

McKay, 396–397. Discusses briefly the theory and procedure of the technique.

Kaluger, G., and C. J. Kolson. 1969. *Reading and learning disabilities.* Columbus, OH: Charles E. Merrill, 267–268. Presents a brief summary and discussion of this and other techniques.

Orton, S. 1937. *Reading, writing, and speech problems in children.* New York: W. W. Norton. Discusses Orton's theory for specific disabilities in reading.

———. 1966. The Orton-Gillingham approach. In *The disabled reader,* edited by J. Money. Baltimore: Johns Hopkins University Press, 119–146. Summarizes Orton's theory and discusses the technique.

Fernald Technique

Purpose

The Fernald technique (Fernald, 1943) has two basic purposes: (1) to teach the student to write and read words correctly; and (2) to extend the student's reading to various materials other than personal compositions.

Rationale

Fernald claims that many cases of reading disability, both "partial" and "extreme," are due to teachers' failure to use methods that allow students to learn in the manner most appropriate to their individual abilities. Fernald claims that the use of limited methods blocks the learning process. As an alternative, Fernald's own procedure, which incorporates a multisensory strategy, purportedly caters to the varied needs of individuals.

Intended Audience

The Fernald technique is intended for use with cases of extreme and partial reading disability. Extreme disability refers to the totally disabled student with zero reading ability. Partial disability refers to the student with some reading skills, who is unable to acquire adequate reading skills within the instructional framework of the class. It is intended that the teacher use the procedure on a one-to-one basis with each student; however, the technique can be adapted for use with groups.

Description of the Procedure

Fernald divides her technique into four stages in accord with varying levels of individual reading ability and development. In the first stage, the student traces the word with a finger, saying each part of the word aloud as it is traced, until it can be written without looking at the copy. By the final stage, the student is eager to read. The student can begin to generalize about words and to identify new ones.

Stage 1   The first stage is highly structured and for this reason will be described in some detail. In this stage, the student selects any word or words that he or she wants to learn, regardless of length. Each word is written with crayon on a strip of paper in large, chalkboard-size cursive writing, or manuscript print. The student then traces the word with finger contact, pronouncing each part of the word as it is traced. This tracing procedure is repeated as many times as necessary until the student can write the word on a separate piece of paper without looking at the copy. As new words are learned in this manner, they are placed in an alphabetized word file by the student.

After several words are taught in this way, the student begins to realize that he or she can read and write words. At this time, "story-writing" activities are introduced. Subsequent learning of words occurs whenever the student cannot write a word for the story. Sometimes the student may have to learn every word by this tracing technique before the story can be written. After the words are learned and the story is written, the story is typed by the teacher within 24 hours. The story is then read by the student, who proceeds to file the words under the proper letter in the word file.

The following points are stressed by Fernald for using this initial stage:

1. For maximum efficiency, unknown words should always be traced with the finger in contact with the paper.
2. In order to avoid breaking the word into meaningless units, the student should write the word from memory rather than from copy.
3. Similarly, if any error or interruption occurs during the student's writing of the word, the word should be rewritten entirely.
4. To ensure that the student understands the meaning of the word, words should always be used in context.

The following dialogue between a student and teacher is presented to illustrate the use of the first stage of the Fernald technique with a totally disabled reader.

TEACHER: Good morning, my name is Mr. Stewart and I'm your teacher. Please sit here at my side.

STUDENT: Oh, all right.

TEACHER: I have a new way of learning to read which I'd like you to try. Many bright people have had the same difficulty you have had in learning to read and have learned easily by this new method. Now, give me any word that you want to learn to read.

STUDENT: Dinosaur.

TEACHER: Dinosaur?

STUDENT: Dinosaur.

TEACHER: Now, watch what I do and listen to what I say. Are you ready?

STUDENT: Yeah.

[The teacher should use a crayon and a piece of paper which is approximately 4 inches by 12 inches.

1. The teacher says the word before writing it.
2. As the word is written, each syllable is said.
3. If the word is written in cursive style (as the word is said again), the *t*'s are crossed and the *i*'s are dotted, etc.
4. As the word is said again, each syllable is underlined.
5. The word is said again.]

TEACHER: Now again, watch what I do and listen to what I say. Are you ready?

STUDENT: Yeah.

TEACHER: [The teacher follows exactly the steps as above, only the teacher uses a finger instead of a crayon.] I want you to do exactly as I did until you think you can write the word without looking at it. Now watch again what I do and listen to what I say. Ready? [Teacher repeats tracing procedure.]

STUDENT: Let me try.

TEACHER: Do what I did and say what I said until you can write the word without looking at it.

STUDENT: [The student traces the word following the procedure demonstrated.]

TEACHER: [Teacher checks student's tracing technique. Whenever the student hesitates or makes an error, the teacher stops the student and, if necessary, demonstrates the technique again. The number of times the student traces the word is recorded.]

STUDENT: (After several tracings): I think I know the word now.

TEACHER: [Teacher removes copy of word and places a blank sheet of paper and a crayon in front of the student.] Write the word on this piece of paper using the same procedure. [If the student makes a mistake, the student is stopped immediately. Do not erase the word. Instead, fold or turn paper over and allow the student to try again.]

STUDENT: [Student writes the word using the same procedure followed when tracing the word.] Finished.

TEACHER: Are you correct?

STUDENT: I sure am.

TEACHER: Check and see if you are correct.

STUDENT: [Student turns over the copy and compares attempt.]

TEACHER: Were you correct?

STUDENT: Yeah.

TEACHER: Do you think you can write it correctly twice? Try writing the word again. [The teacher turns copies of the word down and gives student another blank sheet of paper.]

[Student proceeds to write the word correctly a second time.]

TEACHER: Check to see if you are correct again.

[Student checks word.]

TEACHER: Congratulations! That's great! Now place the word in your word file under the proper letter.

[Student proceeds to place word under the letter *d* in the word file.]

TEACHER: Now tell me another word you wish to learn.

Two, three, or maybe four words might be learned using this same procedure during a single session over each of the first few days. As soon as the student realizes that words can be learned by this procedure, story-writing is started. Words are learned as they are needed for the story the student is writing.

Stage 2   The length of the tracing period (Stage 1) will vary from student to student and is phased out when the student is able to learn without it. This becomes evident when there is a decrease in the number of tracings required to learn a word, and when some words are learned with single or no tracings. At the point when the need for any tracing disappears, the student is ready to embark upon Stage 2. On the average, the tracing period lasts about two months, with a range from one to eight months.

During Stage 2, the student learns words simply by looking at the word while saying it over and over. As with Stage 1, words to be learned are derived from unknown words in stories the student has written. These words are presented to the student in print or in cursive form for study. The word is learned by saying the word several times, over and over again, until it can be written from memory.

Stage 3   Stage 3 is basically the same as Stage 2, except that the student has now reached the stage where learning occurs merely by looking at a word and saying it. The student is permitted to read anything and as much as he or she desires. Whenever an unknown word is met, the student is told the word. At this stage, the student learns directly from the printed page. It has become unnecessary to write or print each new word on a card. The student looks at the word in print, pronounces it a number of times, and then is able to write it from memory. As with the previous stage, new words are reviewed after reading, filed, and, at a later stage, reviewed again.

Stage 4 In Stage 4, the student is able to recognize new words from their resemblance to words or parts of words already learned. As with Stage 3, the student is expected to read a variety of materials. However, unlike Stage 3, the student is able to work out many words. For example, such words might be learned from the context, or from generalizations about words or word parts. The student is told only words for which it is not possible to determine the meaning. For purposes of retention, such words are usually written down by the student.

Fernald emphasizes the need for student involvement in the content of what is being read. For this reason, she suggests that the student be encouraged to survey a paragraph to clear up the meaning of unknown words prior to reading. She argues that this will prevent distraction and enable the student to concentrate on the content of the reading material. Toward the goal of reading for meaning, she discourages the sounding out of words during reading, either by the teacher or by a student, and suggests that any word that the student does not know be provided.

Cautions and Comments

Empirical evidence of the success of the Fernald technique comes from various studies. Kress and Johnson (1970), Berres and Eyer (1970), Enstrom (1970), and Coterell (1972) have all reported positive results with this approach. Fernald herself provides a great deal of documented support for the strategy's success in *Remedial Techniques in Basic School Subjects* (1943).

While there seems to be a consensus that the Fernald technique yields positive results and has several desirable features, there also seems to be agreement that it suffers from some major drawbacks.

On the positive side, the desirable features of the Fernald method include:

1. It reinforces the acquisition of word form cues, and the ability to use context.
2. Methods seem consistent with aims and take into account variations in the child's rate of learning and specific needs and interests.
3. Motivation and reading of interesting materials are emphasized.

On the negative side, objections to the use of the technique include:

1. The procedure tends to be very time-consuming and demanding of the teacher, especially in the early stages. Often more expedient methods for teaching disabled readers can be developed.
2. Reading books is deemed important, but delayed.
3. Syllabic division within words may distort the pronunciation of certain words, e.g., *fat/her.*

4. Readers may develop who are too busy sounding out words to either concentrate on meaning or understand the purposes of reading. In this respect, it can be argued that Fernald suggests the need, but not the methods by which students will read for meaning.

References

Berres, F., and J. T. Eyer. 1970. John. In *Casebook on reading disability,* edited by A. J. Harris. New York: David McKay, 25–47. Describes a case history example of the use of the procedure.

Bond, G. L., and M. A. Tinker. 1973. *Reading difficulties: Their diagnosis and correction.* 3d ed. Englewood Cliffs, NJ: Prentice-Hall, 498–501. Presents a brief discussion on the procedure and its uses.

Chall, J. 1967. *Learning to read: The great debate.* New York: McGraw-Hill, 170–172. Presents a brief discussion of aspects of Fernald's work with disabled readers.

Coterell, G. 1972. A case of severe learning disability. *Remedial Education* 7:5–9. Describes an example of the procedure's successful use.

Enstrom, E. A. 1970. A key to learning. *Academic Therapy* 5:295–297. Describes a successful example using the procedure.

Fernald, G. 1943. *Remedial techniques in basic school subjects.* New York: McGraw-Hill. Presents a detailed description of the procedure and results of its use.

Gearhart, B. R. 1973. *Learning disabilities: Educational strategies.* St. Louis: C. V. Mosby, 76–90. Presents a detailed discussion of the procedure and provides examples of its use through case histories.

Harris, A. J., and E. R. Sipay. 1975. *How to increase reading ability.* 6th ed. New York: David McKay, 393–396. Presents a brief discussion of the procedure and its use with students experiencing reading difficulty.

Kaluger, G., and C. J. Kolson. 1969. *Reading and learning disabilities.* Columbus, OH: Charles E. Merrill, 263–267. Presents a theoretical discussion of the procedure and its use.

Kress, R. A., and M. S. Johnson. 1970. Martin. In *Casebook on reading disability,* edited by A. J. Harris. New York: David McKay, 1–24. Describes an example of the use of the procedure through a case history.

Meyer, C. A. 1978. Reviewing the literature on Fernald's technique of remedial reading. *The Reading Teacher* 31:614–619. Reviews studies examining the effectiveness of Fernald's technique.

Word Identification

UNIT OVERVIEW

No aspect of reading instruction has been the subject of more debate than that dealing with word identification instruction. Unfortunately, these debates may lead one to think that instruction in word identification, particularly in phonics, is the single most important ingredient in the entire reading program. Such arguments seem to disregard the notion that word identification includes skills other than phonic skills. These arguments ignore the notion that word identification and phonics are only a means to an end: reading for understanding. The issue addressed in this unit is not *whether* to teach, but *how* to teach, word identification skills. Of particular concern is the problem of preparing readers to deal with unknown words they encounter as they read.

The unit presents the theoretical bases and procedures for some of the alternative ways to teach word identification. In so doing, it provides a backdrop for examining alternatives. Beyond these descriptions, selected books and articles should be reviewed. In 1990, the Massachusetts Institute of Technology released a report by M. Adams; in 1989, the magazine *Phi Delta Kappan* devoted several issues to this topic. Finally, Stanovich (1991) and Cunningham (1992) provided a review of the literature on word identification and phonics, respectively.

Four strategies designed to improve the reader's word identification skills are presented here. The strategies represent both traditional and contemporary suggestions for developing word identification abilities. A brief summary of the strategies provides a preview of the unit.

Analytic Method. The Analytic Method is among the most widely used of the traditional methods for teaching phonics. This method is designed to have readers use known words to discover strategies for decoding unknown words. In recent years it has been referred to as the implicit method of teaching phonics.

Synthetic Word Families. The Synthetic Word Families approach is another widely used traditional method for developing phonic and word identification abilities. It is designed to serve three purposes: (1) to help readers learn the sounds represented by letters and some methods of blending these sounds into words; (2) to increase the student's sight vocabulary through the use of consonant substitution; and (3) to aid students in word identification skills through the use of blending and minimally contrasting word elements. In recent years it has been referred to as the explicit method of teaching phonics.

Syllabaries.   The Syllabaries strategy has evolved in recent years. This approach is designed to improve word identification skills through the use of the syllable as the unit of pronunciation.

Goodman's Reading Strategy Lessons.   Reading Strategy Lessons represent an attempt to translate the theories of Kenneth Goodman (1967–75) into practice. Advocates of Goodman's psycholinguistic perspective on reading have designed these lessons to help readers focus on and strengthen their use of the syntactic or grammatic, the semantic or meaning, and the graphophonic or sound-symbol cueing systems involved in reading.

References

Adams, M. J. 1990. *Beginning to read: Thinking and learning about print.* Cambridge, MA: MIT Press.

Cunningham, P. M. 1992. What kind of phonics instruction will we have? In *Literacy research, theory, and practice: View from many perspectives,* edited by C. K. Kinzer and D. J. Leu. Forty-first Yearbook of the National Reading Conference (pp. 17–31). Chicago: National Reading Conference.

Stanovich, K. E. 1991. Word recognition: Changing perspectives. In *Handbook of reading research: Volume II,* edited by R. Barr, M. L. Kamil, P. Mosenthal, and P. D. Pearson, 418–452. New York: Longman.

Analytic Method

Purpose

The Analytic Method, or implicit method, of phonics instruction is designed to provide students with strategies for decoding unfamiliar words; in this method, students are encouraged to employ their knowledge of the phonic elements within familiar words.

Rationale

The Analytic Method of phonic instruction is based on the premise that words can be analyzed into their common phonic elements. The student is introduced to a number of common words, from which an analysis of component parts can follow. That is, when the student has a bank of words with the same phonic features, phonics instruction begins. For example, students might be asked to discover this generalization: common sound of the letter *b* as in *bat, ball,* and *boy.*

In essence, this method places stress on meaning and on the importance of building a bank of known words as the basis for acquiring certain phonic understandings. Letter sounds are never learned in isolation, thus avoiding the distorted notion that isolated letters have sounds. Phonic elements are learned through discovery, rather than through rote memorization.

Intended Audience

The Analytic Method of phonics instruction is suggested for use with beginning readers, where the emphasis is placed on learning sound/symbol relationships. The method may be used in conjunction with existing classroom materials or as a substitute for them, either in a group or in an individual situation.

Description of the Procedure

The discussion of the actual teaching of an Analytic phonics lesson focuses on the following steps: (1) auditory and visual discrimination, (2) auditory discrimination, (3) word blending, and (4) contextual application.

1. Auditory and Visual Discrimination   Hearing and seeing the likeness and differences in sound and letters are essential parts of phonics instruction. It is from this base that an analytic phonics lesson begins. If a teacher were to present a phonics lesson concerning the single consonant *d,* the first thing to do would be to put a sentence on the board, underlining the word containing the target element in this way:

The <u>dog</u> bit the boy.

Rather than call attention to the sentence at this time, the teacher writes other words on the board that have the same phonic element. The words should all be known words. Children are asked to look at the words and read them. It is suggested that the students, rather than the teacher, pronounce the words. Since language differences may exist between the teacher and the children, the sounds produced by the teacher may differ from those produced by the children; some confusion may arise.

Words that might be listed could include:

Dick

dot

dig

duck

Emphasis is placed upon the beginning sound as each is pronounced, but the phonic element is never separated from the word. Through questioning and discussion, the teacher would elicit the following from the students: (a) the words all start alike, and (b) the words all sound alike in the beginning.

2. Auditory Discrimination Now that students have seen and heard that the words start alike, the next step is to reinforce further the targeted phonic element through the student's listening vocabulary. A new group of words is read by one of the students, rather than by the teacher, again to avoid possible language confusion caused by differences in sound production between the teacher and students. The students are now asked to decide whether these words begin in the same way as the group of words on the board. The new words are not written on the board. Words that might be used here could include:

    dock   bank   deep

    went   dark   rich

Finally, students are asked to generate words that begin the same way as the targeted phonic element:

    dumb   do   Doug   dear

3. Word Blending If students are successful with the first two steps of the teaching procedure, they will be ready to learn to generalize from known words how the targeted phonic element sounds in new words. A sight word is written on the board, and below this word, another one with the targeted element:

    mad

    dad

Students are asked to focus on the similarities and differences between the word that they know and the new word with the phonic element they are learning. They should observe that: (a) the words end alike; (b) they sound alike at the end; and (c) they differ in the beginning.

Once students have observed the above, the teacher draws their attention to the fact that the new word starts like the group of words on the board.

Students are now asked to interchange the beginning consonant elements; thus, the *m* is replaced with a *d*. Students must remember how words with *d* sound in order to pronounce the new word, *dad*. This process is continued with a few more pairs of words, to ensure that students can use their newly learned phonic element. Other pairs that might be used are:•

    bay   rip   fairy

    day   dip   dairy

4. Contextual Application The last step in this teaching strategy requires that students apply their new learning in an actual reading situation, where phonic learning is more natural than in isolation. Students are now asked to read their newly acquired words in short sentences:

My dad is at work.

What day is today?

Dip your brush in the paint.

Milk comes from a dairy.

After reading these sentences successfully, the students are asked to go back to the original sentence that started the lesson and read it:

The dog bit the boy.

Students may respond to the original sentence in different ways. Some may rhyme *log* with *dog,* substituting the initial consonant; others may have mastered the sound of *d* and use it in conjunction with context clues to decode *dog.* The important thing to remember is that nowhere in the lesson was the *d* separated from real words, thus avoiding any distortion that may result when the students sound letters in isolation.

Cautions and Comments

Substantial claims have been made by proponents of both synthetic and analytic phonics approaches as to which is the better method. Certainly, the more holistic approach taken by analytic phonics seems to be the more appropriate learning strategy. However, at this time there is no well-founded longitudinal research that would enable us to choose between the two approaches. Research that bears on the influence of the variations in these approaches upon oral reading performance has yielded predictable results. As Allington (1984) indicated:

> The errors of children in meaning-emphasis programs continue to reflect greater sensitivity to contextual constraints, while those of readers in code-emphasis programs reflect greater sensitivity to graphemic cues and less awareness of context. (P. 848)

Two comments are in order concerning the use of either analytic or synthetic phonics. First, some professionals argue that the exclusive use of one approach over the other limits students' chances to master phonic principles. Moving back and forth between the two approaches may be a productive procedure if it enhances the students' abilities to deal with the abstract principles of phonics. It also may prove to be nonproductive, causing confusion rather than developing understanding.

Second, no matter which approach is chosen, it must be remembered that the ultimate test of a student's ability to use phonics is whether the student is able to read successfully for meaning and to apply such skills in contextual situations. Regardless of the method used, it is possible that a student would acquire adequate phonic skills and still remain a poor reader. With respect to either the analytic or the synthetic phonic method, it would seem imperative that students' newly acquired phonic understandings be applied to actual reading situations. For a further discussion of this comment, the reader is directed to the Cautions and Comments section under Synthetic Word Families.

References ▮

Allington, R. L. 1984. Oral reading. In *Handbook of reading research,* edited by P. D. Pearson, R. Barr, M. L. Kamil, and P. Mosenthal, New York: Longman. Presents a review of research findings dealing with oral reading including the effects of different phonics approaches.

Durkin, D. 1983. *Teaching them to read.* 4th ed. Boston: Allyn and Bacon, 177–205. Describes both the content of and the various teaching procedures used in phonics.

Johnson, D. D. and P. D. Pearson. 1978. *Teaching reading vocabulary.* New York: Holt. Rinehart & Winston. Examines word identification in both the analytic and the synthetic approaches.

———. 1984. *Teaching reading vocabulary,* 2nd ed. New York: Holt. Rinehart & Winston. A revised edition of their earlier book.

Stahl, S. A. 1992. Saying the "p" word: Nine guidelines for exemplary phonics instruction. *The Reading Teacher* 45:618–625. Discusses guidelines for effective phonics instruction.

Synthetic Word Families ▮

Purpose

The purpose of Synthetic Word Families, or explicit phonics, is to: (1) increase vocabulary through the use of consonant substitution and (2) aid students in word identification skills by employing the strategy of blending letter sounds with contrasting word elements.

Rationale

Word families are word elements that contain both vowel and consonant elements, to which can be synthetically blended an initial consonant element. For instance, the word family *at* can be blended with the sounds of *b, c, f,* and *h* to form *bat, cat, fat,* and *hat.* Word families have also been variously referred to as phonograms, graphemic bases, and spelling patterns; they form the basis for reading systems claiming a linguistic approach.

The use of word families is based upon the principle that English is an alphabetic writing system employing a methodical code that is easily broken. This code consists of many contrasting patterns (word families), which the student can take advantage of when learning to read. Therefore, reading instruction centered around the patterns of language and the contrasting elements that may be generated from those patterns might be highly conducive to success in identifying unknown words and in learning to read. Less importance is placed on learning words in context, since instruction with Synthetic Word Families begins with parts and proceeds to form wholes.

When using word families in conjunction with consonant substitution, the instructor can capitalize on the principle of minimal contrast and the student's knowledge of letter sounds. After a model word (a known word) has been explored for its elements, the word family (vowel and consonant elements) can be used to generate new words through consonant substitution. Learning is accomplished by building on what is already known, varying that known element only minimally. Thus, the identification of new words is centered around maximum similarity and minimum difference—the maximum similarity being the word family, and the minimum difference being the synthetically blended consonant.

Intended Audience

The use of Synthetic Word Families is commonly associated with beginning reading instruction in the primary grades. Although Synthetic Word Families are intended to be used as the total reading program, they may also be used as a supplement for other materials designed to teach word identification skills.

Description of the Procedure

Some background information is in order before dealing with the teaching procedure. The following would be representative of the use of Synthetic Word Families in books known as linguistic readers:

> Nat is a cat
>
> Is Nat fat?
>
> Nat is fat.
>
> Nat is a fat cat.*

The above is a prime example of the use of initial consonant substitution and minimal contrasts within the word family *at*.

Aukerman (1984) has described the variety of ways word families are used in linguistic readers. Synthetic Word Families are built upon a base sound that may be a sound in any position—beginning, medial, or ending. For instance, using the short vowel sound of *a* (aah) with both initial and final consonant substitution, a number of combinations may be generated:

fa (fat)	pa (pal)	na (nab)
da (dad)	sa (sad)	va (van)
ma (mad)	ba (bat)	la (lap)
	or	
at	ax (axe)	ap (apt)
am	ad (add)	ak (ack)
an (ant)	ag	as

Nonsense combinations are encouraged in linguistic material, since they may be parts of meaningful words that the student may meet later.

---

*C. C. Fries, A. C. Fries, R. Wilson, and M. K. Randolph. *Merrill linguistic readers: First reader.* (Columbus, OH: Charles E. Merrill, 1965) 4.

A second method would be to use a medial position and word family, such as *-an,* and build words or nonwords that are larger in length:

ban	bans	band
bant	banx	banp
bang	banz	bank

Using different initial consonant sounds, numerous other combinations may be built, both with and without meaning.

Word pairs may also be used as follows:

lamp	belt	tilt	band
ramp	felt	pilt	cand

On the other hand, if more regularity is desired, an identical base with the five short vowel sounds could be used, to which initial consonant sounds might be added:

b-all	g-all	p-all
c-all	h-all	s-all
f-all	m-all	t-all

or

b-ell	j-ell	p-ell
d-ell	m-ell	s-ell
f-ell	n-ell	t-ell

Used in the previously mentioned ways, the Synthetic Word Family concept can produce innumerable word combinations.

To present a more manageable application of Synthetic Word Families, and to show how they may be fit into a teaching procedure to augment other types of instruction in word identification, we will focus our discussion of Synthetic Word Families on: (1) prior concepts, (2) teacher guidance, and (3) student independence.

1. Prior Concepts   There are certain prior concepts or learnings that students may need to have before the teacher can initiate a Synthetic Word Families approach. These include: (a) a small bank of known words, (b) rhyming words, and (c) consonant sounds.

A first pedagogical principle is that learning proceeds from the known to the unknown. In accordance with this principle, the Synthetic Word Families approach begins with a small bank of known words to serve as a referent from which to generate new words. It is recommended that whole words, rather than elements of words, be used to initiate this procedure. For example, *b-ell* might be easier to learn than *-ell.*

Students must be sensitive to rhyme. They must be able to recognize that words that look alike at their end (possess the same word family) probably rhyme in most cases. In addition, students must know which parts of rhyming words sound alike, and which parts do not. To this end, students should be given auditory discrimination activities to ensure that they can differentiate between the rhyming and nonrhyming words.

Finally, knowledge of individual consonant sounds is necessary, so that students may effectively synthesize these sounds with word families. Needless to say, it will be difficult to rhyme words without a knowledge of consonant sounds.

2. Teacher Guidance   Again, as with most teaching procedures, it must not be assumed that even if students have mastered all necessary prerequisites, they will be able to use word families effectively to improve word identification abilities. The teacher must guide the students toward independence.

Initially, teachers should select a model word that is part of the student's known vocabulary. New words are generated by using: (a) the same word family as the model word and (b) differing beginning consonant sounds, which may be placed next to the model. An example might be:

dog
bog
fog
hog
log

Through observation and teacher encouragement, students will see that the new words look like the model except for the initial consonant. Students who have mastered consonant sounds will be able to read the minimally contrasting words. By doing this, students will recognize that all words sound alike. The teacher may point out that detecting word family elements can aid in pronouncing unfamiliar words.

Exercises as described above should be continued by using other words the students know as a basis and blending known consonant sounds to them. Gradually, the teacher should allow the students to generate new words. Later on, the use of diagraphs and blends as possible initial substitutes should be explored and demonstrated.

By going through these exercises diligently, the teacher can be confident that the students are able to use the concept of Synthetic Word Families in substitution exercises. However, there may not be any transfer to "real" reading and to student independence from these exercises alone.

3. Student Independence   Exercises like these do not necessarily ensure that students will be able to match mentally the word families they know with the unfamiliar words they encounter in reading. To help students gain independence in using word families, Cunningham, Moore, Cunningham, and Moore (1983) have recommended a teaching procedure to aid students in mentally processing word matches to identify unfamiliar words in their reading.

The first step in this strategy is to create five cards with known words for each student. For instance, the five word cards may be: *tell, can, dog, it,* and *bump.* The teacher writes a word on the board, such as *bell,* and students are expected to find a match among their cards. This is followed by the teacher, or more preferably, by a student volunteer, demonstrating how the words look alike (word family) and how they differ (initial consonant), and then pronouncing both words. Searching through their small bank of word cards to secure a match will aid students in eventually gaining the facility to match words on their own when reading print. Word cards are continually added, and this procedure is continued, until students have mastered 15 word cards as well as possible matches.

The second step of this strategy is for students to match a word printed on the board without the aid of the word cards. This is the point where students start to use their total mental processes to provide a match. All 15 words are used in this step.

The third step involves the extension of the 15 words to include all the words the students know. A new model word is given, and students are asked to figure out the unknown word by attempting to match it with a known word in their heads. In this way, they gain further independence in using Synthetic Word Families to decode unknown words.

The fourth and final step is for students to apply this concept to their reading. When a student encounters difficult words, the teacher should encourage the student to think of a word family that ends like the unknown word, to aid in identifying it. It is here that students face the true test of using Synthetic Word Families, i.e., word families to aid in decoding unknown words.

Cautions and Comments

When using Synthetic Word Families as an aid to improving word recognition, teachers need to be aware of some possible problems. For example, using word families in isolation without helping students use them in actual reading situations may be problematic. Students need to be shown the relevance of word families to reading text selections. Indeed, the use of word families may deteriorate into a game of word calling if students are merely asked to play with words, no matter how exciting this activity may become. Furthermore, students taught using synthetic methods may be prone to become overdependent on graphic clues.

Some problems may arise in generating new words using word families. Nonsense words, though advocated by linguistic approaches to reading, should be avoided. By definition, these words are meaningless, despite the linguistic consistency they provide. They are likely to contribute to readers' substituting nonsense words for unknown words in text where real words should apply.

The second area of concern is that of irregular words. For instance, does *bow* rhyme with *cow* or *row?* Furthermore, consonant sounds may become distorted when sounded separately, as with the sound of *b-buh*. Should *bat* be pronounced as *buh-at?*

An alternate use of Synthetic Word Families has been developed by LaPray (1972) for use with poor readers. Those students who have mastered little else in reading except their names are asked to list spontaneously their names and other words they may know. Utilizing the few words generated, new words can be built from their known parts. For example, if a student lists only *Bill, dog, and mom,* new words may be built and learned, first by sound and then by context, by putting them into a short phrase or sentence.

Finally, to leave the reader some food for thought, Kenneth Goodman's (1976) comments on the efficacy of phonic instruction are worthy of note.

You have to put skills in the context of meaning. That's where they have the most value. That's where they maintain their proper proportion. And there they won't lead to the development of problems which eventually interfere with learning to read. In fact, children learn best this way because skills taught in context don't result in incorrect generalizations which then have to be overcome.

Take the common emphasis on phonic skills. When you isolate a letter or a sound, you make it more abstract, and you also change its relative value. If I give kids the sentence, "The girl is in the garden," I can talk about the initial letter of girl and the sound that it relates to. But if I give the lesson backwards, if I start with the sound of g, then I'm saying that each letter has a value—a meaning. That's not true. The value is dependent on the sequence that it's in. And the importance of noticing and using a particular graphic cue is exaggerated because in context it works together with everything else. (P. 7)

References

Aukerman, R. C. 1984. *Approaches to beginning reading,* 2d ed. New York: John Wiley and Sons. 177–220. Discusses the use of Synthetic Word Families as one basic approach to phonics instruction. Also describes, in detail, linguistically oriented materials used in beginning reading instruction.

Cunningham, P. M., S. A. Moore, J. W. Cunningham, and D. W. Moore. 1983. *Reading in elementary classrooms: Strategies and observations.* New York: Longman. Advocates the use of consonant substitution with word families to build sight vocabulary.

Durkin, D. 1983. *Teaching them to read.* 4th ed. Boston: Allyn and Bacon. Describes different phonic approaches, but especially synthetic.

Goodman, K. 1976. *Reading: A conversation with Kenneth Goodman.* Glenview, IL: Scott, Foresman.

LaPray, M. 1972. *Teaching children to become independent readers.* New York: Center for Applied Research in Education. Advocates the use of Synthetic Word Families as a means to establish success-oriented instruction with students experiencing reading difficulties.

Syllabaries

Purpose

The purpose of Syllabaries is to: (1) teach word identification skills through the use of the syllable as the unit of instruction; and (2) use a comparison-contrast strategy to decode words by preceding from known word parts to unknown word parts.

Rationale

The Syllabary Method of improving word recognition skills is based upon the use of the syllable as the unit of pronunciation. It is an alternative to traditional phonics, which is based upon the use of phoneme/grapheme correspondence.

Phonemes, the basic sounds of language, become distorted when pronounced in isolation, i.e., the sound of the letter *b* pronounced in isolation is *buh*. Some students seem to have difficulty learning to pronounce these units and even more trouble blending them together, i.e., *buh-ah-tuh* = *bat*. Although the use of phonics to decode unknown words presents difficulty to some, most students do have the facility to segment words into syllables (Gibson and Levin, 1975).

The Syllabary, seemingly a more natural unit of pronunciation for some students, may provide a sound means to overcome those phonological problems by beginning with those units (syllables) that are more easily recognized and pronounced in isolation (Gleitman and Rozin, 1973). To illustrate this point with the word *paper,* note the difference in ease of pronunciation between *puh-aper* (only first letter sound in isolation) versus *pa-per* (two syllables in isolation). This premise and the use of a comparison-contrast strategy to decode unknown words form the basis of the Syllabary, which was developed as a means to teach word recognition skills.

There are some differences among the teacher strategies advocated by the various materials for teaching beginning readers decoding skills; however, it can be inferred that: (1) certain rules must be applied by readers to identify unfamiliar words, and (2) they must be applied in some certain order. To identify an unknown word, readers are taught to apply an ordered set of syllabication rules and then to apply phonic rules with each of the individual syllables.

Cunningham provides this example with the word *recertify* to illustrate the word identification processes a reader might typically use:

1. Reader decides on the number of syllables by counting the vowels (remembering that the *y* at the end of a word is a vowel): four vowels = four syllables.
2. Reader divides the word in syllables by applying the following ordered rules:

   a. Divide between a root word and a prefix: *re certify.*

   b. Divide between two intervocalic consonants (except final consonant, of course): *re cer tify.*

   c. Divide before a single intervocalic consonant: *re cer ti fy.*

3. Reader applies rules to the letters in each syllable.

   a. *re:* ends in a vowel—long *e* sound; think long *e* sound—blend with *r*—pronounce *rē*.

   b. *cer:c* before *e, i,* or *y* usually has the *s* sound; *e* is controlled by *r.* Blend *c* with *er*—pronounce *ser.*

   c. *ti:* just like first syllable, if it ends in a vowel; try the long sound—pronounce *tī.*

   d. *fy:* when it is a vowel rather than a consonant, *y* can be pronounced as in *cry* or as in *daddy.* Try *fi.*

4. Reader blends all four syllables together: *re ser ti fi.* Reader does not recognize word as one he or she has heard before or knows a meaning for, so reader tries different sound correspondences.

5. Reader tries a different sound for the syllables. Perhaps it is a *y* as in *daddy: rē ser ŭ fē*. Still not a word reader knows; perhaps this is a word the reader has never heard of before?

6. Finally, reader remembers about unaccented syllables and tries a schwa in different places until he happens upon the correct pronunciation: *rē ser t'fǐ*. "Oh, like what happens if you forget to renew your license and have to be recertified to get another license."

7. Reader continues reading (Cunningham 1975–76, 129–130).

Although it may seem difficult, if not impossible, for this process to take place in a reader's mind as he or she attempts to identify an unknown word, this current mode of word identification processes is advocated and taught to elementary school students.

To provide an alternative to the theory that students apply an ordered set of rules in word identification, Cunningham (1975–76) proposes a synthesized theory of mediated word identification, based on these premises:

1. Words and word parts are stored in the human memory.
2. Word identification does not involve the application of teacher-taught rules; rather, it involves a search through this memory-store, comparing the unknown with the known.
3. Unfamiliar words not recognized on sight are segmented into units.
4. These units are compared/contrasted with known words, with word parts, or with fragments, for identification.
5. Recombining the units results in a word for which the reader knows a meaning or a sound referent.
6. Readers form their own rules (they are not taught rules) for decoding unfamiliar words by comparing/contrasting the unknown with the known.

Applying the synthesized theory of word identification to the previous example with *recertify,* it can be assumed that the reader has numerous words and word parts in his memory-store and has also developed the ability to compare the unknown to the known. Segmenting an unfamiliar word occurs not by successively applying adult-taught syllabication rules, but by recognizing known parts in the unknown whole.

The reader can identify the unfamiliar whole *recertify* through a variety of comparisons such as:

1. If *certify* is in the reader's memory-store, along with either the word part *re* or other words beginning with *re* (*reexamine; relay*), the resulting combination of the two parts is tested against words for which the reader has sound and/or meaning referents.
2. If *certify* is not in the reader's store, it might be segmented into more manageable units. For instance, the reader might have *identify* or *sanctify* segmented *tify.* The reader could identify *re* as described. *Cer* might be secured from parts of *certainly* or *ceramics.* Again, the reader would combine parts for comparison against the reader's sound and/or meaning referents.

3. If a wrong match is chosen from the reader's word-store (*recreation* instead of *relay*, or *ceremony* instead of *certainly*), the reader will be unable to identify it as there will be neither sound nor meaning referent. The reader will reenter his or her memory-store for a more appropriate match.

Intended Audience

Gleitman and Rozin (1973) suggested three possible ways to incorporate the use of the Syllabary in reading instruction in the elementary grades. First, it may be used as an introductory system to make phonics utility more accessible to students. Second, the Syllabary may be used as a substitute for teaching many phonics principles, thus minimizing the quantity of instruction in that area. Finally, Gleitman and Rozin recommend that the Syllabary could be used as a remedial approach to word recognition in cases where students cannot master phonics principles. It is the latter use that Cunningham (1975–76) demonstrated successfully in a study investigating the use of the syllable as a means to improve word recognition skills. Therefore, the Syllabary seems most appropriate for augmenting other forms of word recognition instruction for beginning readers or for readers experiencing difficulty with sound/symbol relationships.

Description of the Procedures

To employ the Syllabary strategy to improve readers' word identification skills, the teacher would follow these steps:

1. Teacher-dominated training.
2. Student-oriented practice.
3. Meaningful reading.

1. Teacher-Dominated Training   The teacher must not assume that students will readily grasp the thrust of the Syllabary. Teachers should start with familiar one-syllable words before moving on to less familiar polysyllabic words. Beginning the training with familiar monosyllabic words ensures that students will be able to call upon their own word-store.

The teacher might begin with words like *pen, sill, for,* and *wind* to illustrate how words like *penny, pencil, silly, before, windy, window,* and *windowsill* may be identified. In this way, words or word parts that are known become established in the word-store, enabling the students to use these known words in comparing unknown polysyllabic words. For example, knowledge of the words *wind* and *silly* will enable a student to make the appropriate comparisons to identify the word *windowsill*. Teacher questioning should accompany this step of acquainting students with the use of the Syllabary to ensure the match between syllables and the known word parts. Gleitman and Rozin (1973) have recommended the use of pictures as an aid to identifying unknown words by their syllabic parts. Some examples are shown in Figure 12–1.

FIGURE 12–1. USE OF PICTURES TO IDENTIFY UNKNOWN WORDS

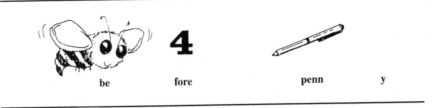

be   fore   penn   y

2. *Student-Oriented Practice* At this point in the strategy, the students are ready to begin more independent work with the concept of the Syllabary. Polysyllabic words are introduced for students to decode using the comparison/contrast strategy. Work may be done individually, but is probably best accomplished in pairs or in small groups until students have a firm grasp of the concept. An illustration of this type of practice follows.

Words like *sleepless, blanket,* and *pillow* might be introduced. The teacher is cautioned that it may be necessary to guide the students through a few practice words before they can work independently. For instance, using the syllabary to decode *sleepless,* the teacher can show children *less,* which might be a word in their memory-store or a word part, as in *unless.*

Again, the teacher is illustrating how to compare unknown words to known words or word parts in the students' word-stores. As students gain skill and confidence in using the comparison/contrast strategy, more complex words may be introduced. It is suggested that as students are exposed to new words, these words be written on word cards for review and reinforcement. The comparisons students have made from their word-stores may be written on the back of the card and may be referred to by the student if any difficulty arises during the review. Review with flash cards may be accomplished by pairing the students.

3. *Meaningful Reading* It is to be remembered that the implementation and usage of the Syllabary has occurred only when unknown words were seen in isolation. The ultimate test of any form of word identification occurs when the student becomes able to decode unknown words from a meaningful context. Hence, the follow-up step in the use of the Syllabary is to develop students' ability to deal with unknown words in story reading.

It is recommended that a short story consisting of a few paragraphs be constructed, using many of the words students have studied in isolation. Variations of those words or similar words should also be incorporated. For example, the polysyllabic words used in Section 2, student-oriented practice, should be used, but the teacher should attempt to use the variations (*sleeping; pill*) as well. In this way, the teacher can be assured that the comparison/contrast word identification strategy is being successfully implemented and has been transferred to real reading. An illustration of a short story using these words is included.

Nim looked very sleepy.
He threw his pillow on the floor.
He removed his blanket.

He had not gotten to sleep.
It had been a sleepless night.

Cautions and Comments

There are apparent merits to a word identification strategy employing the Syllabary; however, there are also a number of cautions of which teachers should be aware. First, although the syllable may be more easily pronounced in isolation than a phoneme, there are thousands of separate syllables in the English language. The task of dealing with each of these units might be overwhelming. For this reason, it should be used in conjunction with sound/symbol relationships.

Second, dialect differences in readers make for differences in syllable pronunciations. What may seem to be an obvious comparison with an individual's word-store may be obvious only to the teacher who also has a particular dialectical pattern. The students may not necessarily be contemplating the obvious comparison because of differences in their speech.

Third, the syllable is very much influenced by the stress it receives, i.e., the sound shifts with the stress (Goodman, 1973). For example, *site* becomes *situate* by adding more meaning units to the original word. This could very easily produce confusion for the younger reader.

Despite these problems, the Syllabary approach has been supported by research. Cunningham (1975–76, 1979) found differences between a group trained to use the Syllabary concept and a control group, when both groups attempted to decode unknown words.

References

Cunningham, P. M. 1975–76. Investigating a synthesized theory of mediated word identification. *Reading Research Quarterly* 11:127–143. Reports the results of an experiment designed to improve the word identification abilities of second graders using a Syllabary approach.

———. 1978. A compare/contrast theory of mediated word identification. *The Reading Teacher* 32:774–778. Reports a follow-up to the earlier study with fourth and fifth grade students.

Gibson, E. J., and H. Levin. 1975. *The psychology of reading*. Cambridge: MIT Press. Describes the use of the syllabic method as a means to learn to read in various languages.

Gleitman, L., and P. Rozin. 1973. Teaching reading by use of a syllabary. *Reading Research Quarterly* 8:447–483. Reports the successful use of the Syllabary with pictures as an introductory method to teach reading to both inner-city and suburban children.

Goodman, K. S. 1973. The 13th easy way to make learning to read difficult. *Reading Research Quarterly* 8:484–493. Challenges the use of the Syllabary as a means of teaching word identification skills.

Rozin, P., and L. R. Gleitman. 1977. The structure and acquisition of reading II: The reading process and the acquisition of the alphabetic principle. In *Toward a psychology of reading*, edited by A. Reber and O. Scarborough. Hillsdale, NJ: Erlbaum, 55–142. Describes research, theory, and practice built around the Syllabary approach.

Goodman's Reading Strategy Lessons

Purpose

The purpose of the Reading Strategy Lessons (Y. Goodman and Burke, 1972) is to increase students' awareness of the language and thought clues available during reading. The lessons are intended to: (1) help readers focus on aspects of written language not being processed effectively, and (2) support and strengthen readers' use of clues already being used.

Rationale

In Unit 1, Whole-Language was partially described and Reading Strategy Lessons were alluded to. Reading Strategy Lessons are based on Kenneth Goodman's (1967, 1975) notions of reading that suggest that there are certain universal reading processes. These processes are applied by all readers with varying levels of proficiency across different reading material. Toward the end of acquiring meaning, these processes include:

1. the reader's selecting the appropriate and necessary language cues to make predictions;
2. the reader's verifying these predictions; and
3. the reader's reprocessing language cues if predictions prove untenable.

A diagram developed by Y. Goodman, Burke, and Sherman (1974), given in Figure 12–2, depicts these notions.

The general goal of the Reading Strategy Lessons is to involve students in a meaningful reading situation that does not distract them from reading with understanding. To this end, some general guidelines are suggested:

1. The language of the material used should be similar to the language of the reader and of worthy literary quality.
2. The language of the material should not be ambiguous.
3. The language of the material should use redundant information naturally.
4. The content of the material used should be both interesting and significant to readers.
5. Lessons should afford students the opportunity to apply learnings from strategy lessons to actual reading situations.
6. Lessons should be related to students' ongoing learning experiences.
7. Lessons should be initiated when students' needs arise and terminate with students' boredom, disinterest, or accomplishment.

Intended Audience

It is suggested that almost all readers can benefit from Reading Strategy Lessons. The lessons may expand proficient readers' actual reading experiences and help them to build

FIGURE 12–2. PROFICIENT SILENT READING MODEL*

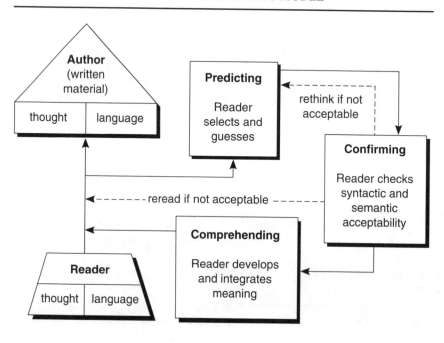

*The reader selects the appropriate language cues in order to *predict* as best he can, based upon his knowledge of language and his background experience. He *confirms* his predictions by testing these hypotheses or predictions. He does this by checking the syntactic and semantic acceptability of what he thinks he is reading against his knowledge of language and the world. Finally, he *compre-hends* those items he believes to be significant. He integrates this new meaning or knowledge into an established meaning system. He then interacts with the print again. The process is continuous, and as we read, we constantly add, alter, or reorganize the meanings. (Y. M. Goodman, Burke, and Sherman 1974, 18; used by permission of the author)

confidence. They can improve and support the strategies used by readers who exhibit evidence of effective, but inconsistent, use of strategies, or for whom the development of effective strategies has been disrupted.

Description of the Procedures

Reading Strategy Lessons are planned situations in which the use and availability of selected reading strategies are highlighted and reinforced. The situations are not intended to be panaceas for reading difficulties. Instead, teacher insight and teacher adaptation of the various strategies are suggested as essential if the needs of students at specific times are to be met.

The following description presents selected and representative strategy lessons. These descriptions have been organized under these headings:

1. Meeting the needs of inefficient readers
2. Meeting the needs of inconsistent readers
3. Meeting the needs of proficient readers

1. Meeting the Needs of Inefficient Readers   Y. Goodman (1975) describes inefficient readers this way:

> They use effective reading strategies occasionally in short phrases or sections of written material, but in most reading situations, these readers tend to omit words they think they do not know; they do not predict acceptable grammatical or semantic structures as they read; they read word for word using sounding out techniques without concern for meaning. They do everything they were taught to do in an isolated and unrelated fashion. They look for little words in big words and find fat/her an acceptable solution for father. They separate words between two middle consonants and often read lit/tul for little and prit/tee for pretty. When they do make occasional effective use of reading strategies, they lack confidence in deciding which strategy is most effective. They regress and correct in situations when it is inefficient to do so. For example, if such a reader reads can't for cannot because of the use of an appropriate predicting strategy, this is corrected when the reader picks up additional graphic cues. Such readers often think that graphic input is the most significant aspect of reading. Reading is not to discover something new or for enjoyment, it is to satisfy another person. (Y. M. Goodman, 1975, 39)*

According to Y. Goodman (1975), inefficient readers need first to realize that they are effective language users and that these abilities can help in reading. To this end, strategy lessons by which students become aware of the utility of their language cueing systems are suggested. For example, cloze procedures similar to the following are suggested to enable students to become more aware of their use of grammatical and meaning cues:

> "Stop!" said John. "Stop! Stop!" He could see that the little red _____ was heading straight for the bridge that had been washed away in the last storm. The driver of the _____ must have heard John. He hit the brakes and the _____ stopped. Its motor stopped and the driver jumped out.

To deal with some of the specific inefficiencies of readers, other strategies are suggested.

a. For readers whose omissions or substitutions result in meaning loss, teachers are urged to encourage them to make meaningful substitutions for omissions. Students might produce words that have some related meaning or words with a close meaning. This might be done incidentally, by encouraging the reader to ask, "What word could go in this spot?" "Why do you think so?" The teacher might take a more systematic approach, too, using exercises like these:

*Copyright 1975 by the National Council of Teachers of English. Reprinted with permission.

1. Present the students a passage with systematic deletions of words or phrases and encourage readers to use the context to suggest alternative possibilities.

   They _____ around the pool.

   _____ enjoyed swimming.

   The children ran for the bus. They had slept late. Just as they arrived at the bus stop,

   _____ .

2. Present the students with a passage containing nonsense words for significant verbs or nouns and have students replace them with real words.

   The buemt hopped through the grass and disappeared into its burrow. The buemt had a little tail of white fur and long ears. The buemt loved to nibble on leaves.

3. Present the students either a passage containing intentional significant miscues, or have the students prepare a passage containing certain intentional miscues. The reader's task would be to locate these miscues.

b. For readers who have developed habitual associations between words or phrases that have close graphic or phonic similarities, such as *for-from, saw-was, though-thought,* lessons using carefully controlled linguistic material are suggested. For example, the students might be asked to read or write stories that use or elicit one of the confused words or use both words nonambiguously.

The following is an example of a suggested method for dealing with students' confusions between *was* and *saw*. First, present the student with sentences containing one of the habitually associated words: for example, "It was father." In this setting, it is not likely that students will produce "It saw father." When the students show evidence of being able to handle one of the habitually associated words, introduce the students to material in which both words are used nonambiguously.

2. Meeting the Needs of Inconsistent Readers   Y. Goodman (1975) describes inconsistent readers in the following statement:

> These readers use effective reading strategies when the material is highly interesting to them or when it is easy because it has a low concept load. However, when these readers find themselves reading material which is complex, they use less efficient reading strategies. They stop searching for meaning and end up sounding out or word calling. When asked how they handle any particular reading problem, such readers often say they sound words out; they may be unaware that they use context to read or they may believe the teacher disapproves of it. Strategy lessons help these readers become aware of the various effective reading strategies they already use when reading easy material, permitting them to transfer effective reading strategies to more difficult reading materials. (Y. M. Goodman 1975, 138)*

As described by Y. Goodman and Burke in the manual *Reading Miscue Inventory* (1972), inconsistent readers include the reader who makes some effective use of reading strategies and the reader who makes moderately effective use of reading strategies. In natural reading situations, it is suggested that these readers be encouraged to make judgments while reading. They should be encouraged to ask self-monitoring questions such as "Does what I am reading make sense?" "If it doesn't, what should I do about it?" If the material is not making sense, it is suggested that the readers be encouraged either to continue to see if the selection will begin to make sense, or to judge whether to move to an alternative selection.

Strategy lessons for these readers are designed to develop their awareness of the transfer value of effective reading strategies from easy to difficult material. For example, in the context of easy material, readers might become aware of the strategies used to deal with unfamiliar words and to differentiate the significance of words.

Here is an example of a strategy lesson serving these purposes. It is taken from Goodman's article "Reading Strategy Lessons: Expanding Reading Effectiveness" (1975). This story uses a concept or word that is probably not well known.

> The boy was looking for Petoskies. He was walking slowly to make sure he wouldn't miss them. He usually found a number of them each time he went looking for them. They were not easy to find because they were the same color as the sand. He enjoyed looking for Petoskies on the beach. He was helping his mother, too, since she used them in her work. She was an artist and made jewelry with them. Petoskies are usually bluish gray in their natural state with the fossils in them somewhat darker. When Petoskies are polished, the gray color becomes lighter and the fossils take on a brown character. Petoskies are found only on the shores of the Great Lakes. (P. 138)

To help students gain meaning for the unknown word, the teacher would:

> Put this story on an overhead projector and use it with a small group of readers. Tell them not to worry about pronouncing every word as they read. Cover the entire story and move the cover down, exposing one more sentence with each move. As each sentence is exposed, ask the children to tell what the word (point to Petoskies) means. After each sentence, ask the children to revise their guesses about the word. Do not pronounce the word for the children, nor should you ask them to pronounce it. If any reader does say the word, the pronunciation should be accepted without comment. Only after the story is completely exposed and the meaning of Petoskies fully discussed should you ask for variations in pronunciation and finally tell the group how you think it may be pronounced. This is an interesting lesson because many teachers may not pronounce Petoskies the same way the people who polish and sell these stones do. (Y. M. Goodman 1975, 138)*

Other strategy lessons for these readers might be to have students judge the significance or insignificance of words, phrases, or sentences contained in a selection. For example, students might be asked to read a selection and either delete or underline redundant words.

3. Meeting the Needs of Proficient Readers   Proficient readers are considered to be using reading strategies effectively. Therefore, Reading Strategy Lessons afford these readers an opportunity to develop confidence in the use of these strategies. Specifically, strategy lessons might broaden and deepen their reading experiences. To deepen the readers' experiences, they might be encouraged to anticipate plot, theme, and events, to perceive subtleties and inferential meaning, to realize the influence of background and experience on interpretation, and to appreciate that other readers have different interpretations about the same reading experience. To broaden their reading experiences, such students might be given the opportunity to read a variety of different types of reading materials in varying literary styles. Obviously, attention should be centered on improving their reading-to-learn abilities.

Cautions and Comments

Reading Strategy Lessons represent an attempt to extend K. Goodman's notions of the reading process to classroom practices. According to this view, learning to read "ought not to be very much more difficult than the process by which one learns the oral mode of language. That is, provided that the same principles of relevance, meaningfulness, and motivation for communication which characterized the learning of oral language have been adhered to" (Cambourne 1976–77, 610). The ramification of this notion for instruction, specifically phonics instruction, lies in the following assumptions: decoding to speech or sound is not a necessary step between grapheme and reading for meaning; a hierarchy of subskills is not a necessary aspect of learning reading; maximizing the internalized knowledge of a reader should be encouraged; beginning readers use the same process as fluent readers and should learn to read as naturally; and phonics analysis is neither useful nor necessary.

In terms of the latter assumption, Goodman has been critical of both the emphasis upon phonics and the methodologies proposed. He has claimed that phonic approaches to reading are preoccupied with the erroneous notion that reading requires precise letter identification. That is, he disagrees with the notion that reading involves exact, detailed, sequential perception and identification of letters, words, and spelling patterns. His main argument is that we do not and cannot read letter by letter. A good reader is so efficient in sampling and predicting that he uses the least available information necessary. A less proficient reader needs the confidence to engage in sampling and predicting; encouraging less proficient readers to use too many cues, to be cautious, may detract from the readers' addressing meaning.

In recent years, the growth of interest in a whole-language orientation to teaching has spurred the development of additional strategy lessons, many of which extend to comprehension. For example, Harste, Short, and Burke (1988) offer several suggestions for strategy lessons as do Watson and Crowley (1987), Kucer and Rhodes (1986), and Atwell and Rhodes (1984). Strategy lessons are not intended to be exhaustive, but to illustrate to teachers ways they might develop their own strategies, based upon a reasonable understanding of the reader and the strategy lessons' rationale. In this regard, the suggestions are sufficiently explicit for appropriate instructional adaptations at most levels. They do need further amplification, though, especially to meet the needs of primary level and advanced high school students. Finally, those teachers needing more background before they construct their own strategy lesson with K. Goodman's ideas are directed to the reference section that follows and the description and references for Whole-Language in Unit 1.

References

Allen, P. D., and D. J. Watson, eds. 1976. *Findings of research in miscue analysis: Classroom implications.* Urbana, IL: National Council of Teachers of English and Educational Resources Information Center. Includes a collection of articles addressing an extended discussion of the research base of Goodman's ideas and its relevance to instruction.

Atwell, N., and L. K. Rhodes. 1984. Strategy lessons as alternatives to skill lessons in reading. *Journal of Reading* 27:700–705. Offer suggestions for planning and implementing strategy lessons.

Cambourne, B. 1976–77. Getting to Goodman: An analysis of the Goodman model of reading with some suggestions for evaluation. *Reading Research Quarterly* 12:605–636. Describes the major features of Goodman's model, its implications, and ways in which it might be reevaluated.

Goodman, K. S. 1965. A linguistic study of cues and miscues in reading. *Elementary English* 42:639–643. Presents aspects of Goodman's research and the bases for Reading Strategy Lessons.

———. 1967. Reading: A psycholinguistic guessing game. *Journal of the Reading Specialist* 6:126–135. Presents Goodman's original definition of reading and describes its ramifications.

———. 1975. The reading process. In *Language and reading,* edited by S. S. Smiley and J. C. Towner. Bellingham: Western Washington State College. Presents an updated model of Goodman's reading process that revises and expands upon the earlier model.

Goodman, K. S., and Y. M. Goodman. 1979. Learning to read is natural. In *Theory and practice of early reading,* edited by L. B. Resnick and P. A. Weaver. Hillsdale, NJ: Erlbaum. Presents a discussion of the rationale behind a wholistic view of reading and teaching reading.

———. 1982. A whole-language comprehension-centered view of reading development. In *Basic skills issues and choices: Approach to basic skills instruction,* Vol. 2, edited by L. Reed and S. Ward. St. Louis: CEMREL. De-

scribes a Whole-Language, comprehension-centered reading program and suggests ways to implement such a program in the classroom, including modifying a basal reader program.

Goodman, Y. M. 1975. Reading strategy lessons: Expanding reading effectiveness. In *Help for the reading teacher: New directions in research,* edited by W. Page. National Council of Teachers of English and Educational Resources Information Center, 34–41. Presents the rationale for and several examples of Reading Strategy Lessons.

Goodman, Y. M., and C. L. Burke. 1972. *Reading miscue inventory.* New York: Macmillan. A manual with suggestions for using strategy lessons, based upon students' identified needs.

———. 1980. *Reading strategies: Focus on comprehension.* New York: Holt, Rinehart & Winston. Presents a resource book of reading strategies for teachers.

———. 1987. Miscue analysis and curriculum development. In *Reading miscue inventory: Alternative procedures.* New York: Richard C. Owens. Offers guidelines for developing an individualized program based on miscue analysis.

Goodman, Y. M., C. L. Burke, and B. Sherman. 1974. *Strategies in reading.* New York: Richard C. Owen. A handbook of reading strategies that provides the theory and practice of strategy lessons.

Harste, J., K. G. Short, and C. Burke. 1988. *Creating classrooms for authors.* Portsmouth, NH: Heinemann. Offers several classroom activities and strategy lessons.

Kucer, S. B., and L. K. Rhodes. 1986. Counterpart strategies. *The Reading Teacher* 40:186–193. Includes various strategies that help students use composing as a means of comprehending.

Watson, D., and P. Crowley. 1987. How can we implement a whole-language approach? In *Reading process and practice,* edited by C. Weaver. Portsmouth, NH: Heinemann. Offers an extended discussion of strategy lessons including several that are oriented to comprehension.

Oral Reading

UNIT OVERVIEW

Current practices seem to indicate that much instructional time in our elementary class-rooms is devoted to oral reading. Although there is value in oral reading for beginning reading instruction, there is some question as to the effectiveness of the way the activity may be conducted in the classroom.

The most frequent oral reading activity is that of "round-robin" or "circle" reading. In this activity, each student in turn reads a small portion aloud to his or her reading group or to the class as a whole, while the other students follow along silently. This practice is used primarily in conjunction with the basal reading program.

Despite its widespread use, research does not support this practice. Research by Anderson, Mason, and Shirey (1984) and research reviews by Allington (1984) and Brulnsma (1981) suggest that the practice of round-robin reading is suspect. They conclude that its use in classrooms is not defensible if comprehension is the goal.

Oral reading is a communication skill. It is a way of delivering information or providing entertainment to listeners. If used in this way, oral reading would seem best done for a specific purpose, and a student's performance would seem best evaluated in terms of its communicative value.

The four strategies discussed in this unit are designed to aid the teacher in planning oral reading activities that have specific purposes. Two of the strategies are mainly developmental in nature and focus on the communicative aspects of oral reading. The other two strategies tend to be used with students who may be having difficulty in reading. As a preview of this unit, a brief summary of the strategies follows.

Choral and Repeated Reading.   Choral and Repeated Reading is a strategy designed to give students practice in reading with the proper expression. Useful as a whole-class reading activity, this strategy provides students with active involvement in print and puts prime emphasis on interpreting meaning.

Radio Reading.   Providing practice for students in both reading and listening, Radio Reading focuses instruction on the ultimate goal of oral reading—communicating a message. It is useful throughout the grades wherever oral reading is one of the teaching methods, particularly as a substitute for round-robin reading.

Echo Reading.   Echo Reading is designed to foster the acquisition of vocabulary and oral fluency. It is most effective in a one-to-one instructional situation and primarily with students in the elementary grades.

Topping's Paired Reading.   In Topping's Paired Reading tutors read along with children and adjust their oral participation to the difficulty the children experience. In this way children not only are given practice in reading but also have a model of fluent reading.

References

Allington, R. L. 1984. Oral reading. In *Handbook of reading research,* edited by P. D. Pearson, R. Barr, M. L. Kamil, and P. Mosenthal. New York: Longman.

Anderson, R. C., J. Mason, and L. Shirey. 1984. The reading group: An experimental investigation of a labyrinth. *Reading Research Quarterly* 20:6–39.

Brulnsma, R. 1981. A critique of "round-robin" oral reading in the elementary classroom. *Reading-Canada-Lecture* 1:78–81.

Choral and Repeated Reading

Purpose

The purpose of Choral and Repeated Reading is to: (1) provide practice for students in reading with the expression necessary to add to meaning; (2) develop self-assurance by giving every student a chance to function as part of a group; and (3) aid students in developing an appreciation for oral expression.

Rationale

Artificial barriers are sometimes created by students and between students when oral reading occurs. For example, poorer readers may not like to read orally, and the shy student who rarely volunteers in any class activity will often be hesitant about oral reading. On the other hand, the overly confident student, if given the opportunity, might dominate an oral reading exercise.

Choral and Repeated Reading provides the teacher with a socialization tool. Poor readers as well as shy ones can use the whole-group format to avoid humiliating corrections while they gain confidence in themselves. The obtrusive student may be tempered through the same whole-group format, which discourages that student from showing off.

In addition, Choral and Repeated Reading can develop students' interest in the creative forms of language such as poetry, whereas previously students might have had negative feelings toward such a medium.

Finally, Choral and Repeated Reading provides students with the opportunity to become actively involved with print, placing the prime emphasis on interpreting and expressing meaning. Many times, words and not meaning are emphasized in reading activities. Choral and Repeated Reading develops students' abilities to read for mean-ing—the eventual goal of the act of reading.

Intended Audience

Choral and Repeated Reading is suitable for any school population. Grade level and achievement level are inconsequential because of the group approach of this strategy. Class size also matters little, as the teacher can divide any large group into smaller, more manageable choral groups.

Description of the Procedures

As a substitute for oral reading as commonly practiced, Choral and Repeated Reading presents the teacher with a unique instructional activity that can unite all readers, regard-less of ability, in a common reading experience. At the same time, this strategy can provide students with entertainment, group involvement, and practice in reading with self-expression.

In order for Choral Reading and Repeated Reading to be carried out effectively, the teacher must be prepared to deal with:

1. Developing rhythmic sensitivity
2. Casting

1. Developing Rhythmic Sensitivity   Before Choral and Repeated Reading can be ac-complished successfully, the students should be guided by the teacher through progressive steps to develop their sensitivity for rhythm. The teacher should not make any assump-tions concerning students' ability in Choral and Repeated Reading. By guiding them through the activity first, the teacher is assured that students have the framework to establish eventual independence in that activity.

The concept of modeling is very appropriate with this activity. One way to impress young children is for the teacher to be an example. By showing students that poetry and other creative forms are enjoyable, by sharing these things with the class, and by demon-strating the desired self-expression, the teacher should find that students experience little difficulty in beginning Choral and Repeated Reading.

A variety of selections should be used to aid students in acquiring a sensitivity for rhythm, mood, and voice modulation. The teacher should demonstrate proper phrasing, tempo, and enunciation with the selections for Choral and Repeated Reading and, through discussion, emphasize the importance of proper expression in conveying a poem's mood and meaning.

Choral and Repeated Reading might begin with short selections, preferably memo-rized. Eventually, longer selections, possibly with the rhythm marked, may be introduced.

To provide additional reinforcement for students, a tape recorder may be used for evaluative purposes. Students may also participate as critical listeners by separating themselves from the choral groups and providing feedback. After a few successful expe-riences, students may begin, and be encouraged, to suggest other ways selections might be interpreted and read. Sound effects and pantomiming may also be used.

Finally, when selecting material for Choral and Repeated Reading, care should be taken to ensure that selections have an easily understandable theme and a distinct rhythm.

2. Casting Casting is a term used in Choral and Repeated Reading to refer to the way a selection is divided into parts and assigned to members of the class for reading. Once the rhythm and tempo of a particular selection are understood, the teacher and students should choose from the following methods of organization for Choral and Repeated Reading:

(a) refrain;

(b) dialogue;

(c) line-a-child or line-a-choir;

(d) cumulative; and

(e) unison.

a. *Refrain.* With certain poems that have a chorus, either the teacher or a designated group can recite the narrative, with the rest of the class responding in the chorus. The refrain provides a good beginning for Choral and Repeated Reading.

b. *Dialogue.* Poems with considerable dialogue (often a question-and-answer format) readily lend themselves to a two-part casting. Alternate responses can be made between boys and girls or between high and low voices.

c. *Line-a-child or line-a-choir.* This arrangement engages three or more individuals or choirs in rhythmic response. Some lines also may be spoken in unison by all participants. This type of Choral and Repeated Reading has variety and provides a challenge for students to respond in the exact tempo.

d. *Cumulative.* In this form of Choral and Repeated Reading, the intent is to create a crescendo effect. Unlike the line-a-choir method, the introduction of a new group to the presentation is permanent, not temporary. This is a more difficult form of Choral and Repeated Reading because voice quality, rather than volume, is necessary to attain a significant climax.

e. *Unison.* This is the most difficult type of Choral and Repeated Reading, even though it has the simplest structure. An entire group or class reads every line together. The potential for problems in blending and timing is very great in unison reading. Monotonous reading often results if the children are inexperienced and insufficient direction has been given by the teacher. This method is best suited for intermediate level students.

The following verse from a poem provides an example of how one type of casting may be used in a Choral and Repeated Reading exercise.

The Triantiwontigongolope*

1ST CHILD: There's a funny insect that you do not often spy,

2ND CHILD: And it isn't quite a spider, and it isn't quite a fly;

---

*"The Triantiwontigongolope" from *A Book for Kids* by C. J. Dennis is reprinted by permission of Angus & Robertson Publishers.

1ST CHILD: It is something like a beetle, and a little like a bee,

2ND CHILD: But nothing like a woolly grub that climbs upon a tree.

1ST CHILD: Its name is quite a hard one, but you'll learn it soon, I hope.

1ST CHILD: So, try:

CHORUS: Tri-

ALL: Tri————anti————wonti————

CHILDREN: Triantiwontigongolope

The refrain in this selection can be used with one group of students reciting the narrative while the other recites the chorus. Individual lines or stanzas of the poem may also be assigned to groups of students and the line-a-choir, cumulative, or unison casting may be implemented, depending on the sophistication of the students.

Cautions and Comments

Choral and Repeated Reading provides students with a unique and valuable language experience, since it integrates reading with two other linguistic skills: listening and speaking. In addition, Choral and Repeated Reading builds positive attitudes toward participation in groups and develops students' imaginative abilities.

However, Choral and Repeated Reading can contribute little to the reading and language development of students if it is not used properly. A common practice has been for the teacher to select a passage for Choral Reading, teach it to students who either read it well or memorize it, assign parts of it to groups, and then drill the students until the passage sounds good according to the teacher's conception of what good Choral and Repeated Reading is.

This practice negates the instructional objectives of: (1) making the selection meaningful to the students, (2) developing creativity, and (3) developing self-expression. Strict, tense drill directed by the teacher does not set the proper learning conditions, but active involvement on the part of the students does.

Another area of concern in Choral and Repeated Reading is maintaining the students' focus on the meaning being conveyed. Students have a tendency to focus attention on their delivery of the selection and sometimes lapse into overdramatics. It must be emphasized that the Choral and Repeated Reading is on display, not the students themselves.

A further meaning-related concern in Choral and Repeated Reading is that all students should have a similar understanding of the selection. This is essential in order to convey effectively, as a group, a depth of feeling and sensitivity to words.

A last area of concern is voice quality. Each word must be enunciated at the same time by the whole group—a difficult task to accomplish for some students. Finally, students must also learn that it is not necessary to read loudly when expressing themselves; rather, they should read with warm but firm voices, and the Choral and Repeated Reading itself will take care of the volume.

References

Dowhower, S. L. 1989. Repeated reading: Research into practice. *The Reading Teacher* 42:502–507. A description of the benefits of Repeated Reading, with suggestions for classroom practice.

Herman, P. A. 1985. The effect of repeated readings on reading rate, speech pauses, and word recognition memory. *Reading Research Quarterly* 20:553–574. Research study demonstrating that repeated practice can increase poor readers' comprehension of text.

Koskinen, P. S., and I. H. Blum. 1985. Paired repeated reading: A classroom strategy for developing fluent reading. *The Reading Teacher* 40:70–75. Describes the use of Choral and Repeated Reading with only a pair of readers.

Lopardo, G., and M. Sadow. 1982. Criteria and procedures for the method of repeated readings. *Journal of Reading* 26:156–160. Describes how to use Repeated Reading in the classroom.

Petty, W. T., D. C. Petty, and M. F. Becking. 1985. *Experiences in language: Tools and techniques for language arts methods.* Boston: Allyn and Bacon. Explores the use of Choral Reading as an enjoyable way to interpret literature.

Temple, C. A., and J. W. Gillett. 1984. *Language arts: Learning processes and teaching practices.* Boston: Little, Brown. Provides examples of using Choral Reading in the language arts program.

Radio Reading

Purpose

The purpose of Radio Reading (Greene, 1979) is to provide help for students in: (1) accurately communicating a message through oral reading; (2) comprehending at the listening level; and (3) summarizing and restating an orally read message.

Rationale

Radio Reading provides the teacher with a viable alternative to the common practice of round-robin reading. Too often, oral reading situations deteriorate into word-attack sessions. Unlike round-robin reading, Radio Reading does not allow for prompting or correction. Rather, it focuses instruction on the ultimate goal of oral reading—to comprehend and communicate a message.

Radio Reading derives its name from the analogy between a radio announcer's talking to a listening audience and the oral reading situation. The reader functions as the radio announcer with a script, and the listeners serve as the audience listening to a radio program. It is the purpose of the reader to communicate accurately a message in oral reading. The listeners respond by discussing and restating the message, and evaluating whether the passage was clearly rendered.

Intended Audience

Radio Reading is appropriate throughout the grades, whenever oral reading is used in instruction. It is particularly suitable in the elementary grades as a substitute for round-robin reading; however, it is also useful in the content areas, especially where interpretive reading is done. Radio Reading may be used in either a one-to-one or a group setting.

Description of the Procedures

Radio Reading creates a safe, nonthreatening atmosphere for the reader, in which comprehension, not word-perfect reading, is the primary instructional goal. In order to implement a Radio Reading lesson properly, Searfoss (1975) recommended that four steps be followed: (1) getting started, (2) communicating the message, (3) checking for understanding, and (4) clarifying an unclear message.

1. Getting Started   In this step of the lesson, the teacher sets the tone for the proper atmosphere by explaining the procedure to the students. The simple ground rules of radio reading are these: the reader reads and the listeners listen.

The teacher leads the activity by explaining the remaining three steps of the strategy to the students. Emphasis is placed on the responsibility of the reader to communicate a message to the listeners, just as a radio announcer communicates to his audience. Since the audience (listeners) will not have a copy of the material, the teacher instructs them to listen closely.

It is also the job of the teacher to select materials for Radio Reading that are appropriate in difficulty and length. The materials should be challenging, though not frustrating, and can be narrative or expository in nature. For example, short stories or selections from basal-type readers would be appropriate. The material should be of reasonable length so as not to overwhelm the listener. As a guideline, Searfoss (1975) recommended that each reader should orally read only a paragraph or two in the lower grades, progressing up to as much as a page in the intermediate grades.

2. Communicating the Message   Since the job of the reader is to convey a clear message, the reader is permitted to change words, insert new words, or omit words where warranted. The role of the reader in this activity is similar to that of the fluent, silent reader; both are attending to meaning rather than to individual words. The reader is responsible, however, for deciding when he or she needs help with an unknown word. Greene (1979) stated that when giving directions for Radio Reading, the teacher should say, "If you come to a word you need and you cannot figure it out, put your finger beside it and ask, 'What is that word?'"

Again, since Radio Reading is comprehension-oriented, and further delay on a word would increase the probability of short-term memory interference, the teacher or other listeners should refrain from prompting or beginning a word-attack lesson. The reader should be given the word immediately so that he or she can continue, with as little interruption as possible, to process meaning.

3. Checking for Understanding   The listening audience has control over the student's oral reading and, if necessary, over rereading. If an accurate message has been communicated by the reader, the check for understanding will be brief. The discussion of what was heard, whether teacher-led or student-initiated, will move quickly. After a quick summary has been volunteered, other listeners can confirm the message. Allowances are made for inferences and rewording, as long as accuracy is maintained.

Thus, the reader earns the right to continue reading by communicating a clear message. In a group situation, the role of the radio reader may rotate to give every reader an opportunity to read.

4. Clarifying an Unclear Message   If the listeners give conflicting information or are able to detect errors during the discussion, the reader has not communicated a clear message. It is the radio readers' responsibility to clear up the confusion by returning to the story and rereading the portions of concern. It is still the reader's job to achieve clarity in the passage. The listener may decide that the reader needs assistance to achieve that goal. However, as before, prompting must be avoided to maintain the necessary atmosphere for radio reading.

Cautions and Comments

Since Radio Reading differs greatly from current oral reading practices, the teacher should be certain the four steps outlined are followed. Two areas of caution warrant discussion to enable the teacher to maintain the proper instructional climate for Radio Reading.

One area of caution concerns the students' response to the procedural steps of Radio Reading. Ideally, the students will quickly understand the rules and follow them. Radio Reading will then be performed smoothly, i.e., the students will read as well as they can, requesting help when necessary. In reality, students may manifest other types of responses to this instructional format, causing possible difficulties for the teacher in its implementation.

One difficulty is for the reader to request help at an inappropriate time. Such an occasion arises when it is apparent that the reader already knows the word or has adequate word-attack skills to decode the word. The only recourse the listener has in this situation is to tell the reader the requested word.

It is most likely correct to assume that the reader is testing the rules concerning the reader's and the listener's responsibilities for unknown words, rather than simply displaying deficiencies in reading. Thus, not responding to a request for help, or prompting the reader, violates the contract between the reader and the listener and makes the rules of Radio Reading worthless. If the reader requests help, it must be immediately supplied.

An additional response that a student may manifest is not to request help when he or she does need it. The reader then will be redirected to render a clear message after the oral reading. On the other hand, failure to respond at all presents the listener with an entirely different situation. In either an individual or a group situation, the appropriate response for the listener, after waiting a reasonable length of time, is simply to say, "What's the rule?"

In an individual situation, it may be necessary for the listener to restate the rule concerning unknown words. If a response is still not elicited, then Radio Reading should be ended for the day. A clarification of the procedural steps is then in order. In a group setting, a no-response situation is much easier to deal with. Anytime the radio announcer (reader) ceases to broadcast, the listeners will tune to a new "station," i.e., the first reader's right to continue reading ceases, and a new radio reader takes over.

A second caution concerning the instructional climate for Radio Reading is the tendency of teachers to prompt, to correct, or to initiate a word-attack lesson when a reader encounters difficulty or requests help. Such tactics are inappropriate with this strategy. It disrupts the process of reading and converts the activity into a word-attack lesson.

If the reader makes an error and the teacher corrects it, the responsibility for correctness shifts to the teacher and deprives the reader of the responsibility for meaningful reading. Prompting also removes from the reader the responsibility for relaying the message.

There is clearly no place for prompting or for correcting in Radio Reading. If an error is made in an oral rendering, the burden of dealing with it rests with the listener, who must be skillful enough to pick it out and remember it until the passage has been read. It is the reader's responsibility alone to render a clear, comprehensible message from the assigned passage.

References

Greene, F. P. 1979. Radio reading. In *Reading comprehension at four linguistic levels,* edited by C. Pennock. Newark, DE: International Reading Association, 104–107. Discusses the concept of Radio Reading and describes the procedure.

Searfoss, L. W. 1975. Radio reading. *The Reading Teacher* 29:295–296. Outlines four basic steps in implementing Radio Reading.

Echo Reading

Purpose

The purpose of Echo Reading is to increase the reading fluency of students who have had difficulty in reading.

Rationale

Echo Reading was originally conceived by Heckelman (1969) and is also known as the "neurological impress method" or the "impress method." Heckelman hypothesized that current reading methods allow a student to commit many mistakes, which become very deeply imprinted and are not easily corrected. Because of the time and difficulty involved in correcting these mistakes, students do not make any progress in reading.

Heckelman believed that implementing a new learning procedure could suppress the older methods of learning and thus enable children to read. As a result of this thinking, the impress—or echo—method was used. Its intent was to expose readers only to accurate, fluid reading patterns. After a certain length of time for instruction, the correct reading patterns would become deeply impressed and would replace previously learned patterns.

Intended Audience

Echo Reading has been used almost exclusively with readers who have had difficulty progressing in reading. The procedure should be employed in a one-to-one instructional situation.

Description of the Procedures

The Echo method is a technique that involves the student's visual, aural, oral, and tactile abilities in the process of learning to read. It is recommended that the procedure be used for 15 minutes a day in consecutive daily sessions. After a total instructional time of 7 to 12 hours, there is often a significant rise in achievement by the reader.

At the start of Echo Reading, the reading material used should be at a level slightly lower than the reader can handle adequately. By using material on which the reader has already experienced success, the teacher increases the probability that the echo method will get off to a successful beginning. Material to be used with the procedure should be varied to maintain the student's interest. Newspapers, magazines, and fiction and nonfiction books might be used.

Before Echo Reading starts, some preliminary instructions are given to the student. The student is told to disregard accompanying pictures in the story. The teacher also indicates to the student not to be concerned with reading at all; rather, the student is asked to do as well as possible in terms of just saying the words. The student is told only to slide his or her eyes smoothly across the line of print without stopping or going back. At no time does the teacher attempt to correct any mistakes the student may make.

As Echo Reading begins, the reader is seated slightly in front of the teacher with both participants jointly holding the reading material. Both read in unison; the voice of the teacher is directed into the reader's ear at this close range. In beginning sessions, the teacher is supposed to read slightly louder and faster than the student. This aspect allows the reader to make maximum use of the aural and visual senses involved in this strategy.

As the student begins to master the material and gains confidence in saying the words, the teacher may choose to read with a softer voice or even lag slightly behind the student. If the student falters, the teacher should resort to immediate reinforcement by increasing loudness and speed.

In the beginning sessions, the goal is to establish a fluent reading pattern. Therefore, it is often necessary for the teacher and student to repeat sentences and paragraphs several times until that goal is reached. Once this is accomplished, the teacher and student may move on to more difficult materials. Usually no more than two or three minutes of repetitive reading is required before a fluent reading pattern is established. It is recommended that the teacher regularly reinforce any success the student meets.

To accompany their voices, the teacher's finger simultaneously moves along the line of print. The finger is placed directly under the word as it is spoken, in a smooth, continual fashion. It is emphasized that the flow of the teacher's finger must coincide with the speed and flow of the oral reading.

Once accustomed to the Echo method, the student can begin to take over this function from the teacher. At first, the teacher may need to help the student by guiding the student's finger until a smooth, continuous movement is established.

The coordination of the movement of the finger with the flow of the oral rendition is essential. It is argued that if the teacher's finger is not placed under the word as it is spoken, the aural and oral sensory modes will not be operating in conjunction with the visual and tactile modes (Heckelman, 1969).

The major concern of the Echo method is the style, not the accuracy, of the oral rendition. At no time during the reading is the student questioned on the material, either for word recognition or comprehension. However, if the student volunteers any information, the teacher permits it.

If success with the method has not been achieved by the fourth hour of its use, the procedure should be terminated. A changeover to another method is then suggested.

Cautions and Comments

Particularly in the beginning stages of Echo Reading, a student may experience some difficulty, due to the novelty of the situation or to the conflict that can arise between aural and visual input. A teacher might counter student complaints of not being able to keep up by urging the student to disregard mistakes and to continue reading. Slowing down slightly to a more comfortable speed or rereading some initial lines may eliminate student discomfort with the technique. However, forcing students to process visual and auditory information concurrently may require them to change their natural processing procedures for these types of input. This change may cause undue difficulty and warrant termination of this time-consuming procedure.

Echo Reading seems to place an undue emphasis on the psychomotor skills involved in reading, rather than upon the reading-thinking processes that direct those skills. If reading-thinking processes direct the use of aural and visual skills, then, logically, reading improvement should begin with these reading-thinking processes. In other words, the emphasis given psychomotor skills within Echo Reading seems misplaced and in danger of detracting from meaningful reading experiences by which the student might acquire visual and aural skills both naturally and incidentally.

References

Heckelman, R. G. 1969. A neurological-impress method of remedial-reading instruction. *Academic Therapy* 4:277–282. Introduces and describes the concept of the impress method.

———. 1986. N.I.M. re-visited. *Academic Therapy* 21:411–420. An update on the impress method.

Hollingsworth, P. M. 1978. An experimental approach to the impress method of teaching reading. *The Reading Teacher* 31:624–626. Describes results from the use of the impress method.

Memory, D. M. 1981. The impress method: A status report of a new remedial reading technique. *Journal of Research and Development in Education* 14:102–114. A review of the literature of the impress method.

Topping's Paired Reading

Purpose

The purpose of Topping's Paired Reading (Topping, 1987a) is to provide a simple system where tutors with little training could improve the reading performance of tutees of lesser reading ability.

Rationale

Originally conceived as a means to use the untapped talents of parents to help improve their children's reading ability, Paired Reading now has expanded to include pairings of adults (Scoble, Topping, and Wigglesworth, 1988) and children (Topping, 1989) in peer tutoring situations. In all cases a tutor of greater reading ability is paired with a reader of lesser ability in a reading-together situation. The tutor provides immediate support to the tutee when an error may occur, which frees the reader from word-by-word decoding and allows him or her to develop fluency. The tutor acts as a participant model in which a continuous prompt for correct reading is given to the reader.

Topping's Paired Reading is thought of as a very inexpensive way to deal with the multitude of people whose reading ability is not adequate. The technique employed is simple to learn and use, therefore, enabling it to be used widely in a variety of learning situations.

Intended Audience

Topping's Paired Reading can be used in virtually unlimited reading situations in which two readers, one of greater and one of lesser ability, work together.

Description of the Procedure

Topping's Paired Reading will be discussed in the following manner. The standard strategy will first be described; then adaptations for peer tutoring with children will be discussed.

1. The Standard Strategy   The Paired Reading session begins with the tutee selecting a book or other reading material at any level of readability that is within the comfort and competence level of the tutor. Thus, the reading interests of both are taken into account to some extent. The tutor also has the responsibility of discussing the book before reading to promote understanding. Additional discussion and questioning may occur throughout the reading.

The pair read out loud together with the tutor adjusting to the tutee's natural reading speed. If the tutee should make an error or gives no response to a word in five seconds, the standard correction procedure is applied. The tutor says the word correctly, and the tutee is required to repeat it before the reading continues. Because the correction procedure is so simple, the possibility of the tutoring situation turning into a word-attack lesson is minimized. At regular intervals the tutor should also praise the tutee for correct reading behavior.

At any point in the reading, or when an easier text is used, a prearranged nonverbal signal to let the tutor know that the tutee wishes to read alone can be used. The tutor can continue to give praise and initiate discussion of the material but does not rejoin the reading until an error is made. As before, the correction procedure is employed and reading together recommences. Figure 13–1 illustrates the procedure for Topping's Paired Reading.

FIGURE 13–1. PAIRED READING PROCEDURE

2. Adaptations for Peer Tutoring   Topping's Paired Reading can easily be employed in the classroom when coupled with the notion of peer tutoring. Tutorial pairs can be trained easily, use the high interest materials available in the classroom, and probably be incorporated into the normal routine without much concern. However, care will need to be given to the organization of this peer tutorial endeavor.

Topping suggests starting with a few pairs and letting others ask to become involved. The ability difference between the tutor and tutee should be neither too large nor too small. Another consideration is to avoid mixing strong and weak personalities. The teacher will also need to have standby tutors available should absences occur; these will need to be particularly competent readers, as they will deal with a variety of less able tutees. Information will probably need to be sent at least to the parents of the tutors communicating the benefits to all participants; permission of the parents may also be needed.

Since the procedure has the advantage of being able to use any reading material the pair is comfortable with, this will probably not be much of a problem. However, some pairs will need extra guidance in book selection as the tutorial sessions begin. Books that are continually too difficult or too easy will be problematic, as would books on the same topic. Time will have to be made to get to the school library as well as gain access to it. Finally, if the teacher decides to let the pair bring in books from outside the school, some form of quick readability check will need to be taught to the students.

Topping suggests that the pairing be continued for a six-week period, with at least three sessions a week for no more than 15 to 30 minutes per session. Training should begin with a demonstration, and students should be provided with written information as a reminder. The teacher will need to circulate around the room to monitor the quality of each pair's session, giving further information or demonstration where necessary. It is also to be remembered that all students doing this procedure simultaneously will result in substantial noise in the classroom.

As the tutorial sessions continue, teachers will need to be sure that problems do not arise with the technique, book choice, the interpersonal relationship of the pairs, or particularly difficult words or concepts. Students should keep a record of their progress in terms of the books read, and this should be monitored by the teacher. Positive behavior by the tutees should also be noted by the tutors. Teachers may also employ group or individual discussions of the tutoring sessions with the tutees and tutors, separately or together.

After the initial six-week period of Paired Reading has concluded, an evaluation should take place. Topping suggests that a feedback and review meeting be held with all participants. Verbal and written feedback should be sought, with suggestions for improvement. Teachers will find that some pairs will wish to continue; others will want a new partner. Some will seek fewer sessions.

Cautions and Comments

Implementing Topping's Paired Reading in a classroom with peer tutoring will not be without difficulty. Topping himself points out that the noise level may be distracting, and students may not feel comfortable with whole ... ; going on. The quality of the tutoring sessions may not be good with less ... children, or they may suffer because some tutors take on an authoritarian r... rs may become bored without constant fine-tuning of the procedure or the m... ly, parents may misunderstand the purpose or the methods and complain.

On the other hand, Topping points out th... en may pick up the procedure more rapidly than some teachers anticipa... ping suggests that successful training in Paired Reading is easiest with... easiest with parents, and most difficult with teachers. Teachers will also ... rience of most pairs is positive, and good relationships prosper beyond the tutoring sessions. Paired Reading in the classroom is inexpensive and easy to set up and monitor because the students and the materials are always on hand. This could make the strategy most appropriate to implement in at-risk schools where students have the most to gain. Finally, since both tutors and tutees improve their skills, it is attractive to implement.

Indeed, extensive research has also been reported by Topping (1987b) that demonstrate gains for all participants in Paired Reading. Additionally, the effects of the strategy seem to continue after termination of the tutoring.

References

Greene, F. P. 1970. *Paired reading*. Unpublished paper, Syracuse University. Discusses the rationale and implementation of another version of Paired Reading.

Rekrut, M. D. 1994. Peer and cross-age tutoring: The lessons of research. *Journal of Reading* 37:356–362. Examines the research on peer and cross-age tutoring, with an emphasis on practice.

Scoble, J., K. Topping, and C. Wigglesworth. 1988. Training family and friends as adult literacy tutors. *Journal of Reading* 31:410–417. Discussion of Paired Reading for use with adult illiterates.

Topping, K. 1987a. Paired reading: A powerful technique for parent use. *The Reading Teacher* 40:608–614. A description of the Paired Reading strategy, with the focus on parents working with children.

———. 1987b. Peer tutored paired reading: Outcome data from ten projects. *Educational Psychology* 7:133–145. Report of various research studies showing the effectiveness of the technique.

———. 1989. Peer tutoring and paired reading: Combining two powerful techniques. *The Reading Teacher* 42:488–494. A discussion of tutoring programs that combine peer tutoring with Paired Reading techniques.

Topping, K., and G. A. Lindsay. 1992. The structure and development of the paired reading technique. *Journal of Research in Reading* 15:120–136. A review of the literature on Paired Reading.

Assessment Strategies for Classrooms, Teachers, and Students

UNIT OVERVIEW

Assessment strategies for classrooms, teachers, and students represent a departure from the types of strategies and practices we have traditionally included in this volume. Some readers may consider this shift to be problematic, since the book has always focused on teaching, not assessment.

Our response to this criticism is tied to our belief that assessment is going through a major reorientation that more clearly connects assessment and teaching. Teachers are being expected to learn to use a repertoire of assessment strategies in conjunction with their teaching; indeed, these assessment strategies are integrated into the teaching and learning within the classroom.

So how did we choose strategies to include in the present unit? A key criterion was that the assessment strategies selected for presentation were those clearly integrated within the fabric of teaching and learning.

Although some of the strategies that we present are not altogether new, most (not all) represent a major shift away from the domination of standardized tests toward redefining assessment in terms of the following:

1. A definition of assessment that is connected with what is going on in the classroom in terms of teaching, learning, the social negotiations of authority, meaning making, and so on.
2. A view of literacy achievement that is upgraded to fit with current views of literacy, current teaching practices, and respect for the complexities and nuances of literacy development.
3. An orientation to assessment practices that is relativistic, intersubjective, jointly negotiated, and context-specific.
4. An orientation to assessment that is driven by concerns for student and teacher empowerment.
5. An orientation to assessment that is concerned with the relevance, meaningfulness, or authenticity of what is assessed.
6. A concern for the teacher's roles (as observer, decision maker, student advocate, educator, interpreter) in ongoing assessment activity in the classroom.
7. A concern for the student as the learner and partner in the assessment activities within the classroom.

Several terms have been suggested to capture some of the goals of some of these kinds of assessment: *authentic, learner-based assessment; performance assessment; context-responsive assessment,* and so on.

In essence these kinds of assessments strive to interconnect teaching, ongoing learning, and student development. Sometimes the interweaving of assessment and teaching and learning may appear invisible; at other times it will be more apparent but not detached, anomalous, disruptive, or overshadowing.

A quick perusal of our listing will indicate that we have not exhausted the possibilities. Indeed, there are a number of other strategies that we might have added ranging from think-aloud and introspective techniques to self-rating scales to logs, questionnaires, interviews, and so on. We apologize for all of these omissions and recognize that what we have done should be viewed as a start and tied to what we deem as a significant shift toward the teacher as observer, "kidwatcher," assessor, collaborator, documenter, and so on.

The strategies:

Performance Assessment: The first practice that is described is perhaps the most encompassing, for Performance Assessment includes a host of possible practices including Portfolios. The purpose of Performance Assessment is to develop assessment tools that are more closely aligned with the goals of the curriculum—an attempt to assess students using activities that are more tied to the nature of the learning with which students are involved rather than traditional assessment formats that may not be considered authentic.

Portfolios: Portfolios have the possibility of serving a multitude of purposes: to engage students in a form of self-assessment of their improvement, efforts, and achievement across a range of activities; to engage students, often in partnership with teachers and parents, in periodical evaluations and goal setting; and to serve as a vehicle whereby teachers or other interested parties can pursue a process for collecting, analyzing, and developing plans or interpretations from a range of primary artifacts of students' work and explorations. We would suggest that Portfolios have the potential of introducing teachers to the power of classroom-based assessment systems that are student-centered, engaging, and empowering.

Anecdotal Records: As teachers assume more responsibility for the assessment and decision making pertaining to their students, they need to learn ways to document student achievement, behavior, and learning as it occurs. To achieve these ends, teachers need to learn ways to observe and document their observations without compromising their ongoing interactions with students. Anecdotal Records provide the mechanisms for such documentation. They represent a way of recording information about a child's literacy as they do literacy in classrooms or other settings. They usually represent information that is collected "on the run" by a teacher or observer.

Running Records: Whereas Anecdotal Records might include a wide array of observations by teachers, Running Records are a means of pursuing a more focused analysis of selected reading behaviors for purposes of monitoring student progress and needs. The Running Records offer teachers procedures for collecting reading behaviors tied to oral reading and ways to analyze these behaviors.

Retelling: Retelling offers an alternative way of observing reading behavior tied to the students' ability to recall what they have read. No approach will ever afford a complete depiction of a student's reading, but these different lenses afford the basis for making some tentative judgments of reading comprehension behaviors and outcomes.

Cloze: Whereas the Cloze procedure has been criticized as a method of assessing comprehension, some have argued that it can only be a useful tool for assessing some facets of reading. Since it is still used extensively by teachers, the present description of Cloze as a testing and teaching tool is described along with several caveats.

Performance Assessment

Purpose

The purpose of Performance Assessment is to develop assessment tools that are more closely aligned with the goals of the curriculum. They represent an attempt to assess students using activities that are more tied to the nature of the learning with which students are involved rather than traditional assessment formats that may not be considered authentic.

Rationale

The development of authentic assessment procedures has its roots in the negative criticisms that have been leveled at traditional means of assessing reading and writing. These criticisms include: concern that multiple-choice items or other forms of "closed" assessment may be inconsistent with constructivist views of reading; questions that the passages used on most standardized tests are unique to those tests; concern that the prepackaged and standardized assessment procedures effect a form of collecting information that is disconcerting for many students and inconsistent with the culture of the classroom; and disagreement with the methods used to measure progress, as well as a growing realization that what is taught may or may not be measured on these tests. As was recently espoused by the Office of Technology Assessment in their summary "Testing in America: Asking the right questions":

> The move toward new methods of student testing has been motivated by new understandings of how students learn as well as changing views of curriculum. These views of learning, which challenge traditional concepts of curricula and teaching, also challenge existing methods of evaluating student competence. For example, it is argued that if instruction ought to be individualized, adaptive, and interactive, then assessment should share these characteristics. In general, educators who advocate performance assessment believe assessment can be made an integral and effective part of teaching. (1992, 16)

Furthermore, as more legislatures (state and federal) and districts use tests as motivations for improving curriculum or as ways to monitor progress toward their goals, the search for assessment tools tied to these goals is increasingly being pursued.

In general, Performance Assessment is tied to the goal that assessment should be clearly linked to the goals of education, meaningful classroom activities, and the nature of the learning itself. In other words, Performance Assessment is woven into the fabric of classroom life. As such, Performance Assessment strives for methods consistent with the nature of behavior and outcomes to which teachers and students are aspiring.

Performance Assessment may cover a broad and diverse range of activities. It may include: observations that students do of their own reading or writing, logs that they keep of their reading and writing, webs generated prior to or after reading and writing, open-ended responses, the actual performance of a task, and so on. The key is that the activities are clearly linked to goals and meaningful activities connected to these goals; furthermore that teachers assess behaviors as directly as possible using criteria grounded in the activities themselves and the goals represented by these activities. These assessments, therefore, may range from the simplest student-constructed response to comprehensive demonstrations or collections of large bodies of work over time (e.g., Portfolios).

As the Office of Technology Assessment, in their summary "Testing in America: Asking the right questions," suggested:

> . . . response to these testing tasks can reveal to the teacher more than just what facts they have learned; they reveal how well the student can put knowledge in context. *Well-crafted classroom performance tasks are useful diagnostic tools that can reveal where a student may be having a problem with the material.* They can also help the teacher gauge the pacing and level of instruction to student responses. At their best, these tasks can be exciting learning experiences in themselves, as when a student, required to create a product or answer that puts knowledge into context, is blessed with that flash inspiration, "Aha! I see how it all comes together now!" In addition, these tests can signal to students what skills and content they should learn, help teachers adjust instruction, and give students clear feedback. (1992, 18)

Intended Audience

Performance Assessment tasks are appropriate for students regardless of age in any setting.

Description of the Procedure

Performance Assessment should have the feel and look of worthwhile teaching and learning activities. Therefore, while Performance Assessment activities may look familiar, recognition or formalization of their use in assessment may be less so. Certainly, teachers are constantly assessing students as they are teaching, and making adjustments or noting performance. Performance Assessment makes the nature of these assessments more visible, perhaps more systematic, and certainly more influential. Above all it creates a relationship between teaching and assessment that is more natural, ongoing, and constructive.

Understandably, the form and complexity of Performance Assessment may vary considerably. For example, it might entail activities such as the following:

> Imagine yourself drafting a letter of appeal to the Vietnamese regarding the release of POWs.
>
> Describe the irony in E. B. White's *Charlotte's Web* and what this made you feel about the different characters and the author.
>
> Draw a map of the town, including locations, for Virginia Hamilton's "Zeeley."
>
> Dramatize the discussions among town folk in response to what they discussed the next day in "Tuesday."
>
> Look back over your journal entries in response to the stories you've read. What do you focus upon? Why? How do your journal entries change over time, and why?
>
> Using your notes, webs, jottings, etc., what steps did you follow in the development of your project? What do you think are the strengths of what you did? What things would you like to do the same or different with other projects?

Sometimes teachers may choose to develop their own sets of activities. These might represent miniteaching activities as a way of exploring with students across a range of different kinds of activities akin to what might be pursued in the class or viewed as a goal.

Such tryouts may take the form of miniprojects. For example,

> a teacher watches how a student pulls together ideas from various sources (different content books) as a way of judging research skills (ability to focus, set purposes, take notes, synthesize material, etc.) en route to preparing for an extended unit of work.
>
> a teacher explores the students' self-questioning and predictions as she or he reads several different kinds of selections.
>
> a teacher debriefs a student in a conference in terms of how he or she selects books to read for pleasure and his or her reading behavior across a number of these books.

Vignettes of Performance Assessment during regular classroom activities:

In the context of a Shared Book Experience, the teacher was noting how different children responded: the types of questions that they asked, their predictions, as well as the comments and responses that were offered among the group. What was particularly noteworthy was the extent to which Nigel offered some of his own ideas and recounted experiences that he had that paralleled the story. This was one of the few times that Nigel had responded in this fashion and the teacher viewed it as significant. As a follow-up, the teacher decided to pull together some books on similar themes and to interact with Nigel and some of his friends around the topic. As a further check she also brought along a couple of selections that dealt with different themes. The teacher was able to note differences across these different materials. For those texts, for which Nigel had had some similar experiences, he self-questioned, made predictions, and embellished. For those for which he had a limited number of related experiences from which to draw, his responses faltered and his self-questioning and predicting were minimal.

Sherry, Michael, and Tony were 16-year-old ninth graders who were having difficulty pulling together ideas for themselves from their reading. The teacher decided to take a closer look at their approach and behaviors as they read. She wanted to get a sense of why they were reading and some of their behaviors as they read—i.e., (1) self-questioning, purpose setting (predictive) capabilities and subsequent modification/confirmation of predictions; (2) developing understandings; (3) use of experiential background; (4) ongoing goals and use of these materials.

In the context of their working on a project on climate, she decided to sit beside them and observe their reading of a passage on weather forecasting excerpted from a science text. At various points the teacher noted what they were doing and asked them to talk about their thinking as they proceeded. She looked to see what they were noting and thinking about and how they planned to incorporate and use those ideas.

The teacher became aware that the students did not approach the text with any of their own questions or a sense of how they might incorporate those ideas into their project. Instead, they read the material as if they were going to be required to answer questions about memorized sections.

Some Advice About Judging, Using, and Scoring Performance Assessment Responses In scoring Performance Assessment, the approach that seems to have the most integrity may require a shift away from scores to trying to see patterns in response and asking yourself, "What does this mean for teaching and learning and ongoing record keeping?" To these ends, an integral part of the scoring or judging might involve student participation in these analyses. Students might be encouraged to suggest how they would judge their responses en route to suggesting ongoing learning goals. It is recommended that you keep your analyses and the responses together so that you can return to the responses either for a second look or a different use. Finally, the goals of the assessment should be kept in mind. Often the analyses of student responses go beyond the needs of the teacher or may not be usable. Teachers and students should ask themselves whether the nature of the return befits the analyses being pursued.

Cautions and Comments

There are many reasons for supporting Performance Assessment. Performance Assessment brings assessment closer to the classroom in which the learning is occurring and instructional decisions are being made. It increases the professionalism of teachers, as well as the value placed upon the teacher's place, including powers of observation and responsibilities in terms of decision making. It also brings to the fore the student's role in assessment—namely, the importance of shifting assessment toward a more learner-based orientation (similar to client-centered).

When the impact upon students and teachers is considered, the value of Performance Assessment is most apparent. Namely, teachers and students are more enthusiastic and more informed from these kinds of assessments. Furthermore, when selected forms of Performance Assessment have been compared with more traditional forms of assessment (multiple-choice items, short-answer questions), the results are different. In particular, students appear to perform differently depending upon the method of assessment. It is noteworthy that the Performance Assessment responses are apt to correspond more closely to teacher judgments of student learning and also apt to be sensitive to differences in curriculum. Whereas traditional forms of assessment may not show any differences in students engaged in dramatically different curricula, Performance Assessment indices will. (See Shavelson, Baxter, and Pine, 1992).

Criticisms directed at Performance Assessment tend to focus on issues of feasibility. In this regard, the Office of Technology Assessment, in their summary "Testing in America: Asking the right questions," suggested the following;

> It is important to recall that the basic concept of direct assessments of student performance is not new. American schools traditionally used oral and written examinations to monitor performance. It was the pressure to standardize those efforts, coupled with the perceived need to test large numbers of children, that led eventually to the invention of multiple-choice format as a proxy for genuine performance. Evidence that these proxies were more efficient in informing administrative decisions rapidly boosted their popularity, despite their less obvious relevance to classroom learning. The modern performance assessment movement is based on the proposition that new testing technologies can be more direct, open ended, and educationally relevant than conventional testing, and also reliable, valid, and efficient. (1992, p. 21).

Nonetheless, there are growing concerns over a number of complex issues:

1. The additional workload that such assessments might demand from teachers
2. The need to improve the capabilities of teachers for developing and interpreting such assessments
3. The development of ways to manage these assessments without detracting from teaching and learning
4. The problems with developing methods of interpreting the responses of students to these tasks
5. The tension between qualitative analyses (which seem more appropriate for such data) and the desire to quantify and simplify these data
6. The possibility that these tests may not be highly correlated with other measures
7. The costs associated with the use of these techniques for large-scale assessment purposes

References

Allington, R., A. Butler, and R. J. Tierney. 1993. *Teacher's guide to evaluation: Assessment handbook.* Celebrate Reading series. Glenview, IL: Scott, Foresman, and Company. This handbook contains performance assessment materials for the reading program specifically but also some general assessment ideas.

Anthony, R. J., T. D. Johnson, N. I. Mickelson, and A. Preece. 1991. *Evaluating Literacy: A Perspective for Change.* Portsmouth, NH: Heinemann. Brings together information about assessment and new assessment practices. Provides forms that can be used in the classroom.

Clay, M. M. 1990. Research currents: What is and what might be in evaluation. *Language Arts,* 67:288–298. A review of current practices in New Zealand elementary schools documents how teachers have developed informal measures that go beyond the standardized tests to evaluate student growth and change. Clay calls for the development of measures at all levels of education that evaluate process and product, and reminds us that such methods empower teachers as well as learners.

Education Department of South Australia. 1991. *Literacy assessment in practice: R-7 language arts.* Adelaide: Education Department of South Australia. Provides a framework for assessment that is being used in Australian schools. Includes samples of forms and children's work.

Johnston, P. 1987. Teachers as evaluation experts. *The Reading Teacher* 40:744–748. Johnston discusses how teachers can most effectively evaluate the process of literacy development by suggesting they become experts at "detecting patterns, knowing classroom procedures, and by listening." He further suggests that such individualized process-centered evaluation not only serves instruction but also allows students and teachers to collaborate in the learning process.

Linn, R. L., E. L. Baker, and S. B. Dunbar. 1991. Complex performance assessment: Expectations and validation criteria. *Educational Researcher* 20:15–21. Discusses issues related to the problems with the validity of Performance Assessment from a traditional testing perspective.

Mehrens, W. A. and I. J. Lehman. 1984. *Measurement and evaluation in education and psychology.* 3rd edition. New York: Holt, Rinehart and Winston. Contains numerous evaluation tools for use by teachers.

Nystrand, M., and J. V. Knapp. 1987. *Review of selected national tests of writing and reading.* Report for Office of Educational Research and Improvement (Grant No. OERI-6008690007). Presents problems with standardized writing assessment.

Office of Technology Assessment. 1992. *Testing in America: Asking the right questions* Congress of the United States, Office of Technology Assessment. Provides a detailed discussion of Performance Assessment and the bases for renewed interest.

Perrone, V., Ed. 1991. *Expanding student assessment.* Alexandria, VA: Association for Supervision and Curriculum Development. This volume includes a range of articles addressing issues and procedures of authentic assessment. These articles raise an array of provocative practical, political, and theoretical issues.

Rhodes, L. K. and N. Shanklin. 1993. *Windows into literacy: Assessing learners K-8.* Portsmouth, NH: Heinemann. Contains many forms of authentic assessment for literacy teachers. Includes sample forms and articles by teachers who actually use them.

Shavelson, R., G. P. Baxter, and J. Pine. 1992. Performance assessment: Political rhetoric and measurement reality. *Educational Researcher* 21:22–27. Presents a study detailing the advantages of Performance Assessment over traditional means of assessment as well as the problems associated with their implementation on a large scale.

Shepard, L. A. 1989. Why we need better assessments. *Educational Leadership* 46:4–9. The large-scale use and limitations of standardized tests are discussed, and the separation of such accountability measures from those that inform instruction is suggested. Problems facing the construction of such accountability tests are noted, and the resulting practices of teaching to the test are discussed. It is suggested that better instructional assessment needs to be developed, which allows assessment to resemble learning tasks and involves the development of portfolios that contain samples of students' work.

Smith, L. M., T. M. Kuhs, and J. M. Ryan. 1993. *Assessment of student learning in early childhood education.* South Carolina Center for Excellence in the Assessment of Student Learning. ERIC Document 358–163. Provides information on several alternatives to testing in the assessment of young children.

Stiggins, R., and N. F. Conklin. 1992. *In teachers' hands: Investigating the practices of classroom assessment.* Albany: SUNY. This book represents several years of exploration of issues of assessment in schools and the shift to legitimizing alternative forms of assessment.

Tierney, R. J. 1993. *Classroom-based assessment systems for literacy.* Glenview, IL: Scott Foresman. Provides a brief discussion of a range of classroom-based assessment procedures from on-the-run assessments to periodical assessments of students using Portfolios and other procedures.

Valencia, S., E. Hiebert, and P. Afflerbach, Eds. *Authentic reading assessment.* Newark, DE: International Reading Association. This volume includes nine case studies representing a range of assessment initiatives from the innovative to the more traditional. The editors provide provocative commentary on some of the issues involved in Portfolios and other authentic assessment practices.

Valencia, S., and P. D. Pearson. 1987. Reading assessment: Time for a change. *The Reading Teacher* 40:726–732. In this article Valencia and Pearson claim that the current view of reading that emphasizes the active role of readers as they construct meaning with a text is not reflected in our present practices.

Valencia, S. W., W. McGinley, and P. D. Pearson. 1990. Assessing reading and writing. In *Reading in the Middle School*, edited by G. G. Duffy. International Reading Association, 124–153. The authors advocate a move to contextualized assessment that views assessment as "continuous, multidimensional, grounded in knowledge and authentic."

Wiggins, G. 1989. Teaching to the (authentic) test. *Educational Leadership* 46:41–47. In this article, Wiggins argues that authentic tests should be truly representative of performance in the field; tied to criteria that make sense; involve student self-assessment, and so on.

Portfolios

Purpose

Portfolios have the possibility of serving a multitude of purposes: to engage students in a form of self-assessment of their improvement, efforts, and achievement across a range of activities; to engage students, often in partnership with teachers and parents, in periodical evaluations and goal setting; to serve as a vehicle whereby teachers or other interested parties can pursue a process for collecting, analyzing, and developing plans or interpretations from a range of primary artifacts of students' work and explorations; to serve as a vehicle for screening students or prospective employees on the basis of a dossier of what they have done.

Rationale

Portfolios have their roots in various professions (e.g., art, journalism, architecture, etc.) in which traditional assessment procedures were obviously unable to adequately represent performance. In their most recent manifestation, portfolio assessment has emerged in response to the criticisms being leveled at traditional assessment procedures, such as standardized tests, and the desire to realign assessment with teaching and learning. In this regard, the rationale undergirding portfolio assessment is that assessment should not be viewed as detached from learning and teaching but inextricably tied to them.

A view of teaching and learning	Some goals for assessment
Dynamic and ongoing	Dynamic and ongoing
Child-centered	Child-centered or client-centered
Interactive	Interactive
Jointly constructed meanings	Jointly constructed assessment
Collaborative	Collaborative
Multifaceted	Multifaceted
Personalized	Personalized
Generative	Generative
Involving taking risks and experimentation	Involving taking risks and experimentation
Nurturing and Facilitative	Nurturing and facilitative
Experiential	Experiential
Context-supported	Context-supported
Based on real texts and meaningful activities	Based on real texts and meaningful activities
Supports multiple literacies	Supports multiple literacies
Encourages self-improvement and ownership	Encourages self-improvement and ownership

Essentially, the portfolio represents some major shifts in some basic tenets of assessment. In conjunction with a shift in views of science away from positivism to constructivism, there has been a movement from absolutism to relativism, as well as an acceptance of subjectivity over objectivity, interpretability over reliability, thickness of description over sampling, collaboration over imposition, emerging over a priori, ongoing over summative and so on. A discussion of traditional versus portfolio classrooms follows.

With traditional assessment students are assessed by some outside person or using what is touted as an "objective" measure. In a portfolio classroom the students are involved in assessing themselves and establishing their own learning goals. To do so, they may work with their peers, teachers, and parents in reviewing their efforts, selecting representative pieces, keeping logs, and developing self-assessments. Admittedly, portfolios may be assessed "subjectively," but fairly—especially considering that the goal is to enhance learning and teaching.

In portfolio classrooms, sameness gives way to diversity. Whereas standardized tests involve the same test's being given at the same time to all students, each student's portfolio provides a unique and multifaceted portrait of a student. Reading-writing portfolios provide a portrait of the range of literacy experiences with which each student has been engaged over time. A portfolio might include a collection of each student's "Sunday best": drafts, pivotal pieces, different kinds of working documents, as well as records and reflections of their efforts, achievements, processes, improvement, and future learning goals. As students using portfolios will say, they provide "a portrait of me, who I am and how I have changed."

Whereas traditional assessment may yield a single score or grade, portfolios yield profiles, tentative goal statements, and interpretative reports or narratives. These profiles, goal statements, and reports serve as the basis for evaluative and planning conferences with the students and the parents of the child. Moreover, they serve as the springboard for the students' negotiations of goals for themselves.

Furthermore, the portfolios represent a form of grounded assessment versus secondary assessment. As a result a portfolio allows a form of assessment that allows the evaluator to return to the actual experiences or data from which evaluations/interpretations are made. In other words, just as historians might return to journals written at the time by participants in an event, so portfolios allow the evaluator to return to the primary sources.

Perhaps the way to begin thinking about assessment is to take a step back and ask yourself, "What do I want in terms of assessment in my classroom?" Be careful not to define yourself in terms of how assessment currently takes place. Think about what it is that you would prefer. So, before jumping to conclusions about the validity of such an approach to assessment or dismissing the use of Portfolios as too radical a departure, ask yourself whether your current assessment practices are serving your purposes. Just how do the assessment practices in your classroom measure up?

Do your assessment practices empower your students' self-understanding and allow them to pursue their own meaningful learning goals? Do they provide you information that you can use in your teaching and to mobilize appropriate support services for each student? Do your assessment practices enhance learning and teaching in your classroom? Is assessment well integrated into your instruction? Do your assessment practices have a relationship with teaching and learning that is ongoing, dynamic, and not disruptive? Do your assessment practices reflect what we know about learning and development? Above all, do your assessment practices empower teachers, students, and parents?

Intended Audience

Portfolio assessment is appropriate for students regardless of age in any setting.

Description of the Procedures

We will provide you a quick glimpse of the Portfolio process and some of the steps involved in implementing portfolio assessment in your classroom. Essentially, students are encouraged to review and examine their current efforts and begin to define their future learning goals. Teachers and students begin by maintaining a file of their work including working drafts, lists of ideas, finished work, notes, logs, and journals. Then they periodically peruse these efforts to check and reflect upon their improvements, the range of experiences, their breakthroughs, new learnings, and future goals.

Is it as simple as it sounds? It is simple, but it is also a major leap in faith. It requires teachers to simultaneously assume a new measure of professionalism and adopt an approach to assessment that is student-centered and classroom-based. The list below offers an overview of the procedure:

PORTFOLIOS Step by Step

1. GETTING STARTED
   - Introduce parents to your plans
   - Share personal portfolio
   - Parent/professional share portfolio, e.g., artist, architect, journalist
   - Develop a class portfolio
   - Brainstorm with students about purposes and possibilities

2. COLLECT AND TAG
   - Develop collections: process, product, seminal pieces, representative pieces, best
   - Be sure to tag each item (e.g., date, significance, pertinent details)
   - Consider home-school connections
   - Ongoing sections: logs, journals, self-appraisals, favorite works, etc.

3. SELECT, SORT, SAVOR
   - Organize to organize
   - Establish possible/tentative guidelines
   - Consider possible samples to include in portfolio
   - Refrain from making final selection until obtaining feedback/input from others
   - Model decision making
   - Conference
   - Adjust or add tags bases for selection

4. SHARE, REFLECT, AND PLAN
   - Conference with peer, parent, teacher, and student
   - Develop overall analysis/narrative, etc.

5. THEN
   2. COLLECT AND TAG, then
   3. SELECT, SAVOR, AND SHARE, then
   4. SHARE AND PLAN, etc.

What do you include in portfolios? Students are usually encouraged to include a range of their writings as well as drafts or other seminal items that may not always look like their best work but may reflect important discoveries or breakthroughs. Students might include what might be labeled as reader response entries. These can run the gamut from time lines to sketches of characters to book reports or journal entries. In addition, students might include logs of their readings, writings, and projects, as well as notes describing their assessments of their progress and future goals. Finally, students might include projects that they work on at home, with or without their parents.

But, then, how does a teacher start?

Several Portfolio advocates encourage teachers to develop their own portfolios. They would encourage teachers to pull together a portfolio of their own reading, writing, and other interests en route to sharing it with someone else or their students. If teachers are hesitant to pull together their own portfolios, there are other ways to introduce the concept to students. Some teachers have enlisted the help of other teachers, parents, or members of the community who maintain portfolios in the course of their profession. For example, some teachers have had art students share their portfolio with their classes. Others have introduced the concept of Portfolio to students by bringing in material representing the range of work of famous individuals such as Leonardo da Vinci. Sometimes teachers have just described what portfolios are and then discussed possible guidelines for students' gathering and selecting materials for their own portfolios. Teachers and their students need to realize that they have access to a great deal of material that can be used as a basis for starting to decide what they might include. In some classes, the teachers and students prescribe a number of particular kinds of material to be included; in other classrooms the material will vary across students. Usually, the students are encouraged to include material other than their Sunday best. For example, students might include thought pieces, breakthrough moments, jot lists, webs, or pivotal pieces.

As students ponder and peruse possible entries, teachers and other students are encouraged to offer support, whether they serve as sounding boards or as facilitators. In addition, students might jot down the basis for their selection of individual pieces by using captions or 3×5 cards and including an extended narrative, Venn diagrams, or profiles describing the whole portfolio. Teachers typically put time aside to have students deliberate over future directions for themselves, and to share their portfolios and plans with the class.

The issue of evaluation of the portfolio is a matter for which there exists a certain amount of disagreement in the field. In the everyday use of Portfolios in classrooms, Tierney, Carter, and Desai (1991) prefer that any assessment of the portfolios be done either by the student or collaboratively between teachers and students. With some exceptions, student self-assessment is a new venture for teachers. It is important to be willing to support students in their own self-assessments and to value their efforts at so doing. Portfolios may not prove beneficial if teachers assume total control of them and are unwilling to enter into the kind of partnership that their use calls for. Accordingly, Tierney, Carter, and Desai strongly encourage having the students discuss their portfolios on their own terms. Although the authors might encourage the teachers to help the students group the material in their portfolios, they prefer that teachers encourage the students to generate their own criteria for judging pieces.

At the risk of being repetitive, Tierney, Carter, and Desai emphasize that the student should be viewed as the client and that the portfolio should be viewed as their property. In several districts, they see portfolios being given to teachers or district personnel by students for use by the district, school, or teacher. They strongly urge schools and districts intent on reviewing student portfolios to either return them or to start up their own portfolios or dossiers especially for those purposes and in partnership with the students. If the portfolios are to be used to assess, the authors would emphasize that portfolios be judged in the spirit with which they were developed. That is, a goal of assessment with portfolios should be to support the students' assessment of their own work, not to supplant their assessment with that of a teacher or an outsider.

In terms of using portfolio assessment for accountability mandates, Tierney, Carter, and Desai would emphasize that we should be careful to respect the integrity of the portfolio and the possibilities that might be forthcoming. Sometimes portfolios are assessed in ways that are not consistent with the complexity they represent. Sometimes rubrics are developed that are imposed upon Portfolios rather than emerging from them. We have found that Portfolios tell us a lot more useful information than an overall achievement level or how well the student performs in specific skill areas. Portfolios provide information on the extent to which students pursue learning activities for a variety of purposes, the nature of the collaborations with which they have been engaged, their investment in different activities, the learning outcomes, and the relevance that they see in these activities, as well as the strategies that they employed. To ignore these multiple facets of learning is to artificially simplify what we know about learning.

In turn, Portfolios are apt to have an impact upon the methods of reporting student performance—especially, report cards and parent-teacher-student conferences. Portfolios lend themselves to jointly constructed narrative descriptions of performance rather than grades. The various dimensions of Portfolios can be portrayed in words much better than in grades. Portfolios have prompted many to question whether the report card (especially those resorting to grades) can ever do justice to the student's achievements, improvement, efforts, and idiosyncrasies. Indeed, they often prompt teachers to move toward the development of interpretative summaries and goal statements in collaboration with students and parents.

Cautions and Comments

The effectiveness of the portfolios as a tool for evaluation is tied partially to how the portfolio process is implemented and the students' developing abilities to pursue self-analyses and trace their development; Portfolios tend to be product-oriented. Portfolio approaches vary significantly along a host of dimensions, especially the extent to which they are prescribed or emerging, for outsiders or for teachers and students. In other words, the label *portfolio* may mean different things in different settings.

Certainly, portfolios have other attributes that other forms of assessment do not. Comparisons that have been made of portfolio assessment and traditional assessment (such as standardized tests and other assessment practices in operation in classrooms) favor Portfolios. Portfolios consistently provide more and better information about student learning. Teachers and parents appear to achieve a fuller understanding of student abilities, interests, and development. Students achieve a fuller and more positive view of themselves and become more invested in their ongoing development.

Student ownership and independence appear to be outgrowths, because they place students in the position of learning to assess themselves, share who they are with others, and set their own learning goals. It has been reported by several authors that students from preschool to adulthood gain immensely from being able to assess themselves and set their own learning goals. They not only learn about their progress as learners, but also how their views on life and social issues have shifted.

Portfolios also help reestablish the students and those in closest contact with the students as primarily responsible for assessment. Assuming that they are defined by students and teachers within classrooms, portfolios ensure that the professionalism of teaching remains intact, and that those most directly involved with the students' learning are recognized. As assessment practices are increasingly removed from the classroom and from the control of students and teachers, the likelihood of mismatches between what should be assessed and what is assessed increases.

Portfolios afford teachers the opportunity to assess students' various activities, strategies, attitudes, interests, and abilities in the context of their work. Whereas standardized tests provide information on students' strategies and abilities on items students meet just once and in rather contrived circumstances, Portfolios enable teachers to see these same features and others as students use them in different and meaningful situations. Sometimes standardized testing descends upon the classroom and, like an unwelcome house guest, requires your making special preparations, involves a great deal of disruption to your life, and often you are glad when it is over.

Portfolios appear to fit into today's classrooms—in fact, Portfolios seem a natural extension of the various learning activities with which students are engaged. Portfolios appear to help teachers and students keep track of, reflect upon, and plan their extended reading and writing projects and activities such as conferencing, journals, and shared book experiences. They also provide an umbrella for the integration of learning. Students are apt to include in their portfolios material from across subject areas as well as activities related to their interests outside of school.

Portfolios appear to: (1) afford students ownership and goal setting; (2) empower students, teachers, parents, and administrators; (3) bring to the fore rather than simplify the complexities of literacies and literacy development; and, (4) enhance the ability of students, teachers, and other interested parties to make effective decisions. In addition, portfolios encourage teachers (1) to be responsive to the nuances of each student's literacy development; (2) encompass rather than retreat from the range of experiences with which students might be engaged; (3) embrace rather than ignore the diverse nature of students' literacies, their approaches, experiences, goals, and interests; and, (4) rethink methods of reporting progress and setting goals with the students and their parents.

At the same time, Portfolios may represent different things to different groups. Indeed, Wile and Tierney (1994) argue that some portfolio assessment practices have a number of pitfalls. They include: (1) imposed versus emerging portfolios; (2) overly rigid and overly prescriptive guidelines for portfolios; (3) formalizing self-assessment; (4) imposed and standardized criteria to guide student evaluations; (5) viewing the portfolio as the end rather than a means of engaging students in reflection, self-assessment, and ongoing goal setting; (6) district and teacher takeover of students' portfolios; (7) methods for evaluation that are not befitting the portfolio purposes, process, elements, and contexts; and (8) prepackaged portfolios. Portfolios are not without their constraints. Specifically, Portfolios should be viewed in terms of what they represent. In this regard, it is important to recognize that Portfolios represent the students' experiences and their perceptions of those experiences; knowledge of context and the interplay of other factors is usually important in assessing student progress via Portfolios; Portfolios trace development but they do not afford a full and in-depth picture.

References

Belanoff, P., and M. Dickson. 1991. *Portfolios: process and product.* Portsmith, NH: Heinemann. This edited volume provides descriptions by several contributors of the use of Portfolios in higher education.

Carter, M., and R. J. Tierney. 1988. *Reading and writing growth: Using portfolios in assessment.* Paper presented at National Reading Conference, Tucson, AZ. Describes the impact of Portfolios upon teachers and students in different classrooms. Specifically, Carter and Tierney present the findings of a study that examines how teachers' awareness of students, teaching practices, and students' views of themselves as readers and writers shifted in conjunction with their use of Portfolios for reading and writing.

Clay, M. M. 1990. Research currents: What is and what might be in evaluation. *Language Arts* 67:288–298. A review of current practices in New Zealand elementary schools documents how teachers have developed informal measures that go beyond the standardized tests to evaluate student growth and change. Clay calls for the development of measures at all levels of education that evaluate process and product, and reminds us that such methods empower teachers as well as learners.

Clemmons, J. L., L. Cooper, D. Aregaldo, and N. Dill, 1993. *Portfolios in the classroom: A teacher's sourcebook.* New York: Scholastic. This publication represents the efforts of a team of educators in Virginia who have amassed a wealth of material and practical suggestions on the implementation of Portfolios.

Courts, P. L., and K. H. McInerney. 1993. *Assessment in higher education: Politics, pedagogy and portfolios.* Westport, CT: Praeger. This volume examines critically aspects of assessment in higher education and the possibilities that Portfolios offer.

Flood, J., and D. Lapp. 1989. Reporting reading progress: A comparison portfolio for parents. *The Reading Teacher* 42:508–514. Flood and Lapp describe the Portfolio as a tool to be used in parent conferences to document student change across time.

Goodman, K. S., Y. M. Goodman, and W. J. Hood. 1989. *The whole language evaluation book.* Portsmouth, NH: Heinemann. Describes various attempts by teachers to develop assessment procedures in line with classroom practices. Among those discussed are Portfolios.

Graves, D., and B. Sunstein. eds. 1992. *Portfolio portraits.* Portsmouth, NH Heinemann. This edited volume captures the intimate and personal descriptions of different teachers' adventures with Portfolios.

Levi, R. 1990. Assessment and educational vision: Engaging learners and parents. *Language Arts* 67:269–273. Using the work of his students, and the words of the students' parents, Levi documents how Portfolios involve students, parents, and teachers as collaborators in the assessment process.

Mathews, J. K. 1990. From computer management to portfolio assessment. *The Reading Teacher* 43(b) 420–421. In this article Mathews details the steps taken and challenges faced as the district begins to move its elementary schools to a portfolio approach to literacy assessment.

Mills, R. P. 1989, December. Portfolios capture rich array of student performance. *The School Administrator* December:8–11. As Vermont's Commissioner of Education, Mills provides an overview of Vermont's struggle to develop a statewide measure of educational performance.

Murphy, S., and M. A. Smith. 1992. *Writing portfolios: a bridge from teaching to assessment.* Markham, Ont.: Pippin. Presents a rich and powerful discussion and description of student involvement in writing Portfolios.

———. 1990. Talking about portfolios. *The Quarterly* 12: Believing that Portfolios can take many forms and that there is no one right way to develop a portfolio, Murphy and Smith suggest that teachers' decisions regarding expectations of the portfolios will have a profound effect on the resulting format and implementation.

Reif, L. 1990. Finding the value in evaluation: Self-assessment in a middle school classroom. *Educational Leadership* 47:24–29. Reif presents a portrait of how Portfolios are used in her seventh- and eighth-grade middle school classes in Durham, NH, by highlighting the portfolio of one of her students.

Shepard, L. A. 1989. Why we need better assessments. *Educational Leadership* 46:4–9. The large-scale use and limitations of standardized tests are discussed, and the separation of such accountability measures from those that inform instruction is suggested. Problems facing the construction of such accountability tests are noted, and the resulting practices of teaching to the test are discussed. It is suggested that better instructional assessment needs to be developed, which allows assessment to resemble learning tasks and involves the development of portfolios that contain samples of students' work.

Simmons, J. 1990. Portfolios as large-scale assessment. *Language Arts* 67:262–267. Based on the work done by his research team in Durham, NH, Simmons discusses a field test of a large-scale model of portfolio assessment involving portfolios collected randomly to represent the district's entire fifth grade. Unlike a one-shot test, portfolios produced profiles of student writers. They also found that while timed tests and portfolio assessments produced the same rank ordering of students, the portfolios more accurately represented the true abilities of all students.

Stowell, L. P., R. J. Tierney, and L. E. Desai. In press. Portfolios in the classroom: What happens when teachers and students negotiate assessment? To appear in *No quick fix: Rethinking literacy lessons in America's elementary schools,* edited by R. Allington, and S. Walmsley. New York: Teachers College Press. Discusses issues of teacher implementation regarding Portfolios. Explores the difficulties and transitions that occur as students and teachers explore portfolio assessment.

Taylor, D. 1990. Teaching without testing. *English Education* 22:4–74. Taylor presents the essence of a project intent on developing biographic literacy profiles from the perspective of the child. She provides a rich description of the features and methods associated with the various objectives of the project: Learning to observe children's literacy behaviors; Learning to develop note-taking procedures to record observations of children reading and writing; Learning to write descriptive biographic literacy profiles; and Learning to increase our awareness of the multiple layers of interpretation that we are incorporating into the children's biographic literacy profiles.

Tierney, R. J. In press. Learner-based assessment: Turning assessment upside down and inside out to make evaluation the right way up and to fit with teaching and learning. To appear in *Language arts in 2000,* edited by L. Morrow. Boston: Allyn & Bacon. A practical summary that can serve as an introductory guide to portfolio implementation.

Tierney, R. J., J. Wile, A. G. Moss, E. W. Reed, J. P. Ribar, and A. Zilversmit. 1993. *Portfolio evaluation as history: Evaluation of the history academy for Ohio teachers.* National Council of History Education, Inc. Occasional Paper. Reports a study dealing with the use of Portfolios to pursue project evaluation. Affords a glimpse at pursuing detailed case studies with Portfolios combined with profiles and quantitative analyses.

Tierney, R. J., M. Carter, and L. Desai. 1991. *Portfolio assessment in the reading writing classroom.* Norwood, MA: Christopher Gordon Publishers, Inc. The first book devoted to a description of the use of Portfolios in literacy classrooms. Provides an extensive discussion of the rationale for and issues related to the implementation of Portfolios. Includes a survey of different portfolio approaches.

Valencia, S., E. Hiebert, and P. Afflerbach. eds. *Authentic reading assessment.* Newark, DE: International Reading Association. This volume includes nine case studies representing a range of assessment initiatives from the innovative to the more traditional. The editors provide provocative commentary on some of the issues involved in Portfolios and other authentic assessment practices.

Valencia, S. 1990. A portfolio approach to classroom reading assessment: The whys, whats, and hows. *The Reading Teacher* 43:338–340. This article highlights the research and instructional practices that make Portfolios a viable form of assessment.

Vavrus, L. 1990. Put portfolios to the test. *Instructor* 100:48–53. Vavrus introduces the concept of Portfolios and outlines several ideas for teachers to consider, including selection of work to go into Portfolios, evaluation, and passing Portfolios on to other teachers. However, the article neglects the importance of developing portfolio processes in conjunction with students.

Wile, J., and R. J. Tierney. 1993. *Analyzing complexity with portfolio techniques: Exploring the schisms between positivistic and constructivistic perspectives.* Paper presented at the annual meeting of the National reading Conference, Charleston. Paper raises various concerns regarding the analysis procedures being espoused for use with Portfolios and explores issues of their validity, comparability, and reliability.

Wolf, D. P. Opening up assessment. *Educational Leadership* 45:24–29. Using the work done through Arts Propel, Wolf discusses the development, by students and teachers of the arts, of holistic and qualitative modes of assessment of students' thinking processes, problem solving, and self-assessment abilities. She focuses on the tools of projects, Portfolios, and reflective interviews, and discusses their ability to provide information for students and teachers about students' development and change across time

————. 1989. Portfolio assessment: Sampling student work. *Educational Leadership* 46:35–39. In this article Wolf discusses in greater detail the development of Propel Portfolios as a tool that accomplishes this goal. The article highlights the characteristics of Portfolios that enable a student to reflect on the process involved in the development of a wide range of his or her own written work, and discusses the impact this form of evaluation has had on teacher abilities to assess their students and themselves.

Yancey, K. B., ed. 1992. *Portfolios in the writing classroom: An introduction.* Urbana, IL: NCTE. The contributors to this volume describe a range of Portfolio efforts. The volume also includes an examination of some pitfalls and limitations pertaining to Portfolios.

Anecdotal Records

Purpose

As a form of assessment, Anecdotal Records are a way of recording information about a child's literacy as they do literacy in classrooms or other settings. They usually represent information that is collected "on the run" by a teacher or observer.

Rationale

Historically, Anecdotal Records have been used to record behaviors of children in the classroom, often for the purpose of making a diagnosis of a problem. Mehrens and Lehman (1984) suggest that they are used to record "social adjustment" (P. 229), while

Locke and Ciechalski (1985) suggest that they are useful for collecting information about children who are being referred for special services.

With the advent of Whole-Language, and particularly, the notion of "kidwatching," the Anecdotal Record has become a way of recording and assessing children's literacy development. Unlike checklists, miscue analyses, and so forth, the Anecdotal Record can be made without anticipating the ways in which children engage with various events in school. Thus, the Anecdotal Record allows the teacher not only to engage in "kidwatching," but it also allows teachers to consider their observations and to use those observations in their future interactions with children and their parents.

Teacher Roles

Yetta Goodman's notion of "kidwatching," which forms the basis of Anecdotal Records, creates an active role for teachers in the process of assessment:

> Teachers screen their observations through their philosophy, their knowledge base, and their assumptions whenever they are involved in kidwatching. Current knowledge about child language and conceptual development guides observations. Not only does it help

FIGURE 14–1. ANECDOTAL RECORDS

teachers know what to look for as signs of growth and development but it also helps teachers become consciously aware of their knowledge, their biases, and their philosophical orientation. . . .

Knowledgeable teachers ready to assume responsibility for observation and evaluation of children play a very significant role in enriching the child's development of language and concepts. (Goodman, 1985, 11)

Thus Anecdotal Records require three roles of teachers:

1. The teacher's ability to draw upon her or his understandings of the child against understandings about literacy development.
2. Recognition of significant events. It is neither possible nor desirable to record every event in the process of a child's acquisition of literacy; the teacher uses the aforementioned knowledge to select events for recording.
3. Instructional practice. The teacher records the event in an appropriate manner, uses the event in a process of analysis and interpretation, and, finally, allows that analysis/interpretation to inform his/her interactions with and about the child.

As Allington, Butler, and Tierney (1993) point out, these three roles for the teacher reflect and enact an ongoing cycle of assessment:

Thus, a set of Anecdotal Records provides the teacher with information that can be used in the classroom, leading ultimately to action and then their collecting more information as events unfold. Assessment is cyclical in nature.

Intended Audience

Anecdotal Records can be used with students of any age.

Description of the Procedure

Anecdotal Records allow the teacher to bring together knowledge of literacy development and the history of a particular child in a process of recognizing events that are significant to that child's development of literacy. In turn, this information leads the teacher to a process of analysis that leads to instructional planning and the generating of new questions for assessment. Figure 14–1 above shows the process of making Anecdotal Records and the roles of the teacher in this assessment procedure. Each aspect of this process is discussed below.

Development of Literacy   Since literacy development is a lifelong process that changes significantly from moment to moment in a person's life, it cannot be easily or briefly summed up. Still, a framework such as that of the Education Department of South Australia (1991) provides a list of aspects of both reading and writing that are part of literacy development. They consider five types of information, under the acronym CAASR:

Concepts about literacy

Attitudes to writing and reading

Aspects of written products and comprehension

Strategies for writing and reading

Range of writing and reading (P. 7)

They then provide an overview of these types of information in relation to both reading and writing, as can be seen below:

CAASR: Reading and Writing Overview	
CONCEPTS ABOUT LITERACY	
Uses for written language Kinds of written products The possible range of audiences The appropriate use of written language The similarities and differences between speech and writing The processes readers and writers use	
ATTITUDES TO READING AND WRITING	
Self-concept Commitment	

CAASR: Reading and Writing Overview   *(Continued)*

ASPECTS OF WRITTEN PRODUCTS	ASPECTS OF READING COMPREHENSION
Ideas/Information ■ Topic knowledge ■ Knowledge of the world ■ Presentation of ideas Organization ■ Kinds of writing ■ Focus ■ Parts ■ Sequences ■ Links ■ Readers' needs Language ■ Vocabulary ■ Sentence ■ Style Mechanics ■ Handwriting ■ Spelling ■ Punctuation ■ Layout ■ Using word processors	Ideas/Information ■ Topic knowledge Organization ■ Fiction texts ■ Nonfiction texts ■ Focus and sequence Language ■ Syntax ■ Word meanings ■ Style Mechanics ■ Letter-sound relationships ■ Directional and positional conventions ■ Devices for showing emphasis or importance ■ Layout conventions
STRATEGIES FOR WRITING	**STRATEGIES FOR READING**
Prewriting ■ Considering possibilities ■ Collecting and connecting ■ Making plans and rehearsing parts Writing ■ Drafting ■ Revising Postwriting ■ Preparing for publishing ■ Presenting to the audience and reflecting on responses	Basic strategies ■ Predict ■ Confirm and check ■ Self-correct Monitoring for congruence Creating worlds Coping strategies
RANGE OF STUDENTS' READING AND WRITING	

Adapted from Education Department of South Australia, Pp. 37–38.

History of Individual Child   Along with the numerous aspects of reading and writing to consider, the teacher must consider the individual child. Anecdotal Records can be used in the process of getting to know the child and his/her literacy development. They can also be used to record unusual events, as Cartwright and Cartwright (1984) point out: "Children behave spontaneously in many ways that often are not anticipated or expected, and the anecdotal record provides a method of recording the observations of these spontaneous behaviors" (P. 114). Obviously, one must either have a sense of a child's history or be interested in working toward that type of understanding in order to know if a behavior is anticipated or not.

Significant Event   What constitutes a significant event? Anthony, Johnson, Mickelson, and Preece (1991) suggest:

> There is usually so much happening in a class that teachers must be highly selective about what to record. Observations can be gathered in two ways: planned or spontaneous.
> Planned observations should be focused on a predetermined area of learning, and this can be signaled by the use of a key word . . . Where do the key words come from? Simply put, they come from the teacher. What do I want to know about the processes of student learning? What will the other stakeholders in the child's education want to know? (P. 73)

Thus, Anecdotal Records can be used in a planned fashion to track literacy acquisition; they can also capture for later consideration spontaneous moments of struggle—or epiphany.

Watson (1985) offers a series of questions about the individual child in relation to literacy development (Figure 14–2); Rhodes and Nathenson-Mejia (1992) provide a teacher-generated observation guide (Figure 14–3).

Rhodes and Nathenson-Mejia (1992) suggest that teachers keep a list of this sort available in their classrooms to remind them of the types of things that might be observed.

Recording Process   There are numerous suggestions for both guidelines for making Anecdotal Records and the actual forms that might be used. Figure 14–4 brings together guidelines from two sources.

Texts on anecdotal record keeping written before the invention of sticky notes encourage teachers to use index cards for Anecdotal Records; more current sources suggest that sticky notes can be carried around on a clipboard and then transferred to a notebook that has ongoing records for each student. With the advent of laptops and hand-held computers with handwriting-recognition software, teachers may soon find word processing to be a viable way of making Anecdotal Records.

Regardless of the recording system, it is important to provide a sufficient amount of detail so that someone else reading the record will have a sense of what happened. Rhodes and Nathenson-Mejia (1992) suggest that detailed descriptions with examples are more helpful in the long run than general descriptions.

Analysis/Interpretation

Most sources on anecdotal record keeping suggest recording the event in the most value-free language possible, keeping interpretive or analytical comments separate from

FIGURE 14–2.

Concepts about Print and Print Settings

1. To what extent does the student attend to print? For example, does the student focus on the print as someone else is reading?
2. How does the student handle books? For example, does the student hold the book right side up, turn pages one at a time, and point to the place where one should begin reading?
3. Does the student expect the print to make sense and have personal meaning? For example, does the student seek out text that will satisfy his/her need for information about feeding hamsters?
4. How does the student use information from the print setting, i.e., where the print is found, its format, who asked that it be read, why it is being read?

Use of Background Knowledge

1. How does the reader bring background knowledge and linguistic information to the reading situation?
2. How does the reader approach text? Is there an effort made to appreciate and live the written experiences by relating the text to his/her own life?
3. How does the reader use memory as a reading aid? For example, when asked to read a familiar song, riddle, or self-authored story, does the reader use memory (i.e., familiarity with the material) as a basis for predicting and making inferences?

Use of Strategies

1. How does the student handle the information-giving systems of language? Does the reader use a flexible strategy that encompasses all language cues (e.g., semantic, grammatical, sound/symbol) to construct meaning or does the reader rely on a single cuing system (e.g., symbol/sound)?
2. Does the reader proficiently sample, predict, and construct meaning from text?
3. Does the student monitor his/her reading by asking, "Am I making sense of what I am reading?"
4. Does the reader self-correct when the flow of language and meaning are interrupted?
5. Is there a dialect or first language influence on the student's reading and how does the student handle this influence?
6. What strategies does the reader use to approach suitable but unfamiliar text?

View of Self as Reader

1. What does the student think of himself/herself as a reader?
2. In what circumstances and how often does the student make the decision to read?
3. What risks are taken by the student as he/she reads?
4. How realistic is the student's judgment of his/her knowledge of concepts and discourse forms needed to read various texts (e.g., science or history materials, poems or drama)?

From Watson, 1985, pp. 119–121.

the record of the event. Cartwright and Cartwright (1984) suggest dividing the record form in half—one half for reporting the incident. Rhodes and Nathenson-Mejia (1992) provide examples in which teachers record the event first and make interpretive comments at the end of the record.

FIGURE 14–3. TEACHER GENERATED OBSERVATION GUIDE

- Functions served in reading/writing
- Engagement in reading/writing
- What appears to impact engagement in reading/writing
- What aspects of text student attends to
- Interactions with others over reading/writing
- Interactions with materials
- Insightful or interesting things students say
- Hypotheses students are trying out in reading/writing
- Misconceptions students have
- Miscues students make while reading
- Changes students make in writing
- How students use text before, during, and after reading
- How a lesson affects students' reading/writing
- Comparisons between what student say and what they do
- Plans students make and whether/how plans are amended
- How, where, and with whom students work
- What students are interested in
- What students say they want to work on in their reading/writing
- What students say about reading/writing done outside of school
- How students generate and solve problems in reading/writing
- Ideas for reading/writing lessons and materials
- How students "symbol weave" (use multiple symbolic forms)
- How students theorize or talk about reading/writing
- How one reading/writing event relates to another
- How students use a variety of resources in reading/writing

From Rhodes and Nathenson-Mejia (1992, 505).

However analytical or interpretive comments are made, there are three aspects of Anecdotal Records to consider: (1) the significance of the single event; (2) the significance of the event in relation to other observed events; and (3) how the information will inform teaching. Anecdotal Records can be analyzed with respect to the three.

Single Event Figure 14–5 shows an example of an Anecdotal Record adapted from Rhodes and Nathenson-Mejia (1992). In this example, the teacher drew on her background knowledge of literacy development and her knowledge of the individual child. The fact that this child began to use letter/sound relationships in her writing was significant, so the teacher chose to record this moment. The teacher recorded the child's actual writing and a translation that would allow her (or others) to read that writing in the future. She also recorded her intervention process (showing child how to "stretch the words" and asking the child what she did that was different).

FIGURE 14–4.   GUIDELINES FOR ANECDOTAL RECORDS

- Describe a specific event or product
- Report rather than evaluate or interpret
- Relate the material to other facts that are known about the child (Thorndike and Hagen as cited in Rhodes and Nathenson-Mejia, 1992)
- Observe children within a variety of settings and at different times in the school day
- Record observations as soon as possible
- Choose a workable recording system
- Protect confidentiality

(Grace and Shores, as cited in Smith, Kuhs, and Ryan, 1993).

In the process of analyzing this particular record, the teacher draws on her knowledge of literacy development to remark about what the child is capable of doing as of this observation, and some possible next steps for this child. In analyzing an event, the teacher might consider the factors that make the event significant as well as the implications of the event for the future.

Several Events Over Time   If the teacher in the example in Figure 14–9 made several Anecdotal Records over time for this particular student, the teacher might find that E. is gaining facility with letter/sound relationships or that E. has a problem with a particular set of letter/sound relationships. She might be able to record the moment when E. starts to understand about word boundaries. In conference with E.'s parents, she will be able to show some rich data about E.'s literacy development.

Rhodes and Nathenson-Mejia (1992) suggest three types of analysis that are possible with Anecdotal Records:

- Making inferences
- Identifying patterns
- Identifying strengths and weaknesses

In addition to tracking the progress of a single child over a period of time, Anecdotal Records can help the teacher improve assessment practices, as Maureen Holland (in Rhodes and Shanklin, 1993) points out:

> While sharing my anecdotal notebook with some colleagues, I discovered that for some students I had copious notes and comments, while for others I had only a few. I had unconsciously collected more notes for those students who were behavior problems and those who were struggling academically. My method of gathering notes had been too haphazard. I determined that a more systematic collection was needed. (P. 39)

She chose a different six students each day to focus on in order to ensure that she didn't leave students out.

FIGURE 14–5. AN EXAMPLE OF AN ANECDOTAL RECORD

PROCESS

Literacy Development	History of Individual Child

Importance of sound/letter relationships to literacy development.
Importance of understanding word boundaries for literacy development.

E. has not demonstrated an understanding of letter/sound relationships in the past.

Significant Event

Child's Writing:
STRDAIPADENBSNO

Recording Process

```
STRDA  = yesterday
I      = I
PAD    = played
EN     = in
B      = the (said "du" and thought she was writing "D")
SNO    = snow
```

Showed her how to stretch her words out like a rubber band—doing it almost on own by SNO. Asked her at end—what she did in writing today that she hadn't done in previous writing. She said, "I listened to sounds." Told her to do it in her writing again tomorrow.

Analysis Interpretation

E. does have a fairly good grasp of sound/letter relationships. However, has a hard time isolating words and tracking words in sentences in her mind.

Use

Invitations to continue to practice letter/sound relationships.
Look for teachable moments for word boundaries.

Use

The information from Anecdotal Records has several possible uses, as Rhodes and Nathenson-Mejia (1992) point out:

- Instructional planning . . . Anecdotal records on children's social behaviors and responses to written language can help teachers plan stimulating situations for the reluctant as well as the enthusiastic reader/writer . . .

- Informing. In addition to using anecdotal records for planning ongoing instruction, teachers also may use them to periodically inform others, including the students themselves, about students' strengths, weaknesses, and progress . . .

- Generating new questions. Analyzing anecdotal records and using them to plan instruction encourages teachers to generate new questions that lead full circle to further assessment of students and of teaching itself. (Pp. 507–8)

Cautions and Comments

Goodman (1985) suggests that kidwatching (and by extension, anecdotal record keeping) can be beneficial to children whose linguistic backgrounds differ from that of the school:

> There are many issues concerning language differences in the areas of both dialect and second language learning which teachers must consider. Too many children have been hurt in the past because of lack of knowledge about language differences. . . . Attitudes such as "these children have no language" or "bilingualism confuses children" are still too prevalent. Kidwatching can help teachers be aware of how such statements are damaging to language growth . . . By observing the language of children in a wide variety of settings such as role playing, retelling of picture books, or playing games during recess or physical education, teachers gain many kinds of information that help to dispel myths about language and language learning.
>
> For example, Sorita, age 6, would use the following types of construction often in oral conversations with other children or during sharing sessions:
>
> "Lots of my friends was at my house . . . "
>
> "We was going to the store . . . "
>
> However, during her narration of "The Three Billy Goats Gruff" which accompanied the acting out of the story by some of her classmates, her teacher heard," "There were three billy goats. . . . " Sorita used this more formal construction throughout the narration. (P. 12)

In this instance, the teacher used her knowledge of an individual child in order to ensure that the child is using both school and home dialect.

Anecdotal Records are potentially a very powerful form of authentic assessment because they create a picture of a child's engagement within a natural setting or settings, rather than the artificial setting of a test. Further, although traditional sources on assessment state that a disadvantage to Anecdotal Records is that they are time-consuming to produce, they can be done within the context of children's engaging with the activities of the school. In other words, Anecdotal Records do not interrupt the child's work for the process of assessment; they are integral to the child's work.

Finally, Anecdotal Records are a form of assessment that acknowledges—and depends on—the teacher's understanding of children and ability to work constructively with them. Unlike behavior checklists (which limit the process of observation) and even Portfolios (which belong to students), Anecdotal Records allow wise teachers who have a great deal of insight into children's behavior and progress to bring all their skills and information to bear in the process of assessment. For this reason, Anecdotal Records can be a strong part of an assessment program—the part that depends mostly on the teacher.

As with any powerful tool, Anecdotal Records have a potential to be harmful. Judgmental language or other implicit judgments in the process of recording can be detrimental to children, particularly if these records become a part of the child's school record. Further, although the teacher may be a wise person, he or she may not have observed the whole event. There may be another side to the story that is missing from the Anecdotal Record, but one that readers of Anecdotal Records may not look for, since it is so easy to assume that the teacher recorded the event accurately. In the case of Anecdotal Records about problematic events, teachers may want to invite children to record their observations and perceptions and to store the children's' records with their own records.

The teachers' Anecdotal Records also depend upon the teachers' understandings of literacy and the nature of literacy development. Oftentimes checklists are used to guide Anecdotal Records and may lead to some practices that are problematic. For example, teachers need to try to describe how the skills and strategies work together in the context of reading and writing. It is not adequate to define the use of a single skill or fail to mention the context within which the skills are used.

Teachers need to be aware that the students' use of skills and strategies are apt to vary from one setting to the next including across story selections. In defining a students' ability, they are apt to find differences from one assignment to the next in terms of the following:

> Nature of engagement (active, curious, passive, etc.)
>
> Strategies (planning, predicting, self-questioning, visualizing, connecting ideas, troubleshooting)
>
> Self-monitoring
>
> Outcomes

Across assignments, they might look for patterns in terms of the following:

> Values and habits
>
> Flexible use of strategies
>
> Self-assessment of needs, goals, achievement
>
> Range of reading and writing pursued

It is key to realize that differences across settings should be expected, but that a pattern might emerge.

Finally, it is very important for teachers to keep this information confidential. Anecdotal Records allow teachers an opportunity to reflect at a very significant level about a child's whole development. These reflections may contribute to a teacher's thoughtful use of instruction and support for children, but this kind of analysis may be harmful to a child if other children (or even other parents) gained access to this information.

References

Allington, R., A. Butler, and R. J. Tierney. 1993. *Teacher's guide to evaluation: Assessment handbook.* Celebrate Reading series. Glenview, IL: Scott, Foresman, and Company. This handbook contains evaluation materials for the reading program specifically but also some general assessment ideas.

Anthony, R. J., T. D. Johnson, N. I. Mickelson, and A. Preece. 1991. *Evaluating literacy: A perspective for change.* Portsmouth, NH: Heinemann. Brings together information about assessment and new assessment practices. Provides forms that can be used in the classroom.

Atwell, N. Making the grade. In *Understanding writing: Ways of observing, learning, and teaching,* 2nd ed., edited by T. Newkirk and N. Atwell, 236–244. Portsmouth, NH: Heinemann. In this article, Atwell discusses the use of conferences to evaluate students' writing.

Barrs, M. 1990. The primary language record: Reflection of issues in evaluation. *Language Arts* 67:244–253. This article discusses the benefits of the Primary Language Record (PLR), an assessment tool developed by the Inner London Education Authority. Barrs briefly discusses several of the strategies incorporated into the observation-based record, including structured observation, samples, error analysis, conferencing, teacher judgment scales, and cumulative records.

Barrs, M., S. Ellis, H. Hester, and A. Thomas. 1988. *The primary language record.* Portsmouth, NH: Heinemann. Developed and piloted as part of an initiative for the Center of Language in primary education, this publication is one of the best sources available for imple-mentable ideas related to analyzing reading and writing.

Cartwright, C. A., and G. P. Cartwright. 1984. *Developing observation skills,* 2nd ed. New York: McGraw-Hill Book Company. Provides teachers with numerous traditional forms of "kidwatching."

Education Department of South Australia. 1991. *Literacy assessment in practice: R-7 language arts.* Adelaide: Education Department of South Australia. Provides a framework for assessment that is being used in Australian schools. Includes samples of forms and children's work.

Goodman, Y. 1985. Kidwatching. In *Observing the language learner,* edited by A. Jaggar and M. T. Smith-Burke. Newark, DE: International Reading Association. Introduces the concept of kidwatching. Provides examples and connects the process of observation with the understanding of children's development.

Jett-Simpson, M., V. Dauer, N. Dussault, B. Gaulke, L. Gerhar, L. Leslie, L. Ruell McClain, J. Pinlott, W. Prentice, and R. Telfer. 1990. *Toward an ecological assessment of reading.* Madison, WI: Wisconsin State Reading Association. This monograph provides a thoughtful discussion of the problems of traditional assessment; suggests guidelines; and describes a host of practices (book selection, observation, response journals, Think-Alouds, interviews, Portfolios) that might be used by classroom teachers.

Johnston, P. 1987. Teachers as evaluation experts. *The Reading Teacher* 40:744–748. Johnston discusses how teachers can most effectively evaluate the process of literacy development by suggesting they become experts at "detecting patterns, knowing classroom procedures, and by listening." He further suggests that such individualized process-centered evaluation not only serves instruction but also allows students and teachers to collaborate in the learning process.

Locke, D. C., and J. C. Ciechalski. 1985. *Psychological techniques for teachers.* Muncie, IN: Accelerated Development, Inc., Publishers. ERIC Document 344–147. Provides several techniques that are based in psychological practice for teachers to use in the classroom, including information on anecdotal records.

Mehrens, W. A., and I. J. Lehman. 1984. *Measurement and evaluation in education and psychology.* 3rd ed. New York: Holt, Rinehart and Winston. Contains numerous evaluation tools for use by teachers.

Rhodes, L. K., and S. Nathenson-Mejia. 1992. Anecdotal records: A powerful tool for ongoing literacy assessment. *The Reading Teacher.* 45:502–509. Describes using Anecdotal Records. Provides examples of records and their analysis.

Rhodes, L. K., and N. Shanklin. 1993. *Windows into literacy: Assessing learners K-8.* Portsmouth, NH: Heinemann. Contains many forms of authentic assessment for literacy teachers. Includes sample forms and articles by teachers who actually use them.

Sharp, Q. Q. 1989. *Evaluation: Whole language checklists for evaluating your children.* New York: Scholastic. Presents an array of charts that teachers might be able to use in conjunction with observations of readers and writers.

Smith, L. M., T. M. Kuhs, and J. M. Ryan. 1993. *Assessment of student learning in early childhood education.* South Carolina Center for Excellence in the Assessment of Student Learning. ERIC Document 358–163. Provides information on several alternatives to testing in the assessment of young children.

Stiggins, R., and N. F. Conklin. 1992. *In teachers' hands: Investigating the practices of classroom assessment.* Albany: SUNY. This book represents several years of exploration of issues of assessment in schools and the shift to legitimizing alternative forms of assessment.

Taylor, D. 1990. Teaching without testing. *English Education* 22:4–74. Taylor presents the essence of a project intent on developing biographic literacy profiles from the perspective of the child.

Tierney, R. J. 1993. *Classroom-based assessment systems for literacy.* Glenview, IL: Scott, Foresman. Provides a brief discussion of a range of classroom-based assessment procedures from on-the-run assessments to periodical assessments of students using Portfolios and other procedures.

Tierney, R. J., L. E. Desai, and L. P. Stowell. 1992. *Dynamic Assessment.* Report prepared for Apple Computer, Inc. Explores the nature of dynamic assessment by teachers in conjunction with the ebb and flow of instruction as well as instructional planning.

Watson, D. 1985. *Watching and listening to children read.* In *Observing the language learner,* edited by A. Jaggar and M. T. Smith-Burke. Newark, DE: International Reading Association. Connects the concept of "kidwatching" with the process of reading. Suggests several types of "kidwatching" and various things to watch for as children engage with print.

Running Records

Purpose

The purpose of Running Records is to "provide an ongoing assessment of the reading strategies being used and developed" (Lyons et al., 1993, 11) as a way of teachers' monitoring a student's reading progress and needs.

Rationale

Advocates for alternative assessment practices proclaim that teachers need to become active constructors of curriculum development and assessment and evaluation programs (e.g., Goodman, et al., 1989; Anthony, et al., 1991). Through these alternative measures, teachers can "look at individual progress while providing specific information on individual pupils' instructional needs and growth" (Routman, 1988, 204). Weaver (1990) asserts that alternative assessment must "evolve from classroom learning and teaching instead of being imposed or supplied from without; they are not prepackaged or immutable" (P. 211), and that these measures "must be selected and developed to suit the needs of themselves and their students" (P. 212). Routman (1991) concurs by stating that "these techniques must focus on meaningful communication in the language process—listening, speaking, reading, and writing—and the individual's day to day progress. As a result, careful teacher observation and teacher judgement becomes crucial; implying there is trust in teachers as professionals" (P. 204).

Running Records is an an alternative assessment technique that purports to contribute to effective instructional planning, ongoing teacher observation of reading behaviors, and other decision making. The Running Record, a form of miscue analysis, was developed by New Zealand educator Marie Clay as an "easy, but precise, way to observe, record, and carefully analyze reading behaviors" (Lyons et al., 1993, 92; Routman, 1988, 205). This technique provides teachers with

> . . . helpful insights about the strategies a child is using to reconstruct meaning while identifying what needs to be learned next. (New Zealand Board of Education, 1985, 121–122)

It is important that students have opportunities to read familiar as well as unfamiliar texts when being assessed through the Running Record.

> Familiar texts reveal whether the difficulty level of the material the child is using is suitable and in what ways the child is making use of the strategies that have been taught. Unfamiliar texts reveal the child's willingness to take risks, and indicates the ability to use and integrate strategies independently. (New Zealand Board of Education, 1985, 121–122)

In addition, this technique serves the following instructional purposes:

- Ongoing assessment by:
  - identifying gradient level of difficulty
  - capturing student strategic processing
  - providing opportunities for observation and detection of "in the head" strategies being developed
- Record keeping by recording:
  - book levels
  - problem-solving strategies

- student progress over time
- evidence of fluent reading in easy or familiar books
- Decision making by:
  - setting the direction for instruction
  - grouping students by strategic processing rather than by ability
  - identifying important strategies to praise, reinforce, or reteach in order to gain control/internalize
  - developing flexibility in reading
  - providing opportunities for students to work within their own Zone of Proximal Development (Vygotsky)
  - ultimately accelerating the reader

Another technique that is closely related to Running Records is the miscue analysis (Goodman, et al., 1987), which is "a tool that has contributed to the development of a comprehensive theory and model of reading; it can be used to reveal the strengths and weaknesses of pupils and the extent to which they are efficient and effective readers" (Goodman, 1973, 4). Differences between these two techniques are illustrated below:

Miscue Analysis	Running Record
lengthy	"on the run"
response sheets	paper, pencil
comprehending	hypothesizing
contrived setting	authentic setting
tape recorded	live/in person
photocopy of unfamiliar text for student	familiar book for student use
hands-on training with manual	hands-on training with practice

Intended Audience

Running Records can be used with students at any grade level. Adaptations to meet individual needs and classroom purposes may be necessary.

Description of the Procedure

Clay (1993) and Lyons et al. (1993) outline the procedures below when administering, recording, and analyzing a running record. An example of a child's running record (i.e., Cory) and its analysis is found in Figure 14–6.

FIGURE 14–6.   CORY'S RUNNING RECORD AND ANALYSIS OF STRATEGIES

Cory's Running Record

Text: _On a Cold Cold Day_   Text Level   3

Scores: Running Words / Error   33 / 10   Error Rate   1 : 3   ACC.   66%   SC Rate   1 : 4

Page	Title and level: On a cold cold day	E	SC	Cues used E	Cues used SC
2	✓On ✓a ✓cold ✓cold ✓day ✓A ✓rat R wears ✓a ✓hat				
3	On|sc a|sc cold|sc cold|sc R A fox wears socks		4	M Ⓢ V / Ⓜ s Ⓥ M Ⓢ V / Ⓜ Ⓢ V M Ⓢ V / Ⓜ Ⓢ V M Ⓢ V / Ⓜ Ⓢ V	
4	✓A ✓giraffe ✓wears ✓a Coat/scarf	1		M Ⓢ V	
5	A/– goat/goats ✓wear ✓coats	2		M Ⓢ V Ⓜ Ⓢ Ⓥ	
6	Kangaroo/Kangaroos ✓wear ✓shoes	1		Ⓜ Ⓢ Ⓥ	
7	A/– Cat/Kittens ✓wear ✓mittens	2		M Ⓢ V Ⓜ Ⓢ Ⓥ	
8	✓And –/Paul ✓wears all/them of/all them/– Ⓦ R	4		M Ⓢ V M Ⓢ V M Ⓢ V M Ⓢ V	

Analysis: Cory's dominant cuing system is structure. Those neglected are meaning and visual. Meaning is cross checked against structure resulting in self correction. (Cold/SC / Socks)

Administration

The teacher and student sit side by side in a comfortable setting. The teacher holds the paper and pencil for recording what occurs during the oral reading session and maintains a neutral observer role. The student holds and controls the book while reading. The reading session is not tape recorded, but the teacher records the entire reading session by looking into the student's copy of the book while marking correct responses with ticks or checkmarks and any miscues (insertions, omissions, repetitions, and substitutions) with a specific symbol notation as described below.

One or two instructional teaching points are identified immediately following the oral reading. These teaching points can be in the form of verbal comments or praise, which signify the presence and use of particular reading strategies that may not yet be internalized, or can be in the form of a direct instruction lesson in which the particular reading behaviors or strategies not being exhibited can be developed through explicit teaching and demonstration. (Clay, 1993, 39). The purpose for teaching is to have students arrive at "an end point in instruction where they have developed a self-extending system which is a set of operations just adequate for reading slightly more difficult text for the precise words and meanings of the author" (Clay, 1993, 39). It is during this time that the teacher wants to build on the strategies already under control while praising and reinforcing those reading strategies that are developing and eventually will become internalized and automatic.

Coding the Running Record

The following notations are used when recording reading behavior on a Running Record. (Clay, 1993, 27–29).

1. Correct words are marked with a checkmark

2. All responses deemed wrong are underlined and written above the word

3. Multiple responses are valued and a MSV coding analysis is required

4. Other codes that will appear on the running record include

   - SC = self-correction
   - — = a hyphen above line omission
   - T = Told
   - R = Repetition
   - — = a hyphen below line insertion
   - A = student appeals for help
   - W = wait (or hesitation, pause)

5. Other guidelines to attend to when counting up errors

   - proper names repeatedly missed is counted as 1 error
   - lowest score for any page read is 0
   - if line or sentence is omitted, count each word as error; if entire page is omitted, deduct number of pages from total score

Using the Running Record to analyze strategies (Clay, 1993)

1. **Searching for cues:** When analyzing errors, the following questions need to be addressed regarding the assumptions of what was going on inside the child's head.

   - Does the child use meaning (M)? Is the student applying his knowledge of the world to his reading?
   - Does the child use structure (S)? Does the student elicit a word that sounds right? What language structure does the child bring to the learning environment?
   - Does the child use visual cues (V)? Does what the student says look visually correct? What part of the word was the child attending to—the beginning, middle, or end? (Pp. 41–42)

2. **Self Correction:** Clay (1993) claims that self-correction reflects that "the student will exhibit reading behaviors such as monitoring, searching by using the three cuing systems, cross-checking using different cues, and will attend to and self-correct miscues.

Asking open ended questions like 'How did you know it was _____ ?' invites students to examine reading behaviors after completing a reading operation successfully" (P. 43).

3. **Cross-Checking Information:** According to Clay (1993), the student, when not satisfied with a response, will exhibit overt behaviors that signal to the observer that something does not make sense and that meaning is lost. Such behaviors include "making another attempt, looking back to previous print, rethinking what was already said, or complaints that a necessary letter is missing" (P. 41). When this occurs, the student is encouraged to cross-check (i.e., visual cues, meaning cues, or structural cues) or use two sources of information—checking one against the other" (P. 41).

4. **Using Running Records to monitor and adjust instructional material:** After taking the Running Record, it is important for the teacher to select appropriate instructional material that will challenge and support the learner. In this regard, a teacher tries to challenge the child with material for which he achieves a 90–94% fluency. As Clay (1993) states,

> The goal of teaching is to assist the child to produce effective strategies for working on text, not to accumulate items of knowledge. It is necessary to develop opportunities for the child to problem solve, predict and accommodate new knowledge. In a literate setting, the most important thing that the child can do when reading is to notice that something is wrong and use his own resources for working on a solution (P. 15).

Beyond 95 percent, the material is viewed as not sufficiently challenging. According to Clay, if a child's instructional program is designed to foster the child's independent level (95–100%), the child most likely will not participate in enough stimulating and challenging opportunities that would encourage, expand, and strengthen his current strategies. There will be little or no authentic opportunities for problem solving, investigating, and taking the initiative to probe and explore.

The opposite will be true for a student with whom instructional learning activities will continually fall within the hard or difficult range (50–89%). If this should occur, the opportunities for the child to utilize, experiment, and risk the few strategies he may have control over will be almost nonexistent. This child needs to be absorbed in authentic, language-rich experiences that will enable him or her to explore what he or she knows while being supported with his or her approximations through scaffolding.

Cory's Running Record results illustrate that he is struggling with reading. Indeed, his teacher might look for material that is not so challenging. Nonetheless, it does appear that he understands what he is reading; however, he relies too much on Meaning (M) and Structure (S) cues without attending to the Visual (V) aspect of words. Although there is evidence he is aware of early reading strategies (directionality, one-to-one matching, searching and monitoring), it appears that Cory has not internalized these strategies enough to initiate them on his own or to utilize these behaviors in a strategic way.

Even though this text (level 3) fell within the hard/difficult range, many positive reading behaviors can be gleaned from this document. For instance, Cory understands storybook language; understands directionality and that words carry the message, not the pictures, but that the pictures are used to assist reading. He is able to locate known words ("here's *a*") but has not yet internalized how this known word can assist him during the reading process; and he understands the functions and forms of language as exhibited in the rhyming of words ("coat/goat and fox/socks match, don't they?").

Cautions and Comments

In the educational arena today, much has been debated regarding the appropriateness and frequency of standardized testing within the school curriculum. Much debate has focused on the aspects of quantitative and qualitative measures. For instance, the standardized test "frequently examines surface behaviors, strategies such as self correction and regressions, which are needed for proficient reading, but are often treated as problematic. Qualitative analysis, on the other hand, evaluates why miscues are made and assumes that they derive from the language and thought that the reader brings to the written material" (Goodman, et al., 1987, 4). With the advent of alternative assessment, many teachers have found ways of implementing these techniques that assist them in tailoring their programs to meet "pupils' instructional needs and growth" (Routman, 1988, 204). In addition, teachers began to participate in decision-making processes that could lead to curriculum development and instructional change. For instance, the success classroom teachers have found with Running Records involves useful, immediate, and diagnostic data that are helpful when reporting school progress to parents (Routman, 1988). Another positive attribute of Running Records involves "observation 'on the run' without time spent in preplanning, tape recording, and photocopying text" (Weaver, 1990, 228) as depicted in miscue analysis.

Running Records are no panacea. They represent a sampling of reading behavior that may or may not give a full or adequate picture. Some students have aversions to oral reading; for others it detracts from their meaning making. Running Records do encourage teachers to be constantly monitoring what students are doing as they are reading en route to making decisions as to appropriate support and materials. Although Running Records may be difficult to manage, as an occasional spot check they afford teachers and the students themselves a teaching tool that is more dynamic than rigid and can be more supportive than intrusive.

References

Anthony, R. J., T. D. Johnson, N. I. Mickelson, and A. Preece. 1991. *Evaluating literacy: A perspective for change.* Portsmouth, NH: Heinemann. This is a practical book that focuses on evaluation strategies that could impact classroom, home, and school populations.

Clay, M. M. 1993. *An observation survey of early literacy achievement* Portsmouth, NH: Heinemann. This text was written for teachers and researchers who work with young readers and writers. This text describes the procedures to follow when administering and scoring the six assessment tasks in the Observation Survey and when utilizing a Running Record.

———. 1993. *Reading recovery: A guidebook for teachers in training.* Portsmouth, NH: Heinemann. This text is used by teachers-in-training. It describes the components and procedures of a Reading Recovery lesson.

Cooper, J. D. 1993. *Literacy: Helping children construct meaning.* Boston: Houghton Mifflin. Provides theoretical and practical techniques in helping teachers guide and facilitate children's literacy development.

Department of Education. 1985. *Reading in junior classes.* Wellington. This handbook offers guidance to teachers while describing the New

Zealand way of teaching reading to young-sters.

Goodman, K. 1973. *Miscue analysis.* Urbana, IL: ERIC Clearinghouse. This text shares several viewpoints on the reading process and miscue analysis and how this procedure can be utilized in classrooms of diversity and grade level.

Goodman, Y. M., D. J. Watson, and C. L. Burke. 1987. *Reading miscue inventory.* New York: Owens. This guidebook describes the steps involved when implementing a miscue analysis. Specific directions, examples, and sample sheets are included.

Goodman, K. S., Y. M. Goodman, and W. J. Hood. 1989. *The whole language evaluation book.* Describes practical and successful alternative evaluation techniques that teachers can utilize in any learning environment.

Lyons, C. A., G. S. Pinnell, and D. E. DeFord. 1993. *Partners in learning: Teachers and children in reading recovery.* New York: Teachers College Press, Columbia University. "This book is written as a text for individuals interested in early or emergent literacy development who want to make a difference in the learning of high-risk children."

Routman, R. 1988. *Transitions from literature to literacy.* Portsmouth, NH: Heinemann. Describes how teachers and school personnel can successfully shift from a more traditional setting to one of an integrated, literature-based language arts program.

———. 1991. *Invitations: changing as teachers and learners K-12.* Portsmouth, NH: Heinemann. An excellent resource to assist teachers when integrating the curriculum and implementing alternative assessments.

Weaver, C. 1988. *The reading process and practice from socio-psycholinguistics to whole language.* Portsmouth, NH: Heinemann. Provides an in-depth study and discussion on the reading process and its relationship to instructional practice.

———. 1991. *Understanding whole language from principles to practice.* Portsmouth, NH: Heinemann. Describes the impact a holistic, integrated, child-centered environment has on literacy learning and the need for authentic means of assessment in relation to literacy learning.

Retelling

Purpose

The purpose of Retelling for classroom assessment is to provide teachers an alternative to asking questions in evaluating students' understanding of what they have read. Using Retelling, students try to recall as much as possible of what they have read, and comprehension performance is judged on the thoroughness of the recall.

Rationale

Critics of the informal reading inventory point out that the question-and-answer format employed by it does not necessarily tap students' understanding of what they read to the fullest extent. Questions, in essence, can function to limit the responses students can make. Retelling, on the other hand, allows students to respond in their own words concerning what they understood from the text. Thus, Retelling can increase both the quantity and the quality of what is comprehended.

Since the procedure involves repetition and rehearsal of what is read, Retelling should add more text information to memory and affect how much is learned. Additionally, the procedure allows for students to make the information gained from the text more personally meaningful than questions and, therefore, should affect the depth of learning.

Intended Audience

Retelling can be used across the curriculum with a variety of grade levels. However, it is most commonly used in elementary level classrooms, particularly those that take a Whole-Language emphasis (see Unit 1).

Description of the Procedures

The procedure for Retelling will be discussed using the following two steps: (1) eliciting the retelling, and (2) scoring the retelling.

1. *Eliciting the Retelling*   Before Retelling is used as a means to assess students' comprehension, they must be familiar with the procedure. Students will have difficulty doing a retelling if they are unfamiliar with the technique and what is expected of them; therefore, they should have had prior practice doing it.

To begin the retelling, make sure that students understand that they will be asked to retell the story. Since the retelling is not for instructional purposes, the story should not be discussed with the student beforehand, nor should there be any prompts during the procedure. After the story has been read, ask the student to retell it as if it were being told to a friend for the first time who had never heard it before. To ensure the accuracy of the assessment, tape-record the retelling.

2. *Scoring the Retelling*   Irwin and Mitchell (1983) have developed a holistic system to score a retelling. Because each student's retelling is individualistic with regard to reaction, personality, and depth of understanding, assessment should be done by examining the whole recall and not its component parts. Only by examining the totality can the richness of the reader's understanding be judged.

To assess a retelling, Irwin and Mitchell developed criteria for establishing five levels of richness, from good to poor, to use in judging a student's recall. Figure 14–7 describes the levels of richness of a retelling while Figure 14–8 is a checklist that compares the principal qualities of the five richness levels.

In using this scoring system, teachers will need to make judgments about the quality of a student's retelling by comparing it to the original story and using the criteria to judge its richness. For instance, if a student's retelling shows that the student did not generalize beyond the story or provide a summarizing statement, only mentioned some major points and a few supporting details, but did show some signs of story coherence and completeness, then the student's retelling would probably be classified as level 2. This, however, would tell the teacher that the student did not do a very good job of comprehending the story. The teacher may then wish to do some further evaluating, such as a probed recall, to gather additional information. All findings should be added to the student's portfolio to get a more comprehensive look at the student's reading.

FIGURE 14–7.   JUDGING RICHNESS OF RETELLINGS

Level	Criteria for Establishing Level
5	Student generalizes beyond text; includes thesis (summarizing statement), all major points, and appropriate supporting details; includes relevant supplementations; shows high degree of coherence, completeness, comprehensibility.
4	Student includes thesis (summarizing statement), all major points, and appropriate supporting details; includes relevant supplementations; shows high degree of coherence, completeness, comprehensibility.
3	Student relates major ideas; includes appropriate supporting details and relevant supplementations; shows adequate coherence, completeness, comprehensibility.
2	Student relates a few major ideas and some supporting ideas; includes irrelevant supplementations; shows some degree of coherence; some degree of completeness; the whole is somewhat comprehensible.
1	Student relates details only; irrelevant supplementations or none; low degree of coherence; incomplete; incomprehensible.

(From Irwin, P. A., and J. N. Mitchell, 1983. A procedure for assessing the richness of retellings. *Journal of Reading,* 26: 391–396. All rights reserved. Reprinted by permission of the International Reading Association.)

FIGURE 14–8.   CHECKLIST FOR JUDGING RICHNESS OF RETELLINGS

	5	4	3	2	1
Generalizes beyond text	X				
Thesis (summarizing statement)	X	X	X		
Major points	X	X	X	?	?
Supporting details	X	X	X	X	?
Supplementations	Relevant	Relevant	Relevant	Irrelevant	Irrelevant
Coherence	High	Good	Adequate	Some	Poor
Completeness	High	Good	Adequate	Some	Poor
Comprehensibility	High	Good	Adequate	Some	Poor

(From Irwin, P. A., and J. N. Mitchell, 1983. A procedure for assessing the richness of retellings. *Journal of Reading,* 26: 391–396. All rights reserved. Reprinted by permission of the International Reading Association.)

Cautions and Comments

Using Retelling enables teachers to get a different look at how students comprehend. A holistic examination helps teachers move away from the small details recalled through questions to look at the richness of a student's retelling and how the student was able to move beyond the story read and how it was related to the student's personal experience. Certainly the global examination of Retelling provides teachers the opportunity to be more consistent in their assessment over time of students' comprehension.

It should be mentioned that the description of the Retelling procedure was based on the student reading a story and orally recalling it. Variations upon this procedure allow teachers to accommodate differences in age, reading ability, culture, and so on, by the teacher's reading the story and having the student retell it or even having the student write his retelling.

It is also cautioned that this description of the Retelling was for assessment, not instruction. If teachers were to use the Retelling as a means for comprehension, the procedure would be modified. Prompts could be added to help students embellish their retellings. Brown and Cambourne (1987) suggested that students be asked to make predictions about the story and that those predictions be shared and discussed before it is read. After their retellings students should compare them with one another to examine others' interpretations of the story. In this way the procedure can be adapted to engage students more fully both before and after reading.

References

Brown, H., and B. Cambourne. 1987. *Read and retell.* Portsmouth, NH: Heinemann. A handbook on the use of Retelling.

Gambrell, L. B., P. S. Koskinen, and B. A. Kapinus. 1991. Retelling and the reading comprehension of proficient and less-proficient readers. *Journal of Educational Research* 84:356–362. Study showing that practice in Retelling improved the comprehension of both good and poor readers.

Glazer, S. M., and C. S. Brown. 1993. *Portfolios and beyond: Collaborative assessment in reading and writing.* Norwood, MA: Christopher-Gordon. Chapter 6 of this text describes the use of Retelling to assess comprehension.

Irwin, P. A., and Mitchell, J. N. 1983. A procedure for assessing the richess of retellings. *Journal of Reading 26:* 391–396. Suggestions of assessing a Retelling.

Morrow, L. M. 1988. Retelling stories as a diagnostic tool. In *Reexamining reading diagnosis: New trends and practices,* edited by S. M. Glazer, L. W. Searfoss, and L. M. Gentile, 128–149. Newark, DE: International Reading Association. A discussion of procedures for using Retelling for assessment purposes.

Cloze

Purpose

Cloze and variations of Cloze are used to assess reading comprehension. However, research has raised serious questions that suggest that Cloze should be used with an understanding that it measures at best sentence level comprehension—specifically, a reader's ability to align him or herself with the language of an author's text.

Rationale

Taylor (1953) described the Cloze procedure as:

> . . . a method of intercepting a message from a "transmitter" (writer or speaker), mutilating its language patterns by deleting parts, and so administer it to "receivers" (readers and lis-

teners) that their attempts to make the pattern whole again potentially yield a considerable number of cloze units. (P. 416)

Since Taylor made such a statement, Cloze has been widely advocated as a method for assessing whether students can comprehend text and as a procedure for improving reading comprehension. It has come to be widely used in tests such as the Degrees of Reading Power as well as standardized tests and tests tied to instructional material. Unfortunately, recent research is equivocal with regard to what exactly Cloze is measuring, and it should not be assumed to be directly associated with reading comprehension. Notable among these studies is the work of Shanahan, Kamil, and Tobin (1982) and Shanahan and Kamil (1983), showing that Cloze is neither sensitive to intersentential aspects of text nor to prior knowledge. On the other hand, these results have been called into question by Gamarra and Jonz (1987). While further research is conducted to further define what the relationship of Cloze to reading comprehension is, we can say with some certainty that Cloze appears to measure—and maybe heighten—a student's use of the syntax of and information presented with individual sentences.

Intended Audience

The Cloze procedure has been recommended for use with readers at all levels for a variety of purposes, such as instructional placement and an assessment of a student's ability to use context clues and to assess the readability level of certain texts. As an instructional tool, its use has been referenced at the first-grade level (Gove, 1975) through college level (Bloomer, 1962; Friedman, 1964; Guice, 1969).

Description of the Procedure

For those who have used the Cloze procedure as a measure of the comprehensibility of printed material, it would be best to note some differences between the use of the technique in those settings and the use of the strategy as an instructional device. Essential differences are summarized in Table 14–1.

Different forms of Cloze have been developed to achieve different assessment ends. For purposes of assessing students' comprehension or to assess the readability of a text, the most common approach to Cloze requires students to generate exact word replacement for a random selection of deleted words. In this form of Cloze test, every fifth word is deleted, regardless of the word. Recommended procedures for constructing such a passage are as follows:

1. Select a representative selection from the material to be assessed or that represents the type of material being assigned to children. Look for an intact section of this text (i.e., a section that could stand alone) of approximately 250–350 words. You should avoid material that depends upon or is obviously linked to previous material.
2. Keep intact the first and last sentence or sentences depending upon the length of the sentence. If the sentence is especially short, you may wish to include more than one sentence.

TABLE 14–1. CLOZE PROCEDURE

Characteristic	As a measuring device	As a teaching tool
Length	(1) 250–350-word selections	(1) Initially, may use single sentences. Later, passages of no more than 150 words
Deletions	(2) Delete every *n*th word with approximately 50 for the total word passage	(2) Make deletions selectively and systematically in accordance with proposed use
Evaluation	(3) With this procedure,, only exact word replacement is correct. Sometimes a teacher may analyze student responses in terms of their syntactic and semantic characteristics	(3) Synonyms or other replacements are appropriate
Follow-up	(4) Usually none	(4) Student and teacher discussion of the exercise helps comprehension

3. Randomly choose one of the first five words in the second sentence. Beginning with this word, omit every fifth word until 50 words are deleted. Dates would be considered single words, certain hyphenated words may be viewed as single words or two words depending upon your rationale.
4. Replace each deleted word by a blank of uniform length.
5. Have students either replace the word in the blank provided or on a separate sheet.

Example Cloze

The Cloze Procedure

The Cloze procedure is based upon the psychological notion of closure (hence, Cloze) and the concept of redundancy within the language. The Cloze has been _____ as a procedure for _____ how well a reader _____ comprehending a text. Research _____ suggest that it measures _____-level comprehension not text-_____ comprehension. It will appear _____ assess how well readers _____ align themselves with the _____ choice of words. Another _____ of Cloze has been _____ assess the readability of _____ text. To this end, _____ following criteria have been _____ : if readers replace more _____ 60 percent of the _____ words accurately then they _____ can handle the material _____ ; if readers replace between _____ and

60 percent of _____ words accurately then they _____ need instructional support when _____ the material; if they _____ below 40 percent the _____ may be too frustrating.

_____ constructing a Cloze passage, _____ a passage of around _____ words in length. Type _____ first sentence intact. _____ with the fifth word _____ the second sentence, delete _____ fifth word until you _____ fifty deletions. Replace each _____ with an underlined blank _____ spaces long. Finish the _____ in which the last _____ occurs, then type one _____ sentence intact. . . .

. . . Since the development of the Cloze, variations such as the Maze procedure have emerged.

Intact Passage from Which Sample Cloze Was Developed

The Cloze Procedure

The Cloze procedure is based upon the psychological notion of closure (hence, Cloze) and the concept of redundancy within the language. The Cloze has been touted as a procedure for assessing how well a reader is comprehending a text. Research would suggest that it measures sentence-level comprehension not text-level comprehension. It will appear to assess how well readers can align themselves with the author's choice of words. Another use of Cloze has been to assess the readability of a text. To this end, the following criteria have been used: if readers replace more than 60 percent of the deleted words accurately then the readers can handle the material independently; if readers replace between 40 and 60 percent of the words accurately then they may need instructional support when reading the material; if they fall below 40 percent the material may be too frustrating.

When constructing a Cloze passage, select a passage of around 300 words in length. Type the first sentence intact. Starting with the fifth word in the second sentence, delete every fifth word until you have fifty deletions. Replace each deletion with an underlined blank fifteen spaces long. Finish the sentence in which the last deletion occurs, then type one more sentence intact. . . .

. . . Since the development of the cloze, variations such as the Maze procedure have emerged.

Guthrie and his colleagues (1974) suggest using Maze to monitor comprehension and assess the level of challenge of the material that they are reading. Unlike Cloze, maze requires the reader to choose among three choices: exact word, a word representing the same part of speech, or a word representing a different part of speech. If students are responding to Maze at a level of 90 percent across three or more passages, then the student seems to be able to read these materials independently. If students are responding at between 60 and 69 percent they are operating at optimal instructional level. Below 60 percent they are likely to be frustrated.

Other assessment uses of Cloze tend to represent variations of the aforementioned approaches or uses of Cloze for specific purposes, such as assessing students' ability to use pronominal references or consonant clues, and so on. Such uses involve forms of Cloze created with these specific tasks in mind and parallel the types of Cloze activities described below for using Cloze for instructional purposes.

Cloze used for instructional purposes Given the questions raised about Cloze, most advocates have shifted away from using Cloze as a method to assess comprehension and instead reserve its use to instructional purposes. Several individuals have attempted to outline systematic procedures for using the Cloze technique as a comprehension-building strategy (Bloomer, 1962; Schell, 1972; Bortnick and Lopardo, 1973; Gove, 1975). The following procedural outline incorporates the thoughts of each of those individuals.

1. *Teacher Preparation*
    a. Selecting materials. Schell (1972) suggests that, in the early stages, materials should be at the students' independent reading level. Teachers can extract written selections from stories and poems in basal readers, from subject matter texts, or from language experience stories the students themselves generate. There are some Cloze-type materials available through several publishers. It is important to note that teachers themselves produce some of the most effective materials.

       As we mentioned earlier, passages should be shorter than passages generally used when Cloze is a testing device. For example, teachers may use single sentences initially with first graders, gradually moving to selections in which 10 to 15 deletions have been made (Gove, 1975).
    b. Designing the Cloze exercise. There appears to be a logical progression in the format for presenting Cloze exercises. Consider the examples that follow only as a guideline for developing Cloze exercises. We present them in order of difficulty, which the teacher should follow.
       1. Sentences in which the teacher deletes one word; a multiple-choice format with two choices. Notice in the following example that the two choices include the correct item and a foil, or an incorrect item that is quite different graphically and is a different part of speech.

          1. monkey

             "We saw a ＿ at the zoo . . .

          2. soon

       2. The same format as above, but with the foil somewhat graphically similar to the correct item and a different part of speech.

          1. mostly

             "We saw a ＿ at the zoo . . .

          2. monkey

       3. Two choices, both the same part of speech.

          1. monkey

             "We saw a ＿ at the zoo . . .

          2. money

4. Three choices that include the correct item, a word of the same part of speech, and a word that represents a different part of speech.*

"We saw a __ at the zoo . . .

1. money

2. mostly

3. monkey

From these highly structured examples, one can move to less structured items. Again, in terms of difficulty, one could progress with exercises of this type:

1. A single graphophonic clue in a sentence where only one word could reasonably fit.
   "I think the square t_____ will look better in the dining room than the round one you considered buying."
2. A single graphophonic clue in a sentence where several choices are possible.
   "We bought a bag of p _____ at the grocery store."

Finally, the teacher could use sentences and passages similar to these, but without the graphophonic rule.*

Again, we suggest this sequence simply to provide a guideline for the development of Cloze activities. Obviously, the teacher must consider the difficulty of the printed materials and the reading sophistication of the students when developing exercises of this type.

The reader may have noticed that each of the examples above contains a noun deletion. Schell (1972) suggests that in the early stages of instruction, the teacher should delete only nouns and verbs. Later, he or she may emphasize categories such as adjectives or adverbs.

2. *Instruction*   In many kindergarten and first grade classrooms, the instructional program might include oral Cloze activities. The following is an example of one such activity:

I am going to say some sentences, but I will leave off the last word of each sentence. See if you can tell me what word I left out. Let's try this one: "At Joe's birthday party on Saturday, we had some ice cream and _____ ." What word(s) make(s) sense there?

Discussion then could center on why students have various answers. Such exercises provide a logical introduction to the use of written Cloze activities.

When initiating written Cloze activities, the teacher might begin with a whole-class activity focused on material presented on an overhead projector. The teacher should direct students to read through the entire sentence or passage before attempting to supply the deleted word(s). A student volunteer could read the material and supply the missing

*This example is similar to a testing strategy, the Maze technique, described by Guthrie et al. (1974).

word(s). One other student who has responded differently could read and provide his or her responses. Class discussion would center on such questions as:

> Why did you choose this word? What word or group of words indicate to you "building" should be placed in the blank? How does your word contribute to the meaning of the passage? When your word is in the sentence, what does the sentence (or passage) mean? How does your word contribute to the meaning in a different way? When your word is in the sentence, does the sentence (or passage) have a different meaning? (Gove, 1975, 38)

Other students could add their suggestions with continued discussion centered on these questions.

Later, the teacher could give the mimeographed Cloze passages to complete individually. In small-group discussions, the teacher asks each student to explain why he or she used a particular word. The small-group discussions would then lead to large-group discussion of some of the more interesting or controversial items.

An exercise such as the following might be used with a group of intermediate level readers. Obviously, the teacher would not type the deleted words on the students' mimeographed copies, but we include the words here for discussion purposes.

> Would you like to find a rich (*gold*) mine? There's one in the Superstition Mountains of Arizona. Jacob Walz, an (*old*) prospector from Germany, was one of the last known persons to (*visit*) the mine. Before Walz died in 1891, he gave (*simple*) directions to the mine. There is also supposed to be a map. But no one has ever been able to find what is now (*called*) "The Lost Dutchman Mine."*

Each of the words in parentheses offers students the opportunity to supply a variety of other words. For example, in place of the word *old,* students might offer replacements such as *elderly, adventurous, interesting, ugly,* or *eccentric.* Discussion then could center on why these choices are feasible, and why words like *young, robust,* and so on are not acceptable.

Jongsma (1980) and others have suggested that this discussion procedure may be the key to the successful use of Cloze as a teaching strategy. There is very little evidence to suggest that Cloze exercises alone will produce better comprehenders.

Cautions and Comments

There appear to be an endless number of ways that teachers can use the Cloze procedure to improve the comprehension skills of readers. For example, Rankin (1959) proposed the use of Cloze exercises to assist readers who have difficulty with text in their content classrooms, and Blachowicz (1977) proposed using the Cloze technique with primary grade students.

Furthermore, there seem to be a number of alternative Cloze formats. Two additional Cloze formats have appeared in research studies and may present possibilities for use in teaching. A limited Cloze technique (Cunningham and Cunningham, 1978) employs the

---

*Smith, R. G., and R. J. Tierney, *Fins and Tales,* Scott, Foresman Basics in Reading. (Glenview, IL: Scott, Foresman, 1978). 72.

traditional deletion pattern of every fifth word with the deleted words randomly ordered and placed in columns on a separate sheet.

Another format, the least-major-constituent limited Cloze (Cunningham and Tierney, 1977), deletes every fifth least-major-constituent (syntactic unit sometimes larger than words) and randomly orders them in columns on a separate sheet.

With the widespread use of Cloze, however, comes the need for caution. As was suggested in the Rationale, Cloze should not be assumed to be directly associated with comprehension. Indeed, it seems that some people are using Cloze haphazardly. The reader should note that merely completing Cloze activities will not result in students' improved comprehension. Rather, comprehension improvement using Cloze depends on the reader's purpose, the text's demands, and the teacher's follow-up during and after a Cloze activity. To this end, teachers should use Cloze selectively with passages and purposes where students' ability to produce replacement words or phrases is a worthwhile activity. For example, Cloze might be inappropriate with text for which a more reader-based understanding is appropriate. Finally, we need to stress the fact that there is very little research that supports the use of Cloze as a procedure either for testing or for developing comprehension.

Johnston (1992) offered a similar view. As he stated:

> There has been considerable debate among researchers about whether the cloze procedure can provide information about a reader's understanding of anything more than a sentence at a time. Some claim that by careful selection of the words to be deleted, the procedure can require the students to know the whole meaning of the text (assuming that only a single meaning can be acceptable). Of course, in order to feel a need to engage in these arguments, you have to feel it is necessary to obtain some numerical indicator of a child's "ability to comprehend." If you do to feel such a need, then the cloze procedure remains a useful instructional technique for helping some children attend more to the use of context to figure out unknown words." (P. 123)

References

Blachowicz, C. L. Z. 1977. Cloze activities for primary readers. *The Reading Teacher* 31: 300–302. Describes how teachers can use variations of Cloze successfully with primary readers.

Bloomer, R. H. 1962. The cloze procedure as a remedial reading exercise. *Journal of Developmental Reading* 5:173–181. Describes the use of the Cloze procedure as a remedial technique for college students.

Bortnick, R. and G. S. Lopardo. 1973. An instructional application of the cloze procedure. *Journal of Reading* 16:296–300. Provides specific direction for using Cloze procedure to improve comprehension. Emphasis is placed on the importance of teacher direction.

Carr, E., P. Dewitz, and J. Patberg. 1989. Using cloze for inference training with expository text. *The Reading Teacher* 42:380–385. Discusses the use of Cloze procedures intended to enhance inferential comprehension and self-monitoring.

Cunningham, J. W., and P. M. Cunningham. 1978. Validating a limited-cloze procedure. *Journal of Reading Behavior* 10:211–213. Presents a variation of the traditional Cloze format.

Cunningham, J. W., and R. J. Tierney. 1977, December. *Comparative analysis of cloze and modified cloze procedures.* Paper presented at National Reading Conference, New Orleans. Provides a comparison of the traditional Cloze format with two modified versions.

Friedman, M. 1964. *The use of the cloze procedure for improving the reading of foreign students at the University of Florida.* Unpublished doctoral diss., University of Florida. Describes an experimental study in which one group received Cloze passages constructed from McCall-Crabbs Standard Test Lessons in Reading.

Gamarra, A. G., and J. Jonz. 1987. Cloze procedure and the sequence of text. In *Research in literacy: Merging perspectives,* edited by J. E. Readence and R. S. Baldwin. Thirty-sixth Yearbook of the National Reading Conference. Rochester, NY: National Reading Conference, 17–24. Calls into question studies that have found Cloze to be unrelated to reading comprehension.

Gove, M. K. 1975. Using the cloze procedure in a first grade classroom. *The Reading Teacher* 29:36–38. Describes how the teacher can use Cloze procedure in conjunction with basal readers and with the language experience approach.

Guice, B. M. 1969. The use of the cloze procedure for improving reading comprehension of college students. *Journal of Reading Behavior* 1:81–92. Provides a description of four groups of college students who received instruction using Cloze passages.

Guthrie, J. T., N. A. Burnham, R. I. Caplan, and M. Seifert. 1974. The maze technique to assess, monitor reading comprehension. *The Reading Teacher* 28:161–168. Presents a multiple-choice-type variation of the Cloze procedure.

Henk, W. 1977–78. A response to Shanahan, Kamil, and Tobin: The case is not yet clozed. *Reading Research Quarterly* 13:508–537. Presents a response to the first study of Shanahan, Kamil, and Tobin, which resulted in a second study by them.

Johnston, P. 1992. *Constructive evaluation of literate activity.* New York: Longmans. Presents a brief discussion of Cloze in the context of a substantial presentation of literacy assessment issues, theories, and practices.

Jongsma, E. 1980. *Cloze instruction research: A second look.* Newark, DE: International Reading Association. Presents descriptions of past research that used the Cloze procedure as a teaching tool; offers suggestions for future Cloze research.

Pikulski, J. J., and A. W. Tobin. 1982. The cloze procedure as an informal assessment technique. In *Approaches to the informal evaluation of reading,* edited by J. J. Pikulski, and T. Shanahan. Newark, DE: International Reading Association, 42–62. Provides an extensive discussion of the research and practical uses of Cloze.

Rankin, E. 1959. Uses of the cloze procedure in the reading clinic. *Proceedings of the International Reading Association* 4:228–232. Suggests ways of using Cloze procedure to bridge the gap between clinical instruction and instruction in the content classroom.

Sampson, M. R. W., W. J. Valmont, and R. V. Allen. 1982. The effects of instructional cloze on the comprehension, vocabulary and divergent production of third grade students. *Reading Research Quarterly* 17:389–399. Presents positive results from a study in which students who received instruction in Cloze with selected deletions outperformed a control group.

Schell, L. M. 1972. Promising possibilities for improving comprehension. *Journal of Reading* 5:415–424. Presents detailed information on the use of Cloze as a teaching technique.

Shanahan, T., and M. Kamil. 1983. A further investigation of sensitivity of cloze and recall to passage organization. In *Searches for meaning in reading/language processing and instruction,* edited by J. A. Niles and L. A. Harris. Thirty-second Yearbook of the National Reading Conference. Rochester, NY: National Reading Conference. In response to Henk's critique, presents a study that further disputes Cloze as a method of improving comprehension.

Shanahan, T., M. Kamil, and A. Tobin. 1982. Cloze as a measure of intersentential comprehension. *Reading Research Quarterly* 17:229–255. Presents a research study that raised serious questions about the use of Cloze as a measure of text comprehension.

Taylor, W. L. 1953. Cloze procedure: A new tool for measuring readability. *Journalism Quarterly* 30:415–453. Provides the first description of the Cloze technique.

Index